Juvenile Delinquency

This book offers a comprehensive introduction to juvenile delinquency by defining and describing juvenile delinquency, examining explanations for delinquent behavior, and considering contemporary efforts to control delinquency through prevention and juvenile justice. The text cultivates an understanding of juvenile delinquency by examining and linking key criminological theories and research. Coverage includes:

- the historical origins and transformation of "juvenile delinquency" and juvenile justice;
- the nature of delinquency, addressing the extent of delinquent offenses, the social correlates of offending and victimization (age, gender, race and ethnicity, and social class), and the developmental patterns of offending;
- theoretical explanations of delinquency, with insights from biosocial criminology, routine activities, rational choice, social control, social learning, social structure, labeling, and critical criminologies;
- evidence-based practice in delinquency prevention and contemporary juvenile justice.

Fully revised and updated, the new edition incorporates the latest theory and research in the field of juvenile delinquency and provides expanded discussion of contemporary juvenile justice reform, evidence-based practice in delinquency prevention, and disproportionate minority contact throughout the juvenile justice process. This book is essential reading for courses on juvenile delinquency and juvenile justice.

The book is supported by a range of compelling pedagogical features. Each chapter includes key terms, learning objectives, an opening case study, box inserts that provide practical application of theory and research, critical thinking questions, suggested reading, useful websites, and a glossary of key terms. A companion website offers an array of resources for students and instructors. For students, this website provides chapter overviews, flashcards of key terms, and useful websites. The instructor site is password protected and offers a complete set of PowerPoint slides and an extensive test bank for each chapter—all prepared by the authors.

James Burfeind is a Professor of Sociology at the University of Montana. He earned a PhD in Criminology and Urban Sociology from Portland State University in Oregon. He is co-author with Ted Westermann of *Crime and Justice in Two Societies: Japan and the United States*, and has received a number of teaching awards, including "Most Inspirational Teaching," a university-wide award chosen by graduating seniors.

Dawn Jeglum Bartusch is an Associate Professor of Sociology and Criminology at Valparaiso University in Indiana. She earned a PhD in Sociology from the University of Wisconsin–Madison. Her research has appeared in *Criminology*, *Social Forces*, *Law and Society Review*, and the *Journal of Abnormal Psychology*.

Whether you are bound for a leadership career in criminal justice or you want to become a star researcher in criminology, *Juvenile Delinquency* in its third edition will make you the expert. This text is the ideal combination of organized and practical to aid mastery, but also intellectually stimulating, to make learning engaging and exciting. This edition is remarkably up to date. Chapter six taught me interesting new facts about developmental criminology!

Terrie Moffitt, *Knut Schmidt Nielsen Professor of Psychology and Neuroscience Psychiatry and Behavioral Sciences, Duke University, Durham, NC*

Burfeind and Bartusch's text provides excellent coverage of key topics and themes that are central to the study of juvenile delinquency. The book is well written, nicely organized and presents juvenile delinquency research in a clear and concise manner that is accessible to students. I have been using the book since its first edition and continue to be pleased with student learning outcomes and feedback on the book.

Dusten Hollist, *University of Montana, Missoula*

Juvenile Delinquency

An integrated approach

Third edition

James Burfeind and
Dawn Jeglum Bartusch

Routledge
Taylor & Francis Group

LONDON AND NEW YORK

Third edition published 2016
by Routledge
2 Park Square, Milton Park, Abingdon, Oxon OX14 4RN

and by Routledge
711 Third Avenue, New York, NY 10017

Routledge is an imprint of the Taylor & Francis Group, an informa business

First edition published by Jones and Bartlett Publishers, Inc. 2006
Second edition published by Jones and Bartlett Publishers, LLC 2011

British Library Cataloguing in Publication Data
A catalogue record for this book is available from the British Library

Library of Congress Cataloguing in Publication Data
Names: Burfeind, James W., 1953– | Bartusch, Dawn Jeglum.
Title: Juvenile delinquency : an integrated approach / James Burfeind
and Dawn Jeglum Bartusch.
Description: Third Edition. | New York : Routledge, 2016. | Revised edition
of the authors' Juvenile delinquency, 2011. Identifiers: LCCN 2015025492 |
ISBN 9781138843196 (hardback) | ISBN 9781138843202 (pbk.) |
ISBN 9781315731094 (ebook)
Subjects: LCSH: Juvenile delinquency. | Juvenile justice, Administration of.
Classification: LCC HV9069 .B79 2016 | DDC 364.36–dc23
LC record available at http://lccn.loc.gov/2015025492

ISBN: 978-1-138-84319-6 (hbk)
ISBN: 978-1-138-84320-2 (pbk)
ISBN: 978-1-315-73109-4 (ebk)

Typeset in Bembo
by Out of House Publishing

Printed and bound by CPI Group (UK) Ltd, Croydon, CR0 4YY

A Companion Website is available for this book at www.routledge.com/cw/
burfeind

To my wonderful wife, Linda. Your love and support is constant, and you make life fun and fulfilling.

– J.B.

To my parents, Patricia and Steven Jeglum, for their support at every stage of my life, and for teaching me the value of hard work and determination.

– D.J.B.

Contents

Figures

Tables

About the authors

James Burfeind is a Professor of Sociology at the University of Montana. He earned a PhD in Criminology and Urban Sociology from Portland State University in Oregon. Professor Burfeind's teaching and research interests are in criminological theory, juvenile delinquency, juvenile justice, and corrections. He has received a number of teaching awards, including "Most Inspirational Teaching," a university-wide award chosen by graduating seniors. He has considerable experience in juvenile probation and parole and adolescent residential care.

Dawn Jeglum Bartusch is an Associate Professor of Sociology and Criminology at Valparaiso University in Indiana. She earned a PhD in Sociology from the University of Wisconsin–Madison. Professor Bartusch's teaching and research interests are in criminological theory, juvenile delinquency, crime and inequality, and social stratification. Her research has appeared in *Criminology*, *Social Forces*, *Law and Society Review*, and the *Journal of Abnormal Psychology*.

Preface

Welcome to the third edition of *Juvenile Delinquency: An integrated approach*. We believe that most students have a natural curiosity about juvenile delinquency. Perhaps they were once involved in delinquency but never caught. Regardless of their personal histories, students come to class with an almost endless list of questions. Why do some kids engage in delinquent acts? Is delinquent behavior a normal part of adolescence? Is the delinquency problem growing worse? Are adolescents becoming more violent? Why is delinquency rampant in some areas? How can we best respond to the problem of juvenile delinquency? Can delinquency be prevented and controlled? As criminologists and authors of this book, we share this interest in understanding juvenile delinquency, and that's why we wrote this text.

As we describe in Chapter 1, the scientific study of delinquent behavior uses two basic tools: theory and research. Theories of delinquency provide a systematic presentation of key causal factors and offer insight into the causes of juvenile delinquency. Delinquency research seeks either to provide sufficient information to develop theory or to test theory. Thus, theory and research go hand-in-hand. The primary purpose of this book is to cultivate an understanding of juvenile delinquency by integrating theory and research.

Organization of the text

Juvenile Delinquency: An integrated approach is divided into four main parts, containing fourteen chapters. The first two parts focus on *defining* and *describing juvenile delinquency*. The third part of the book concentrates on *explaining delinquent behavior*, and the fourth part considers *responses to juvenile delinquency* through efforts at prevention and intervention, and through contemporary juvenile justice systems.

In Part I, "Studying juvenile delinquency," we describe the basic components of theory and the conceptual tools for assessing theory, as well as the research methods and sources of data for studying delinquent behavior. In this part, we also discuss the origins and transformation of juvenile delinquency and juvenile justice.

In Part II, "Describing the nature of delinquency," we present a trilogy of chapters in which we consider the nature of delinquent offenses, offenders, and patterns of offending. We begin by examining the extent of delinquent behavior and the types of offenses in which young people are involved. We then attempt to answer the question "Who are the offenders?" by exploring the social correlates of delinquency: age, gender, race, and social class. We also consider how these four social correlates are related to criminal victimization. Next, we consider patterns of offending, presenting the key elements of the developmental perspective and influential developmental models.

In Part III, "Explaining delinquent behavior," we present the primary biological, psychological, and sociological theories that criminologists have offered to explain delinquency and social responses to it. First, we examine biological and psychological approaches to delinquency – an area of study referred to as "biosocial criminology." Then we explore the "delinquent event," which considers the immediate setting in which delinquency occurs, including the situational aspects of delinquent acts, the routine activities of adolescents that create opportunities for delinquent behavior, and the situational context that surrounds offending decisions. In this part, we also examine sociological perspectives on offending, including social control, social learning, and social structure theories. Finally, we consider social responses to delinquency from the perspectives of labeling theory and critical criminologies.

Part IV, "Responding to juvenile delinquency," considers delinquency prevention and early intervention, and contemporary juvenile justice. We examine the prevention perspective on adolescents "at risk" and describe model prevention programs. Assessment and early intervention seek to identify, classify, and respond to antisocial behavior once it occurs. Our consideration of contemporary juvenile justice describes the structure and process of juvenile justice throughout the United States. Each state has its own juvenile justice system, made up of various components at both the state and local levels and operated by both public and private agencies. As a result, contemporary juvenile justice is hardly a system. Juvenile justice practices and procedures are examined with regard to law enforcement, courts, and corrections, providing a full understanding of contemporary juvenile justice in action.

Distinctive features

In addition to the pedagogical features that we describe in the following section, this text includes the following distinctive features:

Chapter-opening case studies

We begin each chapter with a case study or excerpt that illustrates key ideas addressed in the chapter. These case studies provide students with a compelling introduction to the topic at hand. The cases are not sensationalized accounts of recent high-profile cases – which fail to illustrate the characteristics and true nature of the vast majority of delinquent offenders and acts. Instead, most of the cases we use to open chapters are drawn from classic works in the field of criminology. At the end of each chapter, a critical-thinking question revisits the case study and invites students to consider the case study again in light of what they have read in the chapter.

Application boxes

Application boxes appear throughout this text and enhance understanding of juvenile delinquency by providing students with practical, relevant, and engaging applications of theory and research. We offer four types of applications, which serve distinct purposes.

- *Case in point* applications provide real-life case examples, appellate court cases, or statutory law to illustrate points of discussion.
- *Research in action* applications describe delinquency research, highlighting particular programs of research and offering insight into how researchers actually carry out their work.

For example, these applications often describe the measurement of variables used to test theories.

- *Theory into practice* applications illustrate how theory is translated into policy or practice. These applications describe specific programs or strategies, derived from the theories we discuss, for preventing or reducing delinquency.
- *Expanding ideas* applications elaborate on key points presented in the text, sometimes quoting the scholar(s) who originally presented the idea we are considering.

Emphasis on integration of theory and research

As the title of the book indicates, we emphasize the integration of theory and research in understanding juvenile delinquency. We discuss research within its theoretical context. For example, we consider families, peers, and gangs within the context of the theoretical traditions that most actively address these arenas. This integrated approach helps students understand how social scientists actually do criminology by developing theory and conducting research.

Throughout the book, we present the key theories of delinquent behavior, along with the most relevant research used to test these theories. However, our coverage of research is not encyclopedic. We do not attempt to cite every study in every area of research, but instead we discuss selected research studies thoroughly. This approach provides *depth* of understanding, rather than sheer *breadth* of coverage. Neither do we try to simplify our presentation of theory and research. Much of what is interesting and insightful about delinquency theory and research is lost when it is offered in an abbreviated fashion, and we do not want to lose the richness of this field of study.

Resources to aid learning

Juvenile Delinquency: An integrated approach includes several pedagogical features that will assist students in mastering the material we present.

- **Chapter previews** identify the main topics and themes discussed in each chapter, and provide lists of **theories** and **terms** students should watch for as they read.
- **Learning objectives** alert students to the issues and concepts they should understand after reading each chapter.
- **Application boxes** enhance understanding of juvenile delinquency by providing students with practical, relevant, and engaging applications of theory and research.
- **Chapter summaries and conclusions** draw attention to important points from the chapter, and provide conclusions to chapter materials.
- **Critical-thinking questions** invite readers to *apply* knowledge acquired through reading the chapter and to consider the chapter-opening case study in light of the materials presented in the chapter.
- **Suggested reading** sections offer references to primary sources discussed in each chapter, and to interesting applications of key concepts.
- **Useful websites** present weblinks relevant to each chapter, and invite students to further their understanding of particular topics through additional exploration.
- **Glossaries of key terms** provide definitions and assist students in checking their knowledge of the important terms highlighted in each chapter.

New to the third edition

The student-friendly writing style and the "integrated approach" to the study of delinquency remains the same in this edition. But we would like to draw your attention to some of the revisions we have made in the third edition:

- Throughout the book, we have updated delinquency and juvenile justice data, providing the most current information and statistics.
- We have incorporated recent research, published since the second edition of our text.
- Chapter 2, on the origins and transformation of "juvenile delinquency" and juvenile justice, includes enhanced coverage of contemporary juvenile justice reforms. The reemergence of rehabilitation is the latest "buzz" in juvenile justice reform, fueled by two prominent areas of research: a "developmental approach to juvenile justice reform" and evidence-based practice.
- Several new "Theory into practice" application boxes were added to various chapters. These depict "model programs" that have been substantiated by evaluation research.
- Chapter 13, on delinquency prevention and intervention, was extensively rewritten to incorporate the latest developments in the field – most notably evidence-based practice (ESB). The ESB methodology runs throughout the chapter and is applied to delinquency prevention, assessment, and early intervention.
- Chapter 14, on contemporary juvenile justice, now includes extended discussion of disproportionate minority contact, and this crucial issue is referred to throughout the chapter.

Companion website

A companion website offers an array of resources for students and instructors. For students, this website provides **chapter overviews**, **flashcards of key terms**, and **useful website links** for each chapter. The instructor site is password protected and offers a complete set of **PowerPoint slides** and an extensive **test bank** for each chapter—all prepared by the authors. Visit the companion website at: www.routledge.com/cw/burfeind.

Acknowledgements

We are grateful to the many individuals who have provided thoughtful reviews of our chapters. This edition is much improved as a result of the helpful feedback and suggestions provided by a number of anonymous reviewers.

We were assisted in the revisions for this edition by several very capable students: Eric Speer and Ally Guldborg at the University of Montana; and Erica Gilbert, Carmyn Hamblen, and Elizabeth Hostetler at Valparaiso University. We appreciate their careful work on sometimes tedious tasks.

Thanks also to the American Sociological Association, the American Society of Criminology, National Academies Press, Harvard University Press, the International Association of Chiefs of Police, the National Council of Juvenile and Family Court Judges, Oliver John, the University of Chicago Press, Blueprints, the Institute for Social Research (University of Michigan), Sage, Wiley, and Taylor & Francis for their kind permission to reproduce previously published material in this third edition of the book.

We are especially grateful for the dedication of the team at Routledge/Taylor & Francis Group, who made this third edition possible. Thomas Sutton reached out to us with enthusiasm for this project, and has impressed us at every step in the process of publishing this book. He is a tremendously talented editor, and we are profoundly grateful for his guidance and commitment to this project. We are also extremely grateful to Heidi Lee and Hannah Catterall, who have gently prodded us to keep us on schedule. Heidi was of great help in seeking permissions and in preparing the manuscript for production. We appreciate Heidi and Hannah's efficiency and cheerfulness. We also appreciate the careful copy editing work of Joanna North, and the very capable production work of Emma Hart and Olivia Hatt.

Part I

Studying juvenile delinquency

Chapter 1

The study of juvenile delinquency

Chapter preview

Topics:

- Understanding juvenile delinquency
- Developing and evaluating theories of delinquency
- Purposes of delinquency research
- Causal analysis

Terms:

- juvenile delinquency
- theory
- concepts
- propositions
- level of explanation

- inductive theorizing
- deductive theorizing
- association
- temporal order
- spurious

Chapter learning objectives

After completing this chapter, students should be able to:

- Understand the approach and structure of this book.
- Describe the key components of theory.
- Describe the relationship between theory and research.
- Identify the purposes of research.
- Describe the criteria for establishing cause-and-effect relationships.

They were also drinking →

This activity was behind a bush on court house lawn →

Case in point: Rick, a "delinquent youth"

The youth court "adjudicated" 14-year-old Rick a "delinquent youth" for motor vehicle theft and placed him on formal probation for six months. He and a friend took a car that belonged to Rick's father without permission. They were stopped by the police for driving erratically – a classic case of joyriding.

Rick was already a familiar figure in the juvenile court. When Rick was 12, he was referred to the court for "deviant sex" for an incident in which he was caught engaging in sexual activity with a 14-year-old girl. The juvenile court dealt with this offense "informally." A probation officer met with Rick and his parents to work out an agreement of informal probation, but no petition into court. Not long after this first offense, Rick was taken into custody by the police for curfew violation and later for vandalism – he and his friend had gotten drunk and knocked down numerous mailboxes along a rural road. In both of these instances, Rick was taken to the police station and released to his parents.

Rick was a very personable and likable kid. He expressed a great deal of remorse for his delinquent acts and seemed to genuinely desire to change. He had a lot going for himself; he was goal-directed, intelligent, and athletic. He interacted well with others, including his parents, teachers, and peers. His best friend, an American Indian boy who lived on a nearby reservation, was the same age as Rick and had an offense record very similar to Rick's. In fact, Rick and his friend were often "companions in crime," committing many of their delinquent acts together.

Rick was the adopted son of older parents who loved him greatly and saw much potential in him. They were truly perplexed by the trouble he was in, and they struggled to understand why Rick engaged in delinquent acts and what to do about it. Rick seemed to really care about his parents, and he spent a good deal of time with them.

Rick attended school regularly and earned good grades. He was not disruptive in the classroom or elsewhere in the school. In fact, teachers reported that he was a very positive student both in and out of class and that he was academically motivated. He was also actively involved in several sports.

Rick's six months of formal probation for auto theft turned into a two-year period as he continued to commit delinquent acts. Through regular meetings and enforcement of probation conditions, his probation officer tried to work with Rick to break his pattern of delinquency. Yet Rick continued to offend, resulting in an almost routine series of court hearings that led to the extension of his probation supervision period. The continuing pattern of delinquency included a long list of property and status offenses: minor in possession of alcohol, curfew violations, continued vandalism, minor theft (primarily shoplifting), and continued auto theft.

Rick's "final" offense was criminal mischief, and it involved extensive destruction of property. Once again, Rick and his friend "borrowed" his father's car, got drunk, and drove to a suburb of Minneapolis. For no apparent reason, they parked the car and began to walk. Eventually, they started throwing small rocks toward buildings and ended up breaking numerous windows, causing thousands of dollars' worth of damage.

Because of the scale of damage, Rick faced the possibility of being placed in a state training school. As a potential "loss of liberty case," Rick was provided with representation by an attorney. This time, the juvenile court's adjudication process followed formal procedures, including involvement of a prosecutor and a defense attorney. In the preliminary hearing, Rick admitted to the petition (the formal legal statement of charges against him), and the case was continued to a later date for disposition (sentencing in juvenile court). In the meantime, the judge ordered a predisposition report.

> The predisposition report is designed to individualize the court's disposition to "fit the offender." The investigation for the report uses multiple sources of information, including the arresting officer, parents, school personnel, coaches, employers, friends, relatives, and, most important, the offending youth. The predisposition report tried to describe and explain Rick's persistent pattern of property and status offending, and it offered a recommendation for disposition based on the investigation. The probation officer recommended that Rick be committed to the Department of Corrections for placement at the Red Wing State Training School. Rick was viewed as a chronic juvenile offender, with little hope for reform.

It was one of those formative experiences. I [co-author Jim Burfeind] was fresh out of college and newly hired as a probation officer. I was meeting with two experienced attorneys – one the defense, the other the prosecutor. Almost in unison, they turned to me and asked, "Why did Rick do this? Why did he develop such a persistent pattern of delinquency?" They wanted to make sense of Rick's delinquency, and they wondered how the juvenile court could best respond to his case.

I had become familiar with Rick only in the previous few weeks when his case was reassigned to me as part of my growing caseload as a new probation officer. Now, meeting with the attorneys to gather information for the predisposition report, I was being asked to explain Rick's pattern of delinquency to two legal experts who had far more experience in the juvenile justice system than I did. How could I possibly know enough to offer an explanation? I also had the daunting responsibility of making a recommendation for disposition that the judge would most likely follow completely. Rick's future was at stake, and my recommendation would determine the disposition of the juvenile court.

As I tried to respond to the attorneys, my mind was flooded with questions. The answers to these questions became the basis for my predisposition report. The questions with which I wrestled included the following:

- Is involvement in delinquency common among adolescents; that is, are most youths delinquent? Maybe Rick was just an unfortunate kid who got caught.
- Are Rick's offenses fairly typical of the types of offenses in which youths are involved?
- Will Rick "grow out" of delinquent behavior?
- Is Rick's pattern of offending similar to those of other delinquent youths?
- Do most delinquent youths begin with status offenses and then escalate into serious, repetitive offending? (Status offenses are acts, such as truancy and running away, that are considered offenses when committed by juveniles, but are not considered crimes if committed by adults.)
- Is there a rational component to Rick's delinquency so that punishment by the juvenile court would deter further delinquency?
- Did the fact that Rick was adopted have anything to do with his involvement in delinquency? Might something about Rick's genetic makeup and his biological family lend some insight into his behavior?
- What role did Rick's use of alcohol play in his delinquency?
- Are there family factors that might relate to Rick's involvement in delinquency?
- Were there aspects of Rick's school experiences that might be related to his delinquency?
- What role did Rick's friend play in his delinquent behavior?

- Did the juvenile court's formal adjudication of Rick as a "delinquent youth" two years earlier label him and make him more likely to continue delinquent offending?
- Should the juvenile court retain jurisdiction for serious, repeat offenders like Rick?
- What should the juvenile court try to do with Rick: punish, deter, or rehabilitate?
- Should the juvenile court hold Rick less responsible for his acts than an adult because he has not fully matured?

Perhaps this list of questions seems a little overwhelming to you now. We don't present them here with the expectation that you will be able to answer them. Instead, we present them to prompt you to think about what causes juvenile delinquency and to give you an idea of the types of questions that drive the scientific study of delinquent behavior. Throughout this book, we address these types of questions as we define delinquency; consider the nature of delinquent offenses, offenders, and offending; and present a variety of theories to explain delinquent behavior.

Understanding juvenile delinquency

An understanding of delinquency builds upon explanations offered in theories and findings revealed in research. The primary purpose of this book is to cultivate an understanding of juvenile delinquency by integrating theory and research. Throughout the book, we focus on the central roles that theory and research play in the study of delinquency. These two components form the core of any scientific inquiry.

Before we go any further, we must define "juvenile delinquency." This definition is far more complicated than you might think. In Chapter 2, we discuss the social construction and transformation of the concept of juvenile delinquency. Here we offer a brief working definition of **juvenile delinquency** as actions that violate the law, committed by a person under the legal age of majority.

The questions that shape the scientific study of juvenile delinquency constitute attempts to *define*, *describe*, *explain*, and *respond to* delinquent behavior. Our exploration of juvenile delinquency reflects these four basic tasks. The first two parts of this book are devoted to defining and describing juvenile delinquency, the third part to explaining delinquent behavior, and the final part to contemporary ways of responding to juvenile delinquency. Responses to delinquent behavior, however, should be based on a thorough understanding of delinquency. Thus, an understanding of juvenile delinquency must come first.

Studying juvenile delinquency

The first part of this book describes the historical transformation of the concept of juvenile delinquency and the methods and data sources researchers use to study delinquent behavior. We begin by developing a working understanding of what we commonly call "juvenile delinquency" (Chapter 2). This includes not only the social, political, and economic changes that led to the social construction of juvenile delinquency as a legal term, but also the contemporary transformations that have dramatically altered how we as a society view and respond to delinquency. We then explore how researchers "measure" delinquency (Chapter 3). We describe various methods of gathering data and conducting research on juvenile delinquency and identify sources of data on crime and delinquency.

The nature of delinquency

The second part of this book presents three chapters in which we describe the nature of delinquent offenses, offenders, and patterns of offending. Before criminologists try to explain juvenile delinquency, they must first understand the problem in terms of these three dimensions. Chapters 4 through 6 report research findings that describe the nature and extent of delinquent *offenses* (Chapter 4), the social characteristics of delinquent *offenders* (Chapter 5), and the developmental patterns of delinquent *offending* (Chapter 6).

Explaining delinquent behavior

The third part of this book presents explanations of delinquency that criminologists have proposed in theories and examined in research. These chapters are organized in terms of the major themes that run through different groups of theories. One group of theories, for example, emphasizes the importance of peer group influences on delinquency. These theories, called social learning theories, address how delinquent behavior is learned in the context of peer group relations (Chapter 10). We also consider a number of other key themes: the role of individual factors, including biological characteristics and personality, in explaining delinquent behavior (Chapter 7); whether delinquency is a product of situational influences and the routine activities of adolescents, or whether it results from conscious choice (Chapter 8); the importance of social relationships, especially family relations and school experiences, in controlling delinquency (Chapter 9); the structure of society and how societal characteristics motivate individual behavior (Chapter 11); and the labeling perspective and critical criminologies that focus on how social inequalities shape offending and responses to it (Chapter 12).

Throughout the book, as we present theoretical explanations for delinquency, we weave together theories and the most relevant research that criminologists have conducted to test those theories.

Responding to delinquency

The final part of this book includes two chapters that describe societal responses to delinquency. Chapter 13 addresses the contemporary emphasis on delinquency prevention and the theoretical underpinnings of such efforts. Chapter 14 describes the present-day juvenile justice system. We have deliberately chosen to keep our discussion of juvenile justice to one chapter in order to provide an undivided view of its structure and process. The formal juvenile justice system includes police, courts, and corrections. Yet a substantial amount of juvenile delinquency is dealt with informally, sometimes by agencies outside the "system." Juvenile justice includes efforts at prevention, together with informal and formal actions by the traditional juvenile justice system. Formal procedures, such as taking youths into custody and adjudicating them as delinquent youths, are central to the task of responding to juvenile delinquency. But informal procedures designed to prevent delinquency and divert youths from the juvenile justice system are far more common.

Before launching into these chapters, it is necessary to lay the foundation to the book's emphasis: delinquency theory and research. Our goal is to make these often intimidating terms plain and understandable. In this way, you will be able to more easily grasp the material that follows. Theories of delinquency are no more than explanations, and research tries to provide information to either develop or test theories.

Developing and evaluating theories of delinquency

A **theory** is an explanation that makes a systematic and logical argument about what is important and why. Theories of delinquency try to identify and describe the key causal factors that make up the series of steps through which a person transitions from law-abiding individual to delinquent (Hirschi and Selvin 1995). In doing so, these theories emphasize certain factors as being causally important and then describe how these factors are interrelated in producing delinquent behavior.

Components of theories

Like other scientific theories, theories of delinquency are composed of two basic parts: concepts and propositions. **Concepts** isolate and categorize features of the world that are thought to be causally important (Turner 2003). Different theories of delinquency incorporate and emphasize different concepts. For example, the theories of delinquency we consider in later chapters include concepts such as personality traits, routine activities of adolescents, attachments to others, associations with delinquent friends, and social disorganization of neighborhoods.

Propositions are theoretical statements that tell how concepts are related (Bernard, Snipes, and Gerould 2010). In research, hypotheses are the testable counterpart of propositions, and variables are the measurable counterpart of concepts. Some propositions imply a *positive linear relationship* in which concepts vary in the same direction. In other words, as one concept increases, another concept also increases. Or as one concept decreases, another decreases. For example, some theories propose that the number of delinquent friends is positively related to delinquency: as the number of delinquent friends increases, so does the likelihood of delinquency. In a *negative linear relationship*, concepts vary in opposite directions. For instance, one theory proposes that level of attachment and delinquency are negatively related: as attachment increases, delinquency decreases. Relationships between concepts may also be *curvilinear.* Here, too, the concepts vary together, either positively or negatively. But after reaching a certain level, the relationship moves in the opposite direction. For example, researchers have found that parental discipline is related to delinquency in a curvilinear fashion (Glueck and Glueck 1950). Delinquency is most common when parental discipline is either lax or excessive, but is least common when discipline is moderate.

Different theories may offer competing propositions. One theory may propose that two concepts are related in a particular way, while another theory may claim that they are unrelated. For example, a major issue in delinquency theory is the role of the family in explaining delinquent behavior. One major theory contends that the family is not strongly related to delinquency and that delinquent peers are most important in explaining delinquency (Sutherland, Cressey, and Luckenbill 1992). Another major theory proposes that family relations are strongly related to delinquency, while peer relations are relatively unimportant (Hirschi 1969).

To summarize, a *theory of delinquency* is a set of logically related propositions that explain why and how selected concepts are related to delinquent behavior (Curran and Renzetti 2001). Theories of delinquency offer logically developed arguments that certain concepts are important in causing delinquent behavior. The purpose of theory is to explain delinquency.

Levels of explanation

Theories of delinquency operate at three different **levels of explanation**: individual, microsocial, and macrosocial (Short 1998).[1] At the *individual* level, theories focus on traits and characteristics of individuals, either innate or learned, that make some people more likely than others to engage in delinquency. The *microsocial* level of explanation considers the social processes by which individuals become involved in delinquency. Criminologists have emphasized family relationships and peer group influences at this level. Some microsocial theories also point to the importance of the structural context of social interaction, and how interaction is shaped by factors such as race, gender, and social class (Short 1998; Sampson and Laub 1993; Sutherland et al. 1992). At the *macrosocial* level, societal characteristics such as socioeconomic disadvantage and social cohesiveness are used to explain group variation in rates of delinquency (Akers and Sellers 2013; Cohen 1966). For example, poverty, together with the absence of community social control, is central to several explanations of why gang delinquency is more common in lower-class areas (Shaw and McKay 1969; Cloward and Ohlin 1960; Cohen 1955).

The level of explanation corresponds to the types of concepts incorporated into theories. Individual-level explanations tend to incorporate biological and psychological concepts. Microsocial explanations most often use social psychological concepts, but may incorporate structural concepts that influence social interaction. Macrosocial explanations draw extensively on sociological concepts. Theories can be combined to form "integrated theories," which sometimes merge different levels of explanation into a single theoretical framework. In addition, a similar type of concept may operate differently at different levels of explanation. For example, the effect of single-parent households on individual behavior (a microsocial-level relationship) may not be as strong as the effect of a concentration of single-parent households in a neighborhood on community crime rates (a macrosocial-level relationship).

Assessing theory

We have stated that concepts and propositions are the bare essentials of theory. These components, however, do not automatically produce a valid explanation of delinquency. We can begin to assess the validity of theory – the degree to which it accurately and adequately explains delinquent behavior – by paying attention to several key dimensions of theory (drawn from Cohen 1980: 191–192). We highlight these dimensions in the following list of questions. We invite you to ask yourself these questions as you consider how well the theories we present in later chapters explain delinquency.

1. **Conceptual clarity:** *How clearly are the theoretical concepts identified and defined?* (Shoemaker 2010).
2. **Logical consistency:** *How well do the concepts and propositions fit together – how compatible, complementary, and congruent are they?* (Akers and Sellers 2013; Shoemaker 2010). *Does the theoretical argument develop logically and consistently?*
3. **Parsimony:** *How concise is the theory in terms of its concepts and propositions?* Generally, simpler is better. So if two theories explain delinquency equally well, we should favor the theory that offers the more concise explanation with the smaller number of concepts.
4. **Scope:** *What is the theory attempting to explain?* (Akers and Sellers 2013; Curran and Renzetti 2001). Some theories try to explain a wide variety of delinquent acts and offenders. Others

focus on particular types of offenses or offenders. *What question is the theory designed to answer?* Theories of delinquency usually address one of two basic questions: (1) How and why are laws made and enforced? and (2) Why do some youths violate the law?[2] Far more theories try to answer the second question than the first (Akers and Sellers 2013).[3]

5. **Level of explanation:** *At what level (individual, microsocial, or macrosocial) does the theory attempt to explain delinquency?*

6. **Testability:** *To what extent can the theory be tested – verified or disproved by research evidence?* It is not enough for a theory simply to "make sense" by identifying key concepts and then offering propositions that explain how these concepts are related to delinquency (Akers and Sellers 2013). Rather, theories must be constructed in such a way that they can be subjected to research verification (Stinchcombe 1968).

7. **Research validity:** *To what extent has the theory been supported by research evidence?*

8. **Applicability and usefulness:** *To what extent can the theory be applied practically?* In other words, to what extent is the theory useful in policy and practice?

These questions reflect key concerns in assessing theory. Theory provides the foundation for the accumulation of knowledge and is indispensable for an understanding of delinquency. However, theory must be tested through research. Together, theory and research constitute the two basic components of a scientific approach to juvenile delinquency.

Purposes of delinquency research

Delinquency research serves two vital purposes: to generate or develop theory and to test theory (Stark 2010; Cohen 1980). In Chapter 3, we discuss research methods and sources of data used to study delinquency. Here we briefly describe the two purposes of research as it relates to theory.

Generating theory

Research is sometimes used to gain sufficient information about delinquency to theorize about it (Stark 2010). Research findings require interpretation, and it is this interpretation that yields theory. The development of theoretical explanations of delinquency requires a long, hard look at the "facts" of delinquency (repeated and consistent findings), in order to identify key concepts and then explain how these concepts are related to delinquent behavior. Along this line, Donald Shoemaker (2010: 8) defines theory as "an attempt to make sense out of observations." The difficult task of making theoretical sense of research observations is sometimes called **inductive theorizing** (Babbie 2013; Glaser and Straus 1967). In the process of inductive theorizing, research involves collecting data and making empirical observations, which are then used to develop theory.

For example, Sheldon and Eleanor Glueck, whose work we discuss in later chapters, spent their entire careers trying to uncover the most important empirical findings about delinquency. The Gluecks' work was heavily criticized for being atheoretical, or without theory (Gibbons and Krohn 1991). Their research, however, was intended to provide empirical observations that would allow for the development of a theoretical explanation of delinquency, even though they never developed such a theory (Sampson and Laub 1993; Laub and Sampson 1991). In recent years, their data and findings have become the basis for an important new theory called *life-course theory* (see Chapter 9).

Testing theory

Research also provides the means to evaluate theory and to choose among alternative or competing theories (Cohen 1980). In contrast to inductive theorizing, **deductive theorizing** begins with theoretical statements and then attempts to test the validity of theoretical predictions (Babbie 2013).

As we have already discussed, theories offer explanations of delinquency in which propositions identify certain concepts and describe how they are related to delinquent behavior. These theoretically predicted relationships can be tested through research and either verified or disproved. Throughout this book, we present theories of delinquency along with the research used to test them. Thus, knowledge of the deductive research process will help you better understand the discussions in later chapters.

When testing theory, researchers first identify key theoretical concepts and determine how to measure them. In research, *variables* are the measurable equivalent of concepts. (In "Research in action" boxes throughout this book, we offer examples of variables that researchers have used to measure various concepts.) Next, researchers develop hypotheses or statements about the expected relationships among variables, which are derived from theory. In research, *hypotheses are the testable equivalent of propositions*. Finally, researchers test these hypotheses by collecting and analyzing data, using research strategies we describe in Chapter 3.

Different theories often offer different hypotheses. For example, differential association theory (presented in Chapter 10) and social bond theory (presented in Chapter 9) provide competing hypotheses about the relationships between peers, attitudes, and delinquency. One proposition of differential association theory is that attitudes favoring delinquency are learned in the context of "intimate personal groups" (Sutherland et al. 1992: 88–89). The predicted relationship portrayed here is that youths develop attitudes from peer group relations, and delinquent behavior is then an expression of these attitudes:

peer group relations → delinquent attitudes → delinquent behavior

In contrast, social bond theory contends that attitudes are largely a product of family relationships (Hepburn 1976; Jensen 1972; Hirschi 1969). Delinquent attitudes result in delinquent behavior. Associations with delinquent peers then follow from delinquent behavior as youths seek out friendships with others like themselves. The relationships predicted by social bond theory are as follows:

delinquent attitudes → delinquent behavior → delinquent peer group

If research findings support the theoretical propositions tested, then the theory is verified or confirmed. If research findings are not consistent with the predicted relationships, then the theory is disproved.

Although the relationship between theory and research is complex, it is clear that developing theory and conducting research go hand-in-hand (Gibbons 1994). Both inductive and deductive research processes involve identification of key concepts, hypothesis development, and data collection and analysis. But the order in which these activities occur varies for the two research processes.

Causal analysis

At this point, we must say a few words about causal analysis. In deductive research, criminologists are testing hypotheses derived from theory about the causes of delinquency. But determining that a particular concept or variable is truly a cause of delinquency is more difficult than you might think. Certain criteria must be met before researchers can say that some factor *causes* delinquent behavior.

In a cause-and-effect relationship, the proposed cause is the independent variable, and the proposed effect is the dependent variable. Consider this simple model:

A → B

In this model, "A" is the independent variable, which causes or leads to "B," the dependent variable. "A" might be number of hours spent studying, which causes "B," success in school as measured by grade point average. Rarely, however, does one independent variable alone cause a dependent variable.

Models depicting the causes of delinquency described in theory are far more complex. These theoretical models are difficult to test through research for at least three reasons. First, most theories propose multiple causes of delinquent behavior. Typically, multiple independent variables are measured in relation to delinquency. Second, independent variables are themselves often related in complex ways. In fact, some independent variables "cause" other independent variables, which in turn are related to delinquency. Third, it is difficult to establish cause-and-effect relationships using social science data. Though there have been tremendous advances in data collection and analytic techniques, establishing causation remains a difficult and controversial task for social scientists.

Because there are many causes of delinquency, the causal sequences leading to delinquent behavior are hard to untangle. In "Research in action: establishing cause and effect," we summarize the criteria for establishing cause and effect. Keep these criteria in mind as you consider the causal processes described in various theories in later chapters.

Research in action: establishing cause and effect

In *Delinquency Research: An Appraisal of Analytic Methods*, Hirschi and Selvin (1995) discuss analytical methods used to study delinquency. They offer three criteria for establishing cause and effect.

1. **Association:** The cause and effect are empirically associated. This means that change in one variable is related to change in another. The statistical measure of this associated change is correlation. Though correlation does not prove causation, it is an important first step in establishing a causal connection between an independent variable and a dependent variable. As an example, research shows an association between unstructured socializing activities and delinquency. As the amount of time spent on unstructured activities (e.g., riding around in a car for fun) increases, so does involvement in delinquency.

2. **Temporal order:** The cause precedes the effect in time. The independent variable must precede the dependent variable. As simple as this sounds, it is sometimes difficult to establish which variable occurs first. It is often proposed, for example, that drug use causes delinquency. However, research has established that delinquent acts usually occur before drug use, failing to support the temporal order of the proposition (Elliott, Huizinga, and Menard 1989; Elliott, Huizinga, and Ageton 1985).

3. **Lack of spuriousness:** The relationship between the proposed cause and effect cannot be spurious, or explained away by the influence of some other factor that causes both. Babbie (2013: 94) offers this illustration: "there is a correlation between ice-cream sales and deaths due to drowning: the more ice cream sold, the more drownings, and vice versa. There is, however, no direct link between ice cream and drowning. The third variable at work here is *season* or *temperature*. Most drowning deaths occur during summer – the peak period for ice-cream sales." The correlation between ice cream sales and drowning deaths is spurious because both are related to temperature. Following the same logic, some have proposed that the relationship between drug use and delinquency is spurious because other causal factors, such as having deviant peers, influence both drug use and delinquency (Elliott et al. 1989, 1985).

Summary and conclusions

The scientific study of juvenile delinquency attempts to describe and explain delinquent behavior through theory and research. Theory seeks to provide a systematic and logical argument that specifies what is important in causing delinquency and why. Like other scientific theories, theories of delinquency are composed of concepts and propositions. It is necessary to assess the validity of theories. We provided a series of questions that you can use to evaluate the theories of delinquency presented in later chapters.

The second basic component of the scientific method is research. In relation to theory, research serves two purposes: to generate theory and to test theory. Research is sometimes used to gain sufficient information about juvenile delinquency so that it is possible to theorize about it. The development of theory from research observations is called inductive theorizing. Research is also used to evaluate or test theory in a process called deductive theorizing.

The primary purpose of this book is to cultivate an understanding of juvenile delinquency by integrating theory and research. This chapter offered an overview of the key elements of a scientific approach to delinquency, focusing especially on theory. With this basic understanding of theory and its relationship to research, we can begin our study of delinquency on solid ground. The first two parts of this book present criminologists' efforts to define and describe juvenile delinquency, the third part presents explanations of delinquency that have been offered in theory and tested in research, and the fourth part considers contemporary responses to delinquency. Throughout the book, we present theoretical explanations of delinquency together with the most relevant research that has tested those theories.

Critical-thinking questions

1. Define theory without using the words "concept" or "proposition."
2. Why does a scientific approach to delinquency depend on theory?

3. Develop your own examples of inductive and deductive theorizing.
4. Why is it necessary to demonstrate association, temporal order, and lack of spuriousness to establish a cause-and-effect relationship?
5. As you read Rick's story at the beginning of this chapter, identify the three factors that seem most significant to you in explaining why Rick was delinquent. Explain why you chose these three specific factors.

Suggested reading

Agnew, Robert. 2004. *Why Do Criminals Offend? A General Theory of Crime and Delinquency.* New York: Oxford University Press.
Shoemaker, Donald J. 2010. *Theories of Delinquency: An Examination of Explanations of Delinquent Behavior.* 6th edn. New York: Oxford University Press.

Useful websites

For further information relevant to this chapter, go to the following web sites.

- Office of Juvenile Justice and Delinquency Prevention (www.ojjdp.gov)
- National Criminal Justice Reference Service (www.ncjrs.gov)

Glossary of key terms

Association: In the research process, association exists when change in one variable is related to change in another.
Concepts: Isolated features of the world that are thought to be causally important.
Deductive theorizing: The evaluation of theoretical statements through research.
Inductive theorizing: The development of theory from research observations.
Juvenile delinquency: Actions that violate the law, committed by a person under the legal age of majority.
Level of explanation: The realm of explanation – individual, microsocial, or macrosocial – that corresponds to the types of concepts incorporated into theories.
Propositions: Theoretical statements that tell how concepts are related.
Spurious: The relationship between a proposed cause and effect is considered to be spurious if it can be explained away by the influence of some other factor that causes both.
Temporal order: In establishing a cause-and-effect relationship, the cause (or independent variable) must precede the effect (or dependent variable) in time.
Theory: An explanation that makes a systematic and logical argument about what is important and why.

Notes

1. Some argue that there are only two levels of explanation – microsocial and macrosocial – and that the microsocial level considers both individual-level characteristics and social interaction in small groups. However, we make a distinction between individual and microsocial levels of explanation because we believe that there is a significant difference in the kinds of theories offered at these two levels,

and because this statement of three levels of explanation is consistent with the discussion of levels of explanation by criminologists such as James Short (1998).

2. Renowned criminologist Edwin Sutherland defined *criminology* as the study of law making, law breaking, and law enforcement (Sutherland et al. 1992: 3).

3. Gibbons (1994: 9–11, 73–76) describes two key criminological questions: "Why do they do it?" and "the rates question." The first question addresses "the origins and development of criminal acts and careers," and the second question addresses "organizations, social systems, social structures, and cultures that produce different rates of behaviors of interest."

References

Akers, Ronald L. and Christine S. Sellers. 2013. *Criminological Theories: Introduction, Evaluation, and Application*. 6th edn. New York: Oxford University Press.

Babbie, Earl. 2013. *The Practice of Social Research*. 13th edn. Belmont, CA: Wadsworth/Cengage Learning.

Bernard, Thomas J., Jeffrey B. Snipes, and Alexander L. Gerould. 2010. *Vold's Theoretical Criminology*. 6th edn. New York: Oxford University Press.

Cloward, Richard A. and Lloyd E. Ohlin. 1960. *Delinquency and Opportunity: A Theory of Delinquent Gangs*. New York: Free Press.

Cohen, Albert K. 1955. *Delinquent Boys: The Culture of the Gang*. New York: Free Press.

Cohen, Albert K. 1966. *Deviance and Control*. Englewood Cliffs, NJ: Prentice Hall.

Cohen, Bernard P. 1980. *Developing Sociological Knowledge: Theory and Method*. Englewood Cliffs, NJ: Prentice Hall.

Curran, Daniel J. and Claire M. Renzetti. 2001. *Theories of Crime*. 2nd edn. Boston: Allyn & Bacon.

Elliott, Delbert S., David Huizinga, and Suzanne S. Ageton. 1985. *Explaining Delinquency and Drug Use*. Beverly Hills, CA: Sage.

Elliott, Delbert S., David Huizinga, and Scott Menard. 1989. *Multiple Problem Youth: Delinquency, Substance Use, and Mental Health Problems*. New York: Springer-Verlag.

Gibbons, Don C. 1994. *Talking About Crime and Criminals: Problems and Issues in Theory Development in Criminology*. Englewood Cliffs, NJ: Prentice Hall.

Gibbons, Don C. and Marvin D. Krohn. 1991. *Delinquent Behavior*. 5th edn. Englewood Cliffs, NJ: Prentice Hall.

Glaser, Barney and Anselm L. Straus. 1967. *The Discovery of Grounded Theory*. Chicago: Aldine.

Glueck, Sheldon and Eleanor Glueck. 1950. *Unraveling Juvenile Delinquency*. Cambridge, MA: Harvard University Press.

Hepburn, John R. 1976. "Testing Alternative Models of Delinquency Causation." *Journal of Criminal Law and Criminology* 67: 450–460.

Hirschi, Travis. 1969. *Causes of Delinquency*. Berkeley, CA: University of California Press.

Hirschi, Travis and Hanan C. Selvin. 1995. *Delinquency Research: An Appraisal of Analytic Methods*. Edison, NJ: Transaction.

Jensen, Gary F. 1972. "Parents, Peers, and Delinquent Action: A Test of the Differential Association Perspective." *American Sociological Review* 78: 562–575.

Laub, John H. and Robert J. Sampson. 1991. "The Sutherland–Glueck Debate: On the Sociology of Criminological Knowledge." *American Journal of Sociology* 96: 1402–1440.

Sampson, Robert J. and John H. Laub. 1993. *Crime in the Making: Pathways and Turning Points Through Life*. Cambridge, MA: Harvard University Press.

Shaw, Clifford R. and Henry D. McKay. 1969. *Juvenile Delinquency and Urban Areas: A Study of Rates of Delinquency in Relation to Differential Characteristics of Local Communities in American Cities*. Rev. edn. University of Chicago Press.

Shoemaker, Donald J. 2010. *Theories of Delinquency: An Examination of Explanations of Delinquent Behavior*. 6th edn. New York: Oxford University Press.

Short, James F., Jr. 1998. "The Level of Explanation Problem Revisited." *Criminology* 36: 3–36.

Stark, Rodney. 2010. *Sociology*. 11th edn. Belmont, CA: Thomson/ Wadsworth.

Stinchcombe, Arthur L. 1968. *Constructing Social Theories*. New York: Harcourt, Brace, and World.

Sutherland, Edwin H., Donald R. Cressey, and David F. Luckenbill. 1992. *Principles of Criminology*. 11th edn. Dix Hills, NY: General Hall.

Turner, Jonathan H. 2003. *The Structure of Sociological Theory*. 7th edn. Belmont, CA: Thomson/ Wadsworth.

Chapter 2

"Juvenile delinquency" and juvenile justice
Origins and transformation

Chapter preview

Topics:

- The social construction of "juvenile delinquency"
- Inventing juvenile justice: institutional responses to juvenile delinquency
- Reforming juvenile justice: transformation of juvenile justice philosophy, policy, and practice
- Legal definitions of "juvenile delinquency"

Terms:

- social constructionist perspective
- *parens patriae*
- positivism
- determinism
- Poor laws
- pauperism
- houses of refuge
- placing-out

- reform schools
- child-saving movement
- rehabilitative ideal
- "best interests of the child"
- due process of law
- balanced and restorative justice
- evidence-based practice
- status offense

Chapter learning objectives

After completing this chapter, students should be able to:

- Identify and understand the major historical developments that led to the social construction of "juvenile delinquency" as a social and legal concept.
- Describe the roots of the juvenile court in nineteenth-century developments such as Poor laws, houses of refuge, placing-out, reform schools, and the child-saving movement.
- Explain the character of the original juvenile court – its philosophy, jurisdiction, and procedures.
- Describe the transformation of juvenile justice thought and practice.
- Identify and describe the two major areas of research that fuel contemporary juvenile justice reform.
- Distinguish four legal classifications of juvenile delinquency.

Case in point: "the stubborn child law"

Deuteronomy 21:18–21 (New International Version, 2011)

[18] If a man has a stubborn and rebellious son who does not obey his father and mother and will not listen to them when they discipline him, [19] his father and mother shall take hold of him and bring him to the elders at the gate of his town. [20] They shall say to the elders, "This son of ours is stubborn and rebellious. He will not obey us. He is a profligate and a drunkard." [21] Then all the men of his town shall stone him to death. You must purge the evil from among you. All Israel will hear of it and be afraid.

In November 1646, the governing body of Massachusetts Bay Colony took these verses almost verbatim and made them into law. The colonial codes of Connecticut, Rhode Island, and New Hampshire followed suit. Though substantially amended, the Massachusetts law remained in effect until 1973 (Sutton 1988).

In his book, *Stubborn Children: Controlling Delinquency in the United States, 1640–1981*, John Sutton (1988: 11–12) points out that "the 'stubborn child law' was legally distinctive in three ways: (1) It defined a special legal obligation that pertained to children, but not to adults; (2) it defined the child's parents as the focus of that obligation; and (3) it established rules to govern when public officials could intervene in the family and what actions they could take." While the "bare words" of these stubborn child laws made it a capital offense for a child to disobey parents, they also "established rules to govern when public officials could intervene in the family and what actions they could take." We will explore this new approach to child misconduct in this chapter.

Juvenile delinquency, as we know it today, is a relatively recent concept. Scholars say that juvenile delinquency was **socially constructed** in order to indicate that the concept is a product of sweeping social, political, economic, and religious changes. This transformation of thought and practice eventually led to a series of legal changes at the end of the nineteenth century that created the legal status of "juvenile delinquent" and a separate legal system that included juvenile courts and reformatories (Schlossman 2005; Tanenhaus 2004; Sutton 1988; Platt 1977). The use of a separate legal status and legal system for juveniles spread rapidly throughout the United States in the early twentieth century. It was not long, however, before the legal philosophy of the juvenile court began to be seriously questioned. Beginning in the 1960s, a series of juvenile justice reforms significantly altered contemporary definitions of juvenile delinquency and practices of juvenile justice (Hellum 1979).

This chapter traces the historical origins and recent transformation of juvenile delinquency as a legal concept. We also consider the associated changes in juvenile justice practices. As our perspectives toward juvenile delinquency have changed, so, too, has our legal response to it. Focusing on this correspondence, this chapter examines the social construction of "juvenile delinquency" and the origins and character of the early juvenile court. We then consider a series of juvenile justice reforms since the 1960s that have resulted in significant redefinition of juvenile delinquency and redirection of juvenile justice practice. Lastly, this chapter describes how juvenile delinquency is defined in statutory law – the legal definition of "juvenile delinquency."

The social construction of "juvenile delinquency"

At least three historical developments led to the social construction of "juvenile delinquency": (1) the "discovery" of childhood and adolescence, (2) the English common law doctrine of *parens patriae*, and (3) the rise of positivist criminology. As a result, the concept of juvenile delinquency came to signify a separate and distinct status for young people, both socially and legally. Sociologists use the concept *status* to refer to the position or rank of a person or group within society, with the position being determined by certain individual or group traits. Juvenile delinquency is a status determined both by age (younger than the legal age of majority) and behavior (actions that violate the law).

The discovery of childhood and adolescence

Today, we take for granted that childhood and adolescence are separate stages in life, unique from other stages. However, in his widely cited book, *Centuries of Childhood*, Philippe Aries (1962) argues that the idea of childhood did not emerge until the Renaissance (roughly 1300–1600), and that far greater age distinctions developed during the Enlightenment (mid-1600s to late 1700s) and Industrial Revolution (1760 to mid-1900s). Using a variety of historical records, he argues that attitudes toward children during the Middle Ages were largely "indifferent" and that treatment of children was often harsh and punitive (Aries 1962; Empey and Stafford 1991; deMause 1974; Illick 1974). This changed in the late sixteenth and seventeenth centuries when the special needs of childhood began to be recognized. For example, Aries (1962) notes that a particular type of dress and literature for children emerged during this period. He goes on to point out that although childhood was established as a separate age category by the seventeenth century, it was not distinguished from adolescence until the late eighteenth century.

Family life and childrearing emerged as matters of great importance in Renaissance society. Numerous treatises and manuals were written in the sixteenth and seventeenth centuries, and many remained popular until the eighteenth century. These manuals instructed parents on how to train their children in the "new morality," involving etiquette, obedience, respect for others, self-control, and modesty. The training tools emphasized in these manuals included supervision, strict discipline, and insistence on decency and modesty. These manuals were clear expressions of a new view of children, childhood, and childrearing: children began to be viewed as innocent and vulnerable, and it was the responsibility of parents to protect their children from the evils of a corrupt world and to train them so that they developed moral character and religious faith and devotion (Empey and Stafford 1991; Sommersville 1982; deMause 1974; Illick 1974; Aries 1962).

At the beginning of the Enlightenment, John Locke (1632–1704) published *Some Thoughts Concerning Education*, a treatise on childrearing that went through 26 editions before 1800 (Aries 1962). He used the term "education" not to refer to the importance of schools, but to stress the importance of training by parents in the form of childrearing practices, especially for purposes of supervision, discipline, and moral training. A later Enlightenment philosopher, Jean-Jacques Rousseau (1712–1778), pointed to the "distinctive human plight" confronted by adolescents during the transition from childhood to adulthood – a plight characterized by moral and sexual tensions (Illick 1974: 318–320; Sommerville 1982). Adolescence is actually one of five stages of development that Rousseau advanced in his controversial book, *Emile* (1762). In this work, Rousseau provided the first systematic consideration of the stages of development, emphasizing how these stages differ and how these differences influence learning and necessitate appropriate educational methods (Kaplan 1984).

The slow discovery of childhood and adolescence was not complete until the Enlightenment, when Rousseau's idea of developmental stages led to a growing awareness of age distinctions across the life course. Ideas about the innocence, vulnerability, and dependence of childhood resulted in an increasing emphasis on the family as the key institution of socialization. Gradually, the view developed that young people require protection, nurture, supervision, discipline, training, and education in order to grow and mature into healthy and productive adults (Sommerville 1982; Degler 1980).

The parens patriae doctrine

The development of the English legal doctrine of *parens patriae* coincided with the discovery of childhood and adolescence. This far-reaching legal doctrine emerged slowly in the late fourteenth and early fifteenth centuries in response to a series of cases heard in English chancery courts (Rendleman 1971; Cogan 1970). The resulting law is referred to as *equity law*. Adopted in the United States as a part of the Anglo-Saxon legal tradition of England, *parens patriae* provided the fundamental legal authority for the idea of juvenile delinquency and the early juvenile court.

The Latin phrase **parens patriae** literally means "parent of the country" (*Oxford English Dictionary* 2015). As a legal doctrine, *parens patriae* vested far-reaching power in the king as supreme ruler and guardian over his land and people.[1] Chancery courts were established to provide just settlements to disputes, but to do so in a way that maintained and extended the king's legal authority and power (Feld 1999; Rendleman 1971). These disputes arose mainly with regard to property rights and inheritance. Attached to this authority, however, was a duty that the king had to his subjects in return for the allegiance paid to him. In practice, this duty was concerned primarily with the social welfare of certain dependent groups. Chancery court cases centered on three dependent groups: children, those who were mentally incompetent, and those in need of charity (Curtis 1976; Cogan 1970). Under *parens patriae*, the king was established as protector and guardian of these dependent classes.

With regard to children, *parens patriae* was applied most extensively to cases in which the guardianship of young children who were heirs to an estate or who had already inherited an estate from a deceased father was at issue (Curtis 1976; Cogan 1970). The primary purpose of *parens patriae* legal authority was to award custody and control of these children and their estates to the government. Gradually the chancery courts extended the doctrine of *parens patriae* to include the general welfare of children; the proper care, custody, and control of children was in the "crown's interests" (Cogan 1970). This included the ability of the courts to assume and exercise parental duties – to act *in loco parentis* – when parents failed to provide for the child's welfare (Feld 1999). Implicit in this doctrine are the developmental concepts of childhood and adolescence in which it is the parents' responsibility to protect, nurture, supervise, discipline, train, and educate children. Ensuring the general welfare of children was a means to maintain the power of the monarchy and the feudal structure of English society (Curtis 1976; Rendleman 1971). It is important to note that the chancery courts did not have jurisdiction over children charged with criminal offenses. Juvenile offenders were handled within the framework of the regular court system. As a result, the *parens patriae* doctrine of equity law "embraced the dependent and not the delinquent child" (Curtis 1976: 899; Rendleman 1971; Fox 1970).

Positivist criminology

To say that juvenile delinquency is socially constructed means that it is a product of prevailing thoughts and perspectives. The two historical developments we have considered so far correspond closely in time and perspective. A third historical development took root somewhat later but had an equally strong influence on the idea of juvenile delinquency. Positivist criminology is an approach to the study of crime that emerged in the last half of the nineteenth century and came to dominate the field of study for most of the twentieth century.

Positivist criminology is based on **positivism** – the use of scientific methods to study crime and delinquency (Beirne and Messerschmidt 2011). The scientific method involves systematic observation, measurement, description, and analysis so that scientists can look for, uncover, and draw conclusions about patterns of crime and delinquency and the individual characteristics of offenders (Feld 1999; Platt 1977; Allen 1964). The scientific approach advanced by positivism assumes that crime and delinquency are caused by identifiable factors. This cause-and-effect relationship is called **determinism**. According to positivism, causal factors can be systematically observed and measured, and causal processes can be analyzed and described. As you can imagine, a variety of casual factors were advanced by social scientists in the late 1800s and early 1900s, such as "feeblemindedness," "moral intemperance," poverty, unemployment, and lack of education. We will consider many of these "causal" factors in later chapters. The prospect of a scientific approach to crime and delinquency quickly became very popular because of the hope it offered to better understand and respond to the problem of delinquency.

Armed with scientific methods to discover the causes of delinquency, positivist criminologists sought to use this understanding to bring about change in juvenile offenders and their social environments. Thus, the scientific methods of positivist criminology had a corresponding emphasis on treatment and rehabilitation, which were thought to be especially appropriate to juvenile delinquency, because children and adolescents, in a developmental sense, are not fully matured, and, if given effective treatment and rehabilitation, they are able to be reformed. "Expanding ideas: key elements of positivist criminology" provides a brief summary of positivist criminology.

Expanding ideas: key elements of positivist criminology

Four key elements make up positivist criminology. These elements provide the foundation for most contemporary theories of delinquency and encourage testing theory through scientific methods of research.

- **Determinism:** Crime and delinquency are products of identifiable forces that may be biological, psychological, or sociological. This cause–effect relationship is called determinism.
- **Positivism:** The use of scientific methods to uncover the causes of delinquency through systematic observation, measurement, description, and analysis of data (Gottfredson and Hirschi 1987).
- **Differentiation and pathology:** Delinquents and criminals are fundamentally different from the average person and these differences are so great that they can be called pathological. Early versions of positivist thought emphasized biological and psychological differences, called *individual pathologies*, while later versions emphasized the *social pathologies* of rapid urbanization and industrialization.
- **The "rehabilitative ideal":** The traditional legal philosophy of the juvenile court that emphasizes assessment of the youth and individualized treatment, rather than determination of guilt and punishment (Feld 1999).

Inventing juvenile justice: institutional responses to juvenile delinquency

The concept of "juvenile delinquency" is a clear expression of these three historical developments: the discovery of childhood and adolescence, the English equity law doctrine of *parens patriae*, and the growing dominance of positivist thought in criminology. As a legal term, however, "juvenile delinquency" is tied to the creation of the first juvenile court. In this section, we trace the evolution of thought and practice that led to the origins of juvenile justice in the United States.

Poor laws, charities, and pauperism

Three social institutions were emphasized in colonial America: family, church, and community. David Rothman (1971: 16) writes:

> Families were to raise their children to respect law and authority, the church was to oversee not only family discipline but adult behavior, and the members of the community were to supervise one another, to detect and correct first signs of deviancy.

When these institutions functioned well, towns were orderly and stable, and deviance was kept in check.

Civic responsibility was also a strong obligation in colonial America. It generated individual and social obligation to the less fortunate in a community, especially the poor. The first colonial **poor laws**, legislated in the latter part of the seventeenth century, stipulated a community obligation to support and "relieve" the poor. However, these local statutes merely stated the obligation, without specifying who should be considered "poor" or what provisions were to be provided to the poor (Rothman 1971). Sharing similar philosophy and purpose with the *parens patriae* doctrine, colonial communities, and later cities and states, soon developed a system for protecting poor children and, if necessary, separating them from their "undeserving parents" (Rendleman 1971: 233; Rothman 1971). This system grew to include laws that regulated the poor, charitable organizations and relief societies, and government-sponsored institutions, especially in urban communities. Poor laws provided legal authority for governmental agencies and authorized private philanthropic agencies to separate poor children from their parents and to apprentice these children to local residents. The apprenticeship system kept relief costs down because the child's labor paid for care, education, and training. However, the overall quality of the care and training was questionable, and, in many cases, apprenticeship was merely a "business proposition" in which the child provided slave labor for a term (Rendleman 1971: 212).

This line of thought led to the widely held belief that poverty, if left unchecked, will produce children with "a future of crime and degradation" – a process known throughout much of the nineteenth century as **pauperism** (Fox 1970: 1189). To ward off the ill effects of pauperism, institutions to help the poor were established. Institutional relief efforts included the almshouse, workhouse, and poor house, which sought to motivate the poor out of poverty by hard work and strict discipline (Fox 1970). However, reformers soon realized that these institutional settings could similarly "pauperize" children by exposing them to adults "addicted to idleness and intemperance" (Rendleman 1971: 214).

Houses of refuge and moral reform

test question

In the first quarter of the nineteenth century, the state's parental authority derived from poor laws and institutional efforts to respond to pauperism became increasingly focused on the plight of urban poor children (Mennel 1973). As an expression of this perspective, the New York House of Refuge was established in 1824 by the Society for the Reformation of Juvenile Delinquents. The House of Refuge dealt both with children who were convicted of crimes and those who were vagrant, but in practice almost all of its children were vagrants from pauper families (Rendleman 1971; Rothman 1971; Fox 1970). **Houses of refuge** soon followed in Boston (1825) and Philadelphia (1828), and "for a quarter of a century the activities of these three institutions defined institutional treatment of juvenile delinquents" (Mennel 1973: 4).

Not every vagrant or delinquent child was committed to a house of refuge – only those who could still be "rescued" were admitted. Thus, the main purpose was to protect the "pre-delinquent" (Fox 1970; Pickett 1969). Little distinction was made between "pauper, vagrant, or criminal children" – all required protection and reform.[2] Reformers were convinced that these children were victims rather than offenders and that they needed to be removed from the corrupting influences of urban poverty (Mennel 1973; Fox 1970). Reformers intended the house of refuge to be a sanctuary or haven where children could be isolated from the destructive forces of poverty and where moral reform could take place (Feld 1999; Mennel 1973).

Houses of refuge were intended to provide moral reform, which involved four basic elements: a daily regimen, strict discipline, education, and work (Rothman 1971). Discipline was strictly enforced, based largely on solitary confinement and corporal punishment (Mennel 1973; Rothman 1971). As "Case in point: a typical day at the New York House of Refuge" reveals, education and work consumed the daily life of children in houses of refuge. School in the early mornings and late at night, both before and after work, was intended not only to provide academic skills and achievement, but also to promote self-discipline and to instill morality and religion. Children in houses of refuge were also expected to work long and hard, doing physical labor and repetitive tasks such as making brass nails, finishing shoes, and wicker work. The labor of children was sometimes contracted to manufacturers to provide revenue for houses of refuge. The apprenticeship system was also used, justified as a means for children to develop occupational skills. Apprenticeships accounted for about 90 percent of the children released each year from houses of refuge. The most common apprenticeship placement for boys was with farmers, whereas for girls, maid service was the only socially acceptable form of indenture (Mennel 1973: 21–23).

Case in point: a typical day at the New York House of Refuge

At sunrise, the children are warned, by the ringing of a bell, to rise from their beds. Each child makes his own bed, and steps forth, on a signal, into the Hall. They then proceed, in perfect order, to the Wash Room. Thence they are marched to parade in the yard, and undergo an examination as to their dress and cleanliness; after which, they attend Morning Prayer. The morning school then commences, where they are occupied in summer, until 7 o'clock. A short intermission is allowed, when the bell rings for breakfast; after which, they proceed to their respective workshops, where they labor until 12 o'clock, when they are called from work, and one hour allowed them for washing and eating dinner. At one, they again commence work and continue at it until five in the afternoon, when the labor of the day terminated. Half an hour is allowed for washing and eating their supper, and at half-past five, they are conducted to the school room where they continue at their studies until 8 o'clock. Evening Prayer is performed by the Superintendent; after which, the children are conducted to their dormitories, which they enter, and are locked up for the night, when perfect silence reigns throughout the establishment. The foregoing is the history of a single day, and will answer for every day in the year, except Sundays, with slight variation during stormy weather, and the short days in winter.

Source: Mennel (1973: 18–19).

The enthusiasm of house of refuge reformers was contagious, and numerous institutions of similar design opened across the United States during the 1840s and 1850s (Rothman 1971). The philosophy and authority for placing children in houses of refuge was derived from the English legal doctrine of *parens patriae*. The doctrine of *parens patriae* was introduced into American law in an 1838 Pennsylvania Supreme Court case called *ex parte Crouse*, in which the commitment of a young girl to a house of refuge was contested. Although this case makes only brief mention of the doctrine, the intent and meaning appears deliberate: under the philosophy and purpose of *parens patriae*, the government is granted legal authority to assume custody (guardianship) and parental responsibility (Curtis 1976; Rendleman 1971; Fox 1970). The Pennsylvania Supreme Court held that parental custody and control of children is a natural, but not absolute right, and if parents fail to properly supervise, train, and educate their children, their rights as parents can be taken over by the state.[3]

Placing-out and orphan trains

Even though houses of refuge continued to open during the 1850s, critics began to argue that, rather than being models of care, houses of refuge had become juvenile prisons, unable to nurture and reform children through an institutional approach (Rothman 1971). Beginning in the 1850s, reformers returned to the traditional belief that family homes, not institutions, were the best places for reform (Mennel 1973). Leading this charge was Charles Loring Brace (1826–1890), who founded the New York Children's Aid Society in 1853. He held that urban poverty bred a "dangerous class," prone to crime and violence. Fueled by this fear, the New York Children's Aid Society sought to "drain the city" of poor and delinquent children through a practice called **placing-out** (Mennel 1973: 37). Placing-out involved taking groups of vagrant children west by railroad, on "orphan trains," for placement with farming families. Brace believed that "the best of all Asylums for the outcast child is the farmer's home … the cultivators of the soil are in America our most solid and intelligent class" (Mennel 1973: 37).

Placing-out was apparently well received in many communities. Reports indicate that community members were excited and willing to take these youths into their homes, whether because of the prospect of free farm labor or a sense of civic obligation. Placing-out programs were soon implemented by other organizations, but they were not without critics. Some saw Brace's unabashed faith in the reforming powers of rural family life as naive. Critics contended that it is next to impossible to take a poor, vagrant child off the streets and expect him or her to adjust to rural family life. The solution, according to these critics, was not to do away with the placing-out program, but to use the institutional setting beforehand for discipline and reform (Mennel 1973). The New York Juvenile Asylum and the Pine Farm facility operated by the Boston Children's Aid Society were based upon this more formal placing-out model.

Reform schools

The development of **reform schools**, beginning in the mid-nineteenth century, represents another way in which institutions were used to respond to the problem of dependency and juvenile crime. As the name implies, reform schools emphasized formal schooling. Instead of sandwiching school around a full day of work as houses of refuge did, reform school operated on a traditional school schedule (Mennel 1973).

Many reform schools used a cottage system in which committed youth were divided into "families" of 40 or fewer. Each family had its own cottage, its own matron and/or patron (mother or father), and its own schedule. Cottages were used to make the facility more like a family and less like a prison. Corrective discipline, rather than physical punishment, was used in an effort to generate conformity and instill good citizenship (Schlossman 2005). Cottage reform schools spread across the United States in the latter half of the 1800s, but the degree of emphasis on the family ideal and the roles of school and work varied greatly. Contract labor of children to manufacturers was a part of most reform schools, but after the Civil War, child labor became more exploitative in some schools (Mennel 1973). In addition, as farming opportunities diminished, training in agriculture provided in some rural reform schools became less marketable as a learned trade. Similarly, changes in the nature of work brought on by the Industrial Revolution meant a significant reduction in apprenticeship opportunities – the means by which most children were released from reform schools. In response to this, some reform schools, especially those in the West, began to emphasize vocational education and to deemphasize a family environment. These programs were oriented toward vocational education and often included military drill and organization (Mennel 1973).

Commitment to reform schools was based on the legal authority of the state, under *parens patriae*, to take over parental custody and control. But this legal authority was challenged and overruled in the Illinois Supreme Court case *O'Connell v. Turner* (1870).[4] The court's opinion directly questioned the state's *parens patriae* authority when protective custody was ordered based solely on the parent's ability to care for and supervise the youth. The court's opinion stressed that parents have a right and responsibility to rear and educate their children that cannot be preempted by the government except under "gross misconduct [by the child] or almost total unfitness on the part of the parents" (Fox 1970: 1219).

The child-saving movement

By the late nineteenth century, little enthusiasm and hope remained for the programs and institutions that had once been heralded as places of protection and reform for vagrant and delinquent children (Mennel 1973). The problems of urban poverty and delinquency persisted and, in fact, grew worse. Forces of industrialization, urbanization, and immigration weakened the cohesiveness of communities and the abilities of communities and families to socialize and control children effectively (Feld 1999).

Despite largely unsuccessful efforts to deal with the growing problem of juvenile delinquency, the late nineteenth century was a time of optimism and renewed effort (Feld 1999;

Krisberg and Austin 1993; Sutton 1988). The **child-saving movement** emerged during this period in an effort to mobilize change in how government dealt with dependent, neglected, and delinquency children. The child-saving movement was comprised almost exclusively of women from middle- and upper-class backgrounds, who formed local groups across the United States.

Scholars have long debated the motives behind the child-savers' reform efforts. Traditional explanations of the child-saving movement emphasize the "noble sentiments and tireless energy of middle class philanthropists" (Platt 1977: 10; Tanenhaus 2004). Another point of view holds that child-savers were progressive reformers seeking to alleviate the problems of urban life and to solve social problems by rational, scientific methods (Platt 1977). Still others argue that the child-saving movement was an effort by the ruling class to repress newly arriving immigrants and the urban poor and to preserve its own way of life (Schlossman 2005; Tanenhaus 2004; Platt 1977; Sutton 1988; Rothman 1971). Putting aside assumptions about their motivation, it is safe to say that child-savers were prominent, influential, philanthropic women, who were "generally well educated, widely traveled, and had access to political and financial resources" (Platt 1977: 77, 83). Additionally, child-savers viewed their work as a humanitarian "moral enterprise," seeking to "strengthen and rebuild the moral fabric of society" (Platt 1977: 75). Child-saving was largely women's work. Women involved in the child-saving movement proclaimed that the domestic role of women made them better suited than men to work with dependent and delinquent children (Platt 1977).

Creation of the juvenile court (1899)

The child-savers in the Chicago area were organized as the Chicago Women's Club, and it is this organization that is largely responsible for the creation of the first juvenile court – a separate legal system for children. The child-savers, however, realized that "child-welfare reform could only be accomplished with the support of political and professional organizations" (Platt 1977: 130–131; Tanenhaus 2004; Mennel 1973). Through collaboration between the Chicago Women's Club, the Chicago Bar Association, and the Illinois Conference of Charities, a bill was introduced to the Illinois House of Representatives in February 1899 and shortly thereafter to the Senate. The bill was passed on April 14, the last day of the session (Krisberg and Austin 1978; Platt 1977). "Case in point: excerpts from 'An Act to Regulate the Treatment and Control of Dependent, Neglected, and Delinquent Children' (1899)" provides particularly relevant sections of the Act.

Case in point: excerpts from "An Act to Regulate the Treatment and Control of Dependent, Neglected, and Delinquent Children" (1899)

Section 1. Definitions. This act shall apply only to children under the age of sixteen years. … For the purposes of this act the words **dependent child and neglected child** shall mean any child who for any reason is destitute or homeless or abandoned; or dependent upon the public for support; or has not proper parental care or guardianship; or who habitually begs or receives alms; or who is found living in any house of ill fame or with a vicious or disreputable person;

or whose home, by reason of neglect, or cruelty or depravity on the part of parents, guardian or other person in whose care it may be, is an unfit place for such a child; and any child under the age of eight years who is found peddling or selling any article or singing or playing any musical instrument upon the streets or giving any public entertainment. The words **delinquent child** shall include any child under the age of sixteen who violates any law of the State or any city or village ordinance. ...

Section 3. Juvenile Court. ...A special courtroom, to be designated as the juvenile courtroom, shall be provided for the hearing of such cases, and the findings of the court shall be entered in a book or books to be kept for that purpose and known as the "Juvenile Record," and the court may, for convenience, be called the "Juvenile Court." ...

Section 7. Dependent and Neglected Children. When any child under the age of sixteen (16) years shall be found to be dependent or neglected within the meaning of this act, the court may make an order committing the child to the care of some suitable State institution, or to the care of some reputable citizen of good moral character, or to the care of some training school or an industrial school, as provided by law, or to the care of some association ... embracing in its objects the purpose of caring or obtaining homes for dependent or neglected children....

Section 9. Disposition of Delinquent Children. In the case of a delinquent child the court may continue the hearing from time to time and may commit the child to the care and guardianship of a probation officer duly appointed by the court and may allow said child to remain in its own home, subject to the visitation of the probation officer; such child to report to the probation officer as often as may be required and subject to be returned to the court for further proceeding, whenever such action may appear to be necessary, or the court may commit the child to the care and guardianship of the probation officer, to be placed in a suitable family home, subject to the friendly supervision of such probation officer, ... or the court may commit the child, if a boy, to a training school for boys, or if a girl, to an industrial school for girls. Or, if the child is found guilty of any criminal offense, and the judge is of the opinion that the best interest requires it, the court may commit the child to any institution within said county ... or may commit the child, if a boy over the age of ten years, to the State reformatory, or if a girl over the age of ten years, to the State Home for Juvenile Female Offenders period to end sentence, then ellipsis: State Home for Juvenile Female Offenders....

> *Source*: National Council of Juvenile and Family Court Judges. 1998. "The Illinois Juvenile Court Act of 1899." *Juvenile and Family Court Journal* 49(4): 1–5.

The Illinois Juvenile Court Act of 1899 did not represent radical reform; rather, it consolidated existing practices (Feld 1999; Sutton 1988; Hellum 1979; Platt 1977). In fact, in the years before the bill was drafted, a number of other states already practiced some of the innovations advanced in the Juvenile Court Act. For example, Massachusetts, in 1874, and New York, in 1892, passed laws that provided for separate trials of minors, apart from adults, and Massachusetts developed a system of juvenile probation in 1846 (Platt 1977; Mennel 1973). Nonetheless, the creation of the juvenile court culminated a century-long evolution of thought and practice by which juveniles were differentiated from adults both in terms of development and control (Feld 1999).[5] The new juvenile court established a separate system that is noteworthy in terms of (1) structure and jurisdiction, (2) legal authority under the expansion of *parens patriae*, and (3) legal philosophy and process.

Structure and jurisdiction of the juvenile court

The Illinois Juvenile Court Act of 1899 was the first statutory provision in the United States to provide for an entirely separate system of juvenile justice. As described in Section 3 of the Act, the juvenile court was made up of a designated judge of the circuit court, a "special courtroom," and separate records. The Act specifically refers to this court as the "Juvenile Court." This new court structure was designed to remove children from the adult criminal justice system and to create special programs for delinquent, dependent, and neglected children (Feld 1999; Sutton 1988; Platt 1977). The personnel that made up the first juvenile court were distinct from the personnel that made up the adult court. A substantial portion of the personnel was police officers and truant officers; as a result, the juvenile court provided its own policing machinery and removed many distinctions between the enforcement and adjudication of laws (Platt 1977). The full title of the legislation that created the juvenile court indicates that the new court was granted jurisdiction over both juvenile delinquents and dependent and neglected children. As such, the juvenile court was deliberately created to have broad jurisdiction over almost all juvenile matters. The Act defined a delinquent child as "any child under the age of sixteen who violates any law of the State or any city or village ordinance." The definition of a dependent and neglected child was much longer and far more sweeping, covering a wide range of conditions from which children must be protected, including homelessness, lack of parental care or guardianship, and parental neglect and abuse.

Taken together, the newly established juvenile court was given broad jurisdiction in all matters of dependency, neglect, and delinquency. Such broad jurisdiction, however, blurred the distinctions among dependent, neglected, and delinquent children. Regardless of the reason for referral, the early juvenile court was ready and willing to step in if parents failed to fulfill their proper function (Tanenhaus 2004; Feld 1999; Platt 1977).

Legal authority: parens patriae

A 1905 Pennsylvania Supreme Court case, *Commonwealth v. Fisher,* expressed the legal authority of the new juvenile court under *parens patriae*:

> To save a child from becoming a criminal, or from continuing in a career of crime … the legislatures surely may provide for the salvation of such a child, if its parents or guardians be unable or unwilling to do so, by bringing it into one of the courts of the state without any process at all, for the purpose of subjecting it to the state's guardianship and protection.[6]

Sections 7 and 9 of the Illinois Juvenile Court Act of 1899 prescribe options for "disposition" – court actions or outcomes in dealing with dependent and neglected children, and with delinquent children. A wide variety of "commitment" options are offered in the statute. Commitment refers to the juvenile court's authority to transfer legal custody of the child from the parents to another person or to a public or private agency when the court finds the parents to be inadequate. Regardless of whether cases were dependency and neglect or delinquency, this statute authorized commitment to a probation officer, a "reputable citizen," a training or industrial school, or a private philanthropic association (Ferdinand 1991; Fox 1970; Platt 1977; Mennel 1973). The variety of commitment options specified in the Act clearly reflected and authorized the *parens patriae* doctrine in the early juvenile court (Feld 1999; Platt 1977).

Legal philosophy and process: the "rehabilitative ideal"

In advocating for the juvenile court, the child-savers sought not only a separate legal system for juveniles, but also a legal philosophy and process that distinguished juvenile courts from adult criminal courts. In a 1909 article in the *Harvard Law Review*, Judge Julian Mack, the second judge of the Chicago Juvenile Court, declared:

> Why is it not just and proper to treat these juvenile offenders as we deal with the neglected children, as a wise and merciful father handles his own child whose errors are not discovered by the authorities? Why is it not the duty of the State, instead of asking merely whether a boy or a girl has committed the specific offense, to find out what he is, physically, mentally, morally, and then if it learns that he is treading the path that leads to criminality, to take him in charge, not so much to punish as to reform, not to degrade but to uplift, not to crush but to develop, not to make him a criminal but a worthy citizen.
>
> (Feld 1999: 4)

Legal scholar Barry Feld (1999) refers to this distinctive legal philosophy of the original juvenile court as the **rehabilitative ideal** because of its emphasis on assessment and reform, rather than the determination of guilt and punishment as in adult criminal courts (see also Platt 1977; Allen 1959, 1964). The rehabilitative ideal is clearly founded on *parens patriae*, giving juvenile courts authority and obligation to assume parental responsibility. Rehabilitation became the focus of the new juvenile court, and procedures were developed to reflect and facilitate this ideal. The early juvenile court's rehabilitative ideal and *parens patriae* authority resulted in at least three distinctive legal procedures: (1) diminished criminal responsibility of juveniles, (2) a child welfare approach operating on the concept of the "best interests of the child," and (3) informal and family-like procedures.

1. **Diminished criminal responsibility of juveniles:** Drawn from the developmental concepts of childhood and adolescence, the early juvenile court held that children and adolescents younger than 16 years of age lacked the capacity to commit crime. This presumption of incapacity acknowledged that young people could not be held legally responsible for their offenses because they lacked physical and mental maturity (Brummer 2002). Viewed in this way, juveniles were not charged with or convicted of criminal offenses, and rehabilitation, not punishment, was the appropriate outcome of the juvenile court process.

2. **A child welfare approach – the "best interests of the child":** The child-savers envisioned the juvenile court as a welfare system, rather than a judicial system (Feld 1999). As a result, the prevailing goal of the juvenile court was to protect, nurture, reform, and regulate the dependent, neglected, and delinquent child. The role of the juvenile court was not to determine guilt or innocence, but to ascertain the character and needs of an offender by analyzing his or her social background so that the court could make a full determination of what was in the "**best interests of the child**" (Feld 1999; Platt 1977). The early juvenile court's intense focus on the individual juvenile offender, rather than the offense, coincides with the rise of positivist criminology in the late nineteenth and early twentieth centuries. Using detailed social histories, the juvenile court sought to uncover the causes of a youth's delinquent behavior and thereby provide a "proper diagnosis" or assessment. This assessment was then used to develop a treatment program that was individualized to the child's needs (Feld 1999; Rothman 1971).[7]

Because the juvenile court was primarily interested in determining the "best interests of the child," based upon a scientific assessment of the "total child," it gave little consideration to the reason for referral – dependency, neglect, or delinquency. The referral offense was merely a symptom that the juvenile court had to assess more thoroughly in order to uncover the child's "real needs" (Feld 1999: 66).

3. **Informal and family-like procedures:** In an effort to bring about the rehabilitative ideal, the original juvenile court discarded the rules of criminal procedure that are part of adult criminal courts. Instead, the juvenile court developed an informal process in which the judge, much like a parent, tried to find out all about the child (Feld 1999). Judge Tuthill, the first judge of the Chicago Juvenile Court, described his approach as follows: "I have always felt, and endeavored to act in each case, as I would were it my own son who was before me in the library at home, charged with some misconduct" (Platt 1977: 144).

The physical setting of the juvenile court was intended to facilitate the rehabilitative ideal. The new juvenile court building that opened in Chicago in 1907 was designed to provide an informal, family-like setting for juvenile court hearings:

> The hearings will be held in a room fitted up as a parlor rather than a court, around a table instead of a bench ... The hearing will be in the nature of a family conference, in which the endeavor will be to impress the child with the fact that his own good is sought alone.
>
> (Platt 1977: 143)

Juvenile court reformers also introduced softened legal terminology in order to avoid reference to the harsh, adversarial process of adult criminal courts (Schlossman 2005; Feld 1999). To initiate the juvenile court process, a petition is filed "in the welfare of the child," whereas the formal legal document that initiates the adult criminal process is an indictment or an information. The proceedings of juvenile courts are referred to as "hearings," instead of trials, as in adult courts. Juvenile courts find youths to be "delinquent," rather than guilty of an offense. Finally, juvenile delinquents are given a "disposition," instead of a sentence, as in adult criminal courts.

The juvenile court was clearly an idea ripe for its time. The Illinois Juvenile Court Act of 1899 was a prototype for legislation in a number of other states, including Wisconsin (1901), New York (1901), Ohio (1902), Maryland (1902), and Colorado (1903) (Platt 1977; Mennel 1973). By 1925, all but two states, Maine and Wyoming, had juvenile court laws. The juvenile justice systems that emerged from legislation were composed of newly created juvenile courts together with a collection of private and public institutions and community programs, all embracing the rehabilitative ideal and empowered by *parens patriae* (Ferdinand 1991).

Reforming juvenile justice: transformation of juvenile justice philosophy, policy, and practice

Although the new juvenile court system proved wildly popular and spread rapidly, it was not without critics. Some scholars argued that the child-saver's rhetoric of reform was never really achieved in the newly created juvenile justice systems across the United States (Krisberg and

Austin 1978, 1993; Platt 1977). They contended that the new juvenile justice systems were even more repressive, punitive, and authoritarian than the earlier child welfare systems that were used in combination with adult criminal courts. In addition, the new juvenile justice systems were given extensive, almost unbridled, authority under the rehabilitative ideal and expanded *parens patriae* (Schlossman 2005; Feld 1999; Fox 1970).

Despite occasional criticism, juvenile courts across the United States achieved high regard in the decades following their creation. The few reports of problems were viewed as "minor imperfections soon to be corrected by a continually improving system" (Hellum 1979: 301). In addition, the confidential records and closed hearings of juvenile courts made them inaccessible and beyond accusation.

Challenges to the traditional juvenile court

Shortly after World War II, criticism of the juvenile court began to mount. In 1946, criminologist Paul Tappan (1946) wrote a widely read and influential article entitled "Treatment without Trial?" Tappan criticized the juvenile court's failure to provide due process of law. **Due process of law** refers to the procedural rights established in the Constitution (especially the Bill of Rights) and extended through appellate court decisions, including procedural rights such as notice of charges, legal counsel, and protection from self-incrimination. Under the guise of the rehabilitative ideal and empowered by *parens patriae*, the procedures of the original juvenile court were informal and family-like, making the rules of criminal procedure inapplicable. Beginning in the 1960s and persisting until the 1980s, legal challenges were mounted against the informalities of the juvenile justice system (Hellum 1979). This movement involved a series of Supreme Court cases that radically altered juvenile justice procedures. The most significant cases will be discussed in the next section.

The 1960s also ushered in empirical challenges to the juvenile justice system (Hellum 1979). Most actively in the 1970s, evaluation research seriously questioned the effectiveness of individualized treatment and rehabilitation (Feld 1999; Ferdinand 1991; Hellum 1979; Lerman 1975; Lipton, Martinson, and Wilks 1975). Although this research considered both juvenile and adult correctional methods, it directed significant attention at the rehabilitative ideal of the juvenile court. In his book, *Radical Non-Intervention*, Edwin Schur (1973) argued for a drastic reduction in the juvenile justice system's reliance on treatment and rehabilitation. Instead, he advocated a "return to the rule of law," involving the reduction of discretionary powers of the juvenile court, diversion of less serious offenders, and intervention for only the most serious crimes.

In the years following these challenges, the juvenile justice system was altered dramatically. Prevailing views of juvenile delinquency and the proper approach to juvenile justice changed significantly. Four areas of change have been most pronounced: (1) the due process revolution, (2) enactment of the Juvenile Justice and Delinquency Prevention Act of 1974, (3) initiatives for punishment and accountability, and (4) contemporary juvenile justice reform and the return to rehabilitation.

The due process revolution in juvenile justice

With the purpose of protection and reform, the rehabilitative ideal of the juvenile court made due process protections given to criminal defendants unnecessary (Feld 1999; Ferdinand 1991). In the ten-year period from 1966 to 1975, however, the U.S. Supreme Court took an activist stand in establishing due process requirements in juvenile justice procedures (Feld 2003). Five U.S. Supreme Court decisions handed down during this period dramatically altered the procedures of traditional juvenile justice systems (see "Expanding ideas: a series of U.S. Supreme Court decisions introduced due process into juvenile justice procedures"). The following case summaries are drawn from an overview of significant Supreme Court cases offered by Melissa Sickmund and Charles Puzzanchera (2014: 89–91) from the National Center for Juvenile Justice. The case details provide insight into the dynamics of legal change occurring during the juvenile due process revolution.

Kent v. United States (1966)[8]

In 1961, while on probation from an earlier case, Morris Kent, age 16, was charged with rape and robbery. Kent confessed to the charges as well as to several similar incidents. Assuming that the District of Columbia juvenile court would consider waiving jurisdiction to the adult system, Kent's attorney filed a motion requesting a hearing on the issue of jurisdiction.

The juvenile court judge did not rule on this motion filed by Kent's attorney. Instead, he entered a motion stating that the court was waiving jurisdiction after making a "full investigation." The judge did not describe the investigation or the grounds for the waiver. Kent was subsequently found guilty in criminal court on six counts of housebreaking and robbery and sentenced to 30 to 90 years in prison.

Kent's lawyer sought to have the criminal indictment dismissed, arguing that the waiver had been invalid. He also appealed the waiver and filed a writ of habeas corpus asking the state to justify Kent's detention. Appellate courts rejected both the appeal and the writ, refused to scrutinize the judge's "investigation," and accepted the waiver as valid. In appealing to the U.S. Supreme Court, Kent's attorney argued that the judge had not made a complete investigation and that Kent was denied constitutional rights simply because he was a minor.

The Court ruled the waiver invalid, stating that Kent was entitled to a hearing that measured up to "the essentials of due process and fair treatment," that Kent's counsel should have had access to all records involved in the waiver, and that the judge should have provided a written statement of the reasons for waiver....

In re Gault (1967)[9]

Gerald Gault, age 15, was on probation in Arizona for a minor property offense when, in 1964, he and a friend made a crank telephone call to an adult neighbor, asking her, "Are your cherries ripe today?" and "Do you have big bombers?" Identified by the neighbor, the youths were arrested and detained.

The victim did not appear at the adjudication hearing, and the court never resolved the issue of whether Gault made the "obscene" remarks. Gault was committed to a training school for the period of his minority. The maximum sentence for an adult would have been a $50 fine or 2 months in jail.

An attorney obtained for Gault after the trial filed a writ of habeas corpus that was eventually heard by the U.S. Supreme Court. The issue presented in the case was that Gault's constitutional rights (to notice of charges, counsel, questioning of witnesses, protection against self-incrimination, a transcript of the proceedings, and appellate review) were denied.

The Court ruled that in hearings that could result in commitment to an institution, juveniles have the right to notice and counsel, to question witnesses, and to protection against self-incrimination. The Court did not rule on a juvenile's right to appellate review or transcripts but encouraged the states to provide those rights. The Court based its ruling on the fact that Gault was being punished rather than helped by the juvenile court. The Court explicitly rejected the doctrine of parens patriae as the founding principle of juvenile justice, describing the concept as murky and of dubious historical relevance. The Court concluded that the handling of Gault's case violated the due process clause of the Fourteenth Amendment: "Juvenile court history has again demonstrated that unbridled discretion, however benevolently motivated, is frequently a poor substitute for principle and procedure."

In re Winship (1970)[10]

Samuel Winship, age 12, was charged with stealing $112 from a woman's purse in a store. A store employee claimed to have seen Winship running from the scene just before the woman noticed the money was missing; others in the store stated that the employee was not in a position to see the money being taken.

Winship was adjudicated delinquent and committed to a training school. New York juvenile courts operated under the civil court standard of "preponderance of evidence." The court agreed with Winship's attorney that there was "reasonable doubt" of Winship's guilt but based its ruling on the "preponderance" of evidence.

Upon appeal to the Supreme Court, the central issue in the case was whether "proof beyond a reasonable doubt" should be considered among the "essentials of due process and fair treatment" required during the adjudicatory stage of the juvenile court process. The Court rejected lower court arguments that juvenile courts were not required to operate on the same standards as adult courts because juvenile courts were designed to "save" rather than to "punish" children. The Court ruled that the "reasonable doubt" standard should be required in all delinquency adjudications.

McKeiver v. Pennsylvania (1971)[11]

Joseph McKeiver, age 16, was charged with robbery, larceny, and receiving stolen goods. He and 20 to 30 other youths allegedly chased 3 youths and took 25 cents from them.

McKeiver met with his attorney for only a few minutes before his adjudicatory hearing. At the hearing, the attorney's request for a jury trial was denied by the court. He was subsequently adjudicated and placed on probation.

The state supreme court cited recent decisions of the U.S. Supreme Court that had attempted to include more due process in juvenile court proceedings without eroding the essential benefits of the juvenile court. The state supreme court affirmed the lower court, arguing that, of all due process rights, trial by jury is most likely to "destroy the traditional character of juvenile proceedings."

The U.S. Supreme Court found that the due process clause of the Fourteenth Amendment did not require jury trials in juvenile court. The impact of the Court's *Gault* and *Winship* decisions was to enhance the procedural requirements in the juvenile court's fact-finding stage. In *McKeiver*, the Court argued that juries are not known to be more accurate than judges in the adjudication stage and could be disruptive to the informal atmosphere of the juvenile court, tending to make it more adversarial.

Breed v. Jones (1975)[12]

In 1970, Gary Jones, age 17, was charged with armed robbery. Jones appeared in Los Angeles juvenile court and was adjudicated delinquent on the original charge and two other robberies.

At the dispositional hearing, the judge waived jurisdiction over the case to criminal court. Counsel for Jones filed a writ of habeas corpus, arguing that the waiver to criminal court violated the double jeopardy clause of the Fifth Amendment. The court denied this petition, saying that Jones had not been tried twice because juvenile adjudication is not a "trial" and does not place a youth in jeopardy.

Upon appeal, the U.S. Supreme Court ruled that adjudication in juvenile court, in which a juvenile is found to have violated a criminal statute, is equivalent to a trial in criminal court. Thus, Jones had been placed in double jeopardy. The Court also specified that jeopardy applies at the adjudication hearing when evidence is first presented. Waiver cannot occur after jeopardy attaches.

Expanding ideas: a series of U.S. Supreme Court decisions introduced due process into juvenile justice procedures

Kent v. United States (1966)	Juvenile courts must provide the "essentials of due process" in transferring juveniles to adult courts.
In re Gault (1967)	In hearings that could result in commitment to an institution, juveniles have basic constitutional rights.
In re Winship (1970)	In delinquency matters, the state must prove its case "beyond a reasonable doubt."
McKeiver v. Pennsylvania (1971)	Jury trials are not constitutionally required in juvenile court hearings.
Breed v. Jones (1975)	Waiver of a juvenile to adult criminal court following adjudication in juvenile court constitutes double jeopardy.

Source: Adapted from Sickmund and Puzzanchera (2014: 90).

In the years that followed, the U.S. Supreme Court continued to hear cases that impacted juvenile justice proceedings, but the number and scope of these cases lessened. Taken together, however, these five cases dramatically changed the character and procedures of juvenile justice. The rehabilitative ideal of the traditional juvenile court, together with its *parens patriae* authority, was diminished, making juvenile courts more like criminal courts. Nonetheless, the due process revolution acknowledged the need for a separate system and the need for a distinctive approach to juvenile crime.

The Juvenile Justice and Delinquency Prevention Act of 1974

The Juvenile Justice and Delinquency Prevention (JJDP) Act of 1974 embodied a series of reforms to redefine juvenile delinquency and to redirect the legal philosophy, authority, and procedures of juvenile justice systems across the United States. Three groups directly influenced these reform efforts: the President's Commission on Law Enforcement and Administration of Justice, the National Council on Crime and Delinquency, and the National Advisory Commission on Criminal Justice Standards and Goals (Howell 1997; Crank 1995).

President's Commission on Law Enforcement and Administration of Justice

Established in 1965 by executive order of President Johnson, the President's Commission on Law Enforcement and Administration of Justice was charged, in part, with the tasks of examining the extent of juvenile crime and the workings of juvenile justice systems and then making recommendations for system improvements. Several of the Commission's recommendations significantly challenged prevailing approaches to juvenile justice. These recommendations included: (1) handle minor offenders in the community instead of juvenile courts through diversion and development of community-based programs that provide a variety of services to youth and families; (2) narrow the jurisdiction of the juvenile court to youth who violate the criminal law, thereby eliminating jurisdiction over non-criminal conduct; (3) limit the use of detention and incarceration; and (4) for serious offenders, implement a more formal and punitive system of juvenile justice (President's Commission 1967c: 27; Crank 1995).

National Council on Crime and Delinquency

In 1966, the President's Commission requested that the National Council on Crime and Delinquency (NCCD) survey state and local correctional agencies and institutions across the United States. The survey showed widespread use of detention facilities for juveniles accused of non-criminal conduct (status offenses, dependency, and neglect), often without court petitions. As a result of the survey, the NCCD recommended that "no child be placed in any detention facility unless he is a delinquent or alleged delinquent and there is substantial probability that he will commit an offense dangerous to himself or the community" (President's Commission 1967b: 211; Howell 1997: 18). The NCCD also recommended that non-criminal youths, including dependent and neglected children, should not be placed in detention facilities or committed to institutions with delinquent offenders.

National Advisory Commission on Criminal Justice Standards and Goals

The third group to marshal reform of juvenile justice systems through the JJDP Act was the National Advisory Commission on Criminal Justice Standards and Goals. Established in 1971, this Commission was created to formulate model criminal and juvenile justice standards, goals, and practices. After extensive study, the Commission concluded that "first priority should be given to preventing juvenile delinquency, to minimizing the involvement of young offenders in the juvenile and criminal justice system, and to reintegrating delinquent and young offenders into the community" (National Advisory Commission 1973: 23; Howell 1997). The National Advisory Commission also recommended that the jurisdiction of the juvenile court should be limited to those juveniles who commit acts that violate criminal laws, and that juveniles accused of delinquent acts should not be detained in facilities in which adult offenders are held.

The message coming from these three groups was consistent: The juvenile justice system is not the panacea the child-savers hoped it would be. The findings and recommendations of these three groups formed the basis for the JJDP Act of 1974. This Act was the first major federal initiative to address juvenile delinquency in a comprehensive manner (Raley 1995). While primary responsibility for juvenile justice had historically existed at the state and local levels, the JJDP Act established a leadership role for the federal government through the creation of the Office of Juvenile Justice and Delinquency Prevention (OJJDP). The JJDP Act established juvenile justice goals and policies and committed ongoing financial assistance to aid their implementation at the state and local levels (Shepherd 1999). The most assertive parts of the JJDP Act sought reform in the use of secure detention in four problematic areas: (1) eliminate the use of detention for status offenders who commit offenses such as running away, truancy, and disregard of parents (incorrigibility); (2) separate detained juveniles from adult offenders being held in jails; (3) remove juveniles from adult jail facilities; and (4) reduce the disproportionate rate of minority confinement (Sickmund and Puzzanchera 2014: 87; Crank 1995).

In addition, the JJDP Act called for a preventive approach to the problem of delinquency, as the name of the Act clearly indicates. OJJDP established a grant program for states and communities to develop policies, practices, and programs directed at delinquency prevention in local areas. Communities were encouraged to develop alternatives to the juvenile justice system that included community-based, diversionary, and non-institutional programs aimed at preventing and controlling juvenile delinquency (Sickmund and Puzzanchera 2014; Krisberg et al. 1986).

The juvenile justice reforms initiated by the JJDP Act of 1974 and carried out by the OJJDP are, in many ways, consistent with the juvenile due process revolution that occurred between 1966 and 1975 (Feld 1999). Both reform efforts questioned the rehabilitative ideal and the *parens patriae* authority of the traditional juvenile justice system. The due process changes made the juvenile justice system more like the adult justice system while still acknowledging the need for a separate system. The JJDP Act sought to refine this separate system of justice for juveniles by initiating reforms that sought to regulate juvenile lockup facilities and procedures and to facilitate a preventive approach to juvenile delinquency.

Getting tough: initiatives for punishment and accountability

The 1980s saw a dramatic shift in juvenile justice law and practice at both the federal and state levels. Attention focused on the identification and control of serious, violent, and chronic offenders (Krisberg et al. 1986). The OJJDP began to sponsor research on chronic, violent offenders and funded state and local programs designed to prevent and control violence and the use of drugs (Wilson and Howell 1993; Krisberg et al. 1986). At the state level, legislatures passed laws to crack down on juvenile crime, reflecting a widespread reconsideration of juvenile justice philosophy, jurisdiction and authority, and a more punitive approach to juveniles. Four areas of legal change have been most pronounced: (1) transfer provisions in state law, (2) enhanced sentencing authority for juvenile courts, (3) reduction in juvenile court confidentiality, and (4) balanced and restorative justice efforts (Sickmund and Puzzanchera 2014: 86; Redding 2008).

Transfer provisions

All states have enacted laws that allow juveniles to be tried in adult criminal courts. Although these statutes vary from state to state, the basic idea is that certain types of offenses and offenders, especially violent ones, are beyond the scope of the juvenile court. Transfer provisions fall into three main categories: judicial waiver, concurrent jurisdiction, and statutory exclusion (Sickmund and Puzzanchera 2014; Kupchik 2006).

- **Judicial waiver:** Juvenile court judges are granted statutory authority to waive juvenile court jurisdiction and transfer cases to adult criminal court. States may use terms other than judicial waiver, including certification, remand, or bind over for criminal prosecution.
- **Concurrent jurisdiction:** Revisions in state statutes give prosecutors authority to file certain types of cases in either juvenile or criminal court. Some state statutes, for example, allow prosecutors, at their discretion, to file felony offenses directly in adult criminal courts.
- **Statutory exclusion:** In some states, statutes exclude certain juvenile offenders and offenses from juvenile court jurisdiction, and these cases originate in criminal rather than juvenile court. For example, a number of state statutes specify that violent felony offenses such as homicide, rape, and robbery, when committed by older adolescents, are automatically sent to adult criminal court.

Although judicial waiver is the oldest and most common transfer provision, almost all states have expanded their statutory provisions for transferring juvenile cases to adult court. In addition, a significant number of states (at least 13) have lowered the age of majority to 15, 16, or 17, thereby limiting juvenile court jurisdiction. Youth of the age of majority automatically have their cases heard in adult criminal courts. These statutory law changes are intended to provide procedures whereby serious cases of juvenile crime may be dealt with in adult courts, rather than juvenile courts, in an effort to deter youthful offenders and to administer punishment, rather than rehabilitation. In practice, these provisions reduce juvenile court jurisdiction and lessen its "rehabilitative ideal." The effectiveness of transfer laws, however, has been seriously questioned both in principle and in research findings. Although the research is not entirely conclusive, findings indicate that transfer laws do not seem to prevent serious juvenile crime, nor do they reduce recidivism of youth that were transferred to criminal court (Redding 2008; McGowan et al. 2007; Kupchik 2006; Myers 2005; Sickmund 2003).

Sentencing authority

A second area of transformation in the 1980s was the enactment of state laws that give both criminal and juvenile courts expanded sentencing options in juvenile cases. This change resulted in a more punitive approach to juvenile delinquency. Traditionally, juvenile court dispositions were individualized and based on the background characteristics of the offender. State sentencing laws allowed the juvenile court judge to customize the disposition to fit the offender's needs and situation, with rehabilitation as the primary goal. As states shifted the purpose of their juvenile justice systems away from rehabilitation and toward punishment, accountability, and public safety, juvenile case dispositions began to be based more on the offense than the offender.

Beginning in the mid-1970s, a number of states changed their statutes to allow for punishment in juvenile court disposition. For example, New York's Juvenile Justice Reform Act of 1976 provided for secure confinement and mandatory treatment of serious juvenile offenders, followed by strict parole standards and intensive supervision upon release. By 1997, at least 16 states had followed New York's lead by adding or modifying laws to require minimum periods of incarceration for certain violent or serious offenders (Sickmund and Puzzanchera 2014).

In recent years, 14 states have adopted "blended sentencing" laws that authorize juvenile courts to impose criminal sanctions on certain juvenile offenders (depending on age and criminal history) or for certain types of offenses. As a result of this statutory law change, the sanctioning powers of juvenile courts in these states have been expanded such that some juvenile offenders may receive the same penalties faced by adult offenders, even when those juvenile offenders stay under the jurisdiction of the juvenile court (Sickmund and Puzzanchera 2014: 105–106).

Confidentiality

A third area of juvenile justice transformation concerns the traditional confidentiality of juvenile justice proceedings and records. Even though the first juvenile court was open to the public, confidentiality became the norm over time. Confidentiality of juvenile court proceedings and records was an operating standard in most states until the latter part of the 1980s. In recent years, most states have provided at least some access to juvenile court hearings, although almost half of the states place limits on such access. In addition, most state legislatures have made significant changes in how information about juvenile offenders is treated by the juvenile justice system. Laws allowing for the release of court records to other justice agencies, social service agencies, schools, victims, and the public have been enacted in most states. These laws also establish the circumstances under which media access is allowed. A number of states also permit or even require the juvenile court to notify school districts about juveniles charged with or convicted of serious or violent crimes (Sickmund and Puzzanchera 2014; Tanenhaus 2004).

Balanced and restorative justice

These initiatives for punishment and accountability have replaced the rehabilitative ideal and *parens patriae* authority of the original juvenile court. Sections of state law that declare the purpose of the juvenile court now speak of holding juveniles accountable to victims and communities, having juveniles accept responsibility for their criminal actions, promoting public safety, and deterring potential offenders. Instead of a primary emphasis on rehabilitation, these "purpose clauses" now seek to promote competency development, with the expectation that delinquent youth become responsible citizens. This new orientation of the juvenile court is referred to as **balanced and restorative justice**, and it emphasizes offender accountability, community safety, and offender competency development (OJJDP 2008; Albert 1998; Bazemore and Umbreit 1997; Freivalds 1996; Bazemore and Umbreit 1994).

In the mid-1990s, one leg of this "balanced" approach began to receive more emphasis than the other two: offender accountability. This emphasis was spearheaded by federal legislation called the Balanced Juvenile Justice and Crime Prevention Act of 1996, an Act that promoted a more punitive approach to juvenile justice. This Act was associated with a large federal grant program, the Juvenile Accountability Block Grants Program (JABG), administered by the OJJDP. States requesting funding were required to demonstrate that their laws, policies, and procedures fulfilled a number of federally specified expectations for a more punitive approach to serious delinquency. States used funds from the JABG program to construct and staff juvenile detention and correctional facilities; to hire judges, prosecutors, defense attorneys, and probation officers; and to develop accountability-based sanctioning programs such as drug courts. In addition, the wording of purpose clauses in many state juvenile court acts was changed to adopt balanced and restorative language, as a means of demonstrating an operating philosophy consistent with the requirements of JABG, thereby making these states eligible for federal funds (Sickmund and Puzzanchera 2014; OJJDP 2008; Danegger et al. 1999; Albert 1998). The wording of the "Declaration of Purpose" of the Montana Youth Court Act reflects this balanced and restorative justice orientation (see "Expanding ideas: purpose clause of the Montana Youth Court Act").

Expanding ideas: purpose clause of the Montana Youth Court Act

41–5–102. Declaration of purpose. The Montana Youth Court Act must be interpreted and construed to effectuate the following express legislative purposes:

(1) to preserve the unity and welfare of the family whenever possible and to provide for the care, protection, and wholesome mental and physical development of a youth coming within the provisions of the Montana Youth Court Act;
(2) to prevent and reduce youth delinquency through a system that does not seek retribution but that provides:
    (a) immediate, consistent, enforceable, and avoidable consequences of youths' actions;
    (b) a program of supervision, care, rehabilitation, detention, competency development, and community protection for youth before they become adult offenders;
    (c) in appropriate cases, restitution as ordered by the youth court; and
    (d) that, whenever removal from the home is necessary, the youth is entitled to maintain ethnic, cultural, or religious heritage whenever appropriate;
(3) to achieve the purposes of subsections 1 and 2 in a family environment whenever possible, separating the youth from the parents only when necessary for the welfare of the youth or for the safety and protection of the community;
(4) to provide judicial procedures in which the parties are ensured a fair, accurate hearing and recognition and enforcement of their constitutional and statutory rights.

Source: Montana Code Annotated 2014.

Contemporary juvenile justice reform: return to rehabilitation

Recent reform efforts have been driven by empirical research that seeks to translate research findings into effective juvenile justice practice. Only in the last decade have researchers been able to clearly identify both the developmental processes associated with delinquent behavior and the interventions that consistently reduce the likelihood of its occurrence (Greenwood 2008: 186; National Research Council 2012, 2013). Research in two principal areas has been applied to juvenile justice reform: adolescent development and evidence-based practice.

A *developmental approach* to juvenile justice reform

The get-tough approach is based on the assumption that many present-day delinquents are more adult-like in their offenses than earlier generations and that contemporary juvenile justice is too lenient to be effective (Grisso and Schwartz 2000; Zimring 1998). In the mid-1990s, this assumption and the get-tough initiatives derived from it were drawn into question. Most influential was the work of the MacArthur Foundation's Research Network on Adolescent Development and Juvenile Justice, a group of national experts on juvenile law and developmental psychology. The Network raised two fundamental questions: (1) Do adolescents have the legal competence to be adjudicated in juvenile courts in the same way that adults are tried in criminal courts, or to be tried as adults in criminal courts? (2) Are adolescents less blameworthy for their criminal acts than adults because of their emotional and psychological immaturity? (MacArthur Foundation 2014a, 2014b).

Research sponsored by the Network found that adolescents differ from adults in ways that make them potentially less blameworthy than adults for their criminal acts and less competent in the legal system (MacArthur Foundation 2014b). More specifically, maturation was found to be associated with increasing cognitive and reasoning skills, including the ability to consider long-term consequences, to control impulses, and to resist peer pressure. Based on these findings, the Network argued that developmental immaturity is a mitigating factor in criminal responsibility, or in their terms, youth are "less guilty by reason of adolescence" (MacArthur Foundation 2014b). Immaturity also makes adolescents less competent to negotiate the legal system. The competence to participate in the legal process and to make reasoned and informed decisions is key to ensuring due process of law, especially when the legal procedures of juvenile courts become increasingly formal and punitive, and state laws expand the options to have juvenile cases tried and sentenced in criminal courts (Grisso and Schwartz 2000). The Network concluded that it is justifiable to consider adolescents to be a "special legal category," and to deal with them through a separate system of justice where they are

> treated as responsible but less blameworthy, and where they … receive less punishment and more rehabilitation and treatment than typical adult offenders. The juvenile system does not excuse youths of their crimes; rather, it acknowledges the development stage and its role in the crimes committed, and punishes appropriately.
>
> (MacArthur Foundation 2014b: 4)

Spurred by the Network's findings and approach to juvenile justice reform, the OJJDP asked the National Research Council to organize a committee to review recent research on adolescent development and then to provide implications of the research for juvenile justice reform (National Research Council 2013). In 2013 the Committee released a lengthy report entitled *Reforming Juvenile Justice: A Developmental Approach*. Their review of the research revealed "important behavioral differences between adults and adolescents with direct bearing on the design and operation of the justice system"[13] (National Research Council 2013: 1). Specifically, the Committee concluded that:

- Adolescents are less able to regulate their own behavior in emotionally charged contexts.
- Adolescents are more sensitive to external influences such as peer pressure and immediate rewards.
- Adolescents show less ability to make judgments and decisions that require future orientation (National Research Council 2012: 2, 2013: 91).

The Committee on Juvenile Justice Reform also observed that research consistently shows that most delinquency does not extend beyond the adolescent years and that only a very small proportion of delinquent youth are involved in violent offenses – most are non-serious offenders. Based on these findings, the Committee concluded that a separate system of justice for juveniles is indeed warranted, but that it needs to be reformed using a developmental approach:

> The overarching goal of the juvenile justice system is to support the positive social development of youths who become involved in the system, and thereby assure the safety of communities. The specific aims of juvenile courts and affiliated agencies are to hold youths accountable for wrongdoing, prevent further offending, and treat youths fairly.
>
> (National Research Council 2012: 3)

"Expanding ideas: guiding principles for juvenile justice reform in a developmental approach" briefly describes these three principles advocated by the Committee on Juvenile Justice Reform: accountability, preventing reoffending, and fairness.

Expanding ideas: guiding principles for juvenile justice reform in a developmental approach

Accountability

- Use the justice system to communicate the message that society expects youths to take responsibility for their actions and the foreseeable consequences of their actions.
- Encourage youths to accept responsibility for admitted or proven wrongdoing, consistent with protecting their legal rights.
- Facilitate constructive involvement of family members in the proceedings to assist youths to accept responsibility and carry out the obligations set by the court.
- Use restitution and community service as instruments of accountability to victims and the community.
- Use confinement sparingly and only when needed to respond to and prevent serious reoffending.
- Avoid collateral consequences of adjudication such as public release of juvenile records that reduce opportunities for a successful transition to a prosocial adult life.

Preventing reoffending

- Use structured risk and need assessment instruments to identify low-risk youths who can be handled less formally in community-based settings, to match youths with specialized treatment, and to target more intensive and expensive interventions toward high-risk youths.
- Use clearly specified interventions rooted in knowledge about adolescent development and tailored to the particular adolescent's needs and social environment.
- Engage the adolescent's family as much as possible and draw on neighborhood resources to foster positive activities, prosocial development, and law-abiding behavior.
- Eliminate interventions that rigorous evaluation research has shown to be ineffective or harmful.
- Keep accurate data on the type and intensity of interventions provided and the results achieved.

Fairness

- Ensure that youths are represented throughout the process by properly trained counsel unless the right is voluntarily and intelligently waived by the youth.
- Ensure that youths are adjudicated only if they are competent to understand the proceedings and assist counsel.
- Facilitate participation by youths in all proceedings.
- Intensify efforts to reduce racial and ethnic disparities, as well as other patterns of unequal treatment, in the administration of juvenile justice.
- Ensure that youths perceive that they have been treated fairly and with dignity.
- Establish and implement evidence-based measures of fairness based on both legal criteria and perceptions of youths, families, and other participants.

> *Source*: National Research Council (2013: 324–325). Reprinted with permission from the National Academies Press, © 2013, National Academy of Sciences.

The implementation of juvenile justice reform using a developmental approach is the focus of an initiative launched by the MacArthur Foundation in 2004 called *Models for Change*. The initiative began by providing grant funding for comprehensive juvenile justice policy and practice reform in four states – Illinois, Louisiana, Pennsylvania, and Washington – that could then serve as models for change in other states. Today, Models for Change (n.d.) promotes and sponsors juvenile justice reform in 35 states, targeting a number of key areas:

- **Juvenile aftercare** that provides support, supervision, and services to delinquent youth after custodial placement.
- **Community-based alternatives** to formal court processing and incarceration.
- Coordinated services to "**dual status youth**" – youth involved in both juvenile justice and child welfare systems.
- **Evidence-based practices**, providing programs and services of proven effectiveness to improve behavior.

- **Juvenile indigent defense** that promotes legal counsel to all youth.
- **Mental health collaboration** that provides mental health services without unnecessary juvenile justice involvement.
- **Racial – ethnic fairness** through "data-driven strategies to reduce racial and ethnic disparities" (Models for Change n.d.).
- **Status offense reform** to divert non-delinquent youth from juvenile justice systems, in an effort to provide effective services and community safety.

Models for Change enables state and local juvenile justice reform by providing grant funding and by encouraging coordination with "action networks," resources centers, and federal agencies such as the OJJDP and the Substance Abuse and Mental Health Services Administration (Models for Change n.d.; National Research Council 2013).

Evidence-based practice

Contemporary juvenile justice reform is also being driven by evaluation research that tries to establish whether delinquency prevention and intervention programs effectively reduce the likelihood of offending. Greenwood and Welsh (2012: 495) summarize this approach: "**Evidence-based practice** involves the use of scientific principles to assess the available evidence on program effectiveness and to develop principles for best practice in any particular field." While we will discuss this important development in Chapter 13 when we take up delinquency prevention, assessment, and early intervention, four key points about evidence-based practice are necessary now (Mihalic and Elliott 2015: McKee and Rapp 2014; National Research Council 2013; Greenwood and Welsh 2012; Vincent, Guy, and Grisso 2012; Lipsey et al. 2010; Drake et al. 2009; Lipsey 2009; Greenwood, 2008).

1. Advances in the criteria and methods for assessing program effectiveness through evaluation research provide a growing body of knowledge on program effectiveness – knowledge that has practical usefulness.
2. Several model program guides offer information on the "best practices" in delinquency prevention and intervention:
   - *Blueprints for Healthy Youth Development*, Center for the Study and Prevention of Violence, University of Colorado Boulder;
   - *Model Program Guide*, Office of Juvenile Justice and Delinquency Prevention;
   - *National Registry of Evidence-based Programs and Practices*, Substance Abuse and Mental Health Services Administration.
3. Evidence-based intervention practices increasingly use risk-need assessment instruments to identify the needs of youth and to determine the likelihood of reoffending.
4. Evidence-based practice increasingly involves identification and measurement of the benefits and costs of programs, including those that occur during and after participation in the program.

Each wave of reform that we have discussed seems to have brought about substantial change in juvenile justice philosophy, policy, and practice. While these changes may be enduring, they are also cumulative, transforming how our society defines and responds to delinquency. We now turn to a brief description of how delinquency is defined in statutory law.

Legal definitions of "juvenile delinquency"

In its zeal to save children, the original juvenile court showed little interest in distinguishing the different types of children that came under its jurisdiction (Platt 1977). The juvenile court assumed broad jurisdiction over not only delinquent offenders, but also dependent and neglected children. Although the Juvenile Court Act provided definitions of delinquent and dependent and neglected children, the primary interest of the early court was to act in the "best interests of the child," regardless of the reason the child came before the court. Put simply, the juvenile court focused on the offender, rather than the offense.

Reformers soon realized, however, that restricting the new juvenile court's definition of delinquency to violations of criminal law would make it function like a criminal court (Feld 1999; Sutton 1988). Within two years of the creation of the original juvenile court, amendments to the Illinois Juvenile Court Act broadened the definition of delinquent to include a youth "who is incorrigible" (Feld 1999; Hawes 1971). Barry Feld (1999: 64) observes that this undefined term "introduced a major element of vagueness, imprecision, and subjectivity into the court's inquiry into a youth's 'condition of delinquency.'" This broadened definition of juvenile delinquency now included behavior that was defined by law as illegal only for juveniles. Such non-criminal but illegal acts by juveniles are commonly called **status offenses.** Status offenses include acts such as running away, truancy, ungovernability, and liquor law violations.

Traditionally, juvenile courts have had two primary areas of jurisdiction: (1) juvenile delinquency, which includes violations of criminal law and status offenses; and (2) dependency, neglect, and child abuse (Rubin 1985). The working assumption behind both areas of jurisdiction has been the rehabilitative ideal, using *parens patriae* authority: if parents are unable or have failed to provide proper care for their children, then the juvenile court can assume parental responsibility in the best interests of the child.

In the early 1960s, criticism began to mount over the juvenile court's broad jurisdiction and its failure to distinguish different types of offenses and offenders. This criticism was most pronounced with regard to the sweeping legal definitions of status offenders in state laws, whereby almost all youth could fall under the attention of the juvenile court. The popular solution was for state legislatures to enact laws that legally distinguished status offenses and offenders from those that violated the criminal law. The intent here was to have juvenile courts deal differently with criminal law offenders and status offenders.

In 1961, the California legislature created a separate section of the juvenile code to specify three different areas of jurisdiction for the juvenile court: (1) dependent and neglected children (non-delinquents), (2) juveniles who violate the state criminal code (delinquents), and (3) juveniles who are beyond parental control or who engage in conduct harmful to themselves (status offenders) (Gibbons and Krohn 1991: 15–16). The following year, New York passed legislation that established a family court system with jurisdiction over all areas of family life. In addition, the legislation established a person in need of supervision (PINS) classification to provide a separate designation for status offenders. This legal separation of status and criminal law offenders allowed the juvenile justice system to approach these two groups differently. Following the lead of New York, statutory law in many states soon provided a separate legal category for status offenders. Various acronyms were used: YINS (youth in need of supervision), MINS (minor in need of supervision), CHINS (children in need of supervision), and JINS (juveniles in need of supervision).

This differentiation between status offenders and juvenile criminal law offenders plays an important role in contemporary trends in juvenile justice. The juvenile due process revolution has been applied most extensively to juvenile criminal offenders. Status offenses are normally handled like dependency and neglect cases in terms of both informal procedures and dispositional provisions for social services. Alternatives to the juvenile justice system, in the form of diversion and deinstitutionalization, have been developed most extensively for use with status offenders, while a more punitive approach to juvenile justice has been applied most frequently to serious, violent juvenile offenders.

The state statutes that define juvenile delinquency are similar in form throughout the United States. Contemporary statutes typically use four legal categories, often with varying names but with similar legal conceptualization: "serious delinquent youth," "delinquent youth," "youth in need of supervision," and "dependent and neglected youth." The statutory definitions for these categories under the Montana Youth Court Act illustrate this legal categorization (see "Expanding ideas: adjudication classifications in the Montana Youth Court Act").

Expanding ideas: adjudication classifications in the Montana Youth Court Act

Youth in need of care means a youth who has been adjudicated or determined, after a hearing, to be or to have been abused, neglected, or abandoned.

Youth in need of intervention means a youth who is adjudicated as a youth and who:

(a) commits an offense prohibited by law that if committed by an adult would not constitute a criminal offense, including but not limited to a youth who:

    (i)   violates any Montana municipal or state law regarding alcoholic beverages;

    (ii) continues to exhibit behavior, including running away from home or habitual truancy, beyond the control of the youth's parents, foster parents, physical custodian, or guardian despite the attempt of the youth's parents, foster parents, physical custodian, or guardian to exert all reasonable efforts to mediate, resolve, or control the youth's behavior; or

(b) has committed any of the acts of a delinquent youth but whom the youth court, in its discretion, chooses to regard as a youth in need of intervention.

Delinquent youth means a youth who is adjudicated under formal proceedings under the Montana Youth Court Act as a youth:

(a) who has committed an offense that, if committed by an adult, would constitute a criminal offense; or

(b) who has been placed on probation as a delinquent youth or a youth in need of intervention and who has violated any condition of probation.

Serious juvenile offender means a youth who has committed an offense that would be considered a felony offense if committed by an adult and that is an offense against a person, an offense against property, or an offense involving dangerous drugs.

Source: Montana Code Annotated 2014. 41-3-102. Definitions (34).
41-5-103. Definitions (51), (11), and (38).

Summary and conclusions

Juvenile delinquency is a socially constructed concept. This means that it is a product of sweeping social, political, economic, and religious changes. Three historical developments laid the foundation for the idea of juvenile delinquency: (1) the discovery of childhood and adolescence as separate and distinct stages of life; (2) the emergence of *parens patriae* in English equity law, which gave legal authority to the state for protective control of children when parents failed to fulfill childrearing responsibilities; and (3) the rise of positivist criminology, which introduced scientific methods to the study and control of crime and delinquency.

The creation of the juvenile court in Chicago in 1899 clearly reflected these historical developments. Reformers envisioned a child welfare system, rather than a judicial system. As a result, the prevailing goal of the early juvenile court was to protect, nurture, reform, and regulate the dependent, neglected, and delinquent child. Because the court was pursuing the "best interests of the child," little distinction was made between types of offenders. The legal tradition of *parens patriae*, together with the rehabilitative ideal, provided the new juvenile court with a distinctive legal philosophy, structure, and process.

The traditional juvenile court came under attack shortly after World War II. Criticism centered on its disregard of due process and its failure to provide effective rehabilitation through individualized treatment. Beginning in the 1960s, at least four areas of transformation have dramatically changed the legal concept of juvenile delinquency and the character of juvenile justice systems across the United States: (1) the juvenile due process revolution from 1966 to 1975; (2) the Juvenile Justice and Delinquency Prevention Act of 1974; (3) a growing emphasis on punishment and accountability in the 1980s and 1990s; and (4) contemporary juvenile justice reform that is driven by empirical research on adolescent development and evidence-based practice, resulting in a return to rehabilitation.

Contemporary legal definitions of juvenile delinquency continue to distinguish juvenile offenders from adult criminals and to provide for a separate system and process of justice. Legal definitions continue to emphasize the dependency of children and adolescents and their need for protection and nurture. In addition, the family unit is affirmed as the key institution of socialization, providing "care, protection, and wholesome mental and physical development of a youth."[14] However, contemporary legal definitions of juvenile delinquency commonly specify at least four different legal classifications of juveniles over which the juvenile court maintains jurisdiction: (1) dependent and neglected children; (2) status offenders, sometimes called "youth in need of intervention" or some variant of that term; (3) delinquent youth who violate the criminal code; and (4) serious delinquent offenders who have committed felony offenses.

Critical-thinking questions

1. How does the "invention" of juvenile delinquency and the juvenile court reflect legal innovations suggested in the stubborn child laws of colonial America? (Refer back to the case that opened the chapter.)
2. What does it mean to say that juvenile delinquency has been socially constructed?
3. How was the creation of the juvenile court a culmination of earlier reforms, such as houses of refuge, placing-out, and reform schools?
4. How did the due process revolution change the character of the juvenile justice system?

5. In what ways does contemporary juvenile justice emphasize accountability?
6. How have recent research findings on adolescent development informed juvenile justice reform efforts?
7. What is evidence-based practice?
8. Distinguish the legal categories: "youth in need of care," "youth in need of intervention," "delinquent youth," and "serious delinquent offender."

Suggested reading

Mennel, Robert M. 1973. *Thorns & Thistles: Juvenile Delinquents in the United States 1825–1940.* Hanover, NH: University Press of New England.

National Research Council. 2012. "Reforming Juvenile Justice: A Developmental Approach." Brief Report. Committee on Law and Justice, Division of Behavioral and Social Sciences and Education. Washington, DC: The National Academies.

Platt, Anthony. 1977. *The Child-Savers: The Invention of Delinquency.* 2nd edn. University of Chicago Press.

Schlossman, Steven. 2005. *Transforming Juvenile Justice: Reform Ideals and Institutional Realities, 1825–1920.* DeKalb, IL: Northern Illinois University Press.

Tanenhaus, Daniel. 2004. *Juvenile Justice in the Making.* New York: Oxford University Press.

Useful websites

For weblinks relevant to this chapter, go to the following sites for further information.

- Blueprints for Healthy Youth Development, Center for the Study and Prevention of Violence at the University of Colorado Boulder (www.blueprintsprograms.com/)
- Model Programs Guide, Office of Juvenile Justice and Delinquency Prevention (www.ojjdp.gov/mpg/Home/About)
- Models for Change: Systems Reform in Juvenile Justice, MacArthur Foundation (www.modelsforchange.net/about/index.html)
- *Montana Code Annotated: Youth Court Act* (www.leg.mt.gov/bills/mca_toc/41_5.htm)
- National Registry of Evidence-based Programs and Practices, Substance Abuse and Mental Health Services Administration (www.samhsa.gov/nrepp)

Glossary of key terms

Balanced and restorative justice: A contemporary orientation in juvenile justice that emphasizes offender accountability, community safety, and offender competency development.

"Best interests of the child": The overarching interest of the traditional juvenile court to assess the needs of the youth and then to seek physical, emotional, mental, and social well-being for that youth through court intervention.

Child-saving movement: A collection of locally organized groups of women from middle- and upper-class backgrounds who mobilized change in how governments dealt with dependent, neglected, and delinquent children. One particular child-saving group, the Chicago Women's Club, was largely responsible for the creation of the first juvenile court in Chicago.

Determinism: A cause–effect relationship. Positivist criminology is based on the assumption that the causes of delinquency can be identified through the use of scientific methods.

Due process of law: Procedural rights established in the Constitution (especially the Bill of Rights) and extended through appellate court decisions. They include procedural rights such as notice of charges, legal counsel, and protection from self-incrimination.

Evidence-based practice: The use of evaluation research to assess evidence on program effectiveness and to derive principles for best practice in the field that is being studied (Greenwood and Welsh 2012: 495).

Houses of refuge: The first institutional facilities in the United States for poor, vagrant children. Both private and public refuges sought to protect and reform the "predelinquent."

Parens patriae: Literally means "parent of the country." Refers to the legal authority of courts to assume parental responsibilities when the natural parents fail to fulfill their duties.

Paupersim: The view, popularly held throughout the nineteenth century, that children growing up in poverty, surrounded by depravity in their neighborhood and family, are destined to lives of crime and degradation.

Placing-out: A practice begun in the mid-1800s in which philanthropic groups took vagrant children West by railroad to be placed in farm families.

Poor laws: Laws enacted in colonial America that established a civic duty of private citizens to "relieve" the poor. Legal authority was also granted for governmental agencies or private relief societies to separate poor children from their "undeserving" parents.

Positivism: The use of scientific methods to study phenomena. These methods include observation, measurement, description, and analysis.

Reform school: In the mid-1800s a new form of institution began to replace houses of refuge. These institutions emphasized education and operated with traditional school schedules. Many reform schools also used a cottage system in which children were grouped into "families" of 40 or fewer.

Rehabilitative ideal: The traditional legal philosophy of the juvenile court, which emphasizes assessment of the youth and individualized treatment rather than determination of guilt and punishment.

Social constructionist perspective: An attempt to understand the many social, political, and economic factors that lead to the development of an idea, concept, or view.

Status offense: An act that is illegal for a juvenile but is not a crime if committed by an adult. Status offenses include acts like running away, truancy, ungovernability, and liquor law violations.

Notes

1. The sovereignty of the king and his extensive power to accomplish his interests are referred to as the "king's prerogative," or "*prerogative Regis*" (Curtis 1976; Cogan 1970).
2. Quoting Mary Carpenter, an English penal reformer (Fox 1970: 1193).
3. *Ex parte Crouse*, 4, Wharton (PA) 9 (1838) at 11 (Krisberg and Austin 1993; Pisciotta 1982; Rendleman 1971; Fox 1970).
4. *People ex rel. O'Connell v. Turner*, 55 Ill. (1870) (Rendleman 1971; Fox 1970).
5. Tanenhaus (2004: xxvii) argues that the new juvenile court was not fully formed when it was created; rather it evolved in "structure, rules, and self conception." Nonetheless the early juvenile court was distinctive in terms of the characteristics discussed here.
6. *Commonwealth v. Fisher*, 213 Pennsylvania 48 (1905).

7. Coinciding with the child welfare approach of the juvenile court is the development of child guidance clinics, first implemented in Chicago as the Juvenile Psychopathic Institute under the direction of William Healy (Krisberg 2005; Tanenhaus 2004; Mennel 1973; Hawes 1971).
8. *Kent v. United States*, 383 U.S. 541, 86 S.Ct. 1045 (1966).
9. *In re Gault*, 387 U.S. 1, 87 S.Ct. 1428 (1967).
10. *In re Winship*, 397 U.S. 358, 90 S.Ct. 1068 (1970).
11. *McKeiver v. Pennsylvania*, 403 U.S. 528, 91 S.Ct. 1976 (1971).
12. *Breed v. Jones*, 421 U.S. 519, 95 S.Ct. 1779 (1975).
13. Reprinted with permission from the National Academies Press, Copyright © 2013, National Academy of Sciences.
14. *Montana Code Annotated* 2014, 41-5-102.

References

Albert, Rodney L. 1998. "Juvenile Accountability Incentive Grants Program." Washington, DC: Office of Juvenile Justice and Delinquency Prevention.

Allen, Francis A. 1959. "Legal Values and the Rehabilitative Ideal." *Journal of Law, Criminology, and Police Science* 50: 226–232.

Allen, Francis A. 1964. *The Borderland of Criminal Justice: Essays in Law and Criminology*. University of Chicago Press.

Aries, Philippe. 1962. *Centuries of Childhood: A Social History of Family Life*. Trans. Robert Baldick. New York: Random House.

Bazemore, Gordon and Mark Umbreit. 1994. "Balanced and Restorative Justice: Program Summary." Washington, DC: Office of Juvenile Justice and Delinquency Prevention.

Bazemore, Gordon and Mark Umbreit. 1997. *Balanced and Restorative Justice for Juveniles: A Framework for Juvenile Justice in the 21st Century*. Washington, DC: Office of Juvenile Justice and Delinquency Prevention.

Beirne, Piers and James Messerschmidt. 2011. *Criminology*. 5th edn. New York: Oxford University Press.

Brummer, Chauncey E. 2002. "Extended Juvenile Jurisdiction: The Best of Both Worlds?" *Arkansas Law Review* 54: 777–822.

Cogan, Neil Howard. 1970. "Juvenile Law, Before and After the Entrance of 'Parens Patriae.'" *South Carolina Law Review* 22: 147–181.

Crank, Kathleen Kositzky. 1995. "The JJDP Mandates: Rationale and Summary." Washington, DC: Office of Juvenile Justice and Delinquency Prevention. Available online at: www.ncjrs.gov/txtfiles/fs-9522.txt

Curtis, George B. 1976. "The Checkered Career of *Parens Patriae*: The State as Parent or Tyrant?" *DePaul Law Review* 25: 895–915.

Danegger, Anna E., Carole E. Cohen, Cheryl D. Hayes, and Gwen A. Holden. 1999. *Juvenile Accountability Incentive Block Grants: Strategic Planning Guide*. Washington, DC: Office of Juvenile Justice and Delinquency Prevention.

Degler, Carl. 1980. *At Odds: Women and the Family in America from the Revolution to the Present*. New York: Oxford University Press.

deMause, Lloyd. 1974. "The Evolution of Childhood." Pp. 1–73 in *The History of Childhood*, ed. Lloyd deMause. New York: Psychohistory Press.

Drake, Elizabeth K., Steve Aos, and Marna G. Miller. 2009. "Evidence-Based Public Policy Options to Reduce Crime and Criminal Justice Costs: Implications for Washington State." *Victims & Offenders* 4: 170–196.

Empey, LaMar T. and Mark C. Stafford. 1991. *American Delinquency: Its Meaning and Construction*. 3rd edn. Belmont, CA: Wadsworth.

Feld, Barry C. 1999. *Bad Kids: Race and the Transformation of the Juvenile Court*. New York: Oxford University Press.

Feld, Barry C. 2003. "The Politics of Race and Juvenile Justice: The 'Due Process Revolution' and the Conservative Reaction." *Justice Quarterly* 20: 765–800.

Ferdinand, Theodore N. 1991. "History Overtakes the Juvenile Justice System." *Crime and Delinquency* 37: 204–224.

Freivalds, Peter. 1996. "Balanced and Restorative Justice Project (BARJ)." Washington, DC: Office of Juvenile Justice and Delinquency Prevention.

Fox, Sanford J. 1970. "Juvenile Justice Reform: An Historical Perspective." *Stanford Law Review* 22: 1187–1239.

Gibbons, Don C. and Marvin D. Krohn. 1991. *Delinquent Behavior.* 5th edn. Englewood Cliffs, NJ: Prentice Hall.

Gottfredson, Michael R. and Travis Hirschi. 1987. "The Positive Tradition." Pp. 9–22 in *Positive Criminology*, ed. Michael Gottfredson and Travis Hirschi. Newbury Park, CA: Sage.

Greenwood, Peter W. 2008. "Prevention and Intervention Programs for Juvenile Offenders." *The Future of Children* 18: 185–210.

Greenwood, Peter W. and Brandon C. Welsh. 2012. "Promoting Evidence-Based Practice in Delinquency Prevention at the State Level: Principles, Progress, and Policy Directions." *Criminology & Public Policy* 11: 493–513.

Grisso, Thomas and Robert G. Schwartz. 2000. "Introduction." Pp. 1–5 in *Youth on Trial: A Developmental Perspective on Juvenile Justice*, ed. Thomas Grisso and Robert G. Schwartz. University of Chicago Press.

Hawes, Joseph. 1971. *Children in Urban Society: Juvenile Delinquency in Nineteenth-Century America.* New York: Oxford University Press.

Hellum, Frank. 1979. "Juvenile Justice: The Second Revolution." *Crime and Delinquency* 25: 299–317.

Howell, James C. 1997. *Juvenile Justice and Youth Violence.* Thousand Oaks, CA: Sage.

Howell, James C. 2009. *Preventing and Reducing Juvenile Delinquency: A Comprehensive Framework.* 2nd edn. Thousand Oaks, CA: Sage.

Illick, Joseph E. 1974. "Child-Rearing in Seventeenth-Century England and America." Pp. 303–350 in *The History of Childhood*, ed. Lloyd deMause. New York: Psychohistory Press.

Kaplan, Louise J. 1984. *Adolescence: The Farewell to Childhood.* New York: Simon & Schuster.

Krisberg, Barry. 2005. *Juvenile Justice: Redeeming Our Children.* Newbury Park, CA: Sage

Krisberg, Barry and James Austin. 1978. "History of the Control and Prevention of Juvenile Delinquency in America." Pp. 7–50 in *The Children of Ishmael: Critical Perspectives on Juvenile Justice*, ed. Barry Krisberg and James Austin. Palo Alto, CA: Mayfield.

Krisberg, Barry and James Austin. 1993. *Reinventing Juvenile Justice.* Newbury Park, CA: Sage.

Krisberg, Barry, Ira M. Schwartz, Paul Litsky, and James Austin. 1986. "The Watershed of Juvenile Justice Reform." *Crime and Delinquency* 32: 5–38.

Kupchik, Aaron. 2006. *Judging Juveniles: Prosecuting Adolescents in Adult and Juvenile Courts.* New York University Press.

Lerman, Paul. 1975. *Community Treatment and Control.* University of Chicago Press.

Lipsey, Mark W. 2009. "The Primary Factors That Characterize Effective Interventions with Juvenile Offenders: A Meta-Analytic Overview." *Victims & Offenders* 4: 124–147.

Lipsey, Mark W. and James C. Howell. 2012. "A Broader View of Evidence-Based Programs Reveals More Options for State Juvenile Justice Systems." *Criminology & Public Policy* 11: 515–523.

Lipsey, Mark W., James C. Howell, Marion R. Kelly, Gabrielle Chapman, and Darin Carver. 2010. *Improving the Effectiveness of Juvenile Justice Programs: A New Perspective on Evidence-Based Practice.* Washington, DC: Center for Juvenile Justice Reform.

Lipton, Douglas, Robert Martinson, and Judith Wilks. 1975. *The Effectiveness of Correctional Treatment.* New York: Praeger.

MacArthur Foundation Research Network on Adolescent Development and Juvenile Justice. 2014a. "Adolescent Legal Competence in Court" (Issue Brief 1). Retrieved October 7, 2014 from: www.adjj.org/downloads/9805issue_brief_1.pdf

MacArthur Foundation Research Network on Adolescent Development and Juvenile Justice. 2014b. "Less Guilty by Reason of Adolescence" (Issue Brief 3). Retrieved October 7, 2014 from: www.adjj. org/downloads/6093issue_brief_3.pdf

McGowan, Angela, Robert Hahn, Akiva Liberman, Alex Crosby, Mindy Fullilove, Robert Johnson, Eve Moscicki, LeShawndra Price, Susan Snyder, Farris Tuma, Jessica Lowy, Peter Briss, Stella Cory, and Glenda Stone, Task Force on Community Preventive Services. 2007. "Effects on Violence of Laws and Policies Facilitating the Transfer of Juveniles from the Juvenile Justice System to the Adult Justice System: A Systematic Review." *American Journal of Preventive Medicine* 32: S7–S28.

McKee, Esther Chao and Lisa Rapp. 2014. "The Current Status of Evidence-Based Practice in Juvenile Justice." *Journal of Evidence-Based Social Work* 11: 308–314.

Mennel, Robert M. 1973. *Thorns & Thistles: Juvenile Delinquents in the United States 1825–1940.* Hanover, NH: University Press of New England.

Mihalic, Sharon F. and Delbert S. Elliott. 2015. "Evidence-based Programs Registry: Blueprints for Healthy Youth Development." *Evaluation and Program Planning* 48: 124–131.

Models for Change. n.d. Webpage. Chicago, IL: John D. and Catherine T. MacArthur Foundation, Juvenile Justice. Retrieved September 25, 2014 from: www.modelsforchange.net/index.html

Myers, David. L. 2005. *Boys Among Men: Trying and Sentencing Juveniles as Adults.* Westport, CT: Praeger.

National Advisory Commission on Criminal Justice Standards and Goals. 1973. *Task Force Report on Corrections* (Standard 22.3). Washington, DC: GPO.

National Research Council. 2012. "Reforming Juvenile Justice: A Developmental Approach." Brief Report. Committee on Law and Justice, Division of Behavioral and Social Sciences and Education. Washington, DC: National Academies Press.

National Research Council. 2013. *Reforming Juvenile Justice: A Developmental Approach*, ed. Richard J. Bonnie, Robert L. Johnson, Betty M. Chemers, and Julie A. Schuck. Committee on Law and Justice, Division of Behavioral and Social Sciences and Education. Washington, DC: National Academies Press.

Office of Juvenile Justice and Delinquency Prevention. 2008. *Juvenile Accountability Block Grants Program: 2005 Report to Congress.* Washington, DC: Office of Juvenile Justice and Delinquency Prevention.

Oxford English Dictionary. 2015. "*parens patriae.*" Retrieved April 16, 2015 from: www.oed.com/

Pickett, Robert S. 1969. *House of Refuge: Origins of Juvenile Reform in New York State, 1815–1857.* Syracuse University Press.

Pisciotta, Alexander W. 1982. "Saving the Children: The Promise and Practice of *Parens Patriae*, 1838–98." *Crime and Delinquency* 28: 410–425.

Platt, Anthony. 1977. *The Child Savers: The Invention of Delinquency.* 2nd edn. University of Chicago Press.

President's Commission on Law Enforcement and Administration of Justice. 1967a. *The Challenge of Crime in a Free Society.* Washington, DC: GPO.

President's Commission on Law Enforcement and Administration of Justice. 1967b. *Task Force Report: Corrections.* Washington, DC: GPO.

President's Commission on Law Enforcement and Administration of Justice. 1967c. *Task Force Report: Juvenile Delinquency and Youth Crime.* Washington, DC: GPO.

Raley, Gordon. 1995. "The JJDP Act: A Second Look." *Juvenile Justice Journal* 2: 11–18.

Redding, Richard E. 2008. "Juvenile Transfer Laws: An Effective Deterrent to Delinquency?" *Juvenile Justice Bulletin.* Washington, DC: Office of Juvenile Justice and Delinquency Prevention.

Rendleman, Douglas R. 1971. "*Parens Patriae*: From Chancery to the Juvenile Court." *South Carolina Law Review* 23: 205–259.

Rothman, David J. 1971. *The Discovery of the Asylum: Social Order and Disorder in the New Republic.* Boston: Little, Brown, and Company.

Rubin, H. Ted. 1985. *Juvenile Justice: Policy, Practice, and Law.* 2nd edn. New York: Random House.

Schlossman, Steven. 2005. *Transforming Juvenile Justice: Reform Ideals and Institutional Realities, 1825–1920.* DeKalb, IL: Northern Illinois University Press.

Schur, Edwin M. 1973. *Radical Non-Intervention: Rethinking the Delinquency Problem.* Englewood Cliffs, NJ: Prentice Hall.

Shepherd, Robert E., Jr. 1999. "The Juvenile Court at 100 Years: A Look Back." *Juvenile Justice* 6: 13–21.

Sickmund, Melissa. 2003. "Juveniles in Court." *Juvenile Offenders and Victims National Report Series.* Washington, DC: Office of Juvenile Justice and Delinquency Prevention.

Sickmund, Melissa and Charles Puzzanchera (eds.). 2014. *Juvenile Offenders and Victims: 2014 National Report.* Pittsburgh, PA: National Center for Juvenile Justice.

Sommerville, John. 1982. *The Rise and Fall of Childhood.* Beverly Hills, CA: Sage.

Sutton, John. 1988. *Stubborn Children: Controlling Delinquency in the United States, 1640–1981.* Berkeley, CA: University of California Press.

Tanenhaus, Daniel. 2004. *Juvenile Justice in the Making.* New York: Oxford University Press.

Tappan, Paul. 1946. "Treatment without Trial?" *Social Problems* 24: 306–311.

Vincent, Gina M., Laura S. Guy, and Thomas Grisso. 2012. "Risk Assessment in Juvenile Justice: A Guidebook for Implementation." Models for Change: System Reform in Juvenile Justice. MacArthur Foundation.

Wilson, John J. and James C. Howell. 1993. *Comprehensive Strategy for Serious, Violent, and Chronic Juvenile Offenders: Program Summary.* Washington, DC: Office of Juvenile Justice and Delinquency Prevention.

Zimring, Franklin E. 1998. *American Youth Violence.* New York: Oxford University Press.

Chapter 3

Measuring delinquency

Chapter preview

Topics:

- Research methods for studying crime and delinquency
- Sources of data on crime and delinquency

Terms:

- survey research
- ethnography
- ecological analysis
- Uniform Crime Reporting program
- cross-sectional survey
- longitudinal survey
- validity
- reliability

Chapter learning objectives

After completing this chapter, students should be able to:

- Describe various research methodologies, including ethnography, ecological analysis, survey research, and analysis of data from various sources.
- Explain what types of information various research methodologies are designed to reveal.
- Identify the strengths and weaknesses of the three major sources of data on crime and delinquency: official records, victimization surveys, and self-report surveys.

Case in point: "Indiana Jones" and the temple of the delinquency data archives

The following excerpt describes how Robert Sampson and John Laub discovered data previously collected by Sheldon and Eleanor Glueck, whose work we describe in this chapter. Sampson and

Laub analyzed these data and published the results of their research in the award-winning book, *Crime in the Making: Pathways and Turning Points through Life*.

Eight years ago we stumbled across ... dusty cartons of data in the basement of the Harvard Law School Library. Originally assembled by Sheldon and Eleanor Glueck of Harvard University, these cartons contained the original case files from their classic study, *Unraveling Juvenile Delinquency* (1950). These data, along with the Gluecks' 18-year follow-up of the 1,000 subjects from *Unraveling*, were given to the Harvard Law School Library in 1972. The Gluecks also gave the library their personal papers, correspondence, books, photographs, and the like. The papers and other items were sorted and fully cataloged as part of the Glueck archive. The cartons of data were simply stored in the subbasement of the library.

We sensed that these data were of immense importance. Yet the obstacles to analyzing them were formidable. For example, the data for the 500 delinquent subjects alone were contained in more than fifty 12-by-15 cartons and seemed nearly impenetrable. How could we possibly recode and computerize these data? Moreover, as we began to sort through the case files, we soon discovered that these were not conventional data. And, as we went on, we found out that the Gluecks themselves were not conventional researchers. Nevertheless, after several years of a true group and institutional effort, we reconstructed a good portion of the Gluecks' data. These data are the major source of information analyzed in this book [*Crime in the Making*].

Source: Sampson and Laub (1993: 1). Reprinted by permission of the publisher copyright © 1993 by the President and Fellows of Harvard College.

The scientific study of delinquency is based on the ability to gather accurate and valid data. However, gathering data that accurately represent the occurrence of delinquency is a persistent problem in criminology. Social scientists have used various research methods to obtain data from a variety of sources, including agencies that constitute the juvenile justice system, victims, and offenders themselves. In this chapter, we explore these research methods and sources of data. We begin with examples of various research methods used to study delinquency, including comparison of offenders and non-offenders, ethnography, ecological analysis, and survey research. We then examine sources of data used to study crime and delinquency, including "official data" and data from victimization and self-report surveys. We also compare these three data sources and discuss the strengths and weaknesses of each, focusing on what each source can really tell us about delinquency.

Research methods for studying crime and delinquency

Social scientists have used a variety of research methods to address questions about crime and delinquency. We examine several of these methods to offer a sense of the richness and complexity of the research enterprise and the extent to which theory determines methodology.

Comparing offenders and non-offenders

Sheldon and Eleanor Glueck conducted research on crime and delinquency for forty years (1930–1970) at Harvard University. They searched for the causes of crime and delinquency and assessed the effectiveness of responses to crime, such as confinement (Laub and Sampson

1988). The Gluecks took an interdisciplinary approach, exploring sociological, psychological, and biological factors that might contribute to delinquency.

The Gluecks are best known for *Unraveling Juvenile Delinquency*, a study of the causes of delinquency conducted in the 1940s and published in 1950. In this study, they matched 500 officially defined "delinquent" boys from two correctional facilities in Massachusetts with a control group of 500 non-delinquent boys from Boston public schools. To determine non-delinquent status, the Gluecks used official record checks and interviews with the boys, parents, teachers, police, and others (Sampson and Laub 1993: 26).[1] Comparing delinquents with a matched control group of non-delinquents offered a unique way to isolate the factors leading to delinquency. Both groups contained only white males between the ages of 10 and 17 who had grown up in lower-class Boston neighborhoods. The two samples were matched case by case on age, ethnicity (birthplace of parents), intelligence, and residence in low-income neighborhoods. Thus, as a result of the study design, involvement in delinquency could not be attributed to gender, age, race, ethnicity, IQ, or residence in low-income areas – factors that were taken into account in the matching procedure. "Research in action: Gluecks' matching of delinquents and non-delinquents" provides an excerpt from *Unraveling Juvenile Delinquency*, which demonstrates how closely delinquents and non-delinquents were matched on national origin, age, and IQ. This thoroughness of matching is one of the remarkable features of the Gluecks' study.

Research in action: Gluecks' matching of delinquents and non-delinquents

The following is an excerpt from Appendix B of *Unraveling Juvenile Delinquency* by Sheldon and Eleanor Glueck (1950: 297). In this Appendix, the Gluecks list all pairs of 500 delinquents and 500 non-delinquents in their classic study, matched on national origin, age, and IQ.

Case Number		National Origin		Age*		Total I.Q.	
Delin- quents	Nondelin- quents	Delinquents	Nondelin- quents	Delin- quents	Nondelin- quents	Delin- quents	Nondelin- quents
1	907	Italian	Italian	15 – 3	15 – 4	77	87
2	831	Irish	Irish	14 – 3	13 – 4	117	120
3	581	Italian	Italian	11 – 9	12 – 11	88	93
4	974	English	Scotch	13 – 6	13 – 10	53	58
5	658	Portuguese	Portuguese	14 – 1	13 – 5	75	87
6	845	Irish	Irish	14 – 9	14 – 4	107	107
7	649	Eng. Can.	Eng. Can.	15 – 3	15 – 11	69	73
8	533	Italian	Italian	12 – 8	12 – 11	91	97
9	700	Italian	Italian	14 – 0	13 – 6	93	100
10	524	Italian	Italian	12 – 7	12 – 11	88	98

*Age is represented by year and month. For example, "15 – 5" is 15 years, 5 months old.

Source: Glueck and Glueck (1950: 297). Reprinted by permission of the publisher © 1950 by the President and Fellows of Harvard College.

From 1939 to 1948, the Gluecks and their research team conducted extensive interviews with the boys in both the delinquent and non-delinquent samples, as well as their parents, teachers, neighbors, and employers. They also gathered information from the records of public and private social service agencies, juvenile courts, probation and parole departments, and correctional institutions. The collection of data from multiple sources was one of the strengths of this research project. A second strength was the collection of data about a wide variety of factors thought to be related to delinquency, including family background and family life, school performance, peer relationships, recreational activities, temperament and personality development, body structures, and history of criminal justice system contacts and sanctions (Glueck and Glueck 1950).

The Gluecks also conducted follow-up research on these samples from 1949 to 1963, when the individuals were adults (Glueck and Glueck 1968). With these extensive data, the Gluecks found that family life was the most important factor distinguishing delinquents from non-delinquents. They also discovered the now readily accepted relationship between age and crime (the decline in offending with age), and the stability of offending over the life course of some offenders (Glueck and Glueck 1950, 1968).

Over the years, the Gluecks' research has been criticized on both methodological and substantive grounds.[2] Despite these problems, the Gluecks were interested in the same research questions that shape current criminological debates, particularly those concerning the relationship between age and crime, the stability of crime over the life course, and the value of longitudinal research (in which information is gathered from the same individuals at more than one point in time). In many respects, the Gluecks' work foreshadowed the central concerns of the discipline of criminology today.[3]

Survey research

Survey research is the most common strategy for collecting data in the study of delinquency. It is based on the simple idea that if you want to know what people do or think, you should ask them. Survey research involves asking a series of questions, through questionnaires or interviews. This involves several stages: selecting a sample of respondents, writing and testing questions to be asked, administering the survey to respondents, coding and analyzing the data gathered, and drawing inferences from the sample to the population from which it was selected. In delinquency research, survey questions cover topics such as family background, school experiences and performance, relationships with peers, leisure activities, attitudes and aspirations, and involvement in delinquency.

For most questions that social scientists address, it is not possible to survey everyone in the population of interest. This approach is time-consuming, costly, and unnecessary. Instead, researchers can survey a carefully selected representative sample – a sample that is similar in terms of social characteristics to the population from which it was drawn. For example, suppose we select a sample of adults in the United States that is 80 percent female and 20 percent male. This sample would not be representative of the U.S. population, which is roughly 52 percent female and 48 percent male. By using representative samples, researchers can make inferences about the behaviors or thoughts of the population of interest based on the survey responses of those in the sample.

As an example, suppose we want to know about the relationship between associations with delinquent peers and youths' own involvement in delinquency. We certainly cannot survey all adolescents in America. But we can select a representative sample of adolescents from across the country, ask them about their own involvement in delinquency and that of their friends, analyze the relationship between the two sets of variables, and then make inferences about the relationship between having delinquent peers and youths' own delinquency for the entire population of adolescents in the United States.

The quality of survey research rests on both accurate sample selection and rigorous data analysis. Researchers use a variety of techniques to analyze survey data. Designing the analysis includes three steps: stating hypotheses to test, choosing specific measures or survey questions to use in those tests, and selecting appropriate statistical methods to analyze the data.

Given the complexity of survey research, many sources of error exist in survey analysis. These sources include sample selection, survey questions, interviewers, the coding and entry of data, and data analysis (Fowler and Mangione 1990). For example, the way in which a sample is selected, its size, and the refusal of some individuals included in the sample to participate in the survey or to answer specific questions are all sources of error. Respondents' faulty recollection, misunderstanding of survey questions, and unwillingness to provide accurate answers to some questions also produce error in surveys. For surveys administered through interviews, the interviewers are a potential source of error. For example, they might misread questions or inaccurately record answers. Finally, errors can occur when survey data are incorrectly coded or entered into computer files, and when researchers incorrectly analyze the data or inaccurately interpret their findings.

For decades, criminologists have used surveys to gather information about the frequency and distribution of delinquency and the causes and correlates of offending. We offer two examples of survey research by noted criminologists to provide a sense of how survey analysis is conducted and what it can tell us about delinquency.

The National Youth Survey

Delbert Elliott and his colleagues began the National Youth Survey (NYS) in 1976. This survey was designed to provide a comprehensive assessment of the prevalence and frequency of delinquency and drug use among young people in America. The NYS involved a nationally representative sample of youths who were 11 to 17 years old in 1976, when the study began. Of the original sample of 2,360 youths, 1,725 (or 73 percent) agreed to participate in the study and completed interviews in the first round or "wave" of data collection in 1977 (Elliott, Huizinga, and Ageton 1985: 92). The NYS gathered seven waves of data from the same respondents from 1977 to 1987. Researchers used face-to-face interviews to gather data. In addition to demographic information about respondents, such as age, race, and gender, the survey gathered extensive information about respondents' alcohol and drug use, involvement in delinquency (both minor and serious), and social psychological characteristics. Given the availability of data from the same respondents at multiple points in time, researchers have used NYS data extensively to examine issues of causal ordering and the ability of theoretical variables of interest to predict later drug use and delinquency. "Research in action: the National Youth Survey" describes the NYS in greater detail and provides examples of questions from the survey.

Research in action: the National Youth Survey

The National Youth Survey (NYS) was designed to offer researchers a better understanding of youths' conventional and delinquent behaviors. The NYS contains data on self-reported delinquency and victimization, drug and alcohol use, exposure to delinquent peers, attitudes toward deviance, labeling, family background, parental discipline, parental aspirations for youth, disruptive events in the home, school and work status, community involvement, and perceptions of neighborhood problems, including crime. The following are some of the questions asked in the third wave of NYS data collection.

"Normlessness"

Responses on a five-point scale ranging from "strongly agree" to "strongly disagree."

1. It's important to be honest with your parents, even if they become upset or you get punished.
2. To stay out of trouble, it is sometimes necessary to lie to teachers.
3. Making a good impression is more important than telling the truth to friends.
4. It's okay to lie if it keeps your friends out of trouble.
5. You have to be willing to break some rules if you want to be popular with your friends.

Attitudes toward deviance

Responses on a four-point scale ranging from "very wrong" to "not wrong at all." How wrong is it for someone your age to …

1. Cheat on school tests?
2. Purposely damage or destroy property that does not belong to him or her?
3. Break into a vehicle or building to steal something?
4. Get drunk once in a while?

Exposure to delinquent peers

Responses on a five-point scale ranging from "all of them" to "none of them." Think of your friends. During the last year how many of them have …

1. Cheated on school tests?
2. Used marijuana or hashish?
3. Stolen something worth more than $50?
4. Suggested you do something that was against the law?
5. Gotten drunk once in a while?

Self-reported delinquency

Respondents were asked for their "best estimate of the exact number of times" they had done each of several behaviors during the past year. They were asked about 47 behaviors, not all of which were delinquent. How many times in the last year have you …

1. Purposely damaged or destroyed property belonging to a school?
2. Stolen or tried to steal a motor vehicle, such as a car or motorcycle?

3. Stolen or tried to steal something worth more than $50?
4. Run away from home?
5. Lied about your age to gain entrance or to purchase something, for example, lying about your age to buy liquor or get into a movie?
6. Carried a hidden weapon other than a plain pocket knife?
7. Attacked someone with the idea of seriously hurting or killing him or her?
8. Had sexual intercourse with a person of the opposite sex?
9. Been involved in gang fights?
10. Hit or threatened to hit other students?
11. Sold hard drugs such as heroin, cocaine, and LSD?
12. Used force or strong-arm methods to get money or things from a teacher or other adult at school?

Source: Elliott (1988).

The Community Survey of the Project on Human Development in Chicago Neighborhoods

The Community Survey, begun in 1994, is part of the Project on Human Development in Chicago Neighborhoods (PHDCN).[4] In the Community Survey, researchers divided Chicago into 343 neighborhoods and interviewed 8,782 residents of those neighborhoods (Sampson, Raudenbush, Earls 1997). The goal of the survey was to gather information about the social, economic, organizational, and political structures of Chicago neighborhoods. Respondents were interviewed about a variety of neighborhood factors, including neighborhood cohesion, informal social control, social disorder, availability of programs and services, organizational involvement, and criminal victimization of residents. (See Chapter 11 for a detailed description of the PHDCN and research findings derived from it.)

To analyze data from the Community Survey, researchers have used sophisticated statistical techniques that allow them to examine multiple levels of analysis simultaneously. Many questions of interest to them concern differences across neighborhoods, rather than differences among individuals who reside in a particular neighborhood. Because of the way the survey sample was selected and data were gathered, Community Survey researchers have been able to address these complex questions. For example, in one study, researchers asked: To what extent do informal social control and social cohesion vary across neighborhoods, and how are these characteristics related to neighborhood crime rates? In their multilevel analysis, they examined variation in social control and cohesion *across* neighborhoods and across individuals *within* neighborhoods (Sampson et al. 1997).

Ethnography

Field research has been described as "simply going where the action is and observing it." That is what ethnographers do. **Ethnography** is a form of field study that involves direct, systematic observation of social behavior. Ethnographers typically immerse themselves as participants in the social system they are studying, take extensive field notes about interactions they observe or participate in, often conduct in-depth interviews with key participants in the social system, and then offer a detailed, descriptive analysis of that system. When field studies involve active participation by the researcher, they are called *participant observation*. Elijah Anderson

(1997: 4) describes how ethnographers try to illuminate the social and cultural dynamics of the settings they study by answering questions such as how participants in a particular setting perceive the situation, what assumptions they make, and what consequences result from their choices and behaviors in the setting.

Ethnographic studies are typically based on sustained interactions between the researcher and those whom he or she is studying – interactions that last several months or possibly even years. Participant observation, the primary ethnographic research tool:

> implies that the researcher is closely associated with the daily activities of the subjects under study and is in a position to observe the events involving these subjects as they naturally occur. If enough time is spent in the field there should be sufficient data to establish a pattern that provides an understanding of how, why, and under what conditions certain events (including criminal events) have taken place.
>
> (Jankowski 1995: 81)

The great value of ethnography lies in its description of a particular phenomenon as it truly exists. The artificial qualities of experiments or surveys, for example, are stripped away in ethnographic research. Environments and "subjects" are not controlled or manipulated by the researcher; the ethnographer simply provides a detailed account of naturally occurring interactions and social processes. Ethnography also allows researchers, through direct participation in particular settings, to understand more fully the meanings and definitions shared by participants in those settings that motivate their behavior. The researcher's vantage point from within the setting being studied is the hallmark and primary strength of ethnographic research.

The major drawback to ethnographic research is that everything the ethnographer describes is viewed through the lens of his or her perceptions and subjectivity. When conducting their research, ethnographers must try to set aside their own values and assumptions, and be as objective as possible in describing and analyzing what they see. Although it is often difficult to recognize the influence of one's own assumptions, the quality of ethnographic research depends on the researcher's ability to identify and override those assumptions and to offer a bias-free account of the situation (Anderson 1997).

Another drawback of ethnography is that, because of the amount of time this type of research requires, it is difficult for researchers to observe or interview more than a small number of individuals (Agnew and Brezina 2012). In addition, an observer or interviewer may affect the behavior and ideas of research subjects or even the events that transpire. For example, a researcher studying the functions of violence in gang life might find gang members disinclined to carry out violent acts in his or her presence.

Social scientists have used ethnographic techniques to address diverse questions in the field of criminology. Some have conducted ethnographic studies of street gangs (e.g., Tapia 2014; Totten 2012; Garot 2007; Decker 2001; Venkatesh 1997). Scott Decker (2001), for example, used interviews and direct observations over a three-year period to explore the functions and normative character of gang violence.[5] (See Chapter 10 for a discussion of gangs and Decker's research.)

Elijah Anderson's research is an excellent example of ethnography. He used participant observation and in-depth interviews over a four-year period to explore youth violence in the inner city (Anderson 1997, 1998, 1999). Alienation from social institutions, including the criminal justice system, is common in the context of persistent poverty and deprivation.

Anderson discovered that, for some people living in the most impoverished, crime-ridden areas of the inner city, the "code of the street" – a kind of "people's law" – has replaced the authority of civil law as the standard for acceptable behavior. Particularly for young people, this code or set of informal rules governs behavior, especially concerning the use of violence. In this system of street justice, one gains respect through the display of "nerve," which represents the threat of vengeance for aggression or disrespect. Possession of respect, in turn, shields an individual from violent victimization. Thus the code of the street both fosters and requires violence in some inner–city neighborhoods.

Ecological analysis

Clifford Shaw and Henry McKay used police and juvenile court records to study the ecological distribution of delinquent behavior – the way delinquency rates varied across a city (Shaw and McKay 1931, 1969; Shaw et al. 1929). They were interested in how juvenile delinquents (officially defined) were geographically distributed across the city of Chicago and in the social conditions that characterized areas with high delinquency rates.

To study these issues, Shaw and McKay conducted **ecological analysis** of the geographic distribution of delinquency. They gathered data on approximately 60,000 male delinquents from juvenile court and police records for several time periods from 1900 to 1933 (Shaw and McKay 1969: Chapter 3). Then they plotted the home address of each delinquent on a map of Chicago and observed that delinquency was concentrated in or near areas zoned industrial or commercial.

Shaw and McKay (1969) divided Chicago into 140 "square-mile areas." For each of these areas, they gathered information about community characteristics, including population change, percentage of families receiving government aid, median rent, home ownership, and percentage of immigrant and African American residents. Shaw and McKay then examined the relationship between delinquency rates and community characteristics in each of the 140 square-mile areas. They discovered that delinquency rates were highest in areas characterized by decreasing populations, low rents, high percentages of families receiving government aid, and high percentages of "foreign born" residents (Shaw and McKay 1969: Chapter 6). Shaw and McKay also discovered that delinquency rates in these areas were stable over time, despite population turnover.

The strength of Shaw and McKay's work is that it focused attention on previously neglected community-level factors that contribute to delinquency. By exploring the social characteristics of communities associated with high rates of delinquency, Shaw and McKay literally brought a different level of understanding to the issue of delinquent behavior.

The primary weakness of their work, however, is that it rests on data from police and juvenile court records. Shaw and McKay (1969: 43) defined a male juvenile delinquent as a boy under the age of 17 who was brought before the juvenile court (or another court having jurisdiction) on a delinquency petition, or whose case was disposed of without a court appearance. But as we discuss later in this chapter, not all delinquents are known to police, so official records do not represent all youths who have violated the law. Furthermore, official responses to delinquency vary by class and race – a fact that may have contributed to Shaw and McKay's findings of higher delinquency rates in impoverished, immigrant, and African American neighborhoods. Despite the drawbacks of official data, they represented the best information available for addressing the questions that interested Shaw and McKay.

Contemporary ecological analysis

Criminologist Robert Sampson has led a resurgence of interest in ecological analysis and the study of community-level factors that contribute to high crime rates in some areas (e.g., Sampson 1985, 1988, 2001, 2002, 2006; Sampson and Raudenbush 2004; Sampson et al. 1997; Sampson and Groves 1989; Byrne and Sampson 1986).[6] According to Sampson (1988), a basic assumption of ecological analysis is that social systems, such as neighborhoods, have qualities that exist apart from the characteristics of individuals who constitute those social systems. In several articles, Sampson and his colleagues have used neighborhoods, rather than individuals, as the unit of analysis, and have explored the structural characteristics of communities that are associated with high crime rates.

For example, Sampson (1986) explored the effect of neighborhood family structure (the percentage of households in the neighborhood that are affected by divorce or separation, headed by a woman, or occupied by a single individual) on victimization rates. The reasoning is that family dissolution undermines informal social control, and single-individual households impair guardianship and create increased opportunities for crime. Results indicated that neighborhood family structure strongly affected the risk of victimization. In a separate study, Sampson (1985) examined the relationship between a variety of neighborhood characteristics – unemployment, income inequality, racial composition, residential mobility, population density, and family structure – and rates of criminal victimization. He found that residential mobility, population density, and neighborhood family structure had strong effects on victimization rates.

In more recent work, Sampson and his colleagues examined the community characteristic of collective efficacy (a combination of neighborhood cohesion and informal social control) and its association with violent crime and victimization rates (Sampson et al. 1997; see also Sampson 2001, 2006; Morenoff, Sampson, and Raudenbush 2001; Sampson, Morenoff, and Earls 1999). They found that collective efficacy, measured at the neighborhood level, was negatively related to violence.

Sampson's influential studies, like those of Shaw and McKay, illustrate the value of using communities, rather than individuals, as the unit of analysis. The structural characteristics and dynamics of communities exert powerful influences on the individuals who reside in them. Ecological analysis captures those influences, missed in individual-level research.

Sources of data on crime and delinquency

Data on crime and delinquency come primarily from three sources: "official" records maintained by law enforcement agencies and courts, surveys of individuals who have been victims of crime, and surveys of individuals who self-report involvement in offending. We discuss each of these, comparing the data gathered from these sources, and considering the strengths and weaknesses of each type of data.

"Official data"

"Official data" on juvenile delinquency are gathered by governmental agencies within the criminal justice system. These data reveal the extent of delinquency with which these agencies deal and the characteristics of offenses and offenders they encounter. The two primary sources of official data on delinquency are the Uniform Crime Reporting program and Juvenile Court Statistics.

Uniform Crime Reporting program

The **Uniform Crime Reporting (UCR) program** was begun by the Federal Bureau of Investigation (FBI) in 1930. The UCR program includes "more than 18,000 city, university and college, county, state, tribal, and federal law enforcement agencies voluntarily reporting data on crimes brought to their attention" (FBI 2014). Although participation is voluntary, the vast majority of law enforcement agencies in the United States report crime data to the FBI as part of the UCR program. In 2013, participating agencies represented 98 percent of the total U.S. population (FBI 2014). As the program title implies, the UCR provides uniformity in crime reporting by requiring law enforcement agencies to use standardized offense definitions. In this way, variation in local statutes does not affect the nature or extent of offenses reported.

Offenses included in the UCR are divided into two categories: Part I and Part II offenses. Part I offenses include the violent crimes of murder and non-negligent manslaughter, forcible rape, robbery, and aggravated assault, and the property crimes of burglary, larceny-theft, motor vehicle theft, and arson. Part II offenses include all other criminal and delinquent acts. See Table 3.1 for a list of UCR Part II offenses. Data on both Part I and Part II offenses are gathered and submitted to the FBI on a monthly basis.

The UCR includes primarily four types of information: offenses known to law enforcement, crimes cleared, persons arrested, and police employee data (e.g., number of law enforcement employees throughout the United States). Offenses known to law enforcement are those reported by victims, witnesses, or other sources, or discovered by police officers. "Crimes cleared" are distinct from "offenses known to law enforcement." Crimes are cleared

Table 3.1 Uniform Crime Reporting program Part II offenses

- Simple assaults
- Forgery and counterfeiting
- Fraud
- Embezzlement
- Stolen property offenses (buying, receiving, possessing)
- Vandalism
- Weapons offenses (carrying, possessing, etc.)
- Prostitution and commercialized vice
- Sex offenses (except forcible rape, prostitution, and commercialized vice)
- Drug abuse violations
- Gambling
- Offenses against the family and children (non-violent acts by a family member, such as non-support, neglect, or desertion)
- Driving under the influence
- Liquor law violations
- Drunkenness
- Disorderly conduct
- Vagrancy
- All other offenses ("All violations of state or local laws not specifically identified as Part I or Part II offenses, except traffic violations.")
- Suspicion
- Curfew and loitering law violations (persons under age 18)
- Runaways (persons under age 18)

Source: Federal Bureau of Investigation (2014).

in one of two ways: (1) by arrest of at least one person, who is charged with committing an offense and turned over to the court for prosecution; or (2) by exceptional means when a factor beyond law enforcement control prevents the agency from arresting and formally charging an offender (e.g., death of the offender, or refusal of the victim to cooperate with prosecution after an offender has been identified) (FBI 2014). A law enforcement agency may clear multiple crimes with the arrest of one individual, or it may clear one crime with the arrest of many individuals. In 2013, the nationwide clearance rate was 48 percent for Part I violent crimes and 20 percent for Part I property crimes (FBI 2014). Clearance rates are higher for violent crimes than for property crimes because violent crimes are typically more vigorously investigated than property crimes, and because victims or witnesses of violent crimes often identify the offenders.

For juvenile offenders, a clearance by arrest is recorded "when an offender under the age of 18 is cited to appear in juvenile court or before other juvenile authorities," even though a physical arrest may not have occurred (FBI 2014). The UCR reveals that, in 2013, juvenile offenders accounted for 9 percent of clearances for Part I violent crimes and 11 percent of those for Part I property crimes (FBI 2014).

The third type of data in the UCR is information about persons arrested, such as age, gender, and race. The UCR provides extensive data on crimes committed by various subgroups based on offender characteristics. For example, the UCR presents data separately on offenses committed by juveniles (those under the age of 18) and adults. It also presents data separately for males and females and for different racial and ethnic groups. The total number of persons arrested does not equal the total number of persons who have committed crimes, but rather only the number apprehended by law enforcement personnel. In addition, the number of persons arrested does not equal the number of arrests, because an individual offender may be arrested for multiple crimes. For arrested offenders who have committed multiple Part I crimes, only the most serious offense is recorded in the UCR. This is another reason why the actual amount of crime committed in the United States is higher than the amount revealed by the UCR.

The Bureau of Justice Statistics (BJS) has developed estimates of the total number of arrests nationally, based on UCR arrest statistics (BJS n.d.). These estimates adjust the UCR arrest numbers to take into consideration the size of the population served by each law enforcement agency that reports data to the FBI. The BJS estimates are higher than the number of arrests shown in UCR data. The *Statistical Briefing Book* presented by the Office of Juvenile Justice and Delinquency Prevention (OJJDP) provides extensive estimated arrest data for juvenile offenders (OJJDP 2014).

Redesign of the UCR program

In the early 1980s, law enforcement agencies called for evaluation and modernization of the UCR program. The result was a new UCR program called the National Incident-Based Reporting System (NIBRS). The NIBRS offers detailed information about criminal incidents, including when and where an incident occurred, the type and value of property stolen, the relationship between victim and offender, and the age, gender, and race of both offender and victim. The major differences between the original UCR program and the NIBRS are the greater detail and larger number of offenses included in the NIBRS and the inclusion in the NIBRS of all Part I offenses occurring in a single incident (compared to the UCR, which records only the most serious offense per incident) (FBI 2011).

Strengths of UCR data

The UCR program provides uniform, nationwide data about crime and delinquency. The FBI ensures that law enforcement agencies across the country use consistent definitions and procedures for reporting crimes as part of the UCR program. This uniformity, combined with the nationwide scope of the program, allows researchers to compare crime statistics across jurisdictions and examine the nature and extent of crime for the nation as a whole. Because the UCR program has been in existence for more than 80 years, researchers are also able to use UCR data to explore trends in crime rates over time. Another strength of the UCR program is that it offers information about the demographic characteristics of arrested offenders (age, gender, and race).

Weaknesses of UCR data

The most important weakness of UCR data is the vast number of offenses not included in official statistics. Surveys of crime victims indicate that more than half of the violent and property crime victimizations that occur annually in the United States are not reported to police (Truman and Langton 2014). The majority of offenses are not known to law enforcement and therefore not included in official statistics. In addition, a strong relationship exists between the seriousness of an offense and the likelihood that it will be cleared through an arrest. The less serious the offense, the more likely that it will be excluded from official data. So-called victimless offenses (e.g., drug abuse violations and prostitution) are particularly likely to go unreported to police and thus be excluded from UCR data.

A second weakness of UCR data concerns the effects of policing practices on official statistics. The criteria that influence arrest decisions may vary among law enforcement agencies and within agencies over time. For example, an agency might decide to "crack down" on prostitution, and conduct operations that result in an increased number of vice arrests. Yet this increase does not mean that prostitution has increased in that jurisdiction, or that it is necessarily a greater problem there than in other jurisdictions that show fewer arrests for prostitution. Rather, the increase in arrests reflects only changes in policing practices.

A related criticism is that the criteria governing arrest decisions vary for different segments of the population. For example, race discrimination in the arrest process is well documented and indicates that, for committing the same crimes, blacks are more likely than whites to be arrested (Tapia 2011; Tonry 2010; Beckett et al. 2005; Sealock and Simpson 1998; but see also Engel, Smith, and Cullen 2012). Such discrimination distorts official data, particularly about the characteristics of offenders.

As we noted above, according to the "hierarchy rule" in recording crimes, when an individual is arrested for committing multiple Part I crimes, only the most serious offense is recorded in the UCR. The other offenses in multiple-offenses situations are omitted from UCR data. While there are exceptions to the hierarchy rule for the offenses of justifiable homicide, motor vehicle theft, and arson, this rule clearly results in the underestimation of crime using UCR data (FBI 2014).

Finally, police officers sometimes simply make unintentional errors in recording crime data. In addition, although the FBI works hard to achieve uniformity of data across jurisdictions, some variation in crime coding and recording practices is inevitable, given the huge number of agencies participating in the UCR program. Law enforcement agencies may also intentionally manipulate crime data for political purposes and thus provide an inaccurate picture of crime. For example, an agency may under-report offenses in its jurisdiction to try to show that it has curbed crime.

Juvenile Court Statistics

Juvenile court records provide another official source of data about juvenile delinquency. *Juvenile Court Statistics* is compiled from data that state and county agencies provide to the National Juvenile Court Data Archive (Hockenberry and Puzzanchera 2014). The most recent juvenile court statistics from 2011 regarding delinquency cases are based on individual case-level data from 2,270 jurisdictions in 40 states, and court-level aggregate data from 221 jurisdictions in five states.[7] Together, these jurisdictions contained 85 percent of the juvenile population in the United States in 2011. Juvenile court statistics from 2011 regarding formally handled status offense cases are based on individual case-level and court-level aggregate data from 2,295 jurisdictions containing 79 percent of the juvenile population in the United States in 2011. In 2011, *Juvenile Court Statistics* data were based on 961,632 delinquency cases and 87,122 status offense cases processed (Hockenberry and Puzzanchera 2014: 88). *Juvenile Court Statistics* provides information about offenses charged; age, gender, and race of offenders; referral sources; detention and petitioning decisions; and dispositions ordered. Reporting agencies use their own definitions and coding categories when providing juvenile court data, so the data are not uniform across jurisdictions. However, the National Juvenile Court Data Archive "restructures contributed data into standardized coding categories" (Hockenberry and Puzzanchera 2014: 3).

The "unit of count" in *Juvenile Court Statistics* is the number of "cases disposed." "A 'case' represents a juvenile processed by a juvenile court on a new referral, regardless of the number of law violations contained in the referral" (Hockenberry and Puzzanchera 2014: 1). For example, a youth charged in a single referral with three offenses represents one case. "The fact that a case is 'disposed' means that a definite action was taken as a result of the referral – i.e., a plan of treatment was selected or initiated" (Hockenberry and Puzzanchera 2014: 1). The treatment plan does not have to be completed for a case to be considered disposed. "For example, a case is considered to be disposed when the court orders probation, not when a term of probation supervision is completed" (Hockenberry and Puzzanchera 2014: 1).

Only a portion of juveniles who commit offenses come to the attention of the police, and only a portion of juvenile offenses known to police are processed by juvenile courts. The primary weakness of juvenile court data is that they are available only for juvenile offenders whose cases are handled by juvenile courts. Thus, the offenders included in juvenile court statistics are not representative of all juvenile offenders.

Victimization surveys

Crime data are gathered not only from police agencies and courts, but also from those who have been victimized. Begun in 1972, the National Crime Victimization Survey (NCVS) was developed to overcome problems with data from official sources (O'Brien 2000).[8] Criminologists expected the NCVS data to give a more accurate picture of crime than UCR data because the NCVS provided a systematic way to gather information about offenses unreported to law enforcement personnel and thus excluded from UCR data.

The NCVS is conducted by the U.S. Census Bureau, which selects the national sample and interviews respondents. In 2013, the sample consisted of 90,630 households, and 160,040 persons age 12 or older living in them (Truman and Langton 2014). Households selected as part of the NCVS remain in the sample for three years, and individuals are interviewed twice a year. The first interview is conducted in person, and subsequent interviews are conducted either in person or by phone. The NCVS has a high response rate: in 2013, 84 percent of eligible households and 88 percent of individuals selected to participate in the NCVS actually completed the survey (Truman and Langton 2014).

The NCVS asks respondents about personal crime victimizations (including rape and sexual assault, robbery, aggravated assault, simple assault, and "personal larceny" including purse-snatching and pocket-picking) and property crime victimizations (including burglary, motor vehicle theft, and other theft). During the interview process, one adult answers background questions about the household, such as family income and the number of household members. That same respondent also answers questions about property crime victimizations during the previous six months.[9] Each member of the household age 12 or older is interviewed individually about personal crime victimizations during the previous six months. The NCVS also gathers background information, such as age, gender, and education, for all members of the household. "Research in action: National Crime Victimization Survey" includes sample questions from the NCVS.

Research in action: National Crime Victimization Survey

The following questions are examples of those asked in the National Crime Victimization Survey.

As I go through [these crimes], tell me if any of these happened to you in the last 6 months, that is since _____, 20__.

Was something belonging to YOU stolen, such as –

(a) Things that you carry, like luggage, a wallet, purse, briefcase, book –
(b) Clothing, jewelry, or cellphone –
(c) Bicycle or sports equipment –
(d) Things in your home – like a TV, stereo, or tools –
(e) Things outside your home such as a garden hose or lawn furniture –
(f) Things belonging to children in the household –
(g) Things from a vehicle, such as a package, groceries, camera, or CDs –
OR
(h) Did anyone ATTEMPT to steal anything belonging to you?

(Other than any incidents already mentioned,) since _____, 20__, were you attacked or threatened OR did you have something stolen from you –

(a) At home including the porch or yard –
(b) At or near a friend's, relative's, or neighbor's home –
(c) At work or school –
(d) In places such as a storage shed or laundry room, a shopping mall, restaurant, bank, or airport –

(e)   While riding in any vehicle –
(f)   On the street or in a parking lot –
(g)   At such places as a party, theater, gym, picnic area, bowling lanes, or while fishing or hunting –
OR
(h)   Did anyone ATTEMPT to attack or ATTEMPT to steal anything belonging to you from any of these places?

If respondents answer "yes" to any of these questions, they are then asked (1) how many times the incident occurred, and (2) to describe what happened.

Source: Bureau of Justice Statistics website. Retrieved October 5, 2014 (www.bjs.gov/content/pub/pdf/ncvs1_2012.pdf).

The primary objectives of the NCVS were to estimate the number and types of crimes unreported to police and to gather detailed information about the victims and consequences of crime – information not gathered by the UCR. Victimization surveys were designed to provide data about the following:

- Situational factors, such as where the crime occurred, time of day at which it occurred, how many victims were involved, whether a weapon was used, self-protective actions by the victim, and the results of those actions.
- Victim characteristics, such as gender, age, race, educational attainment, income, marital status, and relationship to the offender.
- Consequences of the victimization, such as whether the victim was injured and cost of medical expenses incurred.

Data from the NCVS enable researchers to estimate the likelihood of victimization for various types of crime for the U.S. population as a whole, as well as for specific demographic subgroups. For example, with data on victim characteristics, researchers can estimate how the likelihood of becoming a robbery victim differs for males and females, or how racial status influences one's chances of becoming a victim of sexual assault.

Strengths of victimization surveys

The primary strength of the NCVS, and of victimization surveys in general, is their ability to provide information about crimes that victims do not report to police. According to NCVS data from 2013, victims reported to police only 36 percent of property crimes, 46 percent of violent crimes, and 61 percent of serious violent crimes (Truman and Langton 2014). By surveying victims directly, the NCVS provides a systematic way to capture offenses unreported to police that would otherwise go unnoticed in crime statistics.

Because the NCVS also gathers information about demographic characteristics of individuals and households that have been victimized, it offers insights into the risks of victimization. Using victimization survey data, researchers can determine how the risks of becoming the victim of various types of crime differ by social characteristics, such as age, gender, race, and social class. (See Chapter 5 for a discussion of the social characteristics of crime victims.)

Weaknesses of victimization surveys

The primary weakness of victimization surveys is that they include a more limited range of offenses than UCR data do. Victimization surveys omit homicide, most crimes classified as Part II offenses in the UCR, "victimless" crimes (e.g., drug use violations, prostitution), and status offenses (e.g., curfew violations, running away) (O'Brien 1985: 66). The NCVS includes questions about all UCR Part I offenses except homicide and arson, but the only Part II offense it includes is simple assault. Thus, by design, it excludes many crimes. Some types of crime, such as employee theft, income tax violations, fraud, and embezzlement, are simply difficult to assess from a victim's perspective.

Some victimizations are omitted from NCVS data not by design, but because survey respondents do not report them. Some offenses may go unreported because the adult answering questions about household victimizations is unaware of all victimizations during the previous six months. Other offenses may go unreported because respondents choose not to reveal them. Despite revisions to the survey instrument, designed to encourage respondents to report personal crimes of violence, offenses such as sexual assault may be particularly likely to be under-reported. Respondents may also under-report offenses because of a relationship between victim and offender. To explore this possibility, one researcher first obtained from police records information about reported crimes and then interviewed the victims of those crimes about recent victimizations. He found that victims reported to the interviewer 76 percent of known incidents when the offender was a stranger to the victim, 57 percent of known incidents when the offender was known to the victim, and only 22 percent of known incidents when the offender was a relative of the victim (Turner 1972).

A second limitation of the NCVS is that it underestimates juvenile victimizations (Wells and Rankin 2001).[10] This is true, in part, because the NCVS excludes victims younger than 12 years of age and, in part, because young respondents appear reluctant to provide interviewers with information about crimes committed against them, especially given that those crimes are likely to have been committed by their peers or a family member (Wells and Rankin 2001).

A third weakness of victimization surveys is that they offer limited information about offenders. Obviously, victimization surveys can provide information about offender characteristics, such as gender, race, and estimated age, only for those offenses involving personal contact between offender and victim. In addition, these data on offender characteristics are reliable only to the extent that victims are able to *accurately* describe these individual characteristics.

Finally, victimization surveys have the shortcomings inherent in the survey method. Perhaps the most important limitation is the problem of recall. Respondents may not accurately recall past victimizations and the details related to them. This problem intensifies as the length of time between the victimization event and the survey interview increases. The NCVS tries to minimize this problem by limiting all interviews after the first one to a six-month time frame, and asking the respondent only about victimizations that have occurred during the previous six months since the last interview. Another problem of survey methodology is that respondents may not provide truthful responses to survey questions, or they may provide what they consider to be "socially desirable" responses. Respondents may also simply misunderstand the questions and so give incorrect answers.

Self-report surveys

Self-report surveys, like UCR data and victimization surveys, are a major source of data on crime and delinquency. Their popularity grew in the 1960s and 1970s as researchers began to recognize the problems associated with official statistics and the ability of self-reports to overcome these problems. Self-report surveys ask individuals directly, through either questionnaires or interviews, about their involvement in crime and delinquency. Thus, these surveys avoid the filter of the criminal justice system and provide information about offenders, regardless of whether those offenders have been arrested or officially processed.

Self-report surveys provide demographic information about offenders, such as age, race, and gender, as well as information – unavailable through official data or victimization surveys – about personal characteristics of offenders, such as family background and social class. Importantly, self-report surveys enable researchers to explore the attitudes, beliefs, and motivations of offenders.

Self-report surveys can be either cross-sectional or longitudinal. A **cross-sectional survey** is one conducted at a single point in time. A cross-sectional design offers researchers a glimpse of a cross-section, or "slice," of the population at a particular time. Researchers must be extremely cautious when using cross-sectional data to try to address questions of causal order or change. A **longitudinal survey**, which gathers information from the same individuals at more than one point in time, is better suited to answer these questions. The National Youth Survey, in which researchers gathered information from respondents at seven points in time, is an example of a longitudinal survey. Longitudinal surveys are relatively expensive and complex to implement compared to cross-sectional surveys. Yet longitudinal designs are popular among researchers interested in processes of change and in crime and delinquency over the life course.

Strengths of self-report data

The primary strength of self-report data is that they offer information about the delinquent acts of those who have not been arrested or officially processed. Thus, they provide a broader and less biased picture of delinquency and crime in the United States than official data do. Self-reports also provide data about relatively minor forms of offending and drug and alcohol use. These behaviors are often omitted from official data because more serious offenses are most likely to lead to arrest. Because self-reports capture both minor and serious forms of offending, apart from the filter of criminal justice system processing, they reveal far more delinquency than do official data.

Self-report data also provide researchers with opportunities to consider questions they would be unable to address with either official or victimization data. In addition to questions about involvement in delinquency and drug use, self-report surveys may include questions regarding respondents' attitudes and beliefs about law violation; perceptions of opportunities for success in school or work; and family interactions, such as parent–child attachment, parental supervision, and disciplinary practices. Answers to these types of questions are needed by researchers interested in testing various theories about the causes of crime and delinquency. Researchers have great flexibility in designing self-report surveys that will provide them with the information they need to test particular theoretical perspectives.

Weaknesses of self-report data

Scholars have raised several concerns about self-report data on crime and delinquency. Among the more serious concerns is the question of whether offenders will candidly report their involvement in crime and delinquency – particularly offenses undetected by police. Some respondents may intentionally under-report their involvement in offending or may simply forget some of the offenses they have committed. The problem of recall may be worse for those who have committed the most offenses (Blumstein et al. 1986). Other respondents may exaggerate or over-report their involvement in offending. A recent study suggests that over-reporting of arrests is almost as likely as under-reporting of arrests among adolescent respondents (Krohn et al. 2013). This study also found that respondents who were arrested more frequently were more likely to under-report their arrests.

A second weakness of self-report surveys concerns sampling design and its potential effects on survey responses. In many self-report studies, samples of respondents are drawn from student populations, and surveys are often conducted in schools. Obviously, in these cases, individuals not attending school – including truants, dropouts, and institutionalized youth – are excluded from the samples. Thus, the individuals excluded may be those most likely to be delinquent. This under-sampling of serious delinquents may result in underestimation of the true amount of delinquency and in an inaccurate picture of the characteristics of offenders (Harris and Shaw 2000; Reiss and Roth 1993).

The selection of samples of respondents in school settings also results in samples that are fairly similar or homogeneous in many respects (Kleck 1982). For example, a researcher who draws a sample from a single high school should not expect much variation among respondents in social class, because students who reside in the same community or neighborhood probably have relatively similar family incomes. The problem with fairly homogeneous samples is that they prevent researchers from exploring the full range of possible responses to some questions. For example, suppose a researcher is interested in the relationship between social class and delinquency and draws a sample of respondents from a school in a lower-class neighborhood. That researcher will be unable to draw conclusions about the offending of middle- and upper-class individuals because the responses to survey questions about social class will be limited mostly to those indicating lower-class status.[11]

A third criticism of self-report surveys is that some fail to capture the full range of delinquent behaviors and focus instead on relatively minor offenses, such as underage drinking, truancy, and petty theft (Morenoff 2005). Minor offenses may be more difficult for offenders to remember than serious offenses, and thus the emphasis on minor offenses is likely to increase the problem of recall error (Kleck 1982). In addition, serious or violent delinquency is relatively rare, so it is difficult to detect many serious or violent offenses with self-reports, even with fairly large samples. The exclusion of serious offenses limits researchers' abilities to address theoretically significant questions and to compare self-reports of offending to official or victimization data, which better represent serious crime and delinquency.

Although the exclusion of serious offenses from self-reports is a legitimate criticism, not all self-report surveys are subject to this problem. The National Youth Survey, for example, was the first self-report survey to incorporate questions about serious offenses, such as rape, assault, and the sale of hard drugs. The volume of serious delinquency revealed by NYS respondents indicates that, even in face-to-face interviews, respondents were willing to report serious delinquent acts they had committed.

Finally, self-report surveys have been criticized for reasons of both validity and reliability. **Validity** is the extent to which a measurement instrument measures what it is supposed to measure (Vogt and Johnson 2011). For example, questions about the number of times a respondent has stolen something or damaged someone else's property would be valid measures of delinquency. Questions about lying to parents, however, would not be valid measures of delinquent behavior, because even though lying might be related to delinquency, it is not itself a delinquent act. The validity of measures is compromised when respondents systematically under-report or over-report their delinquent acts. Validity is also threatened when respondents have limited recall or forget past behaviors or when they misunderstand survey questions. For example, if we ask survey respondents to report the number of times they engaged in delinquency in the past two years, the time frame is probably too long for them to be able to provide accurate responses, and so the measure may not be valid.

To assess the validity of self-reports of delinquency, researchers have compared responses from self-report surveys to official police and court records. These researchers have found relatively strong relationships between official records and self-reported delinquency, indicating that those most likely to report involvement in delinquent behavior were also those most likely to have official records of offending (Thornberry and Krohn 2002; Paschall, Ornstein, and Flewelling 2001; Farrington et al. 1996; Hindelang, Hirschi, and Weis 1981; but see also Kirk 2006). Based on this finding, researchers have concluded that most self-report surveys provide reasonably valid measures of delinquency.

There has been conflicting research, however, about racial differences in the validity of self-reports of delinquency. Early research in the 1980s compared self-reports and official records and suggested that self-reports may be less valid for blacks than for whites because black males tended to under-report their involvement in serious or violent offenses (Huizinga and Elliott 1984, 1986; Hindelang et al. 1981; Hindelang 1981). But more recent research since the mid-1990s shows that the validity of self-reports of delinquency is high for both blacks and whites, particularly when data are collected in computerized ways that enhance the privacy of responses (Piquero, MacIntosh, and Hickman 2002; Thornberry and Krohn 2002; Paschall et al. 2001; Maxfield, Weiler, and Widom 2000; Farrington et al. 1996). For example, Farrington and his colleagues (1996) used a sample of adolescent males in Pittsburgh, and compared juvenile court records with self-reports of offending and arrest. They found that, among those who had juvenile court records, validity was higher for white males in reporting offenses, but higher for black males in reporting arrests. Krohn and his colleagues (2013) found that, once they took into account an individual's number of prior arrests, race had no effect on under-reporting or over-reporting of arrests.

Reliability is the extent to which repeated measurements of a variable produce the same or similar responses over time. Suppose, for example, an individual takes an IQ test once each year for three years. She scores 132 on the first test, 92 on the second test, and 153 on the third. These three tests are not reliable measures of IQ because of the great variation in scores over time.

Reliability is a concern with self-report surveys for two reasons. First, in longitudinal surveys, repeated measurement itself can affect responses, leading to a decline in the reporting of delinquency at later rounds of data collection and therefore to unreliable estimates of the true amount of delinquency (Lauritsen 1998). Second, reliability is related to sample size. The smaller one's sample size, the greater the likelihood of differences in responses due to chance, and the less reliable the measures. Most self-report surveys are conducted with relatively small samples. In addition, serious offenses are relatively rare events, so respondents in a typical self-report survey are unlikely to report involvement in many serious delinquent acts. Thus, small sample sizes, combined with the rarity of serious crime, may decrease the reliability of measures of serious offending in self-report surveys. Although researchers must consider reliability issues when using self-report data, in general, self-report surveys yield "impressive" levels of reliability for delinquency measures (Huizinga and Elliott 1986; Hindelang et al. 1981).

Comparing data sources

What do we see when we compare the pictures of delinquency presented by the three primary data sources?

Comparing UCR and NCVS data

Both UCR and NCVS data are better measures of serious offending than of minor crime and delinquency.[12] The NCVS, by design, includes only relatively serious offenses, and UCR data are available only for offenses known to police, which are likely to be more serious offenses. But because victimization surveys include offenses unknown to police, we should expect them to reveal more offenses than UCR data do. This is, in fact, the case. NCVS estimates suggest that "the actual amount of crime is roughly two to four times higher than official statistics would indicate, depending on the type of crime being considered" (Wells and Rankin 2001: 270). For example, UCR data for 2013 report 79,770 rapes/sexual assaults, 345,031 robberies, and 1,928,465 burglaries (FBI 2014: Table 1). NCVS data for 2013 show far more offenses: 300,170 rapes/sexual assaults, 645,650 robberies, and 3,286,210 household burglaries (Truman and Langton 2014: 2, 3). Research using National Crime Survey and NCVS data suggests that, in recent decades, significant increases have occurred in the likelihood of reporting crimes to the police, for both violent and property offenses (Baumer and Lauritsen 2010).

Comparing self-report data to UCR and NCVS data

Self-report data tend to include relatively minor forms of offending, while UCR and NCVS data tend to include more serious forms of offending. Also, self-report surveys are usually given to samples of respondents of a narrow age range, so these data are more limited than UCR or NCVS data (O'Brien 2000: 75). Given these factors, it is somewhat difficult to compare these data sources. The NYS, however, contains questions about some serious offenses, such as aggravated assault and drug distribution, which have allowed researchers to compare data from the NYS to UCR and NCVS data.

Given that UCR data represent only crimes known to police, it is not surprising that the NYS reveals much higher rates of offending than do UCR data. Robert O'Brien (2000) examined aggravated assault rates in UCR, NCVS, and NYS data for 1980. The NYS revealed an aggravated assault rate of 1,400 per 10,000 (for 15–21-year-olds), whereas the NCVS and UCR showed rates of 90.3 and 29.9 per 10,000, respectively, for the same year. If the NCVS and UCR data were limited to the same ages represented in the NYS (ages 15–21), the aggravated assault rates in these two sources would be much higher. But these rates still would not come close to the self-report rate (O'Brien 2000: 75). Clearly, compared to self-report data, the UCR and NCVS underestimate some types of offenses.

In a 2003 study, David Farrington and his colleagues compared conclusions about delinquent careers derived from official data (court referrals) with those derived from self-reports.

They used longitudinal data from the Seattle Social Development Project, which began in 1985 and included both self-report and court referral data for 808 youths who were aged 11 to 17. The two data sources agreed about some aspects of delinquent careers and disagreed about others. Self-reports and court referrals both showed that the proportion of the sample involved in offending increased during the juvenile years, and that the younger the age at which an individual began offending, the larger the number of offenses committed. When compared to court referral data, however, self-reports showed a higher proportion of the sample involved in offending, a higher frequency of offending among those who committed offenses, offending beginning at younger ages, and less continuity in offending over time (Farrington et al. 2003).

All three data sources (UCR, NCVS, and self-report surveys) reveal similar patterns in the demographic characteristics of those who commit *serious* crimes. For serious crimes, all three data sources show that, relative to their proportions in the population, males, African Americans, and the young commit substantially more offenses than do females, whites, and older persons (O'Brien 2000: 80). (See Chapter 5 for a discussion of the social characteristics of offenders.)

In a recent study, Alex Piquero and his colleagues compared official arrest data with self-reports of arrest over a seven-year period. They found moderate agreement between these two data sources. In addition, this level of agreement was fairly stable over time, and was similar across race, ethnicity, and gender (Piquero, Schubert, and Brame 2014).

Summary and conclusions

In this chapter, we have introduced several sources of data and several research methods. Which methodology is best suited for addressing questions about crime and delinquency? The answer depends on the question at hand and the theory underlying it. A researcher's theoretical perspective suggests a particular research strategy. One must evaluate the adequacy of any research design in terms of its relevance to questions of theory.

Research methods used to study crime and delinquency include comparison of offenders and non-offenders, ethnography, ecological analysis, and survey research. The Gluecks used longitudinal data from multiple sources to compare 500 delinquent boys with 500 non-delinquent boys. They matched these two groups on a case-by-case basis and discovered that family life was a crucial factor distinguishing delinquents from non-delinquents.

Social scientists have also used ethnography to study crime and delinquency. Ethnographic studies involve sustained interaction between the researcher – often acting as a participant-observer – and those whom he or she is studying. Ethnographers provide a detailed account of interactions and social processes as they naturally occur. Anderson used ethnography to explore the "code of the street" governing youth violence in the inner city.

Ecological analysis helps researchers understand the geographic distribution of crime and delinquency. In classic research, Shaw and McKay used official data to plot the home addresses of Chicago delinquents and explore the characteristics of communities with high delinquency rates. In contemporary research, Sampson and his colleagues have revived interest in community-level factors that contribute to high crime rates in some geographic areas.

Survey analysis is the most widely used method in research on crime and delinquency. Surveys often provide detailed information about respondents' behaviors, attitudes, and beliefs.

Many criminologists have used surveys to gather data on the frequency and distribution of delinquency and the causes and correlates of offending. We presented the National Youth Survey and the Community Survey of the Project on Human Development in Chicago Neighborhoods as examples of survey analysis.

In this chapter, we also examined the three primary sources of data on crime and delinquency: agencies within the criminal justice system that provide official data, victimization surveys, and self-report surveys of offenders. We discussed the strengths and weaknesses of each data source and tried to convey how each is best suited to address particular types of questions about crime and offenders. When evaluating data on crime and delinquency, it is important to keep in mind the strengths and weaknesses of the data source and to consider what that source is designed to tell us about crime and delinquency. Official data tell us about crime and delinquency that are recorded by agencies of the juvenile justice system. Victimization surveys tell us about crime and delinquency that people experience as victims. Self-report surveys tell us about delinquent acts that youth themselves report having committed, even if the offenses are not known to police.

Critical-thinking questions

1. How would you determine which research method is best suited for a particular research question?
2. Identify the strengths and weaknesses of the three major sources of data on crime and delinquency: official data, victimization survey data, and self-report survey data. What is each source designed to tell us?
3. What is the primary problem with relying on UCR data to examine crime in America?
4. Suppose you want to understand the nature and extent of violent crime in an impoverished, inner-city neighborhood. What research method would you use to study this problem and why?
5. Explain the relationship between methodology and theory. How does theory influence one's choice of research method? How might methodology influence the development of theory?

Suggested reading

Hindelang, Michael J., Travis Hirschi, and Joseph G. Weis. 1981. *Measuring Delinquency*. Beverly Hills, CA: Sage.

Mosher, Clayton J., Terance D. Miethe, and Timothy C. Hart. 2011. *The Mismeasure of Crime*. 2nd edn. Thousand Oaks, CA: Sage.

O'Brien, Robert M. 2000. "Crime Facts: Victim and Offender Data." Pp. 59–83 in *Criminology: A Contemporary Handbook*, 3rd edn., ed. J. F. Sheley. Belmont, CA: Wadsworth.

Useful websites

For further information relevant to this chapter, go to the following web sites.

- National Youth Survey, Institute of Behavioral Science at the University of Colorado (www.colorado.edu/ibs/NYSFS/)

- Uniform Crime Reporting Program, Federal Bureau of Investigation (www.fbi.gov/about-us/cjis/ucr/ucr)
- Juvenile Court Statistics, National Center for Juvenile Justice (www.ncjj.org/Publication/Juvenile-Court-Statistics-2011.aspx)
- National Crime Victimization Survey, Office of Justice Programs, Bureau of Justice Statistics (www.bjs.gov/index.cfm?ty=dcdetail&iid=245)

Glossary of key terms

Cross-sectional survey: A self-report survey conducted at a single point in time. A cross-sectional research design provides a glimpse of a cross-section of the population at a particular time.

Ecological analysis: A research method used to explore the geographic distribution of crime and delinquency and the social conditions that characterize areas with high rates of crime and delinquency. Geographic areas, such as neighborhoods or cities, rather than the individuals who reside in them, are the units of analysis.

Ethnography: Research method that involves direct, systematic observation of social behavior, which results in a detailed, descriptive analysis of the social system observed.

Longitudinal survey: A self-report survey that gathers information from the same individuals at more than one point in time. A longitudinal research design is better suited than a cross-sectional design to address questions of causal order and change.

Reliability: The extent to which repeated measurements of a variable produce the same or similar responses over time.

Survey research: A research method that involves asking a series of questions through questionnaires or interviews. Includes selecting a sample of respondents, writing and testing questions to be asked, administering the survey to respondents, coding and analyzing the data gathered, and drawing inferences from the sample to the population from which it was selected.

Uniform Crime Reporting program: Provides "official data" on crime and delinquency, voluntarily reported by over 18,000 law enforcement agencies across the United States, and compiled by the Federal Bureau of Investigation. These data reveal the extent of crime and delinquency with which the reporting agencies deal, and the characteristics of offenses and offenders whom they encounter.

Validity: The degree to which a measurement instrument measures what it is supposed to measure.

Notes

1. See Glueck and Glueck (1950: Chapter 4) for a description of the selection and matching of delinquents and non-delinquents.
2. Laub and Sampson (1988) and Sampson and Laub (1993: Chapter 2) provide thorough discussions of the criticisms of *Unraveling Juvenile Delinquency*. See Laub and Sampson (1991) for an analysis of the debate between the Gluecks and Edwin Sutherland, the author of differential association theory.
3. See Laub and Sampson (1991) for an assessment of the Gluecks' contributions to criminology.
4. For information about the PHDCN and publications based on data gathered through it, go to: www.icpsr.umich.edu/icpsrweb/ICPSR/series/206.
5. See Padilla (1992), Hagedorn (1988, 1991), and Vigil (1988), who also use ethnographic methods to examine gangs.

6. For reviews of research on community-level factors and their theoretical importance, see Sampson, Morenoff, and Gannon-Rowley (2002) and Sampson (2000).
7. Individual case-level data include detailed information about "the characteristics of each delinquency and status offense case handled by courts, generally including the age, gender, and race of the youth referred; the date and source of referral; the offenses charged; detention and petitioning decisions; and the date and type of disposition" (Hockenberry and Puzzanchera 2014: 87). Court-level aggregate data "typically provide counts of the delinquency and status offense cases handled by courts in a defined time period (calendar or fiscal year)" (Hockenberry and Puzzanchera 2014: 87). These aggregate data are sometimes abstracted from courts' annual reports.
8. From 1972 to 1990, the NCVS was called the National Crime Survey.
9. O'Brien (1985: 39–61) describes the NCVS sampling and data collection processes.
10. Wells and Rankin (2001) compared NCVS data and self-report victimization data from the National Youth Survey and the Monitoring the Future study, both national samples of young people. Both self-report surveys indicated much higher juvenile victimization rates than did the NCVS.
11. See Kleck (1982: 431–432) for a discussion of class-homogeneous research sites and conclusions about the relationship between social class and crime.
12. The FBI cautions users of UCR data against comparing UCR and NCVS data, stating that these two data sources are intended to complement each other. "Users should not compare crime trends in the UCR Program and the NCVS because of methodology and crime coverage differences. The programs examine the Nation's crime problem from different perspectives, and their results are not strictly comparable. Definitional and procedural differences can account for many apparent discrepancies ..." (FBI 2009). This same report notes, however, that these two data sources use similar offense definitions and measure a similar subset of serious offenses, including forcible rape, robbery, aggravated assault, burglary, theft, and motor vehicle theft. Thus, any attempt to compare UCR and NCVS data must examine only offenses that are similarly measured in both data sources, recognizing the effects of methodological differences in the two sources.

References

Agnew, Robert and Timothy Brezina. 2012. *Juvenile Delinquency: Causes and Control*. 4th edn. New York: Oxford University Press.

Anderson, Elijah. 1997. "Violence and the Inner-City Street Code." Pp. 1–30 in *Childhood and Violence in the Inner City*, ed. J. McCord. New York: Cambridge University Press.

Anderson, Elijah. 1998. "The Social Ecology of Youth Violence." *Crime and Justice* 24: 65–104.

Anderson, Elijah. 1999. *Code of the Street: Decency, Violence, and the Moral Life of the Inner City*. New York: Norton.

Babbie, Earl. 2013. *The Practice of Social Research*. 13th edn. Belmont, CA: Wadsworth/ Cengage Learning.

Baumer, Eric P. and Janet L. Lauritsen. 2010. "Reporting Crime to the Police, 1973–2005: A Multivariate Analysis of Long-Term Trends in the National Crime Survey (NCS) and National Crime Victimization Survey (NCVS)." *Criminology* 48: 131–185.

Beckett, Katherine, Kris Nyrop, Lori Pfingst, and Melissa Bowen. 2005. "Drug Use, Drug Possession Arrests, and the Question of Race: Lessons from Seattle." *Social Problems* 52: 419–441.

Blumstein, Alfred, Jacqueline Cohen, Jeffrey A. Roth, and Christy A. Visher (eds.). 1986. *Criminal Careers and "Career Criminals,"* vol. 1. Washington, DC: National Academy Press.

Bureau of Justice Statistics. n.d. *Arrest Data Analysis Tool*. Retrieved May 28, 2015 (www.bjs.gov/index.cfm?ty=datool&surl=/arrests/index.cfm#).

Byrne, James M. and Robert J. Sampson. 1986. *The Social Ecology of Crime*. New York: Springer-Verlag.

Decker, Scott H. 2001. "Collective and Normative Features of Gang Violence." Pp. 160–181 in *Voices from the Field: Readings in Criminal Justice Research*, ed. C. Pope, R. Lovell, and S. Brandl. Belmont, CA: Wadsworth.

Elliott, Delbert S. 1988. *National Youth Survey (United States): Wave III, 1978,* 2nd ICPSR Edition Codebook. Ann Arbor, MI: Inter-University Consortium for Political and Social Science Research.

Elliott, Delbert S., David Huizinga, and Suzanne S. Ageton. 1985. *Explaining Delinquency and Drug Use*. Beverly Hills, CA: Sage.

Engel, Robin S., Michael R. Smith, and Francies T. Cullen. 2012. "Race, Place, and Drug Enforcement: Reconsidering the Impact of Citizen Complaints and Crime Rates on Drug Arrests." *Criminology and Public Policy* 11: 603–635.

Farrington, David P., Darrick Jolliffe, David J. Hawkins, Richard F. Catalano, Karl G. Hill, and Rick Kosterman. 2003. "Comparing Delinquency Careers in Court Records and Self-Reports." *Criminology* 41: 933–958.

Farrington, David P., Rolf Loeber, Magda Stouthamer-Loeber, Welmoet B. Van Kammen, and Laura Schmidt. 1996. "Self-Reported Delinquency and a Combined Delinquency Seriousness Scale Based on Boys, Mothers, and Teachers: Concurrent and Predictive Validity for African-Americans and Caucasians." *Criminology* 34: 493–517.

Federal Bureau of Investigation. 2009. *Uniform Crime Reporting (UCR) Summary Reporting: Frequently Asked Questions (FAQs)*. Washington, DC: U.S. Department of Justice.

Federal Bureau of Investigation. 2011. *Effects of NIBRS on Crime Statistics*. Washington, DC: U.S. Department of Justice.

Federal Bureau of Investigation. 2012. *Crime in the United States, 2011: Uniform Crime Reports*. Washington, DC: U.S. Department of Justice.

Federal Bureau of Investigation. 2014. *Crime in the United States, 2013: Uniform Crime Reports*. Washington, DC: U.S. Department of Justice. Retrieved November 14, 2014 (www.fbi.gov/about-us/cjis/ucr/crime-in-the-u.s/2013/crime-in-the-u.s.-2013).

Fowler, Floyd J., Jr. and Thomas W. Mangione. 1990. *Standardized Survey Interviewing: Minimizing Interviewer-Related Error*. Newbury Park, CA: Sage.

Garot, Robert. 2007. "'Where You From!' Gang Identity as Performance." *Journal of Contemporary Ethnography* 36: 50–84.

Glueck, Sheldon and Eleanor Glueck. 1950. *Unraveling Juvenile Delinquency*. Cambridge, MA: Harvard University Press.

Glueck, Sheldon and Eleanor Glueck. 1968. *Delinquents and Nondelinquents in Perspective*. Cambridge, MA: Harvard University Press.

Hagedorn, John M. 1988. *People and Folks: Gangs, Crime, and the Underclass in a Rustbelt City*. Chicago: Lakeview Press.

Hagedorn, John M. 1991. "Back in the Field Again: Gang Research in the Nineties." Pp. 240–259 in *Gangs in America*, ed. C. R. Huff. Newbury Park, CA: Sage.

Harris, Anthony R. and James W. Shaw. 2000. "Looking for Patterns: Race, Class, and Crime." Pp. 129–161 in *Criminology*, ed. J. F. Sheley. Belmont, CA: Wadsworth.

Hindelang, Michael J. 1981. "Variations in Sex-Race-Age-Specific Incidence Rates of Offending." *American Sociological Review* 46: 461–474.

Hindelang, Michael J., Travis Hirschi, and Joseph G. Weis. 1981. *Measuring Delinquency*. Beverly Hills, CA: Sage.

Hockenberry, Sarah and Charles Puzzanchera. 2014. *Juvenile Court Statistics 2011*. Pittsburgh, PA: National Center for Juvenile Justice.

Huizinga, David A. and Delbert S. Elliott. 1984. *Self-Reported Measures of Delinquency and Crime: Methodological Issues and Comparative Findings*. Boulder, CO: Behavioral Research Institute.

Huizinga, David A. and Delbert S. Elliott. 1986. "Reassessing the Reliability and Validity of Self-Report Delinquency Measures." *Journal of Quantitative Criminology* 2: 293–327.

Jankowski, Martin Sanchez. 1995. "Ethnography, Inequality, and Crime in the Low-Income Community." Pp. 80–94 in *Crime and Inequality*, ed. J. Hagan and R. D. Peterson. Stanford University Press.

Kirk, David S. 2006. "Examining the Divergence across Self-Report and Official Data Sources on Inferences about the Adolescent Life-Course of Crime." *Journal of Quantitative Criminology* 22: 107–129.

Kleck, Gary. 1982. "On the Use of Self-Report Data to Determine the Class Distribution of Criminal and Delinquent Behavior." *American Sociological Review* 47: 427–433.

Krohn, Marvin D., Alan J. Lizotte, Matthew D. Phillips, Terence P. Thornberry, and Kristin A. Bell. 2013. "Explaining Systematic Bias in Self-Reported Measures: Factors that Affect the Under- and Over-Reporting of Self-Reported Arrests." *Justice Quarterly* 30: 501–528.

Laub, John H. and Robert J. Sampson. 1988. "Unraveling Families and Delinquency: A Reanalysis of the Gluecks' Data." *Criminology* 26: 355–380.

Laub, John H. and Robert J. Sampson. 1991. "The Sutherland–Glueck Debate: On the Sociology of Criminological Knowledge." *American Journal of Sociology* 96: 1402–1440.

Lauritsen, Janet L. 1998. "The Age–Crime Debate: Assessing the Limits of Longitudinal Self-Report Data." *Social Forces* 77: 127–155.

Maxfield, M. G., B. L. Weiler, and C. S. Widom. 2000. "Comparing Self-Reports and Official Records of Arrest." *Journal of Quantitative Criminology* 16: 87–110.

Morenoff, Jeffrey D. 2005. "Racial and Ethnic Disparities in Crime and Delinquency in the United States." Pp. 139–173 in *Ethnicity and Causal Mechanisms*, ed. M. Rutter and M. Tienda. Cambridge University Press.

Morenoff, Jeffrey D., Robert J. Sampson, and Stephen W. Raudenbush. 2001. "Neighborhood Inequality, Collective Efficacy, and the Spatial Dynamics of Urban Violence." *Criminology* 39: 517–559.

O'Brien, Robert M. 1985. *Crime and Victimization Data*. Beverly Hills, CA: Sage.

O'Brien, Robert M. 2000. "Crime Facts: Victim and Offender Data." Pp. 59–83 in *Criminology: A Contemporary Handbook*. 3rd edn., ed. J. F. Sheley. Belmont, CA: Wadsworth.

OJJDP Statistical Briefing Book. Released December 16, 2014. National Center for Juvenile Justice. Retrieved May 28, 2015 (www.ojjdp.gov/ojstatbb/crime/faqs.asp).

Padilla, Felix M. 1992. *The Gang as an American Enterprise*. New Brunswick, NJ: Rutgers University Press.

Paschall, Mallie J., Miriam L. Ornstein, and Robert L. Flewelling. 2001. "African American Male Adolescents' Involvement in the Criminal Justice System: The Criterion Validity of Self-Report Measures in a Prospective Study." *Journal of Research in Crime and Delinquency* 38: 174–187.

Piquero, Alex R., Randall MacIntosh, and Matthew Hickman. 2002. "The Validity of a Self-Reported Delinquency Scale: Comparisons across Gender, Age, Race, and Place of Residence." *Sociological Methods and Research* 30: 492–529.

Piquero, Alex R., Carol A. Schubert, and Robert Brame. 2014. "Comparing Official and Self-Report Records of Offending across Gender and Race/Ethnicity in a Longitudinal Study of Serious Youthful Offenders." *Journal of Research in Crime and Delinquency* 51: 526–556.

Puzzanchera, Charles and Sarah Hockenberry. 2013. *Juvenile Court Statistics 2010*. Pittsburgh, PA: National Center for Juvenile Justice.

Reiss, Albert J., Jr. and J. A. Roth. 1993. *Understanding and Preventing Violence*. Washington, DC: National Academy Press.

Sampson, Robert J. 1985. "Neighborhood and Crime: The Structural Determinants of Personal Victimization." *Journal of Research in Crime and Delinquency* 22: 7–40.

Sampson, Robert J. 1986. "Neighborhood Family Structure and the Risk of Personal Victimization." Pp. 25–46 in *The Social Ecology of Crime*, ed. J. M. Byrne and R. J. Sampson. New York: Springer-Verlag.

Sampson, Robert J. 1988. "Local Friendship Ties and Community Attachment in Mass Society: A Multilevel Systemic Model." *American Sociological Review* 53: 766–779.

Sampson, Robert J. 2000. "Whither the Sociological Study of Crime?" *Annual Review of Sociology* 26: 711–714.

Sampson, Robert J. 2001. "Crime and Public Safety: Insights from Community-Level Perspectives on Social Capital." Pp. 89–114 in *Social Capital and Poor Communities*, ed. S. Saegert, J. P. Thompson, and M. R. Warren. New York: Russell Sage Foundation.

Sampson, Robert J. 2002. "Organized for What? Recasting Theories of Social Dis(Organization)." Pp. 95–110 in *Crime and Social Organization*, ed. E. Waring and D. Weisburd. New Brunswick, NJ: Transaction.

Sampson, Robert J. 2006. "Collective Efficacy Theory: Lessons Learned and Directions for Future Inquiry." Pp. 149–167 in *Taking Stock: The Status of Criminological Theory*, ed. F. T. Cullen, J. P. Wright, and K. R. Blevins. New Brunswick, NJ: Transaction.

Sampson, Robert J. and W. Byron Groves. 1989. "Community Structure and Crime: Testing Social Disorganization Theory." *American Journal of Sociology* 94: 774–802.

Sampson, Robert J. and John H. Laub. 1993. *Crime in the Making: Pathways and Turning Points Through Life*. Cambridge, MA: Harvard University Press.

Sampson, Robert J., Jeffrey D. Morenoff, and Felton Earls. 1999. "Beyond Social Capital: Spatial Dynamics of Collective Efficacy for Children." *American Sociological Review* 64: 633–660.

Sampson, Robert J., Jeffrey D. Morenoff, and Thomas Gannon-Rowley. 2002. "Assessing 'Neighborhood Effects': Social Processes and New Directions in Research." *Annual Review of Sociology* 28: 443–478.

Sampson, Robert J. and Stephen W. Raudenbush. 2004. "Seeing Disorder: Neighborhood Stigma and the Social Construction of 'Broken Windows.'" *Social Psychology Quarterly* 67: 319–342.

Sampson, Robert J., Steven W. Raudenbush, and Felton Earls. 1997. "Neighborhoods and Violent Crime: A Multilevel Study of Collective Efficacy." *Science* 277: 918–924.

Sealock, Miriam D. and Sally S. Simpson. 1998. "Unraveling Bias in Arrest Decisions: The Role of Juvenile Offender Type-Scripts." *Justice Quarterly* 15: 427–457.

Shaw, Clifford R. and Henry D. McKay. 1931. *Social Factors in Juvenile Delinquency: A Study of the Community, the Family, and the Gang in Relation to Delinquent Behavior*. Report of the National Commission on Law Observance and Enforcement, Causes of Crime. Vol. 2. Washington, DC: GPO.

Shaw, Clifford R. and Henry D. McKay. 1969. *Juvenile Delinquency and Urban Areas: A Study of Rates of Delinquency in Relation to Differential Characteristics of Local Communities in American Cities*. Rev. edn. University of Chicago Press.

Shaw, Clifford R., Frederick M. Zorbaugh, Henry D. McKay, and Leonard S. Cottrell. 1929. *Delinquency Areas: A Study of the Geographic Distribution of School Truants, Juvenile Delinquents, and Adult Offenders in Chicago*. University of Chicago Press.

Tapia, Mike. 2011. "Gang Membership and Race as Risk Factors for Juvenile Arrest." *Journal of Research in Crime and Delinquency* 48: 364–395.

Tapia, Mike. 2014. "Latino Street Gang Emergence in the Midwest: Strategic Franchising or Natural Migration." *Crime and Delinquency* 60: 592–618.

Thornberry, Terence P. and Marvin D. Krohn. 2002. "Comparison of Self-Report and Official Data for Measuring Crime." Pp. 43–94 in *Measurement Problems in Criminal Justice Research: Workshop Summary*, ed. J.V. Pepper and C.V. Petrie. Washington, DC: National Academies Press.

Tonry, Michael. 2010. "The Social, Psychological, and Political Causes of Racial Disparities in the American Criminal Justice System." *Crime and Justice* 39: 273–312.

Totten, Mark. 2012. "Gays in the Gang." *Journal of Gang Research* 19: 1–24.

Truman, Jennifer L. and Lynn Langton. 2014. *Criminal Victimization, 2013*. Bureau of Justice Statistics Bulletin. Washington, DC: U.S. Department of Justice.

Turner, A. G. 1972. *The San Jose Methods Test of Known Crime Victims*. National Criminal Justice Information and Statistics Service, Law Enforcement Assistance Administration. Washington, DC: GPO.

Venkatesh, Sudhir Alladi. 1997. "The Social Organization of Street Gang Activity in an Urban Ghetto." *American Journal of Sociology* 103: 82–111.

Vigil, James Diego. 1988. *Barrio Gangs*. Austin, TX: University of Texas Press.

Vogt, W. Paul and R. Burke Johnson. 2011. *Dictionary of Statistics and Methodology: A Nontechnical Guide for the Social Sciences*. 4th edn. Thousand Oaks, CA: Sage.

Wells, Edward L. and Joseph H. Rankin. 2001. "Juvenile Victimization: Convergent Validation of Alternative Measurements." Pp. 267–287 in *Voices from the Field: Readings in Criminal Justice Research*, ed. C. Pope, R. Lovell, and S. Brandl. Belmont, CA: Wadsworth.

Part II

Describing the nature of delinquency

Chapter 4

The extent of offenses

Chapter preview

Topics:

- Prevalence and incidence of delinquent offenses
- Relative frequency of different types of offenses
- Trends in delinquent offenses
- The ecology of juvenile offenses: spatial and temporal distribution

---

Terms:

- prevalence
- incidence
- relative frequency
- ecology of delinquency
- spatial distribution
- temporal distribution

Chapter learning objectives

After completing this chapter, students should be able to:

- Describe the extent to which juveniles are involved in crime.
- Identify the types of delinquent offenses that occur most frequently.
- Give an accurate account of the trends in juvenile crime.
- Describe where and when delinquent offenses occur most frequently.
- Demonstrate interpretive skills developed through exposure to delinquency data presented in tables and figures.

Case in point: country roads

Dave normally worked at his fast-food job on Saturday nights, but he was free for the evening and so were some of his friends. What better way to have fun than to drive around and drink some beer? The beer wasn't hard to get; just wait outside a liquor store until someone was willing to buy it for you. That's what Dave and his buddies did, getting enough beer to last them the night.

Dave and his friends drove out of town on a random country road, having a good time driving, talking, and drinking beer. Having worked throughout his high school years, Dave had finally earned enough money by his junior year to buy a pretty nice car. So he drove and enjoyed the status that came with being the driver, not the "designated driver." As the evening wore on, the guys became more boisterous and animated, trying to think of ways to have fun. Seeing a whole series of mailboxes right along the road gave motive to a simple act of destruction. Hanging out the window, each passenger took turns whacking mailboxes with a baseball bat. It was a lot of fun, especially when Dave increased the speed. It's amazing how many mailboxes can be flayed in a short period of time. But the high speed and loud noise drew neighbors' attention rather quickly, and they called the police. The trail of destruction made it fairly easy to catch the marauding youth. At close to $100 a crack, the price tag for 50 mailboxes added up fast, making the total damage a felony offense.

As a first-time offender, Dave did not have to appear in juvenile court. He was placed on informal probation through an agreement between him, his parents, and a probation officer, made during a visit to the probation department. At the meeting, Dave expressed a great deal of remorse and his parents said that they were stunned that their normally responsible son would engage in such delinquent acts – underage drinking, DUI, and destruction of property – his parents could not believe it. He certainly had never done anything like this before and his parents did not anticipate further trouble.

Are Dave's delinquent acts typical of the type of offenses committed by youth? How about his pattern of offending? Do most youth have a "brush with the law"? These are the types of questions considered in this chapter, which deals with the extent of delinquent offenses.

In Chapter 3, we saw that most offenses committed by juveniles are never reported to authorities and that many juveniles involved in illegal acts are never arrested or officially processed by the juvenile court. Criminologists are also quick to point out that those who do come to the attention of the police or juvenile courts may not be representative of all delinquent offenders (Gibbons and Krohn 1991; Huizinga and Elliott 1987). One of the primary purposes of self-report surveys is to uncover the full extent of delinquency, regardless of whether the illegal acts are reported or whether offenders are arrested or officially processed. Self-report surveys have their limitations, too, including problems of memory and the question of openness and honesty of self-reporting.

This chapter explores the extent of delinquent offenses. Are most juveniles involved in delinquent offenses? If so, how frequently are they involved? What types of delinquent offenses occur most often? Is delinquency increasing, decreasing, or staying the same? Are violent delinquent acts increasing? When and where do most delinquent offenses occur? To address these questions, we rely on data from self-report surveys, but we also turn to juvenile arrest and juvenile court data. The focus here is not on individual offenders or offending, but on juveniles as a group, so that we can obtain a general understanding of delinquent behavior. We will describe four key areas of study with regard to the extent of delinquent offenses: prevalence and incidence, relative frequency, trends, and spatial (place) and temporal (time) distribution. Taken together, these considerations provide a solid understanding of the extent of juvenile delinquency.

Prevalence and incidence of delinquent offenses

One of the most basic considerations regarding delinquency is the extent to which youth engage in delinquent behavior. This consideration begins with the prevalence and incidence of delinquency among adolescents. **Prevalence** refers to the proportion of youth involved in delinquent acts. Prevalence is usually stated in terms of a percentage – the percentage of youth who are involved in delinquent acts. **Incidence**, a measure of the frequency of offending, is the average number of delinquent offenses committed by adolescents in general, or by particular delinquent youth.

When considering the prevalence and incidence of delinquency, remember that juvenile delinquency is a broad legal category which refers to a wide range of offenses, from truancy to homicide. Research will produce very different results depending on the collection of delinquent acts included in the measurement instrument (Mosher, Miethe, and Hart 2011; Hindelang, Hirschi, and Weis 1979). If only minor forms of delinquent behavior are measured through a self-report instrument, delinquency may be found to be incredibly widespread. If, however, only serious delinquent acts are included, or if only arrest data are used, it may appear that relatively few youth are "delinquent."

Self-report data

Self-report studies consistently indicate that the number of youth who commit crimes is far greater than official statistics lead us to believe. A recent nationwide self-report survey, called the National Longitudinal Survey of Youth (NLSY), annually interviewed nearly 9,000 youth, asking them about many aspects of their lives, including law-violating behaviors. A considerable portion of the youth reported involvement in delinquent acts by the time they were 17 years of age (Snyder and Sickmund 2006: 70).

- 33 percent were suspended from school
- 18 percent ran away from home
- 8 percent belonged to a gang
- 37 percent vandalized property
- 43 percent stole something valued at less than $50
- 13 percent stole something valued at more than $50
- 27 percent assaulted with the intent to seriously hurt
- 16 percent sold drugs

Prevalence findings from self-report studies like the NLSY indicate clearly that a sizable portion of youth report involvement in minor acts of misconduct, but relatively few report involvement in serious forms of lawbreaking. The National Youth Survey (NYS), described in Chapter 3, included a comprehensive set of behavioral items that measured the full range of delinquent offenses. Because of the size and representativeness of the sample, the NYS provides some of the most valid and reliable estimates of the prevalence and incidence of delinquency. The NYS revealed that almost two-thirds of the youths reported involvement in less serious offenses like minor theft, minor assault, and property damage, whereas about one-sixth reported involvement in serious forms of assault including aggravated assault, sexual assault, and gang fights (Huizinga and Elliott 1987: 210–211).

To gauge the amount of crime committed by youth, it is also useful to consider the frequency of their involvement. Frequency is usually reported in terms of the incidence of delinquency. Table 4.1 reports both prevalence and incidence findings from the Monitoring the Future survey (MTF) (Bachman, Johnston, and O'Malley 2014). MTF is an annual survey of high school seniors that asks questions about a broad range of activities, including delinquency and drug use in the previous 12-month period. Table 4.1 shows that a significant portion of high school seniors report involvement in delinquent offenses (prevalence). Although most self-reported offenses are minor, a surprising percentage of high school seniors reported involvement in fairly serious offenses. Only 6 percent, however, said they were arrested or taken to the police station. The incidence of self-reported delinquency indicates clearly that delinquent acts are a one- or two-time occurrence. The various behaviors that constitute delinquency are infrequent and sporadic – seldom do youth continue in a repetitive pattern of delinquency (Sickmund and Puzzanchera 2014; Huizinga et al. 2000).[1] For example, while 14 percent of the youth reported that they had participated in a group fight, only 3 percent had been involved three or more times.

Table 4.2 provides prevalence and incidence findings on student drug use from the MTF survey (Johnston et al. 2014). This table reports on not only high school seniors, but also 8th and 10th graders, who were added to the survey in 1991. The prevalence of drug use is indicated by the percentage of youth reporting that they had "ever used." The percentage of students reporting that they used different types of drugs is strikingly high, especially for alcohol and marijuana. The incidence of drug use is represented by the percentage reporting use during the "last 12 months," the "last 30 days," and "daily use." The percentages for daily, 30-day, and annual use drop considerably from those reporting "ever used," indicating that for most forms of drug use frequent use is not common. The glaring exceptions to this observation are alcohol and marijuana use: 39.2 percent of the high school seniors report alcohol consumption in the last 30 days and 22.9 percent report marijuana use in the last 30 days. "Daily use" of marijuana or hashish is reported by 6.5 percent of the seniors. One other startling observation is the high incidence and prevalence of inhalant use by 8th-grade students: 10.8 percent report that they have used inhalants, with 5.2 percent indicating that they have used inhalants in the last 12 months and 2.7 percent indicating inhalant use in the last 30 days.

Self-report data allow us to see that although delinquent acts are common among adolescents, relatively few youths report frequent or repetitive involvement. Nonetheless, a substantial proportion of adolescents report involvement in crime, and some of these offenses are quite serious. Furthermore, of those youths who commit delinquent acts only a small portion come to the attention of the police, relatively few are arrested, and even fewer are processed by juvenile courts.

Official data

Both the Uniform Crime Reporting program and *Juvenile Court Statistics* provide official data relevant to an understanding of the extent of delinquency.

Uniform Crime Reporting program

When juvenile offenders come to the attention of the police and are arrested, they are counted in the Uniform Crime Reporting (UCR) program. As we described in Chapter 3,

Table 4.1 Prevalence and incidence of self-reported delinquency in the Monitoring the Future survey, 2012

In the last 12 months, how often have you ...	Not at all (%)	Once (%)	Twice (%)	3–4 times (%)	> 5 times (%)
Argued or had a fight with either of your parents?	15.0	11.0	13.0	25.4	35.6
Damaged school property on purpose?	92.4	3.9	1.5	1.2	1.1
Gone into some house or building when you weren't supposed to be there?	78.9	10.3	5.6	2.7	2.4
Taken a car that didn't belong to someone in your family without permission of the owner?	96.1	1.9	0.9	0.5	0.5
Taken something from a store without paying for it?	77.9	9.2	4.8	4.0	4.2
Taken something not belonging to you worth under $50?	77.9	11.0	2.0	2.9	3.2
Taken something not belonging to you worth over $50?	92.7	3.7	1.6	0.7	1.4
Used a knife or gun or some other thing (like a club) to get something from a person?	97.3	1.3	0.8	0.2	0.4
Gotten into a serious fight in school or at work?	88.9	7.0	1.9	1.3	1.0
Hurt someone badly enough to need bandages or a doctor?	89.7	6.4	2.0	.08	1.1
Taken part in a fight where a group of your friends were against another group?	85.7	7.1	4.2	1.6	1.4
Been arrested and taken to a police station?	94.4	3.9	1.0	0.5	0.3

Within the LAST 12 MONTHS how many times, if any, have you ...	None (%)	Once (%)	Twice (%)	3 times (%)	> 4 times (%)
Received a ticket (OR been stopped and warned) for moving [traffic] violations?	80.4	12.6	4.3	1.4	1.2
Received a traffic ticket or warning after:					
...drinking alcoholic beverages	94.3	3.8	1.3	0.4	0.3
...smoking marijuana or hashish	93.4	4.4	1.3	0.5	0.4
Involved in a driving accident after:					
...drinking alcoholic beverages	96.0	3.0	0.4	0.2	0.4
...smoking marijuana or hashish	97.1	2.0	0.3	0.2	0.4

Source: Bachman et al. (2014:27–28, 115–117). Retrieved December 24, 2014 (www.monitoringthefuture.org/pubs.html#refvols).

Table 4.2 Prevalence and incidence of drug use: Monitoring the Future survey, 2013

		Ever used (lifetime) (%)	Used in last 12 months (annual) (%)	Used in last 30 days (%)	Daily use (%)
Alcohol: Any Use	8th Grade	27.8	22.1	10.2	0.3
	10th Grade	52.1	47.1	25.7	0.9
	12th Grade	68.2	62.0	39.2	2.2
Alcohol: Been Drunk	8th Grade	12.2	8.4	3.5	0.1
	10th Grade	33.5	27.1	12.8	0.3
	12th Grade	52.5	43.5	26.0	1.3
Marijuana/Hashish	8th Grade	16.5	12.7	6.5	1.1
	10th Grade	35.8	29.8	17.0	4.0
	12th Grade	45.5	36.4	22.9	6.5
Illicit Drug other than Marijuana	8th Grade	9.3	5.8	2.6	–
	10th Grade	15.7	10.9	5.0	–
	12th Grade	24.7	17.3	8.4	–
Inhalants	8th Grade	10.8	5.2	2.7	–
	10th Grade	8.7	3.5	1.4	–
	12th Grade	6.9	2.5	0.9	–
Cigarettes	8th Grade	14.8	–	4.5	1.8
	10th Grade	25.7	–	9.1	4.4
	12th Grade	38.1	–	16.3	8.5
Prescription Drug Misuse	12th Grade	21.5	15.0	7.0	–

Source: Johnston et al. (2014: 55–68).
Retrieved December 28, 2014 (www.monitoringthefuture.org/pubs.html#refvols).

the UCR program primarily gathers three types of information: offenses known to police, crimes cleared, and persons arrested. Of the three types, offenses known to the police provide the clearest picture of the volume and trends of juvenile arrests. When an offense is merely reported and no arrest is made, the age of the offender cannot be determined or recorded, and in these cases specific information on juvenile crimes is unavailable. The extent of juvenile crime, as represented by the UCR, is therefore based on juvenile arrest and clearance data. Keep in mind, however, what these data report. Because these data are collected only when juvenile offenders come to the attention of the police, much juvenile crime goes unrecorded by the UCR. As a result, arrest and clearance data are poor indicators of the extent of juvenile delinquency. Rather, these data reflect police action taken in response to juvenile crime, as well as the proportion of crime known to the police that is attributed to juveniles (Puzzanchera 2014). Nonetheless, these data provide insight into the delinquency problem encountered by the police and the rest of the juvenile justice system.

Population estimates for 2013 reveal that about 73.6 million persons in the United States were under age 18, 23.3 percent of the total population. In most states, these individuals are legally classified as "juveniles" (Sickmund and Puzzanchera 2014). Table 4.3 shows the number, percentage, and rates of arrests for juveniles and adults, as reported in *Crime in the United States, 2013*, the major annual UCR report. Over 875,000 of the arrests recorded involved juveniles, whereas over 8 million arrests involved adults. These numbers indicate the actual number of arrests made by law enforcement, not the number of individuals arrested, because

Table 4.3 Juvenile and adult arrests and arrest rates, by type of crime, 2013

Type of crime	Number of arrests		Percentage of arrests		Arrest rate per 100,000 in age group	
	Juveniles 0–17	Adults	Juveniles 0–17	Adults	Juveniles 13–17	Adults
All crimes	875,262	8,194,730	9.7	90.3	3,909.2	3,378.7
Part I crimes	242,250	1,411,652	14.6	85.4	1,083.6	582.0
Violent crimes	43,651	349,127	11.1	88.9	195.0	143.9
Homicide	614	7,787	7.3	92.7	2.9	3.2
Forcible rape	2,089	11,528	15.3	84.7	8.9	4.8
Robbery	15,932	62,821	20.2	79.8	74.3	25.9
Aggravated assault	25,016	266,991	8.6	91.4	108.8	110.1
Property crimes	198,599	1,062,525	15.7	84.3	888.6	438.1
Burglary	34,760	168,949	17.1	82.9	156.1	69.7
Larceny-theft	151,427	845,068	15.2	84.8	677.6	348.4
Motor vehicle theft	9,469	43,038	18.0	82.0	44.2	17.7
Arson	2,943	5,470	35.0	65.0	10.7	2.3
Part II crimes	633,012	6,783,078	8.5	91.5	2,825.6	2,796.7

Note: Arrest figures based on 11,951 reporting agencies, with 2013 estimated U.S. population of 245,741,701. Population figures from U.S. Census data for 2013: juvenile population = 73,585,872; juvenile population ages 13 – 17 = 20,862,152; adult population = 242,542,967; total population = 316,128,839. See Table 3.1 in Chapter 3 for a list of all Part II crimes.
Sources: Federal Bureau of Investigation (2014: Table 38). Retrieved December 28, 2014 (www.fbi.gov/about-us/cjis/ucr/crime-in-the-u.s/2013/crime-in-the-u.s.-2013/tables/table-38/table_38_arrests_by_age_2013.xls); Puzzanchera et al. (2014). Retrieved December 28, 2014 (www.ojjdp.gov/ojstatbb/ezapop/).

some individuals are arrested more than once in a given year. The number of arrests also does not represent the number of crimes committed "because a series of crimes that one person commits may culminate in a single arrest, and a single crime may result in the arrest of more than one person" (Puzzanchera 2014: 2). Nonetheless, the number of arrests provides a relative representation of the arrests that involve juveniles, as compared to adults.

The percentage of arrests indicates the proportion of arrests that involved juveniles (under the age of 18) and adults (ages 18 and over). In 2013, juveniles accounted for 9.7 percent of all arrests, 14.6 percent of arrests for UCR Part I offenses, and 8.5 percent of arrests for UCR Part II offenses.

To understand the extent of juvenile delinquency, it is most important to consider the ages 13 through 17 – the age range in which juveniles are most involved in crime.[2] In 2013, this group numbered 20.9 million, or about 6.6 percent of the U.S. population (Puzzanchera, Sladky, and Kang 2014). The arrest rates presented in Table 4.3 are stated in terms of the number of arrests per 100,000 juveniles, ages 13 through 17. The juvenile arrest rate of 3,909 for all UCR crimes is substantially higher than the adult arrest rate of 3,379 per 100,000 adults. The disparity in juvenile and adult arrest rates is even more pronounced for certain types of crime such as robbery, burglary, larceny–theft, and motor vehicle theft. That is the topic of discussion in our next section on the relative frequency of delinquent offenses. The conclusion is clear, however: arrest rates for juveniles between the ages of 13 and 17 are considerably higher than arrest rates for adults for most types of crime.

Although UCR data addressing juvenile offenses are based on the number of juvenile arrests, these data provide a sense of the extent of juvenile delinquency in terms of the volume confronted by the juvenile justice system at its entry point – law enforcement. As such, UCR data report *arrest* prevalence, rather than *offense* prevalence. The proportion of youth actually involved in crime is not represented by arrest data.

Juvenile Court Statistics

As we described in Chapter 3, *Juvenile Court Statistics* provides data on cases processed by juvenile courts across the United States. If most crime goes unreported and never comes to the attention of the police, an even smaller portion of juvenile crime is referred to juvenile courts. As a result, neither arrest nor juvenile court data provide accurate estimates of the extent of juvenile delinquency. Nonetheless, data from *Juvenile Court Statistics* provide valuable information on the estimated number of cases processed by juvenile courts. As such, these data represent society's "official" response to the problem of delinquency.

In 2011, juvenile courts handled 1,236,186 delinquency cases and 116,200 petitioned status cases (Hockenberry and Puzzanchera 2014). Note that the number of delinquency cases refers to the number of cases at intake through disposition, while the number of status offense cases counts only those cases that are dealt with by juvenile courts through petitioning, the legal document that initiates formal court hearings. The number of petitioned status offenses does not include status offense cases handled informally by social welfare agencies or juvenile courts without petition. If we conservatively estimate that the number of non-petitioned status offense cases is at least equal to the number that are petitioned, then juvenile courts handle more than 232,000 status offenses each year – about 12 percent of all cases.[3] Thus, status offense cases are a substantial portion of the caseload in most juvenile courts.

Prevalence and incidence in brief

Our analysis of the prevalence and incidence of juvenile delinquency leads to the clear conclusion that a substantial portion of all adolescents are involved in crime. For most youth, however, delinquency is not a frequent or regular activity. Moreover, relatively few youths are dealt with officially by the police or the juvenile courts. The limited frequency of offending suggests that most youths do not develop a persistent pattern of delinquent behavior. The disproportionate involvement of young people in crime, however, is a straightforward indication that there is something distinctive about the adolescent and young adult years that generates high rates of crime for this particular age group. Yet not all adolescents are involved in criminal acts, and most do not develop serious, repetitive patterns of delinquent behavior. So what is it about the adolescent and young adult years that is conducive to criminal involvement for some, but not all, youth? This is a fundamental question for criminology that will be addressed in the chapters that follow.

Relative frequency of different types of offenses

The prevalence and incidence of juvenile delinquency provide a general understanding of the extent to which young people are involved in crime. It is also useful to consider the types of crime that juveniles are most involved in. Relative to each other, what types of juvenile offenses are most common? We refer to this as the **relative frequency** of juvenile offenses. This, too, can be studied by looking at different sources of data to see if identifiable patterns can be observed.

Self-report data

Self-report surveys reveal that a sizable portion of youth report involvement in a wide variety of minor misconduct, but relatively few youths are involved in serious forms of lawbreaking. In addition, only the less serious forms of delinquency are committed with any frequency. More specifically, these self-report data indicate that the most common forms of adolescent misconduct are using alcohol and marijuana, lying about age, skipping school, committing minor theft, damaging the property of others, entering a house or building without permission, engaging in disorderly conduct, making threats of physical harm, and fighting (Bachman et al. 2014; Sickmund and Puzzanchera 2014; Snyder and Sickmund 2006; Huizinga and Elliott 1987). This is not to say that serious violent crime by juveniles is non-existent or unimportant. Self-report data point out that youth are involved in serious crime, but in terms of relative frequency minor delinquency significantly outpaces serious delinquency. As a result, the nature of delinquency is most accurately characterized as minor offenses. This is readily apparent in the MTF data reported in Table 4.1.

Without a doubt, the most common form of illegal activity for youth is drug use. The MTF survey reports that in 2011, 68 percent of all high school seniors have used alcohol, 53 percent have been drunk, 46 percent have used marijuana, and 25 percent have tried an illicit drug other than marijuana (see Table 4.2). Reported drug use in the last 30 days is also substantial. The scope of the drug problem is revealed most visibly when more frequent and excessive drug use among high school seniors is considered. Almost 9 percent report daily cigarette use, 7 percent report daily marijuana use, and 3 percent report daily alcohol use (see Table 4.2). More troubling is the finding that 22 percent of the high school seniors reported drinking five or more drinks in a row in the last two weeks – a measure of binge drinking (Johnston et al. 2014). Since 2005, MTF has gathered data from high school seniors regarding prescription drug misuse – use "without a doctor telling you to use them." A sizable proportion (22 percent) of these youths misused prescription drugs at some point in their lifetime; 15 percent misused prescription drugs in the last year and 7 percent misused them in the last 30 days (see Table 4.2).

It is also important to note that law violations are more common for youth who use drugs than for those who do not (Snyder and Sickmund 2006; Osgood et al. 1988). Youth who use alcohol, marijuana, or other illicit drugs are more likely to be involved in a variety of delinquent acts than are youth who do not use drugs.[4] Like other forms of delinquency, less frequent and less serious forms of drug use are most common among adolescents. As we have seen, although 68 percent of high school seniors have tried alcohol, only 2 percent use it on a daily basis (frequency). Although 46 percent of high school seniors have tried marijuana, far fewer (2 percent) have tried methamphetamine, a drug that has captured much recent attention (seriousness) (Johnston et al. 2014).

Official data

Official data confirm the relative frequency of delinquent offenses that is revealed in self-report data. This is evident in both UCR data and in *Juvenile Court Statistics*.

Uniform Crime Reporting program

Juveniles are arrested for some offenses more frequently than others. In 2013, juveniles accounted for 16 percent of all arrests for property crimes and 11 percent of all arrests for violent crimes. This difference in arrest is revealed more clearly with regard to particular offenses, as shown in Figure 4.1.[5] Clearly, juvenile crime, as indicated by the proportion of arrests involving juveniles, is predominantly property crime and various forms of public order crime. Arrest rates also demonstrate that juvenile crime is predominantly property crime. The juvenile arrest rate for property crimes is 889 per 100,000 adolescents, compared to an arrest rate for violent crimes of 195 per 100,000 adolescents (see Table 4.3).

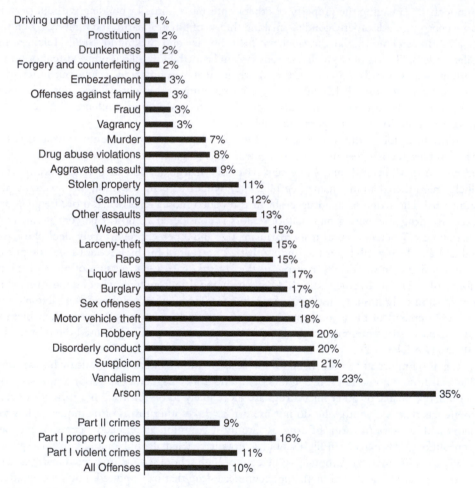

Figure 4.1 Percentage of arrests involving juveniles. In 2013, juveniles were involved in about 1 in 11 arrests for violent crime and 1 in 6 for property crime.
Source: Federal Bureau of Investigation (2014: adapted from Table 38). Retrieved December 28, 2014 (www.fbi.gov/about-us/cjis/ucr/crime-in-the-u.s/2013/crime-in-the-u.s.-2013/tables/table-38/table_38_arrests_by_age_2013.xls).

Table 4.4 Juvenile court delinquency caseload, 2011

	Number of cases 2011	% Change		Offense profile %		
		1985–1997*	1997*–2011	1985	1997*	2011
Total delinquency cases	1,236,186	62	−34	–	–	–
Person offenses	317,473	131	−23	16	23	26
Property offenses	447,473	24	−49	61	47	36
Drug law violations	152,617	146	−19	7	10	12
Public order offenses	318,622	98	−16	17	21	26

* The estimated number of juvenile court cases peaked in 1997 at 1,872,702 cases handled by juvenile courts across the United States.
Source: Sickmund et al. (2014). Retrieved December 29, 2014 (http://ojjdp.ncjrs.gov/ojstatbb/ezajcs/).

Juvenile Court Statistics

Juvenile Court Statistics provides a depiction of the relative frequency of different types of juvenile offenses that is very consistent with self-report and UCR data (Hockenberry and Puzzanchera 2014). Table 4.4 shows that the largest portion of all juvenile court cases are property offenses (36 percent), followed by public order offenses (26 percent) and person offenses (26 percent), and finally drug law violations (12 percent). Although property offenses constitute more than one out of three delinquency cases referred to the juvenile court, this category is a much smaller portion of the court's caseload in 2011 (36 percent) than it was in 1985 (61 percent). Juvenile court cases are concentrated in a few specific offense types: simple assault (18 percent), larceny-theft (18 percent), obstruction of justice (12 percent, a public order offense), disorderly conduct (7 percent, also a public order offense), burglary (6 percent), and vandalism (6 percent) (Hockenberry and Puzzanchera 2014: 7). Data on petitioned status offense cases show that truancy (40 percent) is most common, followed by liquor violations (20 percent), ungovernability (12 percent), curfew violations (10 percent), and runaway (9 percent) (Hockenberry and Puzzanchera 2014: 66).

Relative frequency in brief

All forms of delinquency data confirm that minor forms of delinquent behavior are far more common than serious, violent offenses. Property offenses far exceed violent offenses. Various self-report studies, arrest data (UCR), and juvenile court cases (*Juvenile Court Statistics*) indicate that certain types of delinquency are most common and occur with greater frequency than other offenses: alcohol and marijuana violations; minor theft; property damage and vandalism; disorderly conduct; fighting and simple assault; and truancy. Even though these types of delinquent offenses predominate, delinquent youths rarely specialize in the type of crime they commit (Farrington et al. 2003; Piquero, Farrington, and Blumstein 2003; Farrington 1988; Blumstein et al. 1986; Elliott, Huizinga, and Menard 1989; Elliott, Huizinga, and Ageton 1985; Hamparian et al. 1985). In addition, their involvement is infrequent, sporadic, and non-repetitive (Huizinga et al. 2000).

Trends in delinquent offenses

If we were to ask the general public how juvenile delinquency has changed in recent years, most would respond that juvenile crime is growing increasingly worse (Blumstein 2000). Not only are delinquent offenses growing in number, the general public imagines, but juveniles are also becoming more violent. Is this true? To answer this question, we will examine trends in delinquent offenses.

Self-report data

Monitoring the Future, the annual survey of high school seniors, was designed to chart changes in attitudes, values, and behaviors from one class of seniors to the next, beginning with the class of 1975. Earlier we considered the incidence and prevalence of delinquent activity in the class of 2012. But how do the different classes of high school seniors over the years compare to one another in terms of delinquent acts? The activities included in the MTF survey tend to be relatively minor. Nonetheless, these data provide the only annual depiction of self-reported delinquency that is representative of a sizable segment of American youth. Figure 4.2 shows the 25-year trends in annual prevalence from 1988 through 2012. Represented are the percentages of high school seniors reporting that they had gotten into a serious fight, taken something worth under $50, taken something worth over $50, entered a house or building without permission, and been arrested and taken to a police station. The serious fight and theft questions were chosen because they represent both the most common and serious forms of

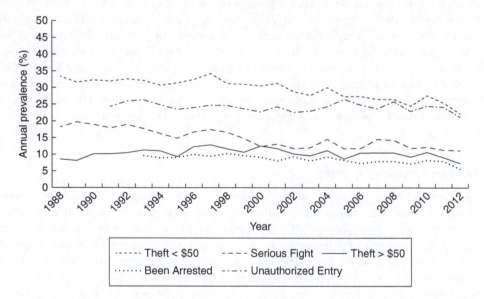

Figure 4.2 Prevalence trends in self-reported delinquency among high school seniors: serious fight, theft, unauthorized entry, and arrest, 1988–2012 (25 years; arrest since 1993; unauthorized entry since 1991).

Source: Bachman et al. (2014: 115–117). Retrieved December 30, 2014 (www. monitoringthefuture.org/pubs.html#refvols). Corresponding published documents reporting questionnaire responses from 1988–1995 were used; data from 1996–2012 are available online at the MTF website noted above.

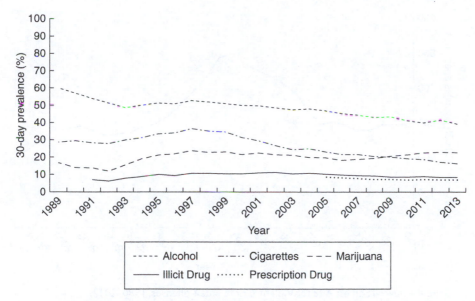

Figure 4.3 Thirty-day prevalence trends in self-reported alcohol, marijuana, illicit drug (other than
marijuana), prescription drug, and cigarette use among high school seniors, 1989–2013
(25 years; prescription drug use since 2005).
Source: Johnston et al. (2014: 55–68).
Retrieved December 28, 2014 (www.monitoringthefuture.org/pubs.html#refvols).

property and violent crime. Less serious theft and unauthorized entry into a house or building are also quite common. Although the data show fluctuations from year to year, the general
trend for these four offenses has been one of decline since 1997, except for unauthorized
entry, which stayed fairly consistent until 2008 and then declined.

We also looked previously at self-reported drug use among high school seniors. Figure 4.3
depicts the 25-year trends in use of alcohol, marijuana, illicit drugs (other than marijuana),
and cigarettes in the last 30 days, and, with data since 2005, prescription drug misuse (use
without a doctor's prescription), as reported by high school seniors. Cigarette and alcohol use
within the last 30 days showed a steady decline since 1997. Illicit drug use in the last 30 days
showed a fairly stable pattern from 1997 until 2005, and then declined modestly. Marijuana
use in the last 30 days declined from 1997 until about 2007, when use began to increase gradually. Prescription drug misuse has declined in this same time period that marijuana use has
increased. It seems as if this recent increase in marijuana use stands in contrast to the decline
in the 30-day prevalence trends of the four other drugs considered here (alcohol, cigarettes,
illicit drugs, and prescription drugs).

Official data

Official data provide important information about the trends in juvenile cases that are dealt
with by agencies in juvenile justice systems throughout the United States. Trends in juvenile
arrests and juvenile court caseloads, for example, are revealed in official data.

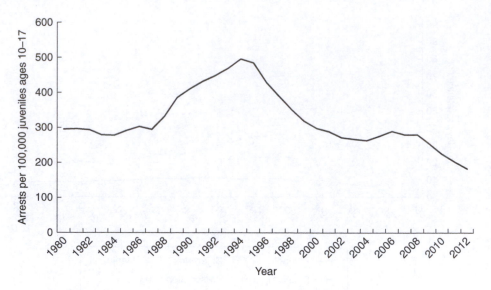

Figure 4.4 Juvenile arrest rate for Violent Crime Index offenses, 1980–2012.
Source: OJJDP Statistical Briefing Book (2014).
Retrieved May 27, 2014 (www.ojjdp.gov/ojstatbb/crime/excel/JAR_2012.xls).

Uniform Crime Reporting program

UCR data can be used to assess trends in the volume of juvenile arrests. The Violent Crime Index is made up of murder and non-negligent manslaughter, forcible rape, robbery, and aggravated assault. The Property Crime Index includes burglary, larceny-theft, motor vehicle theft, and arson. To analyze trends, it is most accurate to express both the Violent Crime Index and the Property Crime Index in terms of arrest rate – the number of juvenile arrests for Index crimes per 100,000 juveniles, ages 10 through 17 (Puzzanchera 2014).

Figure 4.4 shows that, after a rather stable pattern for much of the 1980s, the juvenile Violent Crime Index increased between 1988 and 1994. This increase in juvenile arrest rate drew national attention to the problem of juvenile violence. However, after peaking in 1994, the juvenile arrest rate for violent crimes dropped each year through 2004, followed by a small increase in 2005 and 2006, and then a decline from 2007 to 2012. The Violent Crime Index reached historically low levels from 2009 to 2012; "the rate in 2012 was 63% below the 1994 peak" (Puzzanchera 2014: 6).

The Property Crime Index is another story. Figure 4.5 reveals that, despite a notable dip in 1983 and 1984, the juvenile arrest rate for Property Crime Index crimes was quite stable for the 15-year period from 1980 to 1994. The following 18 years showed a significant drop in the arrest rate for juvenile property crime. In fact, "juveniles were less likely to be arrested for property crimes in 2012 than at any point in the past 33 years" (Puzzanchera 2014: 7).

Juvenile Court Statistics

Trends in the number of juvenile court delinquency cases parallel trends in juvenile arrest for both property and violent crime. Table 4.4 shows that the number of delinquency cases for all categories of offenses has declined since a peak in 1997. The offense profile of delinquency

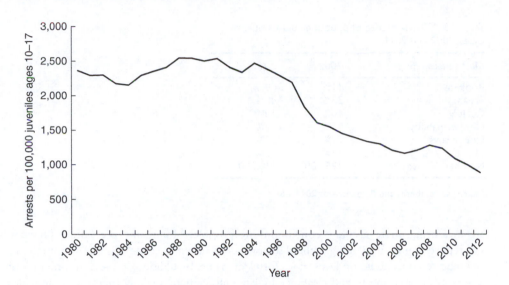

Figure 4.5 Juvenile arrest rate for Property Crime Index offenses, 1980–2012.
  Source: *OJJDP Statistical Briefing Book* (2014).
  Retrieved May 27, 2014 (www.ojjdp.gov/ojstatbb/crime/excel/JAR_2012.xls).

cases in juvenile courts has also changed, with a smaller portion of the cases being property offenses, and a greater portion of the cases being person, drug law, and public order offenses (Hockenberry and Puzzanchera 2014).

The number of petitioned status offense cases in juvenile courts shows a similar rise and fall with a peak in the early 2000s. *Juvenile Court Statistics 2011* indicates that "between 1995 and 2000, the formally handled status offense caseload increased considerably (55%) and then declined 40% through 2011" (Hockenberry and Puzzanchera 2014: 66). The offense profile of petitioned status offense cases has remained relatively constant, except that a larger portion of the caseload involves truancy cases – see Table 4.5 (Hockenberry and Puzzanchera 2014: 66).

In conjunction with this trend in juvenile court cases, there is a growing tendency for police to make referrals to the juvenile court, rather than to deal with juveniles informally through some type of warn-and-release process. In 1972, 51 percent of all juveniles taken into police custody were referred to juvenile court, whereas 45 percent were handled informally within the department. By 2002, police were far more likely to refer cases to juvenile court (73 percent) than to deal with juvenile matters within the police department (18 percent). This trend has subsided in recent years, with 68 percent of the juveniles taken into custody in 2013 referred to the juvenile court and 23 percent of these juveniles handled in the police department (FBI 2014).[6] Thus, trends in the number of juvenile court cases must be tempered by the realization that these trends depict changes in how juvenile offenses are dealt with by the police more than they indicate trends in juvenile delinquency.

Juvenile crime trends in brief

A clear conclusion about trends in juvenile crime is simply not possible because differ-ent sources of data provide different pictures. However, if we keep in mind what the data

Table 4.5 Offense profile of petitioned status offense cases, 2002 and 2011

Most serious offense	2002	2011
Runaway	11%	9%
Truancy	33%	40%
Curfew	10%	10%
Ungovernability	11%	12%
Liquor laws	21%	20%
Miscellaneous	13%	9%
Number of cases	195,300	116,200

Source: Hockenberry and Puzzanchera (2014: 66).

are measuring, more accurate conclusions are possible. Monitoring the Future provides a self-reported indication of high school seniors' involvement in crime. Questions from the survey tend to concentrate on less serious forms of crime. In addition, less serious offenses have low rates of reporting to and clearance by law enforcement, making them more difficult to track with official sources of data, like the UCR. For this reason, self-report surveys are good indicators of trends in less serious juvenile crime, such as less serious forms of violent and property crime, public order offenses, liquor law and drug abuse violations, and status offenses. Reporting is less problematic for violent crime, making arrest data more valid and reliable as a measure of violent juvenile crime trends. With these qualifications, we can draw several conclusions about trends.

Throughout much of the 1990s, juvenile property crime fluctuated, but it is apparent that there was not a substantial increase. In fact, self-reported property offenses tend to reveal a decline since the latter part of the 1990s. Juvenile arrest data for property crime similarly showed a decline after the mid-1990s. Different measures of violent crime committed by juveniles show an increase in the late 1980s and into the 1990s, but since the mid-1990s violent crime has declined, and depending on the measure, sometimes quite substantially. Drug use by adolescents, including the use of alcohol, declined throughout the 1980s and early 1990s, and then increased somewhat in the mid-1990s. This was followed by another decline in the latter part of the decade and into the new century. Based on his analysis of arrest data, Charles Puzzanchera of the National Center for Juvenile Justice concludes that there has been a "substantial reduction in the law-violating behavior of American youth" over the last two decades (Puzzanchera 2009: 5; see also Puzzanchera 2014). His conclusion is also valid when considering the various measures of delinquency.

One of the biggest contemporary controversies in criminology has to do with predictions resulting from the observed increase in juvenile arrests for violent crime from 1988 to 1994, which focused national attention on the problem of juvenile violence. Projections of a growing juvenile population, together with increasing gun violence by juveniles and their involvement in the illicit drug market, led some criminologists and policy analysts to predict a new generation of juvenile offenders, one that was exceedingly violent (Bennett, DiIulio, and Walters 1996; Blumstein 1995a, 1995b; Coordinating Council on Juvenile Justice and Delinquency Prevention 1996; DiIulio 1995). Some criminologists labeled them "superpredators" (Bennett et al. 1996). Many believed that these trends, taken together, provided just the right ingredients for an epidemic of youth violence. The epidemic, however, never materialized, and, as we have seen, violent crime by juveniles has actually declined since the mid-1990s. More recent explanations of trends in juvenile crime address its precipitous drop since the mid-1990s, taking into account changes in the size of the adolescent population, economic conditions, tougher laws and enforcement practices, and patterns of drug use and abuse (Zimring 2005; Levitt 2004; Bernard 1999; Blumstein 2000; Fox 2000; Levitt 1999; Cook and Laub 1998; Steffensmeier and Harer 1999).

The ecology of juvenile offenses: spatial and temporal distribution

One of the oldest observations about crime and delinquency is that offenses are not evenly distributed in place and time (Beirne and Messerschmidt 2011; Beirne 1987). In the 1920s and 1930s, two pioneering sociologists at the University of Chicago, Robert Park and Ernest Burgess, observed that a variety of social problems, including crime and delinquency, were distributed ecologically – in a geographic pattern associated with the growth of cities. Based on this observation, Clifford Shaw and Henry McKay began their extensive study of juvenile delinquency in Chicago. They found that juvenile delinquency varied considerably across the city. Offenses were concentrated in the central part of the city and diminished as distance from the city center increased. Shaw and McKay argued that this "geographic distribution" of delinquency was closely connected to the social characteristics of neighborhoods (Shaw et al. 1929; Shaw and McKay 1969; see also Sampson and Groves 1989; Kornhauser 1978). We describe Shaw and McKay's work more thoroughly in Chapter 11.

Criminologists have maintained a steady interest in the **ecology of delinquency** by examining the **spatial** and **temporal distribution** of offense (Byrne and Sampson 1986). Here we focus on the spatial distribution of delinquent offenses across three areas of different population size: urban, suburban, and rural. We examine the commonly accepted notion that delinquent offenses occur at a much higher rate in urban areas than in rural areas. We also consider the temporal dimension of time of day, or when delinquency occurs.

Self-report data

The National Youth Survey is one of the only self-report surveys that reports urban–rural differences in the prevalence and incidence of delinquent offenses. Across a variety of delinquent acts, including public order offenses, violent offenses, property offenses, and illicit drug use, a greater percentage of urban youth report involvement than do suburban and rural youth (prevalence). As compared to suburban and rural youth, youth from urban areas are also more frequently involved in these various delinquency offenses (incidence). One of the only exceptions to this pattern is that alcohol use was equally distributed in terms of the percentage of youth self-reporting and in terms of frequency of alcohol across different sizes of place (McGarrell and Flanagan 1985: 373–375).

Official data: Uniform Crime Reporting program

UCR data provide juvenile arrest statistics that are categorized in terms of type of community: metropolitan city, suburban, and rural. Table 4.6 shows that juveniles account for a larger portion of the arrests in metropolitan and suburban areas, as compared to rural areas. In rural

Table 4.6 Percentage of arrests involving juveniles, by community type, 2013

Crime Category	Community Type		
	City (%)	Suburban (%)	Rural (%)
Total crime (Part I & II)	10.7	9.3	4.8
Violent crime (Part I)	11.9	10.8	6.2
Property crime (Part I)	16.5	14.5	9.7

Source: Federal Bureau of Investigation (2014: Tables 47, 59, and 65). Retrieved January 8, 2015 (www.fbi.gov/about-us/cjis/ucr/crime-in-the-u.s/2013/crime-in-the-u.s.-2013/persons-arrested/persons-arrested).

areas, 4.8 percent of all arrests involved juveniles, compared to 9.3 percent in suburban areas and 10.7 percent in cities.

Juvenile arrest rates across these population categories would provide a more direct measure of ecological variation than do data on percentage of arrests that involved juveniles. However, the UCR does not provide such information. Some time ago, Howard Snyder and Ellen Nimick, of the National Center for Juvenile Justice, calculated juvenile arrest rates and found that the juvenile property crimes arrest rate was 2,216 (per 100,000 youth ages 10 through 17) for youth in cities, compared to 1,297 for suburban youth, and 625 for youth in rural areas (Jensen and Rojek 1998: 91). These findings indicate that delinquency, as measured by arrest rates, is a much greater problem in urban than in rural areas.

The new generation of UCR data, called the National Incident-Based Reporting System (NIBRS), collects information on each crime reported to law enforcement, including the time the crime was committed. Analysis of this temporal dimension for juvenile and adult violent crime appears in Figures 4.6a and 4.6b. These two graphs reveal that juvenile violence peaks in the after-school hours on school days and in the early evening hours on non-school days – a pattern similar for males and females and for whites and blacks. These findings on the temporal patterns of juvenile violence have spurred a host of after-school programs that provide supervised activity for youth after the school day. Juvenile drug law and weapon law violations reach their highest level during school hours, indicating how often schools are a setting for these crimes and their detection. Temporal patterns of shoplifting are similar on school and non-school days, peaking in the later afternoon hours (Sickmund and Puzzanchera 2014; Snyder and Sickmund 2006).

Ecology of delinquency in brief

The taken-for-granted urban–rural difference in juvenile delinquency is confirmed in findings that use different sources of data. The National Youth Survey, a self-report survey, reveals that a variety of delinquent offenses are more common among urban youth than among suburban or rural youth, and urban youth commit these offenses with greater frequency. UCR arrest data show similar ecological variation in delinquency, with urban and suburban youth accounting for a greater percentage of arrests as compared to rural youth. Juvenile arrest rates are also higher in cities than in suburban or rural areas. The new generation of UCR data (NIBRS) provides a temporal dimension to arrest data, allowing us to see when juvenile crime occurs. The temporal pattern for juvenile crime is distinct from adult crime. Most

(a)

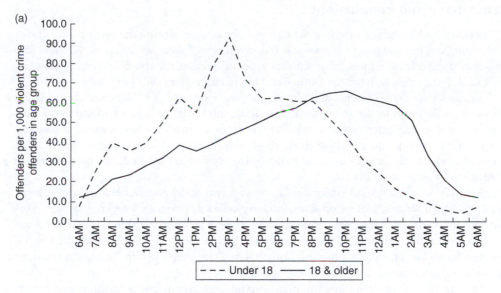

Figure 4.6a Violent crime time-of-day profiles by offender age.

(b)

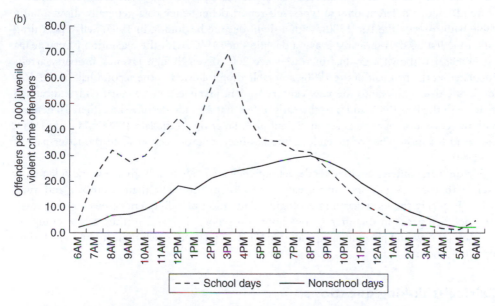

Figure 4.6b Juvenile violent crime time-of-day profiles by type of day.
Source: OJJDP Statistical Briefing Book. Released May 22, 2014.
Retrieved January 8, 2015 (http://ojjdp.gov/ojstatbb/offenders/faqs.asp).

importantly, juvenile violence peaks in the after-school hours on school days and in the early evening on non-school days, and juvenile drug and weapon law violations reach their highest level during school hours. The ecological and temporal variation in delinquency has spawned much research and theory and we will explore these explanations in later chapters (Sampson and Groves 1989; Bursik 1988; Kornhauser 1978).

Summary and conclusions

This chapter addressed the extent of delinquent offenses by exploring the proportion of juveniles involved in delinquent offenses and the frequency of their involvement. We have also examined the relative frequency of different types of offenses, the trends in delinquency, and the ecology of offenses in terms of spatial and temporal distribution.

To understand the extent of delinquency we examined prevalence and incidence. Self-report data lead to the clear conclusion that a substantial portion of adolescents report involvement in delinquent acts, but relatively few indicate that their involvement is frequent or repetitive. Furthermore, among those youth who commit delinquent acts, only a small portion come to the attention of the police, relatively few are arrested, and even fewer are processed by juvenile courts.

Virtually all sources of data indicate that minor forms of delinquent behavior are far more common than serious, violent offenses. Property offenses, especially property damage, vandalism, and theft, are among the most common types of offenses. Alcohol and marijuana use also exceeds serious, violent offenses in prevalence and incidence. Among violent offenses, less serious forms are most common, particularly fighting and simple assault. Truancy is the most common status offense.

Despite data limitations, we can draw certain conclusions about delinquency trends. Because much crime goes unreported, self-report data provide the most accurate indication of trends. Across different offense types, self-report delinquency data generally show a fairly stable pattern since the late 1980s, with a slight decline beginning in 1997. Self-report drug use in the last 30 days similarly shows a decline since 1997, with the exception of marijuana use, which has shown a gradual increase since 2007. Even though juvenile property arrests fluctuated in the first half of the 1990s, a notable drop followed in the second half of the decade – one that persists into the new century. Violent juvenile crime arrest trends indicate an increase in the late 1980s and into the early 1990s, but a steady decline since then. In general, with the exception of an increase in violent juvenile crime in the late 1980s and early 1990s, the trend for most types of juvenile crime has been one of decline since the latter part of the 1990s.

Urban–rural differences in juvenile delinquency are evident in both arrest and self-report data, with urban youth showing greater levels of involvement than suburban and rural youth. Probably the most startling ecological dimension of delinquent offenses is that juvenile violence peaks in the after-school hours on school days and in the early evening on non-school days and juvenile drug and weapon law violations reach their highest levels during school hours.

Critical-thinking questions

1. With regard to juvenile delinquency, to what do the terms *prevalence* and *incidence* refer? What conclusions can be drawn about the prevalence and incidence of delinquent offenses?
2. What types of delinquent offenses are most common? Why do you think these forms of delinquent behavior occur more frequently than others?
3. In recent years, has there been a juvenile crime wave?
4. What is the ecology of delinquency?

5. As depicted in the case that opened this chapter, are Dave's delinquent acts typical of the type of offenses committed by youth? How about his pattern of offending? Do most youth have a "brush with the law"?

Suggested reading

Hockenberry, Sarah and Charles Puzzanchera. 2014. *Juvenile Court Statistics 2011*. Pittsburgh, PA: National Center for Juvenile Justice.

Puzzanchera, Charles. 2014. "Juvenile Arrests 2012." *Juvenile Offenders and Victims National Report Series*. Washington, DC: Office of Juvenile Justice and Delinquency Prevention.

Sickmund, Melissa and Charles Puzzanchera (eds.). 2014. *Juvenile Offenders and Victims: 2014 National Report*. Pittsburgh, PA: National Center for Juvenile Justice.

Useful websites

For further information relevant to this chapter, go to the following websites

- *Crime in the United States*, Federal Bureau of Investigation (www.fbi.gov/about-us/cjis/ucr/crime-in-the-u.s/2013/crime-in-the-u.s.-2013)
- *Statistical Briefing Book*, Office of Juvenile Justice and Delinquency Prevention (www.ojjdp.gov/ojstatbb/default.asp)
- Monitoring the Future, Institute for Social Research, University of Michigan (http://monitoringthefuture.org/)

Glossary of key terms

Ecology of delinquency: The spatial and temporal distribution of delinquent offenses – how offenses vary across place and time.

Incidence: The average number of delinquent offenses committed by adolescents in general or by a delinquent youth.

Prevalence: The proportion of youths involved in delinquent acts.

Relative frequency: In comparison to each other, the types of delinquent offenses that occur most often.

Spatial distribution: The geographic occurrence of delinquency; that is, where delinquency occurs in terms of place.

Temporal distribution: The time aspect of delinquency; that is, when delinquency occurs.

Notes

1. Agnew and Brezina (2015) observe that the MTF survey uses vague response categories. They point out that this is most problematic in the response category "5 or more times," because researchers cannot distinguish someone who committed an act five times from someone who committed the same act many more times.
2. Puzzanchera (2009: 11) argues that the age range 10 through 17 is a more accurate representation of juvenile involvement in crime than the ages 0 through 17 because of the significant size of the population group age 0 through 9 and because of this group's limited involvement in crime.
3. In those states that report both petitioned and non-petitioned status offense cases, it is typical for non-petitioned cases to at least equal the number of petitioned cases, and in a number of states, non-petitioned cases outnumber petitioned cases 2 to 1 (Puzzanchera et al. 2000: 70–92).

4. The tendency for drug use and delinquency to occur together is referred to as *co-occurrence* or the *generality of deviance*, a topic discussed further in Chapter 6 (Huizinga et al. 2000; Elliott et al. 1989; Osgood et al. 1988).
5. Puzzanchera (2014: 2) notes that "a single crime may result in the arrest of more than one person" – a situation fairly common in juvenile law violations because juveniles commonly commit crimes in groups. For this reason, he argues that arrest statistics should not be used to indicate the relative proportions of crime that juveniles commit. Even though the percentage of arrests involving juveniles overestimates the amount of crime committed by juveniles, it depicts the types of crimes that bring juveniles into the system. This representation is useful to understand the relative frequency of different types of juvenile crime.
6. Table 68 of *Crime in the United States, 2013: Uniform Crime Reports* (FBI 2014).

References

Agnew, Robert and Timothy Brezina. 2015. *Juvenile Delinquency: Causes and Control.* 5th edn. New York: Oxford University Press.

Bachman, Jerald G., Lloyd D. Johnston, and Patrick M. O'Malley. 2014. *Monitoring the Future: Questionnaire Responses from the Nation's High School Seniors, 2012.* Ann Arbor, MI: Institute for Social Research.

Beirne, Piers. 1987. "Adolphe Quetelet and the Origins of Positivist Criminology." *American Journal of Sociology* 92: 1140–1169.

Beirne, Piers and James Messerschmidt. 2011. *Criminology.* 5th edn. New York: Oxford University Press.

Bennett, William J., John J. DiIulio, and John P. Walters. 1996. *Body Count: Moral Poverty and How to Win America's War against Crime and Drugs.* New York: Simon & Schuster.

Bernard, Thomas. 1999. "Juvenile Crime and the Transformation of Juvenile Justice: Is There a Juvenile Crime Wave?" *Justice Quarterly* 16: 336–356.

Blumstein, Alfred. 1995a. "Violence by Young People: Why the Deadly Nexus?" *National Institute of Justice Journal* 229 (August): 2–9.

Blumstein, Alfred. 1995b. "Youth Violence, Guns, and the Illicit-Drug Industry." *Journal of Criminal Law and Criminology* 86: 10–36.

Blumstein, Alfred. 2000. "Disaggregating the Violence Trends." Pp. 13–44 in *The Crime Drop in America,* ed. Alfred Blumstein and Joel Wallman. New York: Cambridge University Press.

Blumstein, Alfred, Jacqueline Cohen, Jeffrey A. Roth, and Christy A. Visher (eds.). 1986. *Criminal Careers and "Career Criminals,"* vol. 1. Washington, DC: National Academy Press.

Bursik, Robert J. 1988. "Social Disorganization and Theories of Crime and Delinquency: Problems and Prospects." *Criminology* 26: 519–551.

Byrne, James M. and Robert J. Sampson. 1986. *The Social Ecology of Crime.* New York: Springer-Verlag.

Cook, Philip J. and John Laub. 1998. "The Unprecedented Epidemic in Youth Violence." Pp. 101–138 in *Crime and Justice: A Review of Research* (Vol. 25), ed. Mark H. Moore and Michael Tonry. University of Chicago Press.

Coordinating Council on Juvenile Justice and Delinquency Prevention. 1996. *Combating Violence and Delinquency: The National Juvenile Justice Action Plan.* Washington, DC: Office of Juvenile Justice and Delinquency Prevention.

DiIulio, John J., Jr. 1995. "Arresting Ideas: Tougher Law Enforcement is Driving Down Urban Crime." *Policy Review* 74: 12–16.

Elliott, Delbert S., David Huizinga, and Suzanne S. Ageton. 1985. *Explaining Delinquency and Drug Use.* Beverly Hills, CA: Sage.

Elliott, Delbert S., David Huizinga, and Scott Menard. 1989. *Multiple Problem Youth: Delinquency, Substance Use, and Mental Health Problems.* New York: Springer-Verlag.

Farrington, David P. 1988. "Individual Differences and Offending." Pp. 241–268 in *Handbook of Crime and Punishment,* ed. Michael Tonry. New York: Oxford University Press.

Farrington, David P., Darrick Jolliffe, David J. Hawkins, Richard F. Catalano, Karl G. Hill, and Rick Kosterman. 2003. "Comparing Delinquency Careers in Court Records and Self-Reports." *Criminology* 41: 933–958.

Federal Bureau of Investigation (FBI). 2014. *Crime in the United States, 2013: Uniform Crime Reports.* Washington, DC: U.S. Department of Justice. Available online: www.fbi.gov/about-us/cjis/ucr/crime-in-the-u.s/2013/crime-in-the-u.s.-2013.

Fox, James Alan. 2000. "Demographics and U.S. Homicide." Pp. 288–318 in *The Crime Drop in America,* ed. Alfred Blumstein and Joel Wallman. New York: Cambridge University Press.

Gibbons, Don C. and Marvin D. Krohn. 1991. *Delinquent Behavior.* 5th edn. Englewood Cliffs, NJ: Prentice Hall.

Hamparian, Donna Martin, Joseph M. Davis, Judith M. Jacobson, and Robert E. McGraw. 1985. *The Young Criminal Years of the Violent Few.* Washington, DC: Office of Juvenile Justice and Delinquency Prevention.

Hindelang, Michael J., Travis Hirschi, and Joseph G. Weis. 1979. "Correlates of Delinquency: The Illusion of Discrepancy between Self-Report and Official Measures." *American Sociological Review* 44: 995–1014.

Hockenberry, Sarah and Charles Puzzanchera. 2014. *Juvenile Court Statistics 2011.* Pittsburgh, PA: National Center for Juvenile Justice.

Huizinga, David A. and Delbert S. Elliott. 1987. "Juvenile Offenders: Prevalence, Offender Incidence, and Arrest Rates by Race." *Crime and Delinquency* 33: 206–223.

Huizinga, David A., Rolf Loeber, Terence P. Thornberry, and Lynn Cothern. 2000. "Co-Occurrence of Delinquency and Other Problem Behaviors." *Juvenile Justice Bulletin.* Washington, DC: Office of Juvenile Justice and Delinquency Prevention.

Jensen, Gary F. and Dean G. Rojek. 1998. *Delinquency and Youth Crime.* 3rd edn. Prospect Heights, IL: Waveland Press.

Johnston, Lloyd D., Patrick M. O'Malley, Richard A. Miech, Jerald G. Bachman, and John E. Schulenberg. 2014. *Monitoring the Future National Results on Drug Use: 1975–2013: Overview of Key Findings on Adolescent Drug Use.* Ann Arbor: Institute for Social Research, University of Michigan.

Kornhauser, Ruth Rosner. 1978. *Social Sources of Delinquency: An Appraisal of Analytic Models.* University of Chicago Press.

Levitt, Steven. 1999. "The Limited Role of Changing Age Structure in Explaining Aggregate Crime Rates." *Criminology* 37: 581–599.

Levitt, Steven. 2004. "Understanding Why Crime Fell in the 1990s: Four Factors that Explain the Decline and Six that Do Not." *American Economic Perspectives* 18: 163–190.

McGarrell, Edmund F. and Timothy J. Flanagan (eds.). 1985. *Sourcebook of Criminal Justice Statistics 1984.* Washington, DC: Bureau of Justice Statistics.

Mosher, Clayton J., Terance D. Miethe, and Timothy C. Hart. 2011. *The Mismeasure of Crime.* 2nd edn. Thousand Oaks, CA: Sage.

OJJDP Statistical Briefing Book. 2014. National Center for Juvenile Justice. Available online: http://www.ojjdp.gov/ojstatbb/.

Osgood, D. Wayne, Lloyd D. Johnston, Patrick M. O'Malley, and Jerald G. Bachman. 1988. "The Generality of Deviance in Late Adolescence and Early Adulthood." *American Sociological Review* 53: 81–93.

Piquero, Alex R., David P. Farrington, and Alfred Blumstein. 2003. "The Criminal Career Paradigm." Pp. 359–506 in *Crime and Justice: A Review of Research* (vol. 30), ed. Michael Tonry. University of Chicago Press.

Puzzanchera, Charles. 2009. "Juvenile Arrests 2007." *Juvenile Justice Bulletin.* Washington, DC: Office of Juvenile Justice and Delinquency Prevention.

Puzzanchera, Charles. 2014. "Juvenile Arrests 2012." *Juvenile Offenders and Victims National Report Series.* Washington, DC: Office of Juvenile Justice and Delinquency Prevention.

Puzzanchera, Charles, Anthony Sladky, and Wei Kang. 2014. *Easy Access to Juvenile Populations: 1990–2013*. Available online at www.ojjdp.ncjrs.gov/ojstatbb/ezapop.

Puzzanchera, Charles, Anne L. Stahl, Terrence A. Finnegan, Howard N. Snyder, Rowen S. Poole, and Nancy Tierney. 2000. *Juvenile Court Statistics 1997*. Pittsburgh: National Center for Juvenile Justice.

Sampson, Robert J. and W. Byron Groves. 1989. "Community Structure and Crime: Testing Social Disorganization Theory." *American Journal of Sociology* 94: 774–802.

Shaw, Clifford R. 1930. *Jack-Roller*. University of Chicago Press.

Shaw, Clifford R. and Henry D. McKay. 1931. *Social Factors in Juvenile Delinquency: A Study of the Community, the Family, and the Gang in Relation to Delinquent Behavior*. Report of the National Commission on Law Observance and Enforcement, Causes of Crime, vol. 2. Washington, DC: GPO.

Shaw, Clifford R. and Henry D. McKay. 1969. *Juvenile Delinquency and Urban Areas: A Study of Rates of Delinquency in Relation to Differential Characteristics of Local Communities in American Cities*. Rev. edn. University of Chicago Press.

Shaw, Clifford R., Frederick M. Zorbaugh, Henry D. McKay, and Leonard S. Cottrell. 1929. *Delinquency Areas: A Study of the Geographic Distribution of School Truants, Juvenile Delinquents, and Adult Offenders in Chicago*. University of Chicago Press.

Sickmund, Melissa and Charles Puzzanchera (eds.). 2014. *Juvenile Offenders and Victims: 2014 National Report*. Pittsburgh, PA: National Center for Juvenile Justice.

Sickmund, Melissa, Anthony Sladky, and Wei Kang. 2014. *Easy Access to Juvenile Court Statistics: 1985–2011*. Available online at http://ojjdp.ncjrs.gov/ojstatbb/ezajcs/.

Snyder, Howard N. and Melissa Sickmund. 2006. *Juvenile Offenders and Victims: 2006 National Report*. Washington, DC: Office of Juvenile Justice and Delinquency Prevention.

Steffensmeier, Darrell and Miles D. Harer. 1999. "Making Sense of Recent U.S. Crime Trends, 1980 to 1996/1998: Age Composition Effects and Other Explanations." *Journal of Research in Crime and Delinquency* 36: 235–274.

Zimring, Franklin E. 2005. *American Juvenile Justice*. New York: Oxford University Press.

Chapter 5

The social correlates of offending and victimization

Chapter preview

Topics:

- Age
- Gender
- Race and ethnicity
- Social class
- Victimization

Terms:

- social correlates
- age–crime curve
- crime-prone years
- aging out of crime

- age effect
- age composition effect
- convergence hypothesis

Chapter learning objectives

After completing this chapter, students should be able to:

- Describe how involvement in delinquency is related to age, gender, race, and social class.
- Explain why the relationships between these social characteristics and delinquency differ for different types of data (Uniform Crime Reports, self-reports, victimization data).
- Describe how the likelihood of victimization is related to age, gender, race, and social class.

Case in point: perceptions of criminals in Chestnut Hill – the social correlates of crime and delinquency

Elijah Anderson is an ethnographer who describes the "code of the street" and the ways in which poor inner-city youth use violence or the threat of violence to acquire respect and to shield themselves from further violence. Anderson begins his work with a description of the neighborhood in which he conducted his research.

> Chestnut Hill … is a predominantly residential community consisting mostly of affluent and educated white people, but it is increasingly becoming racially and ethnically mixed. … The business and shopping district along Germantown Avenue draws shoppers from all over the city … You see many different kinds of people – old and young, black and white, affluent, middle class, and working class. …

> Once in a while … a violent incident does occur in Chestnut Hill. A holdup occurred at the bank in the middle of the day not long ago, ending in a shoot-out on the sidewalk. The perpetrators were black, and two black men recently robbed and shot up a tavern on the avenue. Such incidents give the residents here the simplistic yet persistent view that blacks commit crime and white people do not. That does not mean that the white people here think that the black people they ordinarily see on the streets are bound to rob them: many of these people are too sophisticated to believe that all blacks are inclined to criminality. But the fact that black people robbed the bank and that blacks commit a large number of crimes in the area does give a peculiar edge to race relations, and the racial reality of street crime affects the relations between blacks and whites. Because everybody knows that the simplistic view does exist, even middle-class blacks have to work consciously against that stereotype – although the whites do as well. Both groups know the reality that crime is likely to be perpetrated by young black males.

Source: Anderson (1999: 16–17).

To understand theoretical explanations of delinquency, we must first understand the nature of delinquent offenders. Who are the offenders? When you think of delinquent offenders, what picture comes to mind? Young or old? Male or female? Rich or poor? Black, white, or brown? What do age, gender, social class, and race or ethnicity have to do with the likelihood of offending?

The social characteristics that tend to distinguish offenders from non-offenders are often called the **social correlates** of delinquency. Correlation is "the extent to which two or more things or variables are related ('co-related') to one another" (Vogt and Johnson 2011: 77). By social correlates, we mean social characteristics that are statistically associated with each other. Here we are interested in the social characteristics of individuals that are related to delinquency.

In discussing social correlates of delinquency, we place the emphasis on the word *social*. In this chapter, we examine age, gender, race, and social class as social correlates of offending. An individual can be defined according to these characteristics – for example, a young female or a wealthy African American person. But each of these characteristics is fundamentally social, rather than individual, in nature. To be female in contemporary American culture, for example, has meaning far beyond an individual's biological sex. Gender is socially defined, and it determines and defines positions of power – or lack of it – within society. The same is true for race, social class, and age.

Once we have established that age, gender, race, and social class are social correlates of delinquency, the next logical question is, "Why are these characteristics related to offending?" In this chapter, we focus primarily on the social correlates of delinquency and only briefly address the question of why these characteristics are related to delinquency.

Age

There are few factors that criminologists agree are undeniably related to crime. Age is one of those rare factors. A strong link exists between age and involvement in crime. Crime is committed predominantly by the young. Involvement in crime tends to increase with age during the teenage years, peaking in mid-adolescence to early adulthood, and then declines rapidly with age. When we graph the relationship between age and crime, we generally see a bell-shaped curve called the **age–crime curve**. Figure 5.1 shows the age–crime curve for 2013, when the arrest rate increased steadily from about age 10, peaked at ages 19–20, and then declined. The age–crime relationship varies somewhat depending on the type of offense. Compared to arrests for violent offenses, arrests for serious property offenses peak at an earlier age and decline more rapidly. Arrests for violent offenses peak somewhat later and decline more gradually.

Table 5.1 shows, for each type of offense, the proportion of offenders arrested who are juveniles (under the age of 18) and adults (ages 18 and over). In 2013, juveniles accounted for 9.7 percent of all arrests and 14.6 percent of arrests for Uniform Crime Reports (UCR) Part I offenses. These numbers are remarkable when one considers that juveniles in the 13 to 17

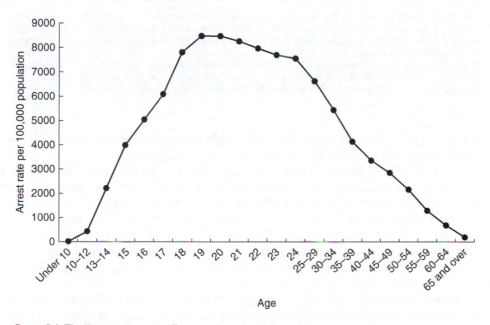

Figure 5.1 The "age–crime curve."

This figure shows the bell-shaped curve one typically sees when graphing the relationship between age and crime. This curve illustrates the consistent finding that crime tends to increase with age during the teenage years, peak in mid-adolescence to early adulthood, and then decline rapidly with age.

Note: This graph is based on arrests for all Part I and Part II offenses. Arrest figures based on 11,951 reporting agencies, with 2013 estimated U.S. population of 245,741,701.

Sources: Federal Bureau of Investigation (2014a: Table 38). Retrieved December 8, 2014 (www.fbi.gov/about-us/cjis/ucr/crime-in-the-u.s/2013/crime-in-the-u.s.-2013/tables/table-38/table_38_arrests_by_age_2013.xls); U.S. Census Bureau (2014). Retrieved December 8, 2014 (www.census.gov/popest/).

Table 5.1 Juvenile and adult arrests and arrest rates, by type of crime, 2013

Type of crime	Number of arrests		Percentage of arrests		Arrest rate per 100,000 in age group	
	Juveniles 0–17	Adults	Juveniles 0–17	Adults	Juveniles 13–17	Adults
All crimes	875,262	8,194,730	9.7	90.3	3,909.2	3,378.7
Part I crimes	242,250	1,411,652	14.6	85.4	1,083.6	582.0
Violent crimes	43,651	349,127	11.1	88.9	195.0	143.9
Homicide	614	7,787	7.3	92.7	2.9	3.2
Forcible rape	2,089	11,528	15.3	84.7	8.9	4.8
Robbery	15,932	62,821	20.2	79.8	74.3	25.9
Aggravated assault	25,016	266,991	8.6	91.4	108.8	110.1
Property crimes	198,599	1,062,525	15.7	84.3	888.6	438.1
Burglary	34,760	168,949	17.1	82.9	156.1	69.7
Larceny-theft	151,427	845,068	15.2	84.8	677.6	348.4
Motor vehicle theft	9,469	43,038	18.0	82.0	44.2	17.7
Arson	2,943	5,470	35.0	65.0	10.7	2.3
Part II crimes	633,012	6,783,078	8.5	91.5	2,825.6	2,796.7

Note: Arrest figures based on 11,951 reporting agencies, with 2013 estimated U.S. population of 245,741,701. Population figures from U.S. Census data for 2013: juvenile population = 73,585,872; juvenile population ages 13–17 = 20,862,152; adult population = 242,542,967; total population = 316,128,839. See Table 3.1 in Chapter 3 for a list of all Part II crimes.
Sources: Federal Bureau of Investigation (2014: Table 38). Retrieved December 28, 2014 (www.fbi.gov/about-us/ cjis/ucr/crime-in-the-u.s/2013/crime-in-the-u.s.-2013/tables/table-38/table_38_arrests_by_age_2013.xls); Puzzancehera et al. (2014). Retrieved December 28, 2014 (www.ojjdp.gov/ojstatbb/ezapop/).

age range (those most likely to be involved in delinquency) constituted only 6.6 percent of the U.S. population in 2013 (Puzzanchera, Sladky, and Kang 2014).

Table 5.1, which focuses primarily on serious UCR Part I offenses, shows that juveniles are more likely to be arrested for property crimes than for violent crimes. Juveniles accounted for 15.7 percent of all persons arrested for Part I property crimes, but only 11.1 percent of those arrested for Part I violent crimes. However, compared to other violent crimes, robbery shows a higher percentage of juvenile arrests. For robbery, 20.2 percent of those arrested were juveniles. Juveniles are disproportionately represented in arrests for arson, for which they account for 35 percent of arrests, and for vandalism (not shown in Table 5.1), for which they account for 23.2 percent of arrests.

Note that statistics on the proportion of arrests attributable to juveniles can be somewhat misleading if a small number of juveniles is responsible for a large percentage of arrests. It may be, for example, that one juvenile is arrested six times for burglary. The percentages in Table 5.1 correctly state the proportions of juvenile and adult arrests, but they mask the reality that a relatively small number of habitual or repeat offenders account for a disproportionate share of crimes and arrests. However, it is also true that more than one offender may be arrested for a single crime.

Arrest rates per age-specific population offer another way to look at juvenile involvement in delinquency. These rates are adjusted to take into account the size of the juvenile and adult populations of potential offenders. The last two columns of Table 5.1 show arrest rates per

100,000 population for selected offenses, for juveniles (ages 13–17) and adults. To calculate juvenile arrest rates, we divided the number of arrests of juveniles by the total juvenile population in the 13–17 age range and then multiplied by 100,000. Similarly, to calculate adult arrest rates, we divided the number of arrests of adults by the total adult population and then multiplied by 100,000.

Column 5 of Table 5.1 presents juvenile (ages 13–17) arrest rates. It shows much higher arrest rates for Part I property offenses (888.6) than for Part I violent offenses (195.0). The high rate for property offenses is driven primarily by the high rate for larceny-theft (677.6). As expected, the juvenile arrest rate for Part II offenses (2,825.6) is significantly higher than the arrest rate for more serious Part I offenses (1,083.6). When we compare arrest rates for juveniles and adults (column 6), we see that, for all Part I offenses combined, the arrest rate is nearly twice as high for juveniles (1,083.6) as for adults (582.0). For Part I violent crimes, arrest rates are substantially higher for juveniles (195.0) than for adults (143.9). For all Part II offenses combined, the arrest rate is almost the same for juveniles (2,825.6) and adults (2,796.7).

Crime-prone years

So far, we have examined arrests of juveniles versus arrests of adults. But this distinction is somewhat artificial and ignores the continuity of crime from adolescence into young adulthood. The age–crime curve is smooth, not disjointed at age 18. The **crime-prone years** are the age period when people are most likely to be involved in crime. They extend into young adult years, with some variation depending on the type of offense.

Table 5.2 shows the ages of individuals arrested for all types of crime combined and for Part I violent and property offenses separately. This table clearly shows the continuity of crime from adolescence into young adulthood. Although individuals in the 13–24 age range constitute only 16.5 percent of the U.S. population, they account for 36.8 percent of arrests for all crimes.

Table 5.2 shows that the crime-prone years are somewhat older for violent crimes than for serious property offenses. Serious property crime is concentrated in the 16–23 age range. Individuals in this age group constituted 11.2 percent of the U.S. population in 2013, yet they accounted for 34.3 percent of all Part I property crime arrests. Serious violent crime is concentrated in the 18–24 age range. Although individuals in this age group constituted 10 percent of the 2013 U.S. population, they accounted for 27.7 percent of all Part I violent crime arrests. Compared to violent crime arrests, property crime arrests show higher percentages of offenders in all age categories through age 20. Then a shift occurs after age 20, and violent crime arrests show higher percentages of offenders in all age categories.

Aging out of crime

Relatively few people who are involved in crime during adolescence and young adulthood continue offending into later adulthood. Most stop committing crime due to sociological, psychological, and biological factors. Criminologists often refer to this process as **aging out of crime**. Even given the continuity of offending from adolescence into young adulthood, the process of aging out of crime is fairly rapid. Arrests for serious property crime, for example, peak at age 18, but then drop off relatively quickly (see Table 5.2). The decline in arrests for

Table 5.2 Percentage of offenders at various ages, by type of crime, 2013

Age	Percentage of U.S. population	All crimes (%)	Part I violent crimes (%)	Part I property crimes (%)
12 and under	16.7	0.7	0.8	1.1
13–14	2.6	2.0	2.4	3.4
15	1.3	1.8	2.1	3.0
16	1.3	2.3	2.7	3.8
17	1.3	2.8	3.1	4.4
18	1.4	3.7	3.7	5.2
19	1.4	4.1	4.0	4.8
20	1.4	4.2	4.0	4.4
21	1.4	4.2	4.2	4.1
22	1.5	4.1	4.1	3.9
23	1.5	3.9	4.0	3.7
24	1.4	3.7	3.7	3.4
25–29	6.8	15.8	16.0	14.6
30–34	6.7	12.7	12.9	11.5
35–39	6.2	8.9	8.9	7.8
40 and over	47.0	25.1	23.5	20.8

Note: Arrest figures based on 11,951 reporting agencies, with 2013 estimated U.S. population of 245,741,701. Due to rounding, columns may not sum precisely to 100 percent.
Sources: Federal Bureau of Investigation (2014: Table 38). Retrieved December 8, 2014 (www. fbi.gov/about-us/cjis/ucr/crime-in-the-u.s/2013/crime-in-the-u.s.-2013/tables/table-38/table_38_ arrests_by_age_2013.xls); U.S. Census Bureau (2014). Retrieved December 8, 2014 (www.census. gov/popest/).

violent crime is more gradual. Violent crime arrests peak at age 21, and then taper off steadily through the 20s.

Victimization surveys and self-reports

So far we have presented official data on age and crime from the Uniform Crime Reporting (UCR) program. Because these data are available only for *arrested* offenders, they may not accurately represent involvement in crime. Studies based on victimization and self-report data, however, do tend to paint a similar picture of age and crime.

Michael Hindelang used data from the National Crime Victimization Survey (NCVS) to examine victims' perceptions of offender age for crimes in which the victim saw the offender (Hindelang 1981). Of course, the reliability of these data depends on victims' abilities to accurately assess offender age. Victimization data, however, were fairly consistent with UCR data. NCVS data revealed that rates of offending were highest for young adults (ages 18–20), followed by adolescents (ages 12–17), and finally older adults (over age 20). Hindelang found that juveniles were less involved than adults in serious crimes – a finding also consistent with UCR data.

Researchers who have used self-reports of delinquency and crime have also found a peak in offending from late adolescence to early adulthood, followed by a decline in criminal involvement (Elliott et al. 1983; Rowe and Tittle 1977). Thus, the relationship between age and crime holds up across all three sources of data.

Age composition effect

Several studies have explored the age composition effect on crime (McCall et al. 2013; Steffensmeier and Harer 1999; Steffensmeier, Streifel, and Harer 1987; Cohen and Land 1987). In these studies, researchers were not interested in the ages of individual offenders, but rather in the age composition of the total population and its effect on overall crime rates. The **age effect** refers to the fact that, although juveniles constitute a small portion of the U.S. population, they commit a disproportionate share of crime. The **age composition effect** attributes changes in crime rates to changes in population demographics, such that crime rates rise as the number of people in the age group most likely to commit crimes (mid-adolescence to early adulthood) increases, and crime rates fall as the number of people in their crime-prone years decreases. For example, some have attributed increases in crime rates in the 1960s and 1970s to the fact that "baby boomers" reached adolescence and early adulthood during those years, and thus the proportion of the population in the crime-prone years increased.

Research has shown that the age composition of the population affects crime rates (Steffensmeier and Harer 1999; Cohen and Land 1987; Steffensmeier et al. 1987). For example, Darrell Steffensmeier and his colleagues (1987) examined UCR data from more than 30 years (1953–1984) and found a large age composition effect on crime rates for Part I offenses. Age composition of the population was a more significant predictor of crime rates than any other factor in their analysis. Crimes increased as the proportion of the population at crime-prone ages increased with the aging of the baby boomers and then declined as baby boomers matured beyond crime-prone ages. In a more recent study, Steffensmeier and Harer (1999) found large effects of age composition on crime rates during the 1980s. They also found smaller age composition effects during the early 1990s, however, and they concluded that recent declines in crime rates cannot be attributed solely to the age composition of the population.

Why are young people disproportionately involved in crime?

Several explanations exist for the relationship between age and crime. First, as individuals mature into young adulthood, they assume more responsible roles (e.g., employment, college attendance, marriage, military service), so they have more to lose if caught committing crime. Though adolescents may be willing to participate in risky offenses, adults who have greater "stakes in conformity" are unlikely to take the same risks. Robert Sampson and John Laub studied the social control effects of job stability and marriage (Sampson, Laub, and Wimer 2006; Sampson and Laub 1990, 1992, 1993; see also McCall et al. 2013). They found that strong social ties achieved through employment and marriage inhibit criminal behavior. Adult entry into the labor market also means that individuals can acquire the financial resources they need in legitimate ways and so have less need to resort to crime (Steffensmeier and Allan 2000).

Second, the legal costs of offending increase with the transition from adolescence to adulthood. The penalties for most offenses are more severe for adults than for juveniles. This should serve as a greater deterrent for adults. In addition, because of the legal costs of offending, many habitual offenders are incarcerated by their mid-20s and unable to commit further crimes.

Third, the structure of opportunities to engage in delinquency and crime changes with the transition from adolescence to adulthood. Although opportunities to participate in offenses such as fraud and embezzlement increase with age, opportunities to engage in more mischievous forms of offending tend to decrease with age. The demands of time that accompany adulthood (e.g., time spent working or attending college classes) mean that less time is available for delinquent activities. Compared to adolescents, adults spend less time just "hanging out" with peers.[1]

Fourth, adolescence is often accompanied by a "party" culture that at least tolerates and often values and reinforces offending (Warr 1993a; Hagan 1991). Status among adolescent peers is sometimes achieved through bravado displayed in offending. Criminal activities are less likely to be rewarded or reinforced in adulthood, when expectations for responsible and productive behavior are greater than in adolescence.

Fifth, some researchers have argued that young people simply have greater physical abilities to commit crimes than do older people. Walter Gove (1985: 138) focuses primarily on "physically demanding crimes" and suggests that "physical strength, energy, psychological drive, and the reinforcement effect of the adrenaline high" can account for the decline in offending with age. He argues that these physical attributes peak at the same ages as offending and that their rapid decline contributes to the rapid decline in offending with age. Research, however, has not supported Gove's hypothesis that the relationship between age and offending can be explained by physical abilities that decline with age (Steffensmeier and Allan 1995).

In a recent study, Gary Sweeten and his colleagues (2013) tried to explain the age–crime relationship using factors drawn from a variety of theories, including social control, social learning, and strain theories. They found that, together, these factors were able to explain a substantial portion of the crime decline from ages 15 to 25.

Gender

Crime and delinquency are committed primarily by males. But the strength of the relationship between gender and crime varies depending on data source (official vs. self-report data) and type of offense.

Official data

UCR data show that males are disproportionately involved in crime and delinquency. Males and females constitute roughly equal shares of the U.S. population, yet 73.4 percent of persons arrested in 2013 were male (Federal Bureau of Investigation 2014a). Table 5.3 presents arrest percentages by gender and age for various offenses. This table illustrates that the proportions of males and females arrested are similar for juveniles and adults. For Part I property crimes, for example, males account for 65.9 percent of juveniles arrested and 61.6 percent of adults arrested.

When we focus only on juveniles (the first three columns of Table 5.3), we see that in 2013 males accounted for 81.3 percent of juvenile arrests for Part I violent crimes and 65.9 percent of juvenile arrests for Part I property crimes. Among juveniles, the gender difference in arrests is largest for murder, rape, robbery, burglary, arson, vandalism, weapons offenses, and sex offenses. For these crimes, more than 84 percent of juveniles arrested in 2013 were male. Although crime in general is a male phenomenon, this is especially true for violent crime.

Table 5.3 Arrests, by gender, age, and type of crime, 2013

Type of crime	Under Age 18			Age 18 and over		
	Total number	Male (%)	Female (%)	Total number	Male (%)	Female (%)
All crimes	875,262	71.1	28.9	8,194,730	73.7	26.3
Part I crimes	242,250	68.7	31.3	1,411,652	66.1	33.9
Violent crimes	43,651	81.3	18.7	349,127	79.7	20.3
Homicide	614	88.1	11.9	7,787	88.3	11.7
Forcible rape	2,089	96.4	3.6	11,528	98.4	1.6
Robbery	15,932	90.4	9.6	62,821	85.7	14.3
Aggravated assault	25,016	74.1	25.9	266,991	77.2	22.8
Property crimes	198,599	65.9	34.1	1,062,525	61.6	38.4
Burglary	34,760	88.4	11.6	168,949	81.8	18.2
Larceny-theft	151,427	59.3	40.7	845,068	56.5	43.5
Motor vehicle theft	9,469	82.6	17.4	43,038	79.6	20.4
Arson	2,943	84.6	15.4	5,470	77.9	22.1
Part II crimes	633,012	72.1	27.9	6,783,078	75.3	24.7
Other assaults	118,253	63.6	36.4	767,569	73.5	26.5
Vandalism	37,678	84.2	15.8	124,390	78.4	21.6
Weapons offenses	16,683	89.6	10.4	95,990	91.6	8.4
Forgery and counterfeiting	850	71.4	28.6	47,976	62.5	37.5
Fraud	3,542	67.5	32.5	109,968	59.9	40.1
Prostitution	655	20.2	79.8	41,455	33.0	67.0
Sex offenses (except forcible rape, prostitution)	8,389	88.6	11.4	38,443	93.0	7.0
Drug abuse violations	94,187	81.8	18.2	1,115,474	78.6	21.4
Curfew violations	47,934	71.7	28.3	–	–	–

Note: Arrest figures based on 11,951 reporting agencies, with 2013 estimated U.S. population of 245,741,701.
Source: Federal Bureau of Investigation (2014: adapted from Tables 39 and 40). Retrieved December 8, 2014 (www.fbi.gov/about-us/cjis/ucr/crime-in-the-u.s/2013/crime-in-the-u.s.-2013/tables/table-39/table_39_arrests_males_by_age_2013.xls and www.fbi.gov/about-us/cjis/ucr/crime-in-the-u.s/2013/crime-in-the-u.s.-2013/tables/table-40/table_40_arrests_females_by_age_2013.xls).

The third column of Table 5.3 shows that the proportions of juvenile females arrested are highest for larceny–theft, simple assault ("other assaults"), forgery and counterfeiting, fraud, prostitution, and curfew violations. Only for prostitution were arrests higher for females than for males (Federal Bureau of Investigation 2014a). Until recently, the UCR also included data for the offense of running away, and for this offense also, arrests were typically higher for females than for males. Females are more likely than males to be arrested for some status offenses, such as running away (Teilmann and Landry 1981; Chesney-Lind 1977), even though males are more likely to report engaging in these offenses (Canter 1982). Meda Chesney-Lind (1977, 1989), a feminist criminologist who has written extensively about why this is the case, argues that juvenile justice officials respond more harshly to status offenses by females than males in an attempt to control female sexual activity.

Research has examined whether official data and victimization survey data show a similar picture of gender and crime (Hindelang 1979). This research shows close agreement between these two data sources regarding female involvement in offending. This similarity demonstrates that the relationship between gender and crime is a consequence of females being less involved in crime, rather than of biases in the criminal justice system that might lead to fewer female arrests.

Self-report data

Self-report studies confirm that crime is a male phenomenon, but the gender difference in offending is generally smaller in self-report studies than in official data (Canter 1982; Smith and Visher 1980; Steffensmeier and Steffensmeier 1980; Jensen and Even 1976).[2] In a widely cited study, Rachelle Canter (1982: 373–374) noted that male-to-female ratios of involvement in delinquency based on UCR data generally range from 3:1 to 7:1, but the ratios based on self-report data range from 1.2:1 to 2.5:1.

Canter (1982) used National Youth Survey (NYS) data to examine the size and pattern of gender differences in self-report delinquency. She found gender differences in overall delinquency, with boys reporting roughly twice as many delinquent acts as girls. These gender differences are due to a higher number of male offenders and a higher frequency of offending among males. Although Canter found consistent gender differences in involvement in delinquency, these differences are far less dramatic than those indicated by official data. Self-report data on arrests reveal that males also have a higher cumulative prevalence of arrest than females (Brame et al. 2014).

Canter also found that males and females generally report involvement in the same types of offenses. The exception to this similarity is for serious offenses, particularly violent ones. Males are substantially more likely than females to report involvement in serious offenses. This finding is consistent with other self-report research and with UCR data (Steffensmeier et al. 2005; Canter 1982; Smith and Visher 1980; Steffensmeier and Steffensmeier 1980; Hindelang 1979). Contrary to UCR data, however, the NYS provides no evidence of greater female involvement in "traditionally female crimes" such as running away (Hindelang, Hirschi, and Weis 1981).[3] Canter attributed this discrepancy between self-report and UCR data to harsher responses by law enforcement officials when females commit such acts than when males do.

Narrowing of the gender gap in delinquency?

Feminist criminologists have advanced a controversial proposition about the relationship between gender and crime. In the mid-1970s, Freda Adler and Rita Simon argued that, as a result of the feminist movement, gender equality would emerge as male and female roles became more similar. This equality across gender would, in turn, lead to more similar crime rates and patterns for males and females, as opportunities for female involvement in crime expanded along with female roles in society (Adler 1975; Simon 1975). In other words, according to this **convergence hypothesis**, the gender gap in crime and delinquency would narrow, and male and female rates of offending would converge as a function of gender equality.

Darrell Steffensmeier and his colleagues have provided a wealth of empirical evidence indicating that the gender gap has not narrowed in the way or to the extent feminist theorists predicted (Steffensmeier et al. 2005; Steffensmeier and Schwartz 2002; Steffensmeier and Allan 1996; Steffensmeier 1978, 1980, 1993; Steffensmeier and Streifel 1992; Steffensmeier and Cobb 1981; Steffensmeier and Steffensmeier 1980). They have shown that females are not "catching up" with males in the commission of serious or violent offenses – the types of crime typically thought of as "masculine." Exploring change over a 30-year period from 1960 to 1990, Steffensmeier (1993: 420) showed that among juvenile offenders the female percentage of arrests decreased 3.1 percent for homicide and increased only 3.6 percent for aggravated assault, 2.8 percent for weapons offenses, and 3.1 percent for robbery. The numbers are similar for adult offenders.

Steffensmeier found, instead, that female arrests have increased most dramatically in recent decades for minor property offenses – larceny-theft, fraud, and forgery. Offenses in these categories include shoplifting, credit card fraud, and writing bad checks. From 1960 to 1990, among juvenile offenders, the female percentage of arrests increased 13.5 percent for larceny-theft, 17.2 percent for fraud, and 9.1 percent for forgery. The figures for adult offenders are 13.2 percent for larceny-theft, 31.1 percent for fraud, and 19.3 percent for forgery (Steffensmeier 1993: 420). In addition, the largest increases in female arrests for minor property crimes were between 1960 and 1975, before the women's movement had a significant impact (Steffensmeier and Allan 1996). Steffensmeier and his colleagues argued that increases among females in minor property crimes do not reflect equality of gender roles or increased opportunities for females in the economic sphere. Instead, they reflect the increasing economic marginalization of females, as rates of divorce, illegitimacy, and female-headed households rise. The economic pressures created by these situations cause increases in "traditional female consumer-based crimes," such as shoplifting and check and welfare fraud (Steffensmeier and Allan 1996; Steffensmeier 1980, 1993; Steffensmeier and Streifel 1992).

Steffensmeier and Streifel (1992: 82) found that changes in the female share of arrests for property crimes were also due to more formal policing, which "tends to increase the visibility of female offending (especially its less serious forms)" and "which has contributed to more 'official' counting of female offending" (Steffensmeier and Streifel 1992: 82).

In more recent research, Steffensmeier and his colleagues (2005, 2006) examined trends in girls' violence from 1980 to 2003 (see also Schwartz et al. 2009). Media accounts of sensational incidents of girls' violence have created the widespread belief that girls' violence is increasing and the gender gap is shrinking. Steffensmeier and his colleagues used UCR data, victimization data from the NCVS, and self-report data from two separate national surveys to see if girls' violent behavior really has increased in recent decades. UCR data clearly indicate an increase in girls' violence (simple assault; aggravated assault; and the Violent Crime Index, which includes homicide, forcible rape, robbery, and aggravated assault). From 1980 to 2000, the female proportion of juvenile arrests increased from 21 to 33 percent for simple assault, from 15 to 24 percent for aggravated assault, and from 10 to 19 percent for the Violent Crime Index (Steffensmeier et al. 2005). However, when Steffensmeier and his colleagues looked at victimization and self-report data, they did not find similar increases in girls' violence. They concluded that several recent shifts in criminal justice policy have increased the likelihood of girls' arrests for violence, fueling the inaccurate perception of increases in girls' violent behavior. These policy shifts include:

first, stretching definitions of violence to include more minor incidents that girls in relative terms are more likely to commit; second, increased policing of violence between intimates and in private settings (for example, home, school) where girls' violence is more widespread; and, third, less tolerant family and societal attitudes toward juvenile females.

(Steffensmeier et al. 2005: 355; see also Zahn et al. 2008;

Chesney-Lind and Paramore 2001)

Steffensmeier's many studies suggest that a true narrowing of the gender gap in crime has not occurred for most offenses. But his finding that UCR and NCVS data lead to different conclusions regarding the gender gap in violence has been challenged by other researchers. Janet Lauritsen and her colleagues examined victimization survey data from 1973 to 2005 and found a narrowing of the gender gap for the crimes of robbery, aggravated assault, and simple assault that is similar to the patterns revealed in UCR arrest data (Lauritsen, Heimer, and Lynch 2009; Heimer, Lauritsen, and Lynch 2009). They also found that the narrowing of the gender gap for these violent crimes was in part a result of larger decreases in male offending than in female offending after the mid-1990s, rather than increases in female offending (see also Rennison 2009). Thus, Lauritsen and her colleagues conclude that the narrowing of the gender gap in violent crime is real, rather than simply an artifact of policy shifts such as those described by Steffensmeier and his colleagues.

Why are males disproportionately involved in crime?

In the last three decades, interest in gender and crime has exploded. Criminologists have tried to determine the extent of the gender gap in crime and delinquency and to develop adequate theories for explaining gender differences in offending.

Traditional theories of crime and delinquency were developed primarily to explain male offending. Criminologists have debated the ability of traditional theories to explain female offending as well (Daigle, Cullen, and Wright 2007). Some have called for separate "gender-specific" theories of female delinquency that take into account the different experiences of girls and boys (Daly 1994; Chesney-Lind 1989; Leonard 1982; Adler 1975). Yet others have demonstrated that the causes of at least minor delinquency are similar across gender and that traditional "gender-neutral" theories can explain male and female delinquency equally well (Moffitt et al. 2001; Liu and Kaplan 1999; Steffensmeier and Allan 1996; Bartusch and Matsueda 1996; Smith and Paternoster 1987). For example, association with delinquent peers and lack of social bonds are important causes of delinquency for both males and females. Yet these causal factors might affect delinquency somewhat differently for males and females, or the level of exposure to these factors might differ by gender. Let's briefly consider some of the causal factors that might vary by gender and partially explain the gender gap in delinquency.

First, a large body of research concerns gender differences in the effects of parent–child relationships on delinquency (e.g., Worthen 2012; Fagan et al. 2011). These studies have focused primarily on parental supervision and attachments between parents and children. Although the results are somewhat mixed, researchers have typically found that parent–child attachment has a stronger preventive effect on delinquency for females than for males (Alarid, Burton, and Cullen 2000; LaGrange and Silverman 1999; Barnes and Farrell 1992; Seydlitz 1990, 1991; Cernkovich and Giordano 1987; Smith and Paternoster 1987; Gove and Crutchfield 1982; Shover et al. 1979). Research has also shown that daughters are subject to higher levels of supervision than are sons, which in part accounts for sons' greater involvement in delinquency (Seydlitz 1991; Cernkovich and Giordano 1987).[4]

Second, relationships with peers differ by gender in ways that may contribute to the gender gap in delinquency. Research has shown that, compared to females, males experience more conflict and more peer pressure in their friendship groups (Giordano, Cernkovich, and Pugh 1986). This pressure to conform to the standards of the group may promote delinquency, through processes described by social learning theory (see Chapter 10). Research also shows that males are more likely than females to be exposed to delinquent peers (Mears,

Ploeger, and Warr 1998). Compared to females, males spend more time with friends, and are about twice as likely to have friends who have broken the law. The causes of association with deviant peers also differ by gender (Chapple, Vaske, and Worthen 2014). In addition, relationships with peers have different effects on delinquency for males and females. Males are more strongly affected by delinquent friends than are females (Piquero et al. 2005; Mears et al. 1998; see also Augustyn and McGloin 2013). Research also shows that having friends of the opposite sex increases the likelihood that females will engage in serious violent delinquency, but decreases the likelihood of involvement in serious violence for males (Haynie, Steffensmeier, and Bell 2007).

Third, strain theorists have suggested that the stresses and strains of adolescence might differ for males and females in ways that contribute to the gender gap in offending (Hay 2003; Broidy and Agnew 1997). Males may have greater exposure than females to the kinds of strain most likely to lead to delinquency, such as physical punishment by parents. The emotional response to strain might also differ by gender (DeCoster and Zito 2010). For example, males may be more likely than females to respond to strain with the emotion of anger, which is conducive to delinquency. Finally, males may be more likely than females to respond to strain with delinquency because they have fewer coping resources for non-delinquent responses or more opportunities for delinquency. For example, males' increased opportunities might be due to less parental supervision or greater reinforcement of delinquency from peers (Hay 2003). Several studies have tested whether these gender differences in strain can explain the gender gap in offending (Posick, Farrell, and Swatt 2013; DeCoster and Zito 2010; Hay 2003; Hoffman and Cerbone 1999; Mazerolle 1998; Hoffman and Su 1997). The results are mixed. Several studies have found few gender differences in strain and its effects on delinquency (Hoffman and Cerbone 1999; Mazerolle 1998; Hoffman and Su 1997). However, a recent study by Hay (2003) suggests that gender differences in the experience of and response to family-related strains contribute to the gender gap in delinquency.

Fourth, some researchers have examined gender differences in the processes of social interaction that lead to delinquency (Heimer and DeCoster 1999; Koita and Triplett 1998; Bartusch and Matsueda 1996; Heimer 1995, 1996). Karen Heimer (1996) explored gender definitions, or "societal definitions of femininity and masculinity," and the extent to which gender definitions contribute to gender differences in offending. She hypothesized that, for girls, feminine gender definitions reduce the likelihood of delinquency because the societal view of femininity is inconsistent with law violation in a way that the societal view of masculinity is not. She also hypothesized that, due to gender differences in socialization experiences, "anticipating disapproval of delinquency from parents and peers should have a larger deterrent effect on girls' than on boys' delinquency because girls are more likely than boys to be affected by others' reactions" (Heimer 1996: 43). Heimer found support for her hypothesis about gender definitions, but not for her hypothesis about anticipated disapproval of delinquency. In a separate study, researchers found that an interactionist model accounted for a substantial portion of the gender gap in delinquency (Bartusch and Matsueda 1996).

Finally, if we use official data to study the gender gap in offending, we might conclude that gender bias in the criminal justice system causes the gap. Research has shown that females are more likely than males to be arrested for some status offenses (Gavazzi, Yarcheck, and Chesney-Lind 2006; Teilmann and Landry 1981; Chesney-Lind 1977), even though males are more likely to report involvement in such offenses (Canter 1982). For more serious forms of delinquency, though, gender bias might operate in the opposite direction. Girls may be less likely than boys to be arrested for serious offenses because police officers, subscribing to traditional notions of appropriate gender-role behavior, treat female delinquents more leniently than males. Also, female involvement in serious delinquency may be less "visible" to police because it contradicts gender stereotypes that portray serious delinquent behavior as a male phenomenon. Research from the 1980s and 1990s provided support for both of these hypotheses (Horowitz and Pottieger 1991; Morash 1984). More recent research, however, suggests that the criminal justice system is currently less tolerant of serious offending than it once was, including serious offending by females (Steffensmeier et al. 2005). Despite evidence of gender bias in the decision to arrest (and in other parts of the criminal justice system), such bias alone cannot account for the gender gap in delinquency. Though the gender gap is smaller when we examine self-report data than when we use official data, it still exists.

Race and ethnicity

The relationship between race and involvement in delinquency is not entirely straightforward. To understand this relationship, one must consider the source of data (official data, victimization survey, or self-report survey) and the biases that exist in different data sources.

In our discussion of race and delinquency, we try to be as racially inclusive as possible. But only limited data on delinquency exist for races other than African Americans and Caucasians. Similarly, data examining delinquency and ethnicity are rather limited. Official data include only five race categories (see Table 5.4) and only two ethnicity categories (see Table 5.5). Recent self-report data on delinquency from the Monitoring the Future survey, for example, are presented only for blacks and whites, and do not include other races or any categories for ethnicity.

Official data

The UCR includes data only for individuals who have been arrested. However, offenses committed by members of some racial or ethnic groups may be more likely to result in arrest, and members of some racial or ethnic groups may be more likely to report offenses to the police (Brame et al. 2014; Tapia 2010; Hawkins et al. 2000). These factors can produce biased estimates of racial differences in offending. Because many factors (such as nature of the offense and demeanor of the suspect) come into play in the arrest process, those who are arrested are not representative of all offenders. In other words, we cannot look at those who have been arrested and accurately assume that others who have offended but avoided arrest are similar in terms of age, gender, race, or other social characteristics. This is an important point to keep in mind when using official data to explore the relationship between delinquency and social characteristics, including race.

UCR data indicate that African Americans are strongly overrepresented in involvement in delinquency. In 2013, African Americans constituted 13.2 percent of the total U.S. population and 15.1 percent of the juvenile population. Whites constituted 73.2 percent of the juvenile population (U.S. Census Bureau 2014). Yet, 34.4 percent of juveniles arrested in 2013 were black and 63 percent were white (see Table 5.4) (Federal Bureau of Investigation 2014a). An

Table 5.4 Juvenile arrests, by race and type of crime, 2013

Type of crime	White		Black		American Indian or Alaska Native		Asian		Hawaiian or other Pacific Islander	
	Number	%	Number	%	Number	%	Number	%	Number	%
All crimes	547,395	63.0	298,425	34.4	12,601	1.5	9,716	1.1	556	0.1
Part I crimes	137,280	57.0	96,638	40.2	3,266	1.4	3,315	1.4	175	0.1
Violent crimes	19,479	44.8	23,195	53.3	389	0.9	386	0.9	46	0.1
Homicide	263	42.9	333	54.3	10	1.6	6	1.0	1	0.2
Forcible rape	1,316	63.7	709	34.3	21	1.0	18	0.9	1	^
Robbery	4,356	27.4	11,351	71.4	63	0.4	111	0.7	22	0.1
Aggravated assault	13,544	54.4	10,802	43.4	295	1.2	251	1.0	22	0.1
Property crimes	117,801	59.7	73,443	37.2	2,877	1.5	2,929	1.5	129	0.1
Burglary	19,948	57.6	13,913	40.2	331	1.0	385	1.1	33	0.1
Larceny-theft	90,606	60.3	54,725	36.4	2,368	1.6	2,431	1.6	83	0.1
Motor vehicle theft	5,090	54.0	4,111	43.6	135	1.4	81	0.9	11	0.1
Arson	2,157	73.7	694	23.7	43	1.5	32	1.1	2	0.1
Part II crimes	410,115	65.3	201,787	32.1	9,335	1.5	6,401	1.0	381	0.1

^ Less than one-tenth of one percent.

Note: Arrest figures based on 11,951 reporting agencies, with 2013 estimated U.S. population of 245,741,701.

Source: Federal Bureau of Investigation (2014: Table 43). Retrieved December 8, 2014 (www.fbi.gov/about-us/cjis/ucr/crime-in-the-u.s/2013/crime-in-the-u.s.-2013/tables/table-43).

Table 5.5 Juvenile arrests, by ethnicity and type of crime, 2013

Type of crime	Hispanic or Latino		Not Hispanic or Latino	
	Number	*%*	*Number*	*%*
All crimes	99,018	21.4	363,565	78.6
Part I crimes	26,982	21.2	100,455	78.8
Violent crimes	5,705	23.4	18,650	76.6
Homicide	89	32.5	185	67.5
Forcible rape	255	14.4	1,520	85.6
Robbery	1,830	21.7	6,614	78.3
Aggravated assault	3,531	25.5	10,331	74.5
Property crimes	21,277	20.6	81,805	79.4
Burglary	5,139	26.6	14,164	73.4
Larceny-theft	14,425	18.6	62,986	81.4
Motor vehicle theft	1,418	29.1	3,451	70.9
Arson	295	19.7	1,204	80.3
Part II crimes	72,036	21.5	263,110	78.5

Note: Arrest figures based on 11,951 reporting agencies, with 2013 estimated U.S. population of 245,741,701.
Source: Federal Bureau of Investigation (2014: Table 43). Retrieved December 8, 2014 (www.fbi.gov/about-us/cjis/ucr/crime-in-the-u.s/2013/crime-in-the-u.s.-2013/tables/table-43).

additional 1.5 percent of juveniles arrested were American Indian or Alaska Native, 1.1 percent were Asian, and 0.1 percent were Hawaiian or Other Pacific Islander.

Racial differences in arrest rates become more stark when we look at specific types of offenses. Table 5.4 compares across race the percentages of juveniles arrested for various offenses. Table 5.4 shows that, given their percentage of the juvenile population, black youth are consistently overrepresented in arrests for UCR Part I and Part II crimes. The disproportionate likelihood of arrest for blacks is most glaring for violent offenses, particularly robbery and homicide. When we look only at arrests for violent crime, we find that African American youth account for 53.3 percent of arrests, while white youth account for 44.8 percent. Black youth constitute 71.4 percent of those arrested for robbery and 54.3 percent of those arrested for homicide. The numbers are less striking for property crimes, but here, too, black juveniles are overrepresented in arrests.

UCR data indicate that juveniles of Hispanic origin are not similarly overrepresented in arrests. In 2013, persons of Hispanic origin constituted 17.1 percent of the total U.S. population and 24.1 percent of the juvenile population (U.S. Census Bureau 2014). The latter percentage is consistent with the percentages of juveniles arrested who are Hispanic or Latino. Table 5.5 shows that 21.4 percent of juveniles arrested in 2013 were Hispanic or Latino. The percentages of juveniles arrested specifically for Part I violent crimes, Part I property crimes, and Part II crimes who are Hispanic or Latino are quite similar (23.4 percent, 20.6 percent, and 21.5 percent, respectively). Juveniles of Hispanic origin are overrepresented in arrests for homicide and motor vehicle theft, and underrepresented in arrests for rape and larceny-theft, given their percentage of the juvenile population.

To know whether the overrepresentation of blacks in UCR data is due to greater involvement in offending or to biases in the processes that lead to arrest, we must compare official statistics to data from other sources, including victimization surveys and self-reports.

Victimization survey data

The NCVS provides data based on victims' perceptions of the characteristics of offenders, regardless of whether the offenses were reported to the police. Thus, information about the race of offenders is available only for crimes involving personal contact between offender and victim, such as rape, robbery, and aggravated assault. As we mentioned in Chapter 3, the reliability of these data on offender characteristics depends on victims' abilities to describe accurately these individual characteristics.

Research shows that patterns of racial differences in serious juvenile offending are similar in victimization survey data and official data (Hawkins et al. 2000).[5] NCVS data indicate that personal crime victims described 51 percent of juvenile offenders as white and 41 percent as black (Snyder and Sickmund 1995). Like official data, victimization survey data indicate that, compared to the percentage of blacks in the general population, blacks are overrepresented among serious violent offenders. We may reach this same conclusion using either official or victimization survey data because both sources provide data primarily on serious types of crime.

Self-report data

Because self-report surveys ask individuals directly about their involvement in delinquency, whether or not their offenses are known to the police, they avoid the potential biases of official and victimization data. Studies from the 1980s using data from the NYS showed that whites and blacks are basically equally likely to engage in delinquency (i.e. equal in prevalence) (Huizinga and Elliott 1987; Hindelang et al. 1981; Elliott and Ageton 1980). One study used NYS data gathered annually from 1976 to 1980 and for various types of offenses and found almost no significant differences between racial groups in the proportions of persons involved in delinquency (Huizinga and Elliott 1987). Another study compared the proportions of black and white youth reporting that they had committed one or more offenses and found no significant differences by race (Elliott and Ageton 1980).

More recent data, however, from a national survey by the Center for Disease Control (2009) and from the Monitoring the Future national survey (2009–2012) show some racial differences in the proportions of persons reporting involvement in delinquency (Bachman, Johnston, and O'Malley 2011, 2014; Eaton et al. 2010; Johnston, Bachman, and O'Malley 2010, 2013; see also Morenoff 2005). The Center for Disease Control survey (called the Youth Risk Behavior Surveillance study) asked high school students about four offenses: drove after drinking alcohol, carried a weapon, carried a gun, and been in a physical fight. Whites were more likely than blacks to report driving after drinking alcohol during the past 30 days; 10.8 percent of white respondents reported engaging in this behavior, compared to 6.4 percent of blacks. Blacks and Hispanics were more likely than whites to report having been in a physical fight during the past year (41.1 percent of black respondents, 36.2 percent of Hispanics, and 27.8 percent of whites said they had been in a fight). Black respondents were also more likely than whites and Hispanics to report carrying a gun during the past 30 days (7.6 percent of black respondents, 5.8 percent of whites, and 5.1 percent of Hispanics said they had carried a gun) (Eaton et al. 2010).

The Monitoring the Future survey asked respondents about 15 delinquent offenses, some of them serious (see Table 5.6). Data from 2009–2012 show racial differences in self-reported offenses against persons (violent offending) and in some property offenses.

Table 5.6 Racial differences in self-reported offending, by offense type: Monitoring the Future, 2009–2012 (four-year average of percentage reporting involvement)

Delinquent activity *(During the last 12 months, have you ...)*	White (%)	Black (%)
Offenses against persons		
Used a weapon to get something from a person	2.1	6.5
Hit an instructor or supervisor	1.9	6.1
Hurt someone badly enough to need bandages or a doctor	10.4	15.5
Gotten into a serious fight in school or at work	9.6	15.6
Taken part in a group fight	14.5	20.5
Argued or had a fight with either of your parents	90.1	74.6
Property offenses		
Set fire to someone's property on purpose	1.9	4.5
Taken part of a car without permission of the owner	2.4	6.7
Taken a car not belonging to your family without permission	3.1	7.0
Damaged property at work on purpose	3.4	4.8
Taken something not belonging to you worth over $50	7.0	12.3
Damaged school property on purpose	8.6	11.2
Gone into some house or building when you weren't supposed to be there	22.9	22.0
Taken something from a store without paying for it	21.2	30.5
Taken something not belonging to you worth under $50	24.2	24.0
Contact with police		
Been arrested or taken to a police station	5.6	11.2

Sources: Bachman et al. (2011, 2014); Johnston et al. (2010, 2013). Retrieved December 8, 2014 (www.monitoringthefuture.org/pubs.html#refvols).

Compared to white respondents, blacks were substantially more likely to report involvement in all offenses against persons except fighting with parents. Black respondents were also more than twice as likely as whites to report setting fire to someone's property, and taking a car or car parts without the owner's permission. Percentages of respondents reporting involvement in theft of items worth less than $50 and in illegal entry of a building were essentially the same for blacks and whites. Black respondents were twice as likely as whites to report having been arrested or taken to a police station (11.2 percent of black respondents, 5.6 percent of whites) (Bachman Johnston, and O'Malley 2011; Bachman et al. 2014; Johnston et al. 2010, 2013).

Self-report surveys thus show mixed results in terms of racial differences in the prevalence of delinquency. Although some show racial differences in the prevalence of some types of offenses, others do not. But self-report surveys show clear differences by race in the *incidence* of serious offending (the average number of offenses committed by delinquent youth) (Elliott and Ageton 1980). Using NYS data, Elliott and Ageton found that, for serious property crimes (vandalism, burglary, auto theft, larceny, stolen goods, fraud, joyriding), blacks reported more than twice as many offenses as whites. The racial difference in frequency of serious violent crimes (sexual assault, aggravated assault, simple assault, robbery) was substantial, but not statistically significant. For serious violent crimes, blacks reported 1.7 times as many offenses as whites. For less serious types of delinquency, there were no significant racial differences in average frequency of offenses (Elliott and Ageton 1980).

Elliott and Ageton found similar percentages of blacks and whites reporting offenses toward the low end of the frequency distribution. But racial differences exist at the high end of the frequency distribution (with high frequency defined as 200 or more offenses for all delinquent offenses combined). For all delinquent offenses combined, 9.8 percent of black respondents reported engaging in 200 or more offenses, whereas only 4.1 percent of white respondents reported this many offenses (Elliott and Ageton 1980). In a separate study, Wolfgang and his colleagues (1972) found that non-whites were five times more likely than whites to be high frequency or "chronic" offenders.[6] In interpreting the effect of these racial differences at the high end of the frequency distribution on the overall relationship between race and delinquency, however, one must consider that high frequency offenders constitute only a small portion of the total number of offenders.[7]

In summary, self-report surveys show that blacks and whites are equally likely to report involvement in *some* types of delinquency, especially property offending. However, recent self-report surveys show racial differences in the prevalence of *violent* offending, with blacks more likely than whites to report involvement. Similarly, self-report surveys show no racial differences in frequency of offending for *minor* forms of delinquency. However, racial differences exist in the frequency of *serious* offenses, with blacks more likely than whites to be high-frequency offenders.

Why are African Americans disproportionately involved in serious crime?

Official and victimization survey data both show that blacks are overrepresented among serious offenders. Self-report data show that blacks are more likely than whites to commit serious offenses at a high frequency. So why do we see these racial differences in serious offending?

Some social scientists have used the concept of subcultural values and norms to explain racial differences in rates of offending (Curtis 1975; Wolfgang and Ferracuti 1967). According to this explanation, blacks are more likely than other racial groups to hold values that are conducive to crime. Results from empirical research on the question of subcultural values that tolerate violence and deviance are mixed. Some studies show that blacks are more likely than whites to condone deviance or the use of violence in some situations (Blumenthal 1972). But a larger body of research provides strong evidence to the contrary (Sampson and Bartusch 1998; Cao, Adams, and Jensen 1997; Erlanger 1974; Rossi et al. 1974). For example, one study found that, compared to whites, blacks and Hispanics are actually less tolerant of deviance (getting into fights, using marijuana, and drinking alcohol and smoking cigarettes as a teenager) (Sampson and Bartusch 1998).

Given the strong relationship in the United States between race and socioeconomic status, some researchers have turned to strain theory (see Chapter 11) for an explanation of racial differences in offending. These researchers have asked whether racial differences in access to legitimate opportunities (for education and employment, for example) can account for racial differences in crime and delinquency. One study examined the effects of opportunities provided by education, employment, income, and family stability on involvement in crime (robbery, burglary, and homicide) and how these effects differ for blacks and whites (LaFree, Drass, and O'Day 1992). The researchers found that, for whites, crime rates declined as legitimate opportunities increased – as predicted by strain theory. For blacks, however, their findings contradicted common assumptions about opportunities and crime. Crime rates for blacks increased as educational attainment and family income increased, and they declined as the percentage of families headed by females increased. A more recent study also showed that strain created by commitment to economic success but lack of legitimate opportunities did not explain crime for blacks (though it did explain crime for whites) (Cernkovich, Giordano, and Rudolph 2000). Robert Agnew and his colleagues have applied general strain theory to racial differences in offending (Kaufman et al. 2008). They argue that, compared to whites, blacks are likely to experience more and different types of strain, and that these strains will lead to higher levels of negative emotions among blacks. They also argue that blacks may be more likely to cope with strain and negative emotions through crime, as a result of social conditions that many blacks experience. Recent research finds racial differences in strain–crime relationships that are consistent with general strain theory (Piquero and Sealock 2010).

Much of the most promising research on racial differences in offending has focused on structural, rather than individual-level, variables. Some criminologists advocate a community-level approach that considers community structures and cultures and how they contribute to different crime rates across groups, including racial groups (Hawkins et al. 2000). Several influential social scientists, including William Julius Wilson and Robert Sampson, have examined community-level factors and have written extensively about differences in the types of communities in which blacks and whites tend to reside. In *The Truly Disadvantaged*, Wilson (1987) details the plight of the American "ghetto underclass," which occupies inner-city neighborhoods characterized by high rates of violent crime, unemployment, out-of-wedlock births, and female-headed households. This underclass consists overwhelmingly of African Americans. Yet Wilson looks beyond racism to "changes in the urban economy" and the "class transformation of the inner city" to locate the origins of this underclass. In *When Work Disappears*, Wilson (1996) discusses the devastating effects on inner-city blacks of diminished opportunities for legitimate employment, brought about by the decline in jobs for low-skilled workers in the mass production system and the transition to a service economy in which some jobs require more training and education and other jobs pay very little. The adverse effects of these labor market changes tend to be concentrated in inner-city neighborhoods where poor blacks reside. This concentration of economic disadvantage contributes to the disintegration of neighborhood institutions that would otherwise serve many functions, including crime control (Sampson and Wilson 1995).

In their theory of "race, crime, and urban inequality," Sampson and Wilson stress the importance of examining communities as the unit of analysis. They argue that differences between the types of communities in which blacks and whites tend to reside may be the real cause of the relationship we see between race and crime. In other words, blacks may be more likely than whites to commit crime because blacks are more likely to live in communities where they are exposed to structural conditions that lead to crime, such as concentrated poverty, family disruption, and residential instability (Sampson and Wilson 1995). Empirical research has supported this explanation of racial differences in offending. For example, one study found that racial differences in offending disappeared once the researchers took into account neighborhood factors (percentage of neighborhood families or households characterized by poverty, female head of household, public assistance, no employed family member, male joblessness, out-of-wedlock births) (Peeples and Loeber 1994). This finding suggests that what has often appeared as racial difference in rates of offending might actually be an artifact of the reality that African Americans are more likely than whites to live in neighborhoods of concentrated disadvantage.

Recent studies of racial differences in offending highlight the important point that race and socioeconomic status are closely intertwined in American society. African Americans are more likely than whites to live in poverty in America. Any thorough analysis of race and crime must consider this context of disadvantage to avoid attributing differences in rates of offending to race when they are actually due to socioeconomic status or community context.

Social class

UCR data do not contain information about the social class of persons arrested. Yet, for decades, criminologists acted under the assumption that delinquency was a "lower-class" phenomenon. Social class is an important factor in many of the theories we present in later chapters. Some of the most influential theories in criminology are based, either directly or indirectly, on the assumption that the disadvantage of a lower-class environment has far-reaching effects on individuals and the communities in which they live (Tittle 1983). For example, lower-class individuals lack opportunities for success normally given to others and experience strain as a result. The strain of poverty and lack of opportunity motivates involvement in crime. Additionally, those from lower-class backgrounds are exposed daily to criminal traditions in the neighborhood, and lower-class communities often lack effective means of social control.

Research from the early 1970s examined social class and offending and seemed to support the assumption that delinquency is a lower-class phenomenon. An influential study by Marvin Wolfgang and his colleagues showed that social class was strongly related to the likelihood of arrest. In this study, almost half (45 percent) of the boys from lower-class census tracts had at least one recorded police contact, while only 27 percent of those from higher-class census tracts had police records. Boys from lower-class census tracts were also more likely than those from higher-class tracts to be chronic offenders (Wolfgang, Figlio, and Sellin 1972).

Self-report data

In the late 1970s, however, a heated and enduring debate emerged in criminology about the relationship between social class and delinquency revealed in self-report data. Though self-reports, like any form of data, are limited in some ways, they provide the best information available to explore the relationship between social class and crime. Self-report surveys in the 1960s and 1970s challenged the assumption that lower-class persons were more likely than others to engage in crime and delinquency. Numerous early studies relying on self-report data showed no relationship between social class and offending (Johnson 1980; Krohn et al. 1980; Williams and Gold 1972; Hirschi 1969). In 1978, Charles Tittle and his colleagues reviewed 35 studies of social class and crime or delinquency and concluded that the relationship between social class and criminality was a "myth" (Tittle, Villemez, and Smith 1978).

This conclusion did not go unchallenged. John Braithwaite (1981), for example, argued that self-reports exaggerate delinquency by the middle class, and that a true relationship does exist between lower-class status and offending. Similarly, Gary Kleck (1982) argued that findings based on self-report data of no class differences in offending were due to "class linked bias in self-report studies" and other problems associated with the self-report method. Kleck argued that lower-class respondents are more likely than middle-class respondents to under-report their delinquency. He also criticized self-report methods for their inclusion of "trivial" offenses that may be hard to recall; their selection of respondents from sites where there is little class variation, such as schools or neighborhoods; and their exclusion of school dropouts, who are more likely than those in school to be lower-class boys and to be delinquent.

However, more recent self-report studies include more than "trivial" offenses and measure social class and delinquency in a variety of ways. So what do these studies tell us about social class and offending?

National Youth Survey

The NYS, begun in 1976, gathered self-report data on both minor and serious offenses that would allow a thorough examination of the class–crime relationship and permit a reasonable comparison between self-reports and official data (Elliott, Huizinga, and Ageton 1985; Elliott and Huizinga 1983; Elliott and Ageton 1980). Using NYS data, Elliott and Ageton developed a general delinquency scale that included the full range of delinquent behaviors. This general scale was developed to parallel UCR measures of both serious and minor offenses for which youth could be arrested. The NYS 46-item general scale included all UCR Part I offenses except murder and 60 percent of UCR Part II offenses (Elliott and Huizinga 1983). Elliott and Ageton also analyzed six subscales of offenses: serious crimes against persons, serious crimes against property, illegal service crimes, public disorder crimes, status offenses, and hard drug use.

Elliott and Ageton (1980) measured social class in terms of the occupational status of the primary wage earner with a variable containing three categories: lower class, working class, or middle class. They found significant class differences in delinquent behavior for the general delinquency scale and the serious crimes against persons subscale. Lower-class youth scored higher on the general delinquency scale than did youth from the working and middle classes. The striking class difference in this study, though, was for serious crimes against persons. For this subscale of violent offenses, "lower-class youth report nearly four times as many offenses as do middle-class youth and one-and-one-half times as many as working-class youth" (Elliott and Ageton 1980: 160). Elliott and Ageton found no class differences for the other five subscales of offenses they examined. The class differences in the general delinquency scale and the crimes against persons subscale were primarily at the high end of the frequency continuum, where lower-class youth were disproportionately found.

Elliott and Huizinga (1983) extended this study to include data gathered annually over a five-year period. They examined both prevalence and incidence of offending for persons from different social classes. (Recall that *prevalence* refers to the proportion of a group involved in delinquency and *incidence* refers to the frequency of offending.) They found no class differences in the prevalence of delinquency when they measured delinquent behavior using a general scale of offenses. But they did find class differences in prevalence for serious offenses (felony assault, felony theft, and robbery), for males only. Middle-class males were less likely to engage in serious offenses than lower- or working-class males. Elliott and Huizinga concluded that, although some class differences existed in prevalence of offending, these differences were generally not strong, nor were they consistent over time or across gender. Regarding incidence of offending, their results are similar to Elliott and Ageton's.

Class differences in delinquency appear greater with incidence than with prevalence measures, and greater for serious violent crimes than for other types of offenses (Elliott and Huizinga 1983). Yet many previous self-report studies have relied on prevalence measures that do not include the most serious offenses. Elliott and Huizinga argue that these weaknesses of early self-report measures might be responsible for the typical, but incorrect, finding of no relationship between class and involvement in crime.

Philadelphia Birth Cohort Study

Like the NYS, the Philadelphia Birth Cohort Study includes self-reports of serious offenses (Wolfgang et al. 1972). In addition, the Philadelphia study includes official measures of offending for the subjects who provided self-report data and thus allows researchers to compare self-reports and official data.

Terence Thornberry and Margaret Farnworth (1982) used data from the Philadelphia study to examine the class–crime relationship. They found that, when similar types of offenses were compared across data sources, self-reports and official data provided fairly similar portrayals of the class–crime relationship. Thornberry and Farnworth also found a negative relationship between social class and adult offending, particularly among blacks (i.e. the lower the social class, the higher the likelihood of offending). This inverse relationship, however, did not hold for juveniles. Neither self-report nor official measures of offending were strongly related to social class among juveniles as measured by father's occupation. However, Thornberry and Farnworth did find that social class is more strongly related to offending when it is measured in terms of the respondent's own class, rather than that of the family of origin.

Rochester Youth Development Study

To explore the class–delinquency relationship, Margaret Farnworth and her colleagues (1994) also used data from the Rochester Youth Development Study, a longitudinal, self-report survey begun in 1988. The researchers measured both social class and delinquency in several ways to see if inadequate measurement accounted for prior findings of no class–delinquency relationship.

This study highlights the impact that alternative measures of class and delinquency can have on research results. The relationship between social class and delinquent behavior varied greatly depending on the measures used. When class was measured in terms of the education and occupation of wage earners in the household – the kinds of variables used most often in prior research – no strong or consistent relationship existed between class and delinquency. But when class was measured in terms of "underclass" status (households below the poverty level, households receiving welfare, unemployment of the principal wage earner), an inverse relationship existed between class and serious street crime (Farnworth et al. 1994).

The measurement of delinquency also affected research results. When Farnworth and her colleagues examined data from a single time point, none of the class measures were significantly related to general or common (minor) delinquency scales. But when they examined persistent economic need and delinquent behavior over time, they found consistent evidence of a class–delinquency relationship. They concluded that, when class and delinquency are measured in ways most consistent with theories of delinquency, the expected negative relationship exists between class and delinquency. "This is especially the case when persistent underclass status is related to persistent delinquency and to victimizing street crimes associated with lifestyles among the urban poor" (Farnworth et al. 1994: 55).

Explaining inconsistencies between theory and research

Criminological theory typically proposes an inverse relationship between socioeconomic status (SES) and delinquency. However, empirical research tends to show little relationship between the two, at least for minor forms of offending. Bradley Entner Wright and his colleagues (1999) proposed that this inconsistency could be reconciled by recognizing that SES both positively and negatively affects delinquency and that these opposite effects might "cancel each other out" and lead to the faulty conclusion that SES and delinquency are not related.

Relying on classic criminological theories, such as anomie and subculture theory (see Chapter 11), Wright and his colleagues (1999) hypothesized that *low* socioeconomic status will increase the likelihood of involvement in delinquency. In this case, SES will have a negative effect on delinquent behavior. The processes mediating between SES and delinquency, according to these theories, include strain caused by limited opportunities, alienation, diminished educational and occupational aspirations, and diminished self-control. Relying on social psychological theories, such as power-control theory (see Chapter 12), Wright and his colleagues hypothesized that *high* socioeconomic status will increase the likelihood of involvement in delinquency. Here, SES will have a positive effect on delinquent behavior. The processes mediating between SES and delinquency, according to these theories, include "taste for risk" or the search for excitement and thrills, absence of parental controls, and perception of limited risk of detection or punishment (all of which are greatest among the upper class, according to power-control theory).

Wright and his colleagues found strong support for these hypotheses. Socioeconomic status affected delinquency indirectly – positively through some intervening variables and negatively through others. Thus, in the end, the positive and negative effects of SES on delinquent behavior "cancelled each other out." These offsetting effects create the illusion that SES is unrelated to delinquency and might explain why prior studies that have not considered these opposing effects have typically found no relationship between SES and delinquent behavior.

Why are the economically disadvantaged so involved in serious delinquency?

Attempts to explain why social class is related to serious delinquency have occurred on several levels. First, researchers have explored the relationship at the individual level, examining social psychological processes that might explain how social class affects crime. Some research has examined individual-level factors, such as parenting practices, to try to explain the class–crime relationship for serious offending. Karen Heimer (1997) used self-report data (NYS) to explore the relationships among social class, parenting practices, and violent delinquency. She hypothesized that, compared to parents of higher SES, parents of lower SES will be more likely to use coercive discipline (e.g., physically punishing, yelling, threatening) and will be less likely to supervise children closely and to disapprove of aggression. Because of these factors, lower SES children will be more likely to associate with aggressive peers, to develop attitudes favoring violence, and therefore to engage in violent delinquency. Heimer found strong support for most of her hypotheses. Her work demonstrates that socioeconomic status affects violent delinquency indirectly through parenting practices, peer associations, and attitude formation.

Second, criminologists have looked to the economic conditions of neighborhoods, attempting to explain higher rates of offending in more impoverished communities. Because race and class are intertwined in America, the community-level processes we discussed earlier in this chapter apply here also. William Julius Wilson's work on the creation of an "underclass" through the concentration of economic disadvantage sheds a great deal of light on the class–crime link (Wilson 1987, 1996). From Wilson's work and the social disorganization model of crime and delinquency (see Chapter 11), researchers have derived hypotheses about the relationship between the socioeconomic composition of neighborhoods and rates of crime (Hay et al. 2006, 2007; Bursik and Grasmick 1993a). Robert Bursik and Harold Grasmick (1993a) found that severe economic deprivation (measured in terms of percentage of families with incomes below the poverty level, unemployment rate, public assistance rate per 100 residents, and percentage of the population that is black) significantly affected delinquency rates, even after other factors were taken into account. The effects of economic deprivation on delinquency rates were both direct and indirect, through variables measuring social disorganization and the ability of residents to control the behavior of those in the neighborhood (e.g., residential mobility, rates of owner occupancy, percentage of children in two-parent households). The measurement of severe economic deprivation in Bursik and Grasmick's study is consistent with Wilson's conceptualization of an urban underclass.

Finally, some criminologists have explored the class–crime relationship from a Marxist perspective, pointing to the capitalist foundations of modern American society to explain the relationship (see Chapter 12). Marxist criminologists locate the origins of crime in capitalism, which creates competing economic classes within society (Colvin and Pauly 1983; Beirne and Quinney 1982; Chambliss and Seidman 1982; Quinney 1980; Spitzer 1975). Divisions among the classes result in attempts by the ruling class to control those who are relatively powerless. This control is accomplished in part through the legal system, which the ruling class uses to define illegitimate behavior among the working class and to protect its own interests. In the Marxist view, both this process of "criminalization" of the actions of the working class, and the responses of workers to ruling class controls, account for higher rates of offending among the working class.

Victimization

The NCVS reveals that almost 23 million crimes occurred in the United States in 2013 (Truman and Langton 2014). As Table 5.7 indicates, the majority of these offenses were property crimes (73.2 percent), rather than violent crimes (26.7 percent). Victimization rates were almost six times greater for property crimes than for violent crimes, primarily because of the relative frequency of theft.

The risks of becoming a victim of crime are not the same for all people. Victimization risk varies by several factors, including age, gender, race, and social class. The social correlates of offending are basically identical to the social correlates of victimization. Those who are most likely to commit offenses are also most likely to become crime victims.

Age

As we have shown, young people are disproportionately involved in crime. They are also more likely than older persons to be victims of crime. Figure 5.2 shows victimization rates (per 1,000 persons age 12 and older) by age for violent crimes (rape/sexual assault, robbery, aggravated assault, and simple assault). Similar to arrest rates (see the age–crime curve in Figure 5.1), rates of violent victimization peak at ages 12–14 (65.1), and then decline by 50 percent by ages 21–24 (32.2) (Bureau of Justice Statistics [BJS] 2014a). NCVS data do not include information about murder, but UCR data show that young people between the ages of 17 and 29, especially males, are disproportionately likely to be victims of homicide (Federal Bureau of Investigation 2014b).

Table 5.7 Number, percentage, and rate of victimizations, by type of offense, 2013

Type of offense	Number	Percentage of all crimes	Victimization rates*
All crimes	22,900,510	100.0	
Violent crimes	6,126,420	26.7	23.2
Rape/sexual assault	300,170	1.3	1.1
Robbery	645,650	2.8	2.4
Aggravated assault	994,220	4.3	3.8
Simple assault	4,186,390	18.3	15.8
Property crimes	16,774,090	73.2	131.4
Household burglary	3,286,210	14.3	25.7
Motor vehicle theft	661,250	2.9	5.2
Theft	12,826,620	56.0	100.5

* Rates per 1,000 persons age 12 and older for personal crimes, and per 1,000 households for property crimes.
Note: Due to rounding, middle column may not sum to 100 percent.
Source: Truman and Langton (2014: 1).

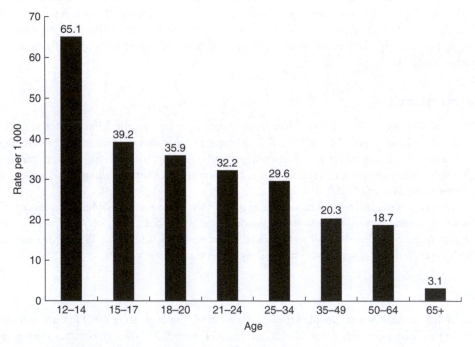

Figure 5.2 Victimization rates for violent crimes, by age, 2013.
This figure shows victimization rates (per 1,000 persons age 12 and older) by age for the violent crimes of rape/sexual assault, robbery, aggravated assault, and simple assault.
Source: Bureau of Justice Statistics (2014a). Generated using the NCVS Victimization Analysis Tool at www.bjs.gov. December 3, 2014.

Gender

Males are more likely than females to commit delinquent or criminal acts. NCVS data reveal that males are also more likely to be victims of certain types of crime. Table 5.8 shows violent crime victimization rates by gender. For all crimes of violence combined (excluding murder), the victimization rate is 23.7 (per 1,000 persons) for males and 22.7 for females (BJS 2014b; see also Lauritsen and Carbone–Lopez 2011). For aggravated assault, the victimization rate for males is substantially higher than the rate for females. Only for the crime of rape are females more likely than males to be victimized. The rape victimization rate in 2013 was nearly seven times greater for females than for males.

Race and ethnicity

Table 5.9 shows victimization rates by race and ethnicity for violent crimes. For all violent crimes combined, blacks are more likely than people of other races to be victims. But variation by race exists when we look at particular types of crime. Whites are more likely than people of other races to be victims of rape. Blacks are more likely than people of other races to be victims of *aggravated* assault, but the likelihood of being a victim of simple assault is essentially the same for blacks (15.6) and whites (15.9) (BJS 2014c). For all violent crimes combined, people of Hispanic origin are more likely than non-Hispanics to be victims.

Table 5.8 Victimization rates for violent crime, by gender, 2013*

Type of offense	Males	Females
All crimes of violence (except homicide)	23.7	22.7
Rape/sexual assault	0.3	2.0
Robbery	2.7	2.2
Aggravated assault	4.7	2.9
Simple assault	16.0	15.7

* Rates per 1,000 persons age 12 and older.
Source: Bureau of Justice Statistics (2014b). Generated using the NCVS Victimization Analysis Tool at www.bjs.gov. December 3, 2014.

Table 5.9 Victimization rates for violent crime, by race and ethnicity, 2013*

Type of offense	Black	White	Other**	Hispanic	Non-Hispanic
Violent crimes	25.2	22.7	11.4	24.8	22.9
Rape/sexual assault	0.7^	1.1	0.3^	0.7^	1.2
Robbery	2.8	2.3	3.8^	3.2	2.3
Aggravated assault	6.2	3.5	0.8^	3.7	3.8
Simple assault	15.6	15.9	6.5	17.3	15.6

* Rates per 1,000 persons age 12 and older.
** Other races include Asians, Native Hawaiians, other Pacific Islanders, Alaska Natives, and American Indians.
^ Based on 10 or fewer sample cases.
Source: Bureau of Justice Statistics (2014c). Generated using the NCVS Victimization Analysis Tool at www.bjs.gov. December 3, 2014.

Victimization rates are higher for Hispanics than for non-Hispanics for the crimes of robbery and simple assault. Victimization rates for these two groups are essentially the same for aggravated assault.

UCR data reveal that blacks are also more likely than whites and those of other races to be victims of homicide. Although blacks constituted 13.2 percent of the U.S. population in 2013, 51.1 percent of homicide victims in 2013 were black and 45.2 percent were white (Federal Bureau of Investigation 2014b; U.S. Census Bureau 2014). The numbers are similar for juvenile homicide victims (those under age 18): in 2013, 46.9 percent were black and 47.9 percent were white (Federal Bureau of Investigation 2014b).

Social class

Table 5.10 shows victimization rates by household income. Economic disadvantage is associated with both violent and property crime victimization. Victimization rates generally decline as household income increases. The decrease in violent victimization as household income increases is clearest for rape and robbery (though the number of cases of rape is small, so the rates may be less reliable and should be viewed with caution). For all violent crimes combined (excluding murder), the victimization rate is 84.0 for those whose household income is less than $7,500, but only 14.4 for those whose household income is $75,000 or more. The decrease in property crime victimization as household income increases is clearest for burglary. For all property crimes combined, the victimization rate is 230.9 for those whose household income is less than $7,500, but 121.4 for those whose household income is $75,000 or more.

Summary and conclusions

In this chapter, we examined age, gender, race, and social class as social correlates of offending. Age and gender, in particular, are strongly and consistently related to involvement in crime, which is primarily a pursuit of young males. Multiple sources of data (UCR and self-report and victimization surveys) all point to the same fact: For most types of offenses, the period

Table 5.10 Victimization rates for violent and property crime, by household income, 2013*

Type of offense	Less than $7,500	$7,500– $14,999	$15,000– $24,999	$25,000– $34,999	$35,000– $49,999	$50,000– $74,999	$75,000 or more
Violent crimes	84.0	62.3	31.8	21.6	22.8	17.8	14.4
Rape/sexual assault	3.3^	2.2^	2.3	1.3^	1.9^	1.5^	0.1^
Robbery	10.0	7.5	4.6	1.7	2.8	1.4	0.6
Aggravated assault	15.2	10.1	5.6	4.4	2.7	1.7	1.9
Simple assault	55.6	42.5	19.3	14.1	15.3	13.3	11.8
Property crimes	230.9	191.7	147.6	165.3	124.1	127.1	121.4
Household burglary	55.4	46.1	34.6	31.0	19.8	24.1	16.1
Motor vehicle theft	6.4	7.3	5.6	9.2	3.1	5.2	4.1
Theft	169.1	138.3	107.3	125.0	101.2	97.8	101.2

* Rates per 1,000 persons age 12 or older for violent crimes, and per 1,000 households for property crimes.
^ Based on 10 or fewer sample cases.
Source: Bureau of Justice Statistics (2014d). Generated using the NCVS Victimization Analysis Tool at www.bjs.gov. December 3, 2014.

of adolescence and young adulthood is the peak time of offending for most individuals. The peak age of offending for violent crimes, however, is somewhat older than for most property offenses.

The gender gap in crime also varies by type of offense and is particularly wide for violent offenses, which are committed overwhelmingly by males. The gap is smaller for status offenses, for which boys and girls are more equally likely to be arrested. All three data sources – official data, victimization surveys, and self-report surveys – show that males are disproportionately involved in crime and delinquency. The gender gap in crime revealed in self-report data, however, is generally smaller than the gap suggested by official data.

Although some theorists predicted that the gender gap in crime would narrow as a function of increasing gender role equality, it appears that this convergence generally has not occurred for offenses other than minor property crimes. Arrests of girls for violent offenses have increased in recent years. But research indicates that changes in criminal justice policy, rather than changes in actual behavior, are primarily responsible for these increases in arrest.

The relationships between race and social class and involvement in crime are less clear-cut than those observed for age and gender. The bulk of evidence suggests that African Americans are disproportionately represented among the population of offenders – at least among those who commit serious offenses. For decades, some social scientists have argued that official data on offenders are suspect because of biases inherent in the criminal justice system. Yet victimization data tend to confirm the conclusions drawn from official data. Both official and victimization data are weighted more heavily toward serious offenses. These data show that blacks are overrepresented among offenders, given their proportion of the general population. However, self-report data, which best capture minor offenses, show that blacks and whites are equally likely to engage in some types of delinquency (prevalence), but blacks are more likely than whites to report involvement in *violent* offending. Self-report data also show racial differences in the frequency of *serious* offending; blacks are more likely than whites to be high-frequency offenders. However, self-report surveys show no racial differences in the frequency of *minor* forms of delinquency.

Self-reports of offending provide the only way to examine the relationship between social class and offending because official data and victimization surveys do not include information about the social class of offenders. The NYS, which includes measures of serious offenses that are comparable to offenses represented in official data, reveals significant class differences in delinquency, particularly in serious crimes against persons. Lower-class youth are more likely than their working- and middle-class counterparts to engage in serious delinquent behavior and to commit a higher frequency of offenses. When we examine more minor forms of offending, however, the class–crime relationship is generally weak. Those of all social classes are equally likely to engage in minor offenses.

We closed this chapter by examining the social correlates of victimization and found a pattern similar to the social correlates of offending. Those who are most likely to be offenders are also most likely to be crime victims. Young people, males, African Americans, and economically disadvantaged persons are more likely than others to be victims of crime.

Critical-thinking questions

1. Why do official statistics and self-report data paint somewhat different pictures of the social correlates of offending?

2.   Given what you have learned about the disproportionate involvement in crime of young people, males, African Americans, and those who are economically disadvantaged, describe the kinds of programs you believe would be most successful in preventing delinquency and crime.
3.   What accounts for the similarities between social correlates of offending and social correlates of victimization? In other words, why are those who are most likely to commit crime also most likely to be victims of it?
4.   Consider the perceptions of criminals in the Chestnut Hill neighborhood, described at the opening of this chapter. How do the social correlates of offending (age, gender, race, and social class) shape people's perceptions of crime and criminals?

Suggested reading

Morenoff, Jeffrey D. 2005. "Racial and Ethnic Disparities in Crime and Delinquency in the United States." Pp. 139–173 in *Ethnicity and Causal Mechanisms*, ed. M. Rutter and M. Tienda. Cambridge University Press.

Sampson, Robert J. and William Julius Wilson. 1995. "Toward a Theory of Race, Crime, and Urban Inequality." Pp. 37–54 in *Crime and Inequality*, ed. J. Hagan and R. D. Peterson. Stanford University Press.

Steffensmeier, Darrell and Emilie Allan. 1996. "Gender and Crime: Toward a Gendered Theory of Female Offending." *Annual Review of Sociology* 22: 459–487.

Steffensmeier, Darrell, Emilie Anderson Allan, Miles D. Harer, and Cathy Streifel. 1989. "Age and the Distribution of Crime." *American Journal of Sociology* 94: 803–831.

Wright, Bradley R. Entner, Avshalom Caspi, Terrie E. Moffitt, Richard A. Miech, and Phil A. Silva. 1999. "Reconsidering the Relationship between SES and Delinquency: Causation but Not Correlation." *Criminology* 37: 175–194.

Useful websites

For weblinks relevant to this chapter, go to the following sites for further information.

*   *Crime in the United States* publications, Federal Bureau of Investigation, Uniform Crime Reports Publications (www.fbi.gov/about-us/cjis/ucr/ucr-publications#Crime)
*   *Criminal Victimization* publications, Office of Justice Programs, Bureau of Justice Statistics (www.bjs.gov/index.cfm?ty=pbse&sid=6)
*   Monitoring the Future study of trends in drug use and delinquency, Institute for Social Research, University of Michigan (http://monitoringthefuture.org/)
*   *Sourcebook of Criminal Justice Statistics*, Hindelang Criminal Justice Research Center, University at Albany (www.albany.edu/sourcebook/about.html)

Glossary of key terms

Age composition effect: Concerns the age composition of the total population and its effects on overall crime rates. This effect traces changes in crime rates with changes in population demographics. Crime rates rise as the number of people in the crime-prone years increases and fall as the number of people in the crime-prone years decreases.

Age–crime curve: The bell-shaped curve observed when one graphs the relationship between age and crime. The age–crime curve typically shows an increase in delinquent involvement during the teenage years, a peak in mid-adolescence to early adulthood, and then a rapid decline.

Age effect: The disproportionate involvement of young people in crime.

Aging out of crime: Termination of involvement in crime following adolescence and young adulthood, due to sociological, psychological, and biological factors.

Convergence hypothesis: The prediction that the gender gap in crime and delinquency would narrow and that male and female rates of offending would converge as a function of increasing gender equality.

Crime-prone years: The age period when people are most likely to be involved in crime. Generally, the crime-prone years range from mid-adolescence into early adulthood.

Social correlates: Social characteristics (such as age, gender, race, and social class) that are statistically related to involvement in delinquency and that tend to distinguish offenders from non-offenders.

Notes

1. But see also Stolzenberg and D'Alessio (2008), who found that patterns of co-offending (offending in the company of others) by age do not account for the age–crime curve.
2. But see also Hindelang et al. (1981: 137–155), who argue that gender differences in delinquency are similar across data sources (self-report and official data), at least for more serious offenses.
3. Hindelang et al. (1981: 141–142) found no gender differences in self-reports of incorrigibility, measured as running away and defying or hitting parents.
4. Hill and Atkinson (1988) found that females were not necessarily subjected to more control than males, but rather that the type of familial control varied by gender.
5. See also Sampson and Lauritsen (1997) and Hindelang (1978), who compared official and victimization survey data on the race of violent offenders and found that the two sources closely matched in terms of racial composition of offenders.
6. But see also a recent study by Piquero and Brame (2008) in which the authors used a sample of *serious* offenders to explore the race–delinquency relationship. They used both official and self-report data on offending and did not find the kinds of racial differences in offending that are typically found with samples that include broad cross-sections of the population.
7. In their classic study, Wolfgang et al. (1972: 247–248) found that "chronic" offenders, defined as those with five or more police contacts, constituted only 18 percent of the total number of offenders in their study.

References

Adler, Freda. 1975. *Sisters in Crime: The Rise of the New Female Criminal*. New York: McGraw-Hill.

Alarid, Leanne Fiftal, Velmer S. Burton, Jr., and Francis T. Cullen. 2000. "Gender and Crime among Felony Offenders: Assessing the Generality of Social Control and Differential Association Theories." *Journal of Research in Crime and Delinquency* 37: 171–199.

Anderson, Elijah. 1999. *Code of the Street: Decency, Violence, and the Moral Life of the Inner City*. New York: Norton.

Augustyn, Megan Bears and Jean Marie McGloin. 2013. "The Risk of Informal Socializing with Peers: Considering Gender Differences across Predatory Delinquency and Substance Use." *Justice Quarterly* 30: 117–143.

Bachman, Jerald G., Lloyd D. Johnston, and Patrick M. O'Malley. 2011. *Monitoring the Future: Questionnaire Responses from the Nation's High School Seniors, 2010*. Ann Arbor, MI: Institute for Social Research, University of Michigan. Retrieved December 8, 2014 (www.monitoringthefuture.org/pubs.html#refvols).

Bachman, Jerald G., Lloyd D. Johnston, and Patrick M. O'Malley. 2014. *Monitoring the Future: Questionnaire Responses from the Nation's High School Seniors, 2012*. Ann Arbor, MI: Institute for Social Research,

University of Michigan. Retrieved December 8, 2014 (www.monitoringthefuture.org/pubs. html#refvols).

Barnes, Grace M. and Michael P. Farrell. 1992. "Parental Support and Control as Predictors of Adolescent Drinking, Delinquency, and Related Problem Behaviors." *Journal of Marriage and the Family* 54: 763–776.

Bartusch, Dawn R. Jeglum and Ross L. Matsueda. 1996. "Gender, Reflected Appraisals, and Labeling: A Cross-Group Test of an Interactionist Theory of Delinquency." *Social Forces* 75: 145–176.

Beirne, Piers and Richard Quinney. 1982. *Marxism and Law*. New York: Wiley.

Blumenthal, Monica D. 1972. "Predicting Attitudes toward Violence." *Science* 176: 1296–1303.

Braithwaite, John. 1981. "The Myth of Social Class and Criminality Reconsidered." *American Sociological Review* 46: 36–57.

Braithwaite, John. 1989. *Crime, Shame and Reintegration*. Cambridge University Press.

Brame, Robert, Shawn D. Bushway, Ray Paternoster, and Michael G. Turner. 2014. "Demographic Patterns of Cumulative Arrest Prevalence by Ages 18 and 23." *Crime and Delinquency* 60: 471–486.

Broidy, Lisa and Robert Agnew. 1997. "Gender and Crime: A General Strain Theory Perspective." *Journal of Research in Crime and Delinquency* 34: 275–306.

Bureau of Justice Statistics. 2014a. *Rates of Violent Victimizations, Serious Violent Victimizations, and Simple Assaults by Age, 2013*. Generated using the NCVS Victimization Analysis Tool at www.bjs.gov. December 3, 2014.

Bureau of Justice Statistics. 2014b. *Rates of Violent Victimizations, Serious Violent Victimizations, Rape/Sexual Assaults, Robberies, Aggravated Assaults, and Simple Assaults by Sex, 2013*. Generated using the NCVS Victimization Analysis Tool at www.bjs.gov. December 3, 2014.

Bureau of Justice Statistics. 2014c. *Rates of Violent Victimizations, Serious Violent Victimizations, Rape/ Sexual Assaults, Robberies, Aggravated Assaults, and Simple Assaults by Race, 2013*; and *Rates of Violent Victimizations, Serious Violent Victimizations, Rape/Sexual Assaults, Robberies, Aggravated Assaults, and Simple Assaults by Hispanic Origin, 2013*. Generated using the NCVS Victimization Analysis Tool at www.bjs.gov. December 3, 2014.

Bureau of Justice Statistics. 2014d. *Rates of Property Victimizations, Household Burglaries, Motor Vehicle Thefts, and Thefts by Household Income, 2013*; and *Rates of Violent Victimizations, Serious Violent Victimizations, Rape/Sexual Assaults, Robberies, Aggravated Assaults, and Simple Assaults by Household Income, 2013*. Generated using the NCVS Victimization Analysis Tool at www.bjs.gov. December 3, 2014.

Bursik, Robert J., Jr. and Harold G. Grasmick. 1993a. "Economic Deprivation and Neighborhood Crime Rates, 1960–1980." *Law and Society Review* 27: 263–283.

Bursik, Robert J., Jr. and Harold G. Grasmick. 1993b. *Neighborhoods and Crime: The Dimensions of Effective Community Control*. New York: Lexington Books.

Canter, Rachelle J. 1982. "Sex Differences in Self-Reported Delinquency." *Criminology* 20: 373–393.

Canter, Rachelle J. 1995. "Family Correlates of Male and Female Delinquency." *Criminology* 20: 149–167.

Cao, Liqun, Anthony Adams, and Vickie J. Jensen. 1997. "A Test of the Black Subculture of Violence Thesis: A Research Note." *Criminology* 35: 367–379.

Cernkovich, Stephen A. and Peggy C. Giordano. 1987. "Family Relationships and Delinquency." *Criminology* 25: 295–321.

Cernkovich, Stephen A., Peggy C. Giordano, and Jennifer L. Rudolph. 2000. "Race, Crime, and the American Dream." *Journal of Research in Crime and Delinquency* 37: 131–170.

Chambliss, William J. and Robert B. Seidman. 1982. *Law, Order, and Power*. 2nd edn. Reading, MA: Addison-Wesley.

Chapple, Constance, Jamie Vaske, and Meredith G. F. Worthen. 2014. "Gender Differences in Associations with Deviant Peer Groups: Examining Individual, Interactional, and Compositional Factors." *Deviant Behavior* 35: 394–411.

Chesney-Lind, Meda. 1973. "Judicial Enforcement of the Female Sex Role: The Family Court and the Female Delinquent." *Issues in Criminology* 8: 51–69.

Chesney-Lind, Meda. 1977. "Judicial Paternalism and the Female Status Offender: Training Women to Know Their Place." *Crime and Delinquency* 23: 121–130.

Chesney-Lind, Meda. 1989. "Girls' Crime and Women's Place: Toward a Feminist Model of Female Delinquency." *Crime and Delinquency* 35: 5–29.

Chesney-Lind, Meda. 1997. *The Female Offender: Girls, Women, and Crime.* Thousand Oaks, CA: Sage.

Chesney-Lind, Meda. 1999. "Challenging Girls' Invisibility in Juvenile Court." *Annals of the American Academy of Political and Social Science* 564: 185–202.

Chesney-Lind, Meda and Vickie V. Paramore. 2001. "Are Girls Getting More Violent? Exploring Juvenile Robbery Trends." *Journal of Contemporary Criminal Justice* 17: 142–166.

Cohen, Lawrence E. and Kenneth C. Land. 1987. "Age Structure and Crime: Symmetry versus Asymmetry and the Projection of Crime Rates through the 1980s." *American Sociological Review* 52: 170–183.

Colvin, Mark and John Pauly. 1983. "A Critique of Criminology: Toward an Integrated Structural-Marxist Theory of Delinquency Production." *American Journal of Sociology* 89: 513–551.

Curtis, Lynn A. 1975. *Violence, Race, and Culture.* Lexington, MA: D. C. Heath.

Daigle, Leah E., Francis T. Cullen, and John Paul Wright. 2007. "Gender Differences in the Predictors of Juvenile Delinquency: Assessing the Generality-Specificity Debate." *Youth Violence and Juvenile Justice* 5: 254–286.

Daly, Kathleen. 1994. *Gender, Crime, and Punishment.* New Haven, CT: Yale University Press.

DeCoster, Stacy and Rena Cornell Zito. 2010. "Gender and General Strain Theory: The Gendering of Emotional Experiences and Expressions." *Journal of Contemporary Criminal Justice* 26: 224–245.

Eaton, Danice K., et al. 2010. "Youth Risk Behavior Surveillance – United States, 2009." *CDC Surveillance Summaries, Morbidity and Mortality Weekly Report* 59, No. SS-5. Washington, DC: USGPO. Cited in *Sourcebook of Criminal Justice Statistics Online*, Table 3.56.2009. Retrieved December 8, 2014 (www.albany.edu/sourcebook/index.html).

Elliott, Delbert S. and Suzanne S. Ageton. 1980. "Reconciling Race and Class Differences in Self-Reported and Official Estimates of Delinquency." *American Sociological Review* 45: 95–110.

Elliott, Delbert S., Suzanne S. Ageton, David Huizinga, B. A. Knowles, and Rachelle J. Canter. 1983. *The Prevalence and Incidence of Delinquent Behavior: 1976–1980: National Estimates of Delinquent Behavior by Sex, Race, Social Class and Other Selected Variables.* Boulder, CO: Behavioral Research Institute.

Elliott, Delbert S. and David Huizinga. 1983. "Social Class and Delinquent Behavior in a National Youth Panel." *Criminology* 21: 149–177.

Elliott, Delbert S., David Huizinga, and Suzanne S. Ageton. 1985. *Explaining Delinquency and Drug Use.* Beverly Hills, CA: Sage.

Erlanger, Howard S. 1974. "The Empirical Status of the Subculture of Violence Thesis." *Social Problems* 22: 280–292.

Fagan, Abigail A., M. Lee Van Horn, Susan Antaramian, and J. David Hawkins. 2011. "How Do Families Matter? Age and Gender Differences in Family Influences on Delinquency and Drug Use." *Youth Violence and Juvenile Justice* 9: 150–170.

Farnworth, Margaret, Terence P. Thornberry, Marvin D. Krohn, and Alan J. Lizotte. 1994. "Measurement in the Study of Class and Delinquency: Integrating Theory and Research." *Journal of Research in Crime and Delinquency* 31: 32–61.

Federal Bureau of Investigation. 2014a. *Crime in the United States, 2013: Uniform Crime Reports.* Washington, DC: U.S. Department of Justice. Retrieved December 8, 2014 (www.fbi.gov/about-us/cjis/ucr/crime-in-the-u.s/2013/crime-in-the-u.s.-2013).

Federal Bureau of Investigation. 2014b. *Expanded Homicide Data Table 2, 2013.* Washington, DC: U.S. Department of Justice. Retrieved December 8, 2014 (www.fbi.gov/about-us/cjis/ucr/crime-in-the-u.s/2013/crime-in-the-u.s.-2013/offenses-known-to-law-enforcement/expanded-homicide/expanded_homicide_data_table_2_murder_victims_by_age_sex_and_race_2013.xls).

Gavazzi, Stephen M., Courtney M. Yarcheck, and Meda Chesney-Lind. 2006. "Global Risk Indicators and the Role of Gender in a Juvenile Detention Sample." *Criminal Justice and Behavior* 33: 597–612.

Giordano, Peggy C., Stephen A. Cernkovich, and M. D. Pugh. 1986. "Friendship and Delinquency." *American Journal of Sociology* 5: 1170–1202.

Gove, Walter R.. 1985. "The Effect of Age and Gender on Deviant Behavior: A Bio-Psychosocial Perspective." Pp. 115–144 in *Gender and the Life Course*, ed. A. S. Rossi. Hawthorne, NY: Aldine.

Gove, Walter R. and Robert D. Crutchfield. 1982. "The Family and Juvenile Delinquency." *Sociological Quarterly* 23: 301–319.

Hagan, John. 1985. *Modern Criminology: Crime, Criminal Behavior and Its Control*. New York: McGraw-Hill.

Hagan, John. 1989. *Structural Criminology*. New Brunswick, NJ: Rutgers University Press.

Hagan, John. 1991. "Destiny and Drift: Subcultural Preferences, Status Attainments, and the Risks and Rewards of Youth." *American Sociological Review* 56: 567–582.

Hagan, John. 1993. "The Social Embeddedness of Crime and Unemployment." *Criminology* 31: 465–491.

Hawkins, Darnell F., John H. Laub, Janet L. Lauritsen, and Lynn Cothern. 2000. *Race, Ethnicity, and Serious and Violent Juvenile Offending*. Washington, DC: Office of Juvenile Justice and Delinquency Prevention.

Hay, Carter. 2001. "Parenting, Self-Control, and Delinquency: A Test of Self-Control Theory." *Criminology* 39: 707–736.

Hay, Carter. 2003. "Family Strain, Gender, and Delinquency." *Sociological Perspectives* 46: 107–135.

Hay, Carter, Edward N. Fortson, Dusten R. Hollist, Irshad Altheimer, and Lonnie M. Schaible. 2006. "The Impact of Community Disadvantage on the Relationship between the Family and Juvenile Crime." *Journal of Research in Crime and Delinquency* 43: 326–356.

Hay, Carter, Edward N. Fortson, Dusten R. Hollist, Irshad Altheimer, and Lonnie M. Schaible. 2007. "Compounded Risk: The Implications for Delinquency of Coming from a Poor Family that Lives in a Poor Community." *Journal of Youth and Adolescence* 36: 593–605.

Haynie, Dana L., Darrell Steffensmeier, and Kerryn E. Bell. 2007. "Gender and Serious Violence: Untangling the Role of Friendship Sex Composition and Peer Violence." *Youth Violence and Juvenile Justice* 5: 235–253.

Heimer, Karen. 1995. "Gender, Race, and the Pathways to Delinquency: An Interactionist Explanation." Pp. 140–173 in *Crime and Inequality*, ed. J. Hagan and R. D. Peterson. Stanford University Press.

Heimer, Karen. 1996. "Gender, Interaction, and Delinquency: Testing a Theory of Differential Social Control." *Social Psychology Quarterly* 59: 39–61.

Heimer, Karen. 1997. "Socioeconomic Status, Subcultural Definitions, and Violent Delinquency." *Social Forces* 75: 799–833.

Heimer, Karen and Stacy DeCoster. 1999. "The Gendering of Violent Delinquency." *Criminology* 37: 277–312.

Heimer, Karen, Janet L. Lauritsen, and James P. Lynch. 2009. "The National Crime Victimization Survey and Gender Gap in Offending: Redux." *Criminology* 47: 427–438.

Hill, Gary D. and Maxine P. Atkinson. 1988. "Gender, Familial Control, and Delinquency." *Criminology* 26: 127–149.

Hindelang, Michael J. 1971. "The Social versus Solitary Nature of Delinquent Involvements." *British Journal of Criminology* 11: 167–175.

Hindelang, Michael J. 1973. "Causes of Delinquency: A Partial Replication and Extension." *Social Problems* 21: 471–487.

Hindelang, Michael J. 1978. "Race and Involvement in Common-Law Personal Crimes." *American Sociological Review* 43: 93–109.

Hindelang, Michael J. 1979. "Sex Differences in Criminal Activity." *Social Problems* 27: 143–156.

Hindelang, Michael J. 1981. "Variations in Sex-Race-Age-Specific Incidence Rates of Offending." *American Sociological Review* 46: 461–474.

Hindelang, Michael J., Travis Hirschi, and Joseph G. Weis. 1979. "Correlates of Delinquency: The Illusion of Discrepancy between Self-Report and Official Measures." *American Sociological Review* 44: 995–1014.

Hindelang, Michael J., Travis Hirschi, and Joseph G. Weis. 1981. *Measuring Delinquency*. Beverly Hills, CA: Sage.

Hirschi, Travis. 1969. *Causes of Delinquency*. Berkeley, CA: University of California Press.

Hirschi, Travis. 1983. "Crime and the Family." Pp. 53–68 in *Crime and Public Policy*, ed. J. Q. Wilson. San Francisco: Institute for Contemporary Studies.

Hirschi, Travis. 1986. "On the Compatibility of Rational Choice and Social Control Theories of Crime." Pp. 105–118 in *The Reasoning Criminal: Rational Choice Perspectives on Offending*, ed. D. B. Cornish and R. V. Clarke. New York: Springer-Verlag.

Hirschi, Travis. 1987. "Review of Explaining Delinquency and Drug Use, by Delbert S. Elliott, David Huizinga, and Suzanne S. Ageton." *Criminology* 25: 193–201.

Hoffman, John P. and Felicia Gray Cerbone. 1999. "Stressful Life Events and Delinquency Escalation in Early Adolescence." *Criminology* 37: 343–373.

Hoffman, John P. and S. Susan Su. 1997. "The Conditional Effects of Stress on Delinquency and Drug Use: A Strain Theory Assessment of Sex Differences." *Journal of Research in Crime and Delinquency* 34: 46–78.

Horowitz, Ruth and Anne E. Pottieger. 1991. "Gender Bias in Juvenile Justice Handling of Seriously Crime-Involved Youths." *Journal of Research in Crime and Delinquency* 28: 75–100.

Huizinga, David A. and Delbert S. Elliott. 1984. *Self-Reported Measures of Delinquency and Crime: Methodological Issues and Comparative Findings*. Boulder, CO: Behavioral Research Institute.

Huizinga, David A. and Delbert S. Elliott. 1986. "Reassessing the Reliability and Validity of Self-Report Delinquency Measures." *Journal of Quantitative Criminology* 2: 293–327.

Huizinga, David A. and Delbert S. Elliott. 1987. "Juvenile Offenders: Prevalence, Offender Incidence, and Arrest Rates by Race." *Crime and Delinquency* 33: 206–223.

Jensen, Gary F. and Raymond Eve. 1976. "Sex Differences in Delinquency: An Examination of Popular Sociological Explanations." *Criminology* 13: 427–448.

Johnson, Richard E. 1979. *Juvenile Delinquency and Its Origins: An Integrated Theoretical Approach*. New York: Cambridge University Press.

Johnson, Richard E. 1980. "Social Class and Delinquent Behavior: A New Test." *Criminology* 18: 86–93.

Johnston, Lloyd D., Jerald G. Bachman, and Patrick M. O'Malley. 2010. *Monitoring the Future: Questionnaire Responses from the Nation's High School Seniors, 2009*. Ann Arbor, MI: Institute for Social Research, University of Michigan. Retrieved December 8, 2014 (www.monitoringthefuture.org/pubs.html#refvols).

Johnston, Lloyd D., Jerald G. Bachman, and Patrick M. O'Malley. 2013. *Monitoring the Future: Questionnaire Responses from the Nation's High School Seniors, 2011*. Ann Arbor, MI: Institute for Social Research, University of Michigan. Retrieved December 8, 2014 (www.monitoringthefuture.org/pubs.html#refvols).

Kaufman, Joanne M., Cesar J. Rebellon, Sherod Thaxton, and Robert Agnew. 2008. "A General Strain Theory of Racial Differences in Criminal Offending." *Australian and New Zealand Journal of Criminology* 43: 421–437.

Kleck, Gary. 1982. "On the Use of Self-Report Data to Determine the Class Distribution of Criminal and Delinquent Behavior." *American Sociological Review* 47: 427–433.

Koita, Kiyofumi and Ruth A. Triplett. 1998. "An Examination of Gender and Race Effects on the Parental Appraisal Process: A Reanalysis of Matsueda's Model of the Self." *Criminal Justice and Behavior* 25: 382–400.

Krohn, Marvin D., Ronald L. Akers, Marcia J. Radosevich, and Lonn Lanza-Kaduce. 1980. "Social Status and Deviance." *Criminology* 18: 303–318.

LaFree, Gary, Kriss A. Drass, and Patrick O'Day. 1992. "Race and Crime in Postwar America: Determinants of African-American and White Rates, 1957–1988." *Criminology* 30: 157–188.

LaGrange, Teresa C. and Robert A. Silverman. 1999. "Low Self-Control and Opportunity: Testing the General Theory of Crime as an Explanation for Gender Differences in Delinquency." *Criminology* 37: 41–72.

Lauritsen, Janet L. and Kristin Carbone-Lopez. 2011. "Gender Differences in Risk Factors for Violent Victimization: An Examination of Individual-, Family-, and Community-Level Predictors." *Journal of Research in Crime and Delinquency* 48: 538–565.

Lauritsen, Janet L., Karen Heimer, and James P. Lynch. 2009. "Trends in the Gender Gap in Violent Offending: New Evidence from the National Crime Victimization Survey." *Criminology* 47: 361–399.

Leonard, Eileen B. 1982. *Women, Crime and Society: A Critique of Theoretical Criminology*. New York: Longman.

Liu, Xiaoru and Howard B. Kaplan. 1999. "Explaining the Gender Difference in Adolescent Behavior: A Longitudinal Test of Mediating Mechanisms." *Criminology* 37: 195–215.

McCall, Patricia, Kenneth Land, Cindy Dollar, and Karen Parker. 2013. "The Age Structure–Crime Rate Relationship: Solving a Long-Standing Puzzle." *Journal of Quantitative Criminology* 29: 167–190.

Mazerolle, Paul. 1998. "Gender, General Strain, and Delinquency: An Empirical Examination." *Justice Quarterly* 15: 65–91.

Mears, Daniel, Matthew Ploeger, and Mark Warr. 1998. "Explaining the Gender Gap in Delinquency: Peer Influence and Moral Evaluations of Behavior." *Criminology* 35: 251–266.

Moffitt, Terrie E., Avshalom Caspi, Michael Rutter, and Phil A. Silva. 2001. *Sex Differences in Antisocial Behavior: Conduct Disorder, Delinquency, and Violence in the Dunedin Longitudinal Study*. Cambridge University Press.

Morash, Merry. 1983. "Gangs, Groups, and Delinquency." *British Journal of Criminology* 23: 309–331.

Morash, Merry. 1984. "Establishment of a Juvenile Record: The Influence of Individual and Peer Group Characteristics." *Criminology* 22: 97–112.

Morenoff, Jeffrey D. 2005. "Racial and Ethnic Disparities in Crime and Delinquency in the United States." Pp. 139–173 in *Ethnicity and Causal Mechanisms*, ed. M. Rutter and M. Tienda. Cambridge University Press.

Peeples, Faith and Rolf Loeber. 1994. "Do Individual Factors and Neighborhood Context Explain Ethnic Differences in Juvenile Delinquency?" *Journal of Quantitative Criminology* 10: 141–157.

Piquero, Alex R. and Robert W. Brame. 2008. "Assessing the Race–Crime and Ethnicity–Crime Relationship in a Sample of Serious Adolescent Delinquents." *Crime and Delinquency* 54: 390–422.

Piquero, Nicole Leeper, Angela R. Gover, John M. MacDonald, and Alex R. Piquero. 2005. "The Influence of Delinquent Peers on Delinquency: Does Gender Matter?" *Youth and Society* 36: 251–275.

Piquero, Nicole Leeper and Miriam D. Sealock. 2010. "Race, Crime, and General Strain Theory." *Youth Violence and Juvenile Justice* 8: 170–186.

Posick, Chad, Amy Farrell, and Marc L. Swatt. 2013. "Do Boys Fight and Girls Cut? A General Strain Theory Approach to Gender and Deviance." *Deviant Behavior* 34: 685–705.

Puzzanchera, Charles, A. Sladky, and W. Kang. 2014. *Easy Access to Juvenile Populations: 1990–2013*. Retrieved December 4, 2014 (www.ojjdp.gov/ojstatbb/ezapop/).

Quinney, Richard. 1980. *Class, State, and Crime*. 2nd edn. New York: Longman.

Rennison, Callie Marie. 2009. "A New Look at the Gender Gap in Offending." *Women and Criminal Justice* 19: 171–190.

Rossi, Peter H., Emily Waite, Christine E. Bose, and Richard E. Berk. 1974. "The Seriousness of Crimes: Normative Structure and Individual Differences." *American Sociological Review* 39: 224–237.

Rowe, A. and Charles Tittle. 1977. "Life Cycle Changes and Criminal Propensity." *Sociological Quarterly* 18: 223–236.

Sampson, Robert J. and Dawn Jeglum Bartusch. 1998. "Legal Cynicism and (Subcultural?) Tolerance of Deviance: The Neighborhood Context of Racial Differences." *Law and Society Review* 32: 777–804.

Sampson, Robert J. and John H. Laub. 1990. "Crime and Deviance over the Life Course: The Salience of Adult Social Bonds." *American Sociological Review* 55: 609–627.

Sampson, Robert J. and John H. Laub. 1992. "Crime and Deviance in the Life Course." *Annual Review of Sociology* 18: 63–84.

Sampson, Robert J. and John H. Laub. 1993. *Crime in the Making: Pathways and Turning Points Through Life*. Cambridge, MA: Harvard University Press.

Sampson, Robert J. and John H. Laub. 1994. "Urban Poverty and the Family Context of Delinquency: A New Look at Structure and Process in a Classic Study." *Child Development* 65: 523–540.

Sampson, Robert J. and John H. Laub. 1997a. "A Life-Course Theory of Cumulative Disadvantage and the Stability of Delinquency." Pp. 133–161 in *Developmental Theories of Crime and Delinquency*, ed. T. P. Thornberry. New Brunswick, NJ: Transaction.

Sampson, Robert J. and John H. Laub. 1997b. "Unraveling the Social Context of Physique and Delinquency: A New, Long-Term Look at the Glueck's Classic Study." Pp. 175–188 in *Biosocial Bases of Violence*, ed. A. Raine, P. Brennan, and D. P. Farrington. New York: Plenum.

Sampson, Robert J. and John H. Laub. 2002. "Life-Course Desisters? Trajectories of Crime among Delinquent Boys Followed to Age 70." *Criminology* 41: 555–592.

Sampson, Robert J. and John H. Laub. 2005a. "The Life-Course View of the Development of Crime." *Annals of the American Academy of Political and Social Science* 602: 12–45.

Sampson, Robert J. and John H. Laub. 2005b. "A General Age-Graded Theory of Crime: Lessons Learned and the Future of Life-Course Criminology." *Advances in Criminological Theory* 15: 165–181. Special issue: "Integrated Developmental and Life Course Theories of Offending," ed. D. P. Farrington.

Sampson, Robert J., John H. Laub, and Christopher Wimer. 2006. "Does Marriage Reduce Crime? A Counterfactual Approach to Within-Individual Causal Effects." *Criminology* 44: 465–508.

Sampson, Robert J. and Janet Lauritsen. 1997. "Racial and Ethnic Disparities in Crime and Criminal Justice in the United States." Pp. 311–374 in *Crime and Justice: An Annual Review of Research*. Vol. 22, ed. M. Tonry. University of Chicago Press.

Sampson, Robert J. and William Julius Wilson. 1995. "Toward a Theory of Race, Crime, and Urban Inequality." Pp. 37–54 in *Crime and Inequality*, ed. J. Hagan and R. D. Peterson. Stanford University Press.

Schwartz, Jennifer, Darrell Steffensmeier, Hua Zhong, and Jeff Ackerman. 2009. "Trends in the Gender Gap in Violence: Reevaluating NCVS and Other Evidence." *Criminology* 47: 401–425.

Seydlitz, Ruth. 1990. "The Effects of Gender, Age, and Parental Attachment on Delinquency: A Test for Interactions." *Sociological Spectrum* 10: 209–225.

Seydlitz, Ruth. 1991. "The Effects of Age and Gender on Parental Control and Delinquency." *Youth and Society* 23: 175–201.

Shover, Neal, Stephen Norland, Jennifer James, and William E. Thornton. 1979. "Gender Roles and Delinquency." *Social Forces* 58: 162–175.

Simon, Rita J. 1975. *Women and Crime*. Lexington, MA: Lexington Books.

Smith, Douglas A. and Raymond Paternoster. 1987. "The Gender Gap in Theories of Deviance: Issues and Evidence." *Journal of Research in Crime and Delinquency* 24: 140–172.

Smith, Douglas A. and Christy A. Visher. 1980. "Sex and Involvement in Deviance/Crime: A Quantitative Review of Empirical Literature." *American Sociological Review* 45: 691–701.

Smith, Douglas A. and Christy A. Visher. 1981. "Street-Level Justice: Situational Determinants of Police Arrest Decision." *Social Problems* 31: 468–481.

Snyder, Howard N. and Melissa Sickmund. 1995. *Juvenile Offenders and Victims: A National Report*. Washington, DC: Office of Juvenile Justice and Delinquency Prevention.

Snyder, Howard N. and Melissa Sickmund. 2006. *Juvenile Offenders and Victims: 2006 National Report*. Washington, DC: Office of Juvenile Justice and Delinquency Prevention.

Spitzer, Steven. 1975. "Toward a Marxian Theory of Deviance." *Social Problems* 22: 638–651.

Steffensmeier, Darrell. 1978. "Crime and the Contemporary Woman: An Analysis of Changing Levels of Female Property Crime, 1960–75." *Social Forces* 57: 566–583.

Steffensmeier, Darrell. 1980. "Sex Differences in Patterns of Adult Crime, 1965–77: A Review and Assessment." *Social Forces* 58: 1080–1108.

Steffensmeier, Darrell. 1993. "National Trends in Female Arrests, 1960–1990: Assessments and Recommendations for Research." *Journal of Quantitative Criminology* 9: 411–440.

Steffensmeier, Darrell and Emilie Allan. 1995. "Age-Inequality and Property Crime: The Effect of Age-Linked Stratification and Status-Attainment Processes on Patterns of Criminality across the Life Course." Pp. 95–115 in *Crime and Inequality*, ed. J. Hagan and R. D. Peterson. Stanford University Press.

Steffensmeier, Darrell and Emilie Allan. 1996. "Gender and Crime: Toward a Gendered Theory of Female Offending." *Annual Review of Sociology* 22: 459–487.

Steffensmeier, Darrell and Emilie Allan. 2000. "Looking for Patterns: Gender, Age, and Crime." Pp. 85–127 in *Criminology*. 3rd edn., ed. J. F. Sheley. Belmont, CA: Wadsworth.

Steffensmeier, Darrell and Michael J. Cobb. 1981. "Sex Differences in Urban Arrest Patterns, 1934–79." *Social Problems* 29: 37–50.

Steffensmeier, Darrell and Miles D. Harer. 1999. "Making Sense of Recent U.S. Crime Trends, 1980 to 1996/1998: Age Composition Effects and Other Explanations." *Journal of Research in Crime and Delinquency* 36: 235–274.

Steffensmeier, Darrell, Cathy Streifel, and Miles D. Harer. 1987. "Relative Cohort Size and Youth Crime in the United States, 1953–1984." *American Sociological Review* 52: 702–710.

Steffensmeier, Darrell and Jennifer Schwartz. 2002. "Trends in Female Crime: Is Crime Still a Man's World." Pp. 95–112 in *The Criminal Justice System and Women: Offenders, Victims, and Workers*, ed. B. Price and N. Sokoloff. New York: McGraw-Hill.

Steffensmeier, Darrell, Jennifer Schwartz, Hua Zhong, and Jeff Ackerman. 2005. "An Assessment of Recent Trends in Girls' Violence Using Diverse Longitudinal Sources: Is the Gender Gap Closing?" *Criminology* 43: 355–405.

Steffensmeier, Darrell and Renee Hoffman Steffensmeier. 1980. "Trends in Female Delinquency: An Examination of Arrest, Juvenile Court, Self-Report, and Field Data." *Criminology* 18: 62–85.

Steffensmeier, Darrell and Cathy Streifel. 1992. "Time-Series Analysis of the Female Percentage of Arrests for Property Crimes, 1960–1985: A Test of Alternative Explanations." *Justice Quarterly* 9: 77–103.

Steffensmeier, Darrell, Hua Zhong, Jeff Ackerman, Jennifer Schwartz, and Suzanne Agha. 2006. "Gender Gap Trends for Violent Crimes, 1980–2003." *Feminist Criminology* 1: 72–98.

Stolzenberg, Lisa and Stewart D'Alessio. 2008. "Co-Offending and the Age-Crime Curve." *Journal of Research in Crime and Delinquency* 45: 65–86.

Sweeten, Gary, Alex Piquero, and Laurence Steinberg. 2013. "Age and the Explanation of Crime, Revisited." *Journal of Youth and Adolescence* 42: 921–938.

Tapia, Michael. 2010. "Untangling Race and Class Effects on Juvenile Arrests." *Journal of Criminal Justice* 38: 255–265.

Teilmann, Katherine S. and Pierre H. Landry, Jr. 1981. "Gender Bias in Juvenile Justice." *Journal of Research in Crime and Delinquency* 18: 47–80.

Thornberry, Terence P. and Margaret Farnworth. 1982. "Social Correlates of Criminal Involvement: Further Evidence on the Relationship between Social Status and Criminal Behavior." *American Sociological Review* 47: 505–518.

Tittle, Charles R. 1980. *Sanctions and Social Deviance*. New York: Praeger.

Tittle, Charles R. 1983. "Social Class and Criminal Behavior: A Critique of the Theoretical Foundation." *Social Forces* 62: 334–358.

Tittle, Charles R., Wayne J. Villemez, and Douglas A. Smith. 1978. "The Myth of Social Class and Criminality: An Empirical Assessment of the Empirical Evidence." *American Sociological Review* 43: 643–656.

Truman, Jennifer L. and Lynn Langton. 2014. "Criminal Victimization, 2013." *Bureau of Justice Statistics Bulletin*. Washington, DC: U.S. Department of Justice.

U.S. Census Bureau. 2014. *Annual Estimates of the Resident Population, 2013*. Retrieved December 8, 2014 (www.census.gov/popest/).

Vogt, W. Paul and R. Burke Johnson. 2011. *Dictionary of Statistics and Methodology: A Nontechnical Guide for the Social Sciences*. 4th edn. Thousand Oaks, CA: Sage.

Warr, Mark. 1993a. "Age, Peers, and Delinquency." *Criminology* 31: 17–40.

Warr, Mark. 1993b. "Parents, Peers, and Delinquency." *Social Forces* 72: 247–264.

Warr, Mark. 1996. "Organization and Instigation in Delinquent Groups." *Criminology* 34: 11–37.

Warr, Mark. 1998. "Life-Course Transition and Desistance from Crime." *Criminology* 36: 183–215.

Warr, Mark. 2002. *Companions in Crime: The Social Aspects of Criminal Conduct.* New York: Cambridge University Press.

Warr, Mark. 2005. "Making Delinquent Friends: Adult Supervision and Children's Affiliations." *Criminology* 43: 77–106.

Williams, Jay R. and Martin Gold. 1972. "From Delinquent Behavior to Official Delinquency." *Social Problems* 20: 209–229.

Wilson, William Julius. 1987. *The Truly Disadvantaged: The Inner City, the Underclass, and Public Policy.* University of Chicago Press.

Wilson, William Julius. 1996. *When Work Disappears.* New York: Knopf.

Wolfgang, Marvin E. and Franco Ferracuti. 1967. *The Subculture of Violence: Toward an Integrated Theory in Criminology.* London: Tavistock.

Wolfgang, Marvin E., Robert M. Figlio, and Thorsten Sellin. 1972. *Delinquency in a Birth Cohort.* University of Chicago Press.

Worthen, Meredith Gwynne Fair. 2012. "Gender Differences in Delinquency in Early, Middle, and Late Adolescence: An Exploration of Parent and Friend Relationships." *Deviant Behavior* 33: 282–307.

Wright, Bradley R. Entner, Avshalom Caspi, Terrie E. Moffitt, Richard A. Miech, and Phil A. Silva. 1999. "Reconsidering the Relationship between SES and Delinquency: Causation but Not Correlation." *Criminology* 37: 175–194.

Zahn, Margaret A., Susan Brumbaugh, Darrell Steffensmeier, Barry C. Feld, Merry Morash, Meda Chesney-Lind, Jody Miller, Allison Ann Payne, Denise C. Gottfredson, and Candace Kruttschnitt, Office of Juvenile Justice and Delinquency Prevention, Girls Study Group. 2008. "Violence by Teenage Girls: Trends and Context." *Understanding and Responding to Girls' Delinquency.* Washington, DC: U.S. Department of Justice.

Chapter 6

Developmental patterns of offending

Chapter preview

Topics:

- "Chronic offenders" and "career criminals"
- The developmental perspective
- Developmental models of delinquency

Theories:

- Developmental theory
- Patterson's early- and late-starter models
- Moffitt's adolescence-limited and life-course-persistent offenders

---

Terms:

- recidivists
- chronic offenders
- criminal career
- participation
- frequency
- career criminals
- age of onset
- behavioral continuity

- escalation
- generality of deviance
- desistance
- early starter
- late starter
- adolescence-limited offenders
- life-course-persistent offenders

Chapter learning objectives

After completing this chapter, students should be able to:

- Describe the age-determined patterning of delinquent behavior.
- Identify the defining characteristics of "chronic offenders" or "career criminals."

- Describe the key elements of the developmental perspective: age of onset of problem behaviors, continuity and change in problem behaviors, progression of seriousness, generality of deviance, and desistance from offending.
- Identify specific models that are good examples of the developmental perspective.

Case in point: the development of delinquency for a chronic offender

This case, from Laub and Sampson's book *Shared Beginnings, Divergent Lives*, briefly describes Michael's childhood and early involvement in delinquency. The case illustrates several elements of the developmental perspective that we discuss in this chapter, including early age of onset of offending, continuity in problem behaviors, and progression of seriousness of offenses.

Michael grew up in a poor section of Boston, an Irish neighborhood in Dorchester south of downtown. ... Michael had one brother and two sisters. His father was a "heavy drinker" and Michael recalled that his father would "take his pay every week and blow it at the track." During Michael's childhood and early adolescence, his family moved excessively (he moved twelve times prior to age 12). ... Michael had a particularly difficult time with school. His mother reported that "he hated school from the first day." Michael repeated second grade several times, and eventually he was placed in a "special class." He scored an 89 on the full-scale Wechsler-Bellevue Intelligence test, a 74 on the verbal test, and a 106 on the performance test. ... Michael's involvement in delinquent activities began at a young age, 6 and 7 years old. In his early years he was involved in smoking, truancy, running away, petty theft, and setting off false alarms. The most serious offense consisted of performing sexual favors for small sums of money. Michael and his friends would hang out in bus stations, train stations, and movie theaters and solicit customers. He was arrested five times as a juvenile and was incarcerated for the first time at age 10. As a juvenile, he served more than two years in reform school.

Source: Laub and Sampson (2003: 2).

The discussion in Chapter 5 of the age–crime relationship implies a patterning to involvement in delinquency that is heavily age determined. In this chapter, we consider the nature of delinquency in terms of developmental patterns of offending. This area of study, which has emerged primarily since the early 1990s, is sometimes referred to as "developmental criminology" or the study of "criminal careers" (Loeber and LeBlanc 1990; Blumstein, Cohen, and Farrington 1988a, 1988b; Blumstein and Cohen 1987; Blumstein et al. 1986). The developmental perspective fills a gap in criminology, which has tended to focus too heavily on the behavior of adolescents alone. Robert Sampson and John Laub, whose life-course perspective on crime and delinquency has made a significant contribution to developmental criminology, write:

The age–crime curve has had a profound impact on the organization and content of sociological studies of crime by channeling research to a focus on adolescents. As a result sociological criminology has traditionally neglected the theoretical significance of childhood characteristics and the link between early childhood behaviors and later adult outcomes.

(Sampson and Laub 1992: 64; see also Sampson and Laub 1990, 1993)

We begin this chapter with research on the small portion of offenders who develop serious patterns of delinquency – "chronic offenders" or "career criminals." This research shares several key elements with the developmental perspective of the last decade. The developmental perspective provides theoretical approaches with which to frame empirical findings regarding criminal careers (Paternoster and Brame 1997). We then discuss the logic of the developmental perspective, focusing on five major themes: age of onset of problem behaviors, continuity of problem behaviors, progression of seriousness, co-occurrence of problem behaviors, and desistance from offending. We illustrate this perspective with two developmental models of delinquent behavior: (1) the work of Gerald Patterson and his colleagues on early- and late-starter routes to delinquency and (2) Terrie Moffitt's work on "adolescence-limited" and "life-course-persistent" offenders.

"Chronic offenders" and "career criminals"

Empirical research demonstrates that a small portion of offenders – those who are repeat or "chronic" offenders – are responsible for a disproportionate number of offenses.

Wolfgang's "chronic offenders"

In 1972, Marvin Wolfgang, Robert Figlio, and Thorsten Sellin published what has become a classic study in criminology: *Delinquency in a Birth Cohort*. In this groundbreaking research, Wolfgang and his colleagues studied the "cohort" of all boys born in 1945 and residing in Philadelphia from at least their tenth to eighteenth birthdays. A *cohort* is a group of people who experience the same event within the same time frame. In this study, the cohort was defined by year of birth, and included 9,945 boys, of whom 3,475 had at least one recorded police contact (Wolfgang et al. 1972: 244). School records provided background information about the boys, including birth date, race, country of origin, IQ scores, achievement level, behavior problems, and highest grade completed. Police records provided information about the number and type of offenses committed by members of the cohort and the disposition of cases (Wolfgang et al. 1972).

With these data, Wolfgang and his colleagues explored the onset and progression of delinquency and the social correlates of offending. Although this study produced many important results, it is probably most noted for its findings regarding "chronic offenders." Wolfgang, Figlio, and Sellin divided the cohort into three groups: non-offenders, one-time offenders, and **recidivists**, or those who committed multiple offenses resulting in police contact. Of the 3,475 boys in the cohort who had at least one police contact, 1,235 boys had two to four contacts and 627 had five or more contacts (Wolfgang et al. 1972: 89). The boys with five or more police contacts were defined as **chronic offenders**.

Table 6.1 shows the classification of offenders and the distribution of their offenses, and it reveals several remarkable findings. First, while almost 35 percent of the cohort had at least one police contact, 65 percent had no police contacts. Second, almost half (46 percent) of those with police contacts were one-time offenders, who accounted for 15.8 percent of recorded offenses. The remaining 54 percent of those with police contacts were classified as recidivists. Third, about one-third (36 percent) of the delinquents had two to four contacts with police. These offenders were labeled non-chronic recidivists, and they accounted for 32.3 percent of recorded offenses. Finally, the most remarkable finding concerns the 627 boys with five or more police contacts. Although these chronic offenders or chronic recidivists

Table 6.1 Classification of offenders and offenses in *Delinquency in a Birth Cohort*

Juveniles	Number of cases	Percentage of original sample	Percentage of delinquent sample	Total number of offenses	Percentage of total offenses
Original sample	9,945				
Delinquents	3,475	34.9		10,214	
One official police contact	1,613	16.2	46.4	1,613	15.8
Two to four police contacts	1,235	12.4	35.6	3,296	32.3
Five or more police contacts	627	6.3	18.0	5,305	51.9

Source: Wolfgang et al. (1972: 89). Reproduced with permission of the publisher.

represented only 6.3 percent of the cohort of 9,945 boys (or 18 percent of the 3,475 boys with police contacts), they were responsible for 51.9 percent of the offenses that resulted in police contact (Wolfgang et al. 1972: 89). This small group of persistent offenders is often called the "chronic 6%."

Chronic offenders not only committed a disproportionate share of offenses, they also committed more serious offenses than did other delinquents, as indicated by their disproportionate involvement in Index offenses. Chronic offenders committed 1,726 Index offenses out of the 2,728 committed by the entire cohort. More specifically, chronic offenders were responsible for:

- 63.3 percent of all Index offenses committed by the cohort
- 71.4 percent of all homicides
- 72.7 percent of all rapes
- 69.9 percent of all robberies
- 69.1 percent of all aggravated assaults (Wolfgang et al. 1972).[1]

The longitudinal design of this study also revealed interesting findings regarding age and its relationship to delinquency. Wolfgang and his colleagues confirmed the age distribution of crime found in prior cross-sectional research. Few offenses were committed by boys under the age of 11; from age 11 to age 16, the proportion of offenses committed increased steadily; and offending peaked at age 16 and then declined rapidly (Wolfgang, Thornberry, and Figlio 1987: 3). Wolfgang and his colleagues also found that boys who began involvement in delinquency at younger ages committed more offenses than boys who began offending later in life.

In a follow-up study, Wolfgang, Thornberry, and Figlio (1987) chose a random sample of the original 1945 birth cohort (975 individuals) and traced them through adulthood to age 30. This study was designed to explore the link between juvenile delinquency and adult criminality. A relationship existed between chronic offending as a juvenile and persistent offending to age 30. Almost half of chronic juvenile offenders were also classified as chronic offenders as adults. The proportion of crimes attributable to chronic offenders in this study is striking. Although chronic offenders represented only 15 percent of the total sample, they accounted for 74 percent of all arrests and 82 percent of index arrests (Wolfgang et al. 1987: 201).

The work of Wolfgang and his colleagues reveals that delinquents who begin offending at a relatively young age tend to accumulate lengthy criminal careers that extend well into adulthood, and that a relatively small number of chronic offenders account for the majority of crimes. These important findings paved the way for the developmental perspective in criminology.

Blumstein's "criminal careers" and "career criminals"

In their research, Alfred Blumstein and his colleagues distinguish between criminal careers and career criminals.

Criminal careers

The criminal career approach, described by Blumstein and his colleagues in 1986, focuses on individual offenders and their patterns of offending over time. Blumstein, Jacqueline Cohen, and David Farrington (1988a: 2) define a **criminal career** as "the longitudinal sequence of offenses committed by an offender who has a detectable rate of offending during some period." A criminal career is characterized by several distinct aspects, including age at which delinquent behavior begins; age at which offending ends; duration of criminal career; and frequency of offending while an individual is an active offender (Blumstein et al. 1988a: 2; Blumstein and Cohen 1987: 986). According to the criminal career paradigm, it is important to distinguish these elements because different causal factors may account for different elements of a criminal career (Piquero, Brame, and Lynam 2004; Piquero, Farrington, and Blumstein 2003; Blumstein et al. 1988a; Blumstein et al. 1986).[2] For example, age at which offending begins may be associated with family influences such as parenting practices or family disruption, whereas age at which offending ends may be related to employment opportunities. Blumstein and his colleagues use and advocate for longitudinal data to study patterns of offending over time and to capture fully all aspects of criminal careers.

It is also important to distinguish those who participate in criminal careers from those who do not. The distinction between participation in offending and frequency of offending is central to the criminal career perspective. **Participation**, sometimes referred to as *prevalence*, is "the proportion of a population who are active offenders at any given time" (Blumstein et al. 1988a: 3). **Frequency** of offending, sometimes referred to as *incidence*, is "the average annual rate at which [the] subgroup of active offenders commits crimes" (Blumstein et al. 1988a: 3).

Research on criminal careers shows that most individuals who participate in offending commit only one or a limited number of offenses during late adolescence or early adulthood, when delinquent behavior is almost normative, and they desist in the young adult years without escalating into serious offending (Blumstein et al. 1988a; Blumstein and Cohen 1987). In other words, the participation rate is high for adolescents and young adults, but frequency of offending is low and criminal career length is short for most delinquents.

As we mentioned earlier, a premise of the criminal career paradigm is that different aspects of criminal activity, such as participation, frequency, and duration of criminal career, may require different causal explanations. In contrast, the general theory of crime (see Chapter 9) contends that different aspects of criminal activity are all caused by a single underlying propensity toward crime, and that a general theory of criminal propensity is sufficient to explain all aspects of criminal activity, including participation, frequency, and persistence. Douglas

Smith and his colleagues tested these competing hypotheses (Smith, Visher, and Jarjoura 1991).[3] Their primary research question was whether different variables were related to participation, frequency, and persistence of offending, or whether the same variables were associated with all three dimensions. Results were somewhat mixed. Contrary to the general theory of crime, a single underlying variable did not account for both participation and frequency of offending. However, the variables associated with different dimensions of offending were not entirely distinct. A "core" set of variables, including exposure to delinquent peers, was related to all three dimensions of offending (Smith et al. 1991).

The distinction in the criminal career approach between participation in offending and frequency of offending also suggests different crime prevention strategies. For example, a neighborhood crime rate may be high because a large proportion of the people who live there each commit a small number of crimes (i.e. high rate of participation, but low frequency of offending) or because a relatively small proportion of the people who live there each commit a large number of crimes (i.e. low rate of participation, but high frequency of offending) or both. A high rate of participation suggests a crime prevention policy of general deterrence aimed at the entire population of the neighborhood. A low rate of participation, but high frequency of offending suggests a crime prevention policy aimed at identifying and treating or controlling those who are heavily involved in crime (Blumstein et al. 1988a).

Career criminals

The distinction of various aspects of criminal careers enables researchers to identify **career criminals**, characterized by "some combination of a high frequency of offending, a long duration of the criminal career, and high seriousness of offenses committed" (Blumstein et al. 1988a: 22). Blumstein's concept of career criminals is consistent with Wolfgang's concept of chronic offenders. These high-rate offenders begin delinquent involvement at a relatively young age and persist in offending after most individuals have aged out of crime in late adolescence or early adulthood. In other words, they are exceptions to the general age–crime curve discussed in Chapter 5. Career criminals constitute a relatively small proportion of all offenders but account for a disproportionate share of offenses, particularly serious ones (Blumstein et al. 1986, 1988a).

The notion of career criminals has been controversial because of its policy implications. If we can identify offenders who are career criminals based on their patterns of offending over time, then presumably we can target them with intervention and crime prevention strategies specific to career criminals. Some have proposed the "selective incapacitation" of career criminals, which involves the incarceration of serious offenders who have high individual rates of offending – ideally, relatively early in their criminal careers. However, this idea has been hotly debated (Blumstein et al. 1988a, 1988b; Gottfredson and Hirschi 1986, 1988).

Theoretical perspectives on criminal careers, career criminals, and chronic offenders

In terms of framing research questions on patterns of offending and guiding discourse on crime prevention policy, the work of Wolfgang, Blumstein, and their colleagues is among the most important research in criminology. In terms of theory, however, the criminal careers construct is not well defined or developed, and criminal careers research has been largely separated from theoretical criminology (Osgood and Rowe 1994). Blumstein and his colleagues acknowledge that "the construct of the criminal career is not a theory of crime" (Blumstein et al. 1988a: 4). Although the criminal career perspective maintains that different causal factors may account for different elements of criminal careers, it does not attempt to determine what those causal factors might be. The criminal career construct, however, has prompted the development of new theoretical approaches that harmonize with the criminal career perspective.[4] Recent developmental and life-course theories of crime, for example, might explain the separate elements of criminal careers – age of onset, duration of career, frequency of offending, and age at termination of offending – identified by Blumstein and others in the criminal career tradition. A great asset of the contemporary developmental perspective is its ability to account theoretically for aspects of offending identified by the empirically rich, but theoretically weak, criminal career perspective.

The developmental perspective

The central tenet of the developmental perspective in criminology is that the development of problem behaviors tends to occur in an "orderly, progressive fashion" that is highly age-determined (Kelley et al. 1997; Thornberry 1997; Nagin, Farrington, and Moffitt 1995; Loeber and LeBlanc 1990). Developmental criminologists examine this age-linked development of problem behaviors and the causal factors that influence this development. The developmental perspective has been supplemented in the past decade by extensive research on the physical maturation of the adolescent brain, especially as this maturation relates to the capacity for self-control. This will be discussed in Chapter 7 as an area of research in biosocial criminology. Our discussion here will focus on the developmental patterns of delinquent offending.

Many years ago, Lee Robins observed that even though "adult antisocial behavior virtually requires childhood antisocial behavior … most antisocial children do not become antisocial adults" (Robins 1978: 611, cited in Thornberry 1997: 3). The developmental perspective attempts to account for this paradoxical finding – simultaneously explaining why antisocial behavior is stable across the life course for some offenders, while it is only a brief adolescent excursion from conformity for most offenders whose "criminal careers" are characterized by change rather than stability (Thornberry 1997).

To address this paradox, developmental theorists speak of variation across individuals in factors that influence involvement in delinquency and crime. They also speak of stability of individual differences over time in both the potential to commit crime and the social factors related to offending. For example, some who engage in delinquency during adolescence have a history beginning in early childhood of difficult and problematic behaviors, and their progression from childhood problem behaviors to adolescent delinquency is characterized by continuity of behaviors in various settings, including home and school. Others who engage in delinquency during adolescence may have no history of problem behaviors prior to their offending in adolescence and show no progression or continuity in offending, but rather may be drawn briefly to delinquent behavior by social or peer influences. Recent research indicates the existence of a third group of offenders as well – those who begin offending in adulthood, with no history of delinquency during adolescence. Developmental criminologists formulate explanations for delinquency that take into account these kinds of individual differences in pathways leading to delinquent and criminal behavior.

In this section, we describe five key themes of the developmental perspective: age of onset of problem behaviors, continuity and change in problem behaviors, progression of seriousness of offenses, generality of deviance or co-occurrence of problem behaviors, and desistance from offending.

Age of onset of problem behaviors

As we discussed in Chapter 5, most offenders begin involvement in delinquency during adolescence, remain active offenders for a relatively brief period of time, and age out of crime in late adolescence or early adulthood. Recognizing this fact, criminologists have typically focused on adolescent offending and ignored problem behaviors that occur earlier in the life course.

Developmental criminologists, however, maintain that some offenders display problem behaviors early in the life course, and that these offenders are the ones most likely to continue problem behaviors into adulthood and to develop stable patterns of offending (e.g., DeLisi et al. 2013; Tzoumakis et al. 2013; LeBlanc and Loeber 1998; Thornberry 1997; Nagin and Farrington 1992a, 1992b; Farrington et al. 1990; Loeber and LeBlanc 1990). Loeber and LeBlanc (1990) provide a thorough review of the research literature on **age of onset** of offending – the age at which an individual begins involvement in delinquent or criminal acts. They conclude that early age of onset is related to the stability and frequency of offending over time and the diversity of offenses committed. Those who begin involvement in problem behaviors early in the life course typically commit offenses at a much higher rate than those who begin offending at a later age. It is important to note that research shows that those who begin offending at a relatively young age do not commit more offenses than those who begin later in life simply because of the longer time span of their offending careers. They commit more offenses in part because of their higher frequency of offending (Loeber and LeBlanc 1990; Tolan 1987).

Research results on the relationship between age of onset of offending and diversity of offenses committed are mixed. Some research shows that early-onset offenders tend to commit a wider variety of offenses than those who begin offending at later ages (Tolan 1987). Other studies, however, suggest that age of onset is not related – or at least not strongly related – to variety of offenses committed or to "offense specialization" (Cohen 1986; Rojek and Erickson 1982).

Studies have also shown that early-onset offenders tend to engage in more serious offenses than do late-onset offenders (e.g., DeLisi 2006; Nagin et al. 1995; Tolan and Thomas 1995; but see also Cohen (1986), who reports contradictory findings). Using data from the NYS, researchers found that early-onset offenders – defined as those who began offending before age 13 – showed significantly higher rates of serious offenses than did late-onset offenders. Among males, rates of serious offending were 2.1 to 2.9 times higher for early- than for late-onset offenders (Tolan and Thomas 1995).

In sum, research suggests that those who begin offending at a relatively young age engage in more frequent offending, a wider variety of offenses, and more serious offenses than do those who begin offending at a later age. These features of offending also characterize chronic offenders or career criminals, for whom early age of onset is typically a defining characteristic. Numerous studies demonstrate that early age of onset of offending is related to chronic offending that persists into adulthood (e.g., DeLisi et al. 2013; DeLisi 2006; Loeber and Farrington 2001; LeBlanc and Frechette 1989).

"How early can we tell?"

In a study of the predictors of conduct disorder and delinquency, Jennifer White and her colleagues (1990) asked, "How early can we tell?" Using data from a longitudinal study of approximately 1,000 subjects in Dunedin, New Zealand, they examined the ability of child characteristics assessed at ages 3 and 5 to predict conduct disorder at age 11 and delinquency at age 15. These preschool characteristics included the following:

*   Behavior problems at age 5, as reported by the mother.
*   "Externalizing" behaviors (hyperactivity and aggression) at age 3, as observed and reported by the research staff.
*   Difficulty managing the child as a baby, as reported by the mother when the child was 3 years old.
*   Two motor skills variables (a measure of perceptual and visual–motor integration, and a measure of physical coordination), assessed at age 5 (White et al. 1990: 522).

Of these characteristics, the first three behavioral variables were most important in predicting conduct disorder at age 11. These preschool characteristics were also able to predict and correctly classify delinquency status at age 15 for the majority of subjects in the study (White et al. 1990). These results suggest that we can "tell" quite early in the life course – adolescent delinquency is foreshadowed in problem behaviors observed as early as ages 3 and 5 (see also Walters 2014).

Continuity and change in problem behaviors

As we noted earlier in this chapter, for *some* offenders, antisocial behavior is stable over time, and their criminal careers are marked by continuity over the life course. For *most* offenders, however, antisocial behavior is not stable over time, and relatively brief involvement in delinquency represents a change in their behavior. Developmental perspectives try to account for both stability and change in patterns of offending.

In explaining stability, developmental perspectives use the concept of **behavioral continuity**, or patterns of behavior that are consistent and stable over time. This continuity pertains to individual attributes and interactional styles, rather than to specific behaviors (Caspi and Bem 1990; Caspi, Bem, and Elder 1989; Caspi 1987). When we say that continuity in behavior exists over time, we are not saying that identical behaviors are displayed over time. Instead, behavioral continuity refers to consistent patterns of behavior. For example, a child may be characterized in infancy as having a difficult temperament and may be aggressive in preschool, have problems interacting with peers and teachers in elementary school, and engage in delinquency in adolescence. This sequence indicates continuity of problem behaviors, though the specific behaviors change over time.

Numerous studies, from the field of developmental psychology and other academic disciplines, provide evidence that antisocial behavior is stable or persistent across the life course (e.g., Piquero and Moffitt 2014; Piquero et al. 2010; Thornberry 2005; Bushway, Brame, and Paternoster 1999; Sampson and Laub 1993; Farrington 1991; Gottfredson and Hirschi 1990; Caspi, Elder, and Bem 1987; Loeber and Stouthamer-Loeber 1987; Elliott, Huizinga, and Ageton 1985). These studies have shown not only continuity in offending from adolescence to adulthood, but also continuity between childhood conduct problems and later involvement in delinquency and crime. For example, in his review of 16 studies, Daniel Olweus (1979) found a strong relationship between early aggressive behavior and involvement in crime later in life.

Recall, however, the paradox stated earlier in this chapter: Antisocial behavior in childhood is a strong predictor of antisocial behavior in adulthood, yet most antisocial children do not become antisocial adults. So while stability characterizes the problem behaviors of some anti-social individuals, change in behavior patterns characterizes far more individuals.

Explaining continuity

What explains continuity for individuals who display problem behaviors that are stable over time? Several possibilities exist. First, there may be persistent differences across individuals in the "underlying potential" or "propensity" to commit antisocial acts (Farrington 1998: 438; Nagin and Paternoster 1991). Shawn Bushway and his colleagues (1999: 24) summarize this "proneness" explanation:

> Individuals vary in the probability with which they will commit crime at all points in time because they differ with respect to some risk factor (impulsivity, criminal propensity, or an antisocial trait, etc.) that is established early in life and remains, at least relatively, stable over time.

A second explanation for continuity in offending suggests that initial involvement in crime has a causal effect on later offending because that initial involvement changes the life chances or personal characteristics of the offender in some way that decreases inhibitions to or increases incentives for future crime (Bushway et al. 1999; see also Bacon, Paternoster, and Brame 2009; Nagin and Paternoster 1991). This interpretation of continuity is more "social" than the first explanation because it takes into consideration the relationship between offenders and their environments. For example, this second explanation is consistent with the scenario that, after committing delinquent acts, one becomes alienated from parents and begins to "hang out" with like-minded delinquent peers who provide incentives for further delinquency. It is also consistent with research which shows that adolescent gang involvement increases the likelihood of economic hardship and family problems in adulthood, which in turn result in sustained criminal involvement (Krohn et al. 2011).

Third, continuity in antisocial behavior may be a function of failure to master "prosocial" developmental tasks from preschool to adolescence. Barbara Kelley and her colleagues (1997) suggest that, to prevent disruptive and delinquent behavior, children must master develop-mental tasks such as being honest, respecting other people (especially authority figures), respecting others' property, and solving interpersonal problems non-aggressively. Because these skills are developed over time, early childhood failure to begin acquiring prosocial skills may set in motion the development over time of patterns of disruptive behaviors in place of prosocial ones.

A fourth explanation for continuity in offending is linked to the labeling process that accompanies involvement in the juvenile justice system. Labeling increases "embeddedness" in criminal social networks, which increases the likelihood of persistent offending (Bernburg, Krohn, and Rivera 2006; Bernburg and Krohn 2003). We discuss the labeling perspective in detail in Chapter 12.

Explaining change

What explains change for individuals whose problem behaviors are less stable over time? Later in this chapter, we present specific developmental models that propose explanations for the lack of continuity for those who offend for brief periods of time. These explanations of the beginnings of involvement in delinquency include peer influences and "social mimicry." Sampson and Laub (1993), in their life-course theory, are interested in behavioral changes in terms of both initiation into offending and desistance from it. They attribute changes in patterns of offending to changes in social bonds and thus in informal social control. For example, desistance from crime may result from strengthened social bonds related to employment, marriage, or educational pursuits.

Progression of seriousness

Few delinquents begin their offending careers with serious delinquent acts. Rather, most individuals who eventually become serious or chronic offenders begin with relatively minor problem behaviors. A key theme of the developmental perspective and a consistent research finding is that progression or escalation in seriousness of offenses characterizes the criminal careers of most serious delinquents (e.g., Kelley et al. 1997; Loeber and LeBlanc 1990). **Escalation** is the tendency for offenders to move from less serious problem behaviors to more serious offenses as offending continues (Blumstein et al. 1986).

Kelley and her colleagues (1997: 3) describe the developmental process relating problem behaviors early in life to delinquency later:

> After birth, the earliest problem noted is generally the infant's difficult temperament. Although activity level is one dimension of temperament, hyperactivity becomes more apparent when children are able to walk. Overt conduct problems, such as aggression, are usually not recognized until age 2 or later, when the child's mobility and physical strength have increased. During the preschool years, the quality of the child's social contacts becomes evident, including excessive withdrawal or poor relationships with peers and/or adults. Academic problems rarely emerge clearly before the child attends first or second grade. Beginning at elementary school age and continuing through early adolescence, covert or concealing conduct problems, such as truancy, stealing, and substance use, become more apparent. ... For youth age 12 and older, the prevalence of delinquency and associated recidivism increases.

This developmental ordering of problem behaviors is illustrated in Figure 6.1. The work of Kelley and her colleagues demonstrates that the precursors of delinquency in adolescence may be observed at very early ages.

Rolf Loeber has conducted extensive research on the development of disruptive and delinquent behaviors. Examining median ages of onset for various behaviors, Loeber and his colleagues (Kelley et al. 1997: 6; Loeber 1996; Loeber et al. 1993; Loeber, Stouthamer-Loeber, and Green 1991) found the following general sequence:

- Stubborn behavior beginning at about age 9.
- Minor "covert" acts (such as shoplifting and frequent lying) beginning at about age 10.
- Defiance and disobedience beginning at about age 11.

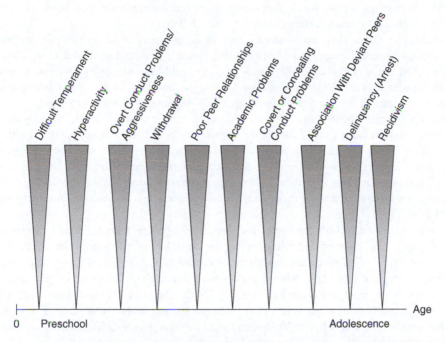

Figure 6.1 Approximate ordering of the different manifestations of disruptive and antisocial behaviors in childhood and adolescence.

This figure, by Kelley and her colleagues, shows continuity over time in problem behaviors. Although specific behavioral manifestations change as children age, a *pattern* of disruptive and antisocial behaviors in interaction with others still exists.

Source: Kelley et al. (1997: 4).

- Minor aggression (such as bullying and annoying others) and property damage (such as vandalism and fire setting) beginning at about age 12.
- Serious aggression involving physical fighting and violence, serious property offenses (such as fraud, burglary, and theft), and "authority avoidance" (such as truancy, running away, and staying out late) beginning at about age 13.

Of course, not all delinquents progress through the entire sequence, or even through the sequence in this order. However, by examining the median ages of onset for various behaviors, researchers can explore the general progression from minor to serious offending.

Other research has also documented the progression of seriousness in delinquency (e.g., MacDonald et al. 2014; Loeber et al. 2008). One study found evidence of escalation in offense seriousness. However, this evidence of escalation diminished when offender background characteristics were taken into consideration, indicating that background characteristics are important predictors of patterns of offending (Armstrong and Britt 2004). Using self-report data from the NYS, Delbert Elliott and his colleagues (1989) found that those who increased involvement in delinquency showed a general progression from "exploratory" to non-serious to serious offenses. A recent study examined escalation in crime seriousness over the life course and found competing processes at work. While aging in adulthood is associated with a de-escalation in crime seriousness, higher numbers of criminal convictions are associated with escalation in crime seriousness (Liu, Francis, and Soothill 2011).

Research also shows that involvement in minor delinquency tends to precede drug use (Wish 1990; Elliott, Huizinga, and Menard 1989; Kandel, Simcha-Fagan, and Davies 1986; Johnston, O'Malley, and Eveland 1978; Kandel, Kessler, and Margulies 1978). Of course, not all youth involved in minor delinquency escalate to drug use, but the transition from delinquency to drugs is much more common than the drugs-to-delinquency transition. One study showed that youth who were arrested most commonly began their criminal careers by committing petty crimes and drinking alcohol and then proceeded to both harder drugs and more serious crimes (Wish 1990). In terms of patterns of escalation in drug use, research shows that the development of serious drug use tends to follow a pattern of escalation from beer or wine to hard liquor, to marijuana, to other illicit drugs (most commonly prescription drugs). This pattern is cumulative in that illicit drug users generally continue to use alcohol and marijuana (Kandel 1988).

In a review of research on the causes and correlates of violent crime, David Farrington (1998) explored the issue of specialization versus versatility in offending: do youth who engage in one type of crime commit other types as well (versatility), or do they "specialize" in a particular type of offending? Several studies have shown that those who engage in serious, violent offenses tend to engage in a variety of both violent and non-violent offenses. In other words, most youth are versatile, rather than specialized, in their offending (Farrington 1998; but see Osgood and Schreck 2007, who found high levels of specialization in violence).

Some recent research suggests that offenders tend to become more specialized in offending as they age, with increasing diversity in offending from adolescence to young adulthood, but then greater specialization in offending during adulthood (Nieuwbeerta et al. 2011; Armstrong 2008; Piquero et al. 1999). Other research suggests, however, that specialization may be short term. Over time, as opportunities and life circumstances change, the types of offenses that individuals commit also change, so that offending patterns over the life course show greater versatility (McGloin, Sullivan, and Piquero 2009; McGloin et al. 2007).

Findings of versatility in offending, particularly in adolescence and young adulthood, combined with the findings of developmental researchers, suggest that offenders who eventually engage in serious or violent delinquency begin the progression toward these offenses with less serious forms of non-violent offending. But the progression from problem behaviors early in life to serious delinquency in adolescence characterizes a relatively small proportion of offenders. Most individuals who engage in delinquency do not progress to the most serious offenses, nor do they necessarily begin to display problem behaviors at young ages. Instead, they experiment with delinquency relatively briefly in adolescence. This brief period may also be marked by a progression of seriousness of offenses, but this progression is characterized neither by "deep developmental roots" of problem behaviors nor by involvement in serious offenses – as the criminal careers of serious, chronic offenders are.

Generality of deviance or co-occurrence of problem behaviors

The **generality of deviance** refers to the extent to which juvenile delinquency is a component of a larger group of problem behaviors, such as drug and alcohol use, mental health problems, and underachievement and behavior problems in school, that tend to occur together or "co-occur." Seriously delinquent youth often appear to suffer difficulties in many areas of life, and their delinquency seems to be part of a more general pattern of problem behaviors.[5] The notion that various problem behaviors tend to co-occur is appealing in a sense because it suggests, from a prevention or intervention perspective, that these problem behaviors can be dealt with collectively.

A good deal of empirical research has explored this issue. Some studies relying on official data show substantial co-occurrence of delinquency and other problem behaviors (Huizinga et al. 2000).[6] For example, recent research shows that there is an overrepresentation of youth with mental health problems in the juvenile justice system. One study reveals that, compared to those without arrest records, arrested juveniles show more mental health problems, such as attention deficit hyperactivity problems and oppositional defiant problems (Hirschfield et al. 2006). However, most youth who are delinquent are never arrested or involved with the juvenile justice system. So a more complete understanding of the co-occurrence of delinquency and other problem behaviors requires the use of self-report data from respondents who are not defined in terms of official responses to delinquency.

Researchers who have used self-report data to explore the co-occurrence of problem behaviors have found that serious delinquency often occurs along with substance use and mental health problems, as well as promiscuous sexual behavior and school failure or dropout (e.g., Farrington 1998; Huizinga and Jakob-Chien 1998; Thornberry, Huizinga, and Loeber 1995; Elliott et al. 1989). Recent research, using self-report data from the National Longitudinal Survey of Youth, showed co-occurrence of substance use (alcohol and marijuana), problem behaviors in school (measured by suspension from school), and serious delinquency. Respondents who drank alcohol or used marijuana in the past 30 days were more likely than those who did not to have been suspended from school and to have been involved in delinquency (vandalism, major theft, assault, carrying a handgun, and gang membership). For example, among those aged 15 to 17, 33 percent of those who had used marijuana in the past 30 days reported vandalizing property within the past 12 months, compared to 11 percent of those who did not use marijuana (McCurley and Snyder 2008). Similarly, Helene White used self-report data and found that several problem behaviors – delinquency, substance use, school misconduct and underachievement, and precocious sexual behavior – tend to "cluster" together (White 1992; White, Pandina, and LaGrange 1987). However, White also found that the clusters of problem behaviors vary somewhat for males and females and that the relationships among specific problem behaviors are not stable over time.

To study the co-occurrence of problem behaviors, David Huizinga and several colleagues used self-report data gathered at three research sites (Rochester, New York; Denver, Colorado; and Pittsburgh, Pennsylvania) as part of the Program of Research on the Causes and Correlates of Delinquency (Thornberry, Huizinga, and Loeber 2004; Huizinga et al. 2000). "Research in action: the Program of Research on the Causes and Correlates of Delinquency" provides a description of this program of research. Huizinga and his associates examined the co-occurrence of persistent serious delinquency with persistent drug use, school problems (subject earned below average grades or dropped out of school), and mental health problems. ("Persistent" problems were defined as those displayed in at least two of the three years examined.)

Research in action: the Program of Research on the Causes and Correlates of Delinquency

The Program of Research on the Causes and Correlates of Delinquency was begun in 1986 by the Office of Juvenile Justice and Delinquency Prevention. This program consists of three coordinated longitudinal projects:

- Denver Youth Survey
- Pittsburgh Youth Study
- Rochester Youth Development Study

These projects were "designed to improve the understanding of serious delinquency, violence, and drug use by examining how youth develop within the context of family, school, peers, and community."

The participants in these studies are from inner cities and are considered to be at high risk for involvement in delinquency and drug use. To gather data, researchers use face-to-face interviews with the youth, their primary caregivers, and in two research sites, their teachers. Researchers also collect data from official agencies, including police, courts, schools, and social services. The surveys include measures of "self-reported delinquency and drug use; community and neighborhood characteristics; youth, family, and peer variables; and arrest and judicial processing histories."

The Denver Youth Survey sample consists of 1,527 children (806 boys and 721 girls), who were 7, 9, 11, 13, or 15 years old in 1987 and lived in a disadvantaged, high-crime neighborhood.

The Pittsburgh Youth Study sample consists of 1,517 boys, who were in the first, fourth, or seventh grade of the Pittsburgh public school system when the study began. This sample includes "the top 30 percent of boys with the most disruptive behavior" and "a random sample of the remaining 70 percent who showed less disruptive behavior."

The Rochester Youth Development Study sample consists of 1,000 children (729 boys and 271 girls), who were in the seventh or eighth grade of the Rochester public school system in 1988. Boys and students from high-crime neighborhoods were "oversampled."

Source: Office of Juvenile Justice and Delinquency Prevention, Program of Research on the Causes and Correlates of Delinquency. Retrieved November 6, 2014 (www.ojjdp.gov/programs/ProgSummary.asp?pi=19).

A primary finding of this study was that a large portion of persistent serious delinquents do not have persistent school or mental health problems and are not persistent drug users (Huizinga et al. 2000). Table 6.2 shows the percentages of persistent serious delinquents who were also characterized by other persistent problems. In Denver and Pittsburgh, about 55–56 percent of the males who were persistent serious delinquents showed no persistent drug use, school problems, or mental health problems. In Rochester, the comparable number was 38.8 percent. The percentages were quite similar for females. When delinquency was combined with another persistent problem behavior, drug use was the most common problem. When researchers examined persistent drug use alone or in combination with other problem behaviors, they found that "among males who were serious delinquents, 34–44% were also drug users; 46–48% of female serious delinquents were also drug users" (Huizinga et al. 2000: 6). Separate research showed that youths who are chronic and multiple drug users report more frequent and more serious delinquent acts. Drug use may be a critical factor

Table 6.2 Co-occurrence of persistent serious delinquency and other persistent problem behaviors

Problem Behavior	Males (%)			Females (%)	
	Denver	Pittsburgh	Rochester	Denver	Rochester
None	55.2	56.4	38.8	54.4	39.9
Drug use only	21.4	24.3	17.7	34.4	3.6
School problems only	4.9	2.9	7.2	0.0	3.6
Mental health problems only	4.6	5.0	5.6	0.0	0.0
Drug use and school problems	6.4	4.3	17.2	11.3	21.7
Drug use and mental health problems	4.9	5.7	3.2	0.0	7.8
School and mental health problems	1.8	0.0	4.7	0.0	8.3
Drug use, school, and mental health problems	0.9	1.4	5.6	0.0	15.1

Notes: Percentages in this table represent persistent serious delinquents who also have other persistent problems. The Pittsburgh Youth Study sample includes males only. Due to rounding, columns may not sum to 100. Source: Huizinga et al. (2000: 5, 6).

in the progression from minor to serious delinquency (Johnson, Crosnoe, and Elder 2001; Inciardi, Horowitz, and Pottieger 1993; Elliott et al. 1989; White et al. 1987).[7]

Although a large portion of serious delinquents in the study by Huizinga and his colleagues were not characterized by other persistent problem behaviors, it is also true that a fairly substantial portion of serious delinquents were. In fact, in the Rochester sample, the majority of those studied showed multiple persistent problem behaviors. Huizinga and his colleagues concluded that the degree of co-occurrence of persistent problem behaviors "suggests that a large number of persistent serious delinquents face additional problems that need to be addressed" (Huizinga et al. 2000: 6).

The general conclusion we can draw from studies of the co-occurrence of problem behaviors is that various forms of deviance often occur together. Delinquency is often part of a more general pattern of problem behaviors. However, these problem behaviors appear to be less closely related than some theorists would have us believe. The relationships among problem behaviors are sometimes weak and vary over time and across groups (e.g., differences for males and females). It is also the case that different problem behaviors follow different developmental paths. For example, delinquency peaks at ages 18–19 and then declines, but drug use increases through adolescence into early adulthood (White 1992). The developmental perspective also suggests the possibility that some adolescents are "multiple problem youth" who participate in several forms of deviance, while others are more limited in their deviant involvement.

Explaining the generality of deviance

How do we explain the co-occurrence of problem behaviors revealed in some studies? Two possible explanations exist. First, causal links may exist between forms of deviance such that involvement in one form leads to involvement in another. For example, drug use may lead to delinquency, which, in turn, may lead to mental health problems. Second, deviant behaviors may be related because of an underlying common cause or "shared influence" (White 1992: 81).

Osgood and his colleagues (1988) tested these competing explanations of the generality of deviance using longitudinal self-reports of alcohol, marijuana, and other illicit drug use; dangerous driving; and other criminal behavior. Their results were somewhat mixed. The first explanation, of causal links between different forms of deviance, received little support. Only the effect of marijuana use on later use of other illicit drugs was significant, and it was significant for one time period in the study, but not for another. Consistent with the second explanation, an underlying common cause accounted for almost all relationships among the various types of deviance. However, contrary to the second explanation, this common cause did not fully explain the stability of separate deviant behaviors over time (Osgood et al. 1988). Osgood and his colleagues concluded that the common cause explanation cannot account completely for the co-occurrence of problem behaviors. Other research supports that conclusion. A study by White and her colleagues (1987), for example, showed that serious delinquency and substance use shared some common causes, but were also affected by unique predictors.

Desistance from offending

At some point, most offenders stop committing crimes. However, criminologists have typically been more interested in the question of why individuals begin offending than why they stop (Laub and Sampson 2001). Recent theory and research, however, consider **desistance** from offending as a key component of the developmental perspective. John Laub and Robert Sampson (2001: 11) define desistance as "the causal process that supports the termination of offending."[8]

Although involvement in offending tends to decline with age (see Chapter 5), desistance does not occur simply as a function of age (Loeber and LeBlanc 1990). Desistance may occur at any age, and it is linked to different factors at different ages (Laub and Sampson 2001). In addition, factors leading to desistance cannot be viewed simply as the opposite of factors leading to involvement in offending. Predictors of desistance are often different from predictors of initiation into offending (Uggen and Piliavin 1998).

So, what accounts for the process of desistance from offending? Laub and Sampson (2001: 3) conducted a thorough review of the literature on desistance and concluded:

> Desistance stems from a variety of complex processes – developmental, psychological, and sociological – and thus there are several factors associated with it. The key elements seem to be aging; a good marriage; securing legal, stable work; and deciding to "go straight," including a reorientation of the costs and benefits of crime.

In their book, *Crime in the Making*, Sampson and Laub (1993) presented an age-graded theory of informal social control to explain crime and deviance over the life course (see Chapter 10). In this theory, they proposed that adult involvement in offending is influenced not only by early life experiences, including delinquency, but also by social ties in adulthood that facilitate informal social control (e.g., family, work, and military service). In other words, they proposed that life-course changes that strengthen social bonds to society in adulthood will lead to desistance from offending. To test their hypotheses, Sampson and Laub used data from the Gluecks' classic study of delinquency and crime (see Chapter 3) (see also Sampson,

Laub, and Wimer 2006; Sampson and Laub 2002; Laub, Nagin, and Sampson 1998). They found that:

> job stability and marital attachment in adulthood were significantly related to changes in adult crime – the stronger the adult ties to work and family, the less crime and deviance ... The major turning points in the life course for men who refrained from crime and deviance in adulthood were stable employment and good marriages.
>
> (Laub and Sampson 2001: 19–20, summarizing the findings of Sampson and Laub 1993)

Other criminologists have also found that marriage is strongly related to desistance from offending, at least for males (e.g., Bersani and Doherty 2013; Doherty and Ensminger 2013; Horney, Tolan, and Weisburd 2012; Piquero et al. 2002; Farrington and West 1995; Horney, Osgood, and Marshall 1995; see also Kreager, Matsueda, and Erosheva 2010).[9]

Sampson and Laub's interpretation of the link between marriage and desistance rests on the assumption that strong ties to conventional institutions create stakes in conformity and thus inhibit crime and delinquency. (This assumption is derived from control theory, which we discuss in Chapter 10.) Mark Warr (1998) interpreted the link between marriage and desistance in a different way. He used data from the NYS to explore the effects of marriage and exposure to delinquent peers on desistance. Like Sampson and Laub, Warr found that marriage contributed to desistance from offending. However, Warr found that this effect occurred through the altering of relationships with delinquent peers.[10] When people marry, they spend less time with friends and their exposure to delinquent peers is reduced (Warr 1998). Reduced interaction with delinquent peers as a result of marriage limits both opportunities and motivation to engage in offending. (This interpretation is consistent with differential association and social learning theories, which we discuss in Chapter 10.)

Peer associations are connected to desistance in other ways, too. Ryan Schroeder and his colleagues (2007) examined the relationship between drug use and desistance among previously institutionalized adolescents. They found that drug use prevented desistance from offending, and that peer networks were an important mechanism through which drug use affected continued offending. Other researchers have also found a strong effect of substance use on persistence of offending (Morizot and LeBlanc 2007).

Recent studies have explored the impact of gang membership on involvement in offending across the life course (Sweeten, Pyrooz, and Piquero 2013; Krohn et al. 2011; Melde and Esbensen 2011). Gang membership can be conceptualized as a turning point in the life course that is related to changes in attitudes, routine activities, and social controls which are conducive to delinquency (Melde and Esbensen 2011). The process of disengaging from gangs is linked to decreases in exposure to antisocial peers, unstructured routine activities, and victimization, and through these mechanisms, is linked to desistance from offending (Sweeten et al. 2013).

Researchers have also examined the effects of employment on desistance, with mixed results. Studies do not consistently show that employment fosters desistance from offending. Christopher Uggen (2000) used data from a national work experiment to compare offenders who were given minimum wage jobs with those who were not. He found that the influence of work on desistance differed depending on the age of offenders. Those aged 27 or older were less likely to report crime and arrest when they were provided with jobs. For those under the age of 27, jobs had no effect on desistance. More recent research found that, contrary to the idea of job entry as a turning point in one's criminal career, most men in the study sample had desisted from offending prior to their employment (Skardhamar and Savolainen 2014).

The Pathways to Desistance study is a multidisciplinary program of research that examines how and why many serious adolescent offenders stop offending (Steinberg, Cauffman, and Monahan 2015; see also Mulvey et al. 2004; Schubert et al. 2004). This research explores the development of psychosocial maturity during adolescence and early adulthood, which includes the ability to control impulses, to take responsibility for one's behavior, and to consider other points of view and long-term consequences of one's actions. Changes in psychosocial maturity over time are linked to the process of desistance from offending. Steinberg and his colleagues (2015: 8) found that "offenders who desisted from antisocial activity during adolescence showed significantly greater growth in psychosocial maturity than those who persisted into adulthood." Less mature individuals were more likely to persist in their offending.

Finally, research has shown that "going straight," or desisting from crime, involves subjective factors, such as offenders' motivation to change, choices to take advantage of opportunities for change that present themselves, changes in perceptions of the risks and rewards of crime, and changes in self-concept (Lebel et al. 2008; Laub and Sampson 2003; Giordano, Cernkovich, and Rudolph 2002; Maruna 2001; Shover 1996). One researcher used life history narratives to explore desistance from offending and found that those who desisted adopted a "new outlook on life" that involved a greater sense of responsibility for their futures and a greater sense of control over their destinies (Maruna 2001; see also Gadd and Farrall 2004). Desistance processes are also connected to age-specific norms regarding what it means to "be a man" and how individuals "do masculinity" at various stages of the life course (Carlsson 2013).

Raymond Paternoster and Shawn Bushway (2009) have developed an "identity theory" of criminal desistance in which they describe how offenders have "working selves" as criminal offenders, but also future or possible selves. These future selves include both positive possibilities (what individuals want or hope to become) and negative possibilities (what individuals fear they may become). Motivation to change and desist from offending is fueled by one's perception that one may actually become the "feared self." This motivation produces changes in preferences and social networks that then stabilize the newly emerging positive self.

Contrary to the view that desistance is driven by subjective factors such as offenders' motivation to change, Laub and Sampson (2003) describe a process of "desistance by default" in which offenders don't necessarily make a conscious or deliberate decision to stop offending. Instead, opportunities for change present themselves (through work or marriage, for example), and individuals simply pursue those opportunities, though not necessarily with the intention of "going straight." Free will or "human agency" are, however, part of the desistance process, because individuals must choose to take advantage of available opportunities.

Developmental models of delinquent behavior

The major components of the developmental perspective have been incorporated into various developmental models of delinquency, including Patterson's early- and late-starter routes to delinquency and Moffitt's work on "adolescence-limited" and "life-course-persistent" offenders. In this section, we describe these models and examine research that has tested them.

Patterson's early- and late-starter models

Gerald Patterson and his colleagues at the Oregon Social Learning Center began the Oregon Youth Study (OYS) in 1984. Longitudinal data for all boys included in the OYS were gathered from multiple sources (parents, teachers, peers, and the boys themselves) using a variety of methods (interviews, questionnaires, home observations, videotapes of family problem-solving, and peer nominations) (Patterson and Yoerger 1993).

Patterson and his colleagues used data from the OYS to develop and test developmental models of delinquent behavior. They propose two routes to delinquency, each characterized by a distinct set of causes and long-term outcomes. What distinguishes these two paths is age at which a child is first arrested. An **early starter** is defined as a child first arrested before age 14. A **late starter** is one who is first arrested at or after age 14 (Patterson and Yoerger 1993:140). For early starters, Patterson and his colleagues (Patterson and Yoerger 1993; Patterson, DeBaryshe, and Ramsey 1989) hypothesize that poor parenting practices lead directly to antisocial behavior in young children, which, in turn, puts them at risk for early arrest. For late starters, the researchers hypothesize that a deviant peer group is the direct determinant of offending and that family processes are only indirectly involved in the process leading to arrest.

Developmental model for early starters

Patterson and his colleagues develop a "coercion model" to explain the antisocial behavior of early starters. This model focuses on poor parenting skills as a primary cause of antisocial behavior in young children (Patterson and Yoerger 1993). Home life for those who become antisocial at early ages is distressing – unskilled parents inadvertently but effectively reinforce children's problem behaviors. Three factors tended to characterize the parenting of antisocial boys: (1) no positive reinforcement for prosocial behaviors, (2) no effective punishment for coercive behaviors, and (3) "a rich supply of reinforcement for coercive behaviors" (Patterson and Yoerger 1993: 141). This reinforcement occurs when an unwanted or disliked behavior is directed at the child (e.g., parent says "no" to a request made by the child), the child responds with coercive behavior (e.g., a temper tantrum), and the initial unwanted behavior gets "turned off" (e.g., parent "gives in" to the child's initial request in order to end the temper tantrum). Thus, the child's coercive behavior is reinforced by parents who give in to him because of it. Coercive behavior "works" for the child in the sense that it allows him to control the situation and stop others' unwanted behaviors. In his research, Patterson found that parental disciplinary practices and monitoring explained a large portion (30 percent) of children's antisocial behavior (Patterson 1986).

Earlier we discussed continuity in problem behaviors and progression of seriousness of offenses as key themes of the developmental perspective. Patterson's model demonstrates both of these elements. The early-starter model assumes that, as antisocial acts in the home become more frequent, "trivial" coercive behaviors escalate to more severe delinquent acts, such as fighting, stealing, and fire setting. If individuals engage in serious delinquency, they are likely to have engaged in more minor forms as well. Patterson's research supports the hypothesis of progression of seriousness (Patterson and Yoerger 1993; Patterson and Bank 1989). Patterson and his colleagues also hypothesize that parents' failure to reinforce prosocial behaviors hinders the development of children's prosocial skills. The presence of antisocial behaviors and absence of social skills early in life produce problems for children that generalize to settings outside the home, leading to problems in school and with peers (Patterson and Yoerger 1993; Patterson et al. 1989). "The child entering school initiates coercive actions, producing a predictable set of reactions from peers and teachers. The peers' and teachers' reactions produce predictable reactions from the problem child, and the sequence continues into adulthood" (Patterson and Yoerger 1993: 145). Thus, according to this early-starter model, poor parenting skills lead to children's antisocial behavior, which, in turn, produces school failure and peer rejection. Rejection by peers contributes to "drift" toward deviant peers, who then become "partners in crime" for the antisocial child (Patterson and Yoerger 1993).

Linking antisocial behavior to age at first arrest, Patterson and Yoerger (1993) reason that children who commit antisocial acts most frequently tend, at relatively young ages, to overwhelm parental attempts to control them and keep them out of the company of deviant peers. Those who commit delinquent acts most frequently are also at greatest risk of being caught. Therefore, childhood antisocial behavior should significantly predict age at first arrest. Research findings support this hypothesis (Patterson, Crosby, and Vuchinich 1992). Patterson and Yoerger also predict that early starters are at greater risk than late starters of chronic offending that lasts into adulthood. Again, research findings support this hypothesis.

Developmental model for late starters

For late starters, the direct cause of delinquency is involvement with a deviant peer group. Family processes that lead to youths' unsupervised time with deviant peers are viewed as indirect causes of delinquency for late starters. Patterson and Yoerger (1993: 162–163; see also Patterson, Capaldi, and Bank 1991; Patterson et al. 1989) list three defining characteristics of late starters:

1. Unlike early starters, they are not considered to be antisocial during assessments in fourth grade.
2. During early adolescence, significant family conflicts result in disrupted parental supervision.
3. They begin involvement with a deviant peer group at about age 13 or 14.

To explain why some families permit adolescents more unsupervised time than others do, Patterson and his colleagues use the idea of "disrupters," which include life events such as family transition (e.g., divorce), unemployment or financial loss, severe illness or death, and change of residence (Patterson and Yoerger 1993). Patterson and Yoerger (1993) also cite studies showing increasing conflict between adolescents and their parents as children age. According to the late-starter model, a lack of parental supervision, caused by family disrupters, along with increases in family conflict, lead to a "flight to peers." Patterson and Yoerger found that family conflict and inadequate supervision together explained the majority (72 percent) of involvement with deviant peers.

According to Patterson's developmental model, late starters are short-term offenders, less at risk for chronic offending than early starters. Patterson's data also reveal a substantially higher frequency of serious offenses (according to self-reports) for early starters than for late starters. This difference in frequency of serious offending exists throughout adolescence, but becomes particularly great at ages 15 and 16 (Patterson and Yoerger 1993; Patterson et al. 1989).

Tests of Patterson's early- and late-starter models

Patterson and his colleagues have conducted numerous tests of their developmental models using OYS data. Other researchers have also tested Patterson's models to see how well they explain delinquency. Ronald Simmons and his colleagues (1994), for example, tested the two routes to delinquency and found strong support for Patterson's models. Consistent with Patterson's early-starter model, they found that, for early starters, the influence of parenting on coercive behavior was key to understanding delinquency. Quality of parenting predicted coercive behavior, which, in turn, predicted association with deviant peers and involvement in the criminal justice system. Consistent with Patterson's late-starter model, Simons and his colleagues found that, for late starters, association with deviant peers was key. Quality of parenting predicted association with deviant peers, which, in turn, predicted involvement in the criminal justice system. For late starters, coercive behavior was unrelated to either association with deviant peers or delinquent behavior.[11]

Moffitt's adolescence-limited and life-course-persistent offenders

Patterson's early- and late-starter models are similar in some ways to the developmental framework offered by Terrie Moffitt (1993, 1997), which tries to explain two contradictory findings in criminology: continuity in antisocial behavior across age, and a dramatic increase in the prevalence of offending during adolescence. Moffitt proposes a pair of developmental theories – one to explain the antisocial behavior of "adolescence-limited" offenders and one to explain the behavior of "life-course-persistent" offenders. **Adolescence-limited offenders** are those who participate in antisocial behavior for a relatively brief period of time during adolescence. For this relatively large group of offenders, involvement in antisocial behavior is temporary and situational. **Life-course-persistent offenders** are those characterized by continuity of antisocial behavior from early childhood through adulthood. For this small group of offenders, antisocial behavior is stable across time and circumstance (Moffitt 1993, 1997). Figure 6.2 illustrates the prevalence and timing of antisocial behavior for these two groups of offenders. This figure shows that a large proportion of individuals engage in antisocial behavior during adolescence (high prevalence for a narrow span of ages), while a small proportion of individuals engage in antisocial behavior at young ages and continue into later adulthood (low prevalence for a wide span of ages).

Life-course-persistent offenders

Life-course-persistent offenders constitute a small proportion of all offenders. Although the antisocial behaviors change with age for these offenders, the underlying disposition that gives rise to them is consistent over time and in diverse situations. Examples of the changing expressions of an antisocial disposition include "biting and hitting at age 4, shoplifting and truancy at age 10, selling drugs and stealing cars at age 16, robbery and rape at age 22, and fraud and child abuse at age 30" (Moffitt 1993: 679).

Moffitt's theory of life-course-persistent offending attributes the early onset of antisocial behavior to a combination of child's neuropsychological deficits and an adverse child-rearing environment. Neuropsychological refers to "anatomical structures and physiological processes within the nervous system [that] influence psychological characteristics such as temperament, behavioral development, cognitive abilities, or all three" (Moffitt 1993: 681).

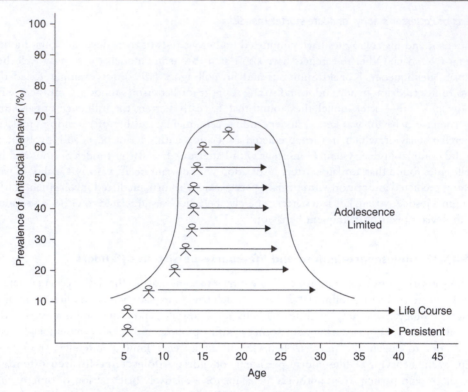

Figure 6.2 Moffitt's adolescence-limited and life-course-persistent offenders.

Terrie Moffitt presents this illustration of "the changing prevalence of participation in antisocial behavior across the life course. The solid line represents the known curve of crime over age. The arrows represent the duration of participation in antisocial behavior by individuals."

Source: Moffitt (1993: 677). Copyright © 1993, American Psychological Association. All rights reserved.

Neuropsychological deficits may begin before or shortly after birth, as a result of, for example, maternal drug use, poor prenatal nutrition, or deprivation of stimulation or affection following birth. Neuropsychological deficits are displayed in problems such as difficult temperament, delays in language and motor development, difficulties with listening and problem-solving, impaired memory, and learning disabilities. Empirical research consistently demonstrates a link between neuropsychological deficits and antisocial behaviors (Moffitt 1990, 1993).

Children with neuropsychological deficits, already disadvantaged by the deficits themselves, also tend to be born into less than ideal family environments. Some of the same problems that contribute to the creation of neuropsychological deficits, such as maternal drug use, also impair the caregiver's ability to provide a supportive environment and deal with the particular challenges posed by a child with these deficits. The pairing of a difficult child with parents who are ill-equipped to deal with the challenges their child presents sets the stage for life-course-persistent antisocial behavior. Moffitt describes a process in which the demands of coping with a difficult child elicit a series of failed parent–child interactions. She calls this evocative interaction – interaction in which children's difficult behaviors evoke particular responses from others (Moffitt 1993; see also Caspi et al. 1987).

Two other types of interaction help explain how the antisocial behavior of life-course-persistent offenders is sustained throughout the life course. Reactive interaction occurs when different children exposed to the same environment interpret it and react to it in ways consistent with their temperament (Moffitt 1993). For example, an antisocial child might interpret the ambiguous situation of being bumped into on the playground as calling for an aggressive response, while another child might interpret it as an accident that requires no response at all. Proactive interaction occurs when children select or create environments that support their temperaments and behaviors (Moffitt 1993). For example, antisocial children might choose friends who are also antisocial. These forms of interaction suggest that antisocial behavior is sustained as children consistently interpret, respond to, and create their own environment in antisocial ways. As they do so, their options for conventional behavior narrow at each stage of development (Moffitt 1993).

Adolescence-limited offenders

Compared to life-course-persistent offenders, adolescence-limited offenders constitute a much larger group. Their pattern of offending is characterized by discontinuity, both over time and across situations (Moffitt 1993). Adolescence-limited offenders have no history of antisocial behavior as children, and are unlikely to continue offending in adulthood. In terms of discontinuity across situations, they may engage in antisocial behavior in the company of their peers, where the behavior is rewarded, but not in the company of parents and teachers.

According to Moffitt (1993), adolescence-limited offenders begin involvement in antisocial behavior because of the "maturity gap" between biological or sexual maturity in early adolescence and social maturity (characterized, for example, by freedom to work, drive, marry, vote, and buy alcohol) in late adolescence or early adulthood. This maturity gap causes adolescents to search for means of achieving status other than those offered in the conventional world. Moffitt hypothesizes that adolescents view antisocial behavior as a way to achieve "mature status," power, and privilege. In attempts to acquire these resources, adolescence-limited delinquents engage in "social mimicry" and imitate the behavior of life-course-persistent offenders, who appear relatively unaffected by the maturity gap (Moffitt 1993). This antisocial behavior is then reinforced by the responses it provokes. According to Moffitt, even responses that at first glance seem "negative," such as disruption of the parent–child relationship, are interpreted by adolescents as positive reinforcers for delinquency, which explain its continued use.

So, why don't all youths become adolescence-limited delinquents? Moffitt (1993) proposes four possible answers to this question. First, some adolescents experience delayed puberty, which limits the maturity gap for them and thereby diminishes motivation for delinquency. Second, some adolescents may have few opportunities to mimic the antisocial behavior of life-course-persistent offenders. For example, the structure of the school setting might limit contact with those who would be models of antisocial behavior. Third, personal characteristics might exclude some adolescents from antisocial peer networks. Finally, some adolescents have "legitimate access to adult privileges" and thus do not need the type of adolescent "power" that accompanies delinquency.

The next obvious question is, "Why do adolescence-limited offenders desist from antisocial behavior in late adolescence or early adulthood?" The answer is that adolescence-limited offenders are able to adapt to changing contingencies. For adolescents caught in the maturity gap, delinquency is reinforced and rewarding. However, as individuals "age out" of the maturity gap and gain access to legitimate adult roles, delinquency becomes costly, rather than rewarding. Adolescence-limited offenders are able to recognize this shift in the consequences of delinquency, and to respond with changes in behavior (Moffitt 1993). They have the "option for change" because, unlike life-course-persistent offenders, they have skills for prosocial behavior and academic success, and they are not restricted by underlying personality traits that entangle them in a life of antisocial behavior.

Tests of Moffitt's developmental theory

Moffitt (2006a, 2006b) recently reviewed the research that has tested her theories of adolescence-limited and life-course-persistent offending. Numerous tests of her developmental approach offer substantial support for her core hypotheses about the existence of two different types of offenders and about the nature of life-course-persistent offending. For example, Bartusch and her colleagues (1997) found strong support for Moffitt's hypothesis that separate factors predict antisocial behavior in childhood and in adolescence. Moreover, the nature of these factors was consistent with Moffitt's explanations of neuropsychological deficits predicting childhood antisocial behavior and peer influence predicting adolescent antisocial behavior. Research suggests that genetic factors also play a role in explaining life-course-persistent offending (Barnes, Beaver, and Boutwell 2011).

Moffitt's explanation of adolescence-limited offending has received fairly consistent support. Consistent with Moffitt's hypothesis that the maturity gap plays a significant role in explaining adolescence-limited offending, research shows that the "rebellious" delinquency that characterizes adolescent offending is explained by a combination of early maturity and the autonomy of peer activities (Piquero and Brezina 2001). A separate study found that, for males, the maturity gap predicted minor forms of delinquency and drug use, but not more serious types of offending. Results, however, were less supportive of Moffitt's theory for females (Barnes and Beaver 2010). Recent research on youth who abstain from delinquency does not support Moffitt's hypothesis that abstainers are socially isolated due to unappealing personal characteristics (Rulison, Kreager, and Osgood 2014; Chen and Adams 2010).

While research provides strong evidence of two types of offenders, consistent with Moffitt's and Patterson's theories, it also indicates that there are additional trajectories of offending. Two comprehensive reviews of research (Jennings and Reingle 2012; Piquero 2008), along with several recent studies, suggest at least three additional types of offenders:

1. Individuals who begin offending relatively early (like life-course-persistent offenders), but then desist without becoming chronic offenders – "childhood-onset desisters" (Stattin, Kerr, and Bergman 2010).
2. Individuals who begin offending in adolescence, but continue into adulthood (Buck et al. 2013; Stattin et al. 2010; Moffitt et al. 2002).
3. Individuals who begin offending in adulthood – a "late-onset" or "adult-onset" group (Piquero, Hawkins, and Kazemian 2012; Zara and Farrington 2009, 2010; Gomez-Smith and Piquero 2005; Eggleston and Laub 2002).

One review of research also differentiates between two groups of chronic offenders – high rate and low rate chronic offenders (Piquero 2008).

To account for the second group of offenders – those who begin offending in adolescence, but continue into adulthood – Moffitt (2006b) has presented a revision of her original typology, suggesting that some youth who begin offending in adolescence become "ensnared" by factors such as involvement with the justice system, drug addiction, and teen pregnancy. These factors prevent individuals from aging out of offending as adolescence-limited offenders typically would. Consistent with this revision by Moffitt, Daniel Nagin and his colleagues (1995) examined self-reports of offending and found that desistance from crime for adolescence-limited offenders is not as clear-cut as Moffitt's original theory suggests. But when they examined official data, they also found that none of the adolescence-limited offenders in their study had been convicted since age 22 (consistent with Moffitt's original predictions). This study reveals an important point about how data sources can shape results. The fact that an individual has no criminal convictions after a particular age does not necessarily mean that he has desisted from offending. Perhaps he simply has not been caught.

Summary and conclusions

The research of Wolfgang and his colleagues produced what some consider one of criminology's most important findings. These researchers found that a small portion of the cohort studied was responsible for over half of the offenses that resulted in police contact and that the offenses of this small group of "chronic offenders" tended to be more serious than those of other offenders. This study also revealed that delinquents who began offending at relatively young ages tended to commit a relatively large number of offenses and to accumulate lengthy criminal careers that extended well into adulthood.

"Chronic offenders" are similar to "career criminals," described by Blumstein and his colleagues. Career criminals are also characterized by a high frequency of offending and a long criminal career, as well as greater seriousness of offenses committed. Like chronic offenders, career criminals constitute a small portion of all offenders but commit a disproportionate share of offenses, especially serious ones. This pattern is a fact that theory should consider.

Blumstein and his colleagues used the term "criminal career" – distinct from "career criminal" – to describe an individual's sequence of offenses during some period of time. Criminal careers are characterized by age of onset, age when offending ends, duration of career, and frequency of offending. Research on criminal careers shows that most offenders commit only one or a limited number of offenses during late adolescence or early adulthood, and they desist in young adulthood without involvement in serious offending. Theory should also consider this non-chronic nature of most delinquency.

The developmental perspective of the 1990s incorporates some of the distinct elements of criminal careers. First, the developmental perspective suggests different patterns of offending based, in part, on age of onset of problem behaviors. Most offenders begin involvement in delinquency during adolescence and relatively quickly age out of crime in late adolescence or early adulthood. Other offenders, however, display problem behaviors early in the life course and are more likely to develop stable patterns of offending into adulthood. Research has shown that, compared to late-onset offenders, early-onset offenders show more stability in offending over time, a higher rate of offending, and more serious offenses.

Second, the developmental perspective considers different patterns of offending based on level of continuity or change in problem behaviors over time. For most offenders, problem behaviors are not stable over time. Involvement in delinquency is brief and represents a change in behavior patterns. However, for a relatively small number of offenders with "extreme" behavior problems, antisocial behavior is stable over time, from childhood through adulthood.

A third pattern that developmental theories consider is progression of seriousness in offending. Research reveals a progression from minor to serious offenses. Most individuals who engage in delinquency do not progress to the most serious offenses. Among those who do become serious delinquents, though, criminal careers tend to start with minor offenses and escalate to more serious ones.

Fourth, the developmental perspective considers the generality of deviance or co-occurrence of problem behaviors. Studies suggest that delinquency is often a component of a larger group of problem behaviors – including drug and alcohol use, mental health problems, behavior problems and underachievement in school, and risky sexual behavior – that tend to co-occur.

Finally, the developmental perspective examines the process of desistance from offending. Research indicates that attachment to law-abiding others (especially a spouse), stable employment, the aging process, and changes in personal identity all influence desistance from crime and delinquency.

We concluded this chapter by presenting two models of delinquency that are excellent examples of the developmental perspective: Patterson's early- and late-starter routes to delinquency, and Moffitt's work on adolescence-limited and life-course-persistent offenders. Both approaches have received considerable empirical support.

Critical-thinking questions

1.   What makes a particular theory or perspective developmental? In other words, what are the defining elements of developmental perspectives?
2.   Think again about Michael's case at the beginning of this chapter. How would you explain his delinquency from a developmental perspective, in terms of age of onset, continuity and change in problem behaviors, and progression of seriousness? Is his pattern of offending typical of most delinquents? Explain.
3.   Explain the distinction between "criminal careers" and "career criminals."
4.   What are the implications of empirical findings regarding chronic offenders for delinquency prevention and intervention strategies? What are the policy implications of the developmental perspective in general?
5.   Think about the relationship between theory and research method. Describe appropriate and adequate methods for conducting research based on a developmental perspective.

Suggested reading

Loeber, Rolf and Marc LeBlanc. 1990. "Toward a Developmental Criminology." Pp. 375–473 in *Crime and Justice: A Review of Research*, ed. M. Tonry and N. Morris. University of Chicago Press.

Moffitt, Terrie E. 1993. "Adolescence-Limited and Life-Course-Persistent Antisocial Behavior: A Developmental Taxonomy." *Psychological Review* 100: 674–701.

Paternoster, Raymond and Robert Brame. 1997. "Multiple Routes to Delinquency? A Test of Developmental and General Theories of Crime." *Criminology* 35: 49–84.

Patterson, Gerald R., Barbara D. DeBaryshe, and Elizabeth Ramsey. 1989. "A Developmental Perspective on Antisocial Behavior." *American Psychologist* 44: 329–335.

Piquero, Alex R., David P. Farrington, and Alfred Blumstein. 2003. "The Criminal Career Paradigm." Pp. 359–506 in *Crime and Justice: A Review of Research, vol.* 30, ed. M. Tonry. University of Chicago Press.

Sampson, Robert J. and John H. Laub. 1992. "Crime and Deviance in the Life Course." *Annual Review of Sociology* 18: 63–84.

Useful websites

For further information relevant to this chapter, go to the following websites.

- National Institute of Justice Study Group on the Transition from Juvenile Delinquency to Adult Crime, Office of Justice Programs, National Institute of Justice (www.nij.gov/topics/crime/Pages/delinquency-to-adult-offending.aspx)
- Pathways to Desistance Study, Center for Research on Health Care, University of Pittsburgh (www.pathwaysstudy.pitt.edu/)
- Program of Research on the Causes and Correlates of Delinquency, Office of Juvenile Justice and Delinquency Prevention (www.ojjdp.gov/Programs/ProgSummary.asp?pi=19)
- Oregon Social Learning Center (www.oslc.org/)
- Terrie Moffitt's research on human development and antisocial behavior (www.moffittcaspi.com/)

Glossary of key terms

Adolescence–limited offenders: Offenders who participate in antisocial behavior for a relatively brief period of time during adolescence.

Age of onset: The age at which an individual begins involvement in delinquent or criminal acts.

Behavioral continuity: Patterns of behavior that are consistent and stable over time, resulting from stable individual attributes or styles of interaction.

Career criminals: Criminals "characterized by some combination of a high frequency of offending, a long duration of the criminal career, and high seriousness of offenses committed" (Blumstein et al. 1988a: 22).

Chronic offenders: The small proportion of offenders who engage in a disproportionate share of offenses, particularly serious and violent ones.

Criminal career: "The longitudinal sequence of offenses committed by an offender who has a detectable rate of offending during some period" (Blumstein et al. 1988a: 2).

Desistance: "The causal process that supports the termination of offending" (Laub and Sampson 2001: 11).

Early starter: A child first arrested before the age of 14, according to the developmental model of Patterson and Yoerger.

Escalation: Progression of seriousness of offenses, or the tendency for offenders to move from less serious problem behaviors to more serious offenses as offending continues.

Frequency: Rate at which an offender or subgroup of active offenders commits crimes. Sometimes called *incidence*.

Generality of deviance: The extent to which problem behaviors, such as juvenile delinquency, drug and alcohol use, mental health problems, behavior problems and underachievement in school, and risky sexual behavior, tend to occur together or "co-occur."

Late starter: A child first arrested at or after the age of 14, according to the developmental model of Patterson and Yoerger.

Life–course–persistent offenders: Offenders characterized by continuity of antisocial behavior from early childhood through adulthood.

Participation: Proportion of a population who are active offenders at any given time. Sometimes called *prevalence*.

Recidivists: Individuals who commit multiple delinquent or criminal offenses, resulting in police contact.

Notes

1. These statistics were derived by combining Table 5.3 on pages 68–69 and Table 6.16 on page 102 in Wolfgang et al. (1972). In 1990, Tracy, Wolfgang, and Figlio published a second birth cohort study that showed results similar to those of the earlier 1945 birth cohort study. In the 1990 study, chronic offenders made up a small portion of the total cohort, but were responsible for a disproportionate share of offenses, especially violent ones.
2. But see Piquero, Moffitt, and Wright (2007), who found support for Gottfredson and Hirschi's (1990) claim that low self-control predicts all dimensions of offending (including participation, frequency, persistence, and desistance).
3. See also Smith and Brame (1994), who examined whether explanatory variables from several theories had different effects on two dimensions of criminal careers: initiation and continuation. They found mixed results. Some variables predicted initiation and continuation decisions similarly, while other variables predicted only one of these decisions.
4. See Paternoster and Brame (1997) and Osgood and Rowe (1994) for discussions of how the criminal career perspective has influenced and is compatible with developmental theories.
5. Junger and Dekovic (2003) offer a review of the literature on the co-occurrence of delinquency, health-endangering behaviors, and other problem behaviors.
6. See Huizinga and Jakob-Chien (1998) for a list of these studies.
7. It is important to note that the number of youth who are both multiple-drug users and serious delinquents is very small. In a study of more than 1,700 youth, Elliott et al. (1989) found just 23 youth (1.4 percent of the sample) who were multiple drug users and serious delinquents.
8. See also Massoglia and Uggen (2007); Bushway, Thornberry, and Krohn (2003); and Bushway et al. (2001), who introduce measures of "subjective" desistance based on individuals' own assessments of their desistance from crime, rather than relying on official measures of desistance.
9. See, for example, Horney et al. (1995); and Farrington and West (1995).
10. See also Giordano, Cernkovich, and Holland (2003), who consider changes in the influence of friends over the life course, and how these changes contribute to the desistance process.
11. In the research of Simons and his colleagues (1994), early starters were defined as those who reported committing two or more serious delinquent acts by the third wave of data collection, when the average respondent age was 14. Late starters were defined as those who reported committing fewer than two serious delinquent acts during the first three waves of data collection.

References

Armstrong, Todd A. 2008. "Are Trends in Specialization Across Arrests Explained by Changes in Specialization Occurring with Age?" *Justice Quarterly* 25: 201–222.
Armstrong, Todd A. and Chester L. Britt. 2004. "The Effect of Offender Characteristics on Offense Specialization and Escalation." *Justice Quarterly* 21: 843–876.
Bacon, Sarah, Raymond Paternoster, and Robert Brame. 2009. "Understanding the Relationship between Onset Age and Subsequent Offending During Adolescence." *Journal of Youth and Adolescence* 38: 301–311.
Barnes, J. C. and Kevin M. Beaver. 2010. "An Empirical Examination of Adolescence-Limited Offending: A Direct Test of Moffitt's Maturity Gap Thesis." *Journal of Criminal Justice* 38: 1176–1185.
Barnes, J. C., Kevin M. Beaver, and Brian B. Boutwell. 2011. "Examining the Genetic Underpinnings to Moffitt's Developmental Taxonomy: A Behavioral Genetic Analysis." *Criminology* 49: 923–954.
Bartusch, Dawn R. Jeglum, Donald R. Lynam, Terrie E. Moffitt, and Phil Silva. 1997. "Is Age Important? Testing a General versus a Developmental Theory of Antisocial Behavior." *Criminology* 35: 13–48.
Bernburg, Jon Gunnar and Marvin D. Krohn. 2003. "Labeling, Life Chances, and Adult Crime: The Direct and Indirect Effects of Official Intervention in Adolescence on Crime in Early Adulthood." *Criminology* 41: 1287–1318.

Bernburg, Jon Gunnar, Marvin D. Krohn, and C. J. Rivera. 2006. "Official Labeling, Criminal Embeddedness, and Subsequent Delinquency: A Longitudinal Test of Labeling Theory." *Journal of Research in Crime and Delinquency* 43: 67–88.

Bersani, Bianca E. and Elaine Eggleston Doherty. 2013. "When the Ties That Bind Unwind: Examining the Enduring and Situational Processes of Change Behind the Marriage Effect." *Criminology* 51: 399–433.

Blumstein, Alfred and Jacqueline Cohen. 1987. "Characterizing Criminal Careers." *Science* 237: 985–991.

Blumstein, Alfred, Jacqueline Cohen, and David P. Farrington. 1988a. "Criminal Career Research: Its Value for Criminology." *Criminology* 26: 1–35.

Blumstein, Alfred, Jacqueline Cohen, and David P. Farrington. 1988b. "Longitudinal and Criminal Career Research: Further Clarifications." *Criminology* 26: 57–74.

Blumstein, Alfred, Jacqueline Cohen, Jeffrey A. Roth, and Christy A. Visher. 1986. *Criminal Careers and "Career Criminals."* Vol. 1. Washington, DC: National Academy Press.

Buck, Nicole, Frank Verhulst, Hjalmar van Marle, and Jan van der Ende. 2013. "Childhood Psychopathology Predicts Adolescence-Onset Offending: A Longitudinal Study." *Crime and Delinquency* 59: 718–737.

Bushway, Shawn D., Robert Brame, and Raymond Paternoster. 1999. "Assessing Stability and Change in Criminal Offending: A Comparison of Random Effects, Semiparametric, and Fixed Effects Modeling Strategies." *Journal of Quantitative Criminology* 15: 23–61.

Bushway, Shawn D., Alex R. Piquero, Lisa M. Broidy, Elizabeth Cauffman, and Paul Mazerolle. 2001. "An Empirical Framework for Studying Desistance as a Process." *Criminology* 39: 491–515.

Bushway, Shawn D., Terence P. Thornberry, and Marvin D. Krohn. 2003. "Desistance as a Developmental Process: A Comparison of Static and Dynamic Approaches." *Journal of Quantitative Criminology* 19: 129–153.

Carlsson, Christoffer. 2013. "Masculinities, Persistence, and Desistance." *Criminology* 51: 661–693.

Caspi, Avshalom. 1987. "Personality in the Life Course." *Journal of Personality and Social Psychology* 53: 1203–1213.

Caspi, Avshalom and Daryl J. Bem. 1990. "Personality Continuity and Change across the Life Course." Pp. 549–575 in *Handbook of Personality: Theory and Research*, ed. L. A. Pervin. New York: Guilford.

Caspi, Avshalom, Daryl J. Bem, and Glen H. Elder, Jr. 1989. "Continuities and Consequences of Interactional Styles across the Life Course." *Journal of Personality* 57: 375–406.

Caspi, Avshalom, Glen H. Elder, Jr., and Daryl J. Bem. 1987. "Moving Against the World: Life-Course Patterns of Explosive Children." *Developmental Psychology* 23: 308–313.

Chen, Xiaojin and Michele Adams. 2010. "Are Teen Delinquency Abstainers Social Introverts? A Test of Moffitt's Theory." *Journal of Research in Crime and Delinquency* 47: 439–468.

Cohen, Jacqueline. 1986. "Research on Criminal Careers: Individual Frequency Rates and Offense Seriousness." Pp. 292–418 in *Criminal Careers and "Career Criminals,"* vol. 1, ed. A. Blumstein, J. Cohen, J. A. Roth, and C. A. Visher. Washington, DC: National Academy Press.

DeLisi, Matt. 2006. "Zeroing in on Early Arrest Onset: Results from a Population of Extreme Career Criminals." *Journal of Criminal Justice* 34: 17–26.

DeLisi, Matt, Tricia K. Neppl, Brenda J. Lohman, Michael G. Vaughn, and Jeffrey J. Shook. 2013. "Early Starters: Which Type of Criminal Onset Matters Most for Delinquent Careers?" *Journal of Criminal Justice* 41: 12–17.

Doherty, Elaine Eggleston and Margaret E. Ensminger. 2013. "Marriage and Offending among a Cohort of Disadvantaged African Americans." *Journal of Research in Crime and Delinquency* 50: 104–131.

Eggleston, Elaine P. and John H. Laub. 2002. "The Onset of Adult Offending: A Neglected Dimension of the Criminal Career." *Journal of Criminal Justice* 30: 603–622.

Elliott, Delbert S., David Huizinga, and Suzanne S. Ageton. 1985. *Explaining Delinquency and Drug Use.* Beverly Hills, CA: Sage.

Elliott, Delbert S., David Huizinga, and Scott Menard. 1989. *Multiple Problem Youth: Delinquency, Substance Use, and Mental Health Problems.* New York: Springer-Verlag.

Farrington, David P. 1991. "Childhood Aggression and Adult Violence: Early Precursors and Later-Life Outcomes." Pp. 5–29 in *The Development and Treatment of Childhood Aggression*, ed. D. Pepler and K. Rubin. Hillsdale, NJ: Lawrence Erlbaum.

Farrington, David P. 1998. "Predictors, Causes, and Correlates of Male Youth Violence." Pp. 421–475 in *Youth Violence*, ed. M. Tonry and M. Harrison Moore. University of Chicago Press.

Farrington, David P., Rolf Loeber, Delbert S. Elliott, J. D. Hawkins, Denise B. Kandel, M. Klein, Joan McCord, David C. Rowe, and Richard E. Tremblay. 1990. "Advancing Knowledge about the Onset of Delinquency and Crime." In *Advances in Clinical Child Psychology*, vol. 13, ed. B. B. Lahey and A. E. Kazdin. New York: Plenum.

Farrington, David P. and Donald J. West. 1995. "Effects of Marriage, Separation, and Children on Offending by Adult Males." Pp. 249–281 in *Current Perspectives on Aging and the Life Cycle*, vol. 4, ed. Z. Blau and J. Hagan. Greenwich, CT: JAI Press.

Gadd, David and Stephen Farrall. 2004. "Criminal Careers, Desistance and Subjectivity: Interpreting Men's Narratives of Change." *Theoretical Criminology* 8: 123–156.

Giordano, Peggy C., Stephen A. Cernkovich, and Donna D. Holland. 2003. "Changes in Friendship Relations over the Life Course: Implications for Desistance from Crime." *Criminology* 41: 293–327.

Giordano, Peggy C., Stephen A. Cernkovich, and Jennifer L. Rudolph. 2002. "Gender, Crime, and Desistance: Toward a Theory of Cognitive Transformation." *American Journal of Sociology* 107: 990–1064.

Gomez-Smith, Zenta and Alex R. Piquero. 2005. "An Examination of Adult Onset Offending." *Journal of Criminal Justice* 33: 515–525.

Gottfredson, Michael R. and Travis Hirschi. 1986. "The True Value of Lambda Would Appear to Be Zero: An Essay on Career Criminals, Criminal Careers, Selective Incapacitation, Cohort Studies, and Related Topics." *Criminology* 24: 213–233.

Gottfredson, Michael R. and Travis Hirschi. 1988. "Science, Public Policy, and the Career Paradigm." *Criminology* 26: 37–55.

Gottfredson, Michael R. and Travis Hirschi. 1990. *A General Theory of Crime*. Stanford University Press.

Hirschfield, Paul, Tina Maschi, Helene Raskin White, and Rolf Loeber. 2006. "Mental Health and Juvenile Arrests: Criminality, Criminalization, or Compassion?" *Criminology* 44: 593–630.

Horney, Julie, D. Wayne Osgood, and Ineke Haen Marshall. 1995. "Criminal Careers in the Short-Term: Intra-Individual Variability in Crime and Its Relation to Local Life Circumstances." *American Sociological Review* 60: 655–673.

Horney, Julie, Patrick H. Tolan, and David Weisburd. 2012. "Contextual Influences." Pp. 86–117 in *From Juvenile Delinquency to Adult Crime: Criminal Careers, Justice Policy and Prevention*, ed. R. Loeber and D. Farrington. New York: Oxford University Press.

Huizinga, David A. and Cynthia Jakob-Chien. 1998. "The Contemporaneous Co-Occurrence of Serious and Violent Juvenile Offending and Other Problem Behaviors." Pp. 47–67 in *Serious and Violent Juvenile Offenders: Risk Factors and Successful Interventions*, ed. R. Loeber and D. Farrington. Thousand Oaks, CA: Sage.

Huizinga, David A., Rolf Loeber, Terence P. Thornberry, and Lynn Cothern. 2000. "Co-Occurrence of Delinquency and Other Problem Behaviors." *Juvenile Justice Bulletin*. Washington, DC: Office of Juvenile Justice and Delinquency Prevention.

Inciardi, James A., Ruth Horowitz, and Anne E. Pottieger. 1993. *Street Kids, Street Drugs, and Street Crime: An Examination of Drug Use and Serious Delinquency in Miami*. Belmont, CA: Wadsworth.

Jennings, Wesley and Jennifer M. Reingle. 2012. "On the Number and Shape of Developmental/Life-Course Violence, Aggression, and Delinquency Trajectories: A State-of-the-Art Review." *Journal of Criminal Justice* 40: 472–489.

Johnson, Monica Kirkpatrick, Robert Crosnoe, and Glen H. Elder, Jr. 2001. "Students' Attachment and Academic Engagement: The Role of Race and Ethnicity." *Sociology of Education* 74: 318–340.

Johnston, Lloyd D., Patrick M. O'Malley, and Leslie K. Eveland. 1978. "Drugs and Delinquency: A Search for Causal Connections." Pp. 137–156 in *Longitudinal Research on Drug Use*, ed. D. B. Kandel. Washington, DC: Hemisphere.

Junger, Marianne and Maja Dekovic. 2003. "Crime as Risk-Taking: Co-Occurrence of Delinquent Behavior, Health-Endangering Behaviors, and Problem Behaviors." Pp. 213–248 in *Control Theories of*

Crime and Delinquency: Advances in Criminological Theory, vol. 12, ed. C. L. Britt and M. R. Gottfredson. New Brunswick, NJ: Transaction.

Kandel, Denise B. 1988. "Issues of Sequencing of Adolescent Drug Use and Other Problem Behaviors." *Drugs and Society* 3: 55–76.

Kandel, Denise B., R. C. Kessler, and R. Z. Margulies. 1978. "Antecedents of Adolescent Initiation into Stages of Drug Use: A Developmental Analysis." *Journal of Youth and Adolescence* 7: 13–40.

Kandel, Denise B., Ora Simcha-Fagan, and Mark Davies. 1986. "Risk Factors for Delinquency and Illicit Drug Use from Adolescence to Young Adulthood." *Journal of Drug Issues* 16: 67–90.

Kelley, Barbara Tatem, Rolf Loeber, Kate Keenan, and Mary DeLamatre. 1997. "Developmental Pathways in Boys' Disruptive and Delinquent Behavior." *Juvenile Justice Bulletin*. Washington, DC: Office of Juvenile Justice and Delinquency Prevention.

Kreager, Derek A., Ross L. Matsueda, and Elena A. Erosheva. 2010. "Motherhood and Criminal Desistance in Disadvantaged Neighborhoods." *Criminology* 48: 221–258.

Krohn, Marvin D., Jeffrey T. Ward, Terence P. Thornberry, Alan J. Lizotte, and Rebekah Chu. 2011. "The Cascading Effects of Adolescent Gang Involvement across the Life Course." *Criminology* 49: 991–1028.

Laub, John H., Daniel S. Nagin, and Robert J. Sampson. 1998. "Trajectories of Change in Criminal Offending: Good Marriages and the Desistance Process." *American Sociological Review* 63: 225–238.

Laub, John H. and Robert J. Sampson. 2001. "Understanding Desistance from Crime." Pp. 1–69 in *Crime and Justice: A Review of Research*, vol. 28, ed. M. Tonry. University of Chicago Press.

Laub, John H. and Robert J. Sampson. 2003. *Shared Beginnings, Divergent Lives: Delinquent Boys to Age 70*. Cambridge, MA: Harvard University Press.

Lebel, Thomas P., Ross Burnett, Shadd Maruna, and Shawn Bushway. 2008. "The 'Chicken and Egg' of Subjective and Social Factors in Desistance from Crime." *European Journal of Criminology* 5: 131–159.

LeBlanc, Marc and Marcel Frechette. 1989. *Male Criminal Activity from Childhood through Youth: Multilevel and Developmental Perspectives*. New York: Springer-Verlag.

LeBlanc, Marc and Rolf Loeber. 1998. "Developmental Criminology Updated." Pp. 115–197 in *Crime and Justice: An Annual Review of Research*, vol. 23, ed. M. Tonry. University of Chicago Press.

Liu, Jiayi, Brian Francis, and Keith Soothill. 2011. "A Longitudinal Study of Escalation in Crime Seriousness." *Journal of Quantitative Criminology* 27: 175–196.

Loeber, Rolf. 1996. "Developmental Continuity, Change, and Pathways in Male Juvenile Problem Behaviors and Delinquency." Pp. 1–27 in *Delinquency and Crime: Current Theories*, ed. J. D. Hawkins. Cambridge University Press.

Loeber, Rolf and David P. Farrington (eds.). 2001. *Child Delinquents: Development, Intervention and Service Needs*. Thousand Oaks, CA: Sage.

Loeber, Rolf, David P. Farrington, Magda Stouthamer-Loeber, and Helene Raskin White. 2008. *Violence and Serious Theft: Development and Prediction from Childhood to Adulthood*. New York: Routledge.

Loeber, Rolf and Marc LeBlanc. 1990. "Toward a Developmental Criminology." Pp. 375–437 in *Crime and Justice: An Annual Review of Research*, vol. 12, ed. M. Tonry and N. Morris. University of Chicago Press.

Loeber, Rolf and Magda Stouthamer-Loeber. 1987. "Prediction." Pp. 325–382 in *Handbook of Juvenile Delinquency*, ed. H. C. Quay. New York: Wiley.

Loeber, Rolf, Magda Stouthamer-Loeber, and Stephanie M. Green. 1991. "Age at Onset of Problem Behavior in Boys, and Later Disruptive and Delinquent Behaviors." *Criminal Behavior and Mental Health* 1: 229–246.

Loeber, Rolf, Phen Wung, Kate Keenan, Bruce Giroux, Magda Stouthamer-Loeber, Welmoet B. Van Kammen, and Barbara Maughan. 1993. "Developmental Pathways in Disruptive Child Behavior." *Development and Psychopathology* 5: 103–133.

McCurley, Carl and Howard N. Snyder. 2008. "Co-Occurrence of Substance Use Behaviors in Youth." *Juvenile Justice Bulletin*. Washington, DC: Office of Juvenile Justice and Delinquency Prevention.

MacDonald, John M., Amelia Haviland, Rajeev Ramchand, Andrew R. Morral, and Alex R. Piquero. 2014. "Linking Specialization and Seriousness in Criminal Careers." *Advances in Life Course Research* 20: 43–55.

McGloin, Jean Marie, Christopher J. Sullivan, and Alex R. Piquero. 2009. "Aggregating to Versatility? Transitions among Offender Types in the Short Term." *British Journal of Criminology* 49: 243–264.

McGloin, Jean Marie, Christopher J. Sullivan, Alex R. Piquero, and Travis C. Pratt. 2007. "Local Life Circumstances and Offending Specialization/Versatility." *Journal of Research in Crime and Delinquency* 44: 321–346.

Maruna, Shadd. 2001. *Making Good: How Ex-Offenders Reform and Reclaim Their Lives.* Washington, DC: American Psychological Association Books.

Massoglia, Michael and Christopher Uggen. 2007. "Subjective Desistance and the Transition to Adulthood." *Journal of Contemporary Criminal Justice* 23: 90–103.

Melde, Chris and Finn-Aage Esbensen. 2011. "Gang Membership as a Turning Point in the Life Course." *Criminology* 49: 513–552.

Moffitt, Terrie E. 1990. "The Neuropsychology of Delinquency: A Critical Review of Theory and Research." Pp. 99–169 in *Crime and Justice: A Review of Research*, vol. 12, ed. M. Tonry and N. Morris. University of Chicago Press.

Moffitt, Terrie E. 1993. "Adolescence-Limited and Life-Course-Persistent Antisocial Behavior: A Developmental Taxonomy." *Psychological Review* 100: 674–701.

Moffitt, Terrie E. 1997. "Adolescence-Limited and Life-Course-Persistent Offending: A Complementary Pair of Developmental Theories." Pp. 11–54 in *Developmental Theories*, ed. T. P. Thornberry. New Brunswick, NJ: Transaction.

Moffitt, Terrie E. 2006a. "Life-Course-Persistent versus Adolescence-Limited Antisocial Behavior." Pp. 570–598 in *Developmental Psychopathology*. 2nd edn, vol. 3: *Risk, Disorder, and Adaptation*, ed. D. Cicchetti and D. J. Cohen. Hoboken, NJ: Wiley.

Moffitt, Terrie E. 2006b. "A Review of Research on the Taxonomy of Life-Course Persistent Versus Adolescence-Limited Antisocial Behavior." Pp. 277–311 in *Taking Stock: The Status of Criminological Theory (Advances in Criminological Theory*, vol. 15, ed. F. Cullen, J. Wright, and K. Blevins. New Brunswick, NJ: Transaction.

Moffitt, Terrie E., Avshalom Caspi, Honalee Harrington, and Barry J. Milne. 2002. "Males on the Life-Course-Persistent and Adolescence-Limited Antisocial Pathways: Follow-Up at Age 26 Years." *Development and Psychopathology* 14: 179–207.

Morizot, Julien and Marc LeBlanc. 2007. "Behavioral, Self, and Social Control Predictors of Desistance from Crime: A Test of Launch and Contemporaneous Effect Models." *Journal of Contemporary Criminal Justice* 23: 50–71.

Mulvey, Edward P., Laurence Steinberg, Jeffrey Fagan, Elizabeth Cauffman, Alex R. Piquero, Carol A. Schubert, Sandra H. Losoya, George P. Knight, Robert Brame, and Thomas Hecker. 2004. "Theory and Research on Desistance from Antisocial Activity among Serious Adolescent Offenders." *Youth Violence and Juvenile Justice* 2: 213–236.

Nagin, Daniel S. and David P. Farrington. 1992a. "The Stability of Criminal Potential from Childhood to Adulthood." *Criminology* 30: 235–260.

Nagin, Daniel S. and David P. Farrington. 1992b. "The Onset and Persistence of Offending." *Criminology* 30: 501–523.

Nagin, Daniel S., David P. Farrington, and Terrie E. Moffitt. 1995. "Life-Course Trajectories of Different Types of Offenders." *Criminology* 33: 111–139.

Nagin, Daniel S. and Raymond Paternoster. 1991. "On the Relationship of Past to Future Participation in Delinquency." *Criminology* 29: 163–189.

Nieuwbeerta, Paul, Arjan A. J. Blokland, Alex R. Piquero, and Gary Sweeten. 2011. "A Life-Course Analysis of Offense Specialization Across Age: Introducing a New Method for Studying Individual Specialization Over the Life Course." *Crime and Delinquency* 57: 3–28.

Olweus, Daniel. 1979. "Stability of Aggressive Reaction Patterns in Males: A Review." *Psychological Bulletin* 86: 852–875.

Osgood, D. Wayne, Lloyd D. Johnston, Patrick M. O'Malley, and Jerald G. Bachman. 1988. "The Generality of Deviance in late Adolescence and Early Adulthood." *American Sociological Review* 53: 81–93.

Osgood, D. Wayne and David C. Rowe. 1994. "Bridging Criminal Careers, Theory, and Policy through Latent Variable Models of Individual Offending." *Criminology* 32: 517–554.

Osgood, D. Wayne and Christopher J. Schreck. 2007. "A New Method for Studying the Extent, Stability, and Predictors of Individual Specialization in Violence." *Criminology* 45: 273–312.

Paternoster, Raymond and Robert Brame. 1997. "Multiple Routes to Delinquency? A Test of Developmental and General Theories of Crime." *Criminology* 35: 49–84.

Paternoster, Raymond and Shawn Bushway. 2009. "Desistance and the 'Feared Self': Toward an Identity Theory of Criminal Desistance." *Journal of Criminal Law and Criminology* 99: 1103–1156.

Patterson, Gerald R. 1986. "Maternal Rejection: Determinant or Product for Deviant Child Behavior?" Pp. 73–94 in *Relationships and Development*, ed. W. W. Hartup and Z. Rubin. Hillsdale, NJ: Lawrence Erlbaum.

Patterson, Gerald R. and Lou Bank. 1989. "Some Amplifying Mechanisms for Pathologic Process in Families." Pp. 167–210 in *Systems and Development: The Minnesota Symposia on Child Psychology*, vol. 22, ed. M. R. Gunnar and E. Thelem. Hillsdale, NJ: Lawrence Erlbaum.

Patterson, Gerald R., Deborah Capaldi, and Lou Bank. 1991. "An Early Starter Model for Predicting Delinquency." Pp. 139–168 in *The Development and Treatment of Childhood Aggression*, ed. D. Pepler and K. Rubin. Hillsdale, NJ: Lawrence Erlbaum.

Patterson, Gerald R., L. Crosby, and Samuel Vuchinich. 1992. "Predicting Risk for Early Police Arrest." *Journal of Quantitative Criminology* 8: 335–355.

Patterson, Gerald R., Barbara D. DeBaryshe, and Elizabeth Ramsey. 1989. "A Developmental Perspective on Antisocial Behavior." *American Psychologist* 44: 329–335.

Patterson, Gerald R. and Karen Yoerger. 1993. "Developmental Models for Delinquent Behavior." Pp. 140–172 in *Mental Disorder and Crime*, ed. S. Hodgins. Newbury Park, CA: Sage.

Piquero, Alex R. 2008. "Taking Stock of Developmental Trajectories of Criminal Activity over the Life Course." Pp. 23–78 in *The Long View of Crime: A Synthesis of Longitudinal Research*, ed. A. M. Liberman. New York: Springer.

Piquero, Alex R., Robert Brame, and Donald Lynam. 2004. "Studying Criminal Career Length through Early Adulthood among Serious Offenders." *Crime and Delinquency* 50: 412–435.

Piquero, Alex R., Robert Brame, Paul Mazerolle, and Rudy Haapenan. 2002. "Crime in Emerging Adulthood." *Criminology* 40: 137–169.

Piquero, Alex R. and Timothy Brezina. 2001. "Testing Moffitt's Account of Adolescence-Limited Delinquency." *Criminology* 39: 353–370.

Piquero, Alex R., David P. Farrington, and Alfred Blumstein. 2003. "The Criminal Career Paradigm." Pp. 359–506 in *Crime and Justice: A Review of Research*, vol. 30, ed. M. Tonry. University of Chicago Press.

Piquero, Alex R., David P. Farrington, Daniel S. Nagin, and Terrie E. Moffitt. 2010. "Trajectories of Offending and Their Relation to Life Failure in Late Middle Age: Findings from the Cambridge Study in Delinquent Development." *Journal of Research in Crime and Delinquency* 47: 151–173.

Piquero, Alex R., J. David Hawkins, and Lila Kazemian. 2012. "Criminal Career Patterns." Pp. 14–46 in *From Juvenile Delinquency to Adult Crime: Criminal Careers, Justice Policy and Prevention*, ed. R. Loeber and D. Farrington. New York: Oxford University Press.

Piquero, Alex R., Terrie E. Moffitt, and Bradley E. Wright. 2007. "Self-Control and Criminal Career Dimensions." *Journal of Contemporary Criminal Justice* 23: 72–89.

Piquero, Alex R., Raymond Paternoster, Robert Brame, Paul Mazerolle, and Charles W. Dean. 1999. "Onset Age and Offense Specialization." *Journal of Research in Crime and Delinquency* 36: 275–299.

Piquero, Nicole Leeper and Terrie E. Moffitt. 2014. "Can Childhood Factors Predict Workplace Deviance?" *Justice Quarterly* 31: 664–692.

Robins, Lee N. 1978. "Sturdy Childhood Predictors of Adult Antisocial Behaviour: Replications from Longitudinal Studies." *Psychological Medicine* 8: 611–622.

Rojek, Dean G. and Maynard L. Erickson. 1982. "Delinquent Careers: A Test of the Career Escalation Model." *Criminology* 20: 5–28.

Rulison, Kelly L., Derek A. Kreager, and D. Wayne Osgood. 2014. "Delinquency and Peer Acceptance in Adolescence: A Within-Person Test of Moffitt's Hypotheses." *Developmental Psychology* 50: 2437–2448.

Sampson, Robert J. and John H. Laub. 1990. "Crime and Deviance over the Life Course: The Salience of Adult Social Bonds." *American Sociological Review* 55: 609–627.

Sampson, Robert J. and John H. Laub. 1992. "Crime and Deviance in the Life Course." *Annual Review of Sociology* 18: 63–84.

Sampson, Robert J. and John H. Laub. 1993. *Crime in the Making: Pathways and Turning Points Through Life.* Cambridge, MA: Harvard University Press.

Sampson, Robert J. and John H. Laub. 2002. "Life-Course Desisters? Trajectories of Crime Among Delinquent Boys Followed to Age 70." *Criminology* 41: 555–592.

Sampson, Robert J., John H. Laub, and Christopher Wimer. 2006. "Does Marriage Reduce Crime? A Counterfactual Approach to Within-Individual Causal Effects." *Criminology* 44: 465–508.

Schroeder, Ryan D., Peggy C Giordano, and Stephen A. Cernkovich. 2007. "Drug Use and Desistance Processes." *Criminology* 45: 191–222.

Schubert, Carol A., Edward P. Mulvey, Laurence Steinberg, Elizabeth Cauffman, Sandra H. Losoya, Thomas Hecker, Laurie Chassin, and geoge P. Knight. 2004. "Operational Lessons from the Pathways to Desistance Project." *Youth Violence and Juvenile Justice* 2: 237–255.

Shover, Neal. 1996. *Great Pretenders: Pursuits and Careers of Persistent Thieves.* Boulder, CO: Westview Press.

Simons, Ronald L., Chyi-In Wu, Rand D. Conger, and Frederick O. Lorenz. 1994. "Two Routes to Delinquency: Differences between Early and Late Starters in the Impact of Parenting and Deviant Peers." *Criminology* 32: 247–276.

Skardhamar, Torbjoern and Jukka Savolainen. 2014. "Changes in Criminal Offending around the Time of Job Entry: A Study of Employment and Desistance." *Criminology* 52: 263–291.

Smith, Douglas A. and Robert Brame. 1994. "On the Initiation and Continuation of Delinquency." *Criminology* 32: 607–629.

Smith, Douglas A., Christy A. Visher, and G. Roger Jarjoura. 1991. "Dimensions of Delinquency: Exploring the Correlates of Participation, Frequency, and Persistence of Delinquent Behavior." *Journal of Research in Crime and Delinquency* 28: 6–32.

Stattin, Haakan, Margaret Kerr, and Lars R. Bergman. 2010. "On the Utility of Moffitt's Typology Trajectories in Long-Term Perspective." *European Journal of Criminology* 7: 521–545.

Steinberg, Laurence, Elizabeth Cauffman, and Kathryn C. Monahan. 2015. "Psychosocial Maturity and Desistance from Crime in a Sample of Serious Juvenile Offenders." *Juvenile Justice Bulletin.* Washington, DC: Office of Juvenile Justice and Delinquency Prevention.

Sweeten, Gary, David C. Pyrooz, and Alex R. Piquero. 2013. "Disengaging from Gangs and Desistance from Crime." *Justice Quarterly* 30: 469–500.

Thornberry, Terence P. 1997. *Developmental Theories of Crime and Delinquency.* New Brunswick, NJ: Transaction.

Thornberry, Terence P. 2005. "Explaining Multiple Patterns of Offending Across the Life Course and Across Generations." *Annals of the Academy of Political and Social Science* 602: 156–195.

Thornberry, Terence P., David Huizinga, and Rolf Loeber. 1995. "The Prevention of Serious Delinquency and Violence: Implications from the Program of Research on the Causes and Correlates of Delinquency." Pp. 213–237 in *Serious, Violent, and Chronic Juvenile Offenders: A Sourcebook,* ed. J. C. Howell, B. Krisberg, J. D. Hawkins, and J. J. Wilson. Thousand Oaks, CA: Sage.

Thornberry, Terence P., David Huizinga, and Rolf Loeber. 2004. "The Causes and Correlates Studies: Findings and Policy Implications." *Juvenile Justice* 9: 3–19.

Tolan, Patrick H. 1987. "Implications of Age of Onset for Delinquency Risk." *Journal of Abnormal Child Psychology* 15: 47–65.

Tolan, Patrick H. and Peter Thomas. 1995. "The Implications of Age of Onset for Delinquency Risk II: Longitudinal Data." *Journal of Abnormal Child Psychology* 23: 157–181.

Tracy, Paul E., Marvin E. Wolfgang, and Robert M. Figlio. 1990. *Delinquency Careers in Two Birth Cohorts*. New York: Plenum Press.

Tzoumakis, Stacy, Patrick Lussier, Marc LeBlanc, and Garth Davies. 2013. "Onset, Offending Trajectories, and Crime Specialization in Violence." *Youth Violence and Juvenile Justice* 11: 143–164.

Uggen, Christopher. 2000. "Work as a Turning Point in the Life Course of Criminals: A Duration Model of Age, Employment, and Recidivism." *American Sociological Review* 65: 529–546.

Uggen, Christopher and Irving Piliavin. 1998. "Asymmetrical Causation and Criminal Desistance." *Journal of Criminal Law and Criminology* 88: 1399–1422.

Walters, Glenn D. 2014. "Pathways to Early Delinquency: Exploring the Individual and Collective Contributions of Difficult Temperament, Low Maternal Involvement, and Externalizing Behavior." *Journal of Criminal Justice* 42: 321–326.

Warr, Mark. 1998. "Life-Course Transition and Desistance from Crime." *Criminology* 36: 183–215.

White, Helene Raskin. 1992. "Early Problem Behavior and Later Drug Problems." *Journal of Research in Crime and Delinquency* 29: 412–429.

White, Helene Raskin, Robert J. Pandina, and Randy L. LaGrange. 1987. "Longitudinal Predictors of Serious Substance Use and Delinquency." *Criminology* 25: 715–740.

White, Jennifer L., Terrie E. Moffitt, Felton Earls, Lee N. Robbins, and Phil A. Silva. 1990. "How Early Can We Tell? Predictors of Childhood Conduct Disorder and Adolescent Delinquency." *Criminology* 28: 507–533.

Wish, Eric. 1990. "U.S. Drug Policy in the 1990s: Insights from New Data from Arrestees." *International Journal of the Addictions* 25: 1–15.

Wolfgang, Marvin E., Robert M. Figlio, and Thorsten Sellin. 1972. *Delinquency in a Birth Cohort*. University of Chicago Press.

Wolfgang, Marvin E., Terence P. Thornberry, and Robert M. Figlio. 1987. *From Boy to Man, From Delinquency to Crime*. University of Chicago Press.

Zara, Georgia and David P. Farrington. 2009. "Childhood and Adolescent Predictors of Late Onset Criminal Careers." *Journal of Youth and Adolescence* 38: 287–300.

Zara, Georgia and David P. Farrington. 2010. "A Longitudinal Analysis of Early Risk Factors for Adult-Onset Offending: What Predicts a Delayed Criminal Career." *Criminal Behaviour and Mental Health* 20: 257–273.

Part III

Explaining delinquent behavior

Chapter 7

Biosocial criminology

Chapter preview

Topics:

- Early biological approaches: focusing on physical characteristics
- Contemporary biological approaches in biosocial criminology
- Personality and biosocial criminology
- Intelligence and delinquency

Terms:

- atavism
- stigmata
- somatotypes
- biological determinism
- environmental determinism
- nature–nurture debate
- biosocial criminology
- nature–nurture interaction
- prefrontal cortex
- executive function
- autonomic system underarousal
- neurotransmitters
- fight-or-flight response
- testosterone
- behavioral genetics
- heritability
- personality
- agreeableness
- conscientiousness
- intelligence quotient (IQ)

Chapter learning objectives

After completing this chapter, students should be able to:

- Provide an overview of the historical development of thought regarding biological factors and criminal behavior.
- Identify a number of physical characteristics associated with criminality that were advanced by early biological approaches.

- Describe nature–nurture interaction as it applies to contemporary biosocial criminology.
  - Identify three contemporary approaches in biosocial criminology that are used to study antisocial behavior.
  - Identify and describe key dimensions of personality and their roles in delinquency causation.
  - Assess the role of intelligence in delinquent behavior.

Case in point: the neurological underpinning of psychopathy

Juvenile delinquency is sometimes attributed to abnormal brain structure and function. The following medical cases, offered by David Rowe in his book *Biology and Crime*, illustrate how the physical structure of the brain affects psychological functioning. This important link between the body's neurological structure – including the central and peripheral nervous systems – and psychological functioning is referred to as *neuropsychology*. This chapter addresses the role of biological and psychological factors in delinquent behavior.

Two medical cases have been studied by the neurologist Antonio Damasio and his colleagues that illustrate a possible neurological underpinning for psychopathy. Their subjects, a man and a woman, had both suffered injuries to the prefrontal cortex during infancy. The prefrontal cortex, located just behind the eye sockets and above the bridge of the nose, is involved in planning a sequence of actions and in anticipating the future. The female subject was run over by a car when she was 15 months old. The male subject had a brain tumor removed from his prefrontal area when he was 3 months old. Both subjects grew up in stable, middle-class families with college-educated parents and had normal biological siblings, but neither made a satisfactory social adjustment; neither had friends and both were dependent on support from their parents. Neither subject had any plans for the future. The woman was a compulsive liar; she stole from her parents and shoplifted; her early and risky sexual behavior led to a pregnancy by age 18. By age 9, the male subject had committed minor theft and aggressive delinquent acts; he had no empathy for others....

Most surprisingly, these brain-injured victims failed to understand the difference between right and wrong; they lacked a sense of social norms and of how to act in social situations. Their moral blindness contrasts with the thought processes of adults who have brain damage in the same region and who display symptoms of psychopathy but understand without any difficulty the moral difference between right and wrong.

Source: Rowe (2002: 69–70).

The individual has long been the center of attention when trying to explain delinquent behavior. Early versions of positivist criminology from the late 1800s and early 1900s adopted the view that delinquents and criminals were fundamentally different from the average person. Using scientific methods, researchers sought to identify these biological and psychological differences. These scholars claimed that criminals were marked by individual "pathologies," such as physiological abnormalities, mental inferiority, insanity, and a lack of "rational and temperate habits" (Beirne 1987: 1159; Walsh 2002; Fishbein 2001; Jacobson and Rowe 2000).

The contemporary study that connects individual traits and characteristics to antisocial behavior is called *biosocial criminology*. The approach is highly interdisciplinary, attempting to consider the biological, psychological, and sociological factors that collectively predispose some individuals to delinquency and crime. This chapter explores scientific efforts to discover biological and psychological forces at work in the individual as they interface with the environment and together influence behavior.

Early biological approaches: focusing on physical characteristics

Early biological approaches tried to identify the physical characteristics that distinguished criminal from non-criminals. Differences in physical appearance, biological make-up, and moral sentiment were thought to be associated with behavior.

Physical appearance and biological differences

Physical appearance was historically thought to reveal the nature and character of the individual. Unusual or atypical physical characteristics were thought to indicate biological defects, abnormalities, and overall inferiority. According to this line of reasoning, criminals have a physical appearance that sets them apart from law-abiding citizens, and this difference is indicative of biological difference between criminals and non-criminals. Criminal behavior, then, is a manifestation of these biological differences. This view of crime was evident, for example, in the work of Italian physician Franz Joseph Gall (1758–1828), who studied the shape of the skull and its link to specific traits and to criminal behavior (Curran and Renzetti 2007).

Search for "criminal man"

Cesare Lombroso (1835–1909), an Italian physician and professor of forensic medicine, is often called "the father of modern criminology" (Wolfgang 1973: 232; Rafter 2008). He, too, argued that there was a relationship between the physical characteristics of individuals and their behavior, but his exploration went much further than Gall's to include the anatomy and physiology of the human body, especially the brain. He also tied objective biological observations to the theory of evolution advanced by Charles Darwin just a few years prior to Lombroso's first major publication. In fact, Darwin was the first to use the term "atavistic man," a concept that Lombroso developed into a theory of crime (Martin, Mutchnick, and Austin 1990).

Lombroso's thesis, as initially advanced in *L'Uomo delinquente* (*Criminal Man*, 1876), was that criminals were physically distinct from non-criminals – criminals were a particular physical type. According to Lombroso, this difference arose because criminals were not as evolved as other individuals and their physical differences represented a reversion to a more primitive stage of evolution. Using Darwin's term, Lombroso referred to this biological reversion as **atavism**, whereby physical traits predisposed certain individuals to crime.

Lombroso's observations on the biological characteristics of criminals were based on extensive study involving autopsies of 66 deceased male criminals and examination of 832 living, serious criminals, both males and females. This latter group of criminals was then compared to non-criminals. Lombroso observed that criminals displayed distinctive physical characteristics, called **stigmata**, which resembled "savages" and lower animals. Criminal stigmata, according to Lombroso, included asymmetry of the face, large jaws and cheekbones, unusually large or small ears that stand out from the head, fleshy lips, abnormal teeth, flattened nose, angular form of the skull, scanty beard but general hairiness of the body, and excessively long arms. Lombroso contended that although these stigmata did not cause criminality, they were useful for identifying individuals with atavism (Beirne and Messerschmidt 2014; Bernard, Snipes, and Gerould 2009; Curran and Renzetti 2007; Lombroso [1911] 1972).

Lombroso expanded his views throughout subsequent editions of *L'Uomo delinquente*. Even though each successive edition gave greater attention to environmental explanations, Lombroso never abandoned the idea of a born criminal type. Gradually, he developed four major categories of criminals: (1) born criminals – people with atavistic characteristics, who accounted for about one-third of all offenders; (2) criminals by passion, who committed crime for anger, love, or honor, being propelled to crime by "irresistible forces"; (3) insane criminals, who committed crime as a "consequence of an alteration of the brain ... [which] makes them unable to discriminate between right and wrong"; and (4) occasional criminals, "who do not seek the occasion for the crime, but are almost drawn into it, or fall into the meshes of the code for very insignificant reasons" (Lombroso, quoted in Martin et al. 1990: 30, 31). This last criminal category was the broadest and included three subtypes: pseudocriminals – those who committed crime involuntarily, such as in self-defense; criminaloids – those whose predisposition to crime was stimulated by environmental circumstances or opportunities; and habitual criminals – those who regularly violated the law as a part of their day-to-day life, with little guilt or remorse (Lilly, Cullen, and Ball 2015; Curran and Renzetti 2007; Martin et al. 1990).

Two of Lombroso's students extended his work into new realms. Raffaele Garofalo (1851–1934) made extensive legal application of Lombroso's theory and Enrico Ferri (1856–1929) developed a sociological perspective on it. Both were famous as criminologists in their own right (Martin et al. 1990).

Legal applications of Lombroso's ideas

During his career, Raffaele Garofalo was a lawyer, prosecutor, magistrate, professor of criminal law, and prominent member of the Italian government. Because of his background in law, Garofalo was most interested in the legal implications of Lombroso's ideas, particularly as they related to legal definitions of crime and appropriate sanctions for criminals. Garofalo, however, was more concerned with psychological deficiencies than with physical anomalies of criminals. He argued that criminals lacked basic moral sentiments because they did not fear punishment and they lacked self-control. He believed that these moral deficiencies were a result of heredity and tradition, and, as a result, the only solution to this evolutionary problem was the incapacitation or elimination of the "unfit" through legislated criminal sanctions (Martin et al. 1990; Garofalo 1914).

Criminal sociology

While Lombroso emphasized biological characteristics of individuals, Enrico Ferri's *Criminal Sociology* gave attention to the interrelatedness of three different sets of causal factors in crime: "those in the physical or geographic environment, those in the constitution of the individual and those in the social environment" (Ferri, quoted in Martin et al. 1990: 38; Ferri 1917). The *physical or geographic environment* included factors such as land forms, natural resources, climate, and vegetation. Drawing from the work of his teacher, Lombroso, Ferri also pointed to the importance of the "*constitution of the individual*," referring to both inherited and acquired traits such as age, sex, and psychological makeup. The *social environment* was composed of factors such as economic status, racial composition, population density, and culture. Because of the interrelatedness of these causal factors, Ferri argued that crime could be controlled by social changes. In particular, he believed that government was responsible for creating better living and working conditions – conditions that would reduce the occurrence of crime (Lilly et al. 2015).

The work of Lombroso, Garofalo, and Ferri pushed the study of crime away from its classical roots to a scientific study of the criminal and the conditions under which crime is committed (Wolfgang 1973). Although Lombroso initially emphasized biological characteristics that distinguished criminals from non-criminals, all three criminologists moved toward "a multi-factor explanation of crime that included not only heredity but also social, cultural, and economic variables" (Lilly et al. 2015: 22).

Physique, temperament, and delinquency

William Sheldon (1898–1977) was perhaps the last great believer in biological determinism, maintaining that the primary determinants of behavior are constitutional and inherited. Sheldon believed that body physique was an accurate and reliable indicator of personality and consequently a predictor of behavior. He spent much of his career as a psychologist developing a classification system of body types and the personality patterns, or temperaments, which are associated with them (Martin et al. 1990). Sheldon identified three primary structures of human physique, or **somatotypes** – *endomorphy*, *mesomorphy*, and *ectomorphy* – which he then connected to personality temperament. The corresponding clusters of temperament were called *viscerotonic*, *somatotonic*, and *cerebrotonic* (Sheldon 1940). These somatotypes and temperaments are described in "Research in action: body physique and temperament."

Research in action: body physique and temperament

Through a series of studies, William Sheldon isolated three primary structures of human physique that he said were associated with three personality temperament types.

Somatotypes	Temperament
Endomorphic: A soft roundness of the body. The digestive system is large and highly developed, whereas other features of the body are weak and underdeveloped. Small bones; short limbs; soft and smooth skin.	**Viscerotonic** is relaxed and outgoing; includes a desire for comfort and gluttony for food and affection.
Mesomorphic: Bone and muscle predominate. The physique is hard, firm, upright, strong, and sturdy. Large blood vessels. Thick skin with large pores.	**Somatotonic** is active, assertive, motivated, and achievement-oriented.
Ectomorphic: Fragile, thin, and delicate. "Poorly muscled extremities" with weak bones. These individuals have "the greatest surface area and hence the greatest sensory exposure to the outside world."	**Cerebrotonic** is introverted, inhibited, restrained. "Cerebrotonic people shrink away from sociality as from too strong a light. They … avoid attracting attention to themselves."

Source: Adapted from Sheldon (1940: 8); Sheldon (1942: 10–11).

Sheldon (1949) applied this two-dimensional classification system to delinquency in *Varieties of Delinquent Behavior*. Here he reported research findings from a ten-year study of 200 delinquent boys placed in the Hayden Goodwill Inn, a small private residential facility in Boston. Sheldon compared these boys to a group of male college students whom he had examined previously. The difference between the two groups was statistically significant, with the delinquent boys being more mesomorphic and less ectomorphic than the male college students. Sheldon went on to compare the delinquency of the boys in residential care with that of their parents. Observing similarity, he concluded that the tendency to become delinquent is inherited (Sheldon 1949; see also Bernard et al. 2009; Curran and Renzetti 2007).

Physique and delinquency

Sheldon and Eleanor Glueck also examined physique in their classic study of 500 delinquents and 500 non-delinquent from lower-class Boston neighborhoods (see Chapter 3 for a description of the study). They found that physique was one of the factors that distinguished these two groups. Using two independent methods of physique classification, the Gluecks found that delinquent boys were disproportionately mesomorphic (Glueck and Glueck 1950: 33, 187; Sampson and Laub 1997).

In light of this finding, the Gluecks (1956) devoted an entire book to the topic of *Physique and Delinquency*. Here they reported that 60 percent of the delinquents, but only 31 percent of the non-delinquents, were mesomorphic (Glueck and Glueck 1956: 9). Their study also considered a large number of personality traits and sociocultural factors in connection with physique and delinquency. The Gluecks observed that mesomorphs were characterized by traits particularly suitable to the commission of aggressive acts, such as physical strength, energy, insensitivity, and the tendency to express tension and frustration in action. Mesomorphs also experienced few inhibitions that would restrain aggressive behavior. Thus, the interaction of mesomorphic physique with an antisocial temperament and a poor social environment created the potential for delinquency (Glueck and Glueck 1956).

Contemporary biological approaches in biosocial criminology

While early biological approaches attempted to connect physical characteristics with behavior, they often acknowledged the importance of environmental conditions. Nonetheless, their heavy biological emphasis made it seem as if all behavior – including criminal behavior – could be reduced to its biological roots. As we have seen, the pioneering versions of positivist criminology sought to identify, through scientific methods, the physical characteristics of criminals that differentiate them from non-criminals and allegedly produce their criminal behavior. This view is referred to as **biological determinism**.

When psychology and sociology came on the positivist scene in the late 1800s and early 1900s, scientific attention turned to environmental conditions. In the years following World War II, emphasis on the biological underpinnings of criminology weakened. The nature emphasis in biological determinism was, to a great degree, replaced with a focus on nurture, in which behavior was seen as a product of social and environmental factors and influences (Jacobson and Rowe 2000). Over the course of this transformation, biological determinism was displaced by **environmental determinism**, which concentrated on the social conditions that cause behavior. The **nature–nurture debate** that ensued was emotionally charged and discipline-driven. Each side adamantly held its ground, alleging that the causes of crime were either biological or environmental, but certainly not both (Rowe 2002; Walsh 2002; Fishbein 1990, 2001; Jacobson and Rowe 2000).

It is now recognized that "the 'nature or nurture' debate on the origins of crime is outdated" (Jacobson and Rowe 2000: 324; see also Burt and Simons 2014; Rowe 2002; Walsh 2002; Fishbein 1990, 2001). As a result, the reductionism of the nature–nurture controversy has faded and contemporary biological perspectives commonly incorporate environmental factors. Sociological theories and research, however, have rarely followed suit by adopting biological elements (Walsh 2002, 2014; Schwartz and Beaver 2011; Brennan and Raine 1997; Udry 1988, 1990, 1995; Gottfredson and Hirschi 1987).

The new, integrated approach of **biosocial criminology** contends that delinquency and other forms of antisocial behavior result from a combination of social, psychological, and biological causes (Brennan and Raine 1997). The approach is deliberately interdisciplinary and integrated, and it includes factors from a variety of disciplines. A biosocial approach points out that biological factors do not operate alone – they are dynamically related to one another and to environmental conditions, all of which interact to influence behavior (Walsh and Beaver 2009; Walsh 2002; Fishbein 2001).

Biosocial research reveals that biological and social variables are often related in complex ways. It is not enough simply to acknowledge that both biology and environment may independently contribute to delinquent behavior; rather, various biological and environmental factors influence each other, and together they affect the likelihood of delinquency. This biosocial process is called **nature–nurture interaction** or *nature–nurture interplay* (Walsh 2014; Walsh and Beaver 2009; Rutter 2006; Moffitt 2005; Caspi et al. 2002; Raine 2002b; Fishbein 1990, 2001; Jacobson and Rowe 2000; Brennan and Raine 1997; Raine, Brennan, and Farrington 1997). "Expanding ideas: nature–nurture interaction, biochemistry plus parenting" provides an example of nature–nurture interaction.

Expanding ideas: nature–nurture interaction, biochemistry plus parenting

In her important book, *Biobehavioral Perspectives in Criminology*, Diana Fishbein offers a number of examples of nature–nurture interaction. This one has to do with a particular neurotransmitter called serotonin and how its influence is affected by parenting.

> Neurotransmitters … are chemical messengers in the brain that allow brain cells and regions to communicate with each other. These chemicals are responsible for a variety of brain functions, from eating and drinking patterns, to memory and learning processes, to emotions and moods. Serotonin is a neurotransmitter of particular interest for its role in impulsivity and aggressiveness. Low levels of activity and metabolism of serotonin have been associated with both, which is perhaps the most reliable finding in the history of psychiatry … Studies further show that poor parenting is associated with low serotonin levels in the child and good parenting techniques may actually raise serotonin activity levels, thereby minimizing the impact of other risk factors for negative behavioral outcomes.

> *Source*: Fishbein (2001: 15, references omitted).

While biological and environmental characteristics and conditions are powerful predictors of antisocial behavior, they are not causal in a deterministic sense. Rather, they are probabilistic, increasing the likelihood or "risk" of antisocial behavior. Antisocial behavior is not an inevitable outcome, but youths who are predisposed by virtue of their biological makeup and who are exposed to an adverse environment are at greater risk. A variety of behavioral outcomes are possible, not just delinquency, and for this reason researchers usually use the general term *antisocial behavior* (Fishbein 2001).

The discussion that follows does not try to inventory all the findings on biological influences in antisocial behavior; instead, we offer just a sampling that points to the major areas of theory and research.[1] In many cases, these biological factors reveal nature–nurture interaction. Key biological influences on antisocial behavior can be categorized into three areas of study: (1) neurological deficits, (2) biochemical factors, and (3) heredity and behavioral genetics. The first two areas of study call for a basic understanding of the human nervous system, described in "Expanding ideas: the human nervous system."

Expanding ideas: the human nervous system

Biosocial criminology studies the human nervous system in relation to criminal behavior. The human nervous system is exceedingly complex and can be divided into two major divisions: the central nervous system and the peripheral nervous system (Fishbein 2001; Fishbein and Pease 1996). Each is composed of cells called *neurons*. The central nervous system (CNS) includes the brain and spinal cord. The peripheral nervous system includes the neural cells emanating from the brain and spinal cord, which carry information to and from the CNS. The peripheral nervous system can be broken down further into two subsystems: somatic and autonomic. The somatic nervous system primarily consists of sensory and motor nerves, providing awareness or consciousness of sensations such as light, touch, sound, and smell and the resulting activation of muscle groups. The autonomic nervous system (ANS) controls bodily functions that are usually beyond people's conscious control, including blood pressure, heart activity, breathing, and hormone levels. The neuronal structures (anatomy) and functions (physiology) of the nervous system have powerful influences on behavior, but these influences must be understood in the context of environmental conditions.

Neurological deficits

Neurological deficits associated with the structure and functioning of the nervous system, especially deficits in the prefrontal cortex and the autonomic nervous system, have received a great deal of interest with regard to delinquency.

The prefrontal cortex and executive functioning

Biosocial scientists who are interested in antisocial behavior focus attention on the **prefrontal cortex** (the outer layer of the cerebrum, see Figure 7.1), because this is the area of the brain that is most responsible for impulses, emotions, and goal-directed actions: "Many individuals with conduct disorders, antisocial behavior, hyperactivity and other traits that place an individual at risk for delinquency or criminal behavior and drug abuse are believed to suffer from defects in the cortex, particularly within the frontal lobes" (Fishbein and Pease 1996: 35; see also

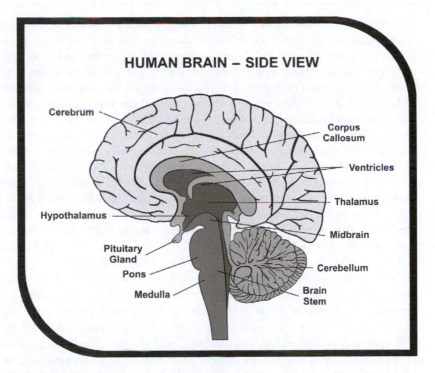

HUMAN BRAIN – SIDE VIEW

Cerebrum

Corpus Callosum

Ventricles

Thalamus

Hypothalamus

Midbrain

Pituitary Gland

Pons

Cerebellum

Medulla

Brain Stem

Figure 7.1 The human brain.

The brain is traditionally divided into three major regions: the hindbrain, the midbrain, and the forebrain (Weiten 2013). The *hindbrain* comprises the cerebellum and two structures found in the lower part of the brain stem: the medulla and the pons. The medulla is involved in unconscious bodily functions such as circulation, breathing, muscle tone, and reflexes, including sneezing, coughing, and salivating. The pons connects the brainstem with the cerebellum. The cerebellum plays a key role in integrating sensory perception and motor control coordination. The *midbrain* is the portion of the brainstem that lies between the hindbrain and the forebrain. This region integrates sensory processes, such as vision and hearing, and it also plays a role in the transmission of dopamine, a neural transmitter, to various higher brain centers. Running through the hindbrain and the midbrain is the reticular formation, which functions as an information filter, arousing and alerting the individual to environmental stimuli. The largest and most complex region of the human brain is the *forebrain*. This includes the cerebrum and a network of structures referred to as the *limbic system*. Although the limbic system is not well-defined anatomically, it is usually recognized to include the thalamus and hypothalamus, the hippocampus, the amygdale, and other brain structures that lie beneath the cerebral cortex (the outer layer of the cerebrum). Collectively these brain structures are theorized to evoke and regulate motivation and emotion (Weiten 2013; Andrews and Bonta 2010; DeLisi, Umphress, and Vaughn 2009b; Wright et al. 2009; Fishbein and Pease 1996). The *cerebral cortex* is the outer layer of the cerebrum, responsible for higher-level intellectual functioning, such as problem-solving, logic, planning, insight, information processing, and decision-making (Fishbein and Pease 1996). The cerebral cortex is referred to as the "thinking" or "higher" brain, because it analyzes and organizes information from other parts of the brain and relays back responses (Walsh 2002: 77).

Peskin et al. 2013; Walsh and Bolen 2012; Wright et al. 2009; Beaver, Wright, and DeLisi 2007; Cauffman, Steinberg, and Piquero 2005; Ishikawa and Raine 2004; Raine 1993, 2002a; Walsh 2002). The prefrontal cortex is about one-quarter of the entire cerebral cortex and serves an integrative and supervisory role in the brain (Weiten 2013; Walsh and Bolen 2012; Walsh 2002). In particular, "deficits in the prefrontal cortex may reduce the **executive function** – that is, the ability to plan and to reflect on one's actions. Impaired executive function implies impulsiveness and disorganized behavior, a focus on the present rather than on the future" (Rowe 2002: 70). Research has consistently found that impaired executive functioning is implicated in the poor self-regulation of impulses, emotions, and behaviors, including delinquency (Peskin et al. 2013; Andrews and Bonta 2010; Syngelaki et al. 2009; Wright et al. 2009; Beaver et al. 2007; Cauffman et al. 2005; Raine et al. 2005; Raine 2002a; Fishbein 2001). The connection between prefrontal cortex impairment and poor executive functioning has been well documented in research using a variety of methods, including brain imagining, electroencephalograph (EEG), and neuro-psychological measures (e.g., verbal and spatial functioning) (Andrews and Bonta 2010; Shannon et al. 2009; Wright et al. 2009; Beaver et al. 2007; Bufkin and Luttrell 2005; Cauffman et al. 2005; Raine et al. 2005; Raine 1993, 2002a; Rowe 2002; Fishbein 2001).[2]

Development of the prefrontal cortex continues throughout adolescence and this may, in part, explain the impulsivity of children and adolescents. Delays in neurophysiological development affect attentiveness and focus, verbal language development, and intelligence. In the past decade, there has been a great deal of research on the physical development of the adolescent brain and its relationship with antisocial behavior, particularly the age-linked patterning of delinquent offending (National Research Council 2013). Research shows, for example that adolescents are less capable of self-regulation than adults in part because "the brain system that influences pleasure-seeking and emotional reactivity develops more rapidly than the brain system that supports self-control"[3] (National Research Council 2013: 97).

Psychologists D. A. Andrews and James Bonta (2010: 170) raise an intriguing question derived from these research findings: "If brain capacity and function is still developing, with frontal lobes developing last, can we hold adolescents responsible for uninhibited, antisocial behavior?" This fundamental question has been the focal point of much research sponsored by the MacArthur Foundation Research Network on Adolescent Development and Juvenile Justice (National Research Council 2013; Grisso and Schwartz 2000). We described in Chapter 2 how this research has influenced calls for juvenile justice reform.

Autonomic system underarousal and low resting heart rate

The autonomic nervous system (ANS) controls involuntary bodily functions such as blood pressure, heart rate, intestinal activity, and hormone levels. Research has shown that the physiological condition of **autonomic system underarousal** is related to antisocial, criminal, and violent behavior in both children and adults (Armstrong et al. 2009; Raine 1993, 2002a; Yaralian and Raine 2001; Jacobson and Rowe 2000). The most common measure of autonomic underarousal is *low resting heart rate* (Raine 2002a; Farrington 1997; Pitts 1997). Psychologist Adrian Raine (2002a) contends that low resting heart rate represents one of the most consistently found, but perhaps least understood, biological correlates of antisocial and aggressive behavior in children and adolescents. Low physiological arousal seems to predispose individuals to antisocial and criminal behavior (Peskin et al. 2013; Bartol and Bartol 2009; Raine 2002a; Jacobson and Rowe 2000). Several explanations have been offered for this often documented relationship (Raine 2002a).

Stimulation-seeking theory contends that low arousal is an unpleasant physiological state and, consequently, some individuals with autonomic underarousal seek stimulation through a

> variety of means, such as risk-taking, sensation-seeking, impulsive action, socializing with many other people, drug abuse, multiplicity of sexual partners, etc. These activities are likely to lead such a person toward criminal activity, but not inevitably; risky sports activities may take the place of criminality in middle- and upper-class persons.
> (Eysenck 1997: 24; see also Raine 2002a; Rowe 2002; Eysenck and Gudjonsson 1989)

Fearlessness theory argues that individuals with low levels of autonomic arousal are relatively fearless in reaction to stress (anxiety reaction). Although antisocial acts, especially violence, require a degree of fearlessness to carry out, underaroused individuals experience little restraint against such acts (Raine 2002a). David Rowe (2002) contends that fearless children are more difficult to socialize than fearful ones because punishment produces less intense emotion and, as a result, lessons are inadequately learned. In contrast, "high levels of autonomic arousal, which produce anxiety and fear of disapproval, encourage childhood socialization" (Bartol and Bartol 2009: 70). Similarly, Hans Eysenck (1997: 24), a well-known English psychiatrist, claims that children with habitually low autonomic arousal "condition poorly" because they do not anticipate punishment. As a result, they fail to develop a conscience that prevents them from committing crime. According to Eysenck, the conscience is a conditioned response that is at the core of socialization.

Reduced right hemisphere functioning has also been implicated in the relationship between low heart rate and antisocial behavior because this is the part of the brain that is dominant for the control of autonomic functions. Low heart rate is indicative of decreased right hemisphere functioning, and poor right hemisphere functioning has been associated with an incapacity to withdraw from aversive and dangerous situations. A weak withdrawal system may make children less averse to dangerous and risky situations, thereby increasing the probability of antisocial behavior (Raine 2002a).

Arousal theories suggest that autonomic system underarousal is "related to low emotionality, poor conditionability, lack of empathy and remorse, and ability to lie easily" (Fishbein 2001: 51). These behavioral characteristics are central to the clinical concept of *psychopathy*, which has been used most extensively to explain persistent and violent adult offenders (Bartol and Bartol 2009). The application of psychopathy to juvenile offenders is controversial, as described in "Expanding ideas: juvenile psychopathy."

Expanding ideas: juvenile psychopathy

Some juvenile delinquents are referred to as *psychopaths* because they lack anxiety and guilt for the wrongs they do. This concept clinically designates a distinctive set of "emotional, interpersonal and neurological characteristics" (Bartol and Bartol 2009: 166). Hervey Cleckley (1959: 567–569) characterized psychopaths as

> chronically antisocial individuals who are always in trouble, profiting neither from experience nor punishment and maintaining no real loyalties to any person, group, or code. They are frequently callous and hedonistic, showing marked emotional immaturity with lack of responsibility, lack of judgment and an ability to rationalize their behavior so that it appears warranted, reasonable and justified.

Psychopathy appears to involve three major areas of personality dysfunction: inter-personal (e.g., deceitful and manipulative), affective (e.g., callous and unemotional), and impulsivity–irresponsibility (Loeber, Burke, and Pardini 2009: 298).

The emergence of psychopathy in juveniles is attributed to "subtle neurobiological deficits" in the prefrontal cortex and limbic system (Loeber et al. 2009: 299). These dysfunctions are related to problems in aversive conditioning, passive avoidance learning, and the processing of negative stimuli (Gao and Tang 2013; Loeber et al. 2009; Shannon et al. 2009). Social factors have also been linked to the development of psychopathic traits in youth, including harsh and inconsistent disci-pline practices and conflicted parent–child communication styles (Loeber et al. 2009).

Although the clinical concept of psychopathy is used in the assessment and treatment of adult offenders, its application to juvenile delinquents is controversial because some of the characteristics associated with adult psychopathy are relatively common during adolescent development, especially callousness and self-centeredness. In addition, the label "psychopathic" is sometimes imposed indiscriminately on youth by juvenile justice professionals, including judges, probation officers, and treatment providers (Bartol and Bartol 2009). Nonetheless, psy-chologist Donald Lynam argues that psychopathy is a reliable and well-validated clinical diag-nostic category that is useful for the assessment and treatment of delinquent youth. Substantial research supports his view, and the concept has received growing attention, especially with regard to persistent juvenile offenders (DeLisi et al. 2009b; Vaughn et al. 2009; Wiebe 2009; Vaughn, Howard, and DeLisi 2008; Lynam et al. 2007; Vaughn et al. 2007; Lynam and Gudonis 2005; Rutter, Moffitt, and Caspi 2006; Vaughn and Howard 2005; Miller and Lynam 2001; Widiger and Lynam 1998).

Biochemical factors

The biochemistry of the human body influences behavior by affecting the central and periph-eral nervous systems. We focus on two key aspects of biochemistry that have been connected most extensively with antisocial behavior: neurotransmitters and the hormone testosterone (Walsh 2002; Fishbein 2001; Fishbein and Pease 1996).

Neurotransmitters

The intricate communication system of the brain is composed of billions of nerve cells called neurons. All thoughts, feelings, emotions and behaviors stem from this system. Each neuron consists of three basic structures.

The *soma* is the cell body, including the nucleus of the cell. *Dendrites* extend from the soma in the form of several branches to receive and respond to electrical activity of other neurons. The *axon* also extends from the soma to transmit electrical activity from the soma to other neurons, muscles, or glands. When an electrical impulse is conducted from the soma down the axon, it will reach the *synapse* which is the gap between cell bodies.

(Fishbein and Pease 1996: 40)

The axon then releases specific chemicals, called **neurotransmitters**, into the synapse. These neurotransmitters carry the signal to a receptor site on the dendrite of the neighboring neuron. After transmitting the signal, the neurotransmitter is released back into the synapse, where it is metabolized or reabsorbed back into the sending neuron.

Three specific neurotransmitters – dopamine, serotonin, and norepinephrine – have been linked to the likelihood of antisocial behavior. In addition, the enzyme monoamine oxidase has also been implicated in antisocial behavior, especially aggression and violence, because of its critical role in regulating neurotransmitter concentrations and activity.

Dopamine affects an individual's ability to associate cues (events or objects) in the environment with rewards and punishments. As a result, conditioned responses are influenced by levels of dopamine. Increased dopamine levels and activity appear to evoke emotions, as part of the **fight–or–flight response**, which, in turn, motivate behavior. As a result, the overproduction of dopamine has been associated with psychotic behavior and with aggression and violence. Antipsychotic drugs that are administered to decrease dopamine levels tend to reduce aggressive behaviors. However, research findings have been inconsistent, and researchers have not uncovered a direct effect of dopamine levels on aggression (Baker, Bezdjian, and Raine 2006; Fishbein 2001; Raine 1993).

Serotonin is an inhibitory neurotransmitter that moderates behaviors. When serotonin is released in the synapse, neuronal activity is reduced, thereby lessening innate drives and impulses (DeLisi 2009). Abnormally low levels of serotonin have been connected with impulsive and aggressive behavior in both juveniles and adults. Although research specifically relates low serotonin activity with impulsivity, the expression of that impulsivity depends on a variety of predisposing and environmental factors: "A deficit in serotonin activity jeopardizes the ability to inhibit urges, increasing the likelihood that underlying hostility or negative mood will lead to aggression or another inappropriate behavior" (Fishbein 2001: 38; Baker et al. 2006; Moffitt et al. 1997, 1998).

Norepinephrine is a neurotransmitter that is produced from dopamine. It has been found to play a central role in the fight-or-flight response by causing the release of stress hormones from the adrenal glands and by stimulating the central and peripheral nervous systems. Generally, norepinephrine is related to arousal, agitated mood states, and behavioral activation. Although several studies seem to establish a link between antisocial behavior, including violence, and levels of norepinephrine, others do not. The "actual behavioral outcome depends upon the circumstance, setting and individual predisposition" (Fishbein 2001: 39; Walsh and Beaver 2009; Raine 2002a).

Monoamine oxidase A (MAOA) is an enzyme responsible for the breakdown of neurotransmitters, including dopamine, serotonin, and norepinephrine. As a result, MAOA plays a vital role in regulating neurotransmitter concentrations and activity levels. Low MAOA activity results in excessive levels of dopamine and norepinephrine, both of which seem to contribute to the fight-or-flight response, aggression, low impulse control, and loss of self-control. Extensive research has linked irregular MAOA levels with antisocial behaviors, including psychopathy, aggression, and violence, especially the "cycle of violence" (Stogner and Gibson 2013; Schwartz and Beaver 2011; Guo et al. 2008a; Caspi et al. 2002; Fishbein 2001; Ellis 1991).

Testosterone

Hormones are chemical compounds secreted into the bloodstream by various glands that comprise the endocrine system. Hormones are carried throughout the body, where they regulate or control certain cells and organs. One particular "sex hormone," **testosterone**, secreted by the testes, ovaries, and adrenal glands, has received the vast majority of attention with regard to antisocial behavior. Sometimes identified as a male sex hormone, testosterone is also produced by females, but in much smaller amounts and with different effects (Mazur 2009; Fishbein 2001). This sex difference in testosterone level is presumed to be partly responsible for higher levels of aggressive and criminal behavior among males (Jacobson and Rowe 2000).

Animal studies have clearly and consistently demonstrated that testosterone plays an important role in the expression of aggressive and violent behavior (Jacobson and Rowe 2000; Brain 1994; Albert et al. 1990). Human research, however, is far less conclusive. In particular, a cause-and-effect relationship between testosterone level and subsequent behavior has not been established, and issues abound with regard to the measurement of such a relationship (Mazur 2009; Jacobson and Rowe 2000; Raine 1993; Brain 1994; Archer 1991; Harris 1985). The most common view among researchers is that testosterone is related primarily to dominant behavior among males, not to aggression (Mazur 2009). As such, testosterone influences responses to "dominance contests" that are a part of everyday life for young males, such as sports competition, academic performance, competition for promotion, and jousting over sexual prowess.

Social variables may intervene in the relationship between testosterone and behavior (Mazur 2009). In a widely cited study, Alan Booth and Wayne Osgood (1993) examined the relationship between testosterone, social integration, prior involvement in juvenile delinquency, and adult deviance. Although testosterone level was strongly associated with adult deviance, the relationship was reduced significantly for individuals who were socially integrated and who were involved in crime as juveniles. These findings indicate that the effect of testosterone on deviance is conditioned by social factors. Similarly, a study of military veterans found that high levels of testosterone were associated with multiple measures of aggression, including retrospective reports of juvenile delinquency, adult crime, and substance abuse. However, this association was true only for veterans from a lower social class, again indicating that the link between testosterone and antisocial behavior is conditioned by social context (Dabbs and Morris 1990).

The role of testosterone in dominance contests is also indicated by research that shows that testosterone levels rise and fall in the course of involvement in competitive sport or in response to a competitive challenge. In one study, levels of testosterone rose prior to a competitive tennis match, declined while the match was being played, and increased dramatically for players who won but dropped for players who lost (Mazur 2009; Mazur and Booth 1998; Booth et al. 1989). Here, too, nature–nurture interaction is revealed in that the role of testosterone in antisocial behavior must be considered within the context of environmental influences.

Behavioral genetics: the heritability of criminal disposition

The common observation that crime runs in families suggests that the tendency for involvement in crime is inherited. A study long ago by Richard Dugsdale traced the lineage of the Juke family from around 1750 until 1870. Dugsdale concluded that the high rate of criminality and "pauperism" among the 709 descendants indicated that crime and poor social adjustment were inherited. More recently, David Farrington's research showed intergenerational criminality across three generations. However, evidence of intergenerational criminality does not necessarily mean that criminal behavior is genetically transmitted because families share a similar lifestyle, making it difficult to say whether criminality is a product of heredity or the environment (Andrews and Bonta 2010; Smith and Farrington 2004).

Despite evidence of intergenerational criminality, the role of genetic influences in criminal behavior has been heavily discounted and, for the most part, ignored by social scientists. Genetic contributions are often misunderstood and sometimes distorted. "Identification of genetic contributions does not reduce behavior to a gene level," nor does identifying the role of genetics in criminal behavior imply that there is a "crime gene" (Fishbein 2001: 26; see also Rutter, Moffitt, and Caspi 2006; Tehrani and Mednick 2000). Moreover, a genetic predisposition toward criminal behavior does not mean that an individual is destined to become criminal, regardless of environmental conditions. Rather, the study of **behavioral genetics** seeks to "estimate the relative contributions of heredity and environment" on individual traits, such as impulsivity, aggressiveness, and negativity (Fishbein 2001: 26; Burt and Simons 2014; Walsh 2002). Whether these traits are given full expression in the form of delinquent and criminal behavior depends on environmental conditions. Thus, as a biosocial approach, behavioral genetics incorporates the basic perspective of nature–nurture interaction (Baker et al. 2006; Walsh 2002).

Behavioral genetics research attempts to sort out influences on aggression and criminal behavior in terms of three sources: shared environmental factors, non-shared environmental factors, and genetic factors. *Shared environmental factors* are conditions and experiences shared by family members. Family structure and socioeconomic status, for example, are shared environmental factors in that they have influence on all family members. *Non-shared environmental factors* are conditions and experiences that family members do not have in common or dissimilar responses of family members to shared experiences. For example, siblings often do not share the same friends, and siblings may respond to divorce in very different ways. *Genetic factors* refer to traits and characteristics that are handed down from parent to child, based on the influence of genes. The measure of this genetic influence is called **heritability** (Beaver et al. 2014; Burt and Simons 2014; Moffitt 2005; Jacobson and Rowe 2000).

Researchers have found it extremely difficult to disentangle environmental and genetic influences by looking just at traditional families. Two research designs – adoption studies and twin studies – are used to control for genetic influences and at the same time consider shared and non-shared environments.

Adoption studies

Adoption studies obtain data from adopted individuals and their adoptive and biological parents. Similarity between adoptive parents and their adopted children is likely due to shared environmental influences, because adoptive parents and their children do not share genes (Jacobson and Rowe 2000). In contrast, if adopted children are similar to their biological parents, then genetic factors are implied for the similarity of traits and behaviors.

The most famous adoption study of antisocial behavior used data from an extensive Danish Adoption Register. These data on 14,427 Danish adoptees and their biological and adoptive parents showed that rates of court convictions were higher for male adoptees when their biological parents were convicted. If neither the biological nor the adoptive parents were convicted, 13.5 percent of the sons were convicted. When the adoptive parents were convicted and the biological parents were not, 14.7 percent of the sons were convicted. In cases where the biological parents were convicted and the adoptive parents were not, 20 percent of the adopted sons were convicted. The highest rates occurred when both biological and adoptive parents had criminal convictions: 24.5 percent of these sons were convicted. The number of convictions for biological parents was also related to the likelihood of criminal convictions for adopted sons in that a greater number of convictions for biological parents were associated with a greater number of convictions for biological sons, but this relationship was much stronger for property offenses than for violent offenses. Thus, the association between adoptees' criminal records and those of their biological parents suggests a heritable component to criminal behavior (Jacobson and Rowe 2000; Tehrani and Mednick 2000; Mednick, Gabrielli, and Hutchings 1984).

Twin studies

Twin studies compare identical twins to fraternal twins. Identical twins, or *monozygotic twins* (MZ), are genetically identical, sharing 100 percent of their genes. Fraternal twins, or *dizygotic twins* (DZ), share, on average, 50 percent of their genes. Genetic influences are implicated to the degree that the similarity observed in MZ twins is greater than that observed in DZ twins. In twin studies, such similarity is referred to as *concordance rates* (Baker et al. 2006; Tehrani and Mednick 2000).

Research examining genetic effects on criminal behavior shows greater concordance rates for criminal behavior among MZ twins than among DZ twins. Some researchers believe that "the twin methodology may be flawed in that MZ twins, in addition to sharing more genetic information than DZ twins, are also more likely to be treated more similarly than DZ twins" (Tehrani and Mednick 2000: 25). One methodological solution to this problem is to study twins reared apart. One group of researchers studied concordance rates of antisocial behavior in a sample of 32 sets of MZ twins that were reared apart, having been adopted by non-relatives shortly after birth (Baker et al. 2006; Grove et al. 1990). MZ twins reared apart displayed concordance in both childhood conduct disorders and adult antisocial behaviors. Although the sample size was small and concordance rates were lower than in previous twin studies, these findings indicate that antisocial behavior has a genetic component (see also Burt and Simons 2014; Niv et al. 2013; Tuvblad et al. 2013).

Molecular genetic studies

Adoption and twin studies suggest that there is a heritable component to individual traits that underlie delinquent and criminal behavior – traits such as impulsivity, negativity, aggressiveness, and low intelligence. These studies, however, do not identify the genetic mechanism that may contribute to these traits (Guo, Roettger, and Cai 2008b; Baker et al. 2006; Fishbein 2001). Studies in molecular genetics attempt to measure more directly genetic influences on behavior and individual traits. Diana Fishbein (2001; see also Baker et al. 2006; Rowe 2002) provides an overview of this contemporary field of research as it relates to delinquent and criminal behavior:

> Characteristics of genes that have been linked to psychological and behavior traits are called *markers*; they "mark" a location of genes that may be actively involved in contributing to a trait. Genetic *variants* are structural differences in genes, also called *polymorphism*. Eventually, when variants and markers have been identified for relevant traits, we will understand better how genes are expressed, or become active, in response to environmental input and how their activity (or lack thereof) contributes to a behavioral trait.
>
> (Fishbein 2001: 29)

Rather than identifying a gene for crime, molecular genetic research shows that complex individual traits, such as self-control, and behavioral tendencies, such as aggression, are products of multiple genes, in combination producing a *polygenic effect* (Beaver 2009; Beaver, Ratchford, and Ferguson 2009b; DeLisi 2009). Genetic influences on antisocial behavior have been studied most extensively in terms of how genes influence neurotransmitter levels and, to a lesser degree, how genes influence brain circuitry, especially circuitry of the prefrontal cortex and amygdala. The challenge to criminology is to "unpack the ways in which genes, the environment and the brain interface to produce undesirable behaviors" (Beaver 2009: 69).

Molecular genetic studies of delinquency are increasingly common (Burt and Simons 2014; Schwartz and Beaver 2011; Beaver 2009; DeLisi 2009). Structural differences in specific genes, called *polymorphism*, have been tied to individual traits such as temperament and intelligence and to behavioral tendencies such as aggressiveness, novelty-seeking, and risk-taking (Beaver 2009; DeLisi 2009; Guo et al. 2008b; Guo, Roettger, and Shih 2007; Rutter 2006). With the advent of datasets providing direct measures, certain genetic polymorphisms have been linked to higher levels of involvement in serious and violent crime among both juveniles and adults. Molecular genetics research also increasingly documents that genetic influences must be understood in terms of gene–environment interaction or interplay. In a recent study, Guo, Roettger, and Cai (2008b) found that genetic polymorphisms in three genes (*DAT1*, *DRD2*, and *MAOA*) interacted with environmental characteristics. For example, the *DRD2* polymorphism that places youth at higher risk for delinquency was effectively neutralized by parental involvement and family connectedness. Put simply, the expression of genes is dependent on environmental conditions, and the influence of environmental conditions is dependent on genetic predispositions. Matt DeLisi (2009: 220) points out that "recent molecular genetic studies are critically important because they are beginning to identify the environmental conditions that suppress or amplify genetic risk factors to produce antisocial behavior" (see also Burt and Simons 2014; Barnes, Boutwell, and Beaver 2013; Brendgen et al. 2013; Shannon et al. 2009; Stogner and Gibson 2013; Beaver et al. 2008a, 2009a, 2009b, 2011; Schwartz and Beaver 2011; Beaver 2010; DeLisi et al. 2009a; Beaver, Wright, and DeLisi 2008b; Vaughn et al. 2009; Guo et al. 2007, 2008b).

"Pulling back the curtain on heritability studies" (Burt and Simons 2014)

Even though behavioral genetic studies consistently indicate gene–environment interplay, the research methodologies that are often used purposely try to determine the relative influence of heredity and the environment on criminal behavior – the portion caused by heritability, compared to the portion caused by the environment (Burt and Simons 2014). The resulting "heritability estimates" are in the 40–60 percent range, meaning that heritability effects account for 40 to 60 percent of the variability in antisocial behavior, with the remaining effects attributed to *shared environmental* and *non-shared environmental factors* (Peskin et al. 2013: 23). Callie Burt and Ronald Simons (2014: 223) have recently taken issue with this approach, contending that reports of such high heritabilities for complex social behaviors such as crime and delinquency are "surprising, and findings indicating negligible shared environmental influences (usually interpreted to include parenting and community factors) seem implausible given extensive criminological research demonstrating their significance." They go on to argue that this methodological effort to partition genetic and environmental influences is fundamentally flawed and is "misguided given the bidirectional, interactional relationship among genes, cells, organisms, and environments" (Burt and Simons 2014: 223). In fact, they contend that heritability studies inaccurately portray genetic effects as separable from the environmental context in which they function. Instead, Burt and Simons (2014: 251) advocate for true biosocial research that focuses on gene–environment interaction in which genetic influences "shape the responses to environmental factors."

Biosocial criminologists do *not* argue that biological factors lead directly to crime and delinquency. Rather, they argue that biological factors, in combination with environmental conditions, produce individual traits that are conducive to involvement in delinquency and crime. As we have seen, the biosocial approach contends that biological characteristics and processes influence individual traits and behavioral tendencies that limit individuals' abilities to respond to the environment in a socially acceptable manner. We now turn to the psychological study of personality, as a key component of biosocial criminology, connecting biological influences with delinquent behavior.[4]

Personality and biosocial criminology

In their 1950 book, *Unraveling Juvenile Delinquency*, Sheldon and Eleanor Glueck itemized the personality traits that distinguish delinquent youth from non-delinquent youth, as indicated by their extensive study of 500 delinquents and 500 non-delinquents.

> On a whole, delinquents are more extroverted, vivacious, impulsive and less self-controlled than the nondelinquents. They are more hostile, resentful, defiant, suspicious and destructive. They are less fearful of failure or defeat than the nondelinquents. They are less concerned about meeting conventional expectations and more ambivalent toward or far less submissive to authority. They are, as a group, more socially assertive. To a greater extent than the control group, they express feelings of not being recognized or appreciated.
>
> (Glueck and Glueck 1950: 275)

Although out of step with dominant sociological approaches of the time, the Gluecks gave extended attention to individual "temperamental traits" and applied these traits to a variety of behaviors, while focusing on delinquency (Glueck and Glueck 1950: 215). In addition, by associating temperament with physique, they suggested that personality traits may have biological roots. Their approach, then, was biosocial and developmental:

> The factors involved [in delinquency] are neither essentially biological nor essentially sociologic, but biosocial. We are concerned, for example, with the results of such a dynamic process as the introjection of certain childhood experiences and the effect of such activity on the development of personality and character.
>
> (Glueck and Glueck 1950: 215)

Contemporary theory and research have, to a great degree, revived the Gluecks' point of view by defining personality in terms of traits and by examining both biological and environmental aspects of personality.

Trait-based personality models

Personality refers to reasonably stable patterns of perceiving, thinking, feeling, and responding to the environment (Kleinmuntz 1982). "Traits are the basic building blocks of personality," providing foundation to thought, emotion, character, and behavior (Miller and Lynam 2001: 767). Contemporary theory and research contend that personality can be characterized along a number of key dimensions, sometimes called "superfactors," that organize the array of personality traits into a limited number of categories according to the interrelatedness of personality traits (John, Naumann, and Soto 2008; Miller and Lynam 2001; Eysenck 1991). Two theoretical models of personality are discussed here because they have been connected most extensively to delinquency. Because these theories group personality traits into a limited number of superfactors, they are referred to as "structural models of personality" or "trait-based personality models" (Miller and Lynam 2001: 767; Caspi et al. 1994: 165).

Eysenck's PEN model

Hans Eysenck, a British psychologist, associated three personality dimensions with crime and delinquency: *extraversion* (E), *neuroticism* (N) and *psychoticism* (P).[5] Each of these superfactors represents a collection of temperament traits that are often expressed together and that typify an individual's responses to environmental stimuli. Eysenck also argued that there is an underlying biological basis to these superfactors.

Eysenck's pioneering work originally advanced a two-factor model consisting of extraversion and neuroticism (Clark and Watson 1999; Eysenck 1964). This basic conceptualization of personality has been used repeatedly. Extraversion is contrasted with introversion and neuroticism is contrasted with emotional stability, resulting in a personality model that can be visualized by two intersecting dimensions lying at right angles. Figure 7.2 depicts the various temperament traits that compose each of the four quadrants. Extraverts high in neuroticism, for example, tend to be touchy, restless, aggressive, and excitable, whereas introverts who are emotionally stable are likely to be passive, careful, thoughtful, and controlled.

Additional analysis led Eysenck to the identification of a third superfactor, *psychoticism*, because certain types of crime and offenders were not adequately captured in the original two-factor model (Clark and Watson 1999). Psychoticism is characterized by social insensitivity, self-centeredness, unemotionality, impersonality, impulsiveness, and aggressiveness.

Eysenck contended that, in general, "crime and antisocial conduct are positively and causally related to high psychoticism, high extraversion, and high neuroticism" (Eysenck and Gudjonsson 1989: 55). Those who engage in crime and antisocial behavior tend to be impulsive, socially insensitive, excitement-seeking, and aggressive. Further, Eysenck theorized that although psychoticism is related to antisocial behavior for all ages, extraversion applies more readily to the antisocial behavior of children and adolescents and neuroticism is more relevant for older offenders (Eysenck and Gudjonsson 1989).

Advancing his personality model as a biosocial theory, Eysenck argues that extraversion and neuroticism have biological roots (Eysenck and Gudjonsson 1989). Extraversion is connected with basic functions of the central nervous system. In particular, he holds that the reticular activating system (RAS) of an extravert excessively filters stimuli, resulting in a habitually underaroused cerebral cortex. (Recall that the cerebral cortex is responsible for thinking, memory, and decision-making.) In the case of introversion, the RAS fails to filter stimuli adequately, resulting in a perpetually overaroused cerebral cortex. Thus, the extravert, who is cortically underaroused, seeks stimulation to achieve an optimally aroused cortex, and the introvert, who is cortically overaroused, tries to avoid stimulation. Earlier we described the two primary results of low cortical arousal: (1) poor conditionability and the inability

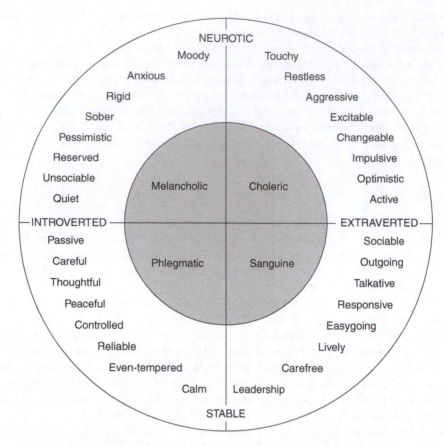

Figure 7.2 Eysenck's superfactors of extraversion and neuroticism.
Extraversion is contrasted with introversion; neuroticism is contrasted with emotional stability. The relationship between these two personality dimensions results in four temperaments identified by ancient Greek physicians.
Source: Ewen (1998: 139). Reproduced with permission of Taylor & Francis Group LLC, rightsholder.

to develop a conscience and (2) sensation-seeking behavior such as crime and delinquency (Ewen 1998; Eysenck 1997; Bartol 1995).

Neuroticism, according to Eysenck, reflects the functioning of the autonomic nervous system. Neuroticism is characterized by an unusually sensitive limbic system in which emotionality is achieved quickly and is long-lasting (Bartol 1995). Such heightened and prolonged emotionality is likely to lead to criminal activity, mainly as a result of individual agitation and excitability. Finally, psychoticism, which relates to impersonality, lack of empathy, aggressiveness, and impulsiveness, is connected to high testosterone levels (Miller and Lynam 2001).

Five-factor model of personality

Using a statistical technique that identifies common dimensions in data (factor analysis), Robert McCrae and Paul Costa (1987, 1997, 2008) derived five basic personality factors, sometimes identified as the "Big Five": extroversion, agreeableness, conscientiousness, neurot-icism, and openness to experience. *Extroversion* indicates positive emotionality as evidenced by being talkative, assertive, energetic, and seeking excitement. *Agreeableness* involves an individ-ual's approach to social relationships, ranging from compliant to antagonistic. *Conscientiousness* relates to one's ability to organize, plan, and complete tasks and to control impulses and delay gratification. *Neuroticism* is contrasted with emotional stability and even-temperedness and is typified by nervousness, anxiety, and insecurity. Negative emotionality characterizes neuroti-cism. *Openness to experience* has to do with intellectual curiosity, imagination, conventionality, and willingness to try new activities (see also Bartol and Bartol 2009; John et al. 2008; Miller and Lynam 2001; John and Srivastava 1999; Ewen 1998).

McCrae and Costa (1987, 1997, 2008) contend that personality can be characterized accu-rately and adequately by measuring the Big Five traits that they have identified (see also John et al. 2008; McCrae and John 1992). Their own personality inventory is called the NEO Personality Inventory. "Research in action: the Big Five Inventory" presents another trait-based inventory, developed by Oliver John, called the Big Five Inventory (BFI).

Research in action: the Big Five Inventory (BFI)

One of the personality questionnaires designed to measure the five-factor model of personal-ity (FFM) is the Big Five Inventory (BFI). The BFI is a 44-item inventory, making it short and efficient.

Instructions: Here are a number of characteristics that may or may not apply to you. For example, do you agree that you are someone who *likes* to spend *time with others*? Please write a number next to each statement to indicate the extent to which you agree or disagree with that statement.

1	2	3	4	5
Disagree strongly	Disagree a little	Neither agree nor disagree	Agree a little	Agree strongly

I see myself as someone who …

_____1. Is talkative
_____2. Tends to find fault with others
_____3. Does a thorough job
_____4. Is depressed, blue
_____5. Is original, comes up with new ideas
_____6. Is reserved
_____7. Is helpful and unselfish with others
_____8. Can be somewhat careless
_____9. Is relaxed, handles stress well
_____10. Is curious about many different things

_____11. Is full of energy
_____12. Starts quarrels with others
_____13. Is a reliable worker
_____14. Can be tense
_____15. Is ingenious, a deep thinker
_____16. Generates a lot of enthusiasm
_____17. Has a forgiving nature
_____18. Tends to be disorganized
_____19. Worries a lot
_____20. Has an active imagination
_____21. Tends to be quiet
_____22. Is generally trusting

_____23. Tends to be lazy

_____24. Is emotionally stable, not easily upset

_____25. Is inventive

_____26. Has an assertive personality

_____27. Can be cold and aloof

_____28. Perseveres until the task is finished

_____29. Can be moody

_____30. Values artistic, aesthetic experiences

_____31. Is sometimes shy, inhibited

_____32. Is considerate and kind to almost everyone

_____33. Does things efficiently

_____34. Remains calm in tense situations

_____35. Prefers work that is routine

_____36. Is outgoing, sociable

_____37. Is sometimes rude to others

_____38. Makes plans and follows through with them

_____39. Gets nervous easily

_____40. Likes to reflect, play with ideas

_____41. Has few artistic interests

_____42. Likes to cooperate with others

_____43. Is easily distracted

_____44. Is sophisticated in art, music, or literature

BFI scale scoring: Reverse score the items labeled "R" and compute scale scores at the mean of the following items:

Extroversion (8 items): 1, 6R, 11, 16, 21R, 26, 31R, 36

Agreeableness (9 items): 2R, 7, 12R, 17, 22, 27R, 32, 37R, 42

Conscientiousness (9 items): 3, 8R, 13, 18R, 23R, 28, 33, 38, 43R

Neuroticism (8 items): 4, 9R, 14, 19, 24R, 34R, 39

Openness (10 items): 5, 10, 15, 20, 25, 30, 35R, 40, 41R, 44.

Although the five-factor model has been criticized as being purely descriptive and providing no explanation of the development of personality, numerous studies have supported this conceptualization of personality, and the five-factor model has become the dominant structural model of personality (John et al. 2008).

Recent studies in behavioral genetics reveal that personality traits are, to a great degree, inherited. Figure 7.3 shows the proportion of each of the Big Five personality traits that is inherited. The relatively small contribution of the shared family environment has led some researchers to conclude that the family environment is relatively unimportant in the personality development of children (Wright and Beaver 2005; Plomin and Caspi 1999).

Personality traits and antisocial behavior

After thorough review of the research findings investigating the relationship between personality traits and antisocial behavior, Joshua Miller and Donald Lynam (2001) concluded that of all the major dimensions of personality *agreeableness* is most strongly associated with antisocial behavior. As one of the Big Five superfactors, *agreeableness* corresponds closely to *psychoticism* in Eysenck's PEN model. A second Big Five superfactor, *conscientiousness*, was also found to be significantly related to antisocial behavior, though less strongly than agreeableness. Miller and Lynam contend that these two dimensions appear to capture and summarize the most important aspects

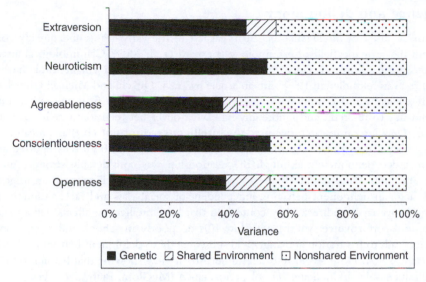

Figure 7.3 The heritability of personality.
Behavioral genetics research reveals that personality traits are, to a great degree, inherited.
Source: Plomin and Caspi (1999: 253) (adapted from Figure 9.1).

of personality in relation to antisocial behavior. Antisocial individuals are low in **agreeableness** and low in **conscientiousness** – they tend to be "hostile, self-centered, spiteful, jealous, and indifferent to others," and "they tend to lack ambition, motivation and perseverance, have difficulty controlling their impulses and hold nontraditional and unconventional values and beliefs" (Miller and Lynam 2001: 780; see also Loeber et al. 2012, Caspi et al. 1994). Well-known psychologist Avshalom Caspi and his colleagues refer to low levels of agreeableness as *negative emotionality* and to lack of conscientiousness as *weak constraint* (Caspi et al. 1994).

Although the research evidence linking these basic dimensions of personality and antisocial behavior is substantial and consistent, the process by which personality leads to antisocial behavior is not well understood. So far, the study of personality traits and antisocial behavior is more descriptive than explanatory (Miller and Lynam 2001). Drawing on previous research in this area, Miller and Lynam suggest that there are three distinctive patterns of social interaction that conceivably explain the connection between personality and antisocial behavior: reactive transactions, evocative transactions, and proactive transactions. During *reactive transactions*, individuals low in agreeableness interpret ambiguous situations as hostile and threatening, requiring an aggressive response. In this way, reactive transactions increase the likelihood of violence. In *evocative transactions*, children who are low in agreeableness and conscientiousness evoke negative reactions from parents because they are difficult to manage. Parents engage in harsh and erratic discipline and, out of frustration, reduce their socialization efforts. These children are also commonly rejected by peers because they are intimidating, self-centered, and indifferent to others. In *proactive transactions*, individuals who are low in conscientiousness have negative educational and occupational histories that will limit future prosocial opportunities (Miller and Lynam 2001).[6]

Intelligence and delinquency

The systematic study of intelligence began in earnest in the early 1900s and quickly connected with the growing field of criminology (Bernard et al. 2009). Criminological attention to intelligence, however, faded by the 1930s and was largely dormant until the late 1970s. Interest was rekindled in 1977 with an article by Travis Hirschi and Michael Hindelang entitled "Intelligence and Delinquency: A Revisionist Review." They first exposed criminology's tendency to discredit and ignore any link whatsoever between low intelligence and delinquency. Drawing on research that used the **intelligence quotient (IQ)** as a measure of intelligence, they claimed that IQ scores were significantly related to both self-reported and officially recorded delinquency, although the relationship was considerably stronger using self-report measures. Hirschi and Hindelang concluded that low intelligence is an important causal factor in delinquent behavior, independent of social class and race, although the relationship is primarily indirect. They contended that low intelligence affects delinquency through school performance: youths with low IQs do poorly in school, and poor school performance leads to frustration and anger and subsequently to delinquent behavior (Hirschi and Hindelang 1977). More recent research supports their view, showing that IQ significantly affects delinquency by influencing school performance (McGloin, Pratt, and Maahs 2004; Ward and Tittle 1993; Denno 1990). "Expanding ideas: IQ as a measure of intelligence and its relationship with delinquency" provides more information about IQ as a measure of intelligence and its connection with delinquency.

Expanding ideas: IQ as a measure of intelligence and its relationship with delinquency

Alfred Binet's original intelligence test was developed to identify students with learning problems – those who did poorly in school. He did not consider the test to be a precise measure of innate intelligence (Bernard, Snipes, and Gerould 2009). Most educators today agree that intelligence quotient (IQ) tests are good measures of children's ability to perform in school. Accordingly, IQ scores are best viewed as representing "a broad set of verbal and problem-solving skills which are better labeled academic aptitude or scholastic readiness" (Simons 1978: 269).

IQ scores also indicate the degree to which a child's socialization experiences are conducive to learning and academic performance (Curran and Renzetti 2007). The availability of books in the home, amount of time spent reading, and parents' encouragement of verbal expression, for example, appear to affect IQ scores (Barrett and Depinet 1999).

Research shows that delinquent youth perform poorly on verbal elements of intelligence tests, while scoring average on performance elements. The so-called "verbal IQ" measures language comprehension, whereas "performance IQ" measures non-verbal, concrete operation skills (Isen 2010). As such, family and school experiences that fail to encourage development of verbal skills are likely to account for some of the discrepancy in these scores for delinquent youth. Herbert Quay (1987) speculates that low verbal abilities may inhibit development of higher-order cognitive processes such as moral reasoning, empathy, and problem-solving.

IQ scores are also influenced by cultural context (Weinberg 1989; Simons 1978). A common complaint about intelligence tests is that they are culturally biased, providing IQ scores that are heavily determined by cultural background. If IQ scores actually measure academic preparedness and aptitude, rather than innate intelligence, then the degree to which a youth's social and cultural contexts are relevant to academic achievement will influence test performance. Similarly, cultures vary in terms of what they hold to be important, what they value as knowledge, the cognitive abilities they encourage, and how they conceptualize time and space. As a result, the degree to which intelligence test questions are culturally biased will affect IQ scores. Supporters of IQ testing claim that since the 1970s test makers have sought to eliminate cultural bias in questions (Curran and Renzetti 2007). Nonetheless, Hirschi and Hindelang (1977) point out that IQ differences between delinquent and non-delinquent youth have not disappeared entirely and seem to have stabilized at a difference of approximately eight IQ points. More recent studies have also found that serious offenders have lower scores than minor offenders and that low IQ scores of young children are related to later offending as adolescents and young adults (Parker and Morton 2009; Koolhof et al. 2007; Rutter, Giller, and Hagell 1998; Bartusch et al. 1997; Lynam and Moffitt 1995; Moffitt, Lynam, and Silva 1994; Moffitt 1990; Farrington 1988; Blumstein, Farrington, and Moitra 1985).

Intelligence, school performance, and delinquency

Although Hirschi and Hindelang argued convincingly that low intelligence influences delinquency indirectly through school failure, the causal connections may be more complex than they suggested. The link between intelligence and delinquency likely begins earlier than the school years. Psychologist Herbert Quay provides an overview of this developmental perspective on intelligence and delinquency:

> Lower intelligence is one of many factors which may put a child at a disadvantage with respect to success in a variety of situations which children face in the process of development. In the early years lower IQ may make a child more vulnerable to poor parenting and, in fact, even act with a predisposed parent to make poor parenting more likely. Such an interaction would be more likely if the IQ deficit was accompanied by a fussy or difficult temperament, motor overactivity and poor inhibitory control. The result of all these forces can be the early onset of troublesome behavior. The affected child is now at a double disadvantage when he does enter school; he has both less intellectual ability, particularly in the verbal sphere, to cope with academic tasks and he has oppositional and aggressive behavior problems that are alienating to teachers and peers. As development proceeds, both are, in combination, likely to lead to school failure, the results of which, in turn, reinforce more conduct-disordered behavior. At the same time, those higher cognitive functions (e.g., verbal self-regulation, social problem solving, and moral judgment) fail to develop adequately. This is likely due both to the limited intellectual capacity and to the mutually reinforcing social interactions that now characterize the child's relations with others. All of these factors and others as well (e.g., deviant parental and peer models) interact to produce behavior which is legally proscribed.
>
> (Quay 1987: 114–115)

Contemporary research also establishes that the relationship between intelligence and delinquency is more complex than Hirschi and Hindelang contended; a variety of factors affect the relationship. For example, the relationship between intelligence and delinquency varies by gender, race, and class; for various types of offenders; and according to temperament (Hampton et al. 2014; Block 1995; Lynam and Moffitt 1995; Lynam, Moffitt, and Stouthamer-Loeber 1993; Denno 1985). In addition, recent research points out that the indirect effect of intelligence on delinquency is also due to the effect of intelligence on self-control and susceptibility to peer pressure. One study found that while the largest indirect effect of IQ on delinquency was through school performance, the indirect effect of IQ on delinquency also occurred through level of self-control and deviant peer pressure. Low IQ contributes to delinquency by inhibiting school performance, decreasing the development of self-control (sometimes called inhibitory deficits), and increasing the likelihood of experiencing pressure from deviant peers (McGloin et al. 2004; see also Loeber et al. 2012; Parker and Morton 2009; Beaver et al. 2007, 2008a, 2008b; Beaver and Wright 2007; Koolhof et al. 2007).

The heritability of intelligence

There is also much debate about the degree to which intelligence is inherited. Earlier in this chapter, we described how genetic influences on delinquent behavior are studied primarily through adoption and twin studies. The same methods are used to try to determine the genetic basis of intelligence (Curran and Renzetti 2007). Some research shows that IQ levels of children more closely resemble those of their biological mothers than those of their adoptive parents, but other research finds that IQ scores of adopted children are influenced significantly by the conditions in which they are reared (Eysenck 1998; Plomin et al. 1997; Scarr and Weinberg 1983, 1994). Twin studies indicate that, although there is likely a heritable component to IQ, the influence of heritability is far less than once believed. Some researchers have claimed that IQ is 70–80 percent inherited. Research on identical twins, however, shows that about half of the similarity in IQ scores is a result of genetic influence (Petrill et al. 1998; Bouchard et al. 1990).

The heritability of intelligence, however, is most accurately viewed as a "genetic potential for intellectual development" (Guo and Stearns 2002: 905). Recent research once again points to the importance of nature–nurture interaction. Although genes provide a potential for intellectual development, the extent to which this potential is realized depends on environmental conditions. More specifically, a disadvantaged environment suppresses the influence of heritability and amplifies the influence of environment on intellectual development.

Summary and conclusions

The roots of positivist criminology are grounded in the scientific study of physical differences between offenders and non-offenders. The nineteenth-century Italian physician Cesare Lombroso, for example, observed physical distinctions between criminals and non-criminals that led him to conclude that criminals were a biological throwback to an earlier stage of evolution. He called such biological reversion *atavism*.

According to early biological approaches, physical differences are inherited, but not a direct cause of criminality. Rather, physical characteristics were commonly connected with the "psychology of the criminal" (Lombroso [1911] 1972). Raffaele Garofalo (1914), a student of Lombroso, argued that criminals lacked basic "moral sentiment" – they did not fear punishment and they lacked self-control. He speculated that these fundamental psychological flaws were a result of heredity and tradition, passed on from one generation to the next. Later attempts by William Sheldon to classify physical characteristics (physique) connected body type to personality temperament, indicating that the temperament associated with a particular body type was the mechanism that made some youths predisposed to delinquent behavior.

Contemporary biosocial criminology contends that delinquency and other forms of anti-social behavior result from a combination of biological, psychological, and social causes. This approach is interdisciplinary and based on the fundamental concept of *nature–nurture inter-action*. Nature–nurture interaction refers to the process by which biological, psychological, and environmental factors influence each other, as together they affect the likelihood of delinquency.

Biosocial criminology includes three major areas of study. First, neurological deficits associated with the prefrontal cortex have been studied extensively in relation to antisocial behavior. Such deficits may reduce executive functioning, resulting in poor self-regulation of impulses, emotions, and behaviors. Another aspect of neurological deficit concerns autonomic system underarousal, which results in risk-taking, sensation-seeking, and impulsive actions. Second, several key neurotransmitters and the hormone testosterone have been associated with anti-social behavior. Neurotransmitters are the chemical compounds that carry signals between neurons in the intricate communication system of the brain. Their concentration and metab-olism play a critical role in how various parts of the brain evoke and regulate behavior, espe-cially as a part of the fight-or-flight response. Levels of testosterone are linked to displays of dominance and control. Third, behavioral genetics seeks to establish the contributions of her-edity and environment to individual traits such as impulsivity, risk-taking, self-control, aggres-siveness, and negative emotionality.

Biosocial criminology does not contend that biological factors have direct effects on delinquency. Rather, biological factors, in combination with environmental conditions, prod-uce personality traits and behavioral tendencies that are conducive to delinquent behavior. Personality theory and research have established clearly that antisocial individuals are low in agreeableness and conscientiousness – they tend to be "hostile, self-centered, spiteful, jealous and indifferent to others" and "they tend to lack ambition, motivation and perseverance, have difficulty controlling their impulses and hold nontraditional and unconventional values and beliefs" (Miller and Lynam 2001: 780).

Intelligence also represents a biological potential in interaction with environmental condi-tions. As a measure of intelligence, IQ scores are most accurately viewed as a measure of aca-demic preparedness and aptitude, rather than innate intellect. As such, low IQ places youth at risk for poor school performance and frustration, leading indirectly to delinquency. Low IQ also contributes to delinquency by inhibiting the development of self-control and increasing the likelihood of experiencing pressure from deviant peers.

Critical-thinking questions

1. According to Lombroso, the physical differences that distinguish criminals from non-criminals are inherited but do not directly cause criminality. What are some of the distinctive physical characteristics of criminals, according to Lombroso? How are these physical characteristics related to crime?
2. Explain nature–nurture interaction and provide an example.
3. How does reduced executive functioning predispose youth to delinquent behavior?
4. What explanations have been offered to account for the relationship between autonomic system underarousal and antisocial behavior?

5. Develop your own working definition of *personality*. What key dimensions of personality are related to delinquency? Explain.
6. According to Hirschi and Hindelang, IQ scores are significantly related to delinquency, but the relationship is indirect. Explain how IQ is related to delinquency through school performance. What other factors influence the IQ–delinquency relationship?

Suggested reading

Burt, Callie and Ronald L. Simons. 2014. "Pulling Back the Curtain on Heritability Studies: Biosocial Criminology in the Postgenomic Era." *Criminology* 52: 223–262.

Caspi, Avshalom, Terrie E. Moffitt, Phil A. Silva, Magda Stouthamer-Loeber, Robert F. Krueger, and Pamela S. Schmutte. 1994. "Are Some People Crime-Prone? Replications of the Personality–Crime Relationship across Countries, Genders, Races and Methods." *Criminology* 32: 163–195.

Guo, Guang, Michael E. Roettger, and Tianji Cai. 2008. "The Integration of Genetic Propensities into Social-Control Models of Delinquency and Violence among Male Youths." *American Sociological Review* 73: 543–568.

Hirschi, Travis and Michael J. Hindelang. 1977. "Intelligence and Delinquency: A Revisionist Review." *American Sociological Review* 42: 571–587.

McGloin, Jean Marie, Travis Pratt, and Jeff Maahs. 2004. "Rethinking the IQ–Delinquency Relationship: A Longitudinal Analysis of Multiple Theoretical Models." *Justice Quarterly* 21: 603–635.

Miller, Joshua D. and Donald Lynam. 2001. "Structural Models of Personality and Their Relation to Antisocial Behavior: A Meta-Analytic Review." *Criminology* 39: 765–798.

Raine, Adrian. 2013. *The Anatomy of Violence: The Biological Roots of Crime*. New York: Pantheon Books.

Useful websites

For further information relevant to this chapter, go to the following websites.

- Center for Disease Control and Prevention: Division of Youth Violence Prevention (www.cdc.gov/ViolencePrevention/youthviolence/index.html)
- MacArthur Foundation Research Network on Adolescent Development and Juvenile Justice (www.adjj.org/content/index.php)
- National Center for Mental Health and Juvenile Justice (www.ncmhjj.com/)

Glossary of key terms

Agreeableness: A dimension of personality that is related strongly to antisocial behavior. Antisocial individuals tend to be hostile, self-centered, spiteful, jealous and indifferent to others. Low *agreeableness* is also referred to as *negative emotionality*.

Atavism: Reappearance in an individual of physical characteristics associated with a more primitive stage of evolution that has been absent in intervening generations. Lombroso claimed that such individuals were "born criminals" because of these characteristics.

Autonomic system underarousal: Arousal refers to the physical activation of the autonomic nervous system (ANS) in response to environmental stimuli. The relatively persistent state of autonomic system underarousal is related to antisocial, criminal, and violent behavior in both children and adults. Because anxiety reaction in anticipation of punishment is the basis for conditioning, individuals with low arousal levels have little desire or ability to avoid punishment. Therefore, they often socialize poorly and engage in antisocial behavior without restraint.

Behavioral genetics: The science that tries to estimate the relative contributions of heredity and environment to personality and behavioral traits such as impulsivity, constraint, aggressiveness, and negative emotionality.

Biological determinism: Identifying, through scientific methods, the biological characteristics of individuals that are the primary causes of behavior. People are the products of their biological makeup.

Biosocial criminology: The approach to the study of criminality that holds that crime and other forms of antisocial behavior result from a combination of social, psychological, and biological causes.

Conscientiousness: A dimension of personality that is related to antisocial behavior. Antisocial individuals tend to lack ambition, motivation, and perseverance; they have difficulty controlling their impulses; and they hold non-traditional values and beliefs. Lack of conscientiousness is also referred to as *weak constraint*.

Environmental determinism: Identifying, through scientific methods, the social conditions that cause behavior. People are the products of their environment.

Executive function: A person's ability to plan and reflect on his or her actions. This involves information processing, memory, assessment, and self-regulation.

Fight-or-flight response: When confronted with environmental stress, the limbic system activates the autonomic nervous system to produce a number of physiological responses, including increased heart rate, blood pressure, respiration, and skin electricity conductance (from stimulated sweat glands), that are designed to motivate and mobilize the body for an efficient and effective behavioral response.

Heritability: The measure of genetic influence.

Intelligence quotient (IQ): The score derived by dividing mental age (determined by the types of mental tasks an individual can perform) by chronological age and then multiplying by 100. IQ is commonly used as a measure of intelligence.

Nature–nurture debate: The argument that grew out of biological determinism and environmental determinism. The causes of behavior are either biological or environmental, but not both.

Nature–nurture interaction: The perspective which holds that it is not enough to say that biological and environmental factors contribute to behavior; rather, each influences the other, as together they produce behavior.

Neurotransmitters: Chemical compounds found in the synapse between nerve cells that carry signals from one neuron to another. Neurotransmitters provide a crucial link in the neural communications system.

Personality: The reasonably stable patterns of perceiving, thinking, feeling, and responding to the environment. Traits are the basic building blocks of personality, providing foundation to thought, emotion, character, and behavior.

Prefrontal cortex: The prefrontal lobes of the cerebral cortex (the outer layer of the cerebrum). The area of the brain that is largely responsible for impulses, emotions, and goal-directed actions. It also serves an integrative and supervisory role, called the *executive function*.

Somatotypes: Body types. William Sheldon identified three somatotypes: endomorphy, mesomorphy, and ectomorphy.

Stigmata: Distinctive physical characteristics observed in criminals that identify atavism.

Testosterone: Hormone that plays an important role in dominance and control.

Notes

1. Several excellent books have been written about biosocial criminology: Walsh and Beaver (2009); Rowe (2002); Walsh (2002); Fishbein (2001). Adrian Raine (2013) offers a very accessible book entitled *The Anatomy of Violence: The Biological Roots of Crime.*
2. In addition, memory functioning associated with the temporal lobe of the cerebral cortex (the hippocampus) has been found to be impaired in murderers, violent offenders, and life-course persistent offenders (Raine et al. 2005).
3. Reprinted with permission from the National Academies Press, Copyright © 2013, National Academy of Sciences.
4. We should note that several areas of study are conspicuously absent from our discussion of psychological approaches to delinquency, including psychoanalytic theory, cognitive and moral development, and "criterion-keyed" personality tests such as the Minnesota Multiphasic Personality Inventory (MMPI) and the California Psychological Inventory (CPI). Although traditionally discussed in juvenile delinquency texts, the study of individual psychological factors has moved in a decidedly different direction to focus on personality traits, and such study has become a key component of biosocial criminology (Miller and Lynam 2001; Steinberg 2001).
5. Eysenck spelled extraversion with an "a," rather than an "o."
6. Moffitt (1993) uses the terms *reactive, evocative,* and *proactive* to describe trait–environment interactions and to explain continuity in antisocial behavior over time.

References

Albert, David J., R. H. Jonik, N. V. Watson, B. B. Gorzalka, and Michael L. Walsh. 1990. "Hormone-Dependent Aggression in Male Rats Is Proportional to Serum Testosterone Concentration but Sexual Behavior Is Not." *Physiology and Behavior* 48: 409–416.

Andrews, D. A. and James Bonta. 2010. *The Psychology of Criminal Conduct.* 5th edn. Cincinnati, OH: Anderson.

Archer, John. 1991. "The Influence of Testosterone on Human Aggression." *British Journal of Psychology* 82: 1–28.

Armstrong, Todd A., Shawn Keller, Travis W. Franklin, and Scott N. MacMillan. 2009. "Low Resting Heart Rate and Antisocial Behavior: A Brief Review of Evidence and Preliminary Results from a New Test." *Criminal Justice and Behavior* 36: 1125–1140.

Baker, Laura A., Serena Bezdjian, and Adrian Raine. 2006. "Behavioral Genetics: The Science of Antisocial Behavior." *Law and Contemporary Problems* 69: 7–46.

Barnes, J. C., Brian B. Boutwell, and Kevin M. Beaver. 2013. "Genetic Risk Factors Correlate with County-Level Violent Crime Rates and Collective Disadvantage." *Journal of Criminal Justice* 41: 50–356.

Barrett, Gerald V. and Robert I. Depinet. 1999. "A Reconsideration of Testing for Competence Rather than Intelligence." *American Psychologist* 46: 1012–1024.

Bartol, Curt R. 1995. *Criminal Behavior: A Psychosocial Approach.* 4th edn. Englewood Cliffs, NJ: Prentice Hall.

Bartol, Curt R. and Anne M. Bartol. 2009. *Juvenile Delinquency and Antisocial Behavior: A Developmental Perspective.* 3rd edn. Upper Saddle River, NJ: Pearson Prentice Hall.

Bartusch, Dawn R. Jeglum, Donald R. Lynam, Terrie E. Moffitt, and Phil Silva. 1997. "Is Age Important? Testing a General Versus a Developmental Theory of Antisocial Behavior." *Criminology* 35: 13–48.

Beaver, Kevin M. 2009. "Molecular Genetics and Crime." Pp. 50–72 in *Biosocial Criminology: New Directions in Theory and Research,* ed. A. Walsh and K. M. Beaver. New York: Routledge.

Beaver, Kevin M. 2010. "The Effects of Genetics, the Environment, and Low Self-Control on Perceived Maternal and Paternal Socialization: Results from a Longitudinal Sample of Twins." *Journal of Quantitative Criminology* 27: 85–105.

Beaver, Kevin M., Matt DeLisi, Michael G. Vaughn, and B. Boutwell. 2008a. "The Relationship between Self-Control and Language: Evidence of a Shared Etiological Pathway." *Criminology* 46: 939–970.

Beaver, Kevin. M., Matt DeLisi, John Paul Wright, and Michael G. Vaughn. 2009a. "Gene–Environment Interplay and Delinquent Involvement." *Journal of Adolescent Research* 24: 147–168.

Beaver, Kevin M., C. Gibson, Matt DeLisi, Michael G. Vaughn, and John Paul Wright. 2011. "The Interaction between Neighborhood Disadvantage and Genetic Factors in the Prediction of Antisocial Outcomes." *Youth Violence and Juvenile Justice* 10: 25–40.

Beaver, Kevin M., Marie Ratchford, and Christopher J. Ferguson. 2009b. "Evidence of Genetic and Environmental Effects on the Development of Low Self-Control." *Criminal Justice and Behavior* 36:1158–1172.

Beaver, Kevin M., Michael G. Vaughn, Matt DeLisi, John Paul Wright, Richard Weibe, H. Harrington Cleveland, and Anthony Walsh. 2014. "The Heritability of Common Risk and Protective Factors to Crime and Delinquency." Pp. 99–114 in *Criminological Theory: A Life-Course Perspective*, 2nd edn., ed. M. DeLisi and K. M. Beaver. Burlington, MA: Jones and Bartlett Learning.

Beaver, Kevin M. and John Paul Wright. 2007. "The Stability of Low Self-Control from Kindergarten through First Grade." *Journal of Crime and Justice* 30: 63–86.

Beaver, Kevin M., John Paul Wright, and Matt DeLisi. 2007. "Self-Control as an Executive Function: Reformulating Gottfredson and Hirschi's Parental Socialization Thesis." *Criminal Justice and Behavior* 34: 1345–1361.

Beaver, Kevin M., John Paul Wright, and Matt DeLisi. 2008b. "Delinquent Peer Group Formation: Evidence of a Gene x Environment Correlation." *Journal of Genetic Psychology* 169: 227–244.

Beirne, Piers. 1987. "Adolphe Quetelet and the Origins of Positivist Criminology." *American Journal of Sociology* 92:1140–1169.

Beirne, Piers and James Messerschmidt. 2014. *Criminology: A Sociological Approach*. 4th edn. New York: Oxford University Press.

Bernard, Thomas J., Jeffrey B. Snipes, and Alexander L. Gerould. 2009. *Vold's Theoretical Criminology*. 6th edn. New York: Oxford University Press.

Block, Jack. 1995. "On the Relation between IQ, Impulsivity and Delinquency: Remarks on the Lynam, Moffitt and Stouthhamer-Loeber (1993) Interpretation." *Journal of Abnormal Psychology* 104: 395–398.

Blumstein, Alfred, David P. Farrington, and Soumyo Moitra. 1985. "Delinquent Careers." Pp. 187–219 in *Crime and Justice: A Review of Research*, vol. 7, ed. Michael H. Tonry and Norval Morris. University of Chicago Press.

Booth, Alan and D. Wayne Osgood. 1993. "The Influence of Testosterone on Deviance in Adulthood: Assessing and Explaining the Relationship." *Criminology* 31: 93–117.

Booth, Alan, G. Shelley, A. Mazur, G. Tharp, and R. Kittok. 1989. "Testosterone, and Winning and Losing in Human Competition." *Hormones and Behavior* 23: 556–571.

Bouchard, J. T., Jr., D. T. Lykken, M. McGue, N. L. Degal, and A. Tellegen. 1990. "Sources of Human Psychological Differences: The Minnesota Study of Twins Reared Apart." *Science* 250: 223–228.

Brain, Paul. 1994. "Hormonal Aspects of Aggression and Violence." Pp. 173–244 in *Understanding and Preventing Violence*, vol. 2, ed. A. J. Reiss, Jr., K. A. Miczek, and J. A. Roth. Washington, DC: National Academy Press.

Brendgen, Mara, Alain Girard, Frank Vitaro, Ginette Dionne, and Michel Boivin. 2013. "Do Peer Group Norms Moderate the Expression of Genetic Risk for Aggression?" *Journal of Criminal Justice* 41: 324–330.

Brennan, Patricia A. and Adrian Raine. 1997. "Biosocial Bases of Antisocial Behavior: Psychophysiological, Neurological and Cognitive Factors." *Clinical Psychology Review* 17: 589–604.

Bufkin, Jana L. and Vickie R. Luttrell. 2005. "Neuroimaging Studies of Aggressive and Violent Behavior Current Findings and Implications for Criminology and Criminal Justice." *Trauma, Violence and Abuse* 6: 176–191.

Burt, Callie and Ronald L. Simons. 2014. "Pulling Back the Curtain on Heritability Studies: Biosocial Criminology in the Postgenomic Era." *Criminology* 52: 223–262.

Caspi, Avshalom, Joseph McClay, Terrie E. Moffitt, Jonathan Mill, Judy Martin, Ian W. Craig, Alan Taylor, and Richie Poulton. 2002. "Role of Genotype in the Cycle of Violence in Maltreated Children." *Science* 297: 851–854.

Caspi, Avashalom, Terrie E. Moffitt, Phil A. Silva, Magda Stouthamer-Loeber, Robert F. Krueger, and Pamela S. Schmutte. 1994. "Are Some People Crime-Prone? Replications of the Personality–Crime Relationship across Countries, Genders, Races and Methods." *Criminology* 32: 163–195.

Cauffman, Elizabeth, Laurence Steinberg, and Alex R. Piquero. 2005. "Psychological, Neuropsychological and Physiological Correlates of Serious Antisocial Behavior in Adolescence: The Role of Self-Control." *Criminology* 43: 133–176.

Clark, Lee Anna and David Watson. 1999. "Temperament: A New Paradigm for Trait Psychology." Pp. 399–423 in *Handbook of Personality: Theory and Research*. 2nd edn., ed. L. A. Pervin and O. P. John. New York: Guilford.

Cleckley, Hervey. 1959. "Psychopathic States." Pp. 567–569 in *American Handbook of Psychiatry*, ed. S. Aneti. New York: Basic Books.

Curran, Daniel J. and Claire M. Renzetti. 2007. *Theories of Crime*. 3rd edn. Boston: Allyn & Bacon.

Dabbs, J. M. and R. Morris. 1990. "Testosterone, Social Class and Antisocial Behavior in a Sample of 4,462 Men." *Psychological Science* 1: 209–211.

DeLisi, Matt. 2009. "Neuroscience and the Holy Grail: Genetics and Career Criminality." Pp. 209–224 in *Biosocial Criminology: New Directions in Theory and Research*, ed. A. Walsh and K. M. Beaver. New York: Routledge.

DeLisi, Matt, Kevin M. Beaver, Michael G. Vaughn, and John Paul Wright. 2009a. "All in the Family: Gene × Environment Interaction between DRD2 and Criminal Father Is Associated with Five Antisocial Phenotypes." *Criminal Justice and Behavior* 36: 1187–1197.

DeLisi, Matt, Zachary R. Umphress, and Michael G. Vaughn. 2009b. "The Criminology of the Amygdala." *Criminal Justice and Behavior* 36: 1241–1252.

Denno, Deborah. 1985. "Sociological and Human Developmental Explanations of Crime: Conflict or Consensus." *Criminology* 23: 141–174.

Denno, Deborah. 1990. *Biology and Violence: From Birth to Adulthood*. New York: Cambridge University Press.

Ellis, Lee. 1991. "Monoamine Oxidase and Criminality: Identifying an Apparent Biological Marker for Antisocial Behavior." *Journal of Research in Crime and Delinquency* 28: 277–251.

Ewen, Robert B. 1998. *Personality: A Topical Approach: Theories, Research, Major Controversies and Emerging Findings*. Mahwah, NJ: Lawrence Erlbaum.

Eysenck, Hans J. 1964. *Crime and Personality*. Boston: Houghton Mifflin.

Eysenck, Hans J. 1991. "Dimensions of Personality: 16, 5, or 3: Criteria for a Taxonomic Paradigm." *Personality and Individual Differences* 8: 773–790.

Eysenck, Hans J. 1997. "Personality and the Biosocial Model of Anti-social and Criminal Behavior." Pp. 21–37 in *Biosocial Bases of Violence*, ed. A. Raine, P. Brennan, and D. P. Farrington. New York: Plenum.

Eysenck, Hans J. 1998. *A New Look at Intelligence*. London: Transaction.

Eysenck, Hans J. and Gisli H. Gudjonsson. 1989. *The Causes and Cures of Criminality*. New York: Plenum.

Farrington, David P. 1988. "Individual Differences and Offending." Pp. 241–268 in *Handbook of Crime and Punishment*, ed. Michael Tonry. New York: Oxford University Press.

Farrington, David P. 1997 "The Relationship between Low Resting Heart Rate and Violence." Pp. 89–105 in *Biosocial Bases of Violence*, ed. A. Raine, P. Brennan, and D. P. Farrington. New York: Plenum.

Ferri, Enrico. 1917. *Criminal Sociology*. Boston: Little, Brown.

Fishbein, Diana. 1990. "Biological Perspectives in Criminology." *Criminology* 28: 27–72.

Fishbein, Diana. 2001. *Biobehavioral Perspectives in Criminology*. Belmont, CA: Wadsworth.

Fishbein, Diana and Susan E. Pease. 1996. *The Dynamics of Drug Abuse*. Boston: Allyn & Bacon.

Gao, Yu and Simone Tang. 2013. "Psychopathic Personality and Utilitarian Moral Judgment in College Students." *Journal of Criminal Justice* 41: 342–349.

Garofalo, Raffaele. 1914. *Criminology*. Trans. R. Millar. Boston: Little, Brown.

Glueck, Sheldon and Eleanor Glueck. 1950. *Unraveling Juvenile Delinquency*. Cambridge, MA: Harvard University Press.

Glueck, Sheldon and Eleanor Glueck. 1956. *Physique and Delinquency*. New York: Harper.

Gottfredson, Michael R. and Travis Hirschi. 1987. "The Positive Tradition." Pp. 9–22 in *Positive Criminology*, ed. M. Gottfredson and T. Hirschi. Newbury Park, CA: Sage.

Grisso, Thomas and Robert G. Schwartz (eds.). 2000. *Youth on Trial: A Developmental Perspective on Juvenile Justice*. University of Chicago Press.

Grove, W. M., E. D. Eckert, L. Heston, T. J. Bouchard, N. Segal, and D. Y. Lykken. 1990. "Heritability of Substance Abuse and Antisocial Behavior: A Study of Monozygotic Twins Reared Apart." *Biological Psychiatry* 27: 1293–1304.

Guo, Guang, Xiao-Ming Ou, Michael Roettger, and Jean C. Shih. 2008a. "The VNTR 2 Repeat in MAOA and Delinquent Behavior in Adolescence and Young Adulthood: Associations and MAOA Promoter Activity." *European Journal of Human Genetics* 16: 626–634.

Guo, Guang, Michael E. Roettger, and Tianji Cai. 2008b. "The Integration of Genetic Propensities into Social-Control Models of Delinquency and Violence among Male Youths." *American Sociological Review* 73: 543–568.

Guo, Guang, Michael E. Roettger, and Jean C. Shih. 2007. "Contributions of the *DAT1* and *DRD2* Genes to Serious and Violent Delinquency among Adolescents and Young Adults." *Human Genetics* 121: 125–136.

Guo, Guang and Elizabeth Stearns. 2002. "The Social Influences on the Realization of Genetic Potential for Intellectual Development." *Social Forces* 80: 881–910.

Hampton, Ashley S., Deborah A. G. Drabick, and Laurence Steinberg. 2014. "Does IQ Moderate the Relation between Psychopathy and Juvenile Offending?" *Law and Human Behavior* 38: 23–33.

Harris, Julie Aitken. 1985. "Review and Methodological Considerations in Research on Testosterone and Aggression." *Aggression and Violent Behavior* 4: 273–291.

Hirschi, Travis and Michael J. Hindelang. 1977. "Intelligence and Delinquency: A Revisionist Review." *American Sociological Review* 42: 571–587.

Isen, Joshua. 2010. "A Meta-Analytic Assessment of Wechsler's P>V Sign In Antisocial Populations." *Clinical Psychology Review* 30: 423–435.

Ishikawa, S. S. and Adrian Raine. 2004. "Prefrontal Deficits and Antisocial Behavior: A Causal Model." Pp. 277–304 in *Causes of Conduct Disorder and Juvenile Delinquency*, ed. B. B. Lahey, T. E. Moffitt, and A. Caspi. New York: Guilford.

Jacobson, Kristen C. and David C. Rowe. 2000. "Nature, Nurture and the Development of Criminality." Pp. 323–347 in *Criminology*. 3rd edn., ed. J. F. Sheley. Belmont, CA: Wadsworth.

John, Oliver P., Laura P. Naumann, and Christopher J. Soto. 2008. "Paradigm Shift to the Integrative Big Five Taxonomy: History, Measurement, and Conceptual Issues." Pp. 114–158 in *Handbook of Personality: Theory and Research*. 3rd edn., ed. O. P. John, R. W. Robins and L. A. Pervin. New York: Guilford.

John, Oliver P. and Sanjay Srivastava. 1999. "The Big Five Taxonomy: History, Measurement and Theoretical Perspectives." Pp. 102–138 in *Handbook of Personality: Theory and Research*. 2nd edn., ed. L. A. Pervin and O. P. John. New York: Guilford.

Kleinmuntz, Benjamin. 1982. *Personality and Psychological Assessment*. New York: St. Martin's Press.

Koolhof, Roos, Rolf Loeber, Evelyn H. Wei, Dustin Pardini, and Annematt Collot D'Escury. 2007. "Inhibition Deficits of Serious Delinquent Boys of Low Intelligence." *Criminal Behaviour and Mental Health* 17: 274–292.

Lilly, J. Robert, Francis T. Cullen, and Richard A. Ball. 2015. *Criminological Theory: Context and Consequences*. 6th edn. Newbury Park, CA: Sage.

Loeber, Rolf, Jeffrey D. Burke, and Dustin A. Pardini. 2009. "Development and Etiology of Disruptive and Delinquent Behavior." *Annual Review of Clinical Psychology* 5: 293–312.

Loeber, Rolf, Barbara Menting, Donald R. Lynam, Terri E. Moffitt, Magda Stouthamer-Loeber, M., Rebecca Stallings, and Dustin Pardini. 2012. "Findings from the Pittsburgh Youth Study: Cognitive Impulsivity and Intelligence as Predictors of the Age–Crime Curve." *Journal of the American Academy of Child and Adolescent Psychiatry* 51: 1136–1149.

Lombroso, Cesare. [1911] 1972. *Criminal Man (L'Uomo delinquente)*. Trans. Gina Lombroso-Ferrero. Montclair, NJ: Patterson Smith.

Lynam, Donald R., Avshalom Caspi, Terrie E. Moffitt, Rolf Loeber, and Magda Stouthamer-Loeber. 2007. "Longitudinal Evidence That Psychopathy Scores in Early Adolescence Predict Adult Psychopathy." *Journal of Abnormal Psychology* 116: 155–165.

Lynam, Donald R. and Lauren Gudonis. 2005. "The Development of Psychopathy." *Annual Review of Clinical Psychology* 1: 381–407.

Lynam, Donald R. and Terrie Moffitt. 1995. "Delinquency and Impulsivity and IQ: A Reply to Block (1995)." *Journal of Abnormal Psychology* 104: 399–401.

Lynam, Donald, Terrie Moffitt, and Magda Stouthamer-Loeber. 1993. "Explaining the Relationship between IQ and Delinquency: Class, Race, Test Motivation, School Failure, or Self-Control?" *Journal of Abnormal Psychology* 102: 187–196.

McCrae, Robert R. and Paul T. Costa, Jr. 1987. "Validation of the Five-Factor Model of Personality across Instruments and Observations." *Journal of Personality and Social Psychology* 52: 81–90.

McCrae, Robert R. and Paul T. Costa, Jr. 1997. "Personality Trait Structure as a Human Universal." *American Psychologist* 52: 509–516.

McCrae, Robert R. and Paul T. Costa, Jr. 2008. "The Five-Factor Theory of Personality." Pp. 159–181 in *Handbook of Personality: Theory and Research*. 3rd edn., ed. O. P. John, R. W. Robins, and L. A. Pervin. New York: Guilford.

McCrae, Robert R. and Oliver P. John. 1992. "An Introduction to the Five-factor Model and Its Applications." *Journal of Personality* 60: 175–215.

McGloin, Jean Marie, Travis Pratt, and Jeff Maahs. 2004. "Rethinking the IQ–Delinquency Relationship: A Longitudinal Analysis of Multiple Theoretical Models." *Justice Quarterly* 21: 603–635.

Martin, Randy, Robert J. Mutchnick, and W. Timothy Austin. 1990. *Criminological Thought: Pioneers Past and Present*. New York: Macmillan.

Mazur, Allan. 2009. "Testosterone and Violence among Young Men." Pp. 190–204 in *Biosocial Criminology: New Directions in Theory and Research*, ed. A. Walsh and K. M. Beaver. New York: Routledge.

Mazur, Allan and Alan Booth. 1998. "Testosterone and Dominance in Men." *Behavior and Brain Science* 21: 353–363.

Mednick, Sarnoff A., William F. Gabrielli, and Bernard Hutchings. 1984. "Genetic Influences in Criminal Conviction: Evidence from an Adoption Cohort." *Science* 224: 891–894.

Miller, Joshua D. and Donald Lynam. 2001. "Structural Models of Personality and Their Relation to Antisocial Behavior: A Meta-Analytic Review." *Criminology* 39: 765–798.

Moffitt, Terrie E. 1990. "The Neuropsychology of Delinquency: A Critical Review of Theory and Research." Pp. 99–169 in *Crime and Justice: A Review of Research*, vol. 12, ed. M. Tonry and N. Morris. University of Chicago Press.

Moffitt, Terrie E. 1993. "Adolescence-Limited and Life-Course-Persistent Antisocial Behavior: A Developmental Taxonomy." *Psychological Review* 100: 674–701.

Moffitt, Terrie E. 2005. "The New Look of Behavioral Genetics in Developmental Psychopathology: Gene–Environment Interplay in Antisocial Behaviors." *Psychological Bulletin* 131: 533–554.

Moffitt, Terrie E., Gary L. Brammer, Avshalom Caspi, Paul Fawcett, Michael Raleigh, Arthur Yuwiler, and Phil Silva. 1998. "Whole Blood Serotonin Relates to Violence in an Epidemiological Study." *Biological Psychiatry* 43: 446–457.

Moffitt, Terrie E., Avshalom Caspi, Paul Fawcett, Gary L. Brammer, Michael Raleigh, Arthur Yuwiler, and Phil Silva. 1997. "Whole Blood Serotonin and Family Background Relate to Male Violence." Pp. 231–249 in *Biosocial Bases of Criminal Behavior*, ed. by S. Mednick and K. O. Christiansen. New York: Gardner.

Moffitt, Terrie E., Donald R. Lynam, and Phil A. Silva. 1994. "Neuropsychological Testing Predicting Persistent Male Delinquency." *Criminology* 32: 277–300.

National Research Council. 2013. *Reforming Juvenile Justice: A Developmental Approach*, ed. Richard J. Bonnie, Robert L. Johnson, Betty M. Chemers, and Julie A. Schuck. *Committee on Law and Justice, Division of Behavioral and Social Sciences and Education.* Washington, DC: National Academies Press.

Niv, Sharon, Catherine Tuvblad, Adrian Raine, and Laura A. Baker. 2013. "Aggression and Rule-Breaking: Heritability and Stability of Antisocial Behavior Problems in Childhood and Adolescence." *Journal of Criminal Justice* 41: 285–291.

Parker, Jennifer S. and Todd L. Morton. 2009. "Distinguishing Between Early and Late Onset Delinquents: Race, Income, Verbal Intelligence and Impulsivity." *North American Journal of Psychology* 11: 273–284.

Peskin, Melissa, Yu Gao, Andrea L. Glenn, Anna Rudo-Hutt, Yaling Yang, and Adrian Raine. 2013. "Biology and Crime." Pp. 22–39 in *The Oxford Handbook of Criminological Theory*, ed. F. T. Cullen and P. Wilcox. New York: Oxford University Press.

Petrill, S. A., R. Plomin, S. Berg, B. Johanson, N. L. Pedersen, F. Ahern, and G. E. McClean. 1998. "The Genetic and Environmental Relationship between General and Specific Cognitive Abilities in Twins Age 80 and Older." *Psychological Science* 9: 183–189.

Pitts, Traci Bice. 1997. "Reduced Heart Rate Levels in Aggressive Children." Pp. 317–320 in *Biosocial Bases of Violence*, ed. A. Raine, P. Brennan, and D. P. Farrington. New York: Plenum.

Plomin, Robert and Avshalom Caspi. 1999. "Behavioral Genetics and Personality." Pp. 251–276 in *Handbook of Personality: Theory and Research.* 2nd edn., ed. L. A. Pervin and O. P. John. New York: Guilford.

Plomin, Robert, D. W. Fulker, R. Corley, and J. C. DeFries. 1997. "Nature, Nurture and Cognitive Development from 1 to 16 years: A Parent–Offspring Adoption Study." *Psychological Science* 8: 442–447.

Quay, Herbert C. 1987. "Intelligence." Pp. 106–117 in *Handbook of Juvenile Delinquency*, ed. H. C. Quay. New York: Wiley.

Rafter, Nicole. 2008. *The Criminal Brain: Understanding Biological Theories of Crime.* New York University Press.

Raine, Adrian. 1993. *The Psychopathology of Crime: Criminal Behavior as a Clinical Disorder.* New York: Academic Press.

Raine, Adrian. 2002a. "Annotation: The Role of Prefrontal Deficits, Low Autonomic Arousal and Early Health Factors in the Development of Antisocial and Aggressive Behavior in Children." *Journal of Child Psychology and Psychiatry* 43: 417–434.

Raine, Adrian. 2002b. "Biosocial Studies of Antisocial and Violent Behavior in Children and Adults: A Review." *Journal of Abnormal Child Psychology* 30: 311–326.

Raine, Adrian. 2013. *The Anatomy of Violence: The Biological Roots of Crime.* New York: Pantheon Books.

Raine, Adrian, Patricia Brennan, and David P. Farrington. 1997. "Biosocial Bases of Violence: Conceptual and Theoretical Issues." Pp. 1–20 in *Biosocial Bases of Violence*, ed. A. Raine, P. Brennan, and D. P. Farrington. New York: Plenum.

Raine, Adrian, Terrie E. Moffitt, Avshalom Caspi, Rolf Loeber, Magda Stouthamer-Loeber, and Don Lynam. 2005. "Neurocognitive Impairments in Boys on the Life-Course Persistent Antisocial Path." *Journal of Abnormal Psychology* 114: 38–49.

Rowe, David C. 2002. *Biology and Crime*. Los Angeles: Roxbury.

Rutter, Michael. 2006. *Genes and Behavior: Nature–Nurture Interplay Explained*. Malden, MA: Blackwell.

Rutter, Michael, Henri Giller, and Ann Hagell. 1998. *Antisocial Behavior by Young People*. Cambridge University Press.

Rutter, Michael, Terrie E. Moffitt, and Avshalom Caspi. 2006. "Gene–Environment Interplay and Psychopathology: Multiple Varieties but Real Effects." *Journal of Child Psychology and Psychiatry* 47: 226–261.

Sampson, Robert J. and John H. Laub. 1997. "Unraveling the Social Context of Physique and Delinquency: A New, Long-Term Look at the Glueck's Classic Study." Pp. 175–188 in *Biosocial Bases of Violence*, ed. A. Raine, P. Brennan, and D. P. Farrington. New York: Plenum.

Scarr, Sandra and Richard A. Weinberg. 1983. "The Minnesota Adoption Studies: Genetic Differences and Malleability." *Child Development* 54: 260–267.

Schwartz, Joseph A. and Kevin M. Beaver. 2011. "Evidence of a Gene × Environment Interaction between Perceived Prejudice and MAOA Genotype in the Prediction of Criminal Arrests." *Journal of Criminal Justice* 39: 378–384.

Shannon, Katherine E., Colin Sauder, Theodore P. Beauchaine, and Lisa M. Gatzke-Kopp. 2009. "Disrupted Effective Connectivity between the Medial Frontal Cortex and the Caudate in Adolescent Boys with Externalizing Behavior Disorders." *Criminal Justice and Behavior* 36: 1141–1157.

Sheldon, William H. 1940. *The Varieties of Human Physique: An Introduction to Constitutional Psychology*. New York: Harper.

Sheldon, William H. 1942. *Varieties of Temperament*. New York: Harper.

Sheldon, William H. 1949. *Varieties of Delinquent Youth*. New York: Harper.

Simons, Ronald L. 1978. "The Meaning of the IQ–Delinquency Relationship." *American Sociological Review* 43: 268–270.

Smith, Carolyn A. and David P. Farrington. 2004. "Continuities in Antisocial Behavior and Parenting across Three Generations." *Journal of Child Psychology and Psychiatry* 45: 230–247.

Steinberg, Laurence. 2001. "Adolescent Development." *Annual Review of Psychology* 52: 83–110.

Stogner, John M. and Chris L. Gibson. 2013. "Stressful Life Events and Adolescent Drug Use: Moderating Influences of the MAOA Gene." *Journal of Criminal Justice* 41: 357–363.

Syngelaki, Eva M., Simon C. Moore, Justin C. Savage, Graeme Fairchild, and Stephanie H. M. Van Goozen. 2009. "Executive Functioning and Risky Decision Making In Young Male Offenders." *Criminal Justice and Behavior* 36: 1213–1227.

Tehrani, Jasmine and Sarnoff A. Mednick. 2000. "Genetic Factors and Criminal Behavior." *Federal Probation* 64: 24–27.

Tuvblad, Catherine, Serena Bezdjian, Adrian Raine, and Laura A. Baker. 2013. "Psychopathic Personality and Negative Parent-to-Child Affect: A Longitudinal Cross-Lag Twin Study." *Journal of Criminal Justice* 41: 331–341.

Udry, Richard J. 1988. "Biological Predispositions and Social Control in Adolescent Sexual Behavior." *American Sociological Review* 53: 709–722.

Udry, Richard J. 1990. "Biosocial Models of Adolescent Problem Behaviors." *Social Biology* 37: 1–10.

Udry, Richard J. 1995. "Sociology and Biology: What Biology Do Sociologists Need to Know?" *Social Forces* 73: 1267–1278.

Vaughn, Michael G., Matt DeLisi, Kevin M. Beaver, and John Paul Wright. 2009. "DAT1 and 5HTT Are Associated with Pathological Criminal Behavior in a Nationally Representative Sample of Youth." *Criminal Justice and Behavior* 36: 1113–1124.

Vaughn, Michael G., Matt DeLisi, Kevin M. Beaver, John Paul Wright, and Matthew O. Howard. 2007. "Toward a Psychopathology of Self-Control Theory: The Importance of Narcissistic Traits." *Behavioral Sciences and the Law* 25: 803–821.

Vaughn, Michael G. and Matthew O. Howard. 2005. "The Construct of Psychopathy and Its Role in Contributing to the Study of Serious, Violent and Chronic Youth Offending." *Youth Violence and Juvenile Justice* 3: 235–252.

Vaughn, Michael G., Matthew O. Howard, and Matt DeLisi. 2008. "Psychopathic Personality Traits and Delinquent Careers: An Empirical Examination." *International Journal of Law and Psychiatry* 31: 407–416.

Walsh, Anthony. 2002. *Biosocial Criminology: Introduction and Integration.* Cincinnati, OH: Anderson.

Walsh, Anthony. 2014. *Biosociology: Bridging the Biolog Sociology Divide.* New Brunswick, NJ: Transaction.

Walsh, Anthony and Kevin M. Beaver (eds.). 2009. *Biosocial Criminology: New Directions in Theory and Research.* New York: Routledge.

Walsh, Anthony and Jonathan D. Bolen. 2012. *The Neurobiology of Criminal Behavior: Gene–Brain–Culture Interaction.* Burlington, VT: Ashgate.

Ward, David A. and Charles R. Tittle. 1993. "Deterrence or Labeling: The Effects of Informal Sanctions." *Deviant Behavior* 14: 43–64.

Weinberg, R. A. 1989. "Intelligence and IQ: Landmark Issues and Great Debates." *American Psychologist* 44: 98–104.

Weiten, Wayne. 2013. *Psychology: Themes and Variation.* 9th edn. Belmont, CA: Wadsworth.

Widiger, Thomas A. and Donald R. Lynam. 1998. "Psychopathy as a Variant of Common Personality Traits: Implications for Diagnosis, Etiology and Pathology." Pp. 171–187 in *Psychopathy: Antisocial, Criminal and Violent Behavior,* ed. T. Million. New York: Guilford.

Wiebe, Richard P. 2009. "Psychopathy." Pp. 225–242 in *Biosocial Criminology: New Directions in Theory and Research,* ed. A. Walsh and K. M. Beaver. New York: Routledge.

Wolfgang, Marvin K. 1973. "Cesare Lombroso." Pp. 232–291 in *Pioneers in Criminology.* 2nd edn., ed. H. Mannheim. Montclair, NJ: Patterson Smith.

Wright, John Paul and Kevin M. Beaver. 2005. "Do Parents Matter in Creating Self-Control in Their Children? A Genetically Informed Test of Gottfredson and Hirschi's Theory of Low Self-Control." *Criminology* 43: 1169–1202.

Wright, John Paul, Danielle Boisvert, Kim Dietrich, and M. Douglas Ris. 2009. "The Ghost in the Machine and Criminal Behavior: Criminology for the 21st Century." Pp. 73–89 in *Biosocial Criminology: New Directions in Theory and Research,* ed. A. Walsh and K. M. Beaver. New York: Routledge.

Yaralian, Pauline S. and Adrian Raine. 2001. "Biological Approaches to Crime." Pp. 57–72 in *Explaining Criminals and Crime,* ed. R. Paternoster and R. Bachman. Los Angeles: Roxbury.

Chapter 8

The delinquent event

Situational aspects, routine activities, and rational choice

Chapter preview

Topics:

- Situational aspects of delinquency
- The experience of delinquency
- Routine activities: opportunities for delinquency
- Drifting into delinquency
- Choosing delinquency: rational choice theory

Theories:

- Situational inducements and commitment to conformity
- Routine activities theory
- Drift theory
- Techniques of neutralization
- Rational choice theory
- Situational action theory

Terms:

- delinquent event
- objective content of situations
- subjective content of situations
- situational inducements
- commitment to conformity
- routine activities
- motivated offenders
- suitable targets
- capable guardians
- hard determinism
- positivist criminology
- soft determinism

- classical criminology
- drift
- subculture of delinquency
- subterranean values
- techniques of neutralization
- will
- criminal propensity
- deterrent effect
- human agency
- morality

Chapter learning objectives

After completing this chapter, students should be able to:

- Identify characteristics of situations that motivate and provide opportunities for delinquency.
- Explain how the adversity of homelessness is related to delinquent behavior.
- Describe how an individual's perception and interpretation of the immediate situation are related to delinquency.
- Describe how adolescents' routine activities provide opportunities for delinquency.
- Distinguish the *subculture of delinquency* from the *delinquent subculture*, and explain how each is relevant to an understanding of delinquent behavior.
- Identify several key factors that enter into offending decisions.
- Explain how criminal propensity is related to offending choices.
- Describe how morality affects an individual's perceptions of "action alternatives" within particular situations.

Case in point: the sneaky thrill of pizza theft – a spontaneous, situational act

In his provocative book *Seductions of Crime*, Jack Katz provides a series of personal accounts of crime that were offered by students in his criminology class. These accounts offer vivid description of the experience of crime – "what it means, feels, sounds, tastes, or looks like to commit a particular crime." The immediate situation of delinquency not only provides sensation, but also elicits interpretation, meaning, and response. Certain situations also motivate and provide opportunity for delinquent behavior. This chapter considers such situational and routine dimensions of delinquent behavior and the perceptions and choices that go into delinquent offending.

> I grew up in a neighborhood where at 13 everyone went to Israel, at 16 everyone got a car and after high school graduation we were all sent off to Europe for the summer. ... I was 14 and my neighbor was 16. He had just gotten a red Firebird for his birthday and we went driving around. We just happened to drive past the local pizza place and we saw the delivery boy getting into his car. ... We could see the pizza boxes in his back seat. When the pizza boy pulled into a high rise apartment complex, we were right behind him. All of a sudden, my neighbor said, "You know, it would be so easy to take a pizza!" ... I looked at him, he looked at me, and without saying a word I was out of the door ... got a pizza and ran back ...
>
> The feeling I got from taking the pizza, the thrill of getting something for nothing, knowing I got away with something I never thought I could, was wonderful. ... I'm 21 now and my neighbor is 23. Every time we see each other, I remember and relive a little bit of that thrill.
>
> *Source*: Katz (1988: 3, 52, 64).

Adolescent behavior in general, and delinquent behavior in particular, is often characterized as impulsive and spontaneous, being driven by the immediate situation. It is also the case that teenagers are not well known for their rational and thoughtful decision-making. They are often criticized for acting without thinking. It is ironic, then, that criminological explanations of delinquency have focused on background characteristics of youth and their surroundings that may lead to delinquency rather than the "immediate setting" in which delinquency occurs (Agnew 1990: 272; Birkbeck and LaFree 1993; Hagan and McCarthy 1997; Sutherland, Cressey, and Luckenbill 1992).

In a well-known study of delinquency, Martin Gold (1970: 92–99) found that most delinquent acts were unplanned and rarely developed into a repetitive pattern of delinquent behavior. In addition, those who participated in delinquent acts had varying levels of commitment and involvement. These observations led Gold (1970: 92) to compare delinquent behavior to a pickup game of basketball in which participation is desired, but casual, unplanned, and short term. Teams are rarely set beforehand, and boys who want to play know where other likely players hang out and where the game is usually played. The game's competitiveness depends on the level of participation of those who play: some players are invested in the game, while others are casual participants. Gold's observations support an image of delinquency that is far more casual and spontaneous than most explanations of delinquency.

This chapter explores the **delinquent event** – the situational context of offending decisions and delinquent acts (Sacco and Kennedy 2002; Lopez 2008; Gottfredson 2005; Agnew 1990; Gottfredson and Hirschi 1989). Our focus on the immediate setting of delinquent events will consider five interrelated areas of study: (1) situational aspects of delinquent acts, (2) the experience of delinquency, (3) routine activities of adolescents, (4) a theoretical view that adolescents "drift" into delinquency, and (5) the rational elements of choosing to engage in delinquent acts. In each of these areas of study, the situational context of delinquent acts is the unit of analysis and immediate circumstances are the center of attention (Matsueda 1989; Gibbons 1971).

Situational aspects of delinquency

The immediate setting of delinquent events "can be described in terms of who is there, what is going on, and where it takes place" (LaFree and Birkbeck 1991: 75; Pervin 1978). Viewed in this way, the situational characteristics of delinquent events provide both motivation and opportunity for delinquent acts. The **objective content of situations** can motivate delinquent behavior by "imposing negative experiences such as frustration, threats, humiliation, and boredom; by offering positive attractions such as money, property, image-building, thrills, and sexual satisfaction; or by providing models to be imitated" (Birkbeck and LaFree 1993: 129–130). Encountering interpersonal conflict, for example, may arouse an aggressive response, and poverty and hunger may necessitate theft of food. Situations can also provide opportunity by affecting the extent to which criminal motivations can be carried out. The possibility of success, absence of detection, availability of goods, and access to victims all relate to the degree to which a situation provides opportunity for delinquency. In this regard, the routine daily activities of some adolescents provide ample opportunity for involvement in delinquency when they spend large amounts of unsupervised time with peers.

Offending situations can also be described in terms of their subjective qualities. The **subjective content of situations** encompasses the "individual's perception and interpretation of the immediate setting" (Birkbeck and LaFree 1993: 129). The various rationalizations that run through a youth's mind before he or she commits a delinquent act are one example of subjective content. Subjective content of situations also includes how delinquent acts are experienced by youths and what these experiences mean to them. Shoplifting, for example, sometimes takes on a game-like quality, pitting the shoplifter against the store clerk. In these cases, shoplifting provides a sense of thrill and accomplishment, rather than the need for the particular item being stolen (Katz 1988).

Situational correlates of aggression

A large body of research, conducted primarily by psychologists, has examined the situational factors that are related to aggressive behavior. Experimental studies have revealed five situational correlates of aggression.[1]

1. **Blocked goals and frustration:** Research has examined the degree to which aggression is a consequence of frustration, commonly identified as the frustration–aggression hypothesis. This research reveals that individuals sometimes respond aggressively to situations that they find frustrating, especially when these frustrations are thought to be intentionally produced by others (Birkbeck and LaFree 1993).[2]
2. **Physical or verbal provocation:** Research has also found that verbal and physical threats and attacks provoke aggressive responses. Daniel Lockwood's (1997) study of 250 violent incidents reported by 110 middle and high school students found that the most common provocation for violence was "offensive touching," including grabbing, pushing, and hitting. Provocations were also non-physical; these included teasing, insulting, and saying something negative about a person to a third party. Typically, these provocations led first to an argument, then escalated into an exchange of insults, and finally resulted in a violent response by one of the youths.
3. **Aggressive models:** Exposure to violent models, particularly in the media, appears to produce aggressive behavior in some individuals. After an extensive review of the literature, Wendy Wood and her associates (1991: 380) conclude: "Our results demonstrate that media violence enhances children's and adolescents' aggression in interaction with strangers, classmates, and friends." However, they point out that the studies they reviewed focused on short-term media effects, because they measured aggressive behavior shortly after the media portrayal of violence. It is also the case that researchers, using experimental methods, have not been able to conclusively establish a causal relationship between media violence and subsequent violent behavior (Freedman 1988; Messner 1986; Snyder 1991). It may be that violent children watch more media violence, identify with violent characters, or believe that violence is a normal part of everyday life, and thus an appropriate response to interpersonal conflict (Bartol and Bartol 2009: 111–112).
4. **Cues for aggression:** In some instances, people or objects may prompt aggressive behavior. "Crimes of obedience" sometimes result from the physical presence or instruction of authority figures. Milgram's (1974) famous experiment found that subjects would administer what they thought to be a near-fatal electric shock to another subject when told to do so by an experimenter. Similarly, delinquent youths often claim that they were just "following the leader" in committing delinquent offenses. Research also indicates that the presence of weapons and certain clothing (e.g., displaying gang colors) may function as a cue for aggression (Birkbeck and LaFree 1993).
5. **Low levels of restraint on aggression:** Situations also vary in the level of restraint on aggression. In some situations, the presence of rules and sanctions, together with the threat of punishment (either physical or non-physical), operate as controls for aggressive action. However, the influence of these situational characteristics on aggressive behavior depends on the perception of the individual. When restraints are perceived as unjust or as lacking authority, restraint is reduced.

Situational inducements

The reluctance of sociological criminologists to consider situational factors in delinquent behavior was first exposed in 1965 by Scott Briar and Irving Piliavin in an article entitled "Delinquency, Situational Inducements, and Commitment to Conformity." They argued that most criminological theories are based on the assumption that some youths develop long-lasting predispositions to engage in delinquent acts because of certain individual, interpersonal, and social characteristics that "propel them into illegal behavior" (Briar and Piliavin 1965: 35). According to Briar and Piliavin (1965: 35), these "motivational theories" share a number of serious problems. Most significant, many youths who experience these conditions never develop delinquent dispositions, and even among youths who do, many never engage in delinquent acts. Most delinquent youths, regardless of whether they develop delinquent predispositions, become law-abiding in late adolescence and early adulthood. Thus, Briar and Piliavin question whether the causal conditions identified by motivational theories adequately explain why some youths become involved in delinquent offenses and others do not, and why most delinquent involvement is short-term.

In contrast to motivational theories, Briar and Piliavin (1965: 36–37) turn to characteristics of the current situation that provide "conflicts, opportunities, pressures, and temptations" that may influence what youth think and do. They refer to these as "situationally induced stimuli of relative short duration," or, more simply, **situational inducements** (Briar and Piliavin 1965: 37, 35). The actions that follow from these situational inducements serve a purpose: they allow youth "to obtain valued goods, to portray courage in the presence of, or be loyal to peers, to strike out at someone who is disliked, or simply to 'get kicks'" (Briar and Piliavin 1965: 36).

Briar and Piliavin also acknowledge that not all youths succumb to such pressures and that situational inducements may not be sufficient in themselves to produce delinquent behavior. All youths experience situational motivation and opportunity to engage in delinquent acts; however, the probability that they will be acted upon depends on the youth's **commitment to conformity** (Briar and Piliavin 1965: 39, 45). Those youths who have little commitment to conformity are heavily influenced by situational inducements, whereas those who are highly committed are not. In addition, commitment to conformity influences the youth's response to adult authority figures and to their choice of friends.

During childhood and adolescence, the development of commitment is most heavily influenced by the youth's relationship with his or her parents (Briar and Piliavin 1965: 41). Affection, discipline, expectations, and willingness to conform to parental authority are key aspects of the relationship between parents and youth. Youth with strong commitments to parents are less likely to act upon situational inducements to deviate than are youths with minimal commitments. Thus, the parent–child relationship, as a primary determinant of commitment, influences the effect that situational pressures have on behavior and the likelihood of involvement in delinquency.

Mean streets: adverse situations and delinquency

The motivational theories of delinquency that Briar and Piliavin criticize have also been taken to task more recently by Bill McCarthy and John Hagan (1992) because of their neglect of situational influences on delinquent behavior. In particular, they draw attention to the adverse situations encountered by homeless youth in their everyday lives. Hagan and

McCarthy (1997: 1) contend that living on the streets provides not only temptations and opportunities for involvement in delinquent behavior, but that these harsh living conditions also produce much strain: "The homeless youth who live on the streets of our cities confront desperate situations on a daily basis. Often without money, lacking shelter, hungry, and jobless, they frequently are involved in crime as onlookers, victims, and perpetrators." Crime is all around them – they see it, experience it, and resort to it as a means of coping with the difficulties of being homeless. It is also the case that street life involves few controls to restrain crime and delinquency. For homeless youth, the freedom of street life goes hand-in-hand with the harsh living conditions of "mean streets." Desperate situations require desperate means, and street crime is an ever-present part of life for homeless youth.

Not only has contemporary criminology neglected the role that adverse situations play in delinquent behavior, it has also failed to study the street youths who disproportionately experience such hardships. The dominance of self-report research methods over the past 50 years has led to a focus on delinquency committed by adolescents living at home and attending school (McCarthy and Hagan 1992; Hagan and McCarthy 1992). As a result, self-report methods may minimize the causal importance of situational factors, especially the strain that results from difficult situations. Hagan and McCarthy's (1997) solution is to take criminology back to the streets, where delinquency research first began. In what are now classic studies, sociologists in the early twentieth century studied whether the social forces of urbanization, immigration, and industrialization were exposing urban youth to conditions that bred crime.

McCarthy and Hagan conducted a survey of 390 homeless youths in the city of Toronto. They deliberately chose not to refer to these street youths as "runaways," because

> it implies that leaving home is inappropriate and that a return is both possible and desirable. Yet previous research reveals that many youths who leave home are forced out by parents or are escaping from abusive environments; not surprisingly, many are unwilling to return home.
>
> (McCarthy and Hagan 1992: 602)

The survey was administered primarily in two contexts: at social service agencies that provided assistance to homeless youths (e.g., hostels, shelters, drop-in centers) and at street locations where homeless youths panhandled or spent the night (e.g., inner-city parks, street corners, and bus stations).

McCarthy and Hagan supplemented their street data with data drawn from a sample of youths living at home and attending school. These data were gathered at three different high schools in the Toronto area from randomly selected 9th- through 12th-grade classes. Using a questionnaire designed to parallel the instrument used with the street youth, 562 students provided information about their families, friends, and school. These data were then combined with those gathered from street youths, allowing the researchers to investigate the factors that compel youths to leave home and "take to the streets" (McCarthy and Hagan 1992: 604, 619–620).

Taking to the streets

McCarthy and Hagan found that the likelihood of leaving home increased with a number of factors: age, coercive controls by parents, sexual abuse, conflict with teachers, and having delinquent friends. Youths who leave home tend to be older, to have little desire to achieve in school, and to have frequent conflict with teachers. Their parents are often divorced and characterized as abusive, both physically and sexually. They are also more likely to have delinquent friends. These empirical findings are supported by the narrative accounts of family and school life offered by homeless youths. Jeremy, a young boy who left home at age 12, describes his situation this way:

> My dad was an alcoholic, and he always abused me – physically. He'd punch me and stuff like that – throw me up against the walls. And like one night we were going at it, and I turned around, like he punched me a couple of times. I turned around and got a baseball bat out of the bedroom, and I hit him in the head, and then he got back up, and he started pounding on me big time. Well, the cops came and they took him, and they said "You can go live with your mother, right?" My mother had already said, "We don't want you," so I said, "Okay, I'm going to go to my mother's" and [instead] I went out in the streets.
>
> (Hagan and McCarthy 1997: 26)

The adversity of homelessness

Youths who leave home are exposed almost immediately to harsh living conditions. One of the first problems they confront is finding a safe place to sleep. The narrative accounts of initial experiences on the street frequently tell of youths walking for hours with no place to go. Jeremy expressed the problem of shelter like this: "I mostly didn't sleep the first couple days. Then I got to a bridge, and I just slept underneath the bridge. Then I kept on walking, sleeping at night in people's sheds and stuff like that" (Hagan and McCarthy 1997: 38). The lack of shelter is an almost immediate strain for most homeless youth: "The worst thing was not knowing where you were going to sleep. Sleeping in a storefront or on the street. Who knows what's going to happen to you?" (Hagan and McCarthy 1997: 41).

It also is not long before homeless youths face the problem of hunger. Hagan and McCarthy (1997: 49) report that over three-quarters of the youths surveyed revealed that they had gone an entire day without eating, and more than half said they frequently went hungry. Without resources of money or employment, homeless youths confront the unrelenting problems of food and shelter. Street crimes – principally theft, robbery, selling drugs, prostitution, and violence – are a means of coping with the adversity of homelessness. "Many street youth … move in and out of these activities to sustain and support their existence on the street" (Hagan and McCarthy 1997: 115).

McCarthy and Hagan's (1991) study of street youth demonstrated that homelessness leads to crime, especially street crimes associated with problems of shelter, hunger, and the lack of legitimate resources (most important, money and employment). A significant proportion of homeless youth were involved in criminal activities only after leaving home. This was true for crimes typically associated with street life, including drug use, theft, and prostitution. The effect of street life on criminal involvement held true for both males and females and was true regardless of age. McCarthy and Hagan concluded that motivation for crime exists in the crime-producing conditions of homelessness, rather than in a person's background.

In a study that followed, McCarthy and Hagan (1992) explored more fully how homelessness was connected to criminal involvement, particularly to the types of crime most commonly associated with street life: theft of food, serious theft, and prostitution. Using the same data provided by homeless youth, they investigated how three specific conditions of homelessness – hunger, lack of shelter, and unemployment – were related to these forms of street crime. A large number of background factors were incorporated into their study, including social class, strain within the family, family structure, parental supervision and controls, school experiences, involvement in delinquency at home, delinquent associates at home and on the streets, and time on the streets. The simultaneous consideration of these background factors, together with conditions of homelessness, allowed the researchers to see whether street crime was a response to the adversity of homelessness or a result of characteristics that homeless youth bring with them to the streets.

McCarthy and Hagan used a statistical method that allowed them to determine whether situational adversity, measured by hunger, lack of shelter, and unemployment, had a measurable direct effect on street crime, independent of a youth's background when living at home. They found that each measure of situational adversity was as strongly associated with street crime as background and developmental variables. They concluded that the adverse situations of homelessness have strong direct effects on street crime.

Situational strains

The daily situations in which adolescents find themselves may involve frustrations and irritations related to fairly immediate social goals such as "being popular with peers, earning good grades, doing well in athletics, being popular with the opposite sex, and getting along well with parents and teachers" (Agnew 1990: 272). Delinquent events may originate in the frustration and anger generated by failing to achieve these immediate goals, such as flunking a test, poor performance on the athletic field, or an argument with a dating partner (Agnew 1990: 273). Similarly, delinquency may be triggered when a youth is unable to avoid undesirable or painful situations such as school, abuse, or undesired attention from certain individuals. These types of frustrations and irritations in the daily lives of adolescents are the focal point of a contemporary theory called *general strain theory*, introduced by Robert Agnew. This theory is discussed in Chapter 11. Agnew claims that many of the strains of adolescence are situationally based, being a product of frustrating circumstances. His research on the situational character of strain reveals that frustrations of social life are primarily relevant to violent crime, vandalism, and running away.

The situation of company

One of the most enduring areas of study in criminology is the role that peers play in learning and reinforcing patterns of delinquent behavior (Warr 2002). Chapter 10 addresses the major questions, issues, and theories related to the nature and extent of peer influences. The consideration of peer influence, however, is based on an explanation that focuses on how delinquent attitudes and behaviors are learned from delinquent peers over time. The peer relationships that produce such strong influence on adolescents are thought to be strong, close, and long-lasting.

A contrasting point of view on peer influence has been offered by LaMar Empey and Steven Lubeck (1968). They contend that situations involving peers – the "situation of company" – generate certain expectations for behavior and that these "normative expectations in group contexts" are the primary mechanisms of peer influence.

Empey and Lubeck's research involved a survey of youths in two different locations: one urban, one rural. The survey instrument included 16 different "situated choices," asking youths what they were "prepared to do." For example: "Suppose when you and your friends were messing around one night, they decided to break into a place and steal some stuff, do you think you would go with them?" (Empey and Lubeck 1968: 761). Those who completed the survey chose one of five response categories for each question: (1) every time, (2) most of the time, (3) about half the time, (4) some of the time, and (5) never. The pattern of responses indicated the degree to which youths were subjected to normative expectations of particular situations.

Empey and Lubeck (1968) found that all youths – both urban and rural, delinquent and non-delinquent – reported a willingness to conform to situational expectations. However, delinquent youth were more inclined than non-delinquent youth to associate with peers in situations in which delinquency was expected. In contrast, urban, non-delinquent youth were least inclined to involve themselves with peers in situations that involve delinquency.[3] Thus, peer expectation within situations is a motivational force for delinquent acts.

The experience of delinquency

The perspectives discussed so far consider characteristics of current situations as if they are entirely objective. Being hungry, homeless, and in the "situation of company," for example, are thought to motivate and provide opportunity for delinquent acts. Characteristics of the situation, however, also include subjective content, relating to the individual's perception and interpretation of the current circumstances – the meaning that situations have for those involved (Birkbeck and LaFree 1993; Sutherland et al. 1992; see also Putnins 2010).

In a provocative book, *Seductions of Crime: Moral and Sensual Attractions in Doing Evil*, sociologist Jack Katz (1988) focuses on the subjective content of crime and delinquency. His central thesis is that delinquent and criminal behavior cannot be understood or explained without grasping how it is experienced or what it means to the offender (Goode 1990: 7). Katz (1988: 3) argues:

> The social science literature contains only scattered evidence of what it means, feels, sounds, tastes, or looks like to commit a particular crime. Readers of research on homicide and assault do not hear the slaps and curses, see the pushes and shoves, or feel the humiliation and rage that may build toward the attack, sometimes persisting after the victim's death. How adolescents manage to make the shoplifting or vandalism of cheap and commonplace things a thrilling experience has not been intriguing to many students of delinquency.

Katz draws attention to the "moral and sensual attraction of doing evil" (the book's subtitle) as experienced by the offender in the criminal event. Central to the "experience of criminality" is one or more "moral emotions: humiliation, righteousness, arrogance, ridicule, cynicism, defilement, and vengeance" (Katz 1988: 9). Katz proposes that the situational dynamics of crime involve three stages. Each stage is necessary for crime to occur, and together the three stages are sufficient to explain crime; however, the content of each stage varies for different types of crime. The three stages are as follows:

1. A *path of action* – distinctive practical requirements for successfully committing the crime.

2. A *line of interpretation* – unique ways of understanding how one is and will be seen by others.
3. An *emotional process* – seduction and compulsions that have special dynamics.

(Katz 1988: 9, emphasis added)

These moral and sensual dynamics of crime situations are difficult to analyze through traditional data; therefore, Katz turns to various accounts of illegal activity, including biographies, autobiographies, ethnographies, observational studies, and journalism (Goode 1990: 7). These stories relate real-life experiences that make his theory remarkably compelling. Several of these stories are offered here in the context of Katz's explanation of the "sneaky thrill" of property crime.

Sneaky thrills: juvenile property crime

According to Katz (1988: 52):

> Various property crimes share an appeal to young people, independent of material gain or esteem from peers. Vandalism defaces property without satisfying a desire for acquisition. During burglaries, young people sometimes break in and exit successfully but do not try to take anything. Youthful shoplifting, especially by older youth, often is a solitary activity retained as a private memory. "Joyriding" captures a form of auto theft in which getting away with something in celebratory style is more important than keeping anything or getting anywhere in particular.

Katz contends that these property offenses are essentially emotional events that provide sneaky thrills. Rather than reflecting a youth's upbringing or material living conditions, property crimes are determined almost exclusively by situational experiences. The sneaky thrill of property crime is created in the three-stage process just described, although the content of these stages is unique to juvenile property crimes.

Constructing an object as seductive

The "path of action" for sneaky thrills often begins with a situation that is simply exciting. Even though juvenile property offenders may set out to commit a crime, there is usually little forethought or planning; rather, spontaneity and excitement prevail. The possibility of property crime emerges when the future offender realizes that an act or an object has appeal, that the act can be done, and that the item can be taken with relative ease:

> There we were, in the most lucrative department Mervyn's had to offer two curious (but very mature) adolescent girls: the cosmetic and jewelry department ... We didn't enter the store planning to steal anything. In fact, I believed we had "given it up" a few weeks earlier; but once my eyes caught sight of the beautiful white and blue necklaces alongside the counter, a spark inside me was once again ignited ... Those exquisite puka necklaces were calling out to me, "Take me! Wear me! I can be yours!" All I needed to do was take them to make it a reality.

(Katz 1988: 54)

Remaining in rational control

The second stage of juvenile property crime – what Katz refers to as "the emergence of practiced reason" – involves an attempt to appear normal and legitimate in an effort to successfully carry out the crime. Efforts to appear normal and legitimate are especially relevant to shoplifting. Katz (1988: 59) provides a recollection of one of his students who shoplifted with her sister while using their mother as "cover":

> I can clearly remember when we coaxed my mom into taking us shopping with the excuse that our summer trip was coming and we just wanted to see what the stores had so we could plan on getting it later. We walked over to the section that we were interested in, making sure that we made ourselves seem "legitimate" by keeping my mom close and by showing her items that appealed to us. We thought "they won't suspect us, two girls in school uniforms with their mom, no way." As we carried on like this, playing this little game "Oh, look how pretty, gee, I'll have to tell dad about all these pretty things."

Avoiding suspicion is a challenge that constantly confronts would-be property offenders. Shoplifters, for example, become extraordinarily conscious of their actions and how they appear to others. Katz (1988: 64) provides the following account of a juvenile shoplifter:

> She [the store clerk] stopped me about 5 ft. from the door, my heart was beating so hard, not fast just hard like it was going to jump out of my chest. The lady asked me "Didn't you find anything you liked?" I knew she was trying to see if I was nervous and to let me know she had seen me earlier. I said no, that I hadn't discovered anything that I couldn't live without. I remember trying to phrase the sentence as grownup as possible so she wouldn't think I was a dumb little kid. Then she said "What about that green necklace I saw you holding." … I said "I simply don't own anything to go with it so I hung it back on the rack." She said "Oh" and started toward the rack, so I continued out the door.

Being thrilled

The third stage to the moral and sensual attraction of juvenile property offending involves the emotional sensation of being thrilled by a delinquent act. Thrill is derived from the secretive and cunning nature of these offenses and the sense of accomplishment after being able to "pull it off." Katz (1988: 69–70) summarizes a lengthy account of non-acquisitive burglary provided by one of his students:

> When she was 13, she would enter neighbors' homes and roam around. Somehow being in a neighbor's house without express permission made the otherwise mundane environment charged. She had been invited into all these homes before but by entering without notice through an unlocked door or an open window, she found that a familiar kitchen or living room was magically transformed into a provocative environment. The excitement was distinctly sensual … But she rarely took anything. Instead she might simply rearrange the furniture. It seems she was not so much "playing house" or decorating to fit her tastes as she was trying to leave evidence that someone had been there.

An assessment of sneaky-thrill property crime

Bill McCarthy (1995) offers an extension to Katz's phenomenological explanation of sneaky-thrill property crime. He acknowledges that criminology has neglected the importance of situational factors, especially the moral and sensual dynamics of the immediate situation that make theft compelling to juveniles. McCarthy contends, however, that Katz's emphasis on the emotional elements of situations is overstated. McCarthy argues that not all people respond to the seductive quality of situations by resorting to shoplifting – some simply purchase the item or wait until later to buy it.

McCarthy proposes that the seductive quality of theft is influenced by an individual's background, including age, gender, and social class. Shoplifting, for example, may be tied to a low socioeconomic status in which the lack of economic means to purchase an item leads to theft. McCarthy also claims that rational thought plays an important role in the degree to which theft is morally and sensually compelling to the individual. Juvenile property crime is not simply an emotional response to an enticing situation, devoid of reason.

Using survey data, McCarthy tested a model of sneaky-thrill property crime that included background and rational choice. Questionnaire items were used to measure background factors, including gender, age, race, socioeconomic status, and strain resulting from lack of opportunity. Other questionnaire items were used to measure rational thought, such as concern for being sanctioned, fear of loss of respect, and moral commitment. Seduction to crime was measured through questions that asked, "How often would you like to take something that does not belong to you?" and "If you were in a situation tomorrow where you had an extremely strong desire or need to, what are the chances that you would take something that does not belong to you?" (McCarthy 1995: 527, 537).

Analysis of the survey data revealed that the reported desire to steal both in the past and in the future was not simply an emotional response to the current situation. Rather, the desire to steal was influenced in important ways by rational thought and by background characteristics of the individual. In terms of rational thought, people who thought that theft was not morally wrong and who felt that their detection would not lead to a loss of respect were more likely to report that they had experienced a desire to commit theft in the past and that they would likely commit theft in the future, given a desire to do so. In addition, having committed theft in the past and having been exposed to sanctions for crime did not inhibit consideration of future theft. In fact, these experiences actually seemed to encourage consideration of future theft.

Gender also influenced involvement in sneaky thrills. Males were more likely than females to report that they experienced a desire to steal in the past and that they would steal given the desire sometime in the future. Thus, the desire or seduction of theft is not simply an emotional response. Rather, it is influenced by rational thought and by an individual's gender.

Routine activities: opportunities for delinquency

Situations are important largely to the degree that they provide opportunity for delinquency (Wilcox et al. 2014; Sacco and Kennedy 2002; Sutherland et al. 1992). Obviously, some situations are more favorable for delinquency than others, but what characteristics of situations provide greater opportunity? Opportunity includes not only the actual possibility of delinquent acts, but also the youth's consideration of whether a delinquent act is likely to bring about an expected reward, and his or her perception of the likelihood of getting caught

(Birkbeck and LaFree 1993).Viewed in this way, opportunity involves choice, but it is a choice prescribed by the situation. Marcus Felson (1986: 119) observes: "People make choices, but they cannot choose the choices available to them."[4] Together with Lawrence Cohen, Felson developed routine activities theory in an attempt to address the characteristics of the situation that influence the range of choices available to individuals (Cullen, Agnew, and Wilcox 2014).

Situations that provide opportunity for crime are not necessarily unique or unusual in any way; rather, what must be considered are the **routine activities** of everyday life (Osgood et al. 1996; Cohen and Felson 1979).[5] Crime and delinquency are more common when the routines of daily living – at home, on the job, and in activities away from home – provide opportunity for crime. Cohen and Felson (1979: 598) point out that significant lifestyle changes since the end of World War II have resulted in "the dispersion of activities away from households." Changes include increases in female workforce participation, in the proportion of households unattended during the day, in out-of-town travel, and in sales of consumer goods. These changes in routine activities are, in turn, related to the rise in predatory crimes such as robbery, burglary, larceny, and murder.

According to routine activities theory, three basic elements of the situation are necessary for crime or delinquency to occur: **motivated offenders** must come in contact with **suitable targets** in the absence of **capable guardians** (Cohen and Felson 1979: 590). Although motivation is one of the three "minimal elements" that must "converge in space and time" for predatory crime to occur, Cohen and Felson assume that people continually pursue what is self-beneficial; therefore, there will always be motivated offenders.[6] What must be explained, then, is change in the other two elements: suitable targets and absence of capable guardians. Cohen and Felson point out that although modern conveniences make life easier, their availability increases opportunity for predatory crime. Electronic goods, for example, have greatly enhanced quality of life, but they are also relatively easy to steal and have high value. Target suitability for crime depends on several key characteristics, including value, physical visibility, access, and "inertia" (weight, size, and protective features) (Cohen and Felson 1979: 591; see also Miethe and Meier 1990). Technological advances have tended to make consumer goods smaller, lighter, and more valuable, thereby increasing opportunity for crime. Greater availability and value have increased consumption of consumer products, making them more available for theft and robbery. Lifestyle changes that move activities away from the home also reduce the level of residential guardianship, making homes vulnerable to predatory property crimes. The proportion of households unattended during the day, for example, has increased dramatically since 1960.

Target suitability for personal crime is similarly enhanced when people spend more time in public spaces, such as restaurants, bars, sidewalks, and parks (Cohen and Felson 1979). Public activities increase the likelihood that potential victims of personal crime will come into contact with motivated offenders, in the absence of capable guardians. Routine activities theory claims that individuals engaged in activities away from home, without family members, are at greater risk of criminal victimization than those who are at home with family. Reduced levels of guardianship in the routine activities of daily life enhance opportunities for crime.

The routine activities of adolescents

Using a routine activities perspective, Wayne Osgood and his colleagues (1996) examined how the routine activities of adolescents are related to a broad range of deviant behavior.

They were especially interested to see if routine activities theory might provide insight into the relationship between age and criminal involvement. Chapter 5 described how criminal involvement is especially prominent in the adolescent and young adult years and rises and falls rapidly before and after these years. Do "age-related changes in the activities of every-day life" account for this age–crime connection (Osgood et al. 1996: 641; see also Osgood and Anderson 2004)? Further, what types of adolescent activities provide opportunity for deviance?

Osgood and his associates frame their study within a revised routine activities theory. Instead of "motivated offenders," the researchers contend that the motivation for deviant behavior resides in the situation rather than in the person. Some situations to which youths are exposed provide both opportunity and reward for deviant behavior. This is referred to as "situational motivation."

Of special importance during the adolescent years is the role that peer influence plays in deviant behavior. Osgood and his colleagues contend that "being with peers can increase the situational potential for deviance by making deviance easier and rewarding" (Osgood et al. 1996: 639). Consequently, they include time with peers as a second key dimension of their routine activities theory.

In applying the "absence of guardian" concept to the adolescent years, Osgood and his associates use another situational factor that they refer to as "the absence of authority figures." Settings of work, school, and family provide authority figures that limit the possibility of deviance. In contrast, situations conducive to deviance are most common in leisure activities with peers, away from authority figures.

The final element of their revised routine activities theory is unstructured activities. Although structured activities such as participation in athletics, clubs, and work often involve authority figures who exercise social control and leave little time for deviant behavior, these activities do not necessarily eliminate opportunity for deviant activity. Participation in athletic activities, for example, has been found to be positively associated with substance use, sexual behavior, and delinquency (Hundleby 1987). Routine activities theory, however, draws attention to activities that provide opportunity for deviant behavior. In particular, opportunity for deviance increases to the degree that activities involve unstructured, unsupervised socializing with peers (Osgood et al. 1996).

Taken together, these four key aspects of adolescents' routine activities demonstrate that:

> situations conducive to deviance are especially prevalent in unstructured socializing activities with peers that occur in the absence of authority figures. The lack of structure leaves time available for deviance; the presence of peers makes it easier to participate in deviant acts and makes them more rewarding; and the absence of authority figures reduces the potential for social control responses to deviance.
>
> (Osgood et al. 1996: 651)

Using longitudinal data from the Monitoring the Future study, Osgood and his colleagues measured 13 different routine activities and five types of deviant behavior: delinquent behavior, heavy alcohol use, marijuana use, use of illicit drugs, and dangerous driving. "Research in action: measuring the routine activities of adolescents" lists the activities that were included in the analysis.

Research in action: measuring the routine activities of adolescents

The next questions ask about the kinds of things you might do. How often do you do each of the following?

(1) Never
(2) A few times a year
(3) Once or twice a week
(4) At least once a week
(5) Almost everyday

_____ Watch TV
_____ Go to movies
_____ Ride around in a car (or motorcycle) just for fun
_____ Participate in community affairs or volunteer work
_____ Do creative writing
_____ Actively participate in sports, athletics, or exercising
_____ Work around the house, yard, garden, car, etc.
_____ Get together with friends, informally
_____ Go shopping or window-shopping
_____ Spend at least an hour of leisure time alone
_____ Read books, magazines, or newspapers
_____ Go to parties or other social affairs

During a typical week, on how many evenings do you go out for fun and recreation?

(1) Less than one   (4) Three
(2) One   (5) Four or five
(3) Two   (6) Six or seven

On the average, how often do you go out with a date (or your spouse, if you are married)?

(1) Never   (4) Once a week
(2) Once a month or less   (5) 2 or 3 times a week
(3) 2 or 3 times a month   (6) Over 3 times a week

Source: Osgood et al. (1996: adapted from Appendix A, p. 653).

Four of these 13 routine activities involve unstructured socializing with peers without authority figures present, as specified by the revised theory: riding around in a car for fun, getting together with friends informally, going to parties, and spending evenings out for fun and recreation. When all 13 of these routine activities were considered together, they explained a significant amount of the variation in involvement in deviant behavior. However, unstructured socializing activities accounted for the largest share of the variation in deviant involvement. The researchers conclude that "it is not merely spending time outside the home or socializing that leads to deviant behavior" (Osgood et al. 1996: 645). Rather, it is the unstructured and unsupervised nature of these activities that is associated with involvement in deviant behavior (see also Bernasco et al. 2013; Miller 2013; Thomas and McGloin 2013).

Further analysis revealed that unstructured socializing activities accounted for a substantial portion of the association that age, sex, and socioeconomic status have with these different types of deviant behaviors (Osgood et al. 1996: 65).[7] This means that much of the reason age, sex, and socioeconomic status are related to deviance is because of their relation to routine activities. These structural characteristics are related to youths' routine activities, and these routine activities are, in turn, linked to level of involvement in deviant acts.

Drifting into delinquency

In his classic book *Delinquency and Drift*, David Matza (1964) challenged the view that delinquent behavior is determined by factors that can be identified through science – a view called **hard determinism** (Agnew 1995). Determinism is a basic element of **positivist criminology**, which emphasizes the use of scientific methods (positivism) to identify the causes of crime and delinquency (determinism) (see Chapter 2; Gottfredson and Hirschi 1987). Hard determinism characterizes delinquent youth as being driven into delinquent acts because of biological or psychological conditions or because of social structural influences, such as the effects of social class, race and ethnicity, family factors, and neighborhood characteristics (Matza 1964). In contrast, Matza advances the concept of drift to convey a far less deterministic view of delinquent youth and their involvement in delinquency – a view he calls **soft determinism**. Soft determinism incorporates the element of choice from **classical criminology**, which holds that individuals choose to engage in crime based upon a consideration of possible gains and losses (Beccaria [1764] 1963: 55–62). "Expanding ideas: key elements of classical thought" provides the major ideas upon which classical criminology is based. Drawing on these ideas, **drift** acknowledges that youths are not entirely free in choosing their behavior, nor are they compelled to commit delinquency by their background and experiences (Matza 1964: 4).

Expanding ideas: key elements of classical criminology

Classical criminology was first advanced by Cesare Beccaria in a short book entitled *On Crimes and Punishments* ([1764] 1963). Four key elements make up classical criminology, as first expressed by Beccaria (see also Beirne 1991).

- **Will:** Acknowledging that humans have a natural tendency to pursue self-interest, Beccaria argued that people choose actions based on rational considerations of gains and losses, pleasure and pain, benefits and costs. Such choices, however, are not entirely free, being influenced by emotion, individual temperament, ignorance, and the characteristics of the situation.
- **Utilitarianism:** Beccaria contended that crime should be defined, classified, and responded to in terms of the harm done to society. *Utilitarianism* refers to the pursuit of the collective good – the "greatest good for the greatest number of people" (Beccaria [1764] 1963: 8).
- **Humanitarianism:** *On Crimes and Punishments* deals mainly with what law and justice ought to be, instead of what law is. In this way, Beccaria advocated for wide-ranging legal reform, including the need for codified and public laws, prohibition on the use of judicial

torture to illicit confessions, the need for public trials, the use of witnesses and evidence, the role of jurors, and sentencing practices, including imprisonment and the death penalty (Phillipson 1970).

- **Legal rationality:** Beccaria argued long and hard that legal systems must be founded on statutory law, in which law is produced from a legislative process and is codified (written down in a systematic manner). Such statutory law defines crime, specifies an impartial and efficient judicial process, and stipulates punishment that is "measured" so that it deters future criminal acts. Legal and just punishment must be "prompt," "certain," and "proportionate to the crime."

Many of Matza's observations about drift and delinquency were developed with Gresham Sykes (Sykes and Matza 1957). *Drift theory* incorporates three fundamental elements: the subculture of delinquency and subterranean values, techniques of neutralization, and the development of a "will" for delinquency.

Subculture of delinquency and subterranean values

A variety of positivist theories of criminology emphasize that some youths engage in delinquent acts simply because they are conforming to the norms and values of a delinquent subculture. Sykes and Matza (1957) reject such hard determinism, reasoning that if delinquent subcultures define delinquency as the expected and "right" thing to do, then delinquent youth should hold values and norms that are in complete opposition to those of conventional society. Instead, they offer four fairly simple observations that question whether delinquent subcultures exert such powerful influence over youths (Sykes and Matza 1957: 664–666; see also Matza 1964: 40–48). First, rather than experiencing pride and fulfillment from following the values and norms of the delinquent subculture, most delinquents experience a sense of guilt and shame over illegal acts. This indicates that delinquents are not completely separated from the standards and expectations of conventional society. Second, delinquent youths often respect and admire honest, law-abiding individuals, suggesting that delinquents do not completely reject the legitimacy and "rightness" of the traditional normative system. Third, delinquents often distinguish between who can be victimized and who cannot. The notions that you "don't steal from friends" and "don't commit vandalism against the church of your own faith" reflect such distinction. Fourth, delinquents are not immune to the demands of conformity made by the dominant social order. Parents, for example, usually agree with "respectable society" and view delinquency as wrong.

Matza (1964: 33) goes on to make what appears to be a very fine distinction: "there is a subculture of delinquency, but it is not a delinquent subculture." In other words, the **subculture of delinquency** does not represent an entirely separate set of values and norms that distinguish delinquents from the rest of society; rather, delinquent traditions consist of less conventional and less publicized standards of behavior that are still a part of the dominant culture.

Contemporary culture, then, is not as simple and uniform as often depicted. It is composed of conventional values and norms, but also of contrasting beliefs and expectations, including those that allow and encourage delinquent acts. Matza and Sykes (1961) refer to these subtle, underlying, and alternative traditions as **subterranean values**. The subculture of delinquency and its subterranean values are embraced by most adolescents, making delinquent activity possible, but not required.

The subculture of delinquency emphasizes and encourages a search for thrills and excitement ("kicks"), a reluctance for work, conspicuous consumption, an image of toughness, and a "taste for aggression"; however, these are also a part of conventional society (Matza and Sykes 1961: 713). It seems that all adolescents are attuned to the subculture of delinquency, but the degree to which delinquent subterranean values influence youths depends on the relevance of those values to particular situations. For example, although violence is generally not socially approved, it can be argued that "the dominant society exhibits a widespread taste for violence in books, magazines, movies, and television" (Matza and Sykes 1961: 717). Additionally, violence may be justified in certain situations in which subterranean values condone or even expect it, such as when a male adolescent has his masculinity questioned. The processes that allow subterranean values to come to the forefront in certain situations are described in a second aspect of drift: techniques of neutralization.

Techniques of neutralization

If the subculture of delinquency does not entirely abandon the values and norms of conventional society, and in fact generally disapproves of delinquent acts, how is it that subterranean values come to have influence in certain situations? According to Sykes and Matza, subterranean values include a number of justifications that can be used prior to delinquent acts in order to neutralize conventional values and norms and thereby render them non-binding. These **techniques of neutralization** are "episodic" and temporary, and they allow a youth to drift out of society's moral constraints and into delinquency (Matza 1964: 69). The use of these techniques depends on how appropriate they are to a given situation. Sykes and Matza (1957) describe five techniques of neutralization.[8]

1. **Denial of responsibility:** Although most people distinguish between harm that results from an accident and that which is intended, denial of responsibility moves beyond the claim that a delinquent act was just an accident. Personal responsibility can also be denied because of unloving parents, bad companions, or a ghetto neighborhood – any contention that makes the delinquent act seem as if it were beyond the offender's control (Sykes and Matza 1957).

2. **Denial of injury:** "For the delinquent ... wrongfulness may turn on the question of whether or not anyone has clearly been hurt by his deviance, and this matter is open to a variety of interpretations. Vandalism, for example, may be defined by the delinquent simply as 'mischief' – after all, it may be claimed, the persons whose property has been destroyed can well afford it. Similarly, auto theft may be viewed as 'borrowing,' and gang fighting may be seen as a private quarrel" (Sykes and Matza 1957: 667).

3. **Denial of the victim:** Even if the delinquent youth admits that his or her actions involve harm or injury, moral responsibility may be neutralized by the youth's insistence that the actions are justified in light of the circumstances, and therefore the harm or injury is also justified. Rightful retaliation moves the delinquent "into the position of an avenger and the victim is transformed into a wrong-doer" (Sykes and Matza 1957: 668).

4. **Condemnation of the condemner:** Similarly, the delinquent may shift the focus of attention from his own delinquent behavior to the motives and actions of those who

disapprove of him or her. The delinquent may claim that these condemners are hypocrites or are motivated by self-righteousness or self-interest. For example, "police ... are corrupt, stupid, and brutal. Teachers always show favoritism and parents always 'take it out' on their children" (Sykes and Matza 1957: 668).

5. **Appeal to higher loyalties:** The delinquent may believe that a group of friends or a gang demands allegiance, even if it means violating the law. The delinquent does not necessarily denounce the law, despite his or her failure to follow it; rather, loyalty to the group takes priority.

Techniques of neutralization theory is based on the assumption that most adolescents generally accept conventional beliefs and that they are subject to the social controls that result from the acceptance of these beliefs. If this is true, delinquent behavior is only possible when the binding power of social control is neutralized. In contrast, if delinquents are actually uncommitted to and uninfluenced by conventional values and norms, then neutralization is unnecessary. This fundamental assumption has resulted in much research.

After reviewing this research, Robert Agnew (1994: 558) concluded that "at minimum, it would appear that there is good reason to believe that the techniques of neutralization may not be relevant to a sizable portion of the individuals engaging in violence." However, "mixed results" and methodological problems in prior neutralization research caused him to not abandon the theory completely. In response, Agnew conducted his own research using longitudinal data from the National Youth Survey and focusing on juvenile violence – specifically on attitudes toward violence and neutralization of conventional beliefs against the use of violence. In contrast to prior research, Agnew found that a vast majority of the youths surveyed disapprove of violence but that a large percentage of these youth accept one or more neutralizations that justify the use of violence in particular situations. As shown in "Research in action: measuring techniques of neutralization that justify the use of violence," four measures of neutralization were used. In terms of Sykes and Matza's (1957) techniques of neutralization, Agnew classified all four measures as "denial of the victim," with the third question also indicating "denial of responsibility." The fairly wide acceptance of these neutralizations implied the existence of subterranean values in which the prevailing beliefs against violence are qualified by beliefs held simultaneously that justify the use of violence in certain situations.

Research in action: measuring the techniques of neutralization that justify the use of violence

The National Youth Survey includes four questions that Robert Agnew used to measure techniques of neutralization. These neutralizations represent beliefs that justify the use of violence in particular situations. Although Agnew found that almost all youth disapprove of violence, a large percentage also accepts one or more neutralizations for violence:

1. It's alright to beat up people if they started the fight.
2. It's alright to physically beat up people who call you names.
3. If people do something to make you really mad, they deserve to be beaten up.
4. If you don't physically fight back, people will walk all over you.

Source: Agnew (1994: 565).

Agnew found that, as Sykes and Matza suggest, neutralization preceded violence among youths who disapprove of violence and contributed to the likelihood of violent behavior. However, youths who had weak conventional beliefs about the appropriateness of violence were more likely to justify their delinquency after they committed the act, rather than before. Thus, neutralization occurs both before and after violent acts. For some youths, the binding power of conventional beliefs must be neutralized before delinquent behavior is even possible. For others, neutralization occurs only after they commit delinquent acts, serving more as a justification for the act than as a contributing factor. Agnew also found that neutralization was most likely to lead to violent behavior among youths who associated with delinquent peers, suggesting that peers play a role in learning techniques of neutralization.

A "will" for delinquency

The image of most delinquents offered by Matza and Sykes is that they are not immune to society's demands for conformity, nor do they wholeheartedly reject conventional beliefs. Modern societies are complex, being composed of conventional beliefs and expectations and of subterranean values that sometimes allow and encourage delinquency. Neutralization allows for the "episodic release" from "moral constraints," resulting in drift, in which the individual is "neither committed nor compelled" to delinquent action (Matza 1964: 69, 28, 181). Matza claims, however, that the "moral vacuum" of drift is not enough to explain the occurrence of delinquency: "Drift makes delinquency possible or permissible by temporarily removing the restraints that ordinarily control members of society," but it does not require delinquent action (Matza 1964: 181). Matza (1964) observes that there is a missing element here: an element of "thrust or impetus" that results in delinquency. He calls this missing element **will**.

Since Matza rejects the hard determinism of positivist criminology, he turns to classical criminology for a less deterministic approach to account for the driving force that leads to delinquency. He finds a close fit to his idea of drift in classical criminology's central concept of will. The potential for delinquent behavior brought on by drift can be realized only when this potential is acted upon. In classical criminology, this decision or desire to engage in crime is referred to as *will*. The choice to engage in a delinquent act may or may not be exercised – it is an option. The concept of will is therefore consistent with Matza's desire to provide for soft determinism in a model of delinquency. However, the classical idea of will fails to account for "how, why, or when the will to crime becomes activated" (Matza 1964: 183).

Matza (1964: 183–191) offers two conditions that activate the will: preparation and desperation. *Preparation* refers to learning through experience that delinquent acts can be done and, in the absence of constraint, may be done. In a state of drift, illegal behavior becomes possible in a sense that youths realize that delinquent acts are something that they are capable of doing and for which there are no moral barriers.

Desperation arises primarily from a "mood of fatalism" – a key component of the subculture of delinquency. This mood of fatalism involves a sense, common among adolescents, that they have little or no control over their surroundings or their destiny – a feeling that they are being "pushed around" (Matza 1964: 188–189). Although the mood of fatalism does not always lead to desperation, it is sufficiently common among adolescents so as to draw them together in peer groups in which desperation is experienced collectively. Together they seek to regain a sense of meaning and control over their lives. Within peer groups, the desperation that they experience serves to neutralize the legal constraints by making delinquency permissible and desirable. In addition, delinquent acts allow desperate youths to gain a sense of accomplishment – to "make something happen" – and thereby to regain a sense of meaning and control over their lives (Matza 1964: 189).

The three elements of Matza's drift theory are not often considered together. However, as we have seen, the subculture of delinquency, with its subterranean values, together with techniques of neutralization and the motivational element of will, provides a view of delinquency that emphasizes the immediate situation.

Choosing delinquency: rational choice theory

The explanations of delinquent events that we have described in this chapter recognize that delinquent events have an element of choice in which potential offenders evaluate the costs and benefits of delinquent acts. Rational choice theory was developed in the 1980s by Derek Cornish and Ronald Clarke (1986: 1) to draw attention to the rational aspect of criminal events – what they call a "measure of rationality." Drawing on classical criminology and the economic principle of "expected utility," the theory argues that offenders act deliberately and are motivated by self-interest.[9] Criminal acts result when the potential for personal gain is greater than the probable cost. They are careful to point out, however, that rationality is limited in that decisions to engage in crime are rarely based on full and accurate information, nor do decision-makers have sufficient time, ability, and reasoning skills for offending choices to be completely rational (Cornish and Clarke 1986: 1; see also Sacco and Kennedy 2002; Agnew 1990; Paternoster 1989). Cornish and Clarke also contend that offending decisions are conditioned by situational influences and opportunities to commit crime (see also Saco and Kennedy 2002; Piquero and Tibbits 1996; Nagin and Paternoster 1993; Agnew 1990). Rational choice theory, then, is an attempt to explain the influences and processes of criminal decisions within particular situational contexts (Clarke and Cornish 2001: 24).

Clarke and Cornish (1985: 24) advance six basic propositions that summarize rational choice theory.

1. Crimes are purposive and deliberate acts, committed with the intention of benefitting the offender.
2. In seeking to benefit themselves, offenders do not always succeed in making the best decisions because of the risks and uncertainty involved.
3. Offender decision making varies considerably with the nature of crimes.
4. Decisions about becoming involved in particular kinds of crime (involvement decisions) are quite different from those relating to the commission of a specific criminal act (event decisions).
5. Involvement decisions can be divided into three stages – becoming involved for the first time (initiation), continued involvement (habituation), and ceasing to offend (desistance) – that must be separately studied because they are influenced by quite different sets of variables.
6. Event decisions include a sequence of choices made at each stage of the criminal act (e.g., preparation, target selection, commission of the act, escape, and aftermath).

Following from these propositions, rational choice theory is composed of four models: initial involvement, the actual crime event, continuing involvement, and desistance. These models isolate different types of criminal decisions and the factors that influence each decision. Each of the four decision models is depicted in a separate "flow diagram" that summarizes the decision-making process (Clarke and Cornish 1985).

The *initial involvement model* depicts the individual's willingness or "readiness" to become involved in crime to satisfy individual needs. Needs launch the involvement decision and include desires such as money, sex, leadership, status, and excitement. The consideration of whether to engage in crime to satisfy these needs is influenced by a variety of factors, especially the individual's background, which includes individual temperament, upbringing, and social and demographic characteristics (e.g., gender, social class, and neighborhood).

Decisions that are part of committing crime make up a second model: the *event model*. These decisions are specific to a particular crime, place, and time. Accordingly, the decision to engage in a particular crime is influenced heavily by the immediate situation – availability of goods, level of opportunity, ease of committing the crime, amount of controls, and chance of detection. The event model suggests that the offender must be ready and willing (initial involvement model); then, if the situation is conducive to crime, the decision to commit crime follows. The implication of the event model is that crime can be prevented by limiting situations that are conducive to crime, such as controlling ease of access, increasing neighbor watch programs, and increasing police patrol.

Continuation and desistance from crime are considered in two additional models. The *continuing involvement model* includes the degree to which skills, knowledge, lifestyle, values, and peer groups either support or discourage criminal involvement. For example, becoming financially dependent on crime encourages continued involvement, as does the development of a criminal peer group. In contrast, the *desistance model* presents a series of "re-evaluations" that relate to life events such as getting married or getting a job, as well as factors more directly related to the crime event that might discourage continued involvement in crime, such as realizing that crime does not pay enough or that the income from crime is too irregular (Cornish and Clarke 1986; Clarke and Cornish 1985).

While rational choice theory has been applied most extensively to adult criminality, juvenile offending also exhibits a rational component. It may be, however, that rational choice operates differently within the adolescent population – a group not known for sophisticated decision-making (Paternoster 1989: 10). Drawing from the theoretical work of Cornish and Clarke, research on rational choice and juvenile delinquency has focused most extensively on the considerations that enter into decisions to offend.

Offending decisions

Criminologist Raymond Paternoster (1989) conducted an insightful study on the role of rational choice in delinquent behavior. He examined the degree to which different factors influence delinquent offending decisions. Beginning with the premise that delinquent behavior is a product of "imperfectly informed choice," he argued that even if delinquency is only minimally rational, offending decisions involve far more than the simple consideration of potential costs of punishment (deterrence theory). Instead, offending decisions involve a variety of considerations including material gain, consistency with moral beliefs, and impact on social relationships.

Paternoster's rational choice model includes six basic considerations ("controls") that enter into offending decisions: formal sanctions (certainty and severity of punishment), affective ties, material considerations, opportunities, informal sanctions, and moral beliefs.[10] Measures of these elements of rational choice are listed in "Research in action: measures of rational choice." The model also includes background factors of gender, household employment, and family structure. Paternoster analyzed whether these background factors influenced offending decisions directly or indirectly through the six basic considerations of rational choice.

Research in action: measures of rational choice

Raymond Paternoster (1989) argues that a variety of considerations are taken up in offending decisions. These include deterrence theory's focus on perceptions of certainty and severity of punishment, as well as material, moral, and affective considerations. His research included six factors with multiple measures. Most of the questions had response categories that ranged from "a little" to "a lot," or from "never" to "always." Response categories that lie along such a continuum are called Likert items.

Affective ties

Attachment to parents:
   If you think your father/mother would disapprove of something you wanted to do, how often would you go ahead and do it anyway?

Attachment to teachers:
   In general, do you like your teachers?

   Do you feel like your teachers understand you?

Material considerations

Grades: Self-reported grades that the respondent *"typically received in school"*
Conventional commitments:
   How much would your chances of getting a good education be hurt if you were arrested for [each of four specific offenses]?

   How much would your chances of having good friends be hurt if you were arrested for [each of four specific offenses]?

Importance of education:
   How important is it that you get good grades in school?

   How important is it that you finish high school?

   How important is it that you get a college degree?

Expected education:
   How likely is it that you will reach your desired educational goals?

Expected employment:
   How likely is it that you will secure the job/career you are aspiring to?

Opportunities

Parental supervision:

> Do your parents know where you are when you are away from home?
>
> Do your parents know who you are with when you are away from home?

Peer involvement and social activities: Measures of proportion of friends that engaged in particular forms of delinquent behavior; amount of time spent with boyfriend or girlfriend and with friends.

Informal sanctions

Parental sanctions: Questions were asked with regard to how their mother and father would react to each of four offenses.

Peer sanctions: For each of the four offenses, questions were asked about whether respondents thought that their friends would feel it is morally wrong and would approve of participation in each of the offenses.

Formal sanctions

Perceived certainty:

> How likely is it that you would be caught by the police if you were to be involved in [each of four specific offenses]?

Perceived severity:

> Would it create a problem if you were caught, taken to court, and punished for [each of four specific offenses]?

Moral considerations

Moral beliefs:

> How wrong do you think it is to [each of four specific offenses]?

Source: Paternoster (1989: 11, 15–19). Reproduced with permission from the publisher.

Paternoster studied four different types of delinquency: marijuana use, drinking, petty theft, and vandalism. Drawing from rational choice theory, Paternoster proposed that the factors that influence offending decisions will vary depending on the type of offense being considered. Decisions regarding these types of offenses were also distinguished in terms of whether involvement was for the first time (initiation) or whether the decision was to continue or to desist involvement. Paternoster (1989: 37) summarized his analytic approach as follows:

> Looking at delinquency as involving a series of offending decisions provides an image of a much more active decision maker than presumed by most pure deterrence models.

The informed decision maker of the rational choice perspective repeatedly evaluates information and makes behavior decisions on the basis of such information, re-evaluates that information, and makes new offending decisions that sometimes differ from ones previously made.

This study showed that certainty of punishment is considered in relatively few offending decisions and that severity of punishment has virtually no effect on offending decisions. For example, during the sophomore and junior years, involvement in marijuana use and vandalism was influenced only modestly by perceived certainty of punishment, whereas perceived severity had no effect on the decision to participate in these acts. When considering the decision to drink and to engage in petty theft, neither perceived certainty nor severity of punishment influenced the decision to offend. In general, the various kinds of offending decisions and offenses that Paternoster studied showed that the deterrent effect of formal sanctions was relatively unimportant to delinquency and that other considerations were far more influential in offending decisions.[11]

Various social factors (unrelated to legal sanctions) were found to influence offending decisions in significant ways. Gender consistently played an important role in delinquent offending decisions; males and females make different offending decisions. Opportunities to engage in delinquency, measured by level of parental supervision and peer involvement, affected several offending decisions, especially decisions to get involved in delinquency. Additionally, attachment to parents (affective ties) influenced some offending decisions when youths were not previously involved in delinquent behavior. Across different types of offenses, moral beliefs had the strongest and most consistent influence on offending decisions. Taken together, these findings indicate that the decisions to offend, to continue offending, and to stop offending (desist) involve social considerations to a far greater degree than they do formal, legal considerations of certainty and severity of punishment (Paternoster 1989: 38).

The study of rational choice in delinquent offending is complex and controversial (Akers and Sellers 2012; Matthews and Agnew 2008; Akers 1990; Paternoster 1987; Williams and Hawkins 1986). Clearly, the decision to engage in delinquency is not a simple "once and for all" choice. Rather, youths make a series of offending decisions over time that involve a variety of non-legal, social factors that are sometimes specific to particular types of crime (Putnins 2010; Paternoster 1989). Furthermore, the deliberation that results in rational choice includes possible rewards as well as risks. These perceptions of risk and reward appear to change over time and vary according to the situation (Piliavin et al. 1986: 115; see also Matthews and Agnew 2008; Paternoster 1987, 1989; Williams and Hawkins 1986). For example, an active social life, in which peers support and encourage delinquent involvement, provides opportunity to engage in delinquent acts and encouragement to do so. One group of researchers concluded that assessments of risk and reward are "to some extent situationally-induced, transitory, and unstable" (Piliavin et al. 1986: 116). Past experience, too, influences perceptions of risk and reward, but the research findings are inconsistent. Some research shows that past involvement in offending and experience with formal sanctions actually reduce perceptions of risk and thereby increase the possibility of future crime and delinquency (Paternoster 1987; Piliavin et al. 1986). In contrast, a study by Matsueda, Kraeger, and Huizinga (2006) revealed that current perceptions of risk of arrest are a function of prior risk perceptions, together with new information drawn from experience with crime and arrest and observations made by peers. Theft and violence were found to be a function of perceived risk of arrest, rewards experienced (including excitement and social status), and perceived opportunities. These contrasting findings provide quite different conclusions about whether punishment reduces future involvement in crime and delinquency. Finally, research shows that social costs in terms of impacted social relationships play a significant role in offending decisions (Wenzel 2004; Piquero and Tibbetts 1996; McCarthy 1995; Grasmick and Bursik 1990). Such social costs include loss of respect and friendship, shame, and embarrassment.

Criminal propensity and choices to offend

Among the factors that may influence the choice to offend is an individual's propensity to crime. James Q. Wilson and Richard Herrnstein (1985: 103) argue that the choice to engage in crime "cannot be understood without taking into account individual predispositions and their biological roots." **Criminal propensity** refers to constitutional characteristics, which are present at birth, that are expressed in a variety of psychological traits. Certain psychological traits make individuals more prone to become involved in crime: "It is likely that the psychological traits involve intelligence and personality and that the activating events include certain experiences within the family, in school, and in the community" (Wilson and Herrnstein 1985: 102–103).

Connecting the choice to offend with criminal propensity, Wilson and Herrnstein contend that individuals differ in how important the future is to them. Because the rewards of crime tend to be immediate, whereas the rewards of "non-crime" are in the future, psychological traits that result in a desire for immediate gain and a tendency to "discount the future" create criminal propensity. Singled out in this regard are low intelligence and a number of personality traits, including impulsiveness, sensation seeking, the inability to learn from punishment, and low anxiety. These psychological characteristics influence perceptions of rewards related to crime and non-crime and result in limited conscience, both of which predispose people to commit crime.

According to Wilson and Herrnstein (1985: 217), family life can restrain or magnify criminal propensity. Socialization processes involving interaction between parent and child influence criminal propensity in three important ways: (1) by instilling, or failing to instill, a desire for the approval of others (attachment); (2) by cultivating internalized constraint – conscience – or the lack of it; and (3) by establishing time horizon – a present or future orientation. Each of these socialization outcomes bears on the individual's calculation of the rewards of crime relative to the rewards of non-crime.

Wilson and Herrnstein also discuss how other institutional contexts influence criminal propensity. Schools may affect criminal involvement by bringing youth together into groups that reinforce the value of crime and by generating a sense of inequality when school experiences fail to provide opportunity or when they are perceived as unfair. Communities also influence the expression of criminal propensity. The presence of criminal or delinquent subcultures in neighborhoods, especially in the form of street gangs, have strong influence on crime and non-crime values, thereby encouraging the expression of individual criminal propensity through criminal acts. The economy, too, has an indirect effect on involvement in crime. The condition of the economy affects both work aspirations and opportunity. The level of employment opportunity leads individuals to adjustment their aspirations, thereby influencing whether criminal propensity is displayed through involvement in crime. Thus, the institutional contexts of school, community, and economy provide either "activating" or inhibiting experiences that affect whether criminal propensity is exhibited through criminal acts.

Wilson and Herrnstein assert that the choice of crime is not entirely rational, but rather involves a variety of biological, psychological, and social influences. This view is consistent with contemporary research on rational choice that emphasizes choice more than rationality. Recent research consistently points to the importance of criminal propensity on offending choices (McGloin et al. 2007; Piquero and Tibbetts 1996; Nagin and Paternoster 1993).

The deterrent effect of punishment in offending decisions

Wilson and Herrnstein's criminal propensity theory has a logical extension to the question of whether punishment deters crime. Their theory suggests that "impulsive, risk-taking, and present-oriented individuals" – those with criminal propensity – are less likely to be deterred by the prospect of punishment, because these individuals focus on immediate benefits rather than on long-term consequences of offending (Wright et al. 2004: 182). In a recent study, Bradley Wright and his colleagues (2004) addressed the varying deterrent effect of perceived punishment on individuals, depending on their level of criminal propensity.[12] Their analysis of longitudinal data allowed for the measurement of: (1) criminal propensity in childhood, adolescence, and early adulthood; (2) deterrence perceptions in late adolescence and early adulthood; and (3) self-reported criminal behavior in early adulthood. In contrast to the predictions of criminal propensity theory, the researchers found that individuals who were most prone to crime because of their impulsive, risk-taking, and present-oriented natures were most deterred from crime by perceptions that crime was costly and risky. When criminal propensity was low, however, the **deterrent effect** of possible punishment was virtually non-existent. The researchers interpreted this to mean that the deterrent effect of punishment was irrelevant when other inhibitions (such as moral beliefs) were strong. They concluded that the offending decisions of crime-prone individuals are influenced by their perceptions of risk of criminal sanctions (Wright et al. 2004: 208; see also Matthews and Agnew 2008; McGloin et al. 2007; Nagin and Paternoster 1993; Piquero and Pogarsky 2002; Pogarsky 2002).

Human agency and situated choice

Wilson and Herrnstein propose that criminal propensity is an inherent trait of individuals, influenced by family socialization and institutional contexts. Thus, the concept minimizes the individual's willful choice of delinquent actions. In a study of crime and criminality over the course of life, John Laub and Robert Sampson (2003) introduce the idea of **human agency** (Sampson and Laub 2005; see also Gottfredson 2005). The notion of human agency borrows a great deal from David Matza's concept of "will" by pointing to the purposeful choice of individuals to engage in delinquency. While the individual offender is an active agent in choosing actions, Sampson and Laub (2005) emphasize that human agency is influenced by the opportunities and constraints of life circumstances and that it is not a perfectly rational process. As a result, "human agency cannot be divorced from the situation or context ... making choice situated or relational rather than a property of the person or even the environment" (Sampson and Laub 2005: 38). Even though offending decisions are situated, offenders often put themselves in situations that are conducive to crime:

> For example, we found persistent offenders to have rather chaotic and unstructured lives across multiple dimensions (such as living arrangements, work, and family). Routine activities of these men were loaded with opportunities for crime and extensive associations with like-minded offenders.
>
> (Laub and Sampson 2003: 38–39)

Situational action theory

Per-Olof Wikström (2006) has offered still another qualification on the role that rational choice plays in delinquent acts. His contemporary theory, called *situational action theory* (SAT), contends that "all human action, including acts of crime and deviance, is mainly a product of individual perceptions of action alternatives and choices. The primary characteristic that affects how individuals perceive their action alternatives is morality" (Antonaccdio and Tittle 2008: 482). Wikström (2006: 75) defines **morality** as "the rules prescribing what is right or wrong to do." Individuals apply morality to particular situations in making choices of action. While the importance of moral beliefs has been advanced in other theories of crime and delinquency – most notably social control and social learning theories – it has not been the focal point of these theories, as it is in situational action theory.

Situational action theory contends that an individual's choice of action depends on the "action alternatives" that arise in particular situations (Wikström and Treiber 2007: 258; Wikström 2006). "In a situation conducive to deviant behavior, morality is the main factor that differentiates whether an individual will choose deviant or conventional action. Morality, it is argued, determines what action alternative the individual will perceive to be the best" (Gallupe and Baron 2014: 285). Youths with "strong personal morality" are unlikely to see crime as an option, even in situations that encourage crime. In contrast, youths with "weak personal morality" are situationally vulnerable to temptations and pressures for crime (Wikström et al. 2012). Situational action theory concludes that "most people abide by the law not because they fear the consequences but because they do not perceive crime as an 'action alternative'" (Wikström, Tseloni, and Karlis 2011: 401).

Researchers are beginning to examine the causal significance of morality relative to other factors advanced in traditional explanations of crime. Situational action theory embraces morality as the "main factor" in misconduct; factors featured in other theories are secondary to morality and, in fact, morality qualifies the effect that other causal factors have on crime. For example, situational action theory holds that when an individual does not consider engaging in crime because of high levels of morality, potential consequences of crime (deterrence) are irrelevant. Similarly, when an individual commits crime habitually because of low levels of morality, there is little consideration of potential consequences (Gallupe and Baron 2014: 286). A growing body of research demonstrates that morality is a significant predictor of criminal involvement, and that its influence persists after controlling for other causal variables. In fact, morality appears to be a stronger predictor of criminal involvement than low self-control or deterrence variables (Gallupe and Baron 2014; Wikström et al. 2011, 2012; Wikström and Trieber 2007, 2009; Antonaccdio and Tittle 2008).

Summary and conclusions

The notion that a youth was "in the wrong place at the wrong time" suggests that the delinquent event has some relevance to how and why delinquency occurs. Yet most delinquency theory and research give little attention to the "immediate setting" of delinquency (Birkbeck and LaFree 1993: 115). The term *event* conveys an episodic quality to delinquent acts – they occur at particular times, in particular places, and involve particular people (Sacco and Kennedy 2002: 8). This chapter focused on the delinquent event in order to better understand the situational context of offending decisions and delinquent acts. Five areas of study were addressed: (1) situational aspects of delinquent acts, (2) the experience of delinquency, (3) routine activities of adolescents, (4) drifting into delinquency, and (5) rational elements of choosing delinquency.

Situational characteristics of delinquent events can be described in terms of their objective and subjective content. The *objective content* of situations sometimes motivates and provides opportunity for delinquency by "imposing negative experiences such as frustration, threats, humiliation, and boredom; by offering positive attractions such as money, property, image-building, thrills, and sexual satisfaction; or by providing models to be imitated" (Birkbeck and LaFree 1993: 129–130). Experiencing adverse situations such as homelessness and abuse, and the situational strains of daily adolescent life can also kindle delinquent acts. Moreover, the normative expectations and badgering of peer pressure are often situational in character.

Delinquent events can also be described in terms of their *subjective qualities*, encompassing the "individual's perception and interpretation of the immediate setting" (Birkbeck and LaFree 1993: 129). Subjective content of situations also includes how delinquent acts are experienced by youths and what these experiences mean to them, in the way Katz (1988) described.

The *routine activities* of adolescents and young adults have been found to be especially conducive to crime, thereby providing explanation for the age–crime connection. Routine activities theory holds that the likelihood of participating in delinquent acts depends on the degree to which the daily routines of everyday life provide opportunity for crime. Involvement in delinquency is more likely to the extent that the routine activities of adolescents lack structure and controls and involve peers.

Drift theory contends that contemporary adolescent life is composed of both conventional beliefs and expectations and of subterranean values that sometimes permit and encourage delinquency. Neutralization allows for the "episodic release" from conventional norms, resulting in drift, in which the individual is neither required to participate in nor restricted from delinquent action. The "moral vacuum" of drift, however, is not enough to explain delinquency events. The motivational element of drift theory rests solely within the individual, in that the desire or decision to engage in delinquency – the will for delinquency – provides the necessary "thrust or impetus" for delinquency to occur (Matza 1964).

Rational choice theory focuses on decisions to engage in delinquency. While the word "rational" implies that delinquent acts are deliberate and motivated by self-interest, rational choice theory contends that a series of offending decisions are made over time, involving a variety of individual, social, and legal factors that are sometimes specific to particular types of crime. Furthermore, perceptions of risk and reward appear to change over time and vary according to the situation. The study of rational choice in delinquent offending considers a broad range of influences relating to material gain, legal costs, the normative controls of relationships, moral beliefs, and guilt and shame. Offending decisions are also subject to individual criminal propensity and morality.

Critical-thinking questions

1. According to the opening vignette, how does the immediate situation provide sensation and meaning, and how does it require interpretation and response?
2. What situational characteristics provide inducements for delinquency?
3. How are adverse situations related to delinquency?
4. In what ways might peer expectations in a given situation encourage delinquency?

5. How does routine activities theory explain criminal opportunity?
6. Provide examples of routine activities of adolescents that provide opportunity for delinquency.
7. Distinguish *subculture of delinquency* from *delinquent subculture*.
8. How does Matza's idea of *will* extend our understanding of delinquent behavior?
9. Provide several examples of how individual perception and interpretation of the immediate situation are related to delinquency.

Suggested reading

Briar, Scott and Irving Piliavin. 1965. "Delinquency, Situational Inducements, and Commitment to Conformity." *Social Problems* 13: 35–45.

Hagan, John and Bill McCarthy. 1997. *Mean Streets: Youth Crime and Homelessness*. Cambridge University Press.

Katz, Jack. 1988. *Seductions of Crime: Moral and Sensual Attractions in Doing Evil*. New York: Basic Books.

Osgood, D. Wayne, Janet K. Wilson, Patrick M. O'Malley, Jerald G. Bachman, and Lloyd D. Johnston. 1996. "Routine Activities and Individual Deviant Behavior." *American Sociological Review* 61: 635–655.

Paternoster, Raymond. 1989. "Decisions to Participate and Desist from Four Types of Common Delinquency: Deterrence and the Rational Choice Perspective." *Law and Society Review* 23: 7–40.

Sykes, Gresham M. and David Matza. 1957. "Techniques of Neutralization: A Theory of Delinquency." *American Sociological Review* 22: 664–670.

Useful websites

For further information relevant to this chapter, go to the following websites.

- "KIDS COUNT Data Book," The Annie E. Casey Foundation (http://datacenter. kidscount.org/publications/databook/2013)
- "Youth Risk Behavior Surveillance System," Center for Disease Control and Prevention (www.cdc.gov/healthyyouth/data/yrbs/index.htm)

Glossary of key terms

Capable guardians: The level of control and protection provided to people and property.

Classical criminology: A viewpoint about crime and justice that emerged in the mid-1700s and dominated criminological thought until the late 1800s. It holds that individuals choose to engage in crime based on a consideration of possible gains and losses. For punishment to be just and to deter crime, it must public, prompt, certain, and proportionate to the crime.

Commitment to conformity: Logical reasons to conform, such as the desire to maintain or even enhance self-image, status, valued relationships, and future activities.

Criminal propensity: Individual predisposition to crime. Individual characteristics, especially low intelligence and certain personality traits (including impulsiveness, risk-taking, present orientation, and low anxiety), that produce a tendency to seek immediate benefit, sometimes through crime.

Delinquent event: The situational context of offending decisions and delinquent acts.

Deterrent effect: The assumption that punishment and other formal sanctions prevent and reduce crime by making the costs outweigh the benefits. It is based on the classical criminology assumption that people are both rational and self-interested.

Drift: A view that youths hold both conventional and deviant values, resulting in both conforming and delinquent behavior.

Hard determinism: A view that delinquent behavior is caused by factors that can be identified by science and, given these factors, delinquency is a predictable outcome.

Human agency: This concept emphasizes that purposeful choice, together with an individual's will, determine continued involvement in or desistence from crime.

Morality: "The rules prescribing what is right or wrong to do" (Wikström 2006: 75). Moral rules are specific to and guide behavior in particular circumstances.

Motivated offenders: The inclination to engage in crime for self-benefit.

Objective content of situations: Characteristics of a given situation that provide motivation and opportunity for crime. Poverty and hunger, for example, may lead to property offending.

Positivist criminology: An approach or school of thought that emerged in the last half of the nineteenth century and flourished for most of the twentieth century. Positivist criminology advances the use of scientific methods (*positivism*) to identify the causes of crime and delinquency (*determinism*). Armed with this understanding, delinquent youth can be assessed, treated, and rehabilitated (the *rehabilitative ideal*).

Routine activities: The repetitive patterns of daily living – at home, school, work, and leisure.

Situational inducements: Characteristics and processes of the immediate situation that make crime and delinquency appealing.

Soft determinism: Delinquent behavior is not reliably predictable because humans have choice and their thoughts, beliefs, and actions are not completely produced by their background, experiences, and present life conditions.

Subculture of delinquency: Refers to values and norms that are less than conventional, balanced between convention and delinquency, and that allow and sometimes encourage delinquent acts. The subcultural standards are usually not publicly acknowledged.

Subjective content of situations: How an individual perceives and interprets his or her immediate setting.

Subterranean values: Group values that lie beneath and in contrast to those of the larger society.

Suitable targets: How advantageous a crime is to commit, depending on value, visibility, access, and ease of committing.

Techniques of neutralization: The mental justifications used to deactivate conventional norms and values, thereby releasing a youth from social controls. Neutralizations are temporary and episodic.

Will: The desire or decision to engage in crime, put into action through past experiences that make crime seem possible (preparation) and by feelings of lacking self-determination (desperation).

Notes

1. This section is based extensively on Birkbeck and LaFree's (1993: 117–119) summary of Argyle, Furnham, and Graham's (1981) literature review of the experimental research on aggression.

2. Robert Agnew has incorporated situational frustration in delinquent events into his general strain theory (see Chapter 11).
3. See also Johnson et al. (1987) for research that explores the situational pressures applied by peers, including dares and coaxing of friends, and McCarthy, Hagan, and Cohen (1998) who consider decisions to co-offend that result from collaboration.
4. Miethe and Meier (1990: 245) refer to this as "structural-choice."
5. Sampson and Wooldredge (1987) argue that this emphasis on routines of daily living – the lifestyles or routine activities – fails to adequately consider the structural context of such activities. Marital status, family disruption (single-parent households), and unemployment influence routine activities and are, in fact, directly related to victimization.
6. Akers and Sellers (2012) point out that most research on routine activities theory has failed to measure variation in motivation for crime or variation in the presence of motivated offenders. Although Cohen and Felson (1979: 605) take motivation as a given, they do not rule out that their approach might be "applied to the analysis of offenders and their inclinations."
7. In contrast, Sampson and Wooldredge (1987) found that demographic and structural factors such as age, marital status, family disruption (single-parent households), and unemployment had larger direct effects on victimization than did factors related to lifestyle.
8. In a later work, Matza (1964) describes the subterranean values of the subculture of delinquency in terms of three encompassing forms of neutralization: the negation of offense; the sense of injustice; and custom, tort, and injustice. These more general forms include the five techniques of neutralization advanced first by Sykes and Matza (1957).
9. The idea of "expected utility" was first advanced by Gary Becker in a 1968 article titled "Crime and Punishment: An Economic Approach." Mary Tuck and David Riley (1986) provide a more psychologically oriented approach by referring to "subjective expected utility." This approach emphasizes individual perception of expected benefits and costs of crime. We will focus on the perceptual literature rather than that which presents economic models. See also Sacco and Kennedy (2002); Paternoster (1989); Clarke and Cornish (1985).
10. By including social costs in his rational choice model, Paternoster draws on social control theory. Social control theory will be discussed more fully in Chapter 9, but in terms of rational choice it is argued that one of the main reasons that people conform is because of commitments they develop in social relationships (Hirschi 1986). The factors that are assumed to influence the decision to participate in an offense are often referred to as the "choice-structuring properties of offenses" (Cornish and Clarke 1987: 935; see also Miethe and Meier 1990; Paternoster 1989).
11. Williams and Hawkins (1986: 568) propose incorporating social and material considerations into deterrence theory, thereby making the approach more useful for crime prevention. However, Paternoster (1987: 211–212) argues that rational choice theory already includes both legal and non-legal factors. Thus, rational choice theory incorporates the deterrent effect of legal or formal sanctions together with non-legal factors, including informal sanctions, affective ties, and material costs.
12. Recent criminological research on offending decisions has tended to conceptualize criminal propensity as low self-control, a concept described in Chapter 9. See Piquero and Tibbetts (1996).

References

Agnew, Robert. 1990. "The Origins of Delinquent Events: An Examination of Offender Accounts." *Journal of Research in Crime and Delinquency* 27: 267–294.

Agnew, Robert. 1994. "The Techniques of Neutralization and Violence." *Criminology* 32: 555–580.

Agnew, Robert. 1995. "Determinism, Indeterminism, and Crime: An Exploration." *Criminology* 33: 83–109.

Akers, Ronald L. 1990. "Rational Choice, Deterrence, and Social Learning Theory in Criminology: The Path Not Taken." *Journal of Criminal Law and Criminology* 81: 653–676.

Akers, Ronald L. and Christine S. Sellers. 2012. *Criminological Theories: Introduction and Evaluation.* 6th edn. New York: Oxford University Press.

Antonaccio, Olena and Charles R. Tittle. 2008. "Morality, Self-Control, and Crime." *Criminology* 46: 479–510.

Argyle, Michael, Adrian Furnham, and Jean Ann Graham. 1981. *Social Situations*. Cambridge University Press.

Bartol, Curt R. and Anne M. Bartol. 2009. *Juvenile Delinquency and Antisocial Behavior: A Developmental Perspective*. 3rd edn. Upper Saddle River, NJ: Pearson Prentice Hall.

Beccaria, Cesare. [1764] 1963. *On Crimes and Punishment*. Trans. Henry Paolucci. Indianapolis, IN: Bobbs-Merrill.

Becker, Gary. 1968. "Crime and Punishment: An Economic Approach." *Journal of Political Economy* 76: 169–217.

Beirne, Piers. 1991. "Inventing Criminology: The 'Science of Man' in Cesare Beccaria's *Dei Delitti e Delle Pene* (1764)." *Criminology* 29: 777–820.

Bernasco, Wim, Stijn Ruiter, Gerben J. N. Bruinsma, Lievan J. R. Pauwels, and Frank M. Weerman. 2013. "Situational Causes of Offending: A Fixed-Effects Analysis of Space–Time Budget Data." *Criminology* 51: 895–926.

Birkbeck, Christopher and Gary LaFree. 1993. "The Situational Analysis of Crime and Deviance." *Annual Review of Sociology* 19: 113–137.

Briar, Scott and Irving Piliavin. 1965. "Delinquency, Situational Inducements, and Commitment to Conformity." *Social Problems* 13: 35–45.

Clarke, Ronald V. and Derek B. Cornish. 1985. "Modeling Offenders' Decisions: A Framework for Research and Policy." Pp. 147–185 in *Crime and Justice: An Annual Review of Research*, vol. 6, ed. Michael Tonry and Norval Morris. University of Chicago Press.

Clarke, Ronald V. and Derek B. Cornish. 2001. "Rational Choice." Pp. 23–42 in *Explaining Criminals and Crime: Essays in Contemporary Criminological Theory*, ed. Raymond Paternoster and Ronet Bachman. Los Angeles: Roxbury.

Cohen, Lawrence E. and Marcus Felson. 1979. "Social Change and Crime Rate Trends: A Routine Activity Approach." *American Sociological Review* 44: 588–608.

Cornish, Derek and Ronald Clarke. 1986. "Introduction." Pp. 1–16 in *The Reasoning Criminal: Rational Choice Perspectives on Offending*, ed. Derek B. Cornish and Ronald V. Clarke. New York: Springer-Verlag, 1986.

Cornish, Derek and Ronald Clarke. 1987. "Understanding Crime Displacement: An Application of Rational Choice Theory." *Criminology* 25: 933–947.

Cullen, Francis T., Robert Agnew, and Pamela Wilcox. 2014. *Criminological Theory: Past to Present – Essential Readings*. 5th edn. New York: Oxford University Press.

Empey, LaMar T. and Steven G. Lubeck. 1968. "Conformity and Deviance in the 'Situation of Company.'" *American Sociological Review* 26: 760–774.

Felson, Marcus. 1986. "Linking Criminal Choices, Routine Activities, Informal Control, and Criminal Outcomes." Pp. 119–128 in *The Reasoning Criminal*, ed. Derek B. Cornish and Ronald V. Clark. New York: Springer-Verlag.

Freedman, Jonathan. 1988. "Effect of Television Violence on Aggression." *Psychological Bulletin* 96: 227–246.

Gallupe, Owen and Stephen W. Baron. 2014. "Morality, Self-Control, Deterrence, and Drug Use: Street Youths and Situational Action Theory." *Crime and Delinquency* 60: 284–305.

Gibbons, Don C. 1971. "Observations on the Study of Crime Causation." *American Journal of Sociology* 77: 262–278.

Gold, Martin. 1970. *Delinquent Behavior in an American City*. Belmont, CA: Brooks-Cole.

Goode, Eric. 1990. "Phenomenology and Structure in the Study of Crime and Deviance: Crime Can be Fun; The Deviant Experience." Review of *Seductions of Crime* by Jack Katz. *Contemporary Sociology* 19: 5–12.

Gottfredson, Michael R. 2005. "Offender Classifications and Treatment Effects in Developmental Criminology: A Propensity/Event Consideration." *Annals of the American Academy of Political and Social Science* 602: 46–56.

Gottfredson, Michael R. and Travis Hirschi. 1987. "The Positive Tradition." Pp. 9–22 in *Positive Criminology*, ed. Michael Gottfredson and Travis Hirschi. Newbury Park, CA: Sage.

Gottfredson, Michael R. and Travis Hirschi. 1989. "A Propensity-Event Theory of Crime." Pp. 57–67 in *Advances in Criminological Theory*, vol. 1, ed. Freda Adler and William S. Laufer. New Brunswick, NJ: Transaction.

Grasmick, Harold G. and Robert J. Bursik, Jr. 1990. "Conscience, Significant Others, and Rational Choice: Extending the Deterrence Model." *Law and Society Review* 24: 837–861.

Hagan, John and Bill McCarthy. 1992. "Streetlife and Delinquency." *British Journal of Sociology* 43: 533–561.

Hagan, John and Bill McCarthy. 1997. *Mean Streets: Youth Crime and Homelessness*. Cambridge University Press.

Hirschi, Travis. 1986. "On the Compatibility of Rational Choice and Social Control Theories of Crime." Pp. 105–118 in *The Reasoning Criminal: Rational Choice Perspectives on Offending*, ed. Derek B. Cornish and Ronald V. Clarke. New York: Springer-Verlag.

Hundleby, John D. 1987. "Adolescent Drug Use in a Behavioral Matrix: A Confirmation and Comparison of the Sexes." *Addictive Behaviors* 12: 103–112.

Johnson, Richard E., Anastasios C. Marcos, and Stephen J. Bahr. 1987. "The Role of Peers in the Complex Etiology of Adolescent Drug Use." *Criminology* 25: 323–339.

Katz, Jack. 1988. *Seductions of Crime: Moral and Sensual Attractions in Doing Evil*. New York: Basic Books.

LaFree, Gary and Christopher Birkbeck. 1991. "The Neglected Situation: A Cross-National Study of the Situational Characteristics of Crime." *Criminology* 29: 73–98.

Laub, John H. and Robert J. Sampson. 2003. *Shared Beginnings, Divergent Lives: Delinquent Boys to Age 70*. Cambridge, MA: Harvard University Press.

Lockwood, Daniel. 1997. "Violence among Middle School and High School Students: Analysis and Implications for Prevention." Washington, DC: National Institute of Justice.

Lopez, Vera. 2008. "Understanding Adolescent Property Crime Using a Delinquent Event Perspective." *Deviant Behavior* 29: 581–610.

McCarthy, Bill. 1995. "Not Just 'For the Thrill of It': An Instrumentalist Elaboration of Katz's Explanation of Sneaky Thrill Property Crimes." *Criminology* 33: 519–538.

McCarthy, Bill and John Hagan. 1991. "Homelessness: A Criminogenic Situation?" *British Journal of Criminology* 31: 393–410.

McCarthy, Bill and John Hagan. 1992. "Mean Streets: The Theoretical Significance of Situational Delinquency among Homeless Youths." *American Journal of Sociology* 98: 597–627.

McCarthy, Bill, John Hagan, and Lawrence E. Cohen. 1998. "Uncertainty, Cooperation and Crime: Understanding the Decision to Co-offend." *Social Forces* 77: 155–184.

McGloin, Jean Marie, Christopher J. Sullivan, Alex R. Piquero, and Travis C. Pratt. 2007. "Local Life Circumstances and Offending Specialization/Versatility: Comparing Opportunity and Propensity Models." *Journal of Research in Crime and Delinquency* 44: 321–346.

Matsueda, Ross L. 1989. "The Dynamics of Moral Beliefs and Minor Delinquency." *Social Forces* 68: 428–457.

Matsueda Ross L., Derek A. Kreager, and David Huizinga. 2006. "Deterring Delinquents: A Rational Choice Model of Theft and Violence." *American Sociological Review* 71: 95–122.

Matthews, Shelley Keith and Robert Agnew. 2008. "Extending Deterrence Theory: Do Delinquent Peers Condition the Relationship Between Perceptions of Getting Caught and Offending?" *Journal of Research in Crime and Delinquency* 45: 91–118.

Matza, David. 1964. *Delinquency and Drift*. New York: Wiley.

Matza, David and Gresham M. Sykes. 1961. "Delinquency and Subterranean Values." *American Sociological Review* 26: 712–719.

Messner, Steven F. 1986. "Television Violence and Violent Crime: An Aggregate Analysis." *Social Problems* 33: 218–235.

Miethe, Terance D. and Robert F. Meier. 1990. "Opportunity, Choice, and Criminal Victimization: A Test of a Theoretical Model." *Journal of Research in Crime and Delinquency* 27: 243–266.

Milgram, Stanley. 1974. *Obedience to Authority*. New York: Harper & Row.

Miller, Joel. 2013. "Individual Offending, Routine Activities, and Activity Settings: Revisiting the Routine Activity Theory of General Deviance." *Journal of Research in Crime and Delinquency* 50: 390–416.

Nagin, Daniel S. and Raymond Paternoster. 1993. "Enduring Individual Differences and Rational Choice Theories of Crime." *Law and Society Review* 3: 467–496.

Osgood, D. Wayne and Amy L. Anderson. 2004. "Unstructured Socializing and Rates of Delinquency." *Criminology* 42: 519–549.

Osgood, D. Wayne, Janet K. Wilson, Patrick M. O'Malley, Jerald G. Bachman, and Lloyd D. Johnston. 1996. "Routine Activities and Individual Deviant Behavior. *American Sociological Review* 61: 635–655.

Paternoster, Raymond. 1987. "The Deterrent Effect of Perceived Certainty and Severity of Punishment: A Review of Evidence and Issues." *Justice Quarterly* 42: 173–217.

Paternoster, Raymond. 1989. "Decisions to Participate and Desist from Four Types of Common Delinquency: Deterrence and the Rational Choice Perspective." *Law and Society Review* 23: 7–40.

Pervin, Lawrence A. 1978. "Definitions, Measurements, and Classifications of Stimuli, Situations, and Environments." *Human Ecology* 6: 71–105.

Phillipson, Coleman. 1970. *Three Criminal Law Reformers: Beccaria, Bentham, and Romilly*. Montclair, NJ: Patterson Smith.

Piliavin, Irving and Scott Briar. 1964. "Police Encounters with Juveniles." *American Journal of Sociology* 70: 206–214.

Piliavin, Irving, Rosemary Gartner, Craig Thornton, and Ross L. Matsueda. 1986. "Crime Deterrence and Choice." *American Sociological Review* 51: 101–119.

Piquero, Alex R. and Greg Pogarsky. 2002. "Beyond Stafford and Warr's Reconceptualization of Deterrence: Personal and Vicarious Experiences, Impulsivity, and Offending Behavior." *Journal of Research in Crime and Delinquency* 39: 153–186.

Piquero, Alex R. and Stephen Tibbetts. 1996. "Specifying the Direct and Indirect Effect of Low Self-Control and Situational Factors in Offenders' Decision-Making: Toward a More Complete Model of Rational Offending." *Justice Quarterly* 13: 481–510.

Pogarsky, Greg. 2002. "Identifying Deterrable Offenders: Implications for Deterrence Research." *Justice Quarterly* 16: 451–471.

Putnins, Aldis L. 2010. "An Exploratory Study of Young Offenders' Self-Reported Reasons for Offending." *Journal of Forensic Psychiatry & Psychology* 21: 950–965.

Sacco, Vincent F. and Leslie W. Kennedy. 2002. *The Criminal Event: Perspectives in Space and Time*. Belmont, CA: Wadsworth.

Sampson, Robert J. and John H. Laub. 2005. "The Life-Course View of the Development of Crime." *Annals of the American Academy of Political and Social Science* 602: 12–45.

Sampson, Robert J. and John D. Wooldredge. 1987. "Linking the Micro- and Macro-Level Dimensions of Lifestyle: Routine Activity and Opportunity Models of Predatory Victimization." *Journal of Quantitative Criminology* 3: 371–393.

Shaw, Clifford. 1930. *The Jack-Roller*. University of Chicago Press,

Snyder, Scott. 1991. "Movies and Juvenile Delinquency: An Overview." *Adolescence* 26: 121–132.

Sutherland, Edwin H., Donald R. Cressey, and David F. Luckenbill. 1992. *Principles of Criminology*. 11th edn. Dix Hills, NY: General Hall.

Sykes, Gresham M. and David Matza. 1957. "Techniques of Neutralization: A Theory of Delinquency." *American Sociological Review* 22: 664–670.

Thomas, Kyle J. and Jean Marie McGloin. 2013. "A Dual-Systems Approach for Understanding Differential Susceptibility to Processes of Peer Influence." *Criminology* 51: 435–474.

Tuck, Mary and David Riley. 1986. "The Theory of Reasoned Action: A Decision Theory of Crime." Pp. 156–169 in *The Reasoning Criminal: Rational Choice Perspectives on Offending*, ed. Derek B. Cornish and Ronald V. Clarke. New York: Springer-Verlag.

Warr, Mark. 2002. *Companions in Crime: The Social Aspects of Criminal Conduct.* New York: Cambridge University Press.

Wenzel, Michael. 2004. "The Social Side of Sanctions: Personal and Social Norms as Moderators of Deterrence." *Law and Human Behavior* 28: 547–567.

Wikström, Per-Olof H. 2006. "Individuals, Settings, and Acts of Crime: Situational Mechanisms and the Explanation of Crime." Pp. 61–107 in *The Explanation of Crime: Context, Mechanism, and Development,* ed. Per-Olof H. Wikström and Robert J. Sampson. Cambridge University Press.

Wikström, Per-Olof H., Dietrich Oberwittler, Kyle Treiber, and Beth Hardie. 2012. *Breaking Rules: The Social and Situational Dynamics of Young People's Urban Crime.* New York: Oxford University Press.

Wikström, Per-Olof H. and Kyle H. Treiber. 2007. "The Role of Self-Control in Crime Causation." *European Journal of Criminology* 4: 237–264.

Wikström, Per-Olof H. and Kyle H. Treiber. 2009. "Violence as Situational Action." *International Journal of Conflict and Violence* 3: 75–96

Wikström, Per-Olof H., Andromachi Tseloni, and Dimitris Karlis 2011. "Do People Comply with the Law because they Fear Getting Caught?" *European Journal of Criminology* 8: 401–420.

Williams, Kirk R. and Richard Hawkins. 1986. "Perceptual Research on General Deterrence: A Critical Review." *Law and Society Review* 20: 545–572.

Wilcox, Pamela, Christopher J. Sullivan, Shayne Jones, and Jean-Louis van Gelder. 2014. "Personality and Opportunity: An Integrated Approach to Offending and Victimization." *Criminal Justice and Behavior* 41: 880–901.

Wilson, James Q. and Richard J. Herrnstein. 1985. *Crime and Human Nature: The Definitive Study of the Causes of Crime.* New York: Simon & Schuster.

Wood, Wendy, Frank Wong, and J. Gregory Chachere. 1991. "Effects of Media Violence on Viewers' Aggression in Unconstrained Social Interaction." *Psychological Bulletin* 109: 371–383.

Wright, Bradley R. Entner, Avshalom Caspi, Terrie E. Moffitt, and Ray Paternoster. 2004. "Does the Perceived Risk of Punishment Deter Criminally Prone Individuals? Rational Choice, Self-Control, and Crime." *Journal of Research in Crime and Delinquency* 41: 180–213.

Chapter 9

Social control theories
Family relations

Chapter preview

Topics:

- Informal social control
- Social control theories
- Characteristics of family life and informal social control

Theories:

- Social bond theory
- Life-course theory
- Self-control theory or a general theory of crime

Terms:

- informal social controls
- formal social controls
- direct controls
- indirect controls
- internalized controls
- attachment
- commitment
- involvement
- belief
- life course
- trajectory or pathway
- transition
- turning point
- social capital
- human agency
- low self-control
- family management
- parental social support
- parental efficacy
- family structure
- family disruption

Chapter learning objectives

After completing this chapter, students should be able to:

- Describe how families operate as institutions of both socialization and social control.
- Distinguish various forms of social control: formal, informal, direct, indirect, and internalized.
- Identify and describe the key concepts of the different versions of control theory: social bond, life course, and self-control.
- Explain how family structure and process are related to delinquent behavior.
- Explain the connections between parents, peers, and delinquent behavior.

Case in point: "brothers in crime" – family life and delinquent behavior

Mark and Mel were "brothers in crime" (Shaw 1930). They engaged in a variety of delinquent acts together, ranging from shoplifting and theft to intimidation and physical violence. They also used drugs and alcohol, usually in the company of one another. While born to the same biological mother and father, they were very different physically and temperamentally. Mark, the younger, was athletic in build, smart, and pleasant. Mel, the older, was thin, not terribly bright, and antagonistic. From the age of 4 on, they grew up with their biological mother and stepfather. Mark and Mel's biological father lived in another state and never saw the boys; as a result, their stepfather became "Dad." Mom and Dad were marginally employed and they eked out a living by working as seasonal employees in orchards. They rarely went on public assistance, but how they managed to get by without it was a matter of much debate among law enforcement officials. Drug dealing was suspected.

Family relations were cool and detached, reflecting a long and persistent pattern of family violence. The pattern was almost invariable: Mom and Dad getting high or drunk, engaging in verbal sparring that escalated to physical violence, followed by one of them going to the hospital – usually the mother, but occasionally the stepfather. When young, Mark and Mel would try to intervene in the physical violence inflicted on their mother by their stepfather. Then they too would become the target of violence. As Mark and Mel grew older, bigger, and stronger, they fought back, sometimes injuring their stepfather and sending him to the hospital. Regardless of who ended up in the hospital, the injured person would initially want to press charges against the family member(s) who inflicted the harm, but once charges were ready to file by the prosecutor's office, the victim would refuse to testify, thereby causing the case to be dropped for lack of evidence.

Mark and Mel learned patterns of social interaction in this family context: loud verbal confrontations, intimidating mannerisms, avoidance of reasoning, and escalation of disagreements to physical violence. Ultimately, interpersonal violence became normalized. It was also the case that the parents failed to provide effective monitoring and supervision for Mark and Mel, and the discipline they imposed was inconsistent and often abusive. Mark and Mel's family situation demonstrates that social relations within the family are foundational to both learning and social control because the family provides the primary group context in which lessons are learned and behaviors are regulated.

Two of the most commonly identified sources of delinquent behavior are family and friends. Intuition tells us that bad families and bad companions produce bad kids. Social relationships have a powerful influence on behavior. Two groups of theory consider social relations to be central to delinquent behavior. One group, called *social learning theories*, adopts the common theme that social relations with delinquent peers motivate and bring about delinquent behavior by providing the primary group context in which delinquent attitudes and behaviors are learned and reinforced. This will be the topic of Chapter 10. A second group of theories emphasizes the importance of social relations in controlling behavior. Referred to as *social control theories*, this group of theories pays close attention to the family as an institution of social control. In fact, considerations about the role of the family in delinquent behavior are left largely to the control perspective (Johnson 1979). The control perspective is distinctive not only because of the important role given to the family, but also because of its attempts to explain conformity rather than what motivates delinquent behavior.

Informal social control

The social controls that originate from family relations are more precisely referred to as **informal social controls**. Informal social controls refer to characteristics of social relations that bring about conformity, including parental supervision, sensitivity to others (their feelings, wishes, and expectations), identification with others, emotional attachment, and informal sanctions (such as withdrawal of affection, disregard, and ridicule). These relational controls can be contrasted with **formal social controls** that are based in institutions such as schools, churches, and justice systems. Institutional controls are established to promote conformity and to sanction deviance. For example, schools establish rules and procedures to suspend students, as do churches to excommunicate members and justice systems to imprison serious offenders. When most people think about social control, they usually have in mind only the bigger picture of formal social control, especially criminal or juvenile justice systems (Janowitz 1975). Sociologists have long claimed, however, that informal social controls are more important in explaining conformity than are formal social controls (Gibbs 1989; Tittle 1980).

Ivan Nye (1958) differentiated three major forms of informal social control, and explained how family relations play a vital role in the development and application of these controls. **Direct controls** are the restrictions and punishments imposed by others that restrict behavior and the rewards that encourage and reinforce positive behavior. **Indirect controls** are based on affectional identification with others, especially parents, such that an individual conforms in order to maintain the relationship bond and to avoid disappointing others. **Internalized controls** are controls originally expressed by significant others and then taken on as one's own – they are internalized and implemented from within the individual through conscience or sense of guilt. Nye also argued that when youths' relational needs are not met within the family, they are more likely to turn outside the family. The absence of family relational controls increases the likelihood of delinquency. Although Nye recognized that some social controls are formal, operating through institutions like the school and the juvenile justice system, he emphasized the informal social controls of family relations. Nye's conceptualization of social control is central to the development of social control theories.

This chapter addresses both the theoretical explanations and empirical findings on informal social control. Three different versions of social control theory are described: social bond theory, life-course theory, and self-control theory. The remainder of the chapter considers how characteristics of family life are related to informal social control, including the quality of parent–child relations; parental monitoring, supervision, and discipline; parental efficacy; family structure; mother's employment; family social class; and parental criminality.

Social control theories

Several social control theories focus on the family as the primary source of attachments, commitments, and discipline in preventing and controlling delinquency (Rankin and Kern 1994). In this way, families inspire children to conform to parental norms and expectations, and to the norms and expectations of the larger society. Parents also provide supervision and discipline to encourage compliance from their children. Among the different social control theories, Travis Hirschi's (1969) social bond theory is arguably most responsible for stimulating interest in the family and delinquent behavior. His theory led to significant developments in theory and research.

Hirschi's social bond theory

In developing his version of social control theory, Hirschi (1969: 19) makes frequent reference to a classic question posed long ago by Thomas Hobbes: "Why do men obey the rules of society?" Hirschi claims that this question has never been adequately answered and that the primary task of delinquency theory is to explain conformity, not delinquent behavior. In fact, this is a basic theme of all social control theories. Hirschi answered the Hobbesian question by advancing four elements of an individual's social bond to society: attachment, commitment, involvement, and belief. These elements provide a "stake in conformity," or the reason to conform.

The thesis of social bond theory is that "delinquent acts result when an individual's bond to society is weak or broken" (Hirschi 1969: 16). Consistent with other control theories, Hirschi does not address what motivates young people to get involved in delinquency; rather, he contends that when the bond to society is weak or broken, they are free to engage in delinquent acts.

The full statement of Hirschi's social bond theory is presented in the book *Causes of Delinquency*, published in 1969. His presentation of social bond theory is unique because he systematically laid out the theory's assumptions, concepts, and propositions. He then developed empirical measures of the major concepts and methodically tested the theory, using data from the Richmond Youth Project, a self-report survey of more than 4,000 youths.[1] His research also evaluated social bond theory in comparison to explanations offered by competing theories.

Attachment

Attachment is generally regarded as the primary element of the social bond (Simons et al. 1994). The essence of attachment is the affectional identification that the youth has with others, through which he or she is sensitive to their opinions, communicates openly with them, mutually respects and identifies with them, and values his or her relationship with them (Hirschi 1969). Hirschi also referred to attachment as the "bond of affection." Attachment results in conformity because of the vested interest that the youth has in a relationship. As such, social control is based in the relationship bond itself, rather than in some process of internalization through which the youth develops self-control or conscience (Hirschi 1969).

Although Hirschi considered three forms of attachment – attachments to parents, to school, and to peers – he presented the relational controls of the parent–child attachment as the most important in inhibiting delinquent behavior. The emphasis on relationship bonds means that direct parental controls, such as monitoring and supervision, are relatively unimportant in bringing about conformity. Rather, relationship attachments bring about sensitivity to the wishes and feelings of parents, and it is this sensitivity that results in social control (Hirschi 1969; see also Larzelere and Patterson 1990; Cernkovich and Giordano 1987; Loeber and Stouthamer-Loeber 1986; Nye 1958).

Hirschi's analysis of parental attachment was based most extensively on two measures: *intimacy of communication* and *affectional identity*. Intimacy of communication included questions about communication from child to parent and from parent to child, such as: "Do you share your thoughts and feelings with your mother [father]?" (Hirschi 1969: 90). Affectional identity was measured using questionnaire items such as: "Would you like to be the kind of person your mother [father] is?" (Hirschi 1969: 92). Using these measures, Hirschi found that youths with strong attachments to their parents were significantly less likely to engage in delinquent acts. This connection was consistent across different social classes and racial groups, and it held true regardless of the number of delinquent friends.

Social bond theory advances two other dimensions of attachment: attachments to school and attachment to peers. Attachment to school is more of an attitudinal social bond than a relational social bond. Hirschi (1969: 121, 123, 129) measured attachment to school through questions that gauged whether the youth liked school and cared what teachers thought of him. Another question addressed the youth's views about the legitimacy of the school's authority. Hirschi found that youths who do poorly in school are usually unattached to school and are frequently involved in delinquent acts. Put in terms of social bond theory, when the social bond of school attachment is weakened, youths are free to commit delinquent acts. "Research in action: schools, social bonds, and delinquency" summarizes research on the relationships between delinquency and various aspects of school experiences.

Research in action: schools, social bonds, and delinquency

More than four decades ago, Travis Hirschi (1969) theorized that attachment to school, commitment to education, and involvement in school-related activities would decrease delinquency:

- **Attachment to school.** Many have argued, from the perspective of social bond theory, that students who are strongly attached to school – who, for example, like school, "feel a part of their school," and care what teachers think of them – are less likely than others to engage in delinquency (see Gottfredson, Wilson, and Najaka 2002; Johnson, Crosnoe, and Elder, Jr. 2001). Numerous studies have supported this hypothesis (e.g., Hirschfield and Gasper 2011; Stewart 2003; Jang 1999; Farnworth, Schweinhart, and Berrueta-Clement 1985). Some researchers found, though, that the relationship between attachment to school and delinquency was reciprocal, meaning that attachment influenced delinquency, but delinquency also affected attachment (Siennick and Staff 2008; Liska and Reed 1985). Research also suggests that school capital and high-quality school environments "serve as substitutes for poor parental attachment and a lack of parental involvement in children's schooling," and thus diminish involvement in delinquency in part "by compensating for high-risk family environments" (Hoffman and Dufur 2008: 29).

- **Commitment to education.** Criminologists have also argued, from a social bond perspective, that weak commitment to education (i.e. weak valuing of educational goals) and low educational aspirations are related to delinquency (Gottfredson et al. 2002). Research has strongly supported this hypothesis, showing that weak school commitment is strongly related to school misconduct and various forms of delinquency, including violence (Siennick and Staff 2008; Stewart 2003; Hawkins et al. 1998; Simons et al. 1998; Jenkins 1995). Commitment to education is likely related to academic performance. Students who perform well academically are likely to be more committed to education and have higher aspirations and expectations for success than those who perform poorly (Siennick and Staff 2008; Wasserman et al. 1996). Research suggests that commitment to education has a greater protective effect in preventing delinquency for boys than for girls (Payne 2009).

- **Involvement in school-related activities.** Research generally has not supported the hypothesis that involvement in school-related activities will inhibit delinquency (Stewart 2003; Hoffman and Xu 2002; Jenkins 1995; see also Guest and McRee 2009). In particular, research has challenged the assumption that participation in high school sports would have a deterrent effect on delinquency. Research shows that being a highly involved athlete tends to be associated with higher levels of delinquency (Kelley and Sokol-Katz 2011), and that sports participation increases involvement in particular types of delinquency, such as drunk driving (Hartmann and Massoglia 2007). Wong (2005) reconceptualized Hirschi's hypothesis regarding involvement by constructing involvement as a social setting variable. Wong (2005: 321) argued that "certain activities provide a social setting favorable to the development of the social bond and the reduction in delinquent association." His research showed that school- and family-related activities strengthened the social bond and thereby reduced delinquency, while peer-related activities reduced the social bond and increased the likelihood of delinquent behavior.

- **Truancy and dropping out of school.** Truancy and dropping out of school are manifestations of weak social bonds to school, especially lack of commitment to academic achievement. Research has shown that truancy is a precursor to more serious delinquency (both violent and non-violent offenses) and is also related to substance abuse and marital and job problems later in life (see Baker, Sigmon, and Nugent 2001). Dropping out of school also indicates weak bonds to school, and some research has shown that dropping out is related to delinquency and crime, including violence (Henry, Knight, and Thornberry 2012; Staff and Kreager 2008; Jarjoura 1993; Rosen et al. 1991; Farrington 1989; see also Sweeten, Bushway, and Paternoster 2009). Research has also shown that school failure, measured in part as dropping out of school, operates as a significant adolescent turning point, amplifying later delinquency (Bersani and Chapple 2007). Being suspended or expelled greatly increases a child's risk of dropping out of school and of being drawn into the juvenile justice system (Monahan et al. 2014; Fabelo et al. 2011). Suspension or expulsion increases the likelihood of arrest, particularly for youth who do not have a history of behavior problems (Monahan et al. 2014).

As it does with attachment to parents and school, social bond theory stresses that peer attachment is "conducive to conformity," not to delinquency (Hirschi 1969). Although Hirschi recognized that delinquent acts are usually committed with companions and that delinquent youth are likely to have delinquent friends, he argued that delinquent behavior is related to weak attachment to peers. His research showed that youth who were strongly attached to friends were least likely to be delinquent. This finding suggests that peer attachment operates as a control against delinquent involvement, not as motivation to it. Hirschi claimed that it is the level of attachment that is related to delinquency, not whether peers are involved in delinquent acts. His research revealed that even for youth who were attached to delinquent peers, the stronger the attachment to those friends, the less likely they were to be delinquent. Taking the argument one step further, Hirschi argued that youth with weak social bonds tend to develop friendships with delinquent youth, like themselves. Furthermore, he portrayed the relationship bond of delinquent youth as weak and therefore uninfluential.

Commitment

Throughout life, most people acquire material possessions, reputations, and positions that they do not want to risk losing through involvement in illegal acts. The more that is acquired, the more invested the individual is in conforming. This is what Hirschi (1969) meant by **commitment** – the "rational component" of the social bond. A bond to society is generated when a person invests time and energy in conventional activities such as school and work. Whatever possible gains come from delinquency must then be weighed against the risk of losing the investment that has been made in conventional behavior. Although commitment may seem to be an attitude, it more specifically refers to attitudes that are put into action. During adolescence, conventional activity most commonly involves actions and aspirations related to school and work.

How is commitment demonstrated in the lives of adolescents? Hirschi (1969) first explored the relationship between commitment to "unconventional activity" (such as smoking, drinking, frequent dating, and the importance of having a car) and delinquent behavior. His findings showed that such commitments were positively related to delinquency: the greater the level of unconventional activity, the greater the number of delinquent acts. Hirschi went on to examine the link between commitment to conventional activity and delinquency. Included here were a youth's aspirations and expectations for education and a high-status occupation, and "achievement orientation" – a measure of how much a youth values good grades and works hard in school and other activities. Social bond theory contends that youth with high aspirations and expectations for educational and occupational success are unlikely to pursue delinquent activities. Hirschi's research findings supported the importance of these various forms of commitment; the more committed a youth is to conventional pursuits, the less likely he or she is to be delinquent. In addition, he found that the educational and occupational expectations of delinquent youth tended to be lower than those of non-delinquent youth. The consistent levels of commitment within social groups suggests that commitment arises in the context of social relationships rather than in long-term, deeply held personal values and attitudes. Hirschi repeatedly emphasized this social, rather than internal aspect of the elements of the social bond.

Involvement

The old adage, "idle hands are the devil's workshop," reflects the belief that too much leisure time provides occasion for delinquent acts (Hirschi 1969: 22). This relates to the popular notion that **involvement** in conventional activities controls delinquency simply by consuming a youth's time and energy. Hirschi did *not* argue, however, that any activity that consumes a youth's time and energy will prevent delinquent behavior. In fact, his data showed that the more time a boy spent working, dating, watching television, reading, and playing games, the more – not less – likely he was to be delinquent (although the relationship was very weak). Hirschi contended that most conventional activities are actually neutral with respect to delinquency – they neither inhibit nor promote it. The reason for this is that most delinquent acts require very little time to commit. Accordingly, Hirschi argued that the type of activity is important in determining the commitment that arises from such involvement and the degree of opportunity for delinquent acts.

Hirschi's research points to two specific types of activities that are related to delinquent behavior: school–educational activities and "working-class adult activities." His primary measure of school–educational activities is the amount of time spent on homework. The relevance to social control is straightforward and is supported by Hirschi's findings: the more time spent on homework, the less involvement in delinquency. Involvement in education-related activities is the primary way that adolescent time is structured, thereby reducing the opportunity for delinquent acts. School-related involvement also reflects the social bond of commitment, through which educational aspirations are turned into conventional action – doing homework.

Hirschi refers to a second group of activities as "working-class adult activities" because they provide adult-like activities for youth with limited educational and occupational aspirations and opportunities. His research measured working-class adult activities in terms of "boys who smoked, drank, dated frequently, rode around in cars, and had feelings of boredom." Boys who were involved in these activities were more likely to commit delinquent acts than boys who did not engage in these activities (Hirschi 1969: 196). Thus, youth who have little interest in education-related activities fall outside of the structure provided by schools and become involved in activities that provide many opportunities for delinquency.

Belief

One of the distinguishing features of control theories is the idea that "delinquency is not caused by beliefs that require delinquency, but rather made possible by the absence of beliefs that forbid delinquency" (Hirschi 1969: 198). Other theories attempt to explain the development of **beliefs** that allow and motivate delinquent behavior. Delinquent peer groups and subcultures, for example, provide beliefs that are opposed to the values and norms of conventional society. Delinquent behavior is a natural outcome when such beliefs are adopted. In contrast, control theories consider the strength of belief in the law and the legal system. As Hirschi notes, "the less a person believes he should obey the rules, the more likely he is to violate them" (Hirschi 1969: 26).

Hirschi argues that the most relevant measure of belief is the individual's attitude about the law, and he provides much analysis based on the questionnaire item: "It is alright to get around the law if you can get away with it." His findings revealed that there is a great deal of variation in the extent to which youth believe they should obey the law, and that the more they believe that they should, the less likely they are to get involved in delinquency. So what determines the degree to which a youth desires to obey the laws of society? Hirschi argues that the level of belief is closely connected to parental attachment and commitment: the youth who is unattached to parents and teachers and who has few aspirations for success is unlikely to feel that the law is to be obeyed.

Connections between elements of the social bond

Hirschi's study established that the four elements of the social bond are additive – the more bonds individuals have, the more likely they are to conform (Krohn 1986). He also found that youth tied to conventional society through one of the social bonds are likely to display other elements of the social bond. This suggests that the elements of the social bond are interrelated and that the social bond cannot be adequately described or understood without considering such interconnections. Hirschi (1969) identifies three combinations of social bond elements that are particularly important. First, attachment and commitment tend to vary together. Those attached to others also tend to be committed to conventional activity. Second, commitment and involvement are closely related. Those who are committed to educational and occupational success are also likely to be involved in related conventional activities, such as doing homework. Third, attachment and belief are interrelated. When considering belief, Hirschi found that youth who are attached to parents and who care what their parents think and feel are likely to express belief in the moral validity of the law.

Research findings on the social bond

As mentioned earlier, one of the unique aspects of Hirschi's social bond theory is the fact that he provided an extensive test of the theory using data from the Richmond Youth Project. Although the relationships among Hirschi's measures of the social bond have been questioned, his analysis provided rich and consistent support for the theory. After its original presentation and testing, social bond theory has been tested by many researchers. The resulting evaluation has generally supported the core concepts of social bond theory but has also provided a number of important qualifications. Nonetheless, social bond theory has come to occupy a central place in criminological theory.

A number of important qualifications to social bond theory have been suggested by research:

- In contrast to the predictions of social bond theory, attachment to peers leads to conformity only when those peers are *not* delinquent. Attachment to delinquent peers is related to delinquent behavior (Elliott, Huizinga, and Ageton 1985; Conger 1976; Hindelang 1973; Linden and Hackler 1973).
- Involvement in delinquent acts appears to precede, not follow, weak school attachment. Youths who are involved in delinquent behavior tend to report less attachment to school following their involvement in delinquency. Weak attachment to school, in turn, influences parental attachment (Liska and Reed 1985; see also Kandel 1996; Krohn et al. 1992; Wiatrowski and Anderson 1987; Wiatrowski, Griswold, and Roberts 1981).
- Research has found only modest support for commitment as an element of the social bond (Agnew 1991; Wiatrowski et al. 1981; Krohn and Massey 1980).
- Organized "leisure activities" (e.g., band, school newspaper, scouts, church activities), "passive entertainment" (e.g., reading, radio, TV, movies), and non-competitive sports (e.g., bike riding, horseback riding, roller skating) are negatively related to delinquent behavior (higher involvement was related to lower levels of delinquency). In contrast, hanging out with friends and unsupervised activities with friends are positively related to delinquent behavior (higher involvement, higher delinquency) (Osgood et al. 1996;

Burton et al. 1995; Agnew and Peterson 1989). The unsupervised nature of some leisure activities seems to be one of the most important factors facilitating participation in delinquency.

- The effect of belief on delinquency appears to be relatively small, especially when compared to the effect of delinquency on belief. Belief is largely a product of participation in delinquency, rather than a cause of deviance (Matsueda 1989; see also Wiatrowski and Anderson 1987; Wiatrowski et al. 1981; Krohn and Massey 1980).
- Researchers have found that the different elements of the social bond may have greater importance at different ages (Leonard and Decker 1994; Agnew 1991; Thornberry 1987; Wiatrowski and Anderson 1987; LaGrange and White 1985; Liska and Reed 1985). Findings indicate that parental attachment is most important in early adolescence; commitment to school is most important in early to middle adolescence; and belief is most important in middle to late adolescence.
- Much research indicates that the elements of the social bond are more strongly related to minor delinquency than to serious delinquency (Agnew 1991; Matsueda 1989; Krohn and Massey 1980).
- Research shows that social bond variables are probably better able to explain female delinquency than male delinquency, and that the elements of the social bond may operate differently for girls than for boys (Booth, Farrell, and Varano 2008; Burton et al. 1998; Rosenbaum and Lasley 1990; Cernkovich and Giordano 1987; Krohn and Massey 1980; Johnson 1979).
- Research using longitudinal data reveals that social bond variables are related to delinquency, but that these relationships are relatively weak (Agnew 1991; Akers and Cochran 1985; Elliott et al. 1985; Matsueda 1982). The effects of social bond variables are weaker than the effects of variables specified by competing theories. This has led scholars to develop alternative causal models which specify that social bond variables are indirectly related to delinquency because they increase the probability that some adolescents will associate with delinquent peers from whom they learn delinquent attitudes and behaviors (Warr 1993; Massey and Krohn 1986; Elliott et al. 1985).

Sampson and Laub's life-course theory

More than 20 years ago, Robert Sampson and John Laub (1993) introduced *life-course theory* by bringing a sense of Indiana Jones-like intrigue to their work when they posed several unsolved criminological "puzzles" and revealed their discovery of some "dusty cartons of data" in the "sub-basement" of the Harvard Law School Library – data that they hoped would shed light on these puzzles. Rich data are to sociologists what artifacts are to archaeologists. Sampson and Laub (1993: 1) conveyed this excitement: "As we began to sort through the case files, we soon discovered that these were not conventional data, and, as we went on, we found out the Gluecks [the original researchers who gathered the data] were not conventional researchers."[2] The data that Sampson and Laub had discovered were from Sheldon and Eleanor Glueck's famous longitudinal and comparative study of 500 delinquents and 500 non-delinquents (described in Chapter 3). The Gluecks published their findings in the 1950 book *Unraveling Juvenile Delinquency*. This far-reaching study provided Sampson and Laub with both the data and perspective for their contemporary life-course theory.

Life-course theory has its roots in familiar ground: "Our general organizing principle is that the probability of deviance increases when an individual's bond to society is weak or broken" (Sampson and Laub 1994: 524). Life-course theory is most extensively advanced in Sampson and Laub's (1993) book *Crime in the Making: Pathways and Turning Points through Life*. Like Hirschi, Sampson and Laub focus on the importance of social bonds as the primary means of informal social control. Rather than elaborating on the elements of the social bond, life-course theory examines social bonds over the course of life, considering how changes influence informal social control, and ultimately, behavior. In brief, Sampson and Laub (1993; Laub and Sampson 1993) refer to their theory as an "age-graded theory of informal social control."

The life-course perspective

Sampson and Laub (1993: 6) argue that sociological criminology has traditionally "concentrated on the teenage years" and thereby "neglected the theoretical significance of childhood characteristics and the link between early childhood behaviors and later adult outcomes." Life-course theory is an attempt to bring childhood and adulthood into the criminological picture. Like the Gluecks, Sampson and Laub seek to study criminal behavior from its beginning to end – what we referred to in Chapter 6 as the criminal career. Thus, the frame of reference is the entire life span, and primary attention is given to the different factors that explain the onset, persistence, and desistance of criminal involvement over the life course. To study these factors, Sampson and Laub adopt the conceptual tools of the life-course perspective and the causal principles of social bond theory (see also Warr 1998). **Life course** refers to the age-graded sequence of culturally defined roles and social transitions (Caspi, Elder, and Herbener 1990). Sociologically, *roles* are behavioral expectations of a given position. These roles are age-graded in that the expectations for behavior are different for children, adolescents, and adults. The life course also involves a general **trajectory**, or **pathway**, which is a long-term pattern of behavior relating to education, work, parenting, conformity or deviance, and the like. The life-course trajectory is marked by significant life events, or **transitions**, that may alter the established behavioral trajectory. When a transition results in significant change in the life-course trajectory, it is referred to as a **turning point**. Sampson and Laub's life-course theory relates these basic concepts to the development and alteration of relationship bonds and to informal social control. In doing so, the theory tries to account for not only the onset of delinquency, but also the continuation of and desistance from criminal behavior.

A sociogenic developmental theory

Basing their conclusions on four decades of research, Sheldon and Eleanor Glueck (1968) argued that child temperament and family socialization were the factors that most distinguished delinquents from non-delinquents in early life. Sampson and Laub's life-course theory adopts this same emphasis and expands upon it. Following the Gluecks, Sampson and Laub (1993) propose four family socialization factors that significantly increase the likelihood of delinquent behavior: (1) erratic, threatening, and harsh or punitive discipline by both mothers and fathers; (2) low parental supervision; (3) parental rejection of the child; and (4) weak emotional attachment of the child to his parents. These key dimensions of family relations influence the likelihood of delinquency mainly because they determine the effectiveness of informal social control. Unlike Hirschi's presentation of social bond theory, which emphasizes the indirect controls of the parent–child relational bond, life-course theory also includes direct controls in the form of discipline and supervision.

Life-course theory also recognizes that parenting styles, especially discipline, and emotional attachment, are responsive to the personality and behavior of the child. While the Gluecks referred to child temperament, Sampson and Laub expanded the notion to include difficult personality ("restless and irritable"); predisposition toward aggression and fighting (where violence was a "predominant mode of response"); and the early beginning, or "onset," of misbehavior. Together, these characteristics are referred to as "early childhood predisposition toward disruptive behavior" (Sampson and Laub 1993: 85–88). Such predisposition establishes a pathway or trajectory to criminal involvement that stretches from early childhood to the adult years, implying not only behavioral continuity, but also progression and escalation of deviance (Sampson and Laub 1993; Simons et al. 1998; Patterson, Reid, and Dishion 1992; White et al. 1990; Loeber 1982).

Sampson and Laub call their theory a "sociogenic developmental theory" – a reference that distinguishes their point of view from that of developmental psychology. Although both views use the idea of developmental stages in the life course, a sociogenic approach also emphasizes the structural context of such developmental stages, rather than the individual's adaptation to these stages. In particular, Sampson and Laub point to the importance of structural factors such as poverty, residential mobility, family disruption, family size, household crowding, and mother or father deviance. They propose that "poverty and structural disadvantage influence delinquency in large part by reducing the capacity of families to achieve effective informal social control" (Sampson and Laub 1994: 523–524; see also Sampson and Laub 1993, 2005a).

Life-course change and informal social control

The continuity of behavior throughout the life course is only half the story. Although early childhood misconduct increases the probability of future delinquency and criminality, the causal sequence is far from being totally deterministic. Research reveals that at least half of all antisocial children do not become delinquent during adolescence (Sampson and Laub 1993; Robins 1978). Furthermore, most antisocial children do not become antisocial adults, and a majority of adult criminals have no history as juvenile delinquents. Behavioral stability is true in a "relatively small number of males whose behavioral problems are quite extreme" (Sampson and Laub 1993: 13; see also Loeber and LeBlanc 1990; Gove 1985; McCord 1980). Because of this potential for change in the pathway to crime, life-course theory attempts to "examine crime and deviance in childhood, adolescence, and adulthood in a way that recognizes the significance of both *continuity* and *change* over the life-course" (Laub and Sampson 1993: 302, emphasis added).

Sampson and Laub's search for an explanation for both continuity and change returned them to the importance of social bonds as the primary vehicle of informal social control. Weak social bonds within the family lessen the informal social control of parents, allowing for childhood misconduct to escalate into adolescent delinquency. The social bonds of adulthood are also central to Sampson and Laub's explanation of adult criminal behavior. Sampson and Laub (1993) introduce the concept of **social capital** to refer to the "obligations and restraints" that are a part of relationship bonds.[3] These obligations and restraints are connected to the institutional roles that are a part of adult life – the behavioral expectations associated with positions in the family, school, work, and community. The result of these role obligations and restraints is informal social control.

Testing life-course theory

The dusty cartons of old data not only provided Sampson and Laub with the intrigue that fueled their development of life-course theory, but also provided the records to test that theory. Sampson and Laub resurrected these data by computerizing, supplementing, and validating them. In an extensive reanalysis of the data, Sampson and Laub (1993, 1994; Laub and Sampson 1988, 1993) found support for their life-course theory.

Using measures of an early childhood predisposition to disruptive behavior (difficult disposition, early onset, and tantrums), family process (supervision, attachment, and discipline), and structural background (residential mobility, family disruption, social class, and parental deviance), Sampson and Laub found that family process variables had a strong and direct influence on delinquent behavior, as did early childhood difficulties. As the theory proposes, early childhood difficulty also influenced parental supervision and discipline. Surprisingly, early childhood difficulties did not affect the emotional bond between parent and child. The data showed that early childhood difficulty was not sufficient in itself to explain delinquent behavior. It was also necessary to consider the effect of childhood difficulty in conjunction with family processes. The effect of structural background variables on delinquency was found to occur indirectly, largely through their influence on family processes. In fact, almost 75 percent of the total effect of structural background variables on delinquent behavior was through their effect on family processes (Sampson and Laub 1993).

Sampson and Laub also considered turning points in adult life that changed social capital and informal social control. They found that social capital in the form of social bonds in marriage (marital attachment) and work (job stability) significantly reduced deviant behavior during adulthood, even among those with a history of delinquent behavior in childhood and adolescence. Both continuity and change in behavior were strongly predicted by prior social bonds and the development of adult social bonds (Sampson, Laub, and Wimer 2006; Sampson and Laub 1993; see also Jang 2013; Eitle, Taylor, and Eitle 2010; Christie-Mizell and Peralta 2009).

Life-course desisters

In a more recent book, *Shared Beginnings, Divergent Lives: Delinquent Boys to Age 70*, Laub and Sampson (2003) report findings from interviews conducted with 52 men from the original sample of delinquent boys, now elderly. The life-history narratives allowed Laub and Sampson to better understand patterns of stability and change in offending over the entire life course. Although they found much variability in the "trajectories of adult crime," one pattern was common among the men interviewed: all desisted from crime. Laub and Sampson explain that significant life events, or turning points, occurred at different points in the lives of these men, influencing when desistence occurred. Involvement in marriage, work, and other institutions produced both informal social controls and commitments to conformity. The interviews also revealed that **human agency** – purposeful choice and individual will – played an important role in desisting from crime (Sampson and Laub 2005a, 2005b). The addition of this concept of human agency to life-course theory acknowledges the importance of individual choices and actions in continued involvement in and desistence from crime. Sampson and Laub (2005a) emphasize that human agency is influenced by the opportunities and constraints of life circumstances and that it is not a perfectly rational process. For example, the choice to continue in adult crime is usually accompanied by the view, drawn from experience, that the system is unfair and corrupt, and therefore conformity is not something to be desired.

Gottfredson and Hirschi's General Theory of Crime: self-control theory

Hirschi's newest version of control theory is a theory of self-control, developed with Michael Gottfredson and presented in their book *A General Theory of Crime* (Gottfredson and Hirschi 1990). The theory is undoubtedly an important contribution to criminological theory; however, it has generated a tremendous amount of controversy because of its emphasis on enduring individual differences and its disregard for social causation (Evans et al. 1997). Consistent with other control theories, *self-control theory* tries to explain conformity, not why people engage in crime. However, this social control theory argues that the critical dimension of control is self-control, an internal control that is instilled largely through effective parenting.

The nature of crime

Gottfredson and Hirschi begin their theoretical argument with the contention that criminologists have oddly ignored studying the nature of crime, which they believe can provide important insight into the nature of criminals (Hirschi and Gottfredson 1993; Gottfredson and Hirschi 1990; see also Evans et al. 1997). After studying the crimes that occur most frequently, Gottfredson and Hirschi (1990: 16–17) claim that a "vast majority of criminal acts are trivial and mundane affairs" that require "little in the way of effort, planning, preparation, or skill." Because most crimes are similar, they argue that it is theoretically unproductive for criminology to make distinctions among crimes. Instead, it is possible, and in fact advantageous, to offer a general theory of crime – a theory that accounts for all types of crime.

Gottfredson and Hirschi (1990: 14) also observe that virtually all crimes are "short lived, immediately gratifying, easy, simple, and exciting." These characteristics make crime appeal to everyone. Self-control theory makes no effort to explain the motivation that is necessary for involvement in crime – crime is appealing by its very nature. Instead, what needs to be explained is what keeps people from getting involved in crime.

The nature of criminality: low self-control

Gottfredson and Hirschi (1990: 14) go on to argue that "the properties of criminal acts are closely connected to the characteristics of people likely to engage in them." Their theory holds that crimes are committed by persons with **low self-control**. Such people are "impulsive, insensitive, physical (as opposed to mental), risk taking, short-sighted, and nonverbal" (Gottfredson and Hirschi 1990: 90). People who lack self-control are "vulnerable to the temptations of the moment" because they are unable to calculate or consider the negative consequences of their acts (Gottfredson and Hirschi 1990: 87).[4] The lack of self-control, however, does not predispose or motivate a person to crime. Rather, the probability that low self-control will lead to crime depends on whether the individual is exposed to opportunities to engage in crime.

As a "general" theory of crime, self-control is used to explain not only crime, but also a variety of "analogous acts" – acts that are like crime, such as accidents, smoking, and alcohol use. Because lack of self-control frees the individual to pursue self-interest and personal gain, crime is just one of many possible behaviors.

Corresponding to involvement in crime and analogous acts are a wide variety of "social consequences" of low self-control. Gottfredson and Hirschi (1990) argue that low self-control fosters failure in interpersonal relations, social activities, and social institutions. Individuals with low self-control have difficulty making and keeping friends, and when they do develop friendships they tend to end up in the company of others who similarly lack self-control and are involved in deviance. In addition, they are less able to succeed in school and the workplace, and they tend to enter into marriages that are destined to fail. Finally, Gottfredson and Hirschi (1990: 157) claim that "people who lack self-control tend to dislike settings that require discipline, supervision, or other constraints on their behavior; such settings include school, work, and for that matter, home. As a result, these people tend to gravitate to 'the street' or, at least in adolescence, to the same-sex peer group" in which opportunities for crime abound. (see also Evans et al. 1997; Laub and Sampson 1993; Sampson and Laub 1993).

The logical conclusion to this line of thought provides self-control theory with a unique viewpoint that has generated considerable controversy: many of the traditional causes of crime are in fact consequences of low self-control (Gottfredson and Hirschi 1990; see also Simons et al. 1998; Brownfield and Sorenson 1987). Traditional causes of crime include such factors as deviant peers, dysfunctional family background, school failure, and weak social bonds. According to Gottfredson and Hirschi, the apparent link between these traditional causes and criminal involvement is actually evidence of the true causal connection between low self-control and these apparent causes. Low self-control is the true cause of crime and of other factors that are typically viewed as causes of crime. The argument here is depicted in Figure 9.1, which shows that low self-control has a variety of consequences that are traditionally viewed as causes of crime. However, low self-control is shown to be the true cause of crime and analogous acts.

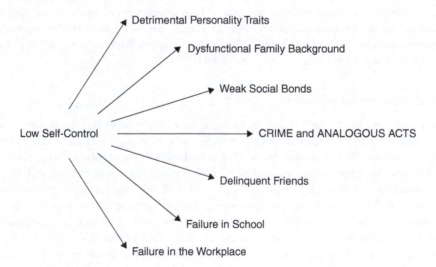

Figure 9.1 The priority of low self-control.

Gottfredson and Hirschi argue that low self-control is the ultimate cause of crime and delinquency. Low self-control also has a wide variety of social consequences that other theories advance as causes of crime.

Origins of self-control

According to Gottfredson and Hirschi, self-control is instilled early in life primarily through effective childrearing. Drawing extensively from Gerald Patterson's (1980, 1982) work on family management skills, self-control theory advances three key components of effective parenting: (1) monitoring of the child's behavior, (2) recognition of deviant behavior when it occurs, and (3) consistent and proportionate punishment of deviance when it is recognized. The influence of these direct controls on self-control is apparent when Gottfredson and Hirschi (1990: 97) state that parents

> who care for the child will watch his behavior, see him doing things he should not do, and correct him. The result may be a child more capable of delaying gratification, more sensitive to the interests and desires of others, more independent, more willing to accept restraints on his activity, and more unlikely to use force or violence to attain his ends.

In contrast, "the characteristics associated with low self-control tend to show themselves in the absence of nurturance, discipline, or training" (Gottfredson and Hirschi 1990: 95).

Self-control theory's emphasis on direct controls is similar to that of life-course theory, which also considers parental supervision and discipline early in life to be central to the development of controls. However, self-control theory, as its name states, emphasizes self-control, whereas life-course theory centers on the informal social controls of relationship bonds. In addition, self-control theory emphasizes that self-control is established early in life and remains stable throughout life. This is called the "stability postulate" (Gottfredson and Hirschi 1990: 118; see also Burt, Simons, and Simons 2006; Hay and Forrest 2006; Winfree et al. 2006; Turner and Piquero 2002). Life-course theory, in contrast, considers the informal social controls of relationship bonds throughout life.

Research findings on self-control theory

Harold Grasmick and his colleagues (1993) developed a widely used attitudinal measure of low self-control made up of six key components: impulsivity, preference for simple rather than complex tasks, risk seeking, preference for physical rather than cerebral activities, self-centered orientation, and a volatile temper. Each of these components was drawn from Hirschi and Gottfredson's definition of low self-control and was measured by several survey questions, as described in "Research in action: measures of low self-control."[5] Grasmick and his colleagues contend that the different components that make up low self-control can best be understood collectively, as a single characteristic of the individual.[6] Consistent with self-control theory, they also argued that these different components of self-control should be considered in conjunction with opportunity for crime.

Research in action: measures of low self-control

In research conducted shortly after self-control theory was introduced, Harold Grasmick and his colleagues (1993: 14–15) advanced a measure of low self-control that was composed of six components: impulsivity, preference for simple rather than complex tasks, risk seeking, preference for physical rather than cerebral activities, self-centered orientation, and a volatile temper. Each of these components was measured by several questions.

Impulsivity

I often act on the spur of the moment without stopping to think.

I don't devote much thought and effort to preparing for the future.

I often do whatever brings me pleasure here and now, even at the cost of some distant goal.

Simple tasks

I frequently try to avoid projects that I know will be difficult.

When things get complicated, I tend to quit or withdraw.

The things in life that are easiest to do bring me the most pleasure.

Risk seeking

I like to test myself every now and then by doing something a little risky.

I sometimes find it exciting to do things for which I might get in trouble.

Excitement and adventure are more important to me than security.

Physical activities

If I had a choice, I would almost always rather do something physical than something mental.

I almost always feel better when I am on the move than when I am sitting and thinking.

I like to get out and do things more than I like to read or contemplate.

Self-centered

I try to look out for myself first, even if it means making things difficult for other people.

I'm not very sympathetic to other people when they are having problems.

If things I do upset people, it's their problem not mine.

Temper

I lose my temper pretty easily.

Often, when I'm angry at people I feel more like hurting them than talking to them about why I am angry.

When I'm really angry, other people better stay away from me.

Source: Grasmick et al. (1993). Copyright © 1993 by Sage.
Reprinted by permission of Sage Publications.

Researchers using this and other measures of self-control have found that low self-control is consistently related to self-reported delinquency, adult crime, and analogous acts, such as cutting classes, drinking, smoking, cyber deviance, and gambling (Holt, Bossler, and May 2012; Pratt and Cullen 2000; LaGrange and Silverman 1999; Piquero and Tibbetts 1996; Burton et al. 1995; Gibbs and Giever 1995; Tremblay et al. 1995; Arneklev et al. 1993; Grasmick et al. 1993; Keane, Maxim, and Teevan 1993; Nagin and Paternoster 1993; Wood, Pfefferbaum, and Arneklev 1993). Recent research has examined the relationship between low self-control and various dimensions of criminal careers. Low self-control has been found to be related to the likelihood of involvement in crime, the frequency of involvement, persistence in crime, and desistance from crime (Piquero, Moffitt, and Wright 2007; see also DeLisi and Vaughan 2008; Doherty 2006; Tittle, Ward, and Grasmick 2004).

Consistent with self-control theory, research by T. David Evans and his colleagues found that low self-control also has a variety of social consequences. These researchers summarize:

> low self-control is related to diminished quality of interpersonal relationships with family and friends, reduced involvement in church, low levels of educational and occupational attainment, and possible poor marriage prospects. ... Further, persons with low self-control are more likely to have criminal associates ... and to internalize criminal values.
>
> (Evans et al. 1997: 493; see also Meldrum, Miller, and Flexon; Wright et al. 1999, 2001)

Besides social consequences, childhood self-control strongly predicts adult success. Using longitudinal data that "followed more than 1,000 people from birth over four decades," Moffitt, Poulton, and Caspi (2013: 353) measured childhood self-control, together with a variety of physical, psychological, and social characteristics over the 38-year period of the study. They found that children with low self-control "grew up to have poorer health, greater substance abuse, more financial difficulties, higher crime conviction rates, and lower parenting skill, even after controlling for the effects of IQ, social class, and sex" (Moffitt et al. 2013: 355).

The most controversial aspect of self-control theory is its assertion that many of the individual and social factors identified by traditional theories as causes of crime are actually consequences of low self-control, which causes both crime and these other factors. It is further argued that these traditional causes of crime will become insignificant in predicting crime when low self-control is considered. Gottfredson and Hirschi (1990) argue that this hypothesis "provides a crucial test" of self-control theory in contrast to traditional criminological theories.

Research directed at this "crucial test" finds that low self-control is not the single, fundamental cause of delinquency, crime, or analogous behavior. Rather, many of the traditional causes of crime (e.g., ineffective parenting, negative school experiences, delinquent attitudes, delinquent peers, and poor neighborhood conditions) are found to be significantly related to delinquent behavior, even after measures of self-control are introduced (Jones, Cauffman, and Piquero 2007; Vazsonyi and Belliston 2007; Unnever, Cullen, and Agnew 2006; Rebellon and Van Gundy 2005; Perrone et al. 2004; Simons et al. 1998; Winfree and Bernat 1998; Evans et al. 1997). Moreover, in at least one study, when the effects of these traditional causes of crime were considered, the relationship between low self-control and delinquent behavior was no longer significant (Simons et al. 1998). It is probably safe to conclude that low self-control is one among many causes of delinquency, though its influence is substantial (Pratt and Cullen 2000).

Still another growing area of research deals with the origins of low self-control. As already mentioned, Gottfredson and Hirschi attribute self-control to effective family management skills – careful monitoring, recognition of problem behaviors, and consistent and proportionate punishment of such behaviors. Although not entirely consistent in results, this research generally indicates that parenting is an important, but not exclusive, determinant of self-control (Vazsonyi and Belliston 2007; Burt et al. 2006; Unnever et al. 2006; Turner, Piquero, and Pratt 2005; Wright and Beaver 2005; Perrone et al. 2004; Gibbs, Giever, and Higgins 2003; Hay 2001; Lynskey et al. 2000; Cochran et al. 1998; Gibbs, Giever, and Martin 1998; Feldman and Weinberger 1994; Polakowski 1994). Recent research, for example, found that exposure to prosocial, self-regulated peers during childhood leads to higher self-control, while exposure to antisocial, poorly-regulated peers reduces self-control. Moreover, this relationship exists even after taking into consideration a child's exposure to positive parenting practices (Meldrum and Hay 2012: 693). Research has also found that self-control is influenced by neighborhood conditions that promote informal social control – the level of caring about what goes on in the neighborhood (Pratt, Turner, and Piquero 2004; see also Simons et al. 2005).

Characteristics of family life and informal social control

All three versions of social control theory point to the central importance of family relations in generating informal social control. In doing so, they try to explain conformity. Despite this common theme, each version of social control theory characterizes the informal social controls of families in a different way, especially in terms of the relative importance of direct and indirect controls.

Social bond theory calls attention to the indirect controls that result from family relationship bonds or "attachments." In fact, Hirschi (1969) argued that direct controls are relatively unimportant. Life-course theory, too, emphasizes indirect controls stemming from family relationship bonds and bonds to other social institutions, such as school, marriage, and work. However, life-course theory also includes direct controls in the form of parental supervision and discipline. In addition, life-course theory incorporates the structural context of informal social controls, especially social class background, residential mobility, family disruption, and parental deviance, arguing that these structural characteristics influence both direct and indirect social controls (Sampson and Laub 1993). The third social control theory, self-control theory, holds that the direct controls of parents in the form of monitoring, supervision, and discipline are foundational to the development of self-control. Even though self-control originates socially, it is an internal, individual characteristic.

Although social control theories are useful in describing how informal social controls within families generate conformity, they fail to fully consider how characteristics of family life influence these informal social controls. Recent research has studied how informal social controls are influenced by a number of family life characteristics, including the quality of the parent–child relationship, family management, parental efficacy, family structure, mother's employment, family social class, and parental criminality.

Quality of the parent–child relationship

Social bond theory and life-course theory contend that the strength of the relationship bond between parent and child is closely related to conforming behavior in the child. This link is attributed to the informal social controls that result from the affectional identification a youth has with parents such that the youth is sensitive to their opinions, desires to please them, values their relationship, identifies with them, and communicates actively and intimately with them. In short, conformity is generated by the desire for social approval. Extensive research reveals that delinquent behavior is associated with low levels of parental acceptance, sense of belonging, identification with parents, parental caring and trust, positive communication, and parental support (Canter 1995; Rankin and Wells 1990; Cernkovich and Giordano 1987; Loeber and Stouthamer-Loeber 1986; Patterson and Stouthamer-Loeber 1984; Loeber and Dishion 1983). The relationship between parental attachment and delinquency, however, is also reciprocal: while parental attachment influences delinquency, delinquency impacts parental attachment as well (Gault-Sherman 2012). Furthermore, other factors may enhance or diminish the effect of the parent–child relationship on delinquency. For example, Petts (2009) found that religion enhances the deterrent effect of parental affection on delinquency and diminishes the increased risk of delinquency among youths in single-parent families.

In contrast to attachment, parent–child relationships characterized by hostility and conflict have been found to result in limited parental control. Rejection of the child by the parent and rejection of the parent by the child are both related to delinquent behavior (Fagan et al. 2011; Li 2011; Sampson and Laub 1993; Henggeler 1989; Loeber and Stouthamer-Loeber 1986; Patterson 1982). Similarly, self-reported delinquency has been found to be associated with high levels of parent–adolescent conflict (Cernkovich and Giordano 1987). In a study of street kids, drugs, and crime in Miami, researchers found that parents of these youth were often aware of their drug use and criminal involvement, and this awareness led to family arguments and conflict, and consequently to a reduction in parental informal controls (Inciardi, Horowitz, and Pottieger 1993).

The relationship between parent–child conflict, ineffective parenting, and delinquent behavior has been studied extensively by Gerald Patterson and his colleagues at the Oregon Social Learning Center. According to Patterson (1982; Patterson et al. 1992), some families are characterized by a high degree of irritable and hostile exchanges between family members due to stress experienced by the family unit. Patterson refers to such family interaction as "coercive family processes." Stress may come from a variety of sources, including economic hardship, parental conflict, health difficulties, and child behavior problems (e.g., difficult temperament, early childhood disruptive and antisocial behavior, and delinquency).[7] Patterson argues that frequent negative exchanges, especially those involving emotional manipulation, hostile interaction, neglect, and abuse, are used in an attempt to control other family members. Such manipulative interaction tends to escalate, leading to a cycle of negative interaction among family members. Because such coercive family processes result in limited informal controls, Patterson advocates for family effectiveness training that centers on direct controls – an approach derived from theory and research on family management skills.

Family management: monitoring, supervision, and discipline

Until recently, the direct controls of parents have been largely dismissed as uninteresting and unimportant (Wells and Rankin 1988). Direct controls, however, have been reconceptualized to go beyond the single consideration of family involvement to the more comprehensive consideration of "**family management**," which has to do with effective parenting practices (Patterson 1980, 1982). Gerald Patterson (1980: 81) contends that effective family management involves seven key skills:

1. Notice what the child is doing.
2. Monitor the child's behavior over long periods.
3. Model social skill behavior.
4. Clearly state house rules.
5. Consistently provide for sane punishments for transgressions.
6. Provide reinforcement for conformity.
7. Negotiate disagreements so that conflicts and crises do not escalate.

Patterson and his colleague, John Reid, founded the Oregon Social Learning Center (OSLC) in an effort to conduct research on developmental patterns of youth and then to apply this knowledge to family intervention programs. Patterson's developmental model was described in Chapter 6. The Oregon Model of Parent Management Training is one of many family intervention programs that OSLC has developed. The evidence-based model program is described in "Theory into practice: Parent Management Training – Oregon Model."

Theory into practice: Parent Management Training – Oregon Model

The Oregon Model of Parent Management Training is a model program in the registry of evidence-based programs called Blueprints for Healthy Youth Development. PMTO is one of only eight model programs that have been evaluated as effective through rigorous evaluation research for preventing delinquency and criminal behavior. Blueprints provides the following program description for the Oregon Model of Parent Management Training.

Parent Management Training – Oregon Model (PMTO) is a group of theory-based parent training interventions that can be implemented in a variety of family contexts. The program aims to teach effective family management skills in order to reduce antisocial and problematic behavior in children who range in age from 3 through 16 years. PMTO is delivered in group and individual family formats, in diverse settings (e.g., clinics, homes, schools, community centers, homeless shelters), over varied lengths of time depending on families' needs. Typically sessions are one week apart to optimize the opportunity for learning and rehearsing new practices. The number of sessions provided in parent groups ranges from 6 to 14; in clinical samples the mean number of individual treatment sessions is 25.

The central role of the PMTO therapist is to teach and coach parents in the use of effective parenting strategies, namely skill encouragement, setting limits or effective discipline, monitoring, problem solving, and positive involvement. In addition to the core parenting practices, PMTO incorporates the supporting parenting components of identifying and regulating emotions, enhancing communication, giving clear directions, and tracking behavior. Promoting school success is a factor that is woven into the program throughout relevant components.

Source: Blueprints for Healthy Youth Development. n.d. Fact Sheet for Parent Management Training (Oregon Model). Retrieved March 10, 2015 (www.blueprintsprograms.com/factSheet.php?pid=c837307a9a2ad4d08ca61 a4f1bd848ba3d6890fc).

Research shows that these direct parental controls are related to low levels of delinquency, even when other causal factors are taken into consideration (Fagan et al. 2011; Wasserman et al. 1996, 2003; Wright and Cullen 2001; Hawkins et al. 2000; Burton et al. 1998; Wells and Rankin 1988; Cernkovich and Giordano 1987; Loeber and Stouthamer-Loeber 1986; Loeber and Dishion 1983). This research also reveals that the direct controls of parents have at least as great an effect on delinquency as do indirect relational controls. Parents who lack effective family management skills also fail to instill self-control in their children, and such parenting appears to foster aggressive attitudes and behaviors in children (Unnever et al. 2006). Furthermore, the direct controls of parents include clear rules and expectations for behavior, covering a range of adolescent-relevant activities including homework, driving, curfew, drugs and alcohol use, and respect for authority (Fagan et al. 2011).

The relationship between direct control and delinquent behavior, however, is not always simple and direct. This is most evident in the case of discipline. Research shows that strict and punitive discipline increases the likelihood of delinquency, as does discipline that is lax and erratic. Consistent and certain discipline, by contrast, is related to lower levels of delinquency (Halgunseth et al. 2013; Burton et al. 1998; Sampson and Laub 1993; Henggeler 1989; Loeber and Stouthamer-Loeber 1986). It is also the case that the direct controls of parents are influenced by characteristics of the child. Individual traits during childhood, such as difficult temperament, tantrums, and early childhood disruptive and antisocial behaviors, have been found to influence parents' direct control efforts, especially efforts to monitor and discipline children (Simons et al. 1998; Sampson and Laub 1993; Lytton 1990; Patterson, DeBaryshe, and Ramsey 1989; Laub and Sampson 1988; Snyder and Patterson 1987). Sampson and Laub (1993), for example, found that parents provided lower levels of supervision of children who were restless and irritable, showed a predisposition to angry and aggressive responses, and engaged in misbehavior at an early age. Such childhood difficulties also predicted parents' use of inconsistent and harsh discipline.

The application of direct controls by parents has been shown to differ for boys and girls. Research shows that females are subjected to greater control and supervision than are males (Hagan 1989; Cernkovich and Giordano 1987). However, research also shows that direct controls are more strongly related to male delinquency than to female delinquency (Burton et al. 1995; Cernkovich and Giordano 1987). Even so, recent research by Fagan and her colleagues (2011: 163) found that "family risk" (encompassing less supervision and monitoring, more family conflict, parental attitudes favorable to offending, and weak parent–child attachment)

> was associated with greater involvement in delinquency and drug use even controlling for other individual and community variables related to offending. The relationship between parenting and offending was significant for both girls and boys and for children in middle and high school.

The research is very clear on one problematic aspect of family life: child maltreatment (physical abuse, sexual abuse, and neglect) is a risk factor for delinquency. A growing body of research shows that maltreated children and adolescents are more likely to be involved in delinquent behavior, especially serious and violent delinquency (Colman et al. 2009; Rebellon and Van Gundy 2005; Thornberry, Huizinga, and Loeber 2004; Wasserman et al. 2003; Ireland, Smith, and Thornberry 2002; Thornberry, Ireland, and Smith 2001; Smith and Thornberry 1995; Zingraff et al. 1993; Widom 1989). However, recent research shows that physical abuse is related to property offending as well as to violence (Rebellon and Van

Gundy 2005). Physical abuse is related to delinquency beyond its impact on self-control and social bonds. Researchers suggest that the negative emotions resulting from physical abuse may increase the probability of delinquency as a coping mechanism. Research also shows that:

> there is a tendency for adults to repeat the abuse they experienced as a child. This phenomenon is often labeled "the cycle of violence." Although most victims of childhood abuse do not go on to abuse their offspring, they are 10 to 15 times more likely to be abusive parents than persons who were not exposed to abusive parenting.
>
> (Simons, Simons, and Wallace 2004: 168–169)

Parental efficacy

Even though social control theories acknowledge the importance of the parent–child relationship bond, they fail to adequately consider the role that social support plays in effective parenting. **Parental social support** has to do with the extent to which parents are warm, trusting, and caring, providing "emotional resources," and the extent to which they are helpful and encouraging, providing "instrumental resources" (Wright and Cullen 2001). A "growing body of psychological research suggests that effective parenting involves both expressing warmth and setting limits" – an approach called "authoritative parenting" (Wright and Cullen 2001: 695–696). Authoritative parents maintain an emotionally close and supportive relationship with their child, and they provide clear rules for their child in an effort to promote prosocial behavior (Baumrind 1991).

The concept of **parental efficacy** has been introduced into criminology by John Wright and Francis Cullen (2001) in an attempt to bolster social control theories by adding the element of parental support. They contend that the social support offered by parents is foundational to both forms of informal social control: indirect and direct. Extensive research shows that parental support is related to parent–child attachment and to the internalization of self-control (Jones et al. 2007; Vazsonyi and Belliston 2007; Perrone et al. 2004; Wright and Cullen 2001). Their argument, then, is that both support and control are necessary for effective parenting, and parental controls are heavily dependent on a supportive parent–child relationship in the task of keeping children out of trouble (Wright and Cullen 2001).

Criminological research has confirmed Wright and Cullen's proposition by showing that parental support is related to the indirect controls of parent–child attachment and the direct controls of parental supervision (Wright and Cullen 2001). Research also indicates that although parental support is related to self-control and, in turn, delinquent behavior, parental support also has an independent effect on delinquency (Jones et al. 2007; Perrone et al. 2004). Additionally, when parental control and parental support are combined as a measure of parental efficacy, parental efficacy has a significant effect on delinquency, and the effect is stronger than when only parental controls are considered (Jones et al. 2007; Vazsonyi and Belliston 2007; Perrone et al. 2004; Wright and Cullen 2001). "Research in action: measuring parental efficacy" provides a measure of parental efficacy that has been used in recent research.

Research in action: measuring parental efficacy

The Adolescent Family Process (AFP) measure was developed by Alexander Vazsonyi and his colleagues to assess six dimensions of family process: closeness, support, monitoring, intimate communication, conflict, instrumental communication, and peer approval. Research indicates that three of the subscales are indicative of parental efficacy: closeness, support, and monitoring. The questionnaire items making up these subscales are listed below.

Closeness

1. My mother often asks about what I am doing in school.
2. My mother gives me the right amount of affection.
3. One of the worst things that could happen to me would be to find out that I let my mother down.
4. My mother is usually proud of me when I finish something at which I've worked hard.
5. My mother trusts me.
6. I am closer to my mother than are a lot of kids my age.

Support

7. My mother sometimes puts me down in front of other people.
8. Sometimes my mother won't listen to me or my opinions.
9. My mother sometimes gives me the feeling that I'm not living up to her expectations.
10. My mother seems to wish I were a different type of person.

Monitoring

11. My mother wants to know who I am with when I go out with friends or on a date.
12. In my free time away from home, my mother knows who I'm with and where I am.
13. My mother wants me to tell her where I am if I don't come home right after school.
14. When I am not at home, my mother knows my whereabouts.

Source: Vazsonyi and Belliston (2007: 524–525). Original AFP measure from Vazsonyi, Hibbert, and Snider (2003). Copyright © 2007 by Sage. Reprinted by Permission of Sage Publications.

Family structure

Family structure refers to various family characteristics that influence relationships within families and how families function. These characteristics include family disruption, family size, and birth order. The key to understanding the relationship between family structure and delinquency is to specify the mechanisms by which family structure influences delinquent behavior. The basic argument of social control theories is that family structure influences family interaction, especially direct and indirect controls within the family, which in turn influences delinquency. Single-parent families, for example, may provide less supervision, monitoring, and discipline, and they may involve weaker relationship bonds between parent and child.

Family disruption

Early social science researchers asserted that the "broken home" was the single most important factor in understanding delinquency (e.g., Monahan 1957). More recent research suggests that **family disruption** is related to delinquency largely because of the effect of such disruption on relationship bonds and parental monitoring and supervision (Demuth and Brown 2004; Wasserman et al. 2003; Rebellon 2002; Thornberry et al. 1999; Van Voorhis et al. 1998; Rankin and Kern 1994; Sampson and Laub 1993; Lamborn et al. 1991; Wells and Rankin 1988, 1991; Cernkovich and Giordano 1987; Gove and Crutchfield 1982).

To more fully understand the effects of disruption on families, researchers have begun to consider variation in family composition together with the multiple outcomes of family disruption. Variation in family composition includes distinctions between two-parent and single-parent families, and consideration of the composition of two-parent families (two-biological-parent, mother–stepfather, father–stepmother) and single-parent families (single-father or single-mother) (Demuth and Brown 2004). In terms of social control theory, family disruption may weaken attachment, commitment, involvement, and belief, and may affect levels of conflict and parental rule-setting, supervision, and monitoring.

Recent research examined the effect of family composition on delinquency by comparing single-mother, single-father, stepfamilies, and two-biological-parent families (Demuth and Brown 2004). Levels of delinquency were highest among adolescents in single-father families and lowest in two-biological-parent families, with single-mother families and stepfamilies in the middle. By itself, the single-parent family structure was not a significant predictor of delinquency; rather, family composition was related to relationship ties and informal social control. The absence of a parent was associated with lower levels of involvement, supervision, monitoring, and closeness. The researchers concluded that the absence of a parent undermines direct and indirect control, which, in turn, accounts for the higher levels of delinquency among adolescents residing in single-parent families, as compared to two-parent families.

Family size and birth order

It has long been noted that delinquents are more likely to come from large families than from small families (Loeber and Stouthamer-Loeber 1986; Rutter 1980; Hirschi 1969; Glueck and Glueck 1968). In addition, middle children are more likely to engage in delinquent acts than are first- or last-born children (Hirschi 1969; McCord and McCord 1959). These two family structural characteristics are thought to be related to delinquency largely because of how they influence the capacity of parents for effective childrearing, especially supervision and discipline. The larger the family, the more limited the parents' time and energy for supervision and discipline. Parents of larger families also have less opportunity for interaction and involvement with their children (Nye 1958). As a result, the attachment between parent and child is diminished. The same can be said for middle children: middle children experience less attachment, supervision, and discipline than do older and younger children (Hirschi 1969; McCord and McCord 1959).

Mother's employment

In 1950, only 16 percent of all children had mothers who worked outside the home, but today almost 70 percent of mothers with dependent children work outside the home (Vander Ven et al. 2001). Some are concerned that working mothers are less able to supervise and nurture their children. From a social control perspective, does mother's employment weaken social bonds within the family and diminish informal social control, thereby increasing the likelihood of delinquency? Most recent research finds little or no connection between maternal employment and delinquency. More specifically, children of working mothers are no less attached than other children, nor are they more likely to display deficits in social, emotional, or behavioral functioning. Further, maternal employment has little or no negative impact on maternal supervision or children's school attachment, and it does not appear to contribute to association with delinquent peers (Vander Ven et al. 2001).

Family social class

Much research and debate have surrounded the relationship between social class and delinquency. This controversy was discussed in Chapter 5. Our concern here is with the link between social class background and different aspects of informal control by parents. Do the informal controls of relationship bonds or the direct controls of monitoring, supervision, and discipline vary by social class? Some argue that many lower-class parents have marginal parenting skills because they experience greater stress and have fewer resources than do middle-class parents (Larzelere and Patterson 1990). Similarly, life-course theory proposes that the effect of social class on delinquency is indirect, operating through diminished parental discipline and monitoring, which, in turn, promotes delinquent behavior. Research supports this causal sequencing (Sampson and Laub 1993, 1994; Larzelere and Patterson 1990; Tittle and Meier 1990; Laub and Sampson 1988).

Parental criminality

Sampson and Laub (1993: 69, references omitted) summarize how control theories view the effects of parental deviance on children's delinquency:

> We argue that parents who commit crimes and drink excessively are likely to use harsh discipline in an inconsistent manner or to be lax in disciplining their children. A central characteristic of deviant and criminal life styles is the rejection of restrictions and duties – especially those that involve planning, patience, and investment in the future. Parenting is perhaps the most demanding of conventional roles, and we expect that deviance in the adult world will manifest itself in disrupted styles of child socialization. Namely, supervision and discipline will be haphazard or nonexistent, and the parent–child/child–parent attachments will be tenuous.

Research has supported this theoretical link between parental criminality and weakened direct and indirect parental controls. Citing numerous researchers, Scott Henggeler (1989) concludes that the association between parental criminality and children's delinquent behavior is one of the most consistent findings in delinquency research. In his interpretation of this finding, he emphasizes that antisocial parents typically lack cognitive and interpersonal skills for positive parenting. Henggeler concludes that delinquency is linked more directly with poor parent–adolescent relationship bonds and the use of ineffective parental control strategies than with the modeling of parental deviance.

Sibling criminality

A small, but growing body of literature has studied similarities between adolescent siblings in a variety of health-related attitudes and behaviors including alcohol and other substance use, risk-taking, delinquency, and sexual activity (Whiteman, Jensen, and Maggs 2014: 687). Behavioral generic studies indicate that concordance rates between siblings for these types of behaviors are not simply due to shared genetics and shared environmental factors, but also arise from social influences (Whiteman et al. 2014: 687). Whiteman and his colleagues recently found that sibling similarity in risky and delinquent behaviors and attitudes was due to mutual modeling, shared friends, and admiration of the older by the younger sibling. Seeking differentiation from a sibling was associated with divergence in sibling behaviors and attitudes.

Parents and peers

Social control theories contend that youth who lack parental support and control are more susceptible to delinquent peer influences, thereby increasing opportunities for involvement in delinquency (Ingram et al. 2007). This basic proposition has been studied extensively, and research consistently shows that weak parent–child attachment is associated with delinquent friendships (Warr 2005). Attachment, however, is usually not found to be directly related to delinquency; rather, parent–child attachment influences level of parental supervision, which, in turn, is related to peer association (Deutsch et al. 2012; Ingram et al. 2007; de Kemp et al. 2006; Warr 1993, 2005; Jang and Smith 1997; Aseltine 1995; Sampson and Laub 1993). In contrast, children with strong social bonds, who have parents who are actively involved in supervising their behavior, are less likely to be drawn to and associate with delinquent peers, which results in greater likelihood of delinquency (Henneberger et al. 2013; Ingram et al. 2007; Warr, 1993, 2005; Dorius et al. 2004).

Summary and conclusions

The essence of informal social control is the extent to which youth are linked to the family and ultimately to society through bonds of attachment and through socially integrative forms of direct control, such as clearly established rules, monitoring, and punishment (Sampson and Laub 1994). Control theories are largely concerned with these mechanisms of informal social control, especially the central role that the family plays in generating and implementing such controls.

This chapter described three different versions of control theory. In social bond theory, Travis Hirschi identified four elements of an individual's social bond to society. Relationship attachments within the family, school, and peer group provide indirect controls, based on affectional identification and the desire for social approval. Commitment, the rational component of the social bond, has to do with an individual's investment in conventional activities or "lines of action." Individuals are controlled to the degree that they desire to participate in conventional activities. Involvement, too, relates to activities, but focuses on what youth actually do with their time. Some activities limit opportunities for involvement in delinquent acts, while others provide few restraints for delinquency. The final element of the social bond, belief, promotes conformity when the youth adopts beliefs that forbid delinquency and when those beliefs are collectively held and reinforced.

Life-course theory also emphasizes the importance of social bonds as the primary vehicle of informal social control. Sampson and Laub's life-course theory examines social bonds over the life course, considering their origins and how changes in these bonds influence informal social control and behavior. Family processes of supervision, attachment, and discipline are key to the development of social bonds in childhood; these family processes are influenced by the family's structural background and by early childhood difficulties (whining, difficult temperament, disruptive and antisocial behavior). Sampson and Laub also considered social bonds in adulthood, which they refer to as "social capital" – a term that more explicitly links relationship bonds to institutional roles within the family, school, work, and community. The informal social controls of social capital involve not only affective attachment, but also social obligations and restraints that are attached to particular roles. Significant changes in life, or turning points (such as marriage, military enlistment, or work), affect social capital and thereby influence informal social control.

Self-control theory veers from this emphasis on the informal controls of relationship bonds to focus on controls within the individual. As a result of effective childrearing practices of monitoring and discipline, some children develop skills to respond to situations that require delayed gratification, planning, sensitivity to others, independence, cognitive and verbal skills, and a willingness to accept restraints on their activities. In contrast, individuals with low self-control are "impulsive, insensitive, physical (as opposed to mental), risk taking, short-sighted, and nonverbal" (Gottfredson and Hirschi 1990: 90). They are unable to resist temptations not only of crime, but also of analogous acts such as reckless driving, smoking, and alcohol and drug use. As a result, low self-control fosters problematic interpersonal relations, social activities, and involvement in social institutions. Individuals with low self-control have difficulty making and keeping friends, are less able to succeed in school and the workplace, and tend to enter into marriages that are destined to fail.

Researchers have assessed the conceptual accuracy and causal arguments of control theories that specify family processes of indirect and direct social control. Social bond theory and life-course theory stress the importance of indirect relational controls, and research supports the importance of attachment to others in preventing delinquency. Life-course theory and self-control theory introduce direct controls such as rule-setting, monitoring, and discipline into the causal equation. Rather than revealing indirect or direct controls as more important, research indicates that both are significant restraints on behavior. Additionally, it is apparent that controls operate at both the social and individual level, and that family structural characteristics influence informal social controls within families.

Critical-thinking questions

1. In the case that opened this chapter, how does the lack of family attachment and parents' ineffective monitoring and supervision pave the way for violent interpersonal interaction outside the family?
2. Distinguish among the various forms of social control – formal, informal, direct, indirect, and internalized – and provide an example of each.
3. In your own words, describe each element of the social bond: attachment, commitment, involvement, and belief. How are these elements of the social bond interconnected?
4. From the life-course perspective, why is it important not to concentrate simply on the adolescent years, as sociological criminology has traditionally done?
5. What do Gottfredson and Hirschi (1990: 119) mean when they say that "many of the traditional causes of crime are in fact consequences of low self-control"?
6. What does Mark Warr (1993: 258) mean when he says that both family and friends exert considerable influence on adolescent behavior, but their influence "does not operate independently of one another"?

Suggested reading

Gottfredson, Michael and Travis Hirschi. 1990. *A General Theory of Crime*. Stanford University Press.

Hirschi, Travis. 1969. *Causes of Delinquency*. Berkeley, CA: University of California Press.

Moffitt, Terrie E., Richie Poulton, and Avshalom Caspi. 2013. "Lifelong Impact of Early Self-Control: Childhood Self-Discipline Predicts Adult Quality of Life." *American Scientist* 101: 352–359.

Sampson, Robert J. and John H. Laub. 1993. *Crime in the Making: Pathways and Turning Points through Life*. Cambridge, MA: Harvard University Press.

Simons, Ronald L., Leslie Gordon Simons, and Lora Ebert Wallace. 2004. *Families, Delinquency, and Crime: Linking Society's Most Basic Institution to Antisocial Behavior*. Los Angeles: Roxbury.

Useful websites

For further information relevant to this chapter, go to the following websites.

*   Incredible Years Parenting Program (http://incredibleyears.com/)
*   Parent Management Training – the Oregon Model (PMTO) (www.isii.net/)
*   Strengthening Families Program (www.extension.iastate.edu/sfp10-14/)

Glossary of key terms

Attachment: The affectional identification one has with others – sensitivity to others' opinions, intimate communication, mutual respect, identification, and valuing of relationship ties.

Belief: The attitudes, values, and norms one has that forbid delinquency.

Commitment (in social bond theory): The investments one has that provide reason to conform – a stake in conformity.

Direct controls: Restrictions and punishments imposed by others that limit behavior and rewards that encourage and reinforce behavior.

Family disruption: Families in which one or both parents are absent due to divorce, separation, desertion, or death.

Family management: Effective parenting practices involving efforts to monitor the child's behavior, model social skill, clearly state family rules, provide consistent and reasonable punishment for inappropriate behavior, provide reinforcement of conformity, and negotiate disagreements (Patterson 1980).

Family structure: Family characteristics that influence relationships within families and how families function. These characteristics include family disruption, family size, and birth order.

Formal social controls: Mechanisms used within the context of institutions such as schools, churches, and justice systems that promote and encourage conformity and sanction deviance.

Human agency: This concept emphasizes that purposeful choice, together with an individual's will, determine continued involvement in or desistence from crime.

Indirect controls: Pressures and reasons to conform that are based on affectional identification with others, especially parents, such that people conform in order to maintain relationship bonds and to avoid disappointing others.

Informal social controls: Characteristics of social relations that bring about conformity, including parental supervision; sensitivity to others (their feelings, wishes, and expectations); identification with others; emotional attachment; and informal sanctions, including withdrawal of affection, disregard, and ridicule.

Internalized controls: A person's adoption of standards of behavior that are exercised from within the individual through conscience or sense of guilt.

Involvement: Conventional activities that not only consume time and energy, but that also inhibit involvement in delinquency.

Life course: The age-graded sequence of culturally defined roles and social transitions.

Low self-control: Individuals characterized as being "impulsive, insensitive, physical (as opposed to mental), risk-taking, short-sighted, and nonverbal" (Gottfredson and Hirschi 1990: 90).

Parental efficacy: The social support offered by parents, together with informal social controls that make effective parenting possible. Social support is foundational to both forms of informal social control: indirect and direct.

Parental social support: The extent to which parents are warm, trusting, and caring, providing "emotional resources," and the extent to which they are helpful and encouraging, providing "instrumental resources."

Social capital: Expectations, obligations, and restraints that are part of adult relationship bonds and that result in informal social control.

Trajectory or pathway: The pattern or direction of life over a number of years, relating to areas of life such as education, work, parenting, and conformity or deviance.

Transition: A significant life event that occurs within the life trajectory or pathway, such as marriage, enlistment in the military, first job, or change in employment.

Turning point: A transition that results in significant change in the life-course trajectory.

Notes

1. Because most of Hirschi's (1969) analysis was conducted on a subsample of 1,588 white males, his reporting of findings makes frequent use of the term "he" and "boys" to refer more specifically to the subsample that was used most.
2. Sampson and Laub (1993: 1). Reproduced with permission of the publisher.
3. The concept of social capital is drawn from Coleman (1988, 1990).
4. See Marcus (2004) for a critique of these personality traits of self-control.
5. For a critique of this measure, see Higgins (2007) and Marcus (2004).
6. Gottfredson and Hirschi (1990) portray self-control as being composed of multiple elements, which are, in essence, one personality trait: low self-control. Marcus (2004) argues that this single-trait construct is at odds with extensive research on the structure of personality, which finds five major dimensions of personality. See also Cochran et al. (1998); Piquero and Rosay (1998); Longshore, Turner, and Stein (1996); Arneklev et al. (1993).
7. See also Conger et al. (1994).

References

Agnew, Robert. 1991. "A Longitudinal Test of Social Control Theory, and Delinquency." *Journal of Research in Crime and Delinquency* 28: 126–156.

Agnew, Robert and David M. Petersen. 1989. "Leisure and Delinquency." *Social Problems* 36: 332–350.

Akers, Ronald L. and John K. Cochran. 1985. "Adolescent Marijuana Use: A Test of Three Theories of Deviant Behavior." *Deviant Behavior* 6: 323–346.

Arneklev, Bruce J., Harold G. Grasmick, Charles R. Tittle, and Robert J. Bursik, Jr. 1993. "Low Self-Control and Imprudent Behavior." *Journal of Quantitative Criminology* 9: 225–247.

Aseltine, Robert H., Jr. 1995. "A Reconsideration of Parental and Peer Influences on Adolescent Deviance." *Journal of Health and Social Behavior* 36: 103–121.

Baker, Myriam L., Jane Nady Sigmon, and M. Elaine Nugent. 2001. "Truancy Reduction: Keeping Students in School." Washington, DC: Office of Juvenile Justice and Delinquency Prevention.

Baumrind, Diana. 1991. "The Influence of Parenting Style on Adolescent Competence and Substance Abuse." *Journal of Early Adolescence* 11: 56–95.

Bersani, Bianca E. and Constance L. Chapple. 2007. "School Failure as an Adolescent Turning Point." *Sociological Focus* 40: 370–391.

Booth, Jeb A., Amy Farrell, and Sean P. Varano. 2008. "Social Control, Serious Delinquency and Risky Behavior: A Gendered Analysis." *Crime and Delinquency* 54: 423–456.

Brownfield, David and Ann Marie Sorenson. 1987. "Latent Structure Analysis of Delinquency." *Journal of Quantitative Criminology* 3: 103–124.

Burt, Callie Harbin, Ronald L. Simons, and Leslie G. Simons. 2006. "A Longitudinal Test of the Effects of Parenting and the Stability of Self-Control: Negative Evidence for the General Theory of Crime." *Criminology* 44: 353–396.

Burton, Velmer S., Jr., Francis T. Cullen, T. David Evans, Leanne Fiftal Alarid, and R. Gregory Dunaway. 1998. "Gender, Self-Control and Crime." *Journal of Research in Crime and Delinquency* 35: 123–147.

Burton, Velmer S., Jr., Francis T. Cullen, T. David Evans, R. Gregory Dunaway, Sesha Kethineni, and Gary Payne. 1995. "The Impact of Parental Controls on Delinquency." *Journal of Criminal Justice* 23: 111–126.

Canter, Rachelle J. 1995. "Family Correlates of Male and Female Delinquency." *Criminology* 20: 149–167.

Caspi, Avshalom, Glen H. Elder, Jr., and Ellen S. Herbener. 1990. "Childhood Personality and the Prediction of Life-Course Patterns." Pp. 13–25 in *Straight and Devious Pathways from Childhood to Adulthood*, ed. L. Robins and M. Rutter. New York: Cambridge University Press.

Cernkovich, Stephen A. and Peggy C. Giordano. 1987. "Family Relationships and Delinquency." *Criminology* 25: 295–321.

Christie-Mizell, C. André and Robert L. Peralta. 2009. "The Gender Gap in Alcohol Consumption during Late Adolescence and Young Adulthood: Gendered Attitudes and Adult Roles." *Journal of Health and Social Behavior* 50: 410–426.

Cochran, John K., Peter B. Wood, Christine S. Sellers, Wendy Wilkerson, and Mitchell B. Chamlin. 1998. "Academic Dishonesty and Low Self-Control: An Empirical Test of a General Theory of Crime." *Deviant Behavior* 19: 227–255.

Coleman, James S. 1988. "Social Capital in the Creation of Human Capital." *American Journal of Sociology* 94: 95–120.

Coleman, James S. 1990. *Foundations of Social Theory*. Cambridge, MA: Harvard University Press.

Colman, Rebecca A., Do Han Kim, Susan Mitchell-Herzfeld, and Therese Shady. 2009. "Delinquent Girls Grown Up: Young Adult Offending Patterns and their Relation to Early Legal, Individual, and Family Risk." *Journal of Youth and Adolescence* 38: 355–366.

Conger, Rand D. 1976. "Social Control and Social Learning Models of Delinquency: A Synthesis." *Criminology* 14: 17–40.

Conger, Rand D., Xiaojia Ge, Glen H. Elder, Jr., Frederick O. Lorenz, and Ronald L. Simons. 1994. "Economic Stress, Coercive Family Process and Developmental Problems of Adolescents." *Child Development* 65: 541–561.

de Kemp, Raymond A. T., Ron H. J. Scholte, Geertjan Overbeek, and Rutger C. M. E. Engels. 2006. "Early Adolescent Delinquency: The Role of Parents and Best Friends." *Criminal Justice and Behavior* 33: 488–510.

DeLisi, Matt and Michael G. Vaughn. 2008. "The Gottfredson–Hirschi Critique Revisited: Reconciling Self-Control Theory, Criminal Careers, and Career Criminals." *International Journal of Offender Therapy and Comparative Criminology* 52: 520–537.

Demuth, Stephen and Susan L. Brown. 2004. "Family Structure, Family Processes, and Adolescent Delinquency: The Significance of Parental Absence versus Parental Gender." *Journal of Research in Crime and Delinquency* 41: 52–81.

Deutsch, Arielle R., Lisa J. Crockett, Jennifer M. Wolff, and Stephen T. Russell. 2012. "Parent and Peer Pathways to Adolescent Delinquency: Variations by Ethnicity and Neighborhood Context." *Journal of Youth and Adolescence* 41: 1078–1094.

Doherty, Elaine Eggleston. 2006. "Self-Control, Social Bonds, and Desistance: A Test of Life-Course Interdependence." *Criminology* 44: 807–833.

Dorius, Cassandra J., Stephen J. Bahr, John P. Hoffmann, and Elizabeth Lovelady Harmon. 2004. "Parenting Practices as Moderators of the Relationship between Peers and Adolescent Marijuana Use." *Journal of Marriage and the Family* 66: 163–178.

Eitle, David, John Taylor, and Tamela Mcnulty Eitle. 2010. "Heavy Episodic Alcohol Use in Emerging Adulthood: The Role of Early Risk Factors and Young Adult Social Roles." *Journal of Drug Issues* 40: 295–320.

Elder, Glen H., Jr. 1998. "The Life Course as Developmental Theory." *Child Development* 69: 1–12.

Elliott, Delbert S., David Huizinga, and Suzanne S. Ageton. 1985. *Explaining Delinquency and Drug Use.* Beverly Hills, CA: Sage.

Evans, T. David, Francis T. Cohen, Velmer S. Burton, Jr., R. Gregory Dunaway, and Michael Benson. 1997. "The Social Consequences of Self-Control: Testing the General Theory of Crime." *Criminology* 35: 475–504.

Fabelo, T., M. D. Thompson, M. Plotkin, D. Carmichael, M. P. Marchbanks, III, and E. A. Booth. 2011. *Breaking Schools' Rules: A Statewide Study of How School Discipline Relates to Students' Success and Juvenile Justice Involvement.* New York: Council of State Governments Justice Center.

Fagan, Abigail A., M. Lee Van Horn, Susan Antaramian, and J. David Hawkins. 2011. "How Do Families Matter? Age and Gender Differences in Family Influences on Delinquency and Drug Use." *Youth Violence and Juvenile Justice* 9: 150–170.

Farnworth, Margaret, Lawrence J. Schweinhart, and John R. Berrueta-Clement. 1985. "Preschool Intervention, School Success and Delinquency in a High-Risk Sample of Youth." *American Educational Review Journal* 22: 445–464.

Farrington, David P. 1989. "Early Predictors of Adolescent Aggression and Adult Violence." *Violence and Victims* 4: 79–100.

Feldman, S. Shirley and Daniel A. Weinberger. 1994. "Self-Restraint as a Mediator of Family Influences on Boys' Delinquent Behavior: A Longitudinal Study." *Child Development* 65: 195–211.

Gault-Sherman, Martha. 2012. "It's a Two-Way Street: The Bidirectional Relationship between Parenting and Delinquency." *Journal of Youth and Adolescence* 4: 121–145.

Gibbs, Jack P. 1989. *Control: Sociology's Central Notion.* Urbana, IL: University of Illinois Press.

Gibbs, John J. and Dennis Giever. 1995. "Control and Its Manifestations among University Students: An Empirical Test of Gottfredson and Hirschi's General Theory." *Justice Quarterly* 12: 231–235.

Gibbs, John J., Dennis Giever, and George E. Higgins. 2003. "A Test of Gottfredson and Hirschi's Generally Theory Using Structural Equation Modeling." *Criminal Justice and Behavior* 30: 441–458.

Gibbs, John J., Dennis Giever, and Jamie S. Martin. 1998. "Parental Management and Self-Control: An Empirical Test of Gottfredson and Hirschi's General Theory." *Journal of Research in Crime and Delinquency* 35: 40–70.

Glueck, Sheldon and Eleanor Glueck. 1968. *Delinquents and Nondelinquents in Perspective.* Cambridge, MA: Harvard University Press.

Gottfredson, Michael R. and Travis Hirschi. 1990. *A General Theory of Crime.* Stanford University Press.

Gottfredson, Denise C., David B. Wilson, and Stacy S. Najaka. 2002. "The Schools." Pp. 149–189 in *Crime: Public Policies for Crime Control.* 2nd edn., ed. J. Q. Wilson and J. Petersilia. Oakland, CA: Institute for Contemporary Studies Press.

Gove, Walter R. 1985. "The Effect of Age and Gender on Deviant Behavior: A Bio-Psychosocial Perspective." Pp. 115–144 in *Gender and the Life Course*, ed. A. S. Rossi. Hawthorne, NY: Aldine.

Gove, Walter R. and Robert D. Crutchfield. 1982. "The Family and Juvenile Delinquency." *Sociological Quarterly* 23: 301–319.

Grasmick, Harold G., Charles R. Tittle, Robert J. Bursik, Jr., and Bruce J. Arneklev. 1993. "Testing the Core Empirical Implications of Gottfredson and Hirschi's General Theory of Crime." *Journal of Research in Crime and Delinquency* 30: 5–29.

Guest, Andrew M. and Nick McRee. 2009. "A School-Level Analysis of Adolescent Extracurricular Activity, Delinquency, and Depression: The Importance of Situational Context." *Journal of Youth and Adolescence* 38: 51–62.

Hagan, John. 1989. *Structural Criminology*. New Brunswick, NJ: Rutgers University Press.

Halgunseth, Linda C., Daniel F. Perkins, Melissa A. Lippold, and Robert L. Nix. 2013. "Delinquent-Oriented Attitudes Mediate the Relation between Parental Inconsistent Discipline and Early Adolescent Behavior." *Journal of Family Psychology* 27: 293–302.

Hartmann, Douglas and Michael Massoglia. 2007. "Reassessing the Relationship between High School Sports Participation and Deviance: Evidence of Enduring, Bifurcated Effects." *Sociological Quarterly* 48: 485–505.

Hawkins, Darnell F., John H. Laub, Janet L. Lauritsen, and Lynn Cothern. 2000. *Race, Ethnicity, and Serious and Violent Juvenile Offending*. Washington, DC: Office of Juvenile Justice and Delinquency Prevention.

Hawkins, J. David, Todd I. Herrenkohl, David P. Farrington, Devon Brewer, Richard F. Catalano, and Tracy W. Harachi. 1998. "A Review of Predictors of Youth Violence." Pp. 106–146 in *Serious and Violent Juvenile Offenders: Risk Factors and Successful Interventions*, ed. R. Loeber and D. P. Farrington. Thousand Oaks, CA: Sage.

Hay, Carter. 2001. "Parenting, Self-Control, and Delinquency: A Test of Self-Control Theory." *Criminology* 39: 707–736.

Hay, Carter and Walter Forrest. 2006. "The Development of Self-Control: Examining Self-Control Theory's Stability Thesis." *Criminology* 44: 739–774.

Henggeler, Scott W. 1989. *Delinquency in Adolescence*. Newbury Park, CA: Sage.

Henneberger, Angela K., Myles I. Durkee, Nancy Truong, Avis Atkins, and Patrick H. Tolan. 2013. "The Longitudinal Relationship between Peer Violence and Popularity and Delinquency in Adolescent Boys: Examining Effects by Family Functioning." *Journal of Youth and Adolescence* 42: 1651–1660.

Henry, Kimberly L., Kelly E. Knight, and Terence P. Thornberry. 2012. "School Disengagement as a Predictor of Dropout, Delinquency, and Problem Substance Use During Adolescence and Early Adulthood." *Journal of Youth and Adolescence* 41: 156–166.

Higgins, George E. 2007. "Examining the Original Grasmick Scale: A Rasch Model Approach." *Criminal Justice and Behavior* 34: 157–178.

Hindelang, Michael J. 1973. "Causes of Delinquency: A Partial Replication and Extension." *Social Problems* 21: 471–487.

Hirschfield, Paul J. and Joseph Gasper. 2011. "The Relationship between School Engagement and Delinquency in Late Childhood and Early Adolescence." *Journal of Youth and Adolescence* 40: 3–22.

Hirschi, Travis. 1969. *Causes of Delinquency*. Berkeley, CA: University of California Press.

Hirschi, Travis and Michael Gottfredson. 1993. "Commentary: Testing the General Theory of Crime." *Journal of Research in Crime and Delinquency* 30: 47–54.

Hoffman, John P. and Mikaela J. Dufur. 2008. "Family and School Capital Effects on Delinquency: Substitutes or Complements?" *Sociological Perspectives* 51: 29–62.

Hoffman, John P. and Jiangmin Xu. 2002. "School Activities, Community Service, and Delinquency." *Crime and Delinquency* 48: 568–591.

Holt, Thomas J., Adam M. Bossler, and David C. May. 2012. "Low Self-Control, Deviant Peer Associations, and Juvenile Cyberdeviance." *American Journal of Criminal Justice* 37: 378–395.

Inciardi, James A., Ruth Horowitz, and Anne E. Pottieger. 1993. *Street Kids, Street Drugs, and Street Crime: An Examination of Drug Use and Serious Delinquency in Miami*. Belmont, CA: Wadsworth.

Ingram, Jason R., Justin W. Patchin, Beth M. Huebner, John D. McCuskey, and Timothy S. Bynum. 2007. "Parents, Friends, and Serious Delinquency: An Examination of Direct and Indirect Effects among At-Risk Early Adolescents." *Criminal Justice Review* 32: 380–400.

Ireland, Timothy O., Carolyn A. Smith, and Terence P. Thornberry. 2002. "Developmental Issues in the Impact of Child Maltreatment on Later Delinquency and Drug Use." *Criminology* 40: 359–399.

Jang, Sung Joon. 1999. "Age-Varying Effects of Family, School, and Peers on Delinquency: A Multilevel Modeling Test of Interactional Theory." *Criminology* 37: 643–685.

Jang, Sung Joon. 2013. "Desistance and Protection from Binge Drinking between Adolescence and Emerging Adulthood: A Study of Turning Points and Insulators. *Sociological Focus* 46: 1–24.

Jang, Sung Joon and Carolyn A. Smith. 1997. "A Test of Reciprocal Causal Relationships among Parental Supervision, Affective Ties, and Delinquency." *Journal of Research in Crime and Delinquency* 34: 307–336.

Janowitz, Morris. 1975. "Sociological Theory and Social Control." *American Journal of Sociology* 81: 82–108.

Jarjoura, G. Roger. 1993. "Does Dropping Out of School Enhance Delinquent Involvement? Results from a Large-Scale National Probability Sample." *Criminology* 31: 149–172.

Jenkins, Patricia H. 1995. "School Delinquency and School Commitment." *Sociology of Education* 68: 221–239.

Johnson, Monica Kirkpatrick, Robert Crosnoe, and Glen H. Elder, Jr. 2001. "Students' Attachment and Academic Engagement: The Role of Race and Ethnicity." *Sociology of Education* 74: 318–340.

Johnson, Richard E. 1979. *Juvenile Delinquency and Its Origins: An Integrated Theoretical Approach*. New York: Cambridge University Press.

Jones, Shayne, Elizabeth Cauffman, and Alex R. Piquero. 2007. "The Influence of Parental Support among Incarcerated Adolescent Offenders: The Moderating Effects of Self-Control." *Criminal Justice and Behavior* 34: 229–245.

Kandel, Denise B. 1996. "The Parental and Peer Contexts of Adolescent Deviance: An Algebra of Interpersonal Influences." *Journal of Drug Issues* 26: 289–315.

Keane, Carl, Paul S. Maxim, and James J. Teevan. 1993. "Drinking and Driving, Self-Control, and Gender: Testing a General Theory of Crime." *Journal of Research in Crime and Delinquency* 30: 30–46.

Kelley, Margaret S. and Jan Sokol-Katz. 2011. "Examining Participation in School Sports and Patterns of Delinquency Using the National Longitudinal Study of Adolescent Health." *Sociological Focus* 44: 81–101.

Krohn, Marvin D. 1986. "The Web of Conformity: A Network Approach to the Explanation of Delinquent Behavior." *Social Problems* 33: 581–593.

Krohn, Marvin D. and James L. Massey. 1980. "Social Control and Delinquent Behavior: An Examination of the Elements of the Social Bond." *Sociological Quarterly* 21: 529–543.

Krohn, Marvin D., Susan Stern, Terence Thornberry, and Sung Joon Jang. 1992. "The Measurement of Family Process Variables: The Effect of Adolescent and Parent Perceptions of Family Life on Delinquent Behavior." *Journal of Quantitative Criminology* 3: 287–315.

LaGrange, Randy and Helen Raskin White. 1985. "Age Differences in Delinquency: A Test of Theory." *Criminology* 23: 19–45.

LaGrange, Teresa C. and Robert A. Silverman. 1999. "Low Self-Control and Opportunity: Testing the General Theory of Crime as an Explanation for Gender Differences in Delinquency." *Criminology* 37: 41–72.

Lamborn, Susie D., Nina S. Mounts, Laurence Steinberg, and Sanford M. Dornbusch. 1991. "Patterns of Competence and Adjustment among Adolescents from Authoritative, Authoritarian, Indulgent, and Neglected Homes." *Child Development* 62: 1049–1065.

Larzelere, Robert E. and Gerald R. Patterson. 1990. "Parental Management: Mediator of the Effect of Socioeconomic Status on Early Delinquency." *Criminology* 28: 301–323.

Laub, John H. and Robert J. Sampson. 1988. "Unraveling Families and Delinquency: A Reanalysis of the Gluecks' Data." *Criminology* 26: 355–380.

Laub, John H. and Robert J. Sampson. 1993. "Turning Points in the Life Course: Why Change Matters to the Study of Crime." *Criminology* 31: 301–325.

Laub, John H. and Robert J. Sampson. 2003. *Shared Beginnings, Divergent Lives: Delinquent Boys to Age 70.* Cambridge, MA: Harvard University Press.

Leonard, Kimberly Kempf and Scott Decker. 1994. "The Theory of Social Control: Does It Apply to the Very Young?" *Journal of Criminal Justice* 22: 89–105.

Li, Spenser D. 2011. "The Religious Context of Parenting, Family Processes, and Alcohol Use in Early Adolescence." *Journal of Drug Issues* 41: 619–648.

Linden, Eric and James Hackler. 1973. "Affective Ties and Delinquency." *Pacific Sociological Review* 16: 27–46.

Liska, Allen E. and Mark D. Reed. 1985. "Ties to Conventional Institutions and Delinquency: Estimating Reciprocal Effects." *American Sociological Review* 50: 547–560.

Loeber, Rolf. 1982. "The Stability of Antisocial Child Behavior: A Review." *Child Development* 53: 1431–1446.

Loeber, Rolf and Thomas J. Dishion. 1983. "Early Predictors of Male Delinquency: A Review." *Psychological Bulletin* 94: 68–99.

Loeber, Rolf and Marc LeBlanc. 1990. "Toward a Developmental Criminology." Pp. 375–437 in *Crime and Justice: An Annual Review of Research*, vol. 12, ed. M. Tonry and N. Morris. University of Chicago Press.

Loeber, Rolf and Magda Stouthamer-Loeber. 1986. "Family Factors as Correlates and Predictors of Juvenile Conduct Problems and Delinquency." Pp. 29–149 in *Crime and Justice: An Annual Review of Research*, vol. 7, ed. M. Tonry and N. Morris. University of Chicago Press.

Longshore, Douglas, Susan Turner, and Judith A. Stein. 1996. "Self-Control in a Criminal Sample: An Examination of Construct Validity." *Criminology* 34: 209–228.

Lynskey, Dana Peterson, L. Thomas Winfree, Finn-Aage Esbensen, and Dennis L. Clason. 2000. "Linking Gender, Minority Group Status and Family Matter to Self-Control Theory: A Multivariate Analysis of Key Self-Control Concepts in a Youth-Gang Context." *Juvenile and Family Court Journal* 51: 1–19.

Lytton, Hugh. 1990. "Child and Parent Effects in Boys' Conduct Disorder: A Reinterpretation." *Developmental Psychology* 26: 683–697.

McCord, Joan. 1980. "Patterns of Deviance." Pp. 157–165 in *Human Functioning in Longitudinal Perspective*, ed. S. B. Sells, R. Crandall, M. Roff, J. S. Strauss, and W. Pollin. Baltimore: Williams and Wilkins.

McCord, William and Joan McCord. 1959. *Origins of Crime: A New Evaluation of the Cambridge–Sommerville Youth Study.* New York: Columbia University Press.

Marcus, Bernd. 2004. "Self-Control in the General Theory of Crime: Theoretical Implications of a Measurement Problem." *Theoretical Criminology* 8: 33–55.

Massey, James L. and Marvin D. Krohn. 1986. "A Longitudinal Examination of an Integrated Social Process Model of Deviant Behavior." *Social Forces* 65: 106–134.

Matsueda, Ross L. 1982. "Testing Control Theory and Differential Association: A Causal Modeling Approach." *American Sociological Review* 47: 489–504.

Matsueda, Ross L. 1989. "The Dynamics of Moral Beliefs and Minor Delinquency." *Social Forces* 68: 428–457.

Meldrum, Ryan. C. and Carter C. Hay. 2012. "Do Peers Matter in the Development of Self-Control? Evidence from a Longitudinal Study of Youth." *Journal of Youth and Adolescence* 41: 691–703.

Meldrum, Ryan C., Holly V. Miller, and Jamie L. Flexon. 2013. "Susceptibility to Peer Influence, Self-Control, and Delinquency." *Sociological Inquiry* 83: 106–129.

Moffitt, Terrie E., Richie Poulton, and Avshalom Caspi. 2013. "Lifelong Impact of Early Self-Control: Childhood Self-Discipline Predicts Adult Quality of Life." *American Scientist* 101: 352–359.

Monahan, Kathryn C., Susan Vanderhei, Jordan Bechtold, and Elizabeth Caufmann. 2014. "From the School Yard to the Squad Car: School Discipline, Truancy, and Arrest." *Journal of Youth and Adolescence* 43: 1110–1122.

Monahan, Thomas P. 1957. "Family Status and the Delinquent Child: A Reappraisal and Some New Findings." *Social Forces* 35: 250–258.

Nagin, Daniel S. and Raymond Paternoster. 1993. "Enduring Individual Differences and Rational Choice Theories of Crime." *Law and Society Review* 3: 467–496.

Nye, Ivan F. 1958. *Family Relationships and Delinquency Behavior*. New York: Wiley.

Osgood, D. Wayne, Janet K. Wilson, Patrick M. O'Malley, Jerald G. Bachman, and Lloyd D. Johnston. 1996. "Routine Activities and Individual Deviant Behavior. *American Sociological Review* 61: 635–655.

Patterson, Gerald R. 1980. "Children Who Steal." Pp. 73–90 in *Understanding Crime*, ed. T. Hirschi and M. Gottfredson. Beverly Hills, CA: Sage.

Patterson, Gerald R. 1982. *Coercive Family Process*. Eugene, OR: Castalia.

Patterson, Gerald R., Barbara D. DeBaryshe, and Elizabeth Ramsey. 1989. "A Developmental Perspective on Antisocial Behavior." *American Psychologist* 44: 329–335.

Patterson, Gerald R., J. G. Reid, and Thomas J. Dishion. 1992. *Antisocial Boys*. Eugene, OR: Castalia.

Patterson, Gerald R. and Magda Stouthamer-Loeber. 1984. "The Correlation of Family Management Practices and Delinquency." *Child Development* 55: 1299–1307.

Payne, Allison Ann. 2009. "Girls, Boys, and Schools: Gender Differences in the Relationships between School-Related Factors and Student Deviance." *Criminology* 47: 1167–1200.

Perrone, Dina, Christopher J. Sullivan, Travis C. Pratt, and Satenik Margaryan. 2004. "Parental Efficacy, Self-Control, and Delinquency: A Test of a General Theory of Crime on a Nationally Representative Sample of Youth." *International Journal of Offender Therapy and Comparative Criminology* 48: 298–312.

Petts, Richard J. 2009. "Family and Religious Characteristics' Influence on Delinquency Trajectories from Adolescence to Young Adulthood." *American Sociological Review* 74: 465–483.

Piquero, Alex R., Terrie E. Moffitt, and Bradley E. Wright. 2007. "Self-Control and Criminal Career Dimensions." *Journal of Contemporary Criminal Justice* 23: 72–89.

Piquero, Alex R. and Andre B. Rosay. 1998. "The Reliability and Validity of Grasmick et al.'s Self-Control Scale: A Comment on Longshore et al." *Criminology* 36: 157–173.

Piquero, Alex R. and Stephen Tibbetts. 1996. "Specifying the Direct and Indirect Effect of Low Self-Control and Situational Factors in Offenders' Decision-Making: Toward a More Complete Model of Rational Offending." *Justice Quarterly* 13: 481–510.

Polakowski, Michael. 1994. "Linking Self- and Social Control with Deviance: Illuminating the Structure Underlying a General Theory of Crime and Its Relation to Deviant Activity." *Journal of Quantitative Criminology* 10: 41–78.

Pratt, Travis C. and Francis T. Cullen. 2000. "The Empirical Status of Gottfredson and Hirschi's General Theory of Crime: A Meta-Analysis." *Criminology* 39: 931–964.

Pratt, Travis C., Michael G. Turner, and Alex R. Piquero. 2004. "Parental Socialization and Community Context: A Longitudinal Analysis of the Structural Sources of Low Self-Control." *Journal of Research in Crime and Delinquency* 41: 219–243.

Rankin, Joseph H. and Roger Kern. 1994. "Parental Attachments and Delinquency." *Criminology* 32: 495–515.

Rankin, Joseph H. and L. Edward Wells. 1990. "The Effect of Parental Attachments and Direct Controls on Delinquency." *Journal of Research in Crime and Delinquency* 27: 140–165.

Rebellon, Cesar J. 2002. "Reconsidering the Broken Homes/Delinquency Relationship and Exploring Its Mediating Mechanism(s)." *Criminology* 40: 103–136.

Rebellon, Cesar J. and Karen Van Gundy. 2005. "Can Control Theory Explain the Link between Parental Physical Abuse and Delinquency? A Longitudinal Analysis." *Journal of Research in Crime and Delinquency* 42: 247–274.

Robins, Lee N. 1978. "Sturdy Childhood Predictors of Adult Antisocial Behaviour: Replications from Longitudinal Studies." *Psychological Medicine* 8: 611–622.

Rosen, Lawrence, Leonard Savitz, Michael Lalli, and Stanley Turner. 1991. "Early Delinquency, High School Graduation and Adult Criminality." *Sociological Viewpoints* 7: 37–60.

Rosenbaum, Jill L. and James R. Lasley. 1990. "School, Community Context and Delinquency: Rethinking the Gender Gap." *Justice Quarterly* 7: 493–513.

Rutter, Michael. 1980. *Changing Youth in a Changing Society: Patterns of Adolescent Development and Disorder.* Cambridge, MA: Harvard University Press.

Sampson, Robert J. and John H. Laub. 1993. *Crime in the Making: Pathways and Turning Points through Life.* Cambridge, MA: Harvard University Press.

Sampson, Robert J. and John H. Laub. 1994. "Urban Poverty and the Family Context of Delinquency: A New Look at Structure and Process in a Classic Study." *Child Development* 65: 523–540.

Sampson, Robert J. and John H. Laub. 2005a. "The Life-Course View of the Development of Crime." *Annals of the American Academy of Political and Social Science* 602: 12–45.

Sampson, Robert J. and John H. Laub. 2005b. "A General Age-Graded Theory of Crime: Lessons Learned and the Future of Life-Course Criminology." *Advances in Criminological Theory* 15: 165–181. Special issue: "Integrated Developmental and Life Course Theories of Offending," ed. D. P. Farrington.

Sampson, Robert J., John H. Laub, and Christopher Wimer. 2006. "Does Marriage Reduce Crime? A Counterfactual Approach to Within-Individual Causal Effects." *Criminology* 44: 465–508.

Shaw, Clifford R. 1930. *Brothers in Crime.* University of Chicago Press.

Siennick, Sonja E. and Jeremy Staff. 2008. "Explaining the Educational Deficits of Delinquent Youths." *Criminology* 46: 609–635.

Simons, Ronald L., Christine Johnson, Rand D. Conger, and Glen Elder, Jr. 1998. "A Test of Latent Trait versus Life-Course Perspectives on the Stability of Adolescent Antisocial Behavior." *Criminology* 36: 217–243.

Simons, Ronald L., Leslie Gordon Simons, Callie Harbin Burt, Gene H. Brody, and Carolyn Cutrona. 2005. "Collective Efficacy, Authoritative Parenting and Delinquency: A Longitudinal Test of a Model Integrating Community- and Family-Level Processes." *Criminology* 43: 989–1029.

Simons, Ronald L., Leslie Gordon Simons, and Lora Ebert Wallace. 2004. *Families, Delinquency and Crime: Linking Society's Most Basic Institution to Antisocial Behavior.* Los Angeles: Roxbury.

Simons, Ronald L., Chyi-In Wu, Rand D. Conger, and Frederick O. Lorenz. 1994. "Two Routes to Delinquency: Differences between Early and Late Starters in the Impact of Parenting and Deviant Peers." *Criminology* 32: 247–276.

Smith, Carolyn A. and Terence P. Thornberry. 1995. "The Relationship between Childhood Maltreatment and Adolescent Involvement in Delinquency." *Criminology* 33: 451–481.

Snyder, J. and Gerald R. Patterson. 1987. "Family Interaction and Delinquent Behavior." Pp. 216–243 in *Handbook of Juvenile Delinquency*, ed. H. C. Quay. New York: Wiley.

Staff, Jeremy and Derek A. Kreager. 2008. "Too Cool for School? Violence, Peer Status and High School Dropout." *Social Forces* 87: 445–471.

Stewart, Eric A. 2003. "School Social Bonds, School Climate and School Misbehavior: A Multilevel Analysis." *Justice Quarterly* 20: 575–604.

Sweeten, Gary, Shawn D. Bushway, and Raymond Paternoster. 2009. "Does Dropping Out of School Mean Dropping into Delinquency?" *Criminology* 47: 47–91.

Thornberry, Terence P. 1987. "Toward an Interactional Theory of Delinquency." *Criminology* 25: 863–891.

Thornberry, Terence P., David Huizinga, and Rolf Loeber. 2004. "The Causes and Correlates Studies: Findings and Policy Implications." *Juvenile Justice* 9: 3–19.

Thornberry, Terence P., T. O. Ireland, and Carolyn A. Smith. 2001. "The Importance of Timing: The Varying Impact of Childhood and Adolescent Maltreatment on Multiple Problem Outcomes." *Development and Psychopathology* 13: 957–979.

Thornberry, Terence P., Carolyn A. Smith, Craig Rivera, David Huizinga, and Magda Stouthamer-Loeber. 1999. "Family Disruption and Delinquency." *Juvenile Justice Bulletin*. Washington, DC: Office of Juvenile Justice and Delinquency Prevention.

Tittle, Charles R. 1980. *Sanctions and Social Deviance*. New York: Praeger.

Tittle, Charles R. and Robert F. Meier. 1990. "Specifying the SES/Delinquency Relationship." *Criminology* 28: 271–299.

Tittle, Charles R., David A. Ward, and Harold G. Grasmick. 2004. "Capacity for Self-Control and Individuals' Interest in Exercising Self-Control." *Journal of Quantitative Criminology* 20: 143–172.

Tremblay, Richard E., Bernard Boulerice, Louise Arseneault, and Marianne Junger Niscale. 1995. "Does Low Self-Control During Childhood Explain the Association Between Delinquency and Accidents in Early Adolescence?" *Criminal Behavior and Mental Health* 5: 439–451.

Turner, Michael G. and Alex R. Piquero. 2002. The Stability of Self-Control. *Journal of Criminal Justice* 30: 457–471.

Turner, Michael G., Alex R. Piquero, and Travis C. Pratt. 2005. "The School Context as a Source of Self-Control." *Journal of Criminal Justice* 33: 327–339.

Unnever, James D., Francis T. Cullen, and Robert Agnew. 2006. "Why Is Bad Parenting Criminogenic? Implications from Rival Theories." *Youth Violence and Juvenile Justice* 4: 3–33.

Van Voorhis, Patricia, Francis T. Cullen, Richard A. Mathers, and Connie Chenoweth Garner. 1998. "The Impact of Family Structure and Quality on Delinquency: A Comparative Assessment of Structural and Functional Factors." *Criminology* 26: 235–261.

Vander Ven, Thomas M., Francis Cullen, Mark A. Carrozza, and John Paul Wright. 2001. "Home Alone: The Impact of Maternal Employment on Delinquency." *Social Problems* 48: 236–257.

Vazsonyi, Alexander T. and Lara M. Belliston. 2007. "The Family → Low Self-Control → Deviance: A Cross-Cultural and Cross-National Test of Self-Control Theory." *Criminal Justice and Behavior* 34: 505–530.

Vazsonyi, Alexander T, Jeffrey R. Hibbert, and J. Blake Snider. 2003. "Exotic Enterprise No More? Adolescent Reports of Family and Parenting Processes from Youth in Four Countries." *Journal of Research on Adolescence* 13: 129–160.

Warr, Mark. 1993. "Parents, Peers, and Delinquency." *Social Forces* 72: 247–264.

Warr, Mark. 1998. "Life-Course Transition and Desistance from Crime." *Criminology* 36: 183–215.

Warr, Mark. 2005. "Making Delinquent Friends: Adult Supervision and Children's Affiliations." *Criminology* 43: 77–106.

Wasserman, Gail A., Kate Keenan, Richard E. Tremblay, John D. Cole, Todd I. Herrenkohl, Rolf Loeber, and David Petechuk. 2003. "Risk and Protective Factors of Child Delinquency." Washington, DC: Office of Juvenile Justice and Delinquency Prevention.

Wasserman, Gail A., Laurie S. Miller, E. Pinner, and B. S. Jaramillo. 1996. "Parenting Predictors of Early Conduct Problems in Urban, High-Risk Boys." *Journal of the American Academy of Child and Adolescent Psychiatry* 35: 1227–1236.

Wells, Edward L. and Joseph H. Rankin. 1988. "Direct Parental Controls and Delinquency." *Criminology* 26: 263–285.

Wells, Edward L. and Joseph H. Rankin. 1991. "Families and Delinquency: A Meta-Analysis of the Impact of Broken Homes." *Social Problems* 38: 71–93.

White, Jennifer L., Terrie E. Moffitt, Felton Earls, Lee N. Robbins, and Phil A. Silva. 1990. "How Early Can We Tell? Predictors of Childhood Conduct Disorder and Adolescent Delinquency." *Criminology* 28: 507–533.

Whiteman, Shawn D., Alexander C. Jensen, and Jennifer L. Maggs. 2014. "Similarities and Differences in Adolescent Siblings' Alcohol-Related Attitudes, Use, and Delinquency: Evidence for Convergent and Divergent Influence Processes." *Journal of Youth and Adolescence* 43: 687–697.

Wiatrowski, Michael D. and Kristine L. Anderson. 1987. "The Dimensionality of the Social Bond." *Journal of Quantitative Criminology* 3: 65–81.

Wiatrowski, Michael D., David B. Griswold, and Mary K. Roberts. 1981. "Social Control Theory and Delinquency." *American Sociological Review* 46: 525–541.

Widom, Cathy S. 1989. "The Cycle of Violence." *Science* 244: 160–166.

Winfree, L. Thomas, Jr. and Frances P. Bernat. 1998. "Social Learning, Self-Control and Substance Abuse by Eighth Grade Students: A Tale of Two Cities." *Journal of Drug Issues* 28: 539–558.

Winfree, L. Thomas, Jr., Terrance J. Taylor, Ni He, and Finn-Aage Esbensen. 2006. "Self-Control and Variability Over Time: Multivariate Results Using a 5-Year, Multisite Panel of Youths." *Crime and Delinquency* 52: 253–286.

Wong, Siu Kwong. 2005. "The Effects of Adolescent Activities on Delinquency: A Differential Involvement Approach." *Journal of Youth and Adolescence* 34: 321–333.

Wood, Peter B., Betty Pfefferbaum, and Bruce J. Arneklev. 1993. "Risk-Taking and Self-Control: Social Psychological Correlates of Delinquency." *Journal of Crime and Justice* 16: 111–130.

Wright, Bradley R. Entner, Avshalom Caspi, Terrie E. Moffitt, and Phil A. Silva. 1999. "Low Self-Control, Social Bonds and Crime: Social Causation, Social Selection, or Both?" *Criminology* 37: 479–514.

Wright, Bradley R. Entner, Avshalom Caspi, Terrie E. Moffitt, and Phil A. Silva. 2001. "The Effects of Social Ties on Crime Vary by Criminal Propensity: A Life-Course Model of Interdependence." *Criminology* 39: 321–351.

Wright, John Paul and Kevin M. Beaver. 2005. "Do Parents Matter in Creating Self-Control in Their Children? A Genetically Informed Test of Gottfredson and Hirschi's Theory of Low Self-Control." *Criminology* 43: 1169–1202.

Wright, John Paul and Francis T. Cullen. 2001. "Parental Efficacy and Delinquent Behavior: Do Control and Support Matter?" *Criminology* 39: 677–705.

Zingraff, M. T., J. Leiter, K. A. Myers, and M. C. Johnsen. 1993. "Child Maltreatment and Youthful Problem Behavior." *Criminology* 31: 173–202.

Chapter 10

Social learning theories
Peer group influences

Chapter preview

Topics:

- Companions in crime: the group character of delinquency
- Theoretical views of peers and delinquency
- Peer group influences
- Street gangs

Theories:

- Differential association
- Social learning

Terms:

- co-offending
- social learning
- differential association
- definitions of the law
- operant conditioning
- differential reinforcement
- imitation

- socialization perspective
- selection perspective
- street gang
- selection model
- social facilitation model
- enhancement model
- group processes

Chapter learning objectives

After completing this chapter, students should be able to:

- Explain the connection between peers and delinquent behavior according to social learning theories.

- Describe and illustrate how peer group association varies in frequency, priority, duration, and intensity.
- Describe how delinquent attitudes and behaviors are acquired.
- Explain the role that modeling and reinforcement play in peer group influences.
- Distinguish the socialization and selection perspectives on peer group involvement.
- Discuss gender differences in peer group influences.
- Explain the role that peers play in drug use.
- Identify the key elements of an adequate definition of street gangs.
- Describe the group processes of street gangs.

Case in point: Sidney's "companions in crime"

The biographical account of Sidney Blotzman's delinquent career, offered by Clifford Shaw in *The Natural History of a Delinquent Career*, provides a good deal of information on his "companions in crime." Criminologist Mark Warr offers a summary of the group nature of Sidney's delinquency:

> Sidney grew up in a highly "deteriorated" neighborhood west of the Loop (downtown Chicago) in a family marked by frequent desertion of the father. He moved with his family to a nearby neighborhood when he was 10 and moved yet again when he was 15. Sidney was first arrested in 1916 (at about age 8) for petty theft and last arrested in 1925 for armed robbery and rape. All but two of the 13 offenses for which he was arrested were committed with accomplices. Over the course of his delinquent career, Sidney was affiliated with three delinquent groups, each of which inhabited the neighborhood in which he resided at the time. Although these groups were fairly large, and although Sidney was arrested with a total of 11 different co-offenders during his career, he never committed an offense with more than three companions on any one occasion. In his first group, which contained six members, Sidney committed offenses with four distinct subsets (triads) of the group. The two groups to which he later belonged were considerably larger (more than a dozen), but in both cases Sidney committed offenses with only a small portion of the group (three members), usually with no more than two of them at any one time.
>
> Shaw and McKay emphasize the fact that the larger groups with which Sidney was affiliated existed before he joined them, that each had its own unique repertoire of offenses, and that Sidney's own history of offending closely paralleled the activities of the groups to which he belonged.

Source: Warr (1996: 15). Drawn from Shaw (1931). Reprinted with permission of the publisher.

One of the distinctive features of the adolescent years is the degree to which peers take on added importance and influence. Therefore, it is no surprise that most delinquent acts are committed with friends. Yet the powerful influence of peers during adolescence is often taken for granted, with little consideration of its extent and nature. We often assume that adolescents spend an inordinate amount of time with friends and that their thoughts and actions are almost totally dictated by peer pressure. In terms of delinquency, we assume that delinquent friends are the major force behind the initiation and persistence of delinquent offending. Although these assumptions may be true, they tell us little about how peers exert their influence.

Companions in crime: the group character of delinquency

Criminologists have long known that delinquency occurs most often in the company of peers (Warr 1996, 2002; Reiss 1988; Erickson and Jensen 1977; Erickson 1971; Hindelang 1971; Shaw et al. 1929; but see also Stolzenberg and D'Alessio 2008).[1] This is known as **co-offending** (Reiss 1988). Empirical study of group offending began in the 1920s with the research of Shaw and McKay, who found that 82 percent of the offenses reported in juvenile court records involved two or more participants (Shaw et al. 1929). More recently, in a review of research on the group character of delinquency, Mark Warr (2002: 32) concluded that "delinquency is predominately group behavior." In his own research, Warr (1996) found that 73 percent of all delinquent offenses were committed in groups. In fact, the offenses committed most frequently by juveniles are the ones most often committed in groups (Warr 2002; Gold 1970). However, not all types of delinquency are typically group offenses. Although some offenses, such as drug and alcohol use, burglary, trespass, and vandalism, are committed almost exclusively in groups, others, such as assault, robbery, shoplifting, and most status offenses, are committed as often, or even more often, by solitary offenders (Weerman 2003; Elliott and Menard 1996; Reiss 1988; Erickson and Jensen 1977). The majority of delinquent careers are characterized by a mix of offenses committed alone and offenses committed with accomplices (Weerman 2003; Warr 1996; Reiss 1988). Nonetheless, juvenile offenders who commit crime with others commit more crime and are involved in more serious offenses, including violence, than juveniles who commit crime alone (Conway and McCord 2002, 2005; Thornberry et al. 1994; Inciardi, Horowitz, and Pottieger 1993; Reiss 1988; Erickson and Jensen 1977; Erickson 1971; Hindelang 1971).

Also relevant to the group character of delinquency is the consistent research finding that adolescents who have delinquent peers are more likely to be delinquent themselves. Hirschi's (1969) research on social bond theory found that 83 percent of youth reporting two or more delinquent acts had at least one close friend who had been picked up by the police, whereas only 25 percent of youth with no delinquent friends had committed a delinquent act. "The number of delinquent friends an adolescent has is the strongest known predictor of delinquent behavior" (Warr 1998: 184; see also Warr 2002; Matsueda and Anderson 1998; Johnson, Marcos, and Bahr 1987; Elliott, Huizinga, and Ageton 1985; Johnson 1979; Erickson and Jensen 1977; Hepburn 1976; Hindelang 1971; Erickson and Empey 1965).

Theoretical views of peers and delinquent behavior

This chapter explores theories that connect peers and delinquent behavior. Differential association and social learning theories point to peer groups as the context in which delinquent behavior is learned and reinforced. In contrast, social control theories argue that peers are largely irrelevant to why youth become delinquent. This theoretical debate gives rise to some important questions regarding peer group influences on delinquency that will also be considered in this chapter. After exploring these questions, we turn to peer influence on offending in street gangs.

Social learning theories

Two versions of social learning theory are described here as the basis for understanding peer group influences on delinquency: Edwin Sutherland's differential association theory and Ronald Akers' social learning theory.

Sutherland's differential association theory

Peer group relations take center stage in *differential association theory*. Edwin Sutherland developed the theory to explain how group relations influence people's attitudes and behavior. The first formal statement of this theory appeared in 1939 in the third edition of Sutherland's textbook, *Principles of Criminology*. A revised version appeared in the fourth edition, published in 1947, and remains the best-known formal statement of the learning processes that occur in delinquent peer groups (Sutherland, Cressey, and Luckenbill 1992; Matsueda 1988).

Differential association theory is stated in the form of nine propositions, each with a brief explanation (see "Expanding ideas: Sutherland's theory of differential association"). The propositions are phrased in terms of criminal behavior, but Sutherland intended his theory to explain a broad range of crimes, including traditional street crime, white-collar crime, and delinquency. In fact, the theory has been applied most extensively to delinquent behavior (Agnew 1991).

Differential association theory is a theory of **social learning**; it holds that criminal behavior is learned (Proposition #1) through social interaction in groups. According to Sutherland, the vehicle for learning is verbal communication (Proposition #2), and learning occurs within intimate personal groups (Proposition #3). Through such inter- action, individuals learn both techniques for committing delinquent acts and attitudes and motivations toward offending (Proposition #4). The theory goes on to state that association with different groups – **differential association** – varies in "frequency, dur- ation, priority, and intensity" (Proposition #7). In other words, the influence of relation- ships within groups is greatest when interaction occurs frequently (frequency), for long periods (duration), and early in life (priority), and when those relationship ties are strong (intensity).

At the heart of the theory are **definitions of the law** (Proposition #6). A person defines the law as favorable or unfavorable – either as rules to obey or as rules to violate – and such definitions are learned through social interaction. The direction of these definitions involves motives and drives that either support obedience to the law or encourage violation of it (Proposition #5).

Sutherland assigned special importance to delinquent peer groups as a context in which adolescents learn "definitions favorable to the violation of the law." In fact, he contended that adolescent peer groups are much more important than the family in teaching delin- quent behavior. The family is important, in Sutherland's view, mainly because where the family lives determines the degree to which the youth is exposed to patterns of delinquency outside of the home. In addition, unpleasant family experiences may drive the youth out of the home and encourage association with delinquent peers. These delinquent peers, in turn, provide the primary group context in which delinquency is learned (Sutherland et al. 1992).

Differential association theory argues that delinquent behavior is learned through inter- action with others. But the theory says little about how such learning occurs other than noting that the "process of learning criminal behavior … involves all the mechanisms that are involved in any other learning" (Proposition #8). *Social learning theory* was developed in an attempt to overcome this shortcoming.

Expanding ideas: Sutherland's theory of differential association

Edwin Sutherland's well-known theory, differential association, is stated in the form of nine propositions. Although only the propositional statements are provided here, Sutherland included a brief explanation for each statement. Differential association theory is one of the most succinct theoretical statements about crime and delinquency. The nine propositions are as follows:

1. Criminal behavior is learned.
2. Criminal behavior is learned in interaction with other persons in a process of communication.
3. The principal part of the learning of criminal behavior occurs within intimate personal groups.
4. When criminal behavior is learned, the learning includes (a) techniques of committing the crime, which are sometimes very complicated, sometimes very simple; and (b) the specific direction of motives, drives, rationalizations, and attitudes.
5. The specific direction of motives and drives is learned from definitions of the legal codes as favorable or unfavorable.
6. A person becomes delinquent because of an excess of definitions favorable to violation of law over definitions unfavorable to violation of law.
7. Differential association may vary in frequency, duration, priority, and intensity.
8. The process of learning criminal behavior by association with criminal and anticriminal patterns involves all the mechanisms that are involved in any other learning.
9. While criminal behavior is an expression of general needs and values, it is not explained by those general needs and values, since noncriminal behavior is an expression of the same needs and values.

Source: Sutherland et al. (1992: 88–90).

Akers' social learning theory

Robert Burgess and Ronald Akers (1966) extended differential association theory and restated it in the form of seven propositions. The revised theory, called *differential association–reinforcement theory*, incorporates principles from behavioral learning theory, especially **operant conditioning**, in which behavior is shaped by rewards and punishments. To emphasize the group context of learning, Burgess and Akers refer to the social processes of rewards and punishments as **differential reinforcement**. Other concepts from behavioral learning theory were also incorporated in the revised propositions, but Sutherland's emphasis on group interaction was maintained.

Ronald Akers continued to develop the theory, which is now called *social learning theory*, by elaborating on the processes of learning that he and Burgess first identified. Akers emphasizes four particular aspects of learning: differential association, definitions, differential reinforcement, and imitation.

The idea of *differential association* builds on Sutherland's use of the term to include not only the group context in which delinquent attitudes and behaviors are learned, but also the group's ability to model and reinforce these attitudes and behaviors. Also drawing on Sutherland's original theory, social learning theory points to the importance of delinquent *definitions.* Attitudes and beliefs that encourage delinquent acts are acquired in groups through imitation and reinforcement. Akers asserts that delinquent definitions are "basically positive or neutralizing. Positive definitions are beliefs or attitudes that make the behavior morally desirable or wholly permissible. Neutralizing definitions favor the commission of crime by justifying or excusing it" (Akers and Sellers 2013: 83, emphasis omitted).

The third aspect of learning is *differential reinforcement.* This term refers to learning processes that involve rewards and punishments. Rewards and punishments may be actual or anticipated, social or non-social (Akers and Sellers 2013; Wood et al. 1997). Clifford Shaw's (1931) case study provides many personal accounts of Sidney's involvement in delinquent acts that were motivated by thrill and excitement (non-social reinforcement) and by the social reinforcement of his companions. Sidney, for example, never committed theft when he was alone. A significant part of the motivation to steal came from the mutual thrill of the act for Sidney and his companions.

The fourth aspect of learning that social learning theory incorporates is **imitation**, in which the behavior modeled by others is copied. Sometimes people behave in particular ways after observing other people's behavior. Imitation may result in new kinds of behavior or serve to maintain current behaviors. In some cases, it can result in the discontinuation of behavior. Akers (1985), for example, argues that imitation is key to learning how to use drugs. Seeing how other people actually take drugs and then observing the effect that they experience provides an important first step into drug use. Similarly, after observing someone take drugs, a person may perceive the effects to be undesirable and refrain or discontinue further drug use.

Akers emphasizes that learning occurs primarily in a group context. Like differential association theory, social learning theory holds that associations will have the greatest influence when they occur early in life (priority), over long periods of time (duration), frequently (frequency), and in the context of valued relationships (intensity) (Akers and Sellers 2013). The processes of learning that social learning theory spells out are nicely illustrated in Shaw's (1931) description of how Sidney learned to shoplift. Sidney's story indicates not only that he learned how to steal by imitating the techniques of a close friend, but that he also learned what to do with the stolen goods and how to respond if he was caught by the store detective. After acquiring these skills, Sidney began to view shoplifting as a means of making money. He also became confident in his abilities and viewed his accomplishments with much pride – shoplifting was a learned skill that was rewarding to him.

Socialization versus selection

Differential association and social learning theories contend that delinquent friends provide the primary group context in which delinquent attitudes and behavior are learned and reinforced. To produce such significant changes in attitudes and behavior, peer group relationships are viewed as strong, cohesive, and long-lasting (Hirschi 1969). It is also apparent that peer group interaction takes place before delinquent attitudes and behavior are acquired. This emphasis on the social processes of learning delinquent behavior through peer group interaction is sometimes referred to as the **socialization perspective** (Thornberry et al. 1993, 1994).[2]

In contrast, social bond theory contends that delinquency is a product of weak social bonds, rather than association with delinquent peers. Youth with weak social bonds, including weak attachment to peers, experience few social controls that would prevent them from getting involved in delinquency. The theory goes on to argue that youth who are involved in delinquency tend to develop friendships with other delinquents – "birds of a feather flock together" (Glueck and Glueck 1950: 164). "Instead of being led into a life of crime by the influence of peers, they [delinquent youth] merely seek out those peers who share their interest in delinquency" (Wilson and Herrnstein 1985: 292). This tendency to seek out individuals like oneself is referred to as the **selection perspective** (Sampson and Laub 1993; Kandel 1978).

The selection perspective holds that individual attitudes, values, beliefs, and behaviors are established early in life, largely through family attachments, and that these characteristics become the criteria for choosing friends, rather than being the products of friendships (Hirschi 1969; see also Gottfredson and Hirschi 1990). Social bond theory also takes issue with "the idea that delinquents have comparatively warm, intimate social relations with each other" (Hirschi 1969: 159). Travis Hirschi contends that this image of delinquent youth having close peer relationships is a "romantic myth"; instead, delinquent youth have relationships that are "cold and brittle." In his later work with Gottfredson, Hirschi describes peer group relations among delinquent peers as "short-lived, unstable, unorganized collectivities, whose members have little regard for one another" (Gottfredson and Hirschi 1990: 159).

Peer group influences

As you probably anticipate, these very different views on peers and delinquent behavior have stimulated much controversy. We explore six questions stemming from this theoretical debate:

1. Is delinquency learned from delinquent peers?
2. How does peer group association influence youth?
3. Are there gender differences in peer group influence?
4. Can peer networks explain racial and ethnic differences in juvenile violence?
5. What is the nature of delinquent groups?
6. What role do peers play in drug use?

Is delinquency learned from delinquent peers?

The lively debate over the role of peers in delinquent behavior has sparked a great deal of research on the question of causal or temporal ordering (Warr 1998; Hirschi 1987). Does association with delinquent peers come before delinquency, as learning theories suggest? Or does delinquency come before association with delinquent peers, as control theories suggest?

Delbert Elliott and Scott Menard (1996) used data from the National Youth Survey to address the question of causal ordering (see also Menard and Elliott 1990). They found that youths typically make delinquent friends before getting involved in delinquency. This general temporal sequence was more true for serious forms of delinquency than it was for minor delinquent acts, and it was more true for younger adolescents than for older adolescents (Elliott and Menard 1996). These findings support the causal ordering offered by social learning theories. However, Elliott and Menard also found that, after a youth is exposed to delinquent acts committed by peers, the youth's own delinquent acts that follow increase the likelihood of association with peers who are more delinquent – a finding that is consistent with control theories. Moreover, Elliott and Menard's analysis revealed that *both* peer association and delinquency increase from early to middle adolescence and decrease in late adolescence and adulthood. This finding indicates a close connection between level of peer group involvement and level of delinquent behavior across the adolescent years (Conway and McCord 2002, 2005; Warr 1993).

So which view is correct? Do delinquents merely seek out friends like themselves, as control theories contend, or do they become delinquent because they associate with delinquent friends, as social learning theories contend (Matsueda and Anderson 1998; Warr 1998)? The most likely answer is that both are partially correct: youth who lack social bonds or self-control are more likely to engage in delinquent acts and then seek out delinquent friends, whereas other youth engage in delinquency only after they have been exposed to such behavior through their peer group relations (Inciardi et al. 1993).

Frank Weerman (2011) studied this complementary process by examining students' social networks and involvement in delinquency. He used a methodology that enabled him to examine simultaneously social network formation and changes in delinquency. Contrary to the selection perspective, he found that similarity in delinquency had no significant effect on the selection of school friends, once other social network dynamics were taken into account (see also Young 2011; McGloin 2009). Consistent with the socialization perspective, friends' involvement in delinquency had a significant effect on individuals' own delinquency (see also Henneberger et al. 2013). Several other studies, however, have found that delinquent peer association and delinquent behavior influence each other. Adolescents tend to choose friends similar to themselves, but friends also influence each other in developing attitudes and behaviors (Seddig 2014; Matsueda and Anderson 1998; Krohn et al. 1996; Thornberry et al. 1994; Akers 1991; Thornberry 1987; Kandel 1978). Mark Warr (2002) notes that outside of criminology, where the matter is less weighed down with theoretical antagonism, social scientists are more likely to agree that behavioral similarity among peers is a combination of both socialization and selection effects (see also Haynie and Osgood 2005).

How does peer group association influence youth?

One of the most consistent findings in delinquency research is that the number of delinquent friends a youth has and the extent of their delinquency are closely related to the level of a youth's own delinquency (Elliott and Menard 1996; Warr 1993; Agnew 1991; Reiss 1988; Matsueda and Heimer 1987; Morash 1983). Peers expose youth to delinquent attitudes and behaviors in a group context. This is the basic tenet of differential association theory: delinquent behavior is learned through group interaction (Proposition #2). Differential association theory goes on to say that group interaction varies in frequency, priority, duration, and intensity (Proposition #7). Such variation in group interaction is referred to as differential association.

Frequency and duration of association

It is usually assumed that more frequent and prolonged exposure to delinquent attitudes and behaviors results in greater likelihood of delinquency. The idea here is that peers provide, or model, both delinquent attitudes and delinquent behaviors. These attitudes and behaviors are then imitated and reinforced by the peer group. Research consistently shows that the more involved a youth is with delinquent friends, the more likely he or she is to engage in delinquent behavior (Megens and Weerman 2012; Miller 2010; Warr 1993; Agnew 1991; Reiss 1988; Elliott et al. 1985; Erickson and Jensen 1977; Short 1960). Going one step further, Robert Agnew found that the influence of delinquent peers on delinquent behavior depends not only on the amount of time spent with friends, but also on the extent to which delinquent behavior patterns are presented in group interaction (Agnew 1991; see also Haynie and Osgood 2005; Menard and Elliott 1994). The more peers are involved in delinquent behavior, the more likely a youth is to engage in similar forms of delinquency. Thus, delinquent behavior is modeled by peers and imitated by the youth. It should also be pointed out that non-delinquent and delinquent youth report very similar levels of contact and stability in their friendships, providing comparable amounts of social interaction within peer groups (Giordano, Cernkovich, and Pugh 1986).

Priority: connecting age and peer group influence

Sutherland's concept of priority refers to association with delinquent peers early in life. Although priority is distinct from duration, Mark Warr found that these concepts are strongly related: youth who associated with delinquent peers early in life did so for longer periods of time. However, he also found that delinquency was more strongly correlated with the delinquency of a youth's current friends than with the delinquency of friends at an early age. He concluded that "it is the *recency*, not the priority, of delinquent friends that affects delinquent behavior at a particular age" (Warr 1993: 34, emphasis in original).

Exposure to delinquent peers changes significantly over the adolescent years. In a study investigating the relationships between age, peers, and delinquency, Warr (1993) found that over the course of adolescence, youth are increasingly exposed to delinquent behaviors by peers. This exposure peaks in middle to late adolescence, and then declines dramatically as individuals leave their teen years and enter young adulthood (Warr 1993; see also Elliott and Menard 1996). Warr found a very strong relationship between exposure to delinquent peers and self-reported delinquency. This pattern of exposure to delinquent peers is strikingly similar to the age curve. Noting this similarity, Warr concluded that the strong connection between age and criminal involvement is explained at least in part by changing levels of peer association (Warr 1993; see also Stolzenberg and D'Alessio 2008; Conway and McCord 2002, 2005; Weerman 2003).

Intensity: the strength of delinquent peer relationships

The strength, or "intensity," of relationships among delinquent peers is critical in determining the extent of peer influence. Peer group relationships can exert influence to the degree that they are strong and cohesive (Giordano et al. 1986). Still, there is heated theoretical debate over this issue.

Learning theories contend that the communication, modeling, imitation, and reinforcement of delinquent attitudes and behaviors are possible only in "intimate personal groups." These groups are characterized by relationships that are close, warm, strong, cohesive, loyal, solidary (united in purpose), and long-lasting. In contrast, control theories offer a far less cohesive and influential view of delinquent peer relationships. According to these theories, delinquent youth lack warm and intimate relationships with their peers, and are therefore incapable of strongly influencing one another.

To address this disagreement about delinquent peer group relationships, Peggy Giordano and her colleagues (1986) carried out an extensive study of relationships among adolescent friends. They found that delinquent youth, at least as much as other adolescents, find their friendships to be meaningful and beneficial. Delinquent and non-delinquent youth reported similar levels of contact, stability, caring and trust, and identity support in their friendships. Compared to non-delinquents, delinquent youth reported higher levels of self-disclosure, rewards from friendships, and influence among friends. The friendships of delinquent youth were also characterized more by conflict and imbalance and less by loyalty than are the friendships of non-delinquent youth. While noting these differences in friendships, the researchers concluded that "overall, we find that youth who are very different in their levels of involvement in delinquency are nevertheless quite similar in the ways in which they view their friendship relations" (Giordano et al. 1986: 1191; see also Inciardi et al. 1993; Kandel and Davies 1991).

A recent study of delinquency and the structure of adolescent peer groups supports the earlier findings of Giordano and her colleagues. Derek Kreager and his colleagues examined how characteristics of friendship groups such as group size, cohesion, stability, and friendship reciprocity might differ between delinquent and non-delinquent groups. They concluded, "Once demographic characteristics are controlled, groups with more delinquent members are of similar size, transitivity, structural cohesion, stability, and centrality as nondelinquent groups" (Kreager, Rulison, and Moody 2011: 121).[3]

Are there gender differences in peer group influence?

Are there differences in the degree to which males and females are exposed to and influenced by delinquent peers? Daniel Mears and his colleagues (1998) considered this twofold question. They found that males are substantially more likely than females to be exposed to delinquent friends. Males spend more time with friends and are roughly twice as likely to have friends who have broken the law. This difference in exposure to delinquent friends *partially* explains gender differences in involvement in delinquency. Mears and his colleagues also found that males are more strongly affected by delinquent friends than are females; having delinquent peers was related to delinquent behavior more strongly for males than it was for females. Recent research supports the findings of Mears and his colleagues, showing gender differences in the predictors of association with deviant peers and in deviant peer pressure (Chapple, Vaske, and Worthen 2014), and gender differences in the effects of unstructured socializing with peers on delinquency (Augustyn and McGloin 2013). Research also reveals that, compared to males, females have a stronger tendency to select friends based on others' behavior. Thus, for females, others' involvement in delinquency is especially important in determining friendship ties (Haynie, Doogan, and Soller 2014).

Why then are males and females affected differently by exposure to delinquent peers? Mears and his associates explore one possible answer: differences in moral evaluation of illegal conduct. Both differential association theory and social bond theory hold that an individual's attitudes toward the law influence the likelihood of delinquent behavior. Carol Gilligan (1982) has suggested that females are socialized in such a way that they are more restrained by moral evaluations of behavior than are males. Using a series of questions that asked how wrong it would be to engage in various delinquent acts ("moral evaluations"), Mears and his colleagues (1998) found that females were consistently more likely than males to rate the offenses as "very wrong." For both males and females, having delinquent friends was less influential for those with high levels of moral disapproval, but this constraint was far greater for females than for males. Females with strong moral disapproval of delinquent acts were immune to the influence of delinquent peers, whereas for males with the same level of belief, the influence of delinquent peers was reduced but not eliminated.

At first glance, these findings seem consistent with differential association theory, because "definitions favorable to the violation of the law" acquired through peer group association are the motivating force behind delinquency. Mears and his colleagues, however, found that moral constraints inhibit delinquency, even when a youth is exposed to delinquent peers. In this way, beliefs operate as a control against involvement in delinquency. This line of thought is more consistent with social bond theory.

Can peer networks explain racial and ethnic differences in juvenile violence?

In Chapter 5, we saw that official and victimization survey data show that blacks are overrepresented among serious offenders and that self-report data show that blacks are more likely than whites to commit serious offenses at a high frequency. Recent research by Dana Haynie and Danielle Payne (2006) tried to explain the racial gap in juvenile violence by exploring the influence of peer group relations or "friendship networks." The researchers argue that

> norms about the appropriateness of violence are more likely to develop when adolescents are enmeshed in friendship networks in which members display deviant and violent behavior. Such a prodelinquent reference group promotes delinquent conceptions of the self as well as pro-violence attitudes, justifications, and motives to engage in violent behavior.
>
> (Haynie and Payne 2006: 777–778, references omitted; see also Haynie, Silver, and Teasdale 2006)

Thus, friendship networks may be an important mechanism for explaining youth violence. Haynie and Payne (2006) used a longitudinal self-report survey of approximately 13,000 students to measure characteristics of friendship networks and involvement in serious violence, including serious physical fights, hurting someone badly enough to need bandages or care from a doctor or nurse, pulling a knife or gun on someone, or shooting or stabbing someone. They found that black and Hispanic youth engage in significantly more violence than their white or Asian counterparts. However, once they considered characteristics of friendship networks, this difference was no longer significant. Friendship networks that were poorly integrated into the school environment, displayed limited orientation toward academic achievement, and were involved in deviance and violence promoted involvement in violence, regardless of race or ethnicity. Thus, racial and ethnic differences in violence can be explained, in part, by the characteristics of adolescent friendship networks.

What is the nature of delinquent groups?

In his research, Mark Warr (1996: 13) tried to discover the "essential features of delinquent groups," using a unique data set called the National Survey of Youth. These data were drawn from interviews that asked about particular offenses and paid close attention to characteristics of co-offenders. Warr found that offenders usually committed offenses with only two or three co-offenders. The composition of these groups changed frequently, and group members were drawn from a larger network of friends. It was unusual for offenders to commit more than three or four offenses with the same group, and, as a result, delinquents tended to belong to multiple groups over the course of their delinquent careers (Warr 1996).[4] These findings led him to describe delinquent groups as "transitory" (Warr 1996: 33; see also McGloin et al. 2008; Weerman 2003; Warr 2002; Reiss and Farrington 1991; Gottfredson and Hirschi 1990; Reiss 1988). Warr also found that the size of delinquent groups decreased with age. By middle and late adolescence, offending groups were made up of only two or three youths (Warr 1996; see also McGloin et al. 2008; Weerman 2003).

Warr's analysis also revealed that most delinquent groups have two distinct types of members, based on their role within the group: instigators and joiners. "Instigators" are identifiable leaders who recruit others to engage in delinquent acts and who coordinate group activities. Other group members can be classified as "joiners." Instigators tend to be older, more experienced, and are emotionally closer to others in the delinquent group than are joiners. Because of the transitory nature of delinquent groups, the role that a youth assumes in one group may not be the same as his or her role in another group.

What role do peers play in drug use?

Nowhere is the controversy over peer influence more evident than with adolescent drug use. Even though association with drug-using friends is the single best predictor of adolescent drug use, the extent of peer influence is better understood than the processes through which peers exert their influence (Kandel and Davies 1991; Marcos, Bahr, and Johnson 1986). The role of peer influence in drug use is the subject of much debate. The socialization perspective draws from social learning theories and holds that drug use most commonly occurs in groups and is best characterized as a group experience. Peers not only supply drugs, but they also define the experience as desirable and pleasant, thereby providing motivation and reinforcement for drug use (Longshore, Chang, and Hsieh 2004; Matsueda and Anderson 1998). The competing selection perspective is based on control theories and contends that both drug use and association with peers who use drugs are a result of weak social bonds or lack of self-control. Instead of being led into drug use by friends, drug-using youth merely seek out those who share their interest in drug use. As a result, the correlation between drug-using friends and drug use is spurious.

Research reveals that both views are partially correct. Youth who use drugs tend to choose friends who also use drugs, and once friendships are established, peer group interaction promotes attitudes and behaviors that encourage continued drug use (Krohn et al. 1996; Kandel, Kessler, and Margulies 1978). In addition, relationships among drug users have been found to be strong and intimate and therefore capable of reinforcing attitudes and behaviors that favor drug use (Kandel and Davies 1991; see also Inciardi et al. 1993; White 1992; Altschuler and Brounstein 1991; Huizinga, Loeber, and Thornberry 1991; Elliott, Huizinga, and Menard 1989; Fagan 1989; Huizinga, Menard, and Elliott 1989; White, Pandina, and LaGrange 1987).

Street gangs

To many people, delinquent groups are synonymous with gangs. Gangs, however, account for only a small fraction of delinquent groups, and obviously not all delinquent behavior occurs in gangs (Warr 1996). Still, there is much evidence that gang membership increases the likelihood, frequency, and seriousness of involvement in crime, as well as levels of victimization (Gordon et al. 2004; Coughlin and Venkatesh 2003; Thornberry et al. 1993, 2003; Venkatesh 2000; Battin et al. 1998; Huff 1998; Thornberry and Burch 1997; Bjerregaard and Smith 1993; Esbensen and Huizinga 1993; Spergel 1990; Fagan 1989). Moreover, gang members commit a disproportionate percentage of both property and violent crimes (Gordon et al. 2004; Battin et al. 1998; Thornberry and Burch 1997; Bjerregaard and Smith 1993; Esbensen and Huizinga 1993; Thornberry et al. 1993).

The scope of the contemporary gang problem is captured in an annual survey of law enforcement agencies across the United States conducted by the National Gang Center. The National Youth Gang Survey (NYGS) asks about the presence and characteristics of local gang problems. Recent survey results estimate that there were approximately 30,700 gangs with 850,000 members in the United States in 2012. Nearly 30 percent of responding law enforcement agencies reported gang activity, which is concentrated primarily in urban areas (Egley, Howell, and Harris 2014: 1). Although gang prevalence has decreased in smaller cities in recent years, it has remained stable in larger cities. Results of the NYGS show that, in each of the four most recent surveys, approximately 85 percent of larger cities, 50 percent of suburban counties, and 15 percent of rural counties reported gang activity. Gang-related homicides, which occur primarily in urban areas, increased substantially in 2012, in part due to agencies in larger cities reporting more complete data than in previous years (Egley et al. 2014: 2).

Defining gangs

Despite social scientists' strong interest in gangs, there is no widely agreed upon definition of *gang*. Nor is there agreement on the point at which a delinquent group becomes a gang. In fact, this question has been debated for decades, with no clear resolution (Warr 1996). As a result, the term *gang* is used with a great deal of variation and imprecision, and it is often used interchangeably with the term *delinquent group* (Decker and Van Winkle 1996; Bursik and Grasmick 1993).

In the first systematic study of delinquent gangs, conducted in the 1920s, Frederic Thrasher (1927: 57) defined the adolescent **gang** as:

> an interstitial group originally formed spontaneously and then integrated through conflict. It is characterized by the following types of behavior: meeting face to face, milling, movement through space as a unit, conflict, and planning. The result of this collective behavior is the development of tradition, unreflective internal structure, esprit de corps, solidarity, morale, group awareness, and attachment to a local territory.

Note that in this definition, Thrasher did not include delinquency as a defining activity of the gang.

Thrasher's definition of gangs was dominant until the mid-1960s. At that time numerous studies sought to describe gangs and their activities in terms of group processes and their wider community context. Robert Bursik and Harold Grasmick (1993: 121) refer to this approach as a "process-based definition" of gangs. Rather than being stable or permanent, gangs were portrayed as constantly changing in terms of membership, activities, structure, and cohesion. Bursik and Grasmick also note that most current research no longer takes this approach.[5] Instead, gangs are defined in terms of involvement in illegal behavior. In fact, Walter Miller (1980) has argued that the term gang should be reserved for a group that is formally organized and engages in serious crime, as opposed to a street group. Bursik and Grasmick (1993: 121) refer to this as a "delinquency-based definition."

In a widely cited study, Walter Miller (1980) tried to determine whether there was any consensus among officials who work with youth as to what constitutes a gang. He surveyed a national sample of police officers, prosecutors, defense attorneys, educators, city council members, state legislators, and even past and present gang members, asking them "What is your conception of a gang?" and "Exactly how would you define gang?" Six characteristics were identified by at least 85 percent of the 309 respondents. Miller (1980: 121) used these to compose the following definition of a gang:

> a self-formed association of peers, bounded together by mutual interests, with identifiable leadership, well-developed lines of authority, and other organizational features, who act in concert to achieve a specific purpose or purposes which generally include the conduct of illegal activity and control over a particular territory, facility or type of enterprise.

Some criminologists have argued that such a definition provides an overly organized picture of gangs. One gang researcher, for example, argues that violent gangs are characterized by diffuse leadership, limited cohesion, impermanence, lack of consensus on norms, shifting membership, and unclear membership expectations (Yablonsky 1959, 1962).

The definitional distinction between the group processes of gangs and their delinquent activity continues to be a source of controversy in the study of gangs (Klein 2011; Curry and Decker 2003; Ball and Curry 1995; Klein 1995; Spergel 1995; Bursik and Grasmick 1993). "Expanding ideas: defining 'gangs' – an irrelevant academic exercise?" describes some of the problems that arise from the difficulty of defining gangs. In an effort to confront this definitional problem, gang researchers from America and Europe held a series of meetings between 1997 and 2005. They came to agreement that a **street gang** is "any durable, street-oriented youth group whose involvement in illegal activity is part of its group identity" (Klein and Maxson 2006: 4). This definition acknowledges that both group processes and illegal activity are central to understanding gangs. Group identity is generated and maintained through group interaction, and such interaction is "durable," indicating that street gangs exist for a period of time. The definition also points to the street orientation of gangs as the locus of gang activity and as the target for gang control.

Expanding ideas: defining "gangs" – an irrelevant academic exercise?

Even though gangs have been a topic of enduring interest, there still is not a widely agreed upon definition of a *gang*. According to Scott Decker and Barrik Van Winkle (1996: 2–3):

> The lack of a consistent definition of gangs creates problems, not the least of which is the ability to compare information about gangs across cities and across different periods of times. For example, many of the groups regarded as gangs in the 1890s would not be so identified at the current time. Since not all of the illegal group activity of young people has a similar motivation or character, it is useful to have a less rigid definition of gangs. In this way, the term can capture variation across time, cities, ethnic, and age groups. However, the lack of consistent definition of gangs creates problems for public officials who must formulate a response to what is perceived as the "gang problem." Without a clear concept of what is a gang and who is a gang member, public officials find themselves responding to an amorphous, ill-defined problem. This often leads, on one hand, to denial that gangs exist or, on the other hand, to the overidentification of gangs.

Street gangs, group processes, and delinquency

"Criminological research has clearly demonstrated that gang members are more likely than nongang members to commit offenses, including serious violent offenses, and to do so with high frequency" (Thornberry et al. 1993: 55; see also Gordon et al. 2004, 2014; Melde and Esbensen 2013, 2014; Thornberry et al. 2003; Venkatesh 2000; Battin et al. 1998; Huff 1998; Thornberry and Burch 1997; Bjerregaard and Smith 1993; Esbensen and Huizinga 1993; Spergel 1990; Fagan 1989). Gang membership increases the likelihood of violent offending, in particular, as well as victimization (Pyrooz, Moule, and Decker 2014b; Melde and Esbensen 2013). The propensity for violence declines substantially after youth leave the gang (Melde and Esbensen 2013). The link between gang involvement and delinquency suggests that membership and social interaction within gangs have strong influence on the behaviors and attitudes of gang members. The question, then, is how do street gangs promote serious and violent crime?

Terrence Thornberry and his colleagues (1993) have advanced three theoretical models that try to explain how street gangs, as social groups, exert influence on their members. The **selection model** argues that gangs recruit and attract youth who are already involved in delinquency or who have a propensity for delinquency. The street gang exerts little influence on these youth other than to provide the social context in which accomplices can be found. These youth are involved in crime before, during, and after gang membership. Gangs are depicted as collections of youth with "shared incapacities" who join together only because they share similar personal problems (Spergel 1990). The **social facilitation model** contends that the link between gang membership and delinquency can best be explained in terms of gang values and expectations that encourage involvement in crime by gang members. Street gang membership provides the social context in which delinquent attitudes and techniques are learned and reinforced. Because delinquency is a product of the group processes of gangs, involvement in crime declines markedly after leaving the gang. The **enhancement model** combines aspects of the selection model and social facilitation model. Youth who are already involved in delinquent acts are attracted to and recruited by gangs because the norms and values of the gang are consistent with their own (Decker and Van Winkle 1996). Once in the gang, violence and a variety of criminal acts are expected, encouraged, and reinforced. In this way, involvement in crime is enhanced (Battin et al. 1998).

Research supports aspects of each model. Thornberry and his colleagues (1993) found that before joining a gang, gang members did not have higher rates of delinquent behavior or drug use than other youth. However, once they became gang members their rates of delinquency increased markedly. Moreover, when gang members left the gang their rates of delinquency and drug use declined (see also Sweeten, Pyrooz, and Piquero 2013). The researchers concluded that the link between gang membership and delinquency can best be explained through gang values and expectations that encourage involvement in crime by gang members – a point of view expressed in the social facilitation model. More recent research, which conceptualizes gang membership as a turning point in the life course, also demonstrates that the onset of gang membership is related to significant changes in attitudes, emotions, and routine activities that are conducive to delinquency (Melde and Esbensen 2011). In contrast, Sara Battin and her colleagues (1998) found that youth who were previously involved in delinquent acts were more likely to have delinquent friends and to join gangs. Once in gangs, youth were increasingly involved in crime, consistent with the values and behavioral expectation of the gang. Battin's research team interpreted their findings as supporting an enhancement model (see also DeLisi et al. 2009, whose research offers support for both the selection and enhancement models).

Desisting from gang involvement is a "drawn-out process" (Decker, Pyrooz, and Moule 2014; see also Pyrooz, Decker, and Webb 2014a; Pyrooz and Decker 2011). Even after gang membership ends, youth who have been involved in gangs, even briefly, continue to be at greater risk of antisocial behavior than they were prior to joining the gang (Melde and Esbensen 2014). Research framed in terms of the life-course perspective has examined the impact of gang membership in adolescence on life chances and criminal behavior in adulthood. The researchers argue that gang involvement will have negative effects on the fulfillment of conventional adult roles in both economic and family spheres, which in turn will lead to sustained involvement in crime in adulthood (Krohn et al. 2011). Marvin Krohn and his colleagues find support for these predictions.

Several **group processes** have been singled out as especially important in promoting delinquency, particularly violence, by street gang members. We focus on three group processes that have received a great deal of attention in gang research: group cohesion, status threats, and threats of violence.

Group cohesion

Although group cohesion is often viewed as an essential attribute of gangs and one that distinguishes gangs from other groups, Malcolm Klein and Lois Crawford (1967) depict the cohesion of gangs as fragile and as generated more by external forces, such as threats from rival gangs, than by internal processes of the group (see also Klein 1971, 1995; Spergel 1995). In their view, what distinguishes gangs from other social groups is not the level of cohesion but rather how cohesion is generated. Social groups derive cohesiveness from internal sources such as interpersonal attraction, common goals, shared norms and values, and stability of membership. Klein and Crawford argue that, in contrast, there are few internal sources of cohesion in gangs. Gangs have few group goals, their membership is unstable, and they have sparse norms and limited role differentiation. Even the names of gangs change often, reflecting minimal group identity.

Especially important in Klein and Crawford's view are the social interactions that promote gang cohesion (see also Papachristos 2013). As an example, they point to the communication involved in delinquent acts, including special jargon, bravado talk, and proudly recounting delinquent escapades engaged in by gang members. Klein and Crawford contend that this type of talk serves to reinforce weak affiliation bonds within the group. Thus, group offending and the social interaction that is a part of it are key to the development of gang cohesion. One of the reasons that gang members are involved in delinquency and violence is that such involvement enhances gang cohesion. A recent study that found "significantly increased mean levels of violence among gangs with relatively low group cohesion" is consistent with this view of violence as a mechanism for enhancing gang cohesion (Hughes 2013: 795).

Status threats

James Short and Fred Strodtbeck (1965) observed that gang leaders acquired and defended their leadership status largely through aggressive responses to verbal or physical challenges to their leadership – what they call "status threats." Status threats sometimes come from within the gang when gang members challenge the leader's authority, but threats may also come from external sources, such as rival gangs or even from larger institutions such as schools and from adults in the neighborhood. Internally, the status of leaders is continually called into question because of changing group membership. On the basis of an analysis of systematic notes drawn from observations by youth workers assigned to delinquent gangs, Short and Strodtbeck conclude that verbal and physical aggression directed outside the gang ("out–group aggression") is one of the few responses available to gang leaders facing status threats from within the gang. Aggressive responses to status threats are an important group process that reaffirms leadership status and generates cohesion in gangs whose structure and boundaries are typically limited and changing.

Threats of violence

Group processes related to violence are central to understanding the formation, growth, and power of gangs. In an important field study of 99 gang members in St. Louis, Scott Decker and Barrik Van Winkle (1996) use the concept of *threat* to refer to the broad and sweeping role that violence plays in the group processes of gangs. They contend that violence is probably the single most important aspect of gang culture and a key ingredient in group processes of gangs.[6] Although violence is part of everyday life for gang members, it does not always result in violent acts. Decker and Van Winkle use the term *threat* to refer to the potential for violence, either in the form of bravado, intimidation, or action. Additionally, threat of violence can be real or perceived – actually expressed through words and action or merely perceived by the gang member. Through interviews and observation, the researchers identified three group processes involving threats of violence that are key to understanding gangs.

First, in keeping with the perspective of Klein and Crawford, the researchers found that threats of violence, whether real or perceived, increase the cohesiveness of gangs (Decker and Van Winkle 1996).[7] Gang members perceive that threats and acts of violence originate primarily outside of the gang, often from rival gangs. External threats serve to strengthen relationship ties among gang members, increase commitment and loyalty to other gang members and to the gang itself, break down constraints against violence, and compel local youth to join neighborhood gangs.

Second, threats of violence have a "contagion" effect that allows gangs to increase in size and territory (Loftin 1984). Some new members join for protection because of threats of violence – threats that are either perceived or experienced. Others join gangs in search of the excitement that violence provides. In either case, violence is a catalyst for gang membership growth. In addition, research has repeatedly shown that gangs seek to maintain or extend their territory ("turf"), especially under the threat of violence by rival gangs (Decker and Van Winkle 1996; Hagedorn 1988; Suttles 1972; Short and Strodtbeck 1965). Here, too, gangs expand as a result of actual or perceived threats of violence by outsiders.

The third group process identified by Decker and Van Winkle (1996) turns the table and deals with threats of violence by gang members to conventional groups and individuals, especially in neighborhoods where gangs operate. In this instance, gangs instigate threats of violence. Such violence isolates gang members from local institutions such as families, schools, and businesses, thereby cutting them off from legitimate activities, roles, and opportunities. Decker and Van Winkle found that, as gang members became increasingly immersed in gang activities, such gang involvement was to the "virtual exclusion of all else." This social isolation, then, results in greater gang cohesiveness.

Cultural context and organizational structure

Field research in various cities and notably different cultural contexts reveals that urban gangs differ significantly in level of organization, leadership, roles, and rules (Coughlin and Vernkatesh 2003; Decker and Van Winkle 1996; Hagedorn 1988; Vigil 1988; Klein 1971; Short and Strodtbeck 1963; Yablonsky 1959, 1962; Thrasher 1927; see also Bouchard and Spindler 2010). Classic studies by Malcolm Klein in Los Angeles and James Short and Fred Strodtbeck in Chicago, for example, revealed that the gangs were only minimally organized. Most activities were not purposive or well organized. Leadership was not firmly established, but was challenged frequently, resulting in limited power and authority. Membership was shifting, and allegiances and loyalty faltered over time. Cohesiveness was largely a product of external, rather than internal, forces (Klein 1971; Short and Strodtbeck 1963).[8]

In contrast, Joan Moore's (1978, 1991) study of gang members in the Mexican American neighborhoods of East Los Angeles found strong ethnic culture influences on the structure and activities of gangs in this area. Moore reported three distinctive characteristics of Chicano gangs. She found that they were (1) territorially based; (2) strongly age-graded, resulting in smaller age cohort groups called "klikas"; and (3) predominated by fighting. The ethnic culture of Chicano gangs resulted in an emphasis on protection of gang territory, or "turf"; physical toughness, or "machismo"; and status, often referred to as "honor." Grounded in this common culture, Moore found that Chicano gangs were highly structured, with distinct leadership and roles, and extensive behavioral expectations (norms). In this case, gang culture and organizational structure appear to go hand-in-hand: cultural cohesiveness provides foundation to the organizational structure of gangs, while gang structure institutionalizes gang culture.

While Moore's research focused on the cultural context of Chicano gangs, Martin Sanchez Jankowski's (1991) ambitious field study included 37 gangs of several different ethnicities: Chicano, Dominican, Puerto Rican, Central American, African American, and Irish. Based on observation of these urban gangs in low-income areas of New York, Boston, and Los Angeles, Jankowski claimed that gangs are more organized than they are traditionally portrayed and that gang culture is the organizing force behind gang structure. He found that low-income neighborhoods revolve around an "intense competition for, and conflict over, the scarce resources that exist in these areas" (Jankowski 1991: 22). With such intense competition, gang members have to be "defiant individualists" who are aggressive and self-reliant, with strong survival skills. Most of the gangs that Jankowski studied displayed a hierarchical structure with leadership and roles, and a system of norms and values that he called "formal codes" and "collective ideology." These mechanisms of internal organization regulated the behavior of gang members and provided them with a common worldview. Unified with an organizational structure, together with common values and norms, Jankowski described gangs as "formal-rational" organizations. In addition, gang structure usually involved organized means for acquiring both legal and illegal income. These urban gangs were in conflict (culturally and economically) not only with rival gangs, but also with legitimate neighborhood organizations, such as schools and churches. Conflict solidified internal organization and generated gang cohesiveness (Klein and Crawford 1967).

Gang culture, however, has not always been found to be the primary force behind gang organizational structure. Ruth Horowitz (1983) studied a single Chicano gang in Chicago, called the "Lions." As Moore found in the gangs of East Los Angeles, Horowitz observed that the Lions placed great emphasis on "honor," achieved primarily through fighting. Given limited educational and occupational opportunities, gang membership provided the primary arena in which honor could be achieved through demonstrations of toughness or machismo. Although the Lions displayed collective goals, distinct roles, and stable membership, there were few membership rules and an unclear structure, especially in terms of leadership. Horowitz characterized the gang as having considerable flexibility, and, at the same time, as being a strong presence in the neighborhood that appeared to reinforce Chicano culture.

Similar to the works of Moore and of Horowitz, James Diego Vigil's (1988) study of Hispanic gang members in Los Angeles found Chicano culture to have a strong influence on barrio (neighborhood) gangs. According to Vigil, barrio youth are "marginalized" from American society because of their low economic status and distinctive Chicano culture. As a result, barrio youth are not socialized into mainstream society and they do not aspire to the "American Dream" of economic success, nor do they have opportunities to achieve success. Instead, barrio youth turn to gangs for identity. Fighting and threats of violence are a constant feature of barrio gang life, primarily because violence provides a means to achieve identity in Chicano culture. Violence is expressed through threats and acts toward both fellow gang members and people outside the gang, sometimes from rival gangs and sometimes from the barrio. As a result, the strong cultural emphasis on violence appeared to limit development of gang structure; barrio gangs display only limited structure in terms of leadership, roles, and rules.

The organizational structure of contemporary gangs is also related to involvement in crime, including both violent crime and drug sales. Scott Decker and his colleagues found that even low levels of gang organization influenced behavior, and even small increases in levels of gang organization were related to increased involvement in offending and victimization (Decker, Katz, and Webb 2008). Earlier research also shows a link between gang organizational structure and the degree to which gangs are involved in drug sales (Howell 1998; Padilla 1992; Taylor 1990). Felix Padilla (1992) conducted an important study of a Puerto Rican Chicago gang, called the "Diamonds," that he described as an "ethnic enterprise" engaged in street drug sales.[9] Although gang members participated in a variety of activities unrelated to crime (e.g., "hanging out" and playing basketball), street drug sales were the primary organizing force of the gang. Drug sales were a collective activity requiring a hierarchical organizational structure with authoritative leadership, distinct roles, and far-reaching rules. Padilla reported that gang members progressed through different roles in drug sales, graduating from "mules," who transported drugs, to "runners," who sold drugs on the street. Leadership was assumed when gang members became involved in the supply of drugs. Career development of gang members was governed by a clear set of rules for drug sales. Among gang members, street drug sales were referred to as "work," and the organizational structure of the gang allowed the work to be conducted like a business. Drug sales, however, did not appear to result in tremendous profit for the gang or individual gang members; instead, proceeds funded typical adolescent pursuits, such as food, clothing, and parties (Padilla 1992; see also Decker and Van Winkle 1996).

Padilla interprets the elaborate organizational structure of the Diamonds as an "ethnic enterprise" because drug trade serves as a "rational" response to the low status and limited opportunities of Puerto Rican youth living in poverty. Like Moore and Vigil, Padilla explains that gang membership provides a viable solution to ethnic youth who are marginalized by Anglo society and by the negative evaluations of schools, neighborhood groups, and even their own families. Gang members saw the decision to join a gang as a constructive decision, not a matter of coercion.

All these studies share an emphasis on the social context in which street gangs emerge and operate. Their existence and persistence are based on a community environment conducive to gangs. As a result, gang prevention and intervention strategies must be directed at the social context of street gangs. "Theory into practice: factors associated with gang membership" lists the key social factors associated with gang membership. "Theory into practice: gang intervention strategies – the Comprehensive Gang Model" summarizes a gang intervention strategy sponsored by the Office of Juvenile Justice and Delinquency Prevention.

Theory into practice: factors associated with gang membership

In recent years, theory and research have identified a number of key factors associated with gang membership. James Howell (1998: 6–7), formerly of the National Youth Gang Center, compiled the following list of factors related to gang membership. The factors are divided into five categories.

Community

- Social disorganization, including poverty and residential mobility
- Organized lower class communities
- Underclass communities
- Presence of gangs in neighborhoods
- Availability of drugs in neighborhoods
- Availability of firearms
- Barriers to and lack of social and economic opportunities
- Lack of social capital
- Cultural norms supporting gang behavior
- Feeling unsafe in neighborhood; high crime
- Conflict with social control institutions

Family

- Family disorganization, including broken homes and parental drug/alcohol abuse
- Troubled families, including incest, family violence, and drug addiction
- Family members in a gang
- Lack of adult male role models
- Lack of parental role models
- Low socioeconomic status
- Extreme economic deprivation, family management problems, parents with violent attitudes, sibling antisocial behavior

School

- Academic failure
- Low educational aspirations, especially among females

- Negative labeling by teachers
- Trouble at school
- Few teacher role models
- Educational frustration
- Low commitment to school, low school attachment, high levels of antisocial behavior in school, low achievement test scores, and identification as being learning disabled

Peer group

- High commitment to delinquent peers
- Low commitment to positive peers
- Street socialization
- Gang members in class
- Friends who use drugs or who are gang members
- Friends who are drug distributors
- Interaction with delinquent peers

Individual

- Prior delinquency
- Deviant attitudes
- Street smartness; toughness
- Defiant and individualistic character
- Fatalistic view of the world
- Aggression
- Proclivity for excitement and trouble
- Locura (acting in a daring, courageous, and especially crazy fashion in the face of adversity)
- Higher levels of normlessness in the context of family, peer group, and school
- Social disabilities
- Illegal gun ownership
- Early or precocious sexual activity, especially among females
- Alcohol and drug use
- Drug trafficking
- Desire for group rewards such as status, identity, self-esteem, companionship, and protection
- Problem behaviors, hyperactivity, externalizing behaviors, drinking, lack of refusal skills, and early sexual activity
- Victimization

Theory into practice: gang intervention strategies – the Comprehensive Gang Model

"The *Comprehensive Gang Model* is the product of a national gang research and development program that OJJDP initiated in the mid-1980s. A national assessment of gang problems and programs provided the research foundation for the Model, and its key components mirror the best features of existing and evaluated programs across the country." Five key strategies guide the Comprehensive Gang Model. Gang intervention programs that have adopted these strategies and have been evaluated as successful are offered as "Best Practices to Address Community Gang Problems":

- **Community mobilization.** Involvement of local citizens, including former gang-involved youth, community groups, agencies, and coordination of programs and staff functions within and across agencies.
- **Opportunities provision.** Development of a variety of specific education, training, and employment programs targeting gang-involved youth.
- **Social intervention.** Involving youth-serving agencies, schools, grassroots groups, faith-based organizations, police, and other juvenile/criminal justice organizations in "reaching out" to gang-involved youth and their families and linking them with the conventional world and needed services.
- **Suppression.** Formal and informal social control procedures, including close supervision and monitoring of gang-involved youth by agencies of the juvenile/criminal justice system and also by community-based agencies, schools, and grassroots groups.
- **Organizational change and development.** Development and implementation of policies and procedures that result in the most effective use of available and potential resources, within and across agencies, to better address the gang problem.

Source: National Youth Gang Center (2008: 1, 2).

Gender, race, and class differences in gang participation

Gangs differ not only in terms of cultural context and organizational structure, but also in terms of the gender, race and ethnicity, and social class of members. Most research in the 1960s and 1970s focused on gangs as homogeneous groups, composed mainly of black, inner-city boys. In the last few decades, gang research has broadened the scope of attention to include female and mixed-sex gangs; Asian, Latino, multiracial, and multiethnic gangs; and suburban and rural gangs (Coughlin and Venkatesh 2003).

The gender composition of gangs takes at least three forms: gangs that have both male and female members (mixed-sex gangs), female gangs that are affiliated with male gangs, and independent "girl gangs." Although the level and nature of female gang involvement varies depending on these gang forms, roughly 30 percent of the overall gang population is female (Coughlin and Venkatesh 2003; Curry and Decker 2003; Bjerregaard and Smith 1993; Esbensen and Huizinga 1993). Even though it is difficult to characterize female participation in gangs, research shows consistently that female gang members are less delinquent than their male counterparts, and this is especially true for gang violence (Coughlin and Venkatesh 2003; Curry and Decker 2003). Female gang members also report less frequent offending than do male gang members for all types of offenses (Bjerregaard and Smith 1993; Esbensen and Huizinga 1993). Nonetheless, gang membership leads to higher rates of offending for females, compared to females not in a gang, as is the case with males (Coughlin and Venkatesh 2003).

Females join gangs for many of the same reasons as males (Bell 2009), yet female gang members are more likely than male gang members to come from dysfunctional families characterized by abuse, conflict, and drug addiction (Miller 2001; Moore and Hagedorn 1996). In addition, females are more likely than males to join gangs as an escape from sexual oppression and exploitation that they have experienced or that they anticipate in the future (Campbell 1984).

Although the racial and ethnic composition of gangs is a matter of much debate among gang researchers, most agree that:

> gangs tend to attract individuals who find themselves at the bottom of the social and economic ladder in society. Just as the gangs of the 1890s and 1920s were composed of Irish and Italian youths, representing groups struggling for inclusion in the economic and social mainstream, Latinos/as and African Americans constitute the modal category of gang membership today.
>
> (Curry and Decker 2003: 80)

Data provided by law enforcement agencies reporting gang problems indicate that, in 2011, 46 percent of gang members were Hispanic, 35 percent were African American, 11 percent were white, and 7 percent were other races or ethnicities (National Gang Center n.d.). Studies based on self-report data find relatively equal numbers of white and black gangs in urban areas (Coughlin and Venkatesh 2003). Thus, minority status, in terms of race and ethnicity, and disadvantaged social class place certain groups of youth at greater risk for street gang involvement (Pyrooz, Fox, and Decker 2010).

Summary and conclusions

Many delinquent acts are committed with peers, and youth who commit crimes with peers commit more offenses and are involved in more serious offenses than youth acting alone. Delinquent youth also tend to have delinquent friends. In fact, the number of delinquent friends a youth has and the extent of their delinquency is one of the best predictors of that youth's delinquency. Despite these clear and consistent findings, the extent and nature of peer influences are subjects of much debate.

Learning theories such as differential association theory and social learning theory contend that peer groups provide an intimate social context in which delinquent behavior is learned. Such learning occurs through communication, modeling, imitation, and reinforcement among peers. Peer group association has the greatest influence when it occurs often, for longer periods, and when relationship ties are strong and intimate. In contrast, control theories minimize the importance of peer group influences, arguing that delinquency results from weak social bonds or from lack of self-control. Delinquent youth seek out peers with similar attitudes and behaviors, and therefore delinquent peers are a result of involvement in delinquency, not a cause.

Analysis of peer group influence partially resolves this debate. Adolescents appear to develop friendships with delinquent peers before becoming involved in delinquent acts. Exposure to delinquent attitudes and behaviors is an important component of peer influence. More frequent and extensive association with delinquent peers leads to greater involvement in delinquency. In addition, the strength of relationship bonds affects the degree to which delinquent peers have influence. Once friendships are established, peer group interaction promotes attitudes and behaviors that encourage continued delinquency.

Although delinquent peers play an important role in the initiation and continuation of delinquency, not all delinquent acts are group offenses. Some offenses such as robbery, shoplifting, and most status offenses are committed as often, or even more often, by solitary offenders.

Even so, the offenses that juveniles commit most frequently, such as alcohol and marijuana violations, minor theft, and vandalism, are most often committed in groups. The delinquent career of most juvenile offenders is characterized by a mix of offenses committed alone and offenses committed with co-offenders.

Because delinquent groups tend to be small and transitory, delinquent youths typically commit offenses with only two or three other youths, and these companions change frequently, being drawn from a larger network of friends. Offenders typically commit only a small number of delinquent acts with the same group and, as a result, delinquents belong to multiple groups over the course of their delinquent careers.

Gangs constitute an important aspect of peer influence. Gang members commit more frequent and more serious crime, compared to delinquent youth who are not gang members. Group processes related to group cohesion, status, and threat of violence are central to understanding how gangs influence the behavior of members. In addition, group characteristics such as gang culture and organizational structure provide the social context for group processes.

Critical-thinking questions

1. As described in the "Case in point" at the beginning of the chapter, what does Sidney's delinquent career tell us about the nature of involvement in delinquent groups?
2. According to differential association theory, how does group association vary? How is this variation important to peer group influences?
3. How does social learning theory extend differential association theory?
4. Distinguish between the *socialization* and *selection* perspectives on peer group involvement.
5. What role do peers play in drug use?
6. What group processes are part of gang involvement?

Suggested reading

Coughlin, Brenda C. and Sudhir Alladi Venkatesh. 2003. "The Urban Street Gang After 1970." *Annual Review of Sociology* 29: 41–64.

Decker, Scott H. and Barrik Van Winkle. 1996. *Life in the Gang: Family, Friends, and Violence.* New York: Cambridge University Press.

Giordano, Peggy C., Stephen A. Cernkovich, and M. D. Pugh. 1986. "Friendship and Delinquency." *American Journal of Sociology* 5: 1170–1202.

Haynie, Dana L, Nathan J. Doogan, and Brian Soller. 2014. "Gender, Friendship Networks, and Delinquency: A Dynamic Network Approach." *Criminology* 52: 688–722.

Kreager, Derek A., Kelly Rulison, and James Moody. 2011. "Delinquency and the Structure of Adolescent Peer Groups." *Criminology* 49: 95–127.

Warr, Mark. 2002. *Companions in Crime: The Social Aspects of Criminal Conduct.* New York: Cambridge University Press.

Useful websites

For further information relevant to this chapter, go to the following web sites.

- Monitoring the Future study of trends in drug use and delinquency, Institute for Social Research at the University of Michigan (http://monitoringthefuture.org/)
- National Gang Center, Office of Juvenile Justice and Delinquency Prevention, and Bureau of Justice Assistance (www.nationalgangcenter.gov/)

- Gang Resistance Education and Training (G.R.E.A.T.), Office of Juvenile Justice and Delinquency Prevention (www.great-online.org/)

Glossary of key terms

Co-offending: Commitment of delinquent acts in the company of peers.

Definitions of the law: A person defines the law as favorable or unfavorable – either as rules to obey or to violate. A person's attitudes and beliefs toward the law, its legitimacy, and authority.

Differential association: Association with different groups. According to differential association theory, association with groups varies in frequency, duration, priority, and intensity.

Differential reinforcement: The social processes and dynamics of rewards and punishments that are the basis of learning.

Enhancement model of gang formation and influence: The view that youth who are already involved in delinquent acts are attracted to and recruited by gangs because the norms and values of the gang are consistent with their own. This model incorporates the selection perspective of peer group relations.

Group processes: The ways in which relationships and interactions within groups influence the attitudes and behaviors of individuals.

Imitation: The copying of behavior displayed or modeled by others.

Operant conditioning: The process by which behavior is shaped by rewards and punishments.

Selection model of gang formation and influence: The view that gangs recruit and attract youth who are already involved in delinquency or who have a propensity for delinquency. The street gang exerts little influence on these youth other than to provide the social context in which accomplices can be found.

Selection perspective: The tendency to seek out individuals like oneself, with similar attitudes, values, beliefs, and behaviors. These characteristics become the criteria for choosing friends, rather than the product of friendship.

Social facilitation model of gang formation and influence: The view that the normative support and group processes of gangs encourage, support, and reinforce commission of crime. The social facilitation model incorporates the socialization perspective of peer group relations.

Social learning: The concept that delinquent and criminal behavior is learned through social interaction in groups.

Socialization perspective: The view that peer group relations are strong, cohesive, and long-lasting and are therefore able to exert strong influence on those involved. Peer group relations and interactions are the context in which attitudes and behavior are learned and reinforced.

Street gang: A durable, street-oriented group of youth whose involvement in illegal activity is part of its group identity (Klein and Maxson 2006: 4).

Notes

1. A recent study by Stolzenberg and D'Alessio (2008) contradicts this well-documented finding, presenting data from seven states which suggest that most juvenile offenses are not perpetrated in the company of others.
2. Haynie and Osgood (2005) refer to this perspective as "normative influence."

3. To explore the issue of intensity of friendships and delinquency, researchers have also examined the influence of one's best friend on delinquency, relative to the influence of the remaining friendship group (Rees and Pogarsky 2011).
4. McGloin et al. (2008) found that although the transitory nature of delinquent groups was true for most offenders, there was considerable individual variation depending on frequency of offending and size of the delinquent group.
5. This observation is based on Hagedorn (1988). See also Spergel (1990).
6. Spergel (1995) and Howell (1998) similarly contend that violence is a distinctive feature of gang life. See also Short (1998) and Short and Strodtbeck (1965).
7. This observation is consistent not only with Klein and Crawford (1967), but also with a wide range of research on gangs, including Hagedorn (1988) and Padilla (1992).
8. See Thornberry et al. (2003) for a different point of view.
9. Similar observations are made by Taylor (1990) in a study of Detroit gangs.

References

Agnew, Robert. 1991. "The Interactive Effects of Peer Variables on Delinquency." *Criminology* 29: 47–72.
Akers, Ronald L. 1985. *Deviant Behavior: A Social Learning Approach.* 3rd edn. Belmont, CA: Wadsworth.
Akers, Ronald L. 1991. "Self-Control as a General Theory of Crime." *Journal of Quantitative Criminology* 7: 201–211.
Akers, Ronald L. and Christine S. Sellers. 2013. *Criminological Theories: Introduction, Evaluation, and Application.* 6th edn. New York: Oxford University Press.
Altschuler, David M. and Paul J. Brounstein. 1991. "Patterns of Drug Use, Drug Trafficking, and Other Delinquency among Inner-City Adolescent Males in Washington, DC." *Criminology* 29: 581–621.
Augustyn, Megan Bears and Jean Marie McGloin. 2013. "The Risk of Informal Socializing with Peers: Considering Gender Differences across Predatory Delinquency and Substance Use." *Justice Quarterly* 30: 117–143.
Ball, Richard A. and G. David Curry. 1995. "The Logic of Definition in Criminology: Purposes and Methods for Defining 'Gangs.'" *Criminology* 33: 225–245.
Battin, Sara R., Karl G. Hill, Robert D. Abbott, Richard F. Catalano, and J. David Hawkins. 1998. "The Contribution of Gang Membership to Delinquency beyond Delinquent Friends." *Criminology* 36: 93–115.
Bell, Kerryn E. 2009. "Gender and Gangs: A Quantitative Comparison." *Crime and Delinquency* 55: 363–387.
Bjerregaard, B. and C. Smith. 1993. "Gender Differences in Gang Participation, Delinquency, and Substance Use." *Journal of Quantitative Criminology* 9: 329–355.
Bouchard, Martin and Andrea Spindler. 2010. "Groups, Gangs, and Delinquency: Does Organization Matter?" *Journal of Criminal Justice* 38: 921–933.
Burgess, Robert L. and Ronald L. Akers. 1966. "A Differential Association–Reinforcement Theory of Criminal Behavior." *Social Problems* 14: 128–147.
Bursik, Robert J., Jr. and Harold G. Grasmick. 1993. *Neighborhoods and Crime: The Dimensions of Effective Community Control.* New York: Lexington Books.
Campbell, Anne. 1984. *The Girls in the Gang.* New York: Basil Blackwell.
Chapple, Constance, Jamie Vaske, and Meredith G. F. Worthen. 2014. "Gender Differences in Associations with Deviant Peer Groups: Examining Individual, Interactional, and Compositional Factors." *Deviant Behavior* 35: 394–411.
Conway, Kevin P. and Joan McCord. 2002. "A Longitudinal Examination of the Relation between Co-Offending with Violent Accomplices and Violent Crime." *Aggressive Behavior* 28: 97–108.
Conway, Kevin P. and Joan McCord. 2005. "Co-Offending and Patterns of Juvenile Crime." *Research in Brief.* Washington, DC: Office of Juvenile Justice and Delinquency Prevention.

Coughlin, Brenda C. and Sudhir Alladi Venkatesh. 2003. "The Urban Street Gang after 1970." *Annual Review of Sociology* 29: 41–64.

Curry, G. David and Scott H. Decker. 2003. *Confronting Gangs: Crime and Community*. 2nd edn. Los Angeles: Roxbury.

Decker, Scott H., Charles M. Katz, and Vincent J. Webb. 2008. "Understanding the Black Box of Gang Organization: Implications for Involvement in Violent Crime, Drug Sales, and Violent Victimization." *Crime and Delinquency* 54: 153–172.

Decker, Scott H., David D. Pyrooz, and Richard K. Moule. 2014. "Disengagement from Gangs as Role Transitions." *Journal of Research on Adolescence* 24: 268–283.

Decker, Scott H. and Barrik Van Winkle. 1996. *Life in the Gang: Family, Friends, and Violence*. New York: Cambridge University Press.

DeLisi, Matt, J. C. Barnes, Kevin M. Beaver, and Chris L. Gibson. 2009. "Delinquent Gangs and Adolescent Victimization Revisited." *Criminal Justice and Behavior* 36: 808–823.

Egley, Arlen, Jr., James C. Howell, and Meena Harris. 2014. "Highlights of the 2012 National Youth Gang Survey." Washington, DC: Office of Juvenile Justice and Delinquency Prevention.

Elliott, Delbert S., David Huizinga, and Suzanne S. Ageton. 1985. *Explaining Delinquency and Drug Use*. Beverly Hills, CA: Sage.

Elliott, Delbert S., David Huizinga, and Scott Menard. 1989. *Multiple Problem Youth: Delinquency, Substance Use, and Mental Health Problems*. New York: Springer-Verlag.

Elliott, Delbert S. and Scott Menard. 1996. "Delinquent Friends and Delinquent Behavior: Temporal and Developmental Patterns." Pp. 28–67 in *Delinquency and Crime*, ed. J. D. Hawkins. New York: Cambridge University Press.

Erickson, Maynard L. 1971. "The Group Context of Delinquent Behavior." *Social Problems* 19: 114–129.

Erickson, Maynard L. and LaMar T. Empey. 1965. "Class Position, Peers, and Delinquency." *Sociology and Social Research* 49: 268–282.

Erickson, Maynard L. and Gary F. Jensen. 1977. "Delinquency Is Still Group Behavior! Toward Revitalizing the Group Premise in the Sociology of Deviance." *Journal of Criminal Law and Criminology* 68: 262–273.

Esbensen, Finn-Aage and David Huizinga. 1993. "Gangs, Drugs, and Delinquency in a Survey of Urban Youth." *Criminology* 31: 565–589.

Fagan, Jeffrey. 1989. "The Social Organization of Drug Use and Drug Dealing among Urban Gangs." *Criminology* 27: 633–669.

Gilligan, Carol. 1982. *In a Different Voice: Psychological Theory and Women's Development*. Cambridge, MA: Harvard University Press.

Giordano, Peggy C., Stephen A. Cernkovich, and M. D. Pugh. 1986. "Friendship and Delinquency." *American Journal of Sociology* 5: 1170–1202.

Glueck, Sheldon and Eleanor Glueck. 1950. *Unraveling Juvenile Delinquency*. Cambridge, MA: Harvard University Press.

Gold, Martin. 1970. *Delinquent Behavior in an American City*. Belmont, CA: Brooks-Cole.

Gordon, Rachel A., Benjamin B. Lahey, Eriko Kawai, Rolf Loeber, Magda Stouthamer-Loeber, and David P. Farrington. 2004. "Antisocial Behavior and Youth Gang Membership: Selection and Socialization." *Criminology* 42: 55–89.

Gordon, Rachel A., Hillary L. Rowe, Dustin Pardini, Rolf Loeber, Helene Raskin White, and David P. Farrington. 2014. "Serious Delinquency and Gang Participation: Combining and Specializing in Drug Selling, Theft, and Violence." *Journal of Research on Adolescence* 24: 235–251.

Gottfredson, Michael R. and Travis Hirschi. 1990. *A General Theory of Crime*. Stanford University Press.

Hagedorn, John M. 1988. *People and Folks: Gangs, Crime, and the Underclass in a Rustbelt City*. Chicago: Lakeview Press.

Haynie, Dana L, Nathan J. Doogan, and Brian Soller. 2014. "Gender, Friendship Networks, and Delinquency: A Dynamic Network Approach." *Criminology* 52: 688–722.

Haynie, Dana L. and D. Wayne Osgood. 2005. "Reconsidering Peers and Delinquency: How do Peers Matter? *Social Forces* 84: 1109–1130.

Haynie, Dana L. and Danielle C. Payne. 2006. "Race, Friendship Networks, and Violent Delinquency." *Criminology* 44: 775–805.

Haynie, Dana L., Eric Silver, and Brent Teasdale. 2006. "Neighborhood Characteristics, Peer Networks, and Adolescent Violence." *Journal of Quantitative Criminology* 22: 147–169.

Henneberger, Angela K., Myles I. Durkee, Nancy Truong, Avis Atkins, and Patrick H. Tolan. 2013. "The Longitudinal Relationship between Peer Violence and Popularity and Delinquency in Adolescent Boys: Examining Effects by Family Functioning." *Journal of Youth and Adolescence* 42: 1651–1660.

Hepburn, John R. 1976. "Testing Alternative Models of Delinquency Causation." *Journal of Criminal Law and Criminology* 67: 450–460.

Hindelang, Michael J. 1971. "The Social versus Solitary Nature of Delinquent Involvements." *British Journal of Criminology* 11: 167–175.

Hirschi, Travis. 1969. *Causes of Delinquency*. Berkeley, CA: University of California Press.

Hirschi, Travis. 1987. "Review of *Explaining Delinquency and Drug Use*, by Delbert S. Elliott, David Huizinga, and Suzanne S. Ageton." *Criminology* 25: 193–201.

Horowitz, Ruth. 1983. *Honor and the American Dream*. New Brunswick, NJ: Rutgers University Press.

Howell, James C. 1998. "Youth Gangs: An Overview." *Juvenile Justice Bulletin: Youth Gang Series*. Washington, DC: Office of Juvenile Justice and Delinquency Prevention.

Huff, C. Ronald. 1998. "Comparing the Criminal Behavior of Youth Gangs and At-Risk Youths." Washington, DC: Office of Justice Programs.

Hughes, Lorine A. 2013. "Group Cohesiveness, Gang Member Prestige, and Delinquency and Violence in Chicago, 1959–1962." *Criminology* 51: 795–832.

Huizinga, David A., Rolf Loeber, and Terence Thornberry. 1991. "Urban Delinquency and Substance Abuse." Washington DC: Office of Juvenile Justice and Delinquency Prevention.

Huizinga, David A., Scott Menard, and Delbert S. Elliott. 1989. "Delinquency and Drug Use: Temporal and Developmental Patterns." *Justice Quarterly* 6: 419–455.

Inciardi, James A., Ruth Horowitz, and Anne E. Pottieger. 1993. *Street Kids, Street Drugs, and Street Crime: An Examination of Drug Use and Serious Delinquency in Miami*. Belmont, CA: Wadsworth.

Jankowski, Martin Sanchez. 1991. *Islands in the Street: Gangs in American Urban Society*. Berkeley, CA: University of California Press.

Johnson, Richard E. 1979. *Juvenile Delinquency and Its Origins: An Integrated Theoretical Approach*. New York: Cambridge University Press.

Johnson, Richard E., Anastasios C. Marcos, and Stephen J. Bahr. 1987. "The Role of Peers in the Complex Etiology of Adolescent Drug Use." *Criminology* 25: 323–339.

Kandel, Denise B. 1978. "Homophily, Selection, and Socialization in Adolescent Friendships." *American Journal of Sociology* 84: 427–436.

Kandel, Denise B. and Mark Davies. 1991. "Friendship Networks, Intimacy, and Illicit Drug Use in Young Adulthood: A Comparison of Two Competing Theories." *Criminology* 29: 441–467.

Kandel, Denise B., R. C. Kessler, and R. Z. Margulies. 1978. "Antecedents of Adolescent Initiation into Stages of Drug Use: A Developmental Analysis." *Journal of Youth and Adolescence* 7: 13–40.

Klein, Malcolm W. 1971. *Street Gangs and Street Workers*. Englewood Cliffs, NJ: Prentice Hall.

Klein, Malcolm W. 1995. *The American Street Gang: Its Nature, Prevalence and Control*. New York: Oxford University Press.

Klein, Malcolm W. 2011. "Who Can You Believe? Complexities of International Street Gang Research." *International Criminal Justice Review* 21: 197–207.

Klein, Malcolm W. and Lois Y. Crawford. 1967. "Groups, Gangs, and Cohesiveness." *Journal of Research in Crime and Delinquency* 4: 63–75.

Klein, Malcolm W. and Cheryl L. Maxson. 2006. *Street Gang Patterns and Policies*. New York: Oxford University Press.

Kreager, Derek A., Kelly Rulison, and James Moody. 2011. "Delinquency and the Structure of Adolescent Peer Groups." *Criminology* 49: 95–127.

Krohn, Marvin D., Alan J. Lizotte, Terence P. Thornberry, Carolyn Smith, and David McDowall. 1996. "Reciprocal Causal Relationships among Drug Use, Peers, and Beliefs: A Five-Wave Panel Model." *Journal of Drug Issues* 26: 405–428.

Krohn, Marvin D., Jeffrey T. Ward, Terence P. Thornberry, Alan J. Lizotte, and Rebekah Chu. 2011. "The Cascading Effects of Adolescent Gang Involvement across the Life Course." *Criminology* 49: 991–1028.

Loftin, Colin. 1984. "Assaultive Violence as a Contagious Process." *Bulletin of the New York Academy of Medicine* 62: 550–555.

Longshore, Douglas, Eunice Chang, and Shih-Chao Hsieh. 2004. "Self-Control and Social Bonds: A Combined Control Perspective on Deviance." *Crime and Delinquency* 50: 542–564.

McGloin, Jean Marie. 2009. "Delinquency Balance: Revisiting Peer Influence." *Criminology* 47: 439–477.

McGloin, Jean Marie, Christopher J. Sullivan, Alex R. Piquero, and Sarah Bacon. 2008. "Investigating the Stability of Co-Offending and Co-Offenders among a Sample of Youthful Offenders." *Criminology* 46: 155–188.

Marcos, Anastasios C., Stephen J. Bahr, and Richard E. Johnson. 1986. "Test of a Bonding/Association Theory of Adolescent Drug Use." *Social Forces* 65: 135–161.

Matsueda, Ross L. 1988. "The Current State of Differential Association Theory." *Crime and Delinquency* 34: 277–306.

Matsueda, Ross L. and Kathleen Anderson. 1998. "The Dynamics of Delinquent Peers and Delinquent Behavior." *Criminology* 36: 269–308.

Matsueda, Ross L. and Karen Heimer. 1987. "Race, Family Structure and Delinquency: A Test of Differential Association and Control Theories." *American Sociological Review* 52: 826–840.

Mears, Daniel, Matthew Ploeger, and Mark Warr. 1998. "Explaining the Gender Gap in Delinquency: Peer Influence and Moral Evaluations of Behavior." *Criminology* 35: 251–266.

Megens, Kim C. I. M. and Frank M. Weerman. 2012. "The Social Transmission of Delinquency: Effects of Peer Attitudes and Behavior Revisited." *Journal of Research in Crime and Delinquency* 49: 420–443.

Melde, Chris and Finn-Aage Esbensen. 2011. "Gang Membership as a Turning Point in the Life Course." *Criminology* 49: 513–552.

Melde, Chris and Finn-Aage Esbensen. 2013. "Gangs and Violence: Disentangling the Impact of Gang Membership on the Level and Nature of Offending." *Journal of Quantitative Criminology* 29: 143–166.

Melde, Chris and Finn-Aage Esbensen. 2014. "The Relative Impact of Gang Status Transitions: Identifying the Mechanisms of Change in Delinquency." *Journal of Research in Crime and Delinquency* 51: 349–376.

Menard, Scott and Delbert S. Elliott. 1990. "Longitudinal and Cross-Sectional Data Collection and Analysis in the Study of Crime & Delinquency." *Justice Quarterly* 7: 11–55.

Menard, Scott and Delbert S. Elliott. 1994. "Delinquent Bonding, Moral Belief, and Illegal Behavior: A Three-Wave Panel Model." *Justice Quarterly* 11: 173–188.

Miller, Holly Ventura. 2010. "If Your Friends Jumped Off of a Bridge, Would You Do It Too? Delinquent Peers and Susceptibility to Peer Influence." *Justice Quarterly* 27: 473–491.

Miller, Jody. 2001. *One of the Guys: Gangs, Girls, and Gender.* New York: Oxford University Press.

Miller, Walter B. 1980. "Gangs, Groups, and Serious Youth Crime." Pp. 115–138 in *Critical Issues in Juvenile Delinquency*, ed. D. Schichor and D. H. Kelly. Lexington, MA: D. C. Heath.

Moore, Joan W. 1978. *Homeboys: Gangs, Drugs, and Prisons in the Barrios of Los Angeles.* Philadelphia: Temple University Press.

Moore, Joan W. 1991. *Going Down to the Barrio: Homeboys and Homegirls in Change.* Philadelphia: Temple University Press.

Moore, Joan W. and John Hagedorn. 1996. "What Happens to Girls in the Gang?" Pp. 205–218 in *Gangs in America*. 2nd edn., ed. C. R. Huff. Thousand Oaks, CA: Sage.

Morash, Merry. 1983. "Gangs, Groups, and Delinquency." *British Journal of Criminology* 23: 309–331.

National Gang Center. n.d. *National Youth Gang Survey Analysis*. Retrieved February 5, 2015 (www.nationalgangcenter.gov/Survey-Analysis/Demographics).

National Youth Gang Center. 2008. "Best Practices to Address Community Gang Problems – OJJDP's Comprehensive Gang Model." Washington, DC: Office of Juvenile Justice and Delinquency Prevention.

Padilla, Felix M. 1992. *The Gang as an American Enterprise*. New Brunswick, NJ: Rutgers University Press.

Papachristos, Andrew V. 2013. "The Importance of Cohesion for Gang Research, Policy, and Practice." *Criminology and Public Policy* 12: 49–58.

Pyrooz, David C. and Scott H. Decker. 2011. "Motives and Methods for Leaving the Gang: Understanding the Process of Gang Desistance." *Journal of Criminal Justice* 39: 417–425.

Pyrooz, David C., Scott H. Decker, and Vincent J. Webb. 2014a. "The Ties That Bind: Desistance from Gangs." *Crime and Delinquency* 60: 491–516.

Pyrooz, David C., Andrew M. Fox, and Scott H. Decker. 2010. "Racial and Ethnic Heterogeneity, Economic Disadvantage, and Gangs: A Macro-Level Study of Gang Membership in Urban America." *Justice Quarterly* 27: 867–892.

Pyrooz, David C., Richard K. Moule Jr., and Scott H. Decker. 2014b. "The Contribution of Gang Membership to the Victim–Offender Overlap." *Journal of Research in Crime and Delinquency* 51: 315–348.

Rees, Carter and Greg Pogarsky. 2011. "One Bad Apple May Not Spoil the Whole Bunch: Best Friends and Adolescent Delinquency." *Journal of Quantitative Criminology* 27: 197–223.

Reiss, Albert J., Jr. 1988. "Co-Offending and Criminal Careers." Pp. 117–170 in *Crime and Justice: A Review of Research*, vol. 10, ed. M. Tonry and N. Morris. University of Chicago Press.

Reiss, Albert J., Jr. and David P. Farrington. 1991. "Advancing Knowledge about Co-Offending: Results from a Prospective Longitudinal Survey of London Males." *Journal of Criminal Law and Criminology* 82: 360–395.

Sampson, Robert J. and John H. Laub. 1993. *Crime in the Making: Pathways and Turning Points Through Life*. Cambridge, MA: Harvard University Press.

Seddig, Daniel. 2014. "Peer Group Association, the Acceptance of Norms and Violent Behaviour: A Longitudinal Analysis of Reciprocal Effects." *European Journal of Criminology* 11: 319–339.

Shaw, Clifford R. 1930. *The Jack-Roller: A Delinquent Boy's Own Story*. University of Chicago Press.

Shaw, Clifford R. 1931. *The Natural History of a Delinquent Career*. University of Chicago Press.

Shaw, Clifford R., Frederick M. Zorbaugh, Henry D. McKay, and Leonard S. Cottrell. 1929. *Delinquency Areas: A Study of the Geographic Distribution of School Truants, Juvenile Delinquents, and Adult Offenders in Chicago*. University of Chicago Press.

Short, James F., Jr. 1960. "Differential Association as a Hypothesis: Problems of Empirical Testing." *Social Problems* 8: 14–25.

Short, James F., Jr. 1998. "The Level of Explanation Problem Revisited." *Criminology* 36: 3–36.

Short, James F., Jr., and Fred L. Strodtbeck. 1963. "The Response of Gang Leaders to Status Threats: An Observation on Group Process and Delinquent Behavior." *American Journal of Sociology* 68: 571–579.

Short, James F., Jr. and Fred L. Strodtbeck. 1965. *Group Process and Gang Delinquency*. University of Chicago Press.

Spergel, Irving A. 1990. "Youth Gangs: Continuity and Change." Pp. 171–275 in *Crime and Justice: A Review of Research*, vol. 12, ed. M. Tonry and N. Morris. University of Chicago Press.

Spergel, Irving A. 1995. *The Youth Gang Problem: A Community Approach*. New York: Oxford University Press.

Stolzenberg, Lisa and Stewart J. D'Alessio. 2008. "Co-Offending and the Age-Crime Curve." *Journal of Research in Crime and Delinquency* 45: 65–86.

Sutherland, Edwin H., Donald R. Cressey, and David F. Luckenbill. 1992. *Principles of Criminology*. 11th edn. Dix Hills, NY: General Hall.

Suttles, Gerald. 1972. *Social Construction of Communities*. University of Chicago Press.

Sweeten, Gary, David C. Pyrooz, and Alex R. Piquero. 2013. "Disengaging from Gangs and Desistance from Crime." *Justice Quarterly* 30: 469–500.

Taylor, Carl. 1990. *Dangerous Society*. East Lansing, MI: Michigan State University Press.

Thornberry, Terence P. 1987. "Toward an Interactional Theory of Delinquency." *Criminology* 25: 863–891.

Thornberry, Terence P. and J. H. Burch. 1997. "Gang Members and Delinquent Behavior." Washington, DC: Office of Juvenile Justice and Delinquency Prevention.

Thornberry, Terence P., Marvin D. Krohn, Alan J. Lizotte, and Deborah Chard-Wierschem. 1993. "The Role of Juvenile Gangs in Facilitating Delinquent Behavior." *Journal of Research in Crime and Delinquency* 30: 55–87.

Thornberry, Terence P., Marvin D. Krohn, Alan J. Lizotte, Carolyn A. Smith, and Kimberly Tobin. 2003. *Gangs and Delinquency in Developmental Perspective*. New York: Cambridge University Press.

Thornberry, Terence P., Alan J. Lizotte, Marvin D. Krohn, Margaret Farnworth, and Sung Joon Jang. 1994. "Delinquent Peers, Beliefs, and Delinquent Behavior: A Longitudinal Test of Interaction Theory." *Criminology* 32: 47–84.

Thrasher, Frederic M. 1927. *The Gang: A Study of 1,313 Gangs in Chicago*. University of Chicago Press.

Venkatesh, Sudhir Alladi. 2000. *American Project: The Rise and Fall of a Modern Ghetto*. Cambridge, MA: Harvard University Press.

Vigil, James Diego. 1988. *Barrio Gangs*. Austin, TX: University of Texas Press.

Warr, Mark. 1993. "Age, Peers, and Delinquency." *Criminology* 31: 17–40.

Warr, Mark. 1996. "Organization and Instigation in Delinquent Groups." *Criminology* 34: 11–37.

Warr, Mark. 1998. "Life-Course Transition and Desistance from Crime." *Criminology* 36: 183–215.

Warr, Mark. 2002. *Companions in Crime: The Social Aspects of Criminal Conduct*. New York: Cambridge University Press.

Weerman, Frank M. 2003. "Co-Offending as Social Exchange: Explaining Characteristics of Co-Offending." *British Journal of Criminology* 43: 398–416.

Weerman, Frank M. 2011. "Delinquent Peers in Context: A Longitudinal Network Analysis of Selection and Influence Effects." *Criminology* 49: 253–286.

White, Helen Raskin. 1992. "Early Problem Behavior and Later Drug Problems." *Journal of Research in Crime and Delinquency* 29: 412–429.

White, Helene Raskin, Robert J. Pandina, and Randy L. LaGrange. 1987. "Longitudinal Predictors of Serious Substance Use and Delinquency." *Criminology* 25: 715–740.

Wilson, James Q. and Richard J. Herrnstein. 1985. *Crime and Human Nature: The Definitive Study of the Causes of Crime*. New York: Simon & Schuster.

Wood, Peter B., Walter R. Gove, James A. Wilson, and John K. Cochran. 1997. "Nonsocial Reinforcement and Habitual Criminal Conduct: An Extension of Learning Theory." *Criminology* 35: 335–366.

Yablonsky, Lewis. 1959. "The Delinquent Gang as a Near Group." *Social Problems* 7: 108–117.

Yablonsky, Lewis. 1962. *The Violent Gang*. New York: Macmillan.

Young, Jacob T. N. 2011. "How Do They 'End Up Together'? A Social Network Analysis of Self-Control, Homophily, and Adolescent Relationships." *Journal of Quantitative Criminology* 27: 251–273.

Chapter 11

Social structure theories
Community, strain, and subcultures

Chapter preview

Topics:

- Social disorganization theory
- Anomie and strain theories

Theories:

- Social disorganization
- Anomie
- Institutional anomie
- Strain
- General strain
- Reaction formation
- Differential opportunity

Terms:

- social structures
- social solidarity
- collective efficacy
- cultural goals
- institutional means
- anomie
- modes of adaptation
- status frustration
- reaction formation

Chapter learning objectives

After completing this chapter, students should be able to:

- Explain how societal characteristics influence individuals.
- Describe how rapid social change influences social integration and social regulation.

- Explain how and why social disorganization leads to a breakdown in social control.
- Summarize the social ecology of delinquency in Chicago as portrayed in the research of Clifford Shaw and Henry McKay.
- Distinguish between anomie and strain theories.
- Describe the "strains" that lead to gang delinquency among urban, lower-class males.

Case in point: living in "delinquent areas"

Clifford Shaw's life history of Sidney Blotzman describes the social forces that led to Sidney's delinquent career. One of Shaw's chief concerns was with the deteriorated and disorganized neighborhoods in which delinquent peer groups flourished. He provided the following description of the neighborhood in which Sidney lived and the lack of control over the behavior of youth in this area.

> [Sidney] lived in one of the most deteriorated and disorganized sections of the city. …The most obvious characteristic of the neighborhood is the marked physical deterioration of its buildings. … Everywhere are unpainted, dilapidated wooden tenements, interspersed with warehouses, junk yards, and factories. With the rapid growth of the city, the central business and industrial district has gradually encroached upon this neighborhood, resulting in physical deterioration and a change in use of the land. …
>
> For the purpose of understanding Sidney's delinquent behavior it is important to draw attention to the social confusion and disorganization which characterize this area. The successive changes in the composition of population, the disintegration of the alien cultures, the diffusion of divergent cultural standards, and the gradual industrialization of the area have resulted in a dissolution of the neighborhood culture and organization. The continuity of conventional neighborhood traditions and institutions is broken. Thus, the effectiveness of the neighborhood as a unit of control and as a medium for the transmission of the moral standards of society is greatly diminished. …
>
> In this area the conventional traditions, neighborhood institutions, and public opinion, through which neighborhoods usually effect a control over the behavior [of the] child, were largely disintegrated. … Neighborhood control was limited largely to the control that was exerted through such formal agencies as the school, the courts, and the police.
>
> This community situation was not only disorganized and thus ineffective as a unit of control, but it was characterized by a high rate of juvenile delinquency and adult crime …Various forms of stealing and many organized delinquent and criminal gangs were prevalent in the area. These groups exercised a powerful influence and tended to create a community spirit which not only tolerated but actually fostered delinquent and criminal practices.

Source: Shaw (1931: 13–15, 229).

Through Sidney's life history, criminologist Clifford Shaw tried to show that some urban neighborhoods lacked social control and that, as a result, their youth were exposed to delinquent and criminal behavior patterns. These neighborhoods had high rates of delinquency, which is why Shaw referred to them as *delinquency areas* (Shaw and McKay [1942] 1969; Shaw 1931; Shaw et al. 1929).

Although Shaw carried out case studies to document "the natural history of a delinquent career," he also conducted empirical studies of delinquency areas with criminologist Henry McKay. Rather than trying to explain an individual's involvement in delinquent acts, these studies examined the social characteristics of communities that were linked to high rates of delinquency. Shaw and McKay ([1942] 1969) identified three key structural characteristics that disrupt community social organization and, in turn, are related to high rates of crime and delinquency: low economic status, ethnic heterogeneity (or diversity), and residential mobility. Sociologists refer to such organizational features of the social environment as **social structures**. Beyond the three structural characteristics that Shaw and McKay emphasized, the concept of social structure also refers to characteristics such as age and gender distributions; cultural traditions; institutions such as the family, school, and church; and statuses and roles.[1] When applied to delinquent behavior, theoretical approaches that emphasize elements of the social structure search for causes that are external to the individual.

Theory and research that focus on structural characteristics of the social environment have their roots in the work of French sociologist Emile Durkheim. Writing in the late 1800s, Durkheim concentrated on the social factors that integrate and regulate individuals and groups. He used the concept of **social solidarity** to refer to the social structures of society that provide integration and regulation. The time period in which Durkheim wrote was a period of rapid urbanization and industrialization; he was especially intrigued with how such rapid social change influenced social integration and undermined regulation. Durkheim ([1893] 1947) referred to the breakdown of societal regulation as *anomie*. Anomie is sometimes simply defined as normlessness. The concept of rapid social change resulting in anomie is an important legacy of Durkheim that appears in social structure theories of delinquency.

Based on Durkheim's work, criminologists have developed a number of theories that emphasize structural features of the social environment that are related to delinquency, rather than individual-level factors (Sampson and Groves 1989; Kornhauser 1978). This chapter describes two prominent theoretical traditions within the structural perspective: social disorganization theories and anomie and strain theories. Social disorganization theories focus on the breakdown of traditional patterns of social life at the neighborhood level as a result of rapid change in urban environments. Anomie and strain theories deal with availability of legitimate opportunities for material success at both the individual and societal levels. Social disorganization and anomie theories are both macrosocial approaches that emphasize organizational features of communities or societies (e.g., the ability of social institutions such as schools and churches to regulate behavior, and the level of commitment to cultural goals such as economic success) to explain variation in rates of crime and delinquency.

Social disorganization theory

Rapid social change and physical deterioration have long been associated with the breakdown in community social control and consequently with high rates of delinquency. This perspective, referred to as *social disorganization theory*, was advanced most extensively by faculty members and others affiliated with the Department of Sociology at the University of Chicago in the early 1900s. As a result, the proponents of social disorganization theory are often referred to as the *Chicago School*.

The Chicago School

In the formative years of the discipline, Chicago sociologists focused on social problems that plagued urban communities and tried to explain these social problems so that practical ways of eliminating them could be developed (Curran and Renzetti 2008; Oberschall 1972). The problems of urban life were associated with rapid population growth, residential mobility, poverty, physical deterioration, and increased cultural diversity. Special attention was given to the poor immigrants and migrants who flocked to the industrial centers of the United States in the late 1800s and early 1900s, hoping to find work and prosperity in major cities. Chicago sociologists believed that this infusion of people, together with the associated increase in cultural diversity and physical deterioration, led to a decline in *moral order*, or what Durkheim had referred to as *solidarity* – the interconnectedness and cohesiveness of people (Bursik 1986; Park and Burgess 1924).

Pioneering Chicago sociologists Robert Park and Ernest Burgess explored patterns of urban growth and the geographic distribution of social problems. Burgess developed the concentric zone model of urban development, in which he argued that urban areas grow through progressive expansion from the central city outwards, in a series of concentric zones associated with different types of land use. As cities expand, business and industry of the central city spill over into adjacent residential areas, producing an area of mixed use. This area just outside the central city is called the *zone in transition*, where newcomers settle, attracted by factory jobs and inexpensive housing. The *zone of workingmen's homes* lies beyond these central areas and is populated by second-generation immigrants who have been able to escape the zone of transition. Further out are the *residential zone* and *commuters' zone*, where white, middle- and upper-class homeowners reside (Burgess [1925] 1967).

Associated with this model of urban development were several identifiable patterns in the distribution of people and their activities. Early sociologists observed that immigrant groups tended to move into the city in waves – first one ethnic group, then another. Often poor, these immigrant groups tended to locate in areas with the least expensive housing and in neighborhoods with individuals of similar ethnicity – in the zone in transition. As individuals achieved greater economic success, they moved into outlying areas, and new immigrant groups moved into the transitional area – a process called *residential succession*. These ecological processes were viewed as common to all cities that experienced rapid urban and industrial growth at the turn of the century (Shaw and McKay [1942] 1969).

Chicago sociologists gathered data and observed that a variety of social problems – alcoholism, mental disorder, crime and delinquency, even infant mortality – were highest in zones closest to the center of the city. The central business district and the zone in transition had the highest rates of social problems, with rates declining progressively in zones farther from the city center. Advocates of the social disorganization perspective argued that characteristics of local neighborhoods, not characteristics of individuals in those areas, were the primary influence on rates of social problems.

More recently, Rodney Stark (1987) advanced five structural characteristics that he believes summarize the idea of social disorganization: (1) density (many people in a small area); (2) poverty; (3) mixed use (a combination of residence, industry, and retail); (4) transience (people moving into and out of the area); and (5) dilapidation (physical deterioration of buildings). Like earlier Chicago sociologists, Stark argues that these key dimensions of social disorganization destroy traditional patterns of social life. Using the concept introduced by Robert Park and Ernest Burgess, Stark describes this breakdown as decline in the moral order of the community. More specifically, he proposes that declining moral order involves moral cynicism (skepticism about others' moral character), increased opportunities for crime and deviance, increased motivation to deviate, and diminished social control. Stark describes these areas of declining moral order as "deviant places."

Shaw and McKay's Delinquency Areas

The application of social disorganization theory to delinquency was primarily the work of Clifford Shaw and Henry McKay. Shaw and McKay were graduate students in sociology at the University of Chicago and were influenced heavily by the writings of Robert Park, Ernest Burgess, W. I. Thomas, and Ellsworth Faris. Drawing on the themes of the Chicago School, Shaw and McKay studied how the urban social environment influenced delinquency rates in the city of Chicago in the first half of the 1900s. They observed that delinquency rates varied extensively across the city, a finding they referred to as the "geographic distribution" of delinquency.

Although their empirical studies documented the geographic distribution of delinquency and identified key community characteristics associated with the ecology of delinquency, Shaw and McKay ([1942] 1969) used autobiographical case studies of delinquent youth to illustrate the social, psychological, and cultural processes that invited involvement in delinquency in those areas with high rates of delinquent offending. These case studies were drawn from the large number of life histories that Shaw compiled through interviews and autobiographies of delinquent youth. The case that opened this chapter was part of one such life history.

The ecology of delinquency

Shaw and McKay's findings on the geographic distribution of delinquency were first presented in the book *Delinquency Areas* (Shaw et al. 1929). The primary purpose of the study was to investigate the *ecological distribution* of delinquent behavior and to discover the community characteristics that were associated with high rates of delinquency. The researchers used Chicago police and juvenile court records to develop measures of delinquency, including truancy, juvenile court appearances, felony adjudications, and recidivism. These measures were depicted geographically on a series of Chicago maps, including: (1) *spot maps*, which depicted offenders' places of residence; (2) *rate maps*, which were graphic representations of delinquency rates in square mile areas; (3) *radial maps*, which provided delinquency rates along radials emanating from the center of the city; and (4) *zone maps*, which depicted delinquency rates in concentric zones. Figure 11.1 shows the zone map for the rate of male juvenile court appearances from 1900 to 1906. The resulting collection of maps – 40 maps in all – is an unparalleled study of the social ecology of delinquency in a particular city.

Shaw and his colleagues (1929: 198–203) drew a number of conclusions from their study. We highlight four here because they speak directly to the link between community characteristics and rates of delinquency:

1. There are marked variations in the rate of school truants, juvenile delinquents, and adult criminals between areas in Chicago. Some areas are characterized by very high rates, while others show very low rates. ...

2. Rates of truancy, delinquency, [recidivism], and adult crime tend to vary inversely in proportion to the distance from the center of the city. In general, the nearer to the center of the city a given locality is, the higher will be its rates of delinquency and crime. ...

3. Differences in rates of truancy, delinquency, and crime reflect differences in community backgrounds. High rates occur in areas which are characterized by physical deterioration and declining population. ...

4. The main high rate areas of the city ... have been characterized by high rates over a long period. ...

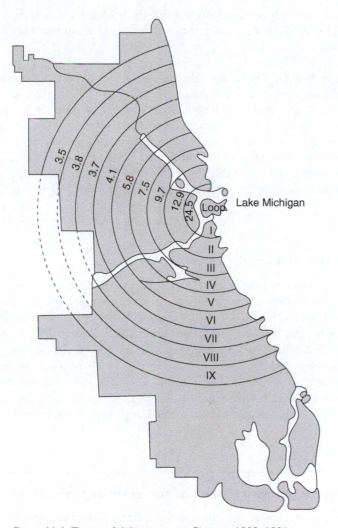

Figure 11.1 Zones of delinquency in Chicago, 1900–1906.

This map identifies the percentage of boys (under the age of 18) in each zone who were brought before the juvenile court from 1900 to 1906. This period covers the first seven years of the juvenile court's existence.

Source: Shaw et al. (1929: 99). Copyright © 1929, University of Chicago Press. All rights reserved. Reproduced with permission of the publisher.

The ecological distribution of delinquency was explored more fully in Shaw and McKay's subsequent work, *Juvenile Delinquency and Urban Areas*, first published in 1942. In this work, Shaw and McKay examined the association between community characteristics and rates of delinquency in several U.S. cities. Their findings in *Juvenile Delinquency and Urban Areas* confirmed their earlier work in *Delinquency Areas*, showing that rates of delinquency varied widely across different areas of cities and that there was stability to such variation – *ecological stability*. As before, they argued that the ecological distribution of delinquency is most closely associated with characteristics of the local community, not with characteristics of individuals:

> It is clear from the data included in this volume that there is a direct relationship between conditions existing in local communities of American cities and differential rates of delinquents and criminals. Communities with high rates have social and economic characteristics which differentiate them from communities with low rates. … Moreover, the fact that in Chicago the rates of delinquents for many years have remained relatively constant in the areas adjacent to centers of commerce and heavy industry, despite successive changes in the nativity and nationality composition of the population, supports emphatically the conclusion that the delinquency-producing factors are inherent in the community.
>
> (Shaw and McKay [1942] 1969: 315)

Social disorganization and the breakdown of social control

Shaw and McKay's basic argument is that processes of urban growth influence community characteristics. Three structural characteristics of communities are especially disruptive of social organization: low economic status, ethnic heterogeneity, and residential mobility (Sampson and Groves 1989; see also Bursik 1988). These community characteristics do not directly affect rates of crime and delinquency. Instead, they limit informal social control and thereby allow high rates of crime and delinquency to occur (Bursik 1988). Thus, juvenile delinquency is a direct consequence of the breakdown of social control in various contexts, such as the family, neighborhood, church, and school. "Research in action: the measurement of social disorganization" provides an example of how social disorganization has been measured in recent research.

Research in action: the measurement of social disorganization

As part of the contemporary resurrection of social disorganization theory, Robert Sampson and W. Byron Groves in 1989 published an influential article in which they empirically tested Shaw and McKay's social disorganization theory. Sampson and Groves hypothesized that structural characteristics of communities, such as low economic status, residential mobility, ethnic heterogeneity, and family disruption, lead to social disorganization, which, in turn, increases rates of crime and delinquency. To test their hypothesis, they used data gathered in two separate national surveys of residents of Great Britain. Each survey included approximately 11,000 respondents. Sampson and Groves found support for their hypothesis and thus for social disorganization theory.

Sampson and Groves clearly distinguished social disorganization from the factors that produce it, which include poverty, ethnic heterogeneity, and residential mobility. Sampson and Groves viewed social disorganization and social organization as two ends of a continuum. Thus, to assess social disorganization, they used three measures:

1. **Sparse local friendship networks.** "Respondents were asked how many of their friends resided in the local community, which was defined as the area within a 15-minute walk of the respondent's home." (Responses were on a five-point scale ranging from none to all.)

> 2. **Low organizational participation.** Respondents were asked about their attendance at meetings of committees or clubs in the week before the interview.
> 3. **Unsupervised youth peer groups.** "Respondents were asked how common it was for groups of teenagers to hang out in public in the neighborhood and make nuisances of themselves." (Responses were on a four-point scale.)
>
> *Source*: Sampson and Groves (1989: 774, 777–778, 783–784).

Although Shaw and McKay did not clearly specify how social disorganization inhibits social control, they identified several social processes that begin with social disorganization and end in diminished social control:

1. Youths fail to acquire internal controls when they are not socialized into the normative expectations of the local community. Instead, youths may be exposed to delinquent and criminal behavior patterns.
2. Youths lack primary relationships with conforming friends and adults, thereby limiting informal controls of relationship bonds.
3. Lack of commitment and involvement in the local community preclude direct controls, especially the supervision that goes along with active community membership.
4. Limited interaction and communication inhibit the development of common community values and norms and hinder community controls and efforts to solve common community problems, including delinquency (Bursik 1988: 521; see also Bursik and Grasmick 1993).

"Research in action: testing the 'broken windows' thesis" discusses a contemporary interpretation of the relationships among disorder, informal social control, and crime. This explanation is called the "broken windows" thesis.

Research in action: testing the "broken windows" thesis

Social disorganization and social and physical disorder are separate but related concepts. *Social disorder* refers to "behavior usually involving strangers and considered threatening, such as verbal harassment on the street, open solicitation for prostitution, public intoxication, and rowdy groups of young males in public." *Physical disorder* refers to "the deterioration of urban landscapes, for example, graffiti on buildings, abandoned cars, broken windows, and garbage in the streets" (Sampson and Raudenbush 1999: 603–604).

Disorder signals to observers both inside and outside the neighborhood that residents are unwilling or unable to exercise informal social control. In other words, disorder can be seen as a symptom or outcome of social disorganization. Recent research suggests that disorder is not only a consequence of a lack of informal social control, but also influences subsequent levels of social control and residential instability (Steenbeek and Hipp 2011).

The "broken windows" thesis, first advanced by James Wilson and George Kelling (1982), proposes that if social and physical disorder in urban neighborhoods goes unchecked, it can lead to serious crime. "The reasoning is that even such minor public incivilities as drinking in the street, spray-painting graffiti, and breaking windows can escalate into predatory crime because prospective offenders assume from these manifestations of disorder that area residents are indifferent to what happens in their neighborhood" (Sampson and Raudenbush 2001: 1).

The broken windows thesis has generated changes in policing strategies in many cities, most notably in New York City, where police have become more vigilant in responding to public signs of disorder, including even minor "incivilities." The goal of these "zero tolerance" policies is to curb serious crime by addressing the disorder that might otherwise promote serious offending.

Sampson and Raudenbush recently tested the broken windows thesis using observational data from the Project on Human Development in Chicago Neighborhoods. The innovative method of gathering these data consisted of having trained observers videotape (using video recorders mounted to a sport utility vehicle) the "face blocks" of more than 23,000 streets in 196 Chicago neighborhoods. A "face block" is defined as a one-block segment on only one side of a street. Trained observers also kept written logs of their observations of each face block. Sampson and Raudenbush refer to this type of measurement as systematic social observation, in which the method of observation is independent of what is being observed. Using this approach, places and actions are observed as they "naturally" occur (Sampson and Raudenbush 1999: 616; 2001: 3).

As an alternative to the broken windows thesis that disorder leads to serious crime, Sampson and Raudenbush propose that "disorder and crime are manifestations of the same phenomenon," and that both stem from structural characteristics of neighborhoods, such as concentrated disadvantage and residential instability, and from low levels of "collective efficacy" among neighbors. Collective efficacy is defined as "cohesion among neighborhood residents combined with shared expectations for informal social control of public space" (Sampson and Raudenbush 2001: 1–2). (See "Research in action: the measurement of collective efficacy," later in this chapter, for a description of collective efficacy.)

In support of their hypothesis and in contrast to the broken windows thesis, Sampson and Raudenbush found that disorder was directly linked only to robbery, but not to other types of crime (see also Boggess and Maskaly 2014). Instead, structural characteristics of neighborhoods (especially concentrated disadvantage) and collective efficacy predicted both disorder and crime. Once collective efficacy and structural characteristics of neighborhoods were taken into account, the relationship between disorder and crime disappeared in most cases.

Sampson and Raudenbush note the implication of their findings for policing policies: "The findings strongly suggest that policies intended to reduce crime by eradicating disorder solely through tough law enforcement tactics are misdirected" (Sampson and Raudenbush 2001: 5; see also Sampson and Raudenbush 2004, and Wilcox et al. 2004).

Cultural aspects of social disorganization

Over the course of their work, Shaw and McKay emphasized different aspects of social disorganization. In its initial form, social disorganization theory emphasized the loss of a common culture in the community – "the customs, codes, taboos, and traditions" of the local neighborhood (Shaw et al. 1929). In their first work, *Delinquency Areas*, Shaw and McKay (1931: 99–100) explained ecological variation in delinquency rates by considering how the lack of a common culture is related to social disorganization:

In the areas close to the central business district, and to a less extent in the areas close to industrial developments, the neighborhood organization tends to disintegrate. For in these areas the mobility of population is so great that there is little opportunity for the development of common attitudes and interests [a common culture].

Robert Bursik (1988: 521) comments that social disorganization in its purest form "refers to the inability of local communities to realize the common values of their residents or solve commonly experienced problems." With regard to delinquent behavior, "the absence of common community ideals and standards prevents cooperative social action ... to ... suppress delinquency" (Shaw and McKay 1931: 102). Shaw's description of Sidney's neighborhood, which introduced this chapter, emphasized the cultural aspects of social disorganization.

Social disorganization and delinquent subcultures

The absence of effective social control in socially disorganized areas allows for the development of delinquent subcultures. These subcultures are the vehicles for transmitting delinquent traditions, values, and expectations, which are passed on through association with delinquent youths and adult criminals in the neighborhood. As Shaw and McKay (1931: 117) observe:

> The presence of a large number of older offenders in a neighborhood is a fact of great significance for the understanding of the problem of juvenile delinquency. It indicates, in the first place, that the possibility of contact between the children and hardened offenders is very great. The older offenders, who are well known and have prestige in the neighborhood, tend to set standards and patterns of behavior for the younger boys, who idolize and emulate them. In many cases the "big shot" represents for the young delinquent an ideal around which his own hopes and ambitions are crystallized. His attainment of this coveted ideal means recognition in his group and the esteem of his fellows.

Shaw and McKay's emphasis on group association clearly foreshadowed the development of *differential association theory*, discussed in Chapter 10, and *subcultural theories* within the strain tradition, which we address later in this chapter. The transmission of a delinquent culture from older youths and adults in the neighborhood to younger, aspiring delinquents implies a level of organization that might seem contrary to the basic idea of social disorganization (Kornhauser 1978). However, the absence of a common culture in socially disorganized neighborhoods and the subsequent breakdown in effective community control provide fertile ground for the emergence of delinquent subcultures which offer plenty of delinquent peers and adult offenders.

Strain in social disorganization theory

So far we have seen that Shaw and McKay's work focused on the consequences of urban growth in terms of culture, social control, group associations, and the development and transmission of delinquent subcultures. The rapid social change associated with urban growth came to an abrupt halt with the nationwide economic collapse (1929–1933) that precipitated the Great Depression. Widespread unemployment resulted in declining immigration and migration to cities and greatly reduced residential mobility. As a result, the ecological processes, such as residential succession, that characterized urban growth in the late nineteenth century and early twentieth century slowed dramatically. With this change, Shaw and McKay gave greater emphasis in their research to issues of poverty, unemployment, and social class. They conceived of social disorganization in inner-city neighborhoods not so much in terms of culture and social control as in terms of lack of economic opportunity, relative deprivation, and the resulting personal frustration and strain that might motivate involvement in criminal and delinquent acts (Shaw and McKay [1942] 1969). Shaw and McKay's point of view here is similar to Robert Merton's anomie theory, discussed later in this chapter.

Testing social disorganization theory in other urban areas

Shaw and McKay's second major ecological study, *Juvenile Delinquency and Urban Areas*, included analysis of Philadelphia, Boston, Cincinnati, Cleveland, and Richmond, Virginia. Shaw and McKay ([1942] 1969) observed that delinquent offenses were distributed in these cities in an ecological pattern similar to the one in Chicago, and that this persistent pattern reflected common conditions of urban communities. Following the work of Shaw and McKay, a number of other researchers conducted area studies in Baltimore, Detroit, and Indianapolis (Schuerman and Kobrin 1986; Chilton 1964; Bordua 1958; Lander 1954). These studies found that while some neighborhood characteristics, such as substandard housing and residential overcrowding, were unrelated to delinquency rates, other socioeconomic characteristics of neighborhoods were consistently related to delinquency rates.

Although researchers have connected the community characteristics associated with social disorganization to high rates of delinquency (for example, Zimmerman and Messner 2010), social disorganization theory has experienced relatively limited direct testing (Sampson and Groves 1989; Kornhauser 1978). Social disorganization theory argues that structural community characteristics affect social organization, especially primary group controls, thereby influencing delinquency rates. According to Robert Sampson and W. Byron Groves (1989), it is this intervening variable of social organization that must be considered to test directly the full theory. Many studies that have tried to test social disorganization theory have measured only whether structural characteristics of communities are related to their crime rates (for example, see Osgood and Chambers 2000). Although valuable, this research does not assess whether these community characteristics are related to the use of social control.

In contrast, Sampson and Groves (1989) developed a causal model of social disorganization in which *community structure* (low economic status, ethnic heterogeneity, residential mobility, family disruption, and urbanization) influences *social organization* (friendship networks, supervision of teenage peer groups, and participation in local organizations). Social organization, in turn, determines level of crime and delinquency. The model is depicted in Figure 11.2. Using two surveys conducted in Great Britain, Sampson and Groves (1989: 799) found that "communities characterized by sparse friendship networks, unsupervised teenage peer groups, and low organizational participation had disproportionately high rates of crime and delinquency."[2] In addition, variation in these dimensions of community social disorganization mediated much of the effects of community structural characteristics on crime and delinquency, as predicted by social disorganization theory.[3]

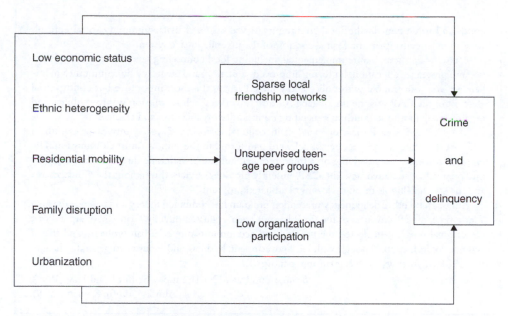

Figure 11.2. Sampson and Groves's model of social disorganization.
Sampson and Groves hypothesized that measures of community structure (listed in the box on the left) influence social disorganization (middle box), which in turn affects the rate of crime and delinquency.
Source: Sampson and Groves (1989: 783).

Delinquency prevention in delinquency areas

The life histories and ecological studies associated with social disorganization theory suggest particular delinquency prevention strategies. Clifford Shaw is responsible for a widely recognized delinquency prevention program called the Chicago Area Project. "Theory into practice: a program based on social disorganization theory – Shaw's Chicago Area Project," provides a description of this program. "Theory into practice: community-based crime prevention strategies" describes elements of contemporary efforts at community-based crime prevention.

Theory into practice: a program based on social disorganization theory – Shaw's Chicago Area Project

Convinced that delinquency prevention could be accomplished only through community organization and "community action," Clifford Shaw established the Chicago Area Project (CAP) in 1932. In philosophy and purpose, the CAP drew from the ecological findings and case histories that are the basis of social disorganization theory. The program grew to include 22 neighborhood centers that promoted community organization, integration, and stability by developing and using community resources and leadership.

The CAP attempted to organize local neighborhoods by having community members participate in various activities and projects. Such involvement was expected to create relationship bonds and investment in the local community. It was assumed that community social controls were more effective than the formal controls of the juvenile justice system.

A range of programs were implemented, including local counseling services, recreation facilities and programs, educational tutoring, improved sanitation, and advocacy by community members for youth in trouble with police and courts. Perhaps the most innovative but controversial element of the CAP was the use of gang "outreach workers" whose mission was to mobilize and organize neighborhood youth in generating community organization and change.

The Chicago Area Project operated in its original form for 25 years, until Shaw's death in 1957. At that time, the project personnel were transferred to the Illinois Youth Commission. The program still exists today, relying on a three-pronged approach, including direct service, community organizing, and advocacy. The CAP presently provides services throughout the Chicago area and the state of Illinois through dozens of affiliated programs.

Although no other delinquency prevention program has combined theory and practice for such a long time, the effectiveness of the CAP has not been evaluated directly. Critics have argued that the original program neglected the political and economic nature of urban problems and that it was not confrontational enough with local government, business, and industry to generate change.

CAP's website: www.chicagoareaproject.org/

Sources: Lundman (2001); Empey, Stafford, and Hay (1999); Alinsky (1960); Kobrin (1959).

Theory into practice: community-based crime prevention strategies

CrimeSolutions.gov is a registry of evidence-based practices, evaluated by the Office of Justice Programs. The website provides information about programs and practices that have been shown, through rigorous research, to be effective or promising for preventing crime. Some of the programs and practices are community-based initiatives.

Community crime prevention programs or strategies target changes in community infrastructure, culture, or the physical environment in order to reduce crime. The diversity of approaches include neighborhood watch, community policing, urban or physical design, and comprehensive or multi-disciplinary efforts. These strategies may seek to engage residents, community and faith-based organizations, and local government agencies in addressing the factors that contribute to the community's crime, delinquency, and disorder.

Examples of effective or promising community-based crime prevention initiatives include:

- Increased police presence (including foot patrols) in crime "hot spots."
- Problem-oriented policing strategies that seek to reduce crimes such as gang violence, illegal gun possession, and gun violence.
- Neighborhood watch programs that involve citizens in efforts to prevent crime in their neighborhood or community.
- School-based comprehensive programs intended to promote anti-drug messages throughout communities and prevent substance use.
- Efforts to reduce crime by improving street lighting.
- Installation of traffic barriers in high-crime neighborhoods to reduce gang drive-by shootings and other violent crimes.

Source: CrimeSolutions.gov (n.d.).

A contemporary version of social disorganization theory: collective efficacy

Social disorganization theory was important in directing criminological attention toward community and societal factors. By the 1970s, however, the theory had lost much of its appeal and influence (Bursik 1988). Beginning in the 1980s, though, renewed interest in social disorganization theory stirred. Robert Sampson has played a leading role in revitalizing social disorganization theory by showing its relevance for understanding and responding to high crime rates in inner-city neighborhoods.[4] He points to the importance of both structural and organizational characteristics of neighborhoods, as well as relationship bonds, social interaction, and social control efforts among neighbors.

Sampson adopts the basic thesis of social disorganization theory that structural features of a community affect its social organization, especially in terms of the ability of primary groups to exercise social control. Poverty, family disruption, and residential instability are structural characteristics that impede relationships among neighbors and reduce their involvement in community organizations. Because of this low social capital, these communities are unable to exert effective collective control in public areas such as streets and parks.[5] In neighborhoods characterized by social disorganization, teenagers are free to roam and become involved in delinquent and criminal groups. High rates of crime and delinquency are a natural consequence.

Working with William Julius Wilson, Sampson also resurrected the cultural emphasis of social disorganization by arguing that structural conditions affect the culture of communities. Sampson and Wilson (1995) consider the concentration of poor African Americans in urban ghetto neighborhoods and its effect on violent crime. The harsh conditions of inner-city life for many African Americans include social isolation – "the lack of contact or of sustained interaction with individuals and institutions that represent mainstream society" (Sampson and Wilson 1995: 51). In this context, cultural norms and values develop that do not necessarily approve of violence and crime, but instead define such actions as an unavoidable expression of ghetto life. The social isolation, lack of opportunity, and fatalistic cultural values of inner-city ghetto areas are experienced disproportionately by African Americans. Sampson and Wilson refer to such structured inequality as *concentrated disadvantage*, which results in the breakdown of community controls needed to restrain criminal behavior. The effects of concentrated disadvantage, however, depend on **collective efficacy** – the willingness of community residents to be involved with each other and to exercise informal control. Communities, then, vary not only in the level of concentrated disadvantage, but also in the cohesiveness of relationships and the collective capacity for informal social control. The degree to which concentrated disadvantage produces crime and delinquency in a community depends on that community's collective efficacy.[6]

Sampson, together with Stephen Raudenbush and Felton Earls, tested this theory of collective efficacy by examining rates of violence across 343 Chicago neighborhoods (Sampson, Raudenbush, and Earls 1997). Three measures of neighborhood social structure were analyzed in conjunction with collective efficacy: concentrated disadvantage (measured by combining a community's poverty, race and age composition, and level of family disruption), immigrant concentration, and residential stability. Sampson, Raudenbush, and Earls found that the social composition of neighborhoods in terms of these three structural characteristics was related strongly to neighborhood rates of violence. This relationship was heavily dependent, however, on the collective efficacy of neighborhoods – the degree to which neighborhood residents were interdependent, cohesive, and willing to exercise informal social control. Neighborhoods that were characterized by collective disadvantage and residential instability, but where residents still maintained cohesive social relationships and engaged readily in informal social control, had low rates of crime and delinquency.[7] Sampson and his associates concluded that the effects of concentrated disadvantage and residential instability on rates of violence are mediated by collective efficacy. "Research in action: the measurement of collective efficacy" lists the measures that Sampson and his colleagues used to assess collective efficacy.

Research in action: the measurement of collective efficacy

Robert Sampson, Stephen Raudenbush, and Felton Earls (1997) developed and tested the theory of collective efficacy using data from the Project on Human Development in Chicago Neighborhoods (PHDCN). The PHDCN includes a community survey of approximately 8,800 residents from all 343 Chicago neighborhoods. In this survey, begun in 1994, residents were interviewed about a variety of neighborhood factors, including neighborhood cohesion, social capital, informal social control, social disorder, and availability of programs and services, as well as activism, organizational involvement, and criminal victimization of residents.

Sampson, Raudenbush, and Earls used the following measures from the PHDCN community survey to construct "informal social control" and "social cohesion and trust" scales that they used to measure collective efficacy, defined as mutual trust among neighbors combined with a willingness to intervene on behalf of the common good using informal methods of social control.

Informal social control

Residents were asked to respond to these questions using a five-point scale, ranging from very likely to very unlikely:
- If a group of neighborhood children were skipping school and hanging out on a street corner, how likely is it that your neighbors would do something about it?
- If some children were spray-painting graffiti on a local building, how likely is it that your neighbors would do something about it?
- If a child was showing disrespect to an adult, how likely is it that people in your neighborhood would scold that child?
- If there was a fight in front of your house and someone was being beaten or threatened, how likely is it that your neighbors would break it up?
- Suppose that because of budget cuts the fire station closest to your home was going to be closed down by the city. How likely is it that neighborhood residents would organize to try to do something to keep the fire station open?

Social cohesion and trust

Residents were asked to respond to these questions using a five-point scale, ranging from strongly agree to strongly disagree:
- People around here are willing to help their neighbors.
- This is a close-knit neighborhood.
- People in this neighborhood can be trusted.
- People in this neighborhood generally don't get along with each other. (This item was reverse coded.)
- People in this neighborhood do not share the same values. (This item was reverse coded.)

Several recent studies have provided additional support for the theory of collective efficacy (MacDonald et al. 2013; Kirk and Matsuda 2011; Mazerolle, Wickes, and McBroom 2010; Simons et al. 2005). For example, research has shown that youth violence is strongly related to neighborhood collective efficacy (MacDonald et al. 2013). Comparative research has also demonstrated the ability of collective efficacy to explain variations in violent crime in settings outside of the United States. Lorraine Mazerolle and her colleagues (2010) used data from Australia and found that collective efficacy was a significant predictor of the distribution of violent victimization.

Other research has provided somewhat mixed support for the theory (Sutherland, Brunton-Smith, and Jackson 2013; Wickes 2010) or has not supported the theory (Wells et al. 2006; Xu, Fiedler, and Flaming 2005; Browning, Feinberg, and Dietz 2004). For example, one study showed that collective efficacy plays a less significant role in controlling crime than does community policing (Xu et al. 2005). Another study showed that the effects of collective efficacy on violence are substantially reduced in neighborhoods with extensive social networks, presumably because social networks provide a source of social capital for offenders as well as law-abiding neighborhood residents (Browning et al. 2004). Despite these findings, collective efficacy remains an important and influential concept in contemporary criminology, supported by numerous studies.

Anomie and strain theories

Although Shaw and McKay emphasized how social disorganization in inner-city neighborhoods disrupted traditional forms of social control and allowed delinquent peer groups to flourish, they also pointed out that legitimate opportunities for success are significantly limited in these areas and that this too is conducive to crime and delinquency:

> The groups in the areas of lowest economic status find themselves at a disadvantage in the struggle to achieve the goals idealized in our civilization. ... Those persons who occupy a disadvantageous position are involved in conflict between the goals assumed to be attainable in a free society and those actually attainable for a large portion of the population. It is understandable, then, that the economic position of persons living in the areas of least opportunity should be translated at times into unconventional conduct, in an effort to reconcile the idealized status and their prospects of attaining this status.
>
> (Shaw and McKay [1942] 1969: 180–181)

This emphasis on cultural goals of success in conjunction with the availability of opportunities for success is the central theme for a second group of social structure theories, referred to as *anomie* and *strain theories*. These terms distinguish two parts to this theoretical tradition: anomie theory explains why societies such as the United States have such high rates of crime and strain theory explains why some people and groups within society are more likely to engage in crime (Cullen, Agnew, and Wilcox 2014).

Anomie theory

The origins of anomie and strain theories can be traced to the work of Robert K. Merton, a famous sociologist. Although Merton did not use these terms to describe his explanations for deviance, others have called the explanations anomie and strain theories (Cullen et al. 2014; Messner and Rosenfeld 1997). In 1938, Merton published a widely read and cited article entitled "Social Structure and Anomie." Merton has revised and extended his anomie theory at least eight times since then (Merton 1997).

Although Merton based his theory on Durkheim's concept of anomie, he significantly reshaped the concept. Durkheim argued that much of what people need or want, such as the desire for status and power, can only be achieved socially, in the context of relationships. As a result, social needs and desires must be regulated externally through social control. When societies change rapidly, however, social control tends to break down, and behavior goes unregulated. Durkheim used the term *anomie* to refer to this societal condition of a breakdown or absence of social regulation.

In comparison, Merton argued that social needs and desires are not only regulated by society, but also defined and established by society. Merton (1938) referred to these culturally defined social aspirations as **cultural goals** – goals that are commonly held to be desirable, worthwhile, and meaningful. Cultural goals are learned socially in the context of families, schools, churches, and through the media. People desire these goals because they are rewarding socially and economically and because they provide influence, power, and control. Merton, however, emphasized that a single cultural goal is most prominent in the United States: the goal of monetary success. Although he used a variety of terms for this cultural goal, he frequently referred to it as "pecuniary success" – the "accumulation of wealth as a symbol of success" (Merton 1938: 675, 680).

A society also defines and regulates the acceptable means of achieving cultural goals. These accepted avenues for achieving goals are referred to as **institutional means**. Like cultural goals, the norms or means for obtaining goals are instilled and enforced within the context of institutions such as the family, schools, and work. Thus, Merton (1938) emphasized the relationship between two aspects of society: cultural goals and institutional means for attaining those goals.

Merton went on to observe that some societies emphasize certain cultural goals without a corresponding emphasis on the institutional means to obtain those goals. This is a societal condition that he called **anomie**. In this sense, *anomie* refers to the normlessness that results when societal goals are stressed to a much greater degree than are the institutionalized means for achieving those goals. According to Merton, it is this inconsistent emphasis on cultural goals and institutional means that explains why some societies have high rates of crime and deviance. Merton (1938: 680, emphasis in original) stated the main idea of anomie theory in one long sentence:

> It is only when a system of cultural values extols, virtually above all else, certain *common* symbols of success [cultural goals] *for the population at large* while its social structure rigorously restricts or completely eliminates access to approved modes of acquiring these symbols *for a considerable part of the same population*, that antisocial behavior ensues on a considerable scale.

"Research in action: the measurement of anomie" provides examples of how anomie has been measured in contemporary and earlier research.

Research in action: the measurement of anomie

In research using data from the community survey portion of the Project on Human Development in Chicago Neighborhoods, Robert Sampson and Dawn Jeglum Bartusch provide a contemporary example of the measurement of anomie.

Consistent with Durkheim's use of the concept, Sampson and Bartusch (1998: 782) define anomie as a "state of normlessness in which the rules of the dominant society (and hence the legal system) are no longer binding in a community or for a population subgroup." According to Sampson and Bartusch (1998: 782), "Normlessness and powerlessness tend ... to go hand in hand, breeding cynicism about the rules of the society and their application." Thus, they view "legal cynicism" as a component of anomie or normlessness. They measure legal cynicism using five variables designed to assess general beliefs about the legitimacy of law and social norms.

Legal cynicism

Residents were asked to respond to these questions using a five-point scale, ranging from strongly agree to strongly disagree.

- Laws were made to be broken.
- It's okay to do anything you want as long as you don't hurt anyone.
- To make money, there are no right and wrong ways anymore, only easy ways and hard ways.
- Fighting between friends or within families is nobody else's business.
- Nowadays a person has to live pretty much for today and let tomorrow take care of itself.

Sampson and Bartusch created their legal cynicism scale by drawing on and modifying an anomie scale created decades earlier by Leo Srole (1956). To measure "anomia" or "interpersonal alienation," Srole used five items, with responses on an agree–disagree scale.

Srole's measures of "anomia"

There's little use writing to public officials because often they aren't really interested in the problems of the average man.

- Nowadays a person has to live pretty much for today and let tomorrow take care of itself.
- In spite of what some people say, the lot of the average man is getting worse, not better.
- It's hardly fair to bring children into the world with the way things look for the future.
- These days a person doesn't really know whom he can count on.

Merton's anomie theory focuses on the relative emphasis a society places on the cultural goal of success and on opportunities for obtaining symbols of success. He argued that, in the United States, economic success is stressed far more than any other goal and that there is not an equivalent emphasis on the institutional means or norms to achieve material success. This is often referred to as a "disjunction" or "imbalance" between goals and means (Bernard, Snipes, and Gerould 2010; Gibbons 1979). Some societies, such as the United States, are characterized by a state of anomie in which individuals' goal-seeking behavior is not well regulated. As a result, people are likely to pursue economic success by whatever means necessary, including crime.

Merton (1938) also points out that anomie associated with an overemphasis on economic success and an underemphasis on the acceptable means to be successful is structured into American society through the class system. The goal of material success is adopted by virtually everyone in the United States, whereas the means to achieve success are not equally available to all classes of people. This structured inequality is what produces a higher rate of crime and delinquency among the lower class. Merton clarifies that poverty in itself does not produce a high rate of criminal behavior, nor does relative deprivation necessarily lead to a high crime rate. Rather, it is only when poverty or relative deprivation is associated with a desire for material success and a lack of opportunity that crime is a likely outcome.

Merton's anomie theory argues that the structural characteristics of American society produce crime. By focusing on these characteristics, he deliberately rejects causal factors at the individual level.

Crime and the American Dream: institutional anomie theory

In their book *Crime and the American Dream*, Steven Messner and Richard Rosenfeld (1997) offer a contemporary version of Merton's anomie theory.[8] Like Merton, Messner and Rosenfeld argue that the United States has a high crime rate because of the disproportionate emphasis on the goal of material success, without a corresponding emphasis on the normative means for achieving such success. This unrestrained pursuit of material success is what they refer to as "the American Dream" – a societal condition that Merton called anomie. Messner and Rosenfeld (1997: 5) state: "In our use of the term 'the American Dream,' we refer to a broad cultural ethos that entails a commitment to the goal of material success, to be pursued by everyone in society, under conditions of open, individual competition."

Four key values form the foundation of the American Dream: achievement, individualism, universalism, and the fetishism of money (or "monetary rewards") (Messner and Rosenfeld 1997). Ideally, the desire to achieve the American Dream is held by all (*universalism*). The American Dream is achieved largely by individuals rather than groups (*individualism*), and it is manifest through the visible accumulation of money (*monetary rewards*).

The American Dream of monetary success has been identified as the "defining characteristic of American culture" (Hochschild 1995: xi). Because of its dominance, the American Dream heavily influences the social organization of American society, especially its institutional structure. As a result, the economy comes to dominate all other institutions, including the political system, the family, and education. As such, non-economic goals, roles, and norms are devalued, and non-economic institutions are influenced by and must accommodate the goals and norms of the economy. Messner and Rosenfeld (1997: 70) offer an example of this:

> Education is regarded largely as a means to occupational attainment, which in turn is valued primarily insofar as it promises economic reward. Neither the acquisition of knowledge nor learning for its own sake is highly valued. A revealing illustration of the devaluation of education relative to purely monetary concerns is provided in an interview with a high school student whose grades dropped when she increased her schedule to thirty hours per week at her two after-school jobs. She described her feelings about the

value of education this way: "School's important but so's money. Homework doesn't pay. Teachers say education is your payment, and that just makes me want to puke."

Messner and Rosenfeld (1997: 68) claim that "the goal of monetary success overwhelms other goals and becomes the principal measuring rod for achievement." Further, the "institutional balance of power" is so centered on the economy that other social institutions are unable to function effectively. In Messner and Rosenfeld's theory, both culture and social structure are important in explaining crime. In terms of culture, the cultural goal of monetary success creates motivations to commit crime. In terms of social structure, the dominance of the economy over other institutions weakens these institutions in their social control functions. They summarize their argument:

> Both of the core features of the social organization of the United States – culture and institutional structure – are implicated in the genesis of high levels of crime. At the cultural level, the dominant ethos of the American Dream stimulates criminal motivations while at the same time promoting a weak normative environment (anomie). At the institutional level, the dominance of the economy in the institutional balance of power fosters weak social control.
>
> (Messner and Rosenfeld 1997: 76–77)

Despite arguments that institutional anomie theory is not easily assessed empirically or open to falsification (Chamlin and Cochran 2007), researchers have begun to test the theory and have provided mixed results (Hirtenlehner, Farrall, and Bacher 2013; Stults and Baumer 2008; Baumer and Gustafson 2007; Schoepfer and Piquero 2006; Maume and Lee 2003). For example, a recent study found no evidence that the cultural constraints of the American Dream or the extent of anomie in a society are linked to cross-national variation in moral misconduct in ways predicted by institutional anomie theory (Hirtenlehner et al. 2013). But other research has shown that the combination of high levels of commitment to monetary success goals and low levels of commitment to legitimate means of achieving those goals predicts both lethal violent crime and instrumental crime rates – consistent with institutional anomie theory (Stults and Baumer 2008; Baumer and Gustafson 2007). In their review of this research, Messner and Rosenfeld (2006) conclude that there is generally more support for the institutional component of the theory than for the cultural component, but that the basic arguments of the theory have not been undermined by research.

Critique of anomie theory

Anomie theory has intuitive appeal, with its commonsense observations about the heavy emphasis on monetary success in American society. The American Dream seems to be an accurate depiction of life in the United States. It is also commonly recognized that not everyone has an equal chance to achieve the American Dream, but this, too, is consistent with anomie theory. Although the intuitive appeal of anomie theory is its strength, some have criticized it (Bernard et al. 2010).

Anomie theory assumes that a single dominant value – monetary success – characterizes American society, and there is widespread consensus regarding this value. But some have argued that American society is more accurately characterized by value diversity and value pluralism (Lemert 1972; see also Agnew 2000). Others have pointed out that individuals and groups may seek a variety of goals, and that goals may vary depending on age, peer group association, social class background, and even individual preference (Agnew 2000; Elliott, Huizinga, and Ageton 1985; Elliott, Ageton, and Cantor 1979). Especially relevant to a discussion of juvenile delinquency is the question of whether adolescents readily adopt the goal of economic success. Some theorists and researchers claim that adolescents tend to be more concerned with immediate rather than long-term goals. Goals related to economic success, such as educational achievement and occupational status, are seen as secondary to more immediate goals, such as popularity, friends, independence, athletic success, and fun (Agnew 2000; Moffitt 1993; Elliott et al. 1985; Greenberg 1977). Thus, some argue, and some research suggests, that the goal of monetary success may not be as universal and strong as anomie theory claims (Agnew 2000; Elliott et al. 1979; Kornhauser 1978).

The broad and sweeping argument of anomie theory has also been criticized for being virtually untestable. Ruth Kornhauser (1978) has led this charge, arguing that anomie is an abstract explanation of crime whose major concepts are difficult to measure and, when they are measured, lack empirical support.[9]

Finally, anomie theory has been criticized as being class-biased. Crime is allegedly concentrated in the lower class due to lack of opportunities (Lilly, Cullen, and Ball 2014). Messner and Rosenfeld (1997) point out that this criticism results from a narrow reading of anomie theory. Merton's primary theoretical depiction of the imbalance between goals and means applies equally to individuals in all social classes. Anomie can explain a variety of crimes, not just lower-class street crime. For example, it can be applied to offenses with a "pecuniary" quality, such as white-collar crime. Nonetheless, Merton contended that crime and delinquency are more likely to be committed by lower-class individuals because they, like individuals from other social classes, desire economic success, but they disproportionately lack opportunities to achieve it. As a result, the lower class should display higher rates of crime and delinquency than other social classes. As we discussed in Chapter 5, however, research has not provided clear, consistent, and conclusive evidence supporting a link between social class and delinquency (Akers and Sellers 2013; Tittle and Meier 1990; Tittle 1983; Tittle, Villemez, and Smith 1978).

Strain theory

Although Merton's theory tries to depict the structural characteristics of society that produce high rates of crime and deviance, it also considers how groups and individuals adapt to those structural characteristics. As we have already seen, this first consideration is referred to as anomie theory while the second consideration is sometimes distinguished as strain theory (Cullen et al. 2014; Cullen 1983). Although many criminologists use the terms *anomie* and *strain* interchangeably, it is useful to make the distinction between these theories.[10]

Building on anomie theory, strain theory explains how groups and individuals adapt to the condition of anomie in society. Anomie refers to the imbalance between goals and institutional means, in which the goal of monetary success is emphasized without clear normative standards for achieving success. In addition, anomie theory states that the acceptable means to success are unavailable to a considerable part of the population. Anomie is a structural characteristic of society, not an individual characteristic. Merton proposed that people experience strain when the accepted means for achieving success are unclear or unavailable and they must adapt to this societal condition of anomie. Although blocked opportunities for success might seem to be the primary source of strain, strain theory centers on an individual's response to anomie in terms of acceptance or rejection of cultural goals and the institutional means to reach those goals. In its most basic form, strain theory argues that "delinquency results when individuals cannot get what they want through legitimate channels" (Agnew 1995: 113). In this way, strain is seen as the motivation for delinquent acts. Although strain is experienced at the individual level, it results from structural factors, especially social class placement and the resulting level of opportunity (Farnworth and Leiber 1989).

Merton's modes of adaptation

According to Merton, there is not only one possible response to structurally induced strain. Merton (1938) proposed five possible **modes of adaptation**, which are individual responses to the goals–means disjunction of anomie. Three of the adaptations are considered deviant, but the other two usually are not. Because crime represents only one of many possible adaptations to strain, criminologists must address the question of why crime is chosen as the solution to strain. The five modes of adaptation are shown in "Expanding ideas: Merton's typology of adaptations to anomie." Merton (1938) pointed out that a person may shift from one adaptation to another.

Expanding ideas: Merton's typology of adaptations to anomie

Adaptation	Cultural goals	Means	Comments
Conformity	+	+	The most common adaptation in all social classes. The individual adopts both cultural goals and institutional means.
Innovation	+	−	With the accepted means to success underemphasized or unavailable, some individuals turn to illegitimate means. Although this adaptation explains crime by all classes of people, crime is most common among the lower class because of disproportionate lack of opportunity.
Ritualism	−	+	An almost compulsive following of the rules. More common among the lower middle class because of their strict patterns of socialization.
Retreatism	−	−	The least common adaptation. Individuals who accept the goals and means, but because the goals and means are unattainable, they become frustrated and drop out of society. For example, drug addicts and "drunkards."
Rebellion	+ −	+ −	Individuals who reject cultural goals and means and then replace them with new ones. This may be a collective adaptation, involving organized struggle for change.

Source: Merton (1938: adapted from p. 676).

Conformity, which represents an acceptance of cultural goals and the institutional means to obtain those goals, is the most common adaptation to anomie. In fact, conformity is the basis for stability and order in society. The existing social structure is supported and reaffirmed, and behavior is controlled to the degree that people accept cultural goals and the means that have been institutionalized to obtain those goals. According to Merton, conformity is spread widely across all social classes. Most people conform because they accept the cultural goals and the means that have been established to obtain success, regardless of whether these means are available to them or not.

Innovation involves the use of illegitimate means to achieve cultural goals. With the accepted means to success underemphasized or unavailable, some individuals turn to illegitimate means. Although this adaptation explains a wide variety of crime by all classes of people, Merton argued that crime is most common among the lower class because of the lack of opportunity afforded its members.

Ritualism involves rigid compliance with rules, without a clear commitment to the goals. Ritualism typically does not result in deviant behavior. In fact, it may produce "over conformity" and the lowest rates of deviance among the five modes of adaptation. A youth who lives within the law but makes little effort in school and has few aspirations displays ritualism in his or her daily life. The routines of institutional norms provide youth with a sense of security, even without the adoption of success goals (Merton 1968). Merton contended that ritualism is most common among the lower middle class because strict patterns of socialization encourage individuals to follow the rules of society.

Retreatism is the least common adaptation. Some individuals initially accept the goals and means, but because the means are unattainable, they eventually drop out of society. Merton says that these frustrated individuals are "aliens" in society. "Not sharing the common frame of orientation," they are "in the society but not of it" (Merton 1938: 677). Merton included vagrants, chronic drunkards, and drug addicts in this adaptation.

Rebellion depicts individuals who not only reject cultural goals and means, but replace them with new ones. Merton noted that this adaptation is so different from the others that it must be distinguished and set apart. (His original table actually had a line separating rebellion from the other modes of adaptation.) This form of adaptation "involves an effort to change the existing structure" of goals and means. Rebellion can involve collective adaptation in an organized struggle for change such as the Vietnam War protests and the Civil Rights movement of the 1960s.

Research on strain

The social psychological character of strain is most frequently depicted as the imbalance between *aspirations* (an individual's goals) and *expectations* (an individual's perception of opportunities) – the discrepancy between what people want and what they expect to get (Cullen et al. 2014; Agnew 2000; Burton et al. 1994; Burton and Cullen 1992; Farnworth and Leiber 1989). According to strain theory, youth who adopt goals of economic success, but who feel that they are unable to reach those goals because of limited opportunities, are more likely than others to experience emotional strain in the form of frustration or anger, and this, in turn, motivates delinquency (Agnew 1995).

Research testing this basic premise of strain theory has provided only limited empirical support (Agnew 2000; Jensen 1995; Burton et al. 1994; Burton and Cullen 1992; Kornhauser 1978). Travis Hirschi conducted one of the most widely cited assessments of strain theory.

In his social bond theory, which stands in contrast to strain theory, Hirschi argued that high aspirations to conventional goals actually constrain delinquency, and that delinquent youth lack commitment to conventional goals. Hirschi argued that the discrepancy between aspirations and expectations does not provide any additional explanation for delinquency beyond that offered by the social bond of commitment. Using measures of educational aspirations and educational expectations, Hirschi found that commitment to educational aspirations decreased the likelihood of delinquent behavior, regardless of the level of perceived expectations. In contrast to strain theory, Hirschi (1969: 172, emphasis in original) observed that *"those boys whose educational or occupational aspirations exceed their expectations are no more likely to be delinquent than those boys whose aspirations and expectations are identical."*[11]

Research findings have also provided only limited support for the proposition that strain results when goals for success go unfulfilled because of blocked opportunities (Agnew 2000; Burton et al. 1994). Contrary to strain theory's predictions, Ruth Kornhauser's (1978) review of the empirical research on strain revealed that delinquents showed both low aspirations and low expectations, indicating that they are not under social psychological strain and have little motivation to engage in delinquency.

Margaret Farnworth and Michael Leiber (1989) contend that the lack of empirical support for strain theory has more to do with the way in which strain has been measured than with the theory's lack of legitimacy. They argue that Merton's depiction of strain is most appropriately measured as the difference between economic goals (the desire to make lots of money) and educational expectations (how much school one expects to complete). The reliance on educational measures of both aspirations and expectations, as Hirschi used, neglects Merton's emphasis on economic aspirations as the primary goal in American society.

Farnworth and Leiber (1989) examined various measures of aspirations and expectations. They found that, consistent with Hirschi's findings, educational aspirations alone are significantly related to delinquency and that the strain of unequal educational aspirations and educational expectations provides no additional explanation. However, they also found that when economic aspirations are used as a measure of goals, instead of educational aspirations, the strain that results from an imbalance between aspirations and expectations is a better predictor of delinquency than are financial aspirations alone. They conclude that "the empirical findings to date are not sufficient to falsify the basic postulates of Merton's theory of strain and deviance" (Farnworth and Leiber 1989: 272).

More recently, Scott Menard (1995) analyzed data from the National Youth Survey and found that nearly all youth adopted the goal of economic success, as measured by a question about the importance of getting a good job or career. Furthermore, there were far more youth who desired success than there were who expected success. This discrepancy between aspirations and expectations indicates a societal condition of anomie. Also consistent with Merton's strain theory, Menard found that innovators and retreatists had higher rates of minor and serious offending than did conformists or ritualists. Throughout the adolescent years, ritualists had the lowest rate of offending. Findings for marijuana and drug use were also consistent with Merton's strain theory, showing that retreatists had the highest rate of drug offending, followed by innovators.

The strain of adolescence: general strain theory

Even though research has not been overly supportive of strain theory, its major theme remains influential in delinquency theory and research: delinquent acts are motivated by the strain or frustration that results when goals cannot be achieved and go unfulfilled. Revisions of classic strain theory continue to adopt this basic theme but sometimes expand the notion of goals beyond the goal of economic success that Merton emphasized. Some have argued that adolescents pursue a variety of goals in addition to monetary success. Goals such as popularity, friends, freedom and independence, athletic success, and having fun take on great importance during the adolescent years, and these more immediate goals are perhaps more influential than the long-term goal of monetary success (Agnew 2000; Moffitt 1993; Elliott et al. 1985; Greenberg 1977).

Robert Agnew's revised strain theory, *general strain theory*, follows a different avenue. Rather than expanding the number and variety of goals that adolescents pursue, Agnew focuses on the central importance of strain as a motivation for delinquency. Crime and delinquency are viewed as adaptations to strain, and Agnew's revised theory identifies several sources of strain beyond that offered by classic strain theory, which points to the lack of legitimate means for achieving economic goals as the single source of strain. Drawing on frustration aggression and social learning theories, Agnew (1995) claims that strain also results from an individual's efforts to avoid unpleasant or painful situations. In other words, strain results not only from goal seeking, but also from undesirable situations and outcomes.

Agnew's theory emphasizes the social psychological aspects of strain, rather than the structural limitation of low social class and lack of opportunity. In particular, he focuses on the strain that results from negative social relationships in which an individual is not being treated as he or she would like to be. He describes three general types of strain: (1) individuals may be unable to achieve their goals, (2) individuals may lose something they value, and (3) individuals may be treated in an aversive or negative manner by others (Agnew 1992, 2006).

Strain resulting from failure to achieve goals

The first source of strain includes the traditional emphasis that classic strain theory places on the disjunction between aspirations and expectations as the primary motivation for delinquency. This form of strain, however, has been heavily criticized. Agnew (1995: 115) points to social psychological research that shows that "people tend to (a) pursue a variety of goals, (b) place most importance on those goals they are best able to achieve, and (c) exaggerate or distort their actual and expected levels of goal achievement." To illustrate, he refers to his own research that showed that the goals adolescents set for themselves are often exaggerated. "Adolescents doing poorly in school ... often described themselves as good students who expected to attend college" (Agnew 1995: 115). Agnew concludes that the disjunction between aspirations and expectations is probably not a major source of strain because virtually all adolescents believe they are achieving at least some of their goals, and they often make social psychological adjustments when their goals seem unachievable. According to Agnew and Brezina (2015), adolescents pursue a variety of goals, including money, status and respect, thrills and excitement, and autonomy from adults.

Within this first category of strain, Agnew (1992) adds two more sources of strain that emerge in the context of negative social relationships. Both sources of strain draw from social psychological research on justice and equity in interpersonal relations. First, a gap between expectations and actual achievements can lead to feelings of anger, unfairness, and disappointment. Similar to goals, beliefs about what is achievable – expectations – are developed in reference groups. In comparison with others, youth develop a sense of what they can reasonably expect to achieve. Strain results when actual achievement falls short of these expectations, especially when an individual sees that others are successful.

Second, strain can result from an inconsistency between perceptions of "fair outcomes" and actual outcomes. Once again, the context of this source of strain is within social relations, but the emphasis is on the fairness or equity of interactions among people. If interpersonal exchange is viewed as unequal in terms of either what one puts into it or what one gets out of it, the individual may experience "distress." A possible reaction to this distress is deviance.

Strain resulting from the loss of something valued

A second category of strain involves the experience of stressful life events or conditions associated with the loss of something or someone an individual values, such as the separation or divorce of parents, parental rejection, the loss of a boyfriend or girlfriend, moving, the death of a friend, or suspension from school (Agnew 1992). The stress of adolescence is often related to such loss. Psychologists have developed numerous inventories of stressful life events and have found that the number of these events experienced by youth is related to delinquency.

Strain resulting from negative treatment by others

The third category of strain relates to another set of stressful life events or conditions – those involving negative actions by others toward the youth (Agnew 1992). Experiences such as harsh or erratic discipline, child abuse, criminal victimization, or negative relations with parents, teachers, or peers are a source of strain. These "noxious stimuli" may lead to delinquency as the adolescent tries to avoid them, compensate for them, or seek revenge.

Explaining the effects of strain

Agnew's general strain theory tries to expand and categorize the sources of strain that result from negative relationships with others (Agnew 2001, 2012). These negative relationships increase the likelihood that individuals will experience anger or frustration. Anger is an especially important emotional reaction because it provides motivation and justification for delinquency, and it breaks down constraints. In this way, delinquency can be seen as a "coping response to interpersonal problems" (Brezina 1996: 41–42; Agnew 1992; Agnew and White 1992).

As in classic strain theory, Agnew acknowledges that strain does not lead all adolescents to crime. Delinquency is only one possible adaptation to strain. A variety of "predispositions" and "constraints" influence the likelihood that a youth will turn to delinquency as a solution to strain. Predispositions and constraints include "the adolescent's temperament, problem-solving skills, self-efficacy, self-esteem, level of conventional social support, attributions regarding the causes of strain, level of social control, and association with delinquent peers" (Agnew and White 1992: 477; see also Agnew 1992, 2006). Agnew and his colleagues (2002) found that youth characterized by personality traits of negative emotionality and low constraint were more likely than others to react to strain with delinquency. In a recent extension of general strain theory, Agnew (2013: 653) argues that several factors must come together before strain is likely to lead to crime: "individuals must (a) possess a set of characteristics that together create a strong propensity for criminal coping, (b) experience criminogenic strains, which are perceived as unjust and high in magnitude, and (c) be in circumstances conducive to criminal coping."

General strain theory holds that strain can be experienced by anyone, regardless of social class, gender, race, or ethnicity.[12] As a result, the negative pressure or motivation toward delinquency crosses social boundaries. Unlike classic strain theory, general strain theory tries to explain delinquency generally, not as an adaptation concentrated in the lower class.

Various sources of strain are associated with school experiences and characteristics. "Research in action: schools, strain, and delinquency" summarizes research on the relationships between delinquency and school-related strains.

Research in action: schools, strain, and delinquency

Various school experiences and characteristics are sources of strain and have been linked through empirical research to delinquency.

School experiences

The relationships between delinquency and the following school experiences can be explained in terms of strain theory:

- **Poor academic performance.** Maguin and Loeber (1996) analyzed more than 100 studies of the relationship between academic performance and delinquency. They found that poor academic performance consistently predicted delinquent behavior. Specifically, children who performed poorly academically committed more frequent, serious, and violent offenses and persisted longer in their offending than children with higher academic achievement (Maguin and Loeber 1996). A more recent study by Felson and Staff (2006), however, suggests that the relationship between poor academic performance and delinquency is spurious and due to the effects of self-control on both academic performance and delinquent behavior. On the flip side, strong academic performance by incarcerated delinquents appears to serve as a turning point, contributing to a return to school following incarceration and a decrease in the likelihood of re-arrest (Blomberg, Bales, and Piquero 2012; see also Hoffman, Erickson, and Spence 2013).
- **Poor relationships with teachers.** Delinquents are more likely than non-delinquents to report that they dislike their teachers and have negative relationships with them (Agnew 1985).
- **Limited educational and occupational goals.** Compared to non-delinquents, delinquents have more limited educational and occupational aspirations and expectations (Agnew and Brezina 2015; Carroll et al. 2013). A recent study found that, compared to at-risk and not at-risk adolescents, "delinquent adolescents reported fewest goals, set fewer challenging goals, had a lower commitment to their goals, and reported lower levels of academic and self-regulatory efficacy" (Carroll et al. 2013: 431). Research shows that educational expectations combined with effort in school explain delinquents' lower educational attainment (Siennick and Staff 2008). Research also reveals that youth in more affluent communities have greater access to both educational and employment opportunities, and that these opportunities are related to higher grades and greater expectations to succeed (Chung, Mulvey, and Steinberg 2011).

School characteristics

Robert Agnew and Timothy Brezina (2015: 279–280) list the following school characteristics that contribute to lower rates of in-school delinquency:

- Small schools with good resources.
- Schools with good discipline. (Rules for behavior are clear, and rules are consistently enforced in a fair manner.)
- Schools that provide opportunities for student success and praise student accomplishments.
- Schools with high expectations for students.
- Schools with pleasant working conditions for students.
- Schools with good cooperation between the administration and teachers.
- Schools with strong community involvement.

From a strain theory perspective, we might explain the relationship between these school characteristics and delinquency in this way: schools with these characteristics are less likely to create strain for students because they are perceived as pleasant and fair, students are likely to achieve their success goals, and students are likely to have positive relationships with teachers and others in the school (Agnew and Brezina 2015; see also National Research Council 2013).

Research on general strain theory

Agnew's general strain theory has generated a great deal of research designed to test it and has received strong empirical support. The theory receives indirect support from a wide variety of research findings showing that:

> delinquency is associated with such strains as negative relations with parents and teachers, child abuse, conflict with peers, criminal victimization, neighborhood problems, and a range of stressful life events – like parental divorce, family financial problems, and changing schools. Further, certain studies indicate that these strains increase the likelihood of delinquency by increasing the individual's level of anger and frustration.
>
> (Agnew 2000: 356)

More direct tests of the theory have constructed summary measures of strain (Paternoster and Mazerolle 1994; Agnew and White 1992). Robert Agnew and Helene White (1992), for example, focused on two categories of strain presented in the theory: the loss of positive stimuli and the presence of negative stimuli. They measured strain through responses to questions about recent negative experiences, such as the loss of a close friend through death; the divorce of parents; not getting along with classmates, parents, and teachers; and experience of various types of crime. Adolescents who scored high on this composite measure of strain were far more likely to engage in delinquent acts than those who scored lower. Thus, the experience of strain pressured or motivated youth to engage in delinquency. Agnew and White also found that the effects of strain depended on association with delinquent peers and self-efficacy – factors that general strain theory acknowledges will play a role in producing delinquent responses to strain.

Timothy Brezina (1996, 1999, 2000) has studied the degree to which delinquent acts are a coping response to strain. He used data drawn from the Youth in Transition survey, a nationally representative sample of almost 2,000 male public high school students. Adopting a measure of strain similar to Agnew and White's, Brezina (1996) found that the experience of strain was associated with feelings of anger, resentment, anxiety, and depression. He concluded that involvement in delinquency enables adolescents to minimize the negative emotional consequences of strained social relationships. This helps to explain the appeal that delinquency has for many adolescents and why delinquent behavior is not easily changed.

More recent studies also provide support for general strain theory and demonstrate its value in explaining both juvenile and adult offending and its applicability to offending in the United States and other countries (Sigfusdottir, Kristjansson, and Agnew 2012; Piquero and Sealock 2004, 2010; Carson et al. 2009; Moon et al. 2009; Rebellon et al. 2009; Sigfusdottir et al. 2008; Froggio and Agnew 2007; Hay and Evans 2006; Ostrowsky and Messner 2005; Baron 2004; Hoffmann and Ireland 2004). For example, some studies show that victimization is a source of strain that increases the likelihood of drug use and delinquency (Watts and McNulty 2013; Carson et al. 2009; Manasse and Ganem 2009; Hay and Evans 2006). Research on family-based victimization reveals that adolescent maltreatment is related to general delinquency, serious delinquency, and substance use, and that negative emotions are key intervening mechanisms between maltreatment and delinquency (Hollist, Hughes, and Schaible 2009; see also Watts and McNulty 2013). Peer rejection, as a source of strain, is also related to involvement in crime and delinquency, at least among males (Higgins, Piquero, and Piquero 2011). Researchers have also examined the loss of positive stimuli that results when a romantic relationship ends. Consistent with general strain theory, males who experience romantic loss are more likely to engage in crime and drug use. For females, the breakup of a romantic relationship leads to greater alcohol and marijuana use (Larson and Sweeten 2012).

Some research suggests that the strain of stressful life events has a stronger effect on offending among adolescents than among young adults (Hoffmann 2010). This research also suggests that peers play an important role in the relationship between strain and delinquent or criminal behavior. Associations with delinquent or criminal peers diminish the effects of stressful life events on offending (Hoffmann 2010).

Other recent studies explore emotions, such as anger and depression, which mediate the effects of strain on delinquency. These studies support Agnew's hypothesis that strain influences delinquent behavior, in part through its effects on negative emotional states, especially anger (Moon et al. 2009; Hay and Evans 2006). This process operates somewhat differently across gender. Research suggests that males and females tend to experience different types of negative life events and that the effects of strain on emotions are somewhat different for males and females. While negative life events lead to similar levels of anger among boys and girls, they predict depressed mood more strongly for girls than for boys (Sigfusdottir and Silver 2009). Emotions also lead to different types of deviance across gender (fighting for males and cutting oneself for females) (Posick, Farrell, and Swatt 2013).

Research supports Agnew's hypothesis that perceptions of injustice increase the likelihood of delinquency, and that situational anger mediates this relationship (Rebellon et al. 2012). Finally, research has examined the "constraints" that influence the likelihood that strain will lead to delinquency. One study, for example, shows that social support decreases individuals' delinquent responses to strain (Robbers 2004). Other recent studies have demonstrated more mixed support for general strain theory (Peck 2013; Botchkovar, Tittle, and Antonaccio 2009; Tittle, Broidy, and Gertz 2008).

Strain and gang subcultures

Criminologists have used the idea of strain to explain gang delinquency among urban, lower-class males in two important extensions of Merton's strain theory: Albert Cohen's *reaction formation theory* and Richard Cloward and Lloyd Ohlin's *differential opportunity theory*. In both applications, the lack of opportunity and relative deprivation that virtually all lower-class boys experience results in strain and ultimately leads to gang delinquency. However, the key link between strain and gang delinquency is the adoption of subcultural values and norms that encourage and support delinquent acts (Hagan et al. 1998).

Cohen's reaction formation theory

Writing in 1955, Albert Cohen observed that much of the delinquent activity in inner-city areas was committed by gang members and that most of these acts were done not for economic gain, but "for the hell of it." He described gang delinquency as "nonutilitarian, malicious, and negativistic" – it appeared to serve little purpose and was often hostile, cruel, and contemptuous. Cohen's influential book, *Delinquent Boys: The Culture of the Gang*, attempts to account for the character of gang delinquency and to explain the development of gangs and the values and norms they embrace.

Like Merton, Cohen (1955) claimed that delinquency is ultimately caused by blocked goals. However, he argued that lower-class boys are not concerned only with the goal of monetary success. Instead, they want to achieve the broader goal of middle-class status, which involves not only monetary success, but also respect from others. Lower-class boys are disadvantaged in their efforts to achieve status, however, especially status in conventional institutions like schools.[13]

Cohen (1955) distinguished *ascribed status* from *achieved status*. Ascribed status is tied to the social position of one's family, and achieved status is earned through effort and accomplishment. Inner-city boys typically have low ascribed status because their families are lower class, and they are at a competitive disadvantage to earn achieved status because their early socialization fails to equip them with the characteristics and skills necessary to be successful in school, the institution in which competition for achieved status first occurs.

According to Cohen (1955: 98–100), lower-class parents are "easy-going" and "permissive," whereas middle-class parents are "rational, deliberate, and demanding." Lower-class parents also do not model attitudes and behaviors that encourage achievement. Thus, Cohen contends that social class placement structures children's socialization experiences. As a result, lower-class boys fail to learn the values, traits, and skills upon which status in school is judged. Skills relevant to future economic achievement and standards such as ambition, responsibility, deferred gratification, "rationality" in terms of planning, control of physical aggression, and courtesy, manners, and "personability" are rarely taught or stressed through the casual parenting of lower-class parents. Due to inadequate socialization, lower-class boys inevitably fail in school because teachers impose "middle-class measuring rods" (Cohen 1955). School failure, in turn, breeds **status frustration** – the dominant type of strain experienced by lower-class boys.

Cohen argued that most people adapt to strain collectively, by joining with others to find solutions to problems they share. Confronted with the problem of status frustration, lower-class boys turn to each other to achieve status. Cohen claims that three different adaptations are likely. The *corner boy* accepts the low status ascribed to those from the lower class and disengages from the competitive struggle for status. Instead, he turns to the "sheltering community of like-minded peers" – the corner boy subculture of the lower class (Cohen 1955: 129). The *college boy* is able to achieve academic success despite the competitive disadvantage that confronts lower-class youth. Relatively few lower-class boys are able to compete in the middle-class arena of education, but the few who are able to master unfamiliar academic and social skills achieve status in school and continue on into college. The final adaptation – the *delinquent boy* – is the focus of Cohen's book. Cohen argues that the delinquent subculture begins and is maintained as a solution to the status problem common among lower-class boys.

According to Cohen, lower-class boys often join gangs in order to deal with their collective problem of status frustration experienced in schools. The delinquent subculture provides criteria of status that lower-class youth can meet, and delinquent gangs offer a social context in which lower-class boys can gain status. In a psychological process called **reaction formation**, lower-class boys in gangs develop alternative values that allow them to experience success and thereby gain status (at least in the eyes of their peers).

Delinquent acts easily fulfill the values of the gang subculture. Cohen describes these acts and the delinquent subculture as non-utilitarian, malicious, negativistic, versatile, and hedonistic, and as providing group autonomy. He claims that much of the property crime committed by gang members yields little apparent gain. It is also commonly observed that gang members acquire status, even pleasure, from the harm and trouble they cause others, and that they take pride in reputations of meanness and toughness. Gang delinquency also occurs spontaneously, with little planning, and includes a wide range of illegal activities. Finally, the criminal acts of the gang provide definition, cohesiveness, and autonomy to the delinquent subculture.

Criticism of Cohen's strain theory has focused more on its logical completeness than on its adequacy as tested through research (Gibbons 1979; see also Akers and Sellers 2013; Agnew 1999; Bordua 1961; Kitsuse and Dietrick 1959). Concern over the theory has been raised primarily by pointing to a number of unresolved questions:

- Do lower-class boys desire middle-class status as achieved through interpersonal respect and economic success?
- Does school failure produce status frustration? Is this strain enough to explain the development of gang subcultures?
- Do youth seek collective responses to problems?
- Does the gang subculture constitute a wholesale rejection of middle-class culture? Is the gang subculture unique, or do delinquent gangs partially reflect the dominant culture? Do subcultures approve of crime?
- Are the delinquent acts of gangs non-utilitarian, malicious, and negativistic? Does this character of gang delinquency promote group autonomy?
- How is the gang subculture maintained over time?

Cloward and Ohlin's differential opportunity theory

Like Cohen, Richard Cloward and Lloyd Ohlin (1960) offer a strain theory that tries to explain how delinquent gang subcultures arise and persist in lower-class neighborhoods. Building on Merton's strain theory, they state their thesis as follows:

> The disparity between what lower-class youth are led to want and what is actually available to them is the source of a major problem of adjustment. Adolescents who form delinquent subcultures ... have internalized an emphasis upon conventional goals. Faced with limitation of legitimate avenues of access to these goals, and unable to revise their aspirations downward, they experience intense frustrations; the exploration of nonconformist alternatives may be the result.
>
> (Cloward and Ohlin 1960: 86)

Cloward and Ohlin also claim that education is central to upward mobility, but there are significant barriers to this *legitimate opportunity* for success. The strain that results from this lack of opportunity is experienced most intensely by adolescent males from urban, lower-class environments. However, just as legitimate opportunities are unequally available, so, too, are the *illegitimate opportunities* that youth turn to out of frustration. Legitimate opportunities to achieve cultural goals include the availability of quality education and employment options. Illegitimate opportunities include criminal means of achieving economic goals (e.g., through theft or selling drugs), of gaining status (e.g., through the use of violence), or of pursuing excitement and fun (e.g., through drug use). Because Cloward and Ohlin's theory points to the existence of both legitimate and illegitimate opportunities for success, it is called *differential opportunity theory*. According to Cloward and Ohlin, gang delinquency is ultimately an expression of the structure of opportunities, both legitimate and illegitimate.

Cloward and Ohlin claim that lower-class areas are characterized by different types of criminal patterns and traditions. They identify three distinct delinquent subcultures that reflect the type of illegitimate opportunity available in the surrounding community: criminal, conflict, and retreatist. A *criminal subculture* exists in neighborhoods that are well organized for crime, where norms all but require criminal involvement and where values support, validate, and rationalize involvement in crime. Criminal role models are readily available, and possibilities for involvement in crime are everywhere. Delinquent gangs that develop within such a tradition of crime are "devoted to theft, extortion, and other illegal means of securing income" (Cloward and Ohlin 1960: 1).

Conflict subcultures predominate in areas that lack criminal traditions. Without criminal patterns to follow and without readily available opportunities for crime, conflict and violence become the primary means of gaining status. Threats and the use of force dominate the activities of these "warrior" groups.

The *retreatist subculture* is culturally and socially detached from the lifestyle and everyday preoccupations of the conventional world. In their place, the retreatist subculture stresses "the continuous pursuit of the 'kick'" (Cloward and Ohlin 1960: 26). The extensive use of drugs for fun and pleasure is encouraged and expected within this subculture.

Differential opportunity theory became the cornerstone of a delinquency prevention program called Mobilization for Youth, begun in New York City in the early 1960s. This was a comprehensive program that tried to increase legitimate opportunities for lower-class youth through a variety of economic and education reforms. Components included preschool programs, tutoring, in-service teacher training to increase teacher–parent communication and enhance cultural awareness of lower-class communities, vocational training, job placement programs, community organization through neighborhood councils and associations, services to youth and families, and a detached worker program to respond to gangs.

Neither this practical application of differential opportunity theory, nor the theory itself, was subject to thorough empirical testing. As a result, criticism focused more on the accuracy and logical completeness of the theory's explanation than on the amount of empirical support for the theory or the program. Differential opportunity theory assumes that blocked educational and economic opportunities make lower-class youth receptive to illegitimate avenues for success – opportunities that are largely illegal. This reflects the common assumption of strain theories that crime and delinquency are committed mainly by lower-class individuals. As we described in Chapter 5, however, research has failed to provide clear and consistent evidence that delinquency is a lower-class activity (Tittle and Meier 1990; Tittle 1983; Tittle et al. 1978). Moreover, when blocked educational opportunities are added to the causal explanation, the link between social class and delinquency becomes even more tenuous. School failure is related to delinquent behavior in all social classes, not just the lower class (Wiatrowski et al. 1982; Wiatrowski, Griswold, and Roberts 1981; Johnson 1979).

Differential opportunity theory also proposes that three types of delinquent subcultures are most common in lower-class areas, depending on the organization of the neighborhood and the availability of illegitimate opportunities for success. Yet, research has not verified these three distinct subcultures nor shown that delinquent gangs specialize in the types of acts suggested by the theory (Esbensen and Huizinga 1993; Thornberry et al. 1993; Farrington, Snyder, and Finnegan 1988; Short and Strodbeck 1965). Instead, delinquent gangs engage in a wide variety of criminal offenses. Moreover, boys in delinquent gangs spend most of their time involved in non-delinquent activities.

Summary and conclusions

Social structure theories attempt to identify and account for the social and societal characteristics that integrate and regulate people's daily lives. Sociologists refer to these organizational features of the social environment as *social structures*. Social structure theories consider societal characteristics such as cultural traditions; institutionalized social relations within the context of families, schools, and employment; and ecological dimensions, such as population mobility and the residential concentration of ethnic groups and social classes. When these societal characteristics disrupt social organization, social control breaks down, and crime and delinquency flourish. The thesis that rapid social change results in the breakdown of primary group controls is particularly important to many social structure theories. This lack of social regulation is called *anomie*.

Shaw and McKay's theory of social disorganization emphasizes three structural characteristics of urban environments that disrupt social organization: *low economic status*, *ethnic heterogeneity*, and *residential mobility*. Urban areas characterized by these structures typically lack effective social control mechanisms and, as a result, experience high rates of crime and delinquency. These delinquency areas often have strong criminal traditions, or subcultures, in which involvement in illegal activity is a way of life, passed on from adults to youth and youth to youth. Delinquency areas also lack legitimate economic opportunities, resulting in personal frustration, or strain, that can motivate involvement in delinquency.

Robert Sampson has recently revitalized *social disorganization theory* by advancing his own theory called *collective efficacy*. He argues that structural characteristics related to the social composition of neighborhoods, including concentrated disadvantage, immigrant concentration, and residential stability, are strongly related to rates of violence. The influence of these structural features of neighborhoods, however, depends on the degree to which local residents are interdependent, cohesive, and willing to exercise informal social control. This essential neighborhood characteristic of interconnectedness is called collective efficacy.

Delinquency theories that focus on the lack of regulation in society are referred to as *anomie theories*. Robert Merton argued that the *cultural goal* of economic success permeates all of American society, but that the *institutional means* or norms to achieve success are neither stressed to the same degree nor equally available to all people. This social structural characteristic of anomie frees people to pursue economic success by whatever means necessary, including crime.

Messner and Rosenfeld's *institutional anomie theory* adds another structural feature to the anomie equation: institutions. They argue that the economy has come to dominate all institutions in the United States because of the ever-increasing emphasis on economic success – "the American Dream." Institutions such as the political system, the family, and education are declining in influence. Domination by the economy prevents these other institutions from functioning effectively to socialize and control the behavior of individuals. Both the culture and institutional structures of American society generate high levels of crime.

Building on anomie theory, the strain perspective explains how groups and individuals adapt to the condition of anomie in society. Merton argued that individuals experience *strain* when the acceptable means to economic success are unclear or unavailable, and that they must adapt to such strain. He proposed five modes of adaptation as being most common: conformity, ritualism, innovation, retreatism, and rebellion. Deviant behavior occurs as part of the last three adaptations.

Robert Agnew's *general strain theory* identifies additional sources of strain beyond the structural feature of anomie. In particular, he focuses on strain that results from negative social relationships and efforts to avoid unpleasant or painful situations. As such, he emphasizes the social psychological aspect of strain.

Strain has also been used as the fundamental explanation for gang delinquency among urban, lower-class males. Albert Cohen's version of strain theory is referred to as either *status frustration theory* or *reaction formation theory* because of the central role these two processes play in his argument. Cohen argued that, due to inadequate socialization, lower-class boys are poorly equipped to do well in school. As a result, they experience status frustration, which leads them to seek collective solutions through involvement in delinquent gangs. The delinquent subculture develops values that stand in sharp contrast to middle-class goals. This process is referred to as *reaction formation*. These alternative values allow lower-class boys to experience success and gain status, at least in the eyes of their peers.

Cloward and Ohlin's strain theory of gang delinquency also points to the importance of blocked educational and economic opportunities in producing delinquent subcultures in lower-class urban areas. When *legitimate opportunities* are unavailable, youth turn to *illegitimate opportunities*. However, like legitimate opportunities, illegitimate opportunities are not always available or accessible. The criminal traditions, values, and norms of lower-class neighborhoods determine the availability of illegitimate opportunities and, in turn, the types of delinquent subcultures that develop. According to Cloward and Ohlin, three types of delinquent gangs are found in lower-class areas: *criminal subcultures*, *conflict subcultures*, and *retreatist subcultures*.

Critical-thinking questions

1. Consider the case of Sidney Blotzman presented at the beginning of this chapter. Explain, in terms of the social structure theories discussed in this chapter, how the characteristics of Sidney's neighborhood may have influenced his involvement in delinquency.

2. Sociologists first proposed social disorganization theory in 1929 and anomie and strain theories in 1938. Discuss the relevance of these theories in contemporary American society. Are these theories as applicable today as when they were first proposed? Why or why not?
3. How accurate is the characterization of American society that anomie and strain theories provide? Are these theories relevant or useful for explaining crime in societies with different economic and political structures?
4. Discuss the ways in which the social structural processes described in social disorganization and anomie theories influence behavior at the individual level.
5. Suppose you were asked to design delinquency prevention efforts based on Sampson, Raudenbush, and Earls' theory of collective efficacy. What components would that delinquency prevention program include, and why?

Suggested reading

Agnew, Robert. 1992. "Foundation for a General Strain Theory of Crime and Deviance." *Criminology* 30: 47–87.

Mazerolle, Lorraine, Rebecca Wickes, and James McBroom. 2010. "Community Variations in Violence: The Role of Social Ties and Collective Efficacy in Comparative Context." *Journal of Research in Crime and Delinquency* 47: 3–30.

Merton, Robert K. 1938. "Social Structure and Anomie." *American Sociological Review* 3: 672–682.

Sampson, Robert J. 2013. "The Place of Context: A Theory and Strategy for Criminology's Hard Problems." *Criminology* 51: 1–31.

Sampson, Robert J., Steven W. Raudenbush, and Felton Earls. 1997. "Neighborhoods and Violent Crime: A Multilevel Study of Collective Efficacy." *Science* 277: 918–924.

Warner, Barbara D. 2007. "Directly Intervene or Call the Authorities? A Study of Forms of Neighborhood Social Control within a Social Disorganization Framework." *Criminology* 45: 99–129.

Useful websites

For further information relevant to this chapter, go to the following websites.

*   Community Crime Prevention, Office of Justice Programs, National Institute of Justice (www.crimesolutions.gov/)
*   Chicago Area Project (www.chicagoareaproject.org/)
*   Project on Human Development in Chicago Neighborhoods, Inter-University Consortium for Political and Social Research, The University of Michigan (www.icpsr. umich.edu/icpsrweb/PHDCN/)
*   Communities That Care (Social Development Research Group), The Center for Communities That Care, University of Washington (www.communitiesthatcare.net/)
*   National Public Radio, "Reconsidering the 'Broken Windows' Theory" (www.npr.org/ templates/story/story.php?storyId=4520866)

Glossary of key terms

Anomie: According to Merton, a societal emphasis on certain cultural goals without a corresponding emphasis on the institutional means to obtain those goals.

Collective efficacy: The willingness of community residents to be involved with each other and to exercise informal social control; it influences the degree to which concentrated disadvantage produces crime and delinquency in a community.

Cultural goals: Goals that are socially learned and commonly held to be desirable, worthwhile, and meaningful.

Institutional means: Accepted avenues for achieving cultural goals.

Modes of adaptation: Individual responses to the goals–means disjunction of anomie: conformity, ritualism, innovation, retreatism, and rebellionism.

Reaction formation: A psychological process of rejecting conventional goals and means for success and substituting alternative goals and means.

Social solidarity: Social structures of society that integrate and regulate individuals and groups.

Social structures: Organizational features of the social environment, such as neighborhood socioeconomic status, ethnic heterogeneity, residential mobility, cultural traditions, and age and gender distributions.

Status frustration: According to Cohen, the dominant type of strain that lower-class boys experience. It results from school failure brought about by inadequate socialization to the values, traits, and skills that teachers use to judge success in school.

Notes

1. In a brief, but important statement, Kroeber and Parsons (1958) tried to make clear the distinction between the concepts of culture and social structure. *Culture*, they argued, should be limited to dimensions such as values, beliefs, and knowledge, whereas *social structure* should refer to relational or interactional dimensions of the social system. Later, Ruth Kornhauser (1978) criticized delinquency theory for failing to keep these concepts distinct. She argued that social disorganization theory and anomie theory mingle these concepts and thereby make them indistinguishable and of limited analytic usefulness. Although Kornhauser's point is well taken, the concepts simply cannot be neatly separated. They refer to different aspects of the same underlying social phenomenon: mechanisms of social organization. See also Messner and Rosenfeld (1997: 50).
2. See Lowenkamp, Cullen, and Pratt (2003) for a replication of Sampson and Groves' findings.
3. See Kingston, Huizinga, and Elliott (2009), who also provide a full test of social disorganization theory that includes structural community characteristics, neighborhood social processes, and delinquency rates. Another recent study examined the extent to which neighborhood characteristics influence residents' use of informal social control, but did not incorporate crime or delinquency rates into the analysis (Warner 2007).
4. See Sampson (2006); Sampson, Morenoff, and Earls (1999); Sampson et al. (1997); Elliott et al. (1996); Sampson and Wilson (1995); Sampson and Groves (1989). See also Kubrin and Weitzer (2003).
5. The concept of social capital is drawn from the work of James S. Coleman (1988, 1990).
6. See Sampson (2006, 2013) for discussions of the current state and future of collective efficacy theory and the importance of contextual approaches to the study of crime and delinquency.
7. Research by Sampson et al. (1999) found that residential stability and concentrated advantage, rather than concentrated disadvantage, predict collective efficacy. Further, their findings indicate that the extent to which neighborhood collective efficacy is able to control crime and delinquency is dependent on the "neighborhood's relative spatial position in the larger city," especially with regard to the collective efficacy of surrounding neighborhoods (Sampson et al. 1999: 657).
8. See Messner, Thome, and Rosenfeld (2008), who present clarifications and elaborations of institutional anomie theory.
9. See Bernard (1984) for a very different interpretation of these same studies.
10. But see Baumer (2007), who argues that Merton's anomie perspective reflects one multilevel theory, rather than two analytically distinct theories of anomie and strain.

11. See Jensen (1995) and Johnson (1979) for findings consistent with Hirschi's. See Bernard (1984) for a reinterpretation of the theoretical and empirical adequacy of control theory's criticism of strain theory.
12. Kaufman et al. (2008) discuss how general strain theory might be applied to explain racial differences in offending. Perez, Jennings, and Gover (2008) explore strains experienced by Hispanics and the effects of these strains on violent delinquency; they find support for general strain theory.
13. Cohen (1955) actually referred to "working-class" boys rather than "lower-class" boys. However, the particular group on which he focused was inner-city boys who today would be more commonly classified as lower class.

References

Agnew, Robert. 1985. "A Revised Strain Theory of Delinquency." *Social Forces* 64: 151–167.

Agnew, Robert. 1992. "Foundation for a General Strain Theory of Crime and Deviance." *Criminology* 30: 47–87.

Agnew, Robert. 1995. "The Contribution of Social-Psychological Strain Theory to the Explanation of Crime and Delinquency." Pp. 113–137 in *The Legacy of Anomie Theory*, ed. F. Adler and W. S. Laufer. New Brunswick, NJ: Transaction.

Agnew, Robert. 1999. "A General Strain Theory of Community Differences in Crime Rates." *Journal of Research in Crime and Delinquency* 36: 123–155.

Agnew, Robert. 2000. "Sources of Criminality: Strain and Subcultural Theories." Pp. 349–371 in *Criminology*. 3rd edn., ed. J. F. Sheley. Belmont, CA: Wadsworth.

Agnew, Robert. 2001. "Types of Strain Most Likely to Lead to Crime and Delinquency." *Journal of Research in Crime and Delinquency* 38: 319–361.

Agnew, Robert. 2006. *Pressured into Crime: An Overview of General Strain Theory*. Los Angeles: Roxbury.

Agnew, Robert. 2012. "Reflection on 'A Revised Strain Theory of Delinquency.'" *Social Forces* 91: 33–38.

Agnew, Robert. 2013. "When Criminal Coping Is Likely: An Extension of General Strain Theory." *Deviant Behavior* 34: 653–670.

Agnew, Robert and Timothy Brezina. 2015. *Juvenile Delinquency: Causes and Control*. 5th edn. New York: Oxford University Press.

Agnew, Robert, Timothy Brezina, John Paul Wright, and Francis T. Cullen. 2002. "Strain, Personality Traits, and Delinquency: Extending General Strain Theory." *Criminology* 40: 43–72.

Agnew, Robert and Helene Raskin White. 1992. "An Empirical Test of General Strain Theory." *Criminology* 30: 475–499.

Akers, Ronald L. and Christine S. Sellers. 2013. *Criminological Theories: Introduction, Evaluation, and Application*. 6th edn. New York: Oxford University Press.

Alinsky, Saul. 1960. *Reveille for Radicals*. New York: Free Press.

Baron, Stephen W. 2004. "General Strain, Street Youth and Crime: A Test of Agnew's Revised Theory." *Criminology* 42: 457–484.

Baumer, Eric P. 2007. "Untangling Research Puzzles in Merton's Multilevel Anomie Theory." *Theoretical Criminology* 11: 63–93.

Baumer, Eric P. and Regan Gustafson. 2007. "Social Organization and Instrumental Crime: Assessing the Empirical Validity of Classic and Contemporary Anomie Theories." *Criminology* 45: 617–663.

Bernard, Thomas. 1984. "Control Criticisms of Strain Theories: An Assessment of Theoretical and Empirical Adequacy." *Journal of Research in Crime and Delinquency* 21: 353–372.

Bernard, Thomas J., Jeffrey B. Snipes, and Alexander L. Gerould. 2010. *Vold's Theoretical Criminology*. 6th edn. New York: Oxford University Press.

Blomberg, Thomas G., William D. Bales, and Alex R. Piquero. 2012. "Is Educational Achievement a Turning Point for Incarcerated Delinquents across Race and Sex?" *Journal of Youth and Adolescence* 41: 202–216.

Boggess, Lyndsay N. and Jon Maskaly. 2014. "The Spatial Context of the Disorder–Crime Relationship in a Study of Reno Neighborhoods." *Social Science Research* 43: 168–183.

Bordua, David J. 1958. "Juvenile Delinquency and 'Anomie': An Attempt at Replication." *Social Problems* 6: 230–238.

Bordua, David J. 1961. "Delinquent Subcultures: Sociological Interpretations of Gang Delinquency." *Annals of the American Academy of Political and Social Science* 338: 119–136.

Botchkovar, Ekaterina V., Charles R. Tittle, and Olena Antonaccio. 2009. "General Strain Theory: Additional Evidence Using Cross-Cultural Data." *Criminology* 47: 131–176.

Brezina, Timothy. 1996. "Adapting to Strain: An Examination of Delinquent Coping Responses." *Criminology* 34: 39–60.

Brezina, Timothy. 1999. "Teenage Violence toward Parents as an Adaptation to Strain: Evidence from a National Survey of Male Adolescents." *Youth and Society* 30: 416–444.

Brezina, Timothy. 2000. "Delinquent Problem-Solving: An Interpretive Framework for Criminological Theory and Research." *Journal of Research in Crime and Delinquency* 37: 3–30.

Browning, Christopher R., Seth L. Feinberg, and Robert D. Dietz. 2004. "The Paradox of Social Organization: Networks, Collective Efficacy, and Violent Crime in Urban Neighborhoods." *Social Forces* 83: 503–534.

Burgess, Ernest W. [1925] 1967. "The Growth of the City." Pp. 47–62 in *The City*, ed. R. E. Park, E. W. Burgess, and R. D. McKenzie. University of Chicago Press.

Bursik, Robert J., Jr. 1986. "Ecological Stability and the Dynamics of Delinquency." Pp. 35–66 in *Communities and Crime, Crime and Justice: A Review of Research*, vol. 8, ed. A. J. Reiss, Jr. and M. Tonry. University of Chicago Press.

Bursik, Robert J., Jr. 1988. "Social Disorganization and Theories of Crime and Delinquency: Problems and Prospects." *Criminology* 26: 519–551.

Bursik, Robert J., Jr. 1993. *Neighborhoods and Crime: The Dimensions of Effective Community Control*. New York: Lexington Books.

Burton, Velmer S., Jr. and Francis T. Cullen. 1992. "The Empirical Status of Strain Theory." *Crime and Justice* 15: 1–13.

Burton, Velmer S., Jr., Francis T. Cullen, T. David Evans, and R. Gregory Dunaway. 1994. "Reconsidering Strain Theory: Operationalization, Rival Theories, and Adult Criminality." *Journal of Quantitative Criminology* 10: 213–239.

Carroll, Annemaree, Kellie Gordon, Michele Haynes, and Stephen Houghton. 2013. "Goal Setting and Self-Efficacy among Delinquent, At-Risk and Not At-Risk Adolescents." *Journal of Youth and Adolescence* 42: 431–443.

Carson, Dena C., Christopher J. Sullivan, John K. Cochran, and Kim M. Lersch. 2009. "General Strain Theory and the Relationship between Early Victimization and Drug Use." *Deviant Behavior* 30: 54–88.

Chamlin, Mitchell B. and John K. Cochran. 2007. "An Evaluation of the Assumptions that Underlie Institutional Anomie Theory." *Theoretical Criminology* 11: 39–61.

Chilton, Roland J. 1964. "Continuity in Delinquency Area Research: A Comparison of Studies in Baltimore, Detroit, and Indianapolis." *American Sociological Review* 29: 71–83.

Chung, He Len, Edward P. Mulvey, and Laurence Steinberg. 2011. "Understanding the School Outcomes of Juvenile Offenders: An Exploration of Neighborhood Influences and Motivational Resources." *Journal of Youth and Adolescence* 40: 1025–1038.

Cloward, Richard A. and Lloyd E. Ohlin. 1960. *Delinquency and Opportunity: A Theory of Delinquent Gangs*. New York: Free Press.

Cohen, Albert K. 1955. *Delinquent Boys: The Culture of the Gang*. New York: Free Press.

Coleman, James S. 1988. "Social Capital in the Creation of Human Capital." *American Journal of Sociology* 94: 95–120.

Coleman, James S. 1990. *Foundations of Social Theory*. Cambridge, MA: Harvard University Press.

CrimeSolutions.gov. n.d. Office of Justice Programs. Retrieved March 10, 2015 (www.crimesolutions. gov/TopicDetails.aspx?ID=10).

Cullen, Francis T. 1983. *Rethinking Crime and Deviance Theory: The Emergence of a Structuring Tradition*. Totowa, NJ: Rowman & Allanheld.

Cullen, Francis T., Robert Agnew, and Pamela Wilcox. 2014. *Criminological Theory: Past to Present*. 5th edn. New York: Oxford University Press.

Curran, Daniel J. and Claire M. Renzetti. 2008. *Theories of Crime*. 3rd edn. Boston: Allyn & Bacon.

Durkheim, Emile. [1893] 1947. *The Division of Labor in Society*. Trans. George Simpson. New York: Free Press.

Elliott, Delbert S., Suzanne S. Ageton, and Rachelle J. Cantor. 1979. "An Integrated Theoretical Perspective on Delinquent Behavior." *Journal of Research in Crime and Delinquency* 16: 3–17.

Elliott, Delbert S., David Huizinga, and Suzanne S. Ageton. 1985. *Explaining Delinquency and Drug Use*. Beverly Hills, CA: Sage.

Elliott, Delbert S., William Julius Wilson, David Huizinga, Robert J. Sampson, Amanda Elliott, and Bruce Rankin. 1996. "Effects of Neighborhood Disadvantage on Adolescent Development." *Journal of Research in Crime and Delinquency* 33: 389–426.

Empey, LaMar T., Mark C. Stafford, and Carter H. Hay. 1999. *American Delinquency: Its Meaning and Construction*. 4th edn. Belmont, CA: Wadsworth.

Esbensen, Finn-Aage and David Huizinga. 1993. "Gangs, Drugs, and Delinquency in a Survey of Urban Youth." *Criminology* 31: 565–589.

Farnworth, Margaret and Michael J. Leiber. 1989. "Strain Theory Revisited: Economic Goals, Educational Means, and Delinquency." *American Sociological Review* 54: 263–274.

Farrington, David P., Howard N. Snyder, and Terrence A. Finnegan. 1988. "Specialization in Juvenile Court Careers." *Criminology* 26: 461–488.

Felson, Richard B. and Jeremy Staff. 2006. "Explaining the Academic Performance–Delinquency Relationship." *Criminology* 44: 299–320.

Froggio, Giacinto and Robert Agnew. 2007. "The Relationship between Crime and 'Objective' Versus 'Subjective' Strains." *Journal of Criminal Justice* 35: 81–87.

Gibbons, Don C. 1979. *The Criminological Enterprise: Theories and Perspective*. Englewood Cliffs, NJ: Prentice Hall.

Greenberg, David F. 1977. "Delinquency and the Age Structure of Society." *Contemporary Crisis* 1: 66–86.

Hagan, John, Gerd Hefler, Cabriele Classen, Klaus Boehnke, and Hans Merkens. 1998. "Subterranean Sources of Subcultural Delinquency beyond the American Dream." *Criminology* 36: 309–341.

Hay, Carter and Michelle M. Evans. 2006. "Violent Victimization and Involvement in Delinquency: Examining Predictions from General Strain Theory." *Journal of Criminal Justice* 34: 261–274.

Higgins, George E., Nicole Leeper Piquero, and Alex R. Piquero. 2011. "General Strain Theory, Peer Rejection, and Delinquency/Crime." *Youth and Society* 43: 1272–1297.

Hirschi, Travis. 1969. *Causes of Delinquency*. Berkeley, CA: University of California Press.

Hirtenlehner, Helmut, Stephen Farrall, and Johann Bacher. 2013. "Culture, Institutions, and Morally Dubious Behaviors: Testing Some Core Propositions of the Institutional-Anomie Theory." *Deviant Behavior* 34: 291–320.

Hochschild, Jennifer. 1995. *Facing Up to the American Dream: Race, Class, and the Soul of the Nation*. Princeton University Press.

Hoffmann, John P. 2010. "A Life-Course Perspective on Stress, Delinquency, and Young Adult Crime." *American Journal of Criminal Justice* 35: 105–120.

Hoffmann, John P., Lance D. Erickson, and Karen R. Spence. 2013. "Modeling the Association between Academic Achievement and Delinquency: An Application of Interactional Theory." *Criminology* 51: 629–660.

Hoffmann, John P. and Timothy O. Ireland. 2004. "Strain and Opportunity Structures." *Journal of Quantitative Criminology* 20: 263–292.

Hollist, Dusten R., Lorine A. Hughes, and Lonnie M. Schaible. 2009. "Adolescent Maltreatment, Negative Emotion, and Delinquency: An Assessment of General Strain Theory and Family-Based Strain." *Journal of Criminal Justice* 37: 379–387.

Jensen, Gary F. 1995. "Salvaging Structure through Strain: A Theoretical and Empirical Critique." Pp. 139–158 in *The Legacy of Anomie Theory*, ed. F. Adler and W. S. Laufer. New Brunswick, NJ: Transaction.

Johnson, Richard E. 1979. *Juvenile Delinquency and Its Origins: An Integrated Theoretical Approach*. New York: Cambridge University Press.

Kaufman, Joanne M., Cesar J. Rebellon, Sherod Thaxton, and Robert Agnew. 2008. "A General Strain Theory of Racial Differences in Criminal Offending." *The Australian and New Zealand Journal of Criminology* 41:421–437.

Kingston, Beverly, David Huizinga, and Delbert S. Elliott. 2009. "A Test of Social Disorganization Theory in High-Risk Urban Neighborhoods." *Youth and Society* 41: 53–79.

Kirk, David S. and Mauri Matsuda. 2011. "Legal Cynicism, Collective Efficacy, and the Ecology of Arrest." *Criminology* 49: 443–472.

Kitsuse, John I. and David C. Dietrick. 1959. "Delinquent Boys: A Critique." *American Sociological Review* 24: 208–215.

Kobrin, Solomon. 1959. "The Chicago Area Project: A 25 Year Assessment." *Annals of the American Society of Political and Social Science* 322: 20–29.

Kornhauser, Ruth Rosner. 1978. *Social Sources of Delinquency: An Appraisal of Analytic Models*. University of Chicago Press.

Kroeber, A. L. and Talcott Parsons. 1958. "The Concepts of Culture and Social System." *American Sociological Review* 23: 582–583.

Kubrin, Charis E. and Ronald Weitzer. 2003. "New Directions in Social Disorganization Theory." *Journal of Research in Crime and Delinquency* 40: 374–402.

Lander, Bernard. 1954. *Toward an Understanding of Juvenile Delinquency*. New York: Columbia University Press.

Larson, Matthew and Gary Sweeten. 2012. "Breaking Up Is Hard to Do: Romantic Dissolution, Offending, and Substance Use During the Transition to Adulthood." *Criminology* 50: 605–636.

Lemert, Edwin M. 1972. *Human Deviance, Social Problems, and Social Control*. 2nd edn. Englewood Cliffs, NJ: Prentice Hall.

Lilly, J. Robert, Francis T. Cullen, and Richard A. Ball. 2014. *Criminological Theory: Context and Consequences*. 6th edn. Thousand Oaks, CA: Sage.

Lowenkamp, Christopher T., Francis T. Cullen, and Travis C. Pratt. 2003. "Replicating Sampson and Groves' Test of Social Disorganization Theory: Revisiting a Criminological Classic." *Journal of Research in Crime and Delinquency* 40: 351–373.

Lundman, Richard. 2001. *Prevention and Control of Juvenile Delinquency*. 3rd edn. New York: Oxford University Press.

MacDonald, John, Robert J. Stokes, Ben Grunwald, and Ricky Bluthenthal. 2013. "The Privatization of Public Safety in Urban Neighborhoods: Do Business Improvement Districts Reduce Violent Crime among Adolescents?" *Law and Society Review* 47: 621–652.

Maguin, Eugene and Rolf Loeber. 1996. "Academic Performance and Delinquency." Pp. 145–264 in *Crime and Justice: A Review of Research*, vol. 20, ed. Michael Tonry. University of Chicago Press.

Manasse, Michelle Eileen and Natasha Morgan Ganem. 2009. "Victimization as a Cause of Delinquency: The Role of Depression and Gender." *Journal of Criminal Justice* 37: 371–378.

Maume, Michael O. and Matthew R. Lee. 2003. "Social Institutions and Violence: A Sub-National Test of Institutional Anomie Theory." *Criminology* 41: 1137–1172.

Mazerolle, Lorraine, Rebecca Wickes, and James McBroom. 2010. "Community Variations in Violence: The Role of Social Ties and Collective Efficacy in Comparative Context." *Journal of Research in Crime and Delinquency* 47: 3–30.

Menard, Scott. 1995. "A Developmental Test of Mertonian Anomie Theory." *Journal of Research in Crime and Delinquency* 32: 136–174.

Merton, Robert K. 1938. "Social Structure and Anomie." *American Sociological Review* 3: 672–682.

Merton, Robert K. 1968. *Social Theory and Social Structure*. 2nd edn. New York: Free Press.

Merton, Robert K. 1997. "On the Evolving Synthesis of Differential Association and Anomie Theory: A Perspective from the Sociology of Science." *Criminology* 35: 517–525.

Messner, Steven F. and Richard Rosenfeld. 1997. *Crime and the American Dream*. 2nd edn. Belmont, CA: Wadsworth.

Messner, Steven F. and Richard Rosenfeld. 2006. "The Present and Future of Institutional-Anomie Theory." Pp. 127–154 in *Taking Stock: The Status of Criminological Theory*, ed. F. T. Cullen, J. P. Wright, and K. R. Blevins. New Brunswick, NJ: Transaction.

Messner, Steven F., Helmut Thome, and Richard Rosenfeld. 2008. "Institutions, Anomie, and Violent Crime: Clarifying and Elaborating Institutional-Anomie Theory." *International Journal of Conflict and Violence* 2: 163–181.

Moffitt, Terrie E. 1993. "Adolescence-Limited and Life-Course-Persistent Antisocial Behavior: A Developmental Taxonomy." *Psychological Review* 100: 674–701.

Moon, Byongook, Merry Morash, Cynthia Perez McCluskey, and Hye-Won Hwang. 2009. "A Comprehensive Test of General Strain Theory: Key Strains, Situational- and Trait-Based Negative Emotions, Conditioning Factors, and Delinquency." *Journal of Research in Crime and Delinquency* 46: 182–212.

National Research Council. 2013. *Reforming Juvenile Justice: A Developmental Approach*, ed. Richard J. Bonnie, Robert L. Johnson, Betty M. Chemers, and Julie A. Schuck. Committee on Law and Justice, Division of Behavioral and Social Sciences and Education. Washington, DC: National Academies Press.

Oberschall, Anthony. 1972. "The Institutionalization of American Sociology." Pp. 187–251 in *The Establishment of Empirical Sociology*, ed. A. Oberschall. New York: Harper & Row.

Osgood, D. Wayne and Jeff M. Chambers. 2000. "Social Disorganization outside the Metropolis: An Analysis of Rural Youth Violence." *Criminology* 38: 81–115.

Ostrowsky, Michael K. and Steven F. Messner. 2005. "Explaining Crime for a Young Adult Population: An Application of General Strain Theory." *Journal of Criminal Justice* 33: 463–476.

Park, Robert E. and Ernest W. Burgess. 1924. *Introduction to the Science of Sociology*. 2nd edn. University of Chicago Press.

Paternoster, Raymond and Paul Mazerolle. 1994. "General Strain Theory and Delinquency: A Replication and Extension." *Journal of Research in Crime and Delinquency* 31: 235–263.

Peck, Jennifer H. 2013. "Examining Race and Ethnicity in the Context of General Strain Theory, Depression, and Delinquency." *Deviant Behavior* 34: 706–726.

Perez, Deanna M., Wesley G. Jennings, and Angela R. Gover. 2008. "Specifying General Strain Theory: An Ethnically Relevant Approach." *Deviant Behavior* 29: 544–578.

Piquero, Nicole Leeper and Miriam D. Sealock. 2004. "Gender and General Strain Theory: A Preliminary Test of Broidy and Agnew's Gender/GST Hypotheses." *Justice Quarterly* 21: 125–158.

Piquero, Nicole Leeper and Miriam D. Sealock. 2010. "Race, Crime, and General Strain Theory." *Youth Violence and Juvenile Justice* 8: 170–186.

Posick, Chad, Amy Farrell, and Marc L. Swatt. 2013. "Do Boys Fight and Girls Cut? A General Strain Theory Approach to Gender and Deviance." *Deviant Behavior* 34: 685–705.

Rebellon, Cesar J., Michelle E. Manasse, Karen T. Van Gundy, and Ellen S. Cohn. 2012. "Perceived Injustice and Delinquency: A Test of General Strain Theory." *Journal of Criminal Justice* 40: 230–237.

Rebellon, Cesar J., Nicole Leeper Piquero, Alex R. Piquero, and Sherod Thaxton. 2009. "Do Frustrated Economic Expectations and Objective Economic Inequity Promote Crime? A Randomized Experiment Testing Agnew's General Strain Theory." *European Journal of Criminology* 6: 47–71.

Robbers, Monica L. P. 2004. "Revisiting the Moderating Effect of Social Support on Strain: A Gendered Test." *Sociological Inquiry* 74: 546–569.

Sampson, Robert J. 2006. "Collective Efficacy Theory: Lessons Learned and Directions for Future Inquiry." Pp. 149–167 in *Taking Stock: The Status of Criminological Theory*, ed. F.T. Cullen, J. P.Wright, and K. R. Blevins. New Brunswick, NJ: Transaction.

Sampson, Robert J. 2013. "The Place of Context: A Theory and Strategy for Criminology's Hard Problems." *Criminology* 51: 1–31.

Sampson, Robert J. and Dawn Jeglum Bartusch. 1998. "Legal Cynicism and (Subcultural?) Tolerance of Deviance: The Neighborhood Context of Racial Differences." *Law and Society Review* 32: 777–804.

Sampson, Robert J. and W. Byron Groves. 1989. "Community Structure and Crime: Testing Social Disorganization Theory." *American Journal of Sociology* 94: 774–802.

Sampson, Robert J., Jeffrey D. Morenoff, and Felton Earls. 1999. "Beyond Social Capital: Spatial Dynamics of Collective Efficacy for Children." *American Sociological Review* 64: 633–660.

Sampson, Robert J. and Stephen W. Raudenbush. 1999. "Systematic Social Observation of Public Spaces: A New Look at Disorder in Urban Neighborhoods." *American Journal of Sociology* 105: 603–651.

Sampson, Robert J. and Stephen W. Raudenbush. 2001. "Disorder in Urban Neighborhoods: Does It Lead to Crime?" *Research in Brief*. Washington, DC: National Institute of Justice.

Sampson, Robert J. and Stephen W. Raudenbush. 2004. "Seeing Disorder: Neighborhood Stigma and the Social Construction of 'Broken Windows.'" *Social Psychology Quarterly* 67: 319–342.

Sampson, Robert J., Steven W. Raudenbush, and Felton Earls. 1997. "Neighborhoods and Violent Crime: A Multilevel Study of Collective Efficacy." *Science* 277: 918–924.

Sampson, Robert J. and William Julius Wilson. 1995. "Toward a Theory of Race, Crime, and Urban Inequality." Pp. 37–54 in *Crime and Inequality*, ed. J. Hagan and R. D. Peterson. Stanford University Press.

Schoepfer, Andrea and Nicole Leeper Piquero. 2006. "Exploring White-Collar Crime and the American Dream: A Partial Test of Institutional Anomie Theory." *Journal of Criminal Justice* 34: 227–235.

Schuerman, Leo A. and Solomon Kobrin. 1986. "Community Careers in Crime." Pp. 67–100 in *Communities and Crime, Crime and Justice: A Review of Research*, vol. 8, ed. A. J. Reiss, Jr. and M. Tonry. University of Chicago Press.

Shaw, Clifford R. 1931. *The Natural History of a Delinquent Career*. University of Chicago Press.

Shaw, Clifford R. and Henry D. McKay. 1931. *Social Factors in Juvenile Delinquency: A Study of the Community, the Family, and the Gang in Relation to Delinquent Behavior*. Report of the National Commission on Law Observance and Enforcement, Causes of Crime, vol. 2. Washington, DC: GPO.

Shaw, Clifford R. and Henry D. McKay. [1942] 1969. *Juvenile Delinquency and Urban Areas: A Study of Rates of Delinquency in Relation to Differential Characteristics of Local Communities in American Cities*. Rev. edn. University of Chicago Press.

Shaw, Clifford R., Frederick M. Zorbaugh, Henry D. McKay, and Leonard S. Cottrell. 1929. *Delinquency Areas: A Study of the Geographic Distribution of School Truants, Juvenile Delinquents, and Adult Offenders in Chicago*. University of Chicago Press.

Short, James F., Jr. and Fred L. Strodtbeck. 1965. *Group Process and Gang Delinquency*. University of Chicago Press.

Siennick, Sonja E. and Jeremy Staff. 2008. "Explaining the Educational Deficits of Delinquent Youths." *Criminology* 46: 609–635.

Sigfusdottir, Inga Dora, Bryndis Bjork Asgeirsdottir, Gisli H. Gudjonsson, and Jon Fridrik Sigurdsson. 2008. "A Model of Sexual Abuse's Effects on Suicidal Behavior and Delinquency: The Role of Emotions as Mediating Factors." *Journal of Youth and Adolescence* 37: 699–712.

Sigfusdottir, Inga Dora, Alfgeir Logi Kristjansson, and Robert Agnew. 2012. "A Comparative Analysis of General Strain Theory." *Journal of Criminal Justice* 40: 117–127.

Sigfusdottir, Inga Dora and Eric Silver. 2009. "Emotional Reactions to Stress among Adolescent Boys and Girls: An Examination of the Mediating Mechanisms Proposed by General Strain Theory." *Youth and Society* 40: 571–590.

Simons, Ronald L., Leslie Gordon Simons, Callie Harbin Burt, Gene H. Brody, and Carolyn Cutrona. 2005. "Collective Efficacy, Authoritative Parenting and Delinquency: A Longitudinal Test of a Model Integrating Community- and Family-Level Processes." *Criminology* 43: 989–1029.

Srole, Leo. 1956. "Social Integration and Certain Corollaries: An Exploratory Study." *American Sociological Review* 21: 709–716.

Stark, Rodney. 1987. "Deviant Places: A Theory of the Ecology of Crime." *Criminology* 25: 893–909.

Steenbeek, Wouter and John R. Hipp. 2011. "A Longitudinal Test of Social Disorganization Theory: Feedback Effects among Cohesion, Social Control, and Disorder." *Criminology* 49: 833–871.

Stults, Brian J. and Eric P. Baumer. 2008. "Assessing the Relevance of Anomie Theory for Explaining Spatial Variation in Lethal Criminal Violence: An Aggregate-Level Analysis of Homicide within the United States." *International Journal of Conflict and Violence* 2: 215–247.

Sutherland, Alex, Ian Brunton-Smith, and Jonathan Jackson. 2013. "Collective Efficacy, Deprivation and Violence in London." *British Journal of Criminology* 53: 1050–1074.

Thornberry, Terence P., Marvin D. Krohn, Alan J. Lizotte, and Deborah Chard-Wierschem. 1993. "The Role of Juvenile Gangs in Facilitating Delinquent Behavior." *Journal of Research in Crime and Delinquency* 30: 55–87.

Tittle, Charles R. 1983. "Social Class and Criminal Behavior: A Critique of the Theoretical Foundation." *Social Forces* 62: 334–358.

Tittle, Charles R., Lisa M. Broidy, and Marc G. Gertz. 2008. "Strain, Crime, and Contingencies." *Justice Quarterly* 25: 283–312.

Tittle, Charles R. and Robert F. Meier. 1990. "Specifying the SES/Delinquency Relationship." *Criminology* 28: 271–299.

Tittle, Charles R., Wayne J. Villemez, and Douglas A. Smith. 1978. "The Myth of Social Class and Criminality: An Empirical Assessment of the Empirical Evidence." *American Sociological Review* 43: 643–656.

Warner, Barbara D. 2007. "Directly Intervene or Call the Authorities? A Study of Forms of Neighborhood Social Control within a Social Disorganization Framework." *Criminology* 45: 99–129.

Watts, Stephen J. and Thomas L. McNulty. 2013. "Childhood Abuse and Criminal Behavior: Testing a General Strain Theory Model." *Journal of Interpersonal Violence* 28: 3023–3040.

Wells, William, Joseph A. Schafer, Sean P. Varano, and Timothy S. Bynum. 2006. "Neighborhood Residents' Production of Order: The Effects of Collective Efficacy on Responses to Neighborhood Problems." *Crime and Delinquency* 52: 523–550.

Wiatrowski, Michael D., David B. Griswold, and Mary K. Roberts. 1981. "Social Control Theory and Delinquency." *American Sociological Review* 46: 525–541.

Wiatrowski, Michael D., Stephen Hansell, Charles R. Massey, and David L. Wilson. 1982. "Curriculum Tracking and Delinquency." *American Sociological Review* 47: 151–160.

Wickes, Rebecca L. 2010. "Generating Action and Responding to Local Issues: Collective Efficacy in Context." *Australian and New Zealand Journal of Criminology* 43: 423–443.

Wilcox, Pamela, Neil Quisenberry, Debra T. Cabrera, and Shayne Jones. 2004. "Busy Places and Broken Windows? Toward Defining the Role of Physical Structure and Process in Community Crime Models." *Sociological Quarterly* 45: 185–207.

Wilson, James Q. and George Kelling. 1982. "The Police and Neighborhood Safety: Broken Windows." *Atlantic Monthly* 249: 29–38.

Xu, Yili, Mora L. Fiedler, and Karl H. Flaming. 2005. "Discovering the Impact of Community Policing: The Broken Windows Thesis, Collective Efficacy, and Citizens' Judgment." *Journal of Research in Crime and Delinquency* 42: 147–186.

Zimmerman, Gregory M. and Steven F. Messner. 2010. "Neighborhood Context and the Gender Gap in Adolescent Violent Crime." *American Sociological Review* 75: 958–980.

Chapter 12

Labeling and critical criminologies

Chapter preview

Topics:

- The labeling perspective
- Critical criminologies
- Feminist criminology

Theories:

- Theory of reintegrative shaming
- Integrated structural–Marxist theory
- Power-control theory
- Greenberg's Marxist interpretation of delinquency

Terms:

- labeling perspective
- critical criminologies
- dramatization of evil
- primary deviance
- secondary deviance
- reflected appraisals of self
- reintegrative shaming
- stigmatization
- interdependency
- communitarianism

- deviance amplification
- stigma
- patriarchal families
- egalitarian families
- masculine status anxiety
- feminism
- liberal feminism
- radical feminism
- patriarchy

Chapter learning objectives

After completing this chapter, students should be able to:

- Explain what distinguishes the labeling perspective and critical criminologies from more traditional approaches to delinquency.
- Describe the consequences of formal and informal labeling processes.
- Identify the major themes of critical criminologies.
- Describe specific theories that take a critical approach to delinquency.
- Identify the defining features of feminist approaches in criminology.
- Describe how feminist perspectives have been applied to delinquency.

Case in point: labeling Rocky "delinquent"

Robert Sampson and John Laub, in their book *Crime in the Making: Pathways and Turning Points Through Life*, describe a movie about Rocky Sullivan and Jerry Connelly – two childhood friends and companions in crime whose lives follow very different courses. The story told in this movie suggests that it is Rocky's experience of being caught by the police and thrust into the juvenile justice system, as well as Jerry's ability to get away and avoid both the justice system and the label "delinquent," that is responsible for the very different paths their lives take.

The movie was *Angels with Dirty Faces* and starred James Cagney, Pat O'Brien, Humphrey Bogart, Ann Sheridan, and, of course, the Dead End Kids. James Cagney played the role of Rocky Sullivan, who was by contemporary definitions a high-rate, chronic offender – in other words, a "career criminal." Pat O'Brien played the role of Jerry Connelly, who became a priest in the local neighborhood parish. Both men were childhood friends, committed petty crime together, and were in fact products of the same slum environment. Yet both obviously had very different life experiences with respect to serious and persistent criminal activity. ...

At the beginning of the film the young boys, James Cagney (Rocky Sullivan) and Pat O'Brien (Jerry Connelly), break into a box car to steal some pens. The police come and both boys run to avoid getting caught. One boy, Jerry, is a little quicker and gets away. Rocky, slower of foot, gets caught. Of course, Rocky does not squeal on his best friend, and he is the one who turns out to be a criminal later in life. The explanation offered in the film is that "reform school made a criminal out of Rocky," "there but for the grace of God go I," and "Rocky was a good kid gone bad." At the end of the film, after Rocky Sullivan is executed for several homicides, Pat O'Brien in the role of Jerry Connelly sadly remarks: "Let's say a prayer for a boy who couldn't run as fast as I could."

Source: Sampson and Laub (1993: 64, 97). Reprinted by permission of the publisher copyright © 1993 by the President and Fellows of Harvard College.

Over four decades ago, Edwin Schur (1971: 7) observed that "deviance and social control always involve processes of social definition." We often take for granted that "delinquency" is behavior that violates the law. The **labeling perspective** does not make this common assumption. Instead, labeling theorists maintain that definitions of what actions are delinquent and who is delinquent result from dynamic social processes. Instead of asking, "Why do they do it?" and attempting to explain individuals' involvement in delinquency, proponents of the labeling perspective ask the question: how and why do certain behaviors and individuals get labeled "deviant," "delinquent," or "criminal?" In Chapter 2, we explored how the legal concept of delinquency first emerged and how it has changed over time. In this chapter, we examine how the label "delinquent" is imposed legally in the juvenile justice system and socially in the context of relationships. We also consider consequences of the labeling process.

The labeling perspective focuses on social and societal reactions to delinquent behavior. The same is true of **critical criminologies**, or conflict theories, which consider why society defines crime and reacts to crime and criminals the way it does. Critical criminologies explore the structural bases of inequality in society and the way in which inequality and social status influence definitions of crime and criminals, and societal reactions to specific behaviors. We consider several applications of critical approaches to delinquency, including integrated structural-Marxist theory, power-control theory, and a Marxist interpretation of juvenile delinquency in capitalist societies (Hagan 1989; Hagan, Simpson, and Gillis 1987; Hagan, Gillis, and Simpson 1985; Colvin and Pauly 1983; Greenberg 1981). We also examine feminist approaches to crime and delinquency, which focus on the role gender plays in creating crime and delinquency and in structuring reactions to offending. We focus on liberal and radical feminist perspectives.

The labeling perspective

In simplest terms, the labeling perspective is concerned with how and why behavior is labeled "deviant." The focus is on the definition or social construction of deviance, rather than on its causes. Labeling theorists do not view deviance as an inherent quality of particular acts. Instead, they see deviance as derived from the social creation of rules that define particular acts as "deviant" and from the application of those rules to particular people. The labeling perspective explicitly recognizes that definitions of deviance are not universal, but rather are unique to particular times, places, and cultures or subcultures (Schur 1971). For example, consider the evolution of the concept of delinquency in the United States that we described in Chapter 2.

Labeling theory has its theoretical roots in both symbolic interactionism and the conflict perspective (Paternoster and Iovanni 1989; Schur 1971). From symbolic interactionism, labeling theorists drew the idea that the imposition of labels (formal or informal) has consequences for those labeled. Through social interaction, individuals recognize and respond to the labels attached to them, often with behavior that is consistent with those labels. From the conflict perspective, labeling theorists drew the idea that definitions of what constitutes deviant behavior are determined by those with sufficient power and resources to make and enforce the rules. We explore these origins of labeling theory in more detail later in this chapter.

In this section, we discuss original statements of labeling theory, which consider how the labels "deviant" or "delinquent" are imposed, and what consequences those labels have for those who bear them. We examine both formal labels imposed through the juvenile justice system and informal labels imposed in the context of interactions with others, such as parents and peers.

Imposing the label of "deviant" or "delinquent"

Early statements of the labeling perspective focused on the consequences for individuals of societal reactions to deviance.

Formal societal reactions to deviance: dramatizing evil

Frank Tannenbaum is typically credited with providing the first statement of the principles of labeling theory, although these principles were not recognized as a formal theory until the 1960s. In *Crime and the Community*, Tannenbaum (1938: 17) argues that youth often engage in acts that they consider to be "play, adventure ... mischief, fun," but that others, including agents of formal social control, consider to be delinquent or "evil." Others react to these actions and to the youths as "bad" or "evil," and this process of definition has negative and lasting consequences for youths' self-images and subsequent behavior. In a process that Tannenbaum (1938: 17–18) calls the **dramatization of evil**, "the young delinquent becomes bad because he is defined as bad and because he is not believed if he is good." In other words, the labeling of individuals as "bad" results in a self-fulfilling prophecy in which youths become what they are said to be.

Once individuals are formally labeled "delinquent," they are isolated from law-abiding groups and drawn together with other children who are similarly defined (Tannenbaum 1938). In this way, because of the formal labeling process, initial acts of mischief evolve into serious delinquency. Thus, according to Tannenbaum, crime and delinquency are created through the dramatization of evil. Tannenbaum's (1938: 20) recommendation for dealing with juveniles is "a refusal to dramatize the evil. The less said about it the better."

Primary and secondary deviance: identity and self-fulfilling prophecy

In 1951, Edwin Lemert expanded on Tannenbaum's ideas about labeling and deviance with the concepts of primary and secondary deviance. **Primary deviance** refers to initial acts of deviance, many of which go undetected. Lemert (1951, 1972) attributes primary deviance to a variety of causes, including cultural, situational, psychological, and even physiological factors. Self-report studies suggest that primary deviance is relatively common. Many individuals engage in delinquency but are never caught and processed by the juvenile justice system. The most important aspect of primary deviance is that it has no significant impact on self-concept or social status. Individuals who engage in primary deviance are able to rationalize their behavior as part of a socially acceptable role and continue to view themselves as something other than deviants. For example, adolescents might skip school and engage in acts of vandalism, but still not define themselves as "delinquents." Primary deviance is often seen as "a problem of everyday life" and dealt with in the context of established relationships (Lemert 1972).

In some cases, however, societal reactions to primary deviance include elements of social control, punishment, and stigmatization that change how primary deviants view themselves. According to Lemert (1951, 1972), the application of "deviant" or "delinquent" labels through formal responses to primary deviance has significant consequences for social status, self-concept, and subsequent deviance. **Secondary deviance** refers to deviance that occurs in response to problems created by societal reactions to primary deviance. Formal societal reactions to primary deviance cause "deviant" individuals to change their self-concepts and social roles in ways that acknowledge the labels that others have applied to them. Deviance may become a central element of identity for those whose primary deviance has received official sanction. These changes in identity and social roles that occur in response to societal reactions are part of a lengthy process in which individuals gradually adjust their behaviors to be consistent with the deviant label. In the creation of secondary deviance, the reasons for primary deviance are overshadowed by the importance of the disapproving and isolating societal reactions to that deviance.

The fundamental distinction between primary and secondary deviance lies in the acceptance of a deviant identity. Secondary deviance occurs in response to changes in identity, which are based on societal reactions, whereas primary deviance occurs without effect on identity. Through the process Lemert describes, deviance becomes a self-fulfilling prophecy. Over time, as others respond to acts of primary deviance, individuals come to see themselves as deviants and behave in accord with that label. A criticism of the labeling perspective has been that it focuses on the continuation of deviance that results from societal reactions, but it tends to ignore the causes of primary deviance, which sets in motion the labeling process.

The emergence of "labeling theory"

The works of Tannenbaum and Lemert stood for many years as relatively isolated statements of the consequences of societal reactions to deviance, but in the 1960s and early 1970s an identifiable school of thought emerged in a series of writings that conveyed a unified theme, known as "labeling theory" (Schur 1969, 1971; Erikson 1962, 1966; Becker 1963; Goffman 1961, 1963; Kitsuse 1962).[1] The common core of these writings was a focus on how definitions of deviance are applied to individuals and groups and on the consequences of social control through the application of deviant labels.

Scholars have noted that, during the 1960s, intellectuals were particularly open to the critique of political authority and government power offered by labeling theory (Beirne and Messerschmidt 2011). Francis Cullen and his colleagues (Cullen, Agnew, and Wilcox 2014: 256) remind us of the historical events:

> Recall that during the 1960s and early 1970s, the United States was greeted with revelation after revelation of the government abusing its power – from Civil Rights demonstrators being beaten, to inmates being gunned down at Attica, to students being shot at Kent State, to Viet Nam, to Watergate, and on and on. As trust in the state plummeted – especially on university campuses – a theory that blamed the government for causing more harm than good struck a chord of truth. Labeling theory, of course, did precisely this in arguing that the criminal justice system stigmatized offenders and ultimately trapped them in a criminal career.

And so the popularity of the labeling perspective grew.

"Theory into practice: juvenile justice system reforms based on the labeling perspective" provides a brief description of juvenile justice policies promoted by the labeling perspective in the 1960s.

Theory into practice: juvenile justice system reforms based on the labeling perspective

LaMar Empey, Mark Stafford, and Carter Hay (1999) describe four reforms of the juvenile justice system in the 1960s and 1970s that were based, at least in part, on the labeling perspective: decriminalization, diversion, due process, and deinstitutionalization.

Decriminalization

"The first reform suggested that status offenses such as running away, defying parents, sexual promiscuity, and truancy should be decriminalized." Labeling theorists believed that responses of the juvenile justice system to minor status offenses produced more harm than good. They proposed that status offenses be dealt with in ways other than legal intervention. In 1967, the President's Commission on Law Enforcement and Administration of Justice concluded that "serious consideration should be given [to] complete elimination from the court's jurisdiction of conduct illegal only for a child" (President's Commission 1967a: 27).

Diversion

"A second reform – diversion – was closely related to decriminalization. It, too, was based on the premise that the evils of children have been overdramatized. To avoid labeling and stigmatization, potential arrestees or court referrals should be diverted from the juvenile justice system into other, less harmful agencies." This policy represented an attempt to respond to the problem behaviors of youth, but without the adverse effects of juvenile court processing. Suggestions for accomplishing this included: (1) the creation of community agencies and Youth Services Bureaux that would provide various services, such as counseling, tutoring, and recreational services, to young people – both delinquents and non-delinquents; and (2) the employment of juvenile specialists in police departments, who would decide which juveniles might be diverted from the juvenile court.

Due process

"The third reform stressed the importance of due process in juvenile court proceedings ... In [*Kent v. United States*] and subsequent decisions, the Supreme Court concluded that except for jury trials, children should receive most of the [constitutional] protections that adults receive." (See Chapter 2 for a discussion of *Kent v. United States* and the due process revolution in juvenile justice.)

"One of the main themes of labeling theory was evident in the actions of the Supreme Court: the need to limit the discretion of child savers and control their power over young people. Because all delinquent acts could not be decriminalized and some offenders could not be diverted, those who were referred to juvenile court should be protected by constitutional procedures."

Deinstitutionalization

"The fourth reform to which labeling theory contributed was deinstitutionalization – the removal of children from detention centers, jails, and reformatories. Like diversion, the goal of deinstitutionalization was to limit the destructive effects of legal processing."

The President's Commission wrote, "Institutions tend to isolate offenders from society, both physically and psychologically, cutting them off from schools, jobs, families, and other supportive influences and increasing the probability that the label of criminal will be indelibly impressed upon them. The goal of reintegration is likely to be furthered much more readily by working with offenders in the community than by incarceration" (President's Commission 1967b: 165).

Sources: Empey et al. (1999: 263–265); President's Commission on Law Enforcement and Administration of Justice (1967a, 1967b).

The creation and enforcement of social rules

One of the most frequently cited works on the social construction of deviance that emerged during the 1960s is Howard Becker's book *Outsiders*. Becker (1963: 9, emphasis in original) describes the process through which deviance is socially constructed:

> *Social groups create deviance by making the rules whose infraction constitutes deviance*, and by applying those rules to particular people and labeling them as outsiders. From this point of view, deviance is *not* a quality of the act the person commits, but rather a consequence of the application by others of rules and sanctions to an "offender." The deviant is one to whom that label has successfully been applied; deviant behavior is behavior that people so label.

In other words, deviance is "in the eye of the beholder."

Becker's work moves beyond the writings of Tannenbaum and Lemert by considering how groups are able to create and enforce the rules that others are selectively called upon to follow. In other words, as we try to understand why some people are labeled deviant or delinquent, Becker invites us to consider not only societal reactions to their behaviors, but also the creation of rules that direct attention to those behaviors.

Becker often refers to those who create rules as *moral crusaders*, who are attempting to correct some "evil" in the world. Moral crusaders are typically individuals of high social status (like the child-savers described in Chapter 2), and this status helps them to convince others of the legitimacy of their position. Thus, according to Becker, it is generally the worldview of influential individuals and groups that is imposed through rules on those who are less powerful. In his book *Outsiders*, Becker (1963) describes the creation of the Marihuana Tax Act in 1937, which outlawed marijuana use, as an example of a "moral crusade."

Once created, rules tend to be applied more to some individuals than to others. Whether rules are enforced depends on who commits deviant acts and who is harmed by them. For example, the process of labeling acts and individuals as deviant may be affected by the race, social class, and gender of the offender and the victim (see Chapter 5); the demeanor of the offender; the attitudes of law enforcement officers; and the characteristics of observers (Becker 1963). To illustrate this point, Becker (1963: 12–13) uses studies of juvenile delinquency and social class:

> Boys from middle-class areas do not get as far in the legal process when they are apprehended as do boys from slum areas. The middle-class boy is less likely, when picked up by the police, to be taken to the station; less likely when taken to the station to be booked; and it is extremely unlikely that he will be convicted and sentenced. This variation occurs even though the original infraction of the rule is the same in the two cases.

Most labeling theorists of the 1960s and 1970s, including Becker, were concerned primarily with the application and consequences of *formal* labels – those applied through formal agencies of social control, such as the juvenile justice system. In the late 1970s, labeling theory began to fall out of favor among criminologists for several reasons: much early empirical research did not support it, it generally ignores the causes of primary deviance, and it assumes that the labeling process has only negative effects and does not consider factors that might lead to deterrent effects of labeling (Reid 2012; Paternoster and Iovanni 1989). In the late 1980s and 1990s, however, the labeling perspective generated renewed interest, particularly in the works of John Braithwaite and Ross Matsueda.

Informal reactions: labeling as an interpersonal process

In the 1990s, Matsueda and his colleagues began to consider the effects of *informal* labels – those applied in the context of interaction with others, such as parents and teachers (Matsueda and Heimer 1997; Bartusch and Matsueda 1996; Heimer and Matsueda 1994; Matsueda 1992). Drawing on symbolic interactionism, Matsueda developed a theory of how self-concept arises and guides behavior, including delinquency. He conceptualized the self, in part, as an individual's perceptions of how others view him or her. These perceptions are developed through the process of role-taking, which, according to symbolic interactionism, is the mechanism through which individuals influence one another in social interaction. Role-taking consists of putting oneself in the role of other persons and assessing oneself, the situation, and possible lines of action from the perspective of those others. Matsueda and his colleagues argue that role-taking serves as a mechanism of social control, as individuals view themselves and potential lines of action from the standpoint of others and adjust their behavior accordingly (Bartusch and Matsueda 1996; Heimer and Matsueda 1994; Matsueda 1992).

Matsueda (1992) uses the term **reflected appraisals of self** to refer to the view of self that one develops by taking the role of others and appraising oneself from the perspective of those others. He argues that reflected appraisals of self result in part from the actual appraisals made by others. Reflected appraisals are important in the study of delinquency because they are a mechanism of self-control; individuals tend to behave in ways that are consistent with their reflected appraisals of self. For example, reflected appraisals of self as "bad kids" may free individuals to behave according to that label. If they perceive that others already see them as "bad kids," they have "nothing to lose" by actually behaving that way. Matsueda hypothesizes that those who see themselves (from the perspective of others) as "rule violators" are more likely to engage in delinquency.

To test his interactionist theory of delinquency, Matsueda used data from the National Youth Survey. "Research in action: the measurement of parents' appraisals and youths' reflected appraisals" presents Matsueda's measures of parents' actual appraisals of their children and youths' reflected appraisals of self.

Research in action: the measurement of parents' appraisals and youths' reflected appraisals

Ross Matsueda (1992) used variables from the National Youth Survey to measure parents' appraisals of their children and youths' reflected appraisals of self. This dataset contains measures of four distinct dimensions of "the self" – as sociable, distressed, rule violator, and likely to succeed.

Parents' appraisals

Each parent respondent was asked, "I'd like more information about how you see your son or daughter. I will read you a list of words or short phrases. Please listen carefully and tell me ... how much you agree or disagree with each of the words or phrases as a description of your son or daughter." Five response categories ranged from strongly agree to strongly disagree.

Parent appraisal as sociable:

My son or daughter is well liked.

My son or daughter gets along well with other people.

Parent appraisal as distressed:

My son or daughter is often upset.

My son or daughter has a lot of personal problems.

Parent appraisal as a rule violator:

My son or daughter gets into trouble.

My son or daughter breaks rules.

Parent appraisal as likely to succeed:

My son or daughter is likely to succeed.

Youths' reflected appraisals

Each youth respondent was asked, "I'd like to know how your parents, friends, and teachers would describe you. I'll read a list of words or phrases and for each will ask you to tell me how much you think your parents would agree with that description of you. I'll repeat the list twice more, to learn how your friends and your teachers would describe you." Five response categories ranged from strongly agree to strongly disagree.

Reflected appraisal as sociable:

Parents agree I am well liked.

Friends agree I am well liked.

Teachers agree I am well liked.

Parents/friends/teachers agree I get along well with other people.

Reflected appraisal as distressed:

Parents/friends/teachers agree I am often upset.

Parents/friends/teachers agree I have a lot of personal problems.

Reflected appraisal as a rule violator:

Parents/friends/teachers agree I get into trouble.

Parents/friends/teachers agree I break rules.

Reflected appraisal as likely to succeed:

Parents/friends/teachers agree I am likely to succeed.

Matsueda (1992) specified several hypotheses, which are illustrated in Figure 12.1. First, prior delinquent behavior was expected to influence both parents' actual appraisals of their children and youths' reflected appraisals of self from the standpoint of significant others. This hypothesis is consistent with the concept of primary deviance setting the labeling process in motion. Second, parents' appraisals of their children were expected to influence youths' reflected appraisals of themselves. Third, youths' reflected appraisals of self (especially as "rule violator") were expected to influence their later involvement in delinquency. Parents' appraisals or labels were expected to influence youths' future delinquency, but only indirectly, through their effects on youths' reflected appraisals of self.

In his research, Matsueda (1992) found general support for these hypotheses. Most important, parents' labels strongly influenced youths' reflected appraisals of self, and youths' reflected

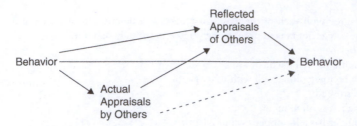

Figure 12.1 Matsueda's model of reflected appraisals and behavior.
Matsueda's interactionist model shows that actual appraisals by others and reflected appraisals of self result in part from prior behavior. Actual appraisals by others influence reflected appraisals, which, in turn, influence subsequent behavior. The dashed path from actual appraisals to subsequent behavior indicates that actual appraisals should have no effect on later behavior, except through their effect on reflected appraisals.
Source: Matsueda (1992: 1585). Copyright © 1992, University of Chicago Press. All rights reserved. Reproduced with permission of the publisher.

appraisals (especially as a rule violator) strongly influenced subsequent delinquency. Youths who perceive that others see them as rule violators engage in more delinquent acts. However, contrary to his theory, Matsueda also found that parents' appraisals of their children as rule violators directly affected youths' delinquent behavior, regardless of youths' perceptions of those appraisals.[2] A later study showed that this direct effect of parental labels on youths' delinquency disappeared once association with delinquent peers was taken into consideration. In other words, "youths who are appraised negatively by parents are likely to commit subsequent delinquent acts, in part because of their perceptions of the appraisal [reflected appraisals] and in part because they are more likely to come into contact with peers who are delinquent" (Heimer and Matsueda 1994: 378). Matsueda's research provides support for labeling theory, and highlights the significance of the informal labeling process.

Braithwaite's theory of reintegrative shaming

Like Matsueda, John Braithwaite has played a significant role in the revival of the labeling perspective in the past two decades. In 1989, Braithwaite presented his *theory of reintegrative shaming*, which begins with several traditional theories of crime (control, subcultural, differential association, strain, and labeling theories), and then introduces a new concept – *reintegrative shaming* – to draw those theories together into an integrated framework. The novel part of this theory is the distinction between two types of shaming – one that increases subsequent offending through its stigmatizing effects (stigmatization) and another that deters subsequent offending through the reintegration of the offender into the community (reintegrative shaming).

Braithwaite (1989: 100) defines *shaming* as "all social processes of expressing disapproval which have the intention or effect of invoking remorse in the person being shamed and/or condemnation by others who become aware of the shaming." **Reintegrative shaming** is "shaming which is followed by efforts to reintegrate the offender back into the community of law-abiding or respectable citizens through words or gestures of forgiveness or ceremonies to decertify the offender as deviant" (Braithwaite 1989: 100–101). Throughout the process of reintegrative shaming, there is an effort to maintain respect for the offender. This type of shaming involves condemnation of deviant behavior, but not condemnation of the individual. According to Braithwaite's theory, reintegrative shaming reduces or controls crime.

Crime prevention through reintegrative shaming is accomplished in several ways. Shaming has a specific deterrent effect on offenders who want to avoid the public humiliation associated with detection of their crimes. Shaming also has a general deterrent effect on others who want to avoid being subjected to the shaming process and therefore choose not to engage in crime. Both of these deterrent effects are greater for persons with strong attachments to others, because these attachments increase the potential social costs of offending. Reintegrative shaming also prevents crime by leading people to think of crime as "unthinkable." The process of reintegrative shaming affirms and builds commitment to the criminal law, and thus makes future crime (by the offender being shamed and by others) less likely. According to Braithwaite, the element of repentance in reintegrative shaming is key to this affirmation of law. Finally, reintegrative shaming involves citizen participation, which is important for both specific and general deterrence (Braithwaite 1989).

In contrast to reintegrative shaming, **stigmatization** is "disintegrative shaming in which no effort is made to reconcile the offender with the community" (Braithwaite 1989: 101). Rather than drawing offenders back into the community, stigmatization propels offenders toward deviant subcultures and increases crime by providing opportunities and reinforcements for criminal behavior. Braithwaite derives the concept of stigmatization from labeling theory.

Braithwaite contends that people vary in susceptibility to shaming based on their level of **interdependency**. The concept of interdependency is similar to attachment, commitment, and social bonding in control theory. Interdependency is "the extent to which individuals participate in networks wherein they are dependent on others to achieve valued ends and others are dependent on them" (Braithwaite 1989: 98, 100). Those who are most interdependent are most affected by the shaming process. Braithwaite's theory proposes that levels of interdependency are influenced by individual characteristics such as age, gender, marital status, and educational and employment aspirations. **Communitarianism** is the societal-level counterpart to interdependency. According to Braithwaite's theory, shaming is more widespread and effective in communitarian societies (such as Japan, where the culture emphasizes obligations to others) than in other societies (such as the United States, where the culture is more individualistic) (Westermann and Burfeind 1991). Communitarianism is influenced by characteristics such as urbanization and residential mobility.

Recent tests of reintegrative shaming theory have provided somewhat mixed results. Some studies show strong support for reintegrative shaming theory. For example, Eliza Ahmed and John Braithwaite (2005) examined the influence of reintegrative shaming and forgiveness on bullying. They found that both decreased subsequent bullying, but the effect of forgiveness was stronger than the effect of reintegrative shaming. Cesar Rebellon and his colleagues (2010) explored the effect of potential shaming by family and friends on criminal intent. Their research revealed that the prospect of shaming has a stronger effect on criminal intent than do factors derived from learning, control, strain, and deterrence theories. Kristina Murphy and her colleagues (Murphy and Helmer 2013; Murphy and Harris 2007) studied tax offenders and found that stigmatizing shaming did not reduce subsequent offending. Reintegrative responses and forgiveness, however, played a significant role in reducing repeat offending.

Other research offers more mixed support (Kim and Gerber 2012; Schaible and Hughes 2011; Losoncz and Tyson 2007; Zhang and Zhang 2004). In one study, researchers measured reintegrative shaming as a combination of disapproval of delinquency (shaming) and forgiveness of the offender (reintegration) by parents and peers (Zhang and Zhang 2004). Although parental forgiveness and peer shaming alone decreased subsequent predatory offending, reintegrative shaming by parents and peers did not influence offending. Although the findings of this study provide some support for Braithwaite's theory, they do not support its key hypothesis that reintegrative shaming decreases future offending. In a more recent study, Kim and Gerber (2012) compared the effects of traditional court processing of juvenile offending with those of a reintegrative shaming approach (restorative justice conferencing). Contrary to reintegrative shaming theory, they found no significant relationship between restorative justice conferencing and offenders' perceptions of the prevention of future offending. But consistent with reintegrative shaming theory, they also found effects of restorative justice conferencing on feelings of repentance and on repayment of the victim and society.

The theory of reintegrative shaming has been very influential in the development of the restorative justice approach, which is intended to make offenders face the harms they have caused to their victims, to allow victims to describe how the offenses have affected them and to have input into the punishment of offenders, and to use a non-adversarial process to determine how to "restore" the situation for both offenders and victims (see Chapter 14).

Consequences of labeling: stigma or deterrence?

The labeling perspective contends that societal reactions to initial acts of deviance may lead to the development of a deviant identity that increases the likelihood of subsequent deviance among those who have been labeled "deviant." In other words, the labeling process has a stigmatizing effect that ultimately results in **deviance amplification**. Erving Goffman (1963) describes **stigma** as a deeply discrediting attribute or "spoiled identity," which can result from being labeled for prior deviant behavior, such as delinquency, or for personal characteristics that others sometimes perceive as deviant, such as mental illness. The stigma associated with a negative label can limit an individual's legitimate opportunities (e.g., ineligibility for particular jobs because of a criminal record), influence an individual's personal relationships (e.g., alienation from parents as a result of delinquent behavior), and affect an individual's self-concept as he or she accepts the deviant identity associated with the negative label. John Hagan (1993) uses the concept of "social embeddedness" to describe how punishment and its accompanying stigma "embed" individuals in relationships and social institutions that make success in the conventional realm (such as employment) less likely and continued deviance more likely.

The stigmatizing effect of societal reactions that labeling theorists describe is contrary to the deterrent effect proposed by classical criminologists (see Chapter 8). Deterrence theory argues that societal reactions to delinquency constitute a form of punishment that deters future delinquency. According to deterrence theory, negative reactions will increase individuals' perceptions of risk associated with future offending, which, in turn, will deter subsequent delinquency (Ward and Tittle 1993). Figure 12.2 depicts the competing models offered by the labeling perspective and deterrence theory of the effects of sanctions or societal reactions on future deviance.

Over the past 25 years, numerous studies have explored the consequences of societal reactions to deviance and delinquency (e.g., Ward, Krohn, and Gibson 2014; Morris and Piquero 2013; Lopes et al. 2012; DeLisi et al. 2011; Stewart et al. 2002, De Li 1999; Adams, Johnson, and Evans 1998; Bartusch and Matsueda 1996; Smith and Brame 1994; Ward and Tittle 1993;

Deterrence Theory:

Deviance $\xrightarrow{+}$ Sanctions $\xrightarrow{+}$ Perception of risk $\xrightarrow{-}$ Future deviance

Labeling Perspective:

Deviance $\xrightarrow{+}$ Sanctions $\xrightarrow{+}$ Labeling $\xrightarrow{+}$ Deviant Identity $\xrightarrow{+}$ Future Deviance

Figure 12.2 Competing models of sanctions and future deviance.
Ward and Tittle illustrate the alternative views of sanctions and subsequent deviance offered by deterrence theory and the labeling perspective. Deterrence theory contends that sanctions or societal reactions decrease the likelihood of future deviance by increasing the perception of risk associated with deviant behavior. The labeling perspective maintains that societal reactions increase the likelihood of future deviance by leading individuals to adopt deviant identities and behave in accord with them. In the figures, plus signs indicate positive relationships and minus signs indicate negative ones.
Source: Based on Ward and Tittle (1993: 44–45).

Smith and Gartin 1989). We briefly review research that has considered the effects of formal and informal reactions.

Formal sanctions: stigma or deterrence?

Initially, labeling theorists focused on the role of formal organizations, such as police or juvenile courts, in creating deviance and delinquency. Much early research on the labeling perspective concentrated on the effects of labeling that occurs in the process of official responses to delinquency, such as arrest or juvenile court processing.[3]

In a 1989 study, Douglas Smith and Patrick Gartin asked whether arrest amplified future offending (as labeling theory predicts) or deterred future offending (as deterrence theory predicts). They considered two groups of offenders: those who had contact with police but were released without arrest and those who were arrested. Smith and Gartin compared subsequent criminal activity (measured by future police contacts) for the two groups and found that those arrested were less likely than those who were released without arrest to have subsequent contact with police. Smith and Gartin also found that the influence of arrest on future offending differed for "novice" offenders (those with only one or two police contacts) and "experienced" offenders with more established criminal careers. Novice offenders were more likely than experienced offenders to stop their criminal activity as a result of arrest. Smith and Gartin (1989) interpreted their results as supporting deterrence theory.

The broad body of later research on the effects of formal sanctions, however, has been more supportive of the labeling perspective and shows effects of formal labels on subsequent delinquency and crime, educational attainment, labor market participation, and psychological well-being (e.g., Ward et al. 2014; Wiley, Slocum, and Esbensen 2013; Lopes et al. 2012; DeLisi et al. 2011; Kurlychek, Brame, and Bushway 2007; Siennick 2007; Bernburg, Krohn, and Rivera 2006; Sweeten 2006; Johnson, Simons, and Conger 2004; Bernburg and Krohn 2003; Stewart et al. 2002). Consistent with the labeling perspective, researchers have found negative consequences of contacts with police (Ward et al. 2014; Wiley et al. 2013; Lopes et al. 2012), arrests (Wiley et al. 2013; Lopes et al. 2012), convictions for delinquent offenses (De

Li 1999), and juvenile confinement (DeLisi et al. 2011). One study showed that intervention by the juvenile justice system increases subsequent involvement in serious delinquency indirectly, through its effect on involvement with delinquent peers and street gangs (Bernburg et al. 2006).

A study of the effects of contacts with police showed that such contacts increase the likelihood of subsequent violent offending, particularly for offenders who were on a low violent-offending trajectory (Ward et al. 2014). Another study examined the effects of legal sanctions (measured as convictions for delinquent offenses) on self-reported delinquency, later delinquency convictions, and achievements in education and work. Results indicated that conviction at an early age (10 to 13 years old) had particularly strong effects, increasing later delinquency, convictions, and unemployment, and decreasing later educational and occupational achievements (De Li 1999).

> Overall, convictions seem to have a strong adverse effect on legitimate opportunities for adolescents: Youths who were labeled by the juvenile justice system were more likely to develop antisocial attitudes and unconventional behaviors. They were also more likely to exhibit low educational achievement, low occupational status, and unstable job records.
>
> (De Li 1999: 391)

Matt DeLisi and his colleagues (2011) examined the consequences of juvenile confinement and found an effect of confinement on later arrests for murder, even after they took into account factors such as juvenile violent offending, juvenile felony adjudications, and career arrests. These findings are consistent with the labeling perspective, which suggests that the stigma associated with delinquent labels has wide-ranging consequences.

Other research offers qualified support for the labeling perspective. Robert Morris and Alex Piquero (2013) examined the effects of arrest on subsequent crime, asking the question, for whom do formal sanctions deter and for whom do they increase future offending? Their results revealed that, for higher risk youth, arrest increases subsequent delinquency. This effect of arrest, however, did not exist for lower risk youth. Another study suggests that the labeling perspective may be less relevant in certain settings. In the context of disadvantaged urban communities, arrests are relatively common among adolescent males and thus carry little stigma. Paul Hirschfield (2008) found that, in this context, arrests do not have an effect consistent with the labeling perspective.

The results of research supportive of the labeling perspective can be interpreted within the developmental framework proposed by Robert Sampson and John Laub (1993, 1997). Sampson and Laub consider the stability of delinquency and crime over time and the way in which labeling contributes to that stability. They use the term "cumulative disadvantage" to describe how delinquency disrupts various aspects of life, including family and peer relationships, success in school, and employment opportunities. Sampson and Laub argue that official sanctions contribute to the process of cumulative disadvantage and play a role in sustaining delinquency. "The theory specifically suggests a 'snowball' effect – that adolescent delinquency and its negative consequences (e.g., arrest, official labeling, incarceration) increasingly 'mortgage' one's future, especially later life chances molded by schooling and employment" (Sampson and Laub 1997: 147). The stigma associated with official sanctions prevents individuals from establishing strong ties to conventional lines of action. Thus, Sampson and Laub propose that the effects of official sanctions on future offending are indirect, operating through the disruption of social relationships and legitimate opportunities. In support of this perspective, Sampson and his colleague, David Kirk, found that arrest has a significant effect on dropping out of high school and on college enrollment, and that disruptions in students' educational trajectories, rather than social psychological factors, account for the relationship between arrest and educational attainment (Kirk and Sampson 2013).

Sampson and Laub's (1997) research supports this view of official sanctions and subsequent delinquency. Other research is also consistent with the theory that official reactions to delinquency have a cumulative effect and contribute to the stability of delinquent behavior by closing off opportunities and relationships (e.g., Bernburg et al. 2006; Stewart et al. 2002; De Li 1999).

Informal reactions: stigma or deterrence?

During the 1990s, researchers began to look beyond official reactions to delinquency and focus on the consequences of informal labels (Triplett and Jarjoura 1994; Wellford and Triplett 1993). Earlier, we described studies by Matsueda and his colleagues, who found that informal labeling affects youths' subsequent involvement in delinquency (Bartusch and Matsueda 1996; Heimer and Matsueda 1994; Matsueda 1992). Other criminologists studying the consequences of youths' perceptions of informal labels have also found support for the labeling perspective (e.g., Adams et al. 2003; Liu 2000; Smith and Brame 1994; Ward and Tittle 1993). Douglas Smith and Robert Brame, for example, examined whether the factors that explain initial involvement in delinquency are the same as those that explain continuation of offending. Consistent with the hypothesis of deviance amplification, they found that youths' perceptions of negative labels by parents and peers contribute to continuity of offending, but not to initiation into delinquency.

> Youths who feel that their parents and peers view them negatively are not at increased risk to begin delinquency. However, among those who have offended in the past, this same negative labeling is associated with a significantly higher probability of continued delinquency.
>
> (Smith and Brame 1994: 624)[4]

Other researchers have explored the effect on delinquency of youths' perceptions of informal labels by teachers. Mike Adams and David Evans (1996) found that students' perceptions of negative labeling by teachers, like their perceptions of labeling by parents in other studies, increased youths' subsequent delinquency. When Adams and Evans took into account youths' associations with delinquent peers, though, the direct effect of teacher labeling on youths' delinquent behavior was no longer significant. Instead, the effect was largely mediated by associations with delinquent peers.

Other research by Adams and his colleagues suggests that the effects of informal labeling vary by race. Prior research indicated that formal labeling by the criminal justice system is more detrimental for whites than it is for blacks (Harris 1975). But Adams and his associates (1998) found that informal labeling has a greater effect on delinquency for blacks than it does for whites.

Who is labeled, and based on whose rules?

As we noted earlier in this chapter, labeling theory is grounded, in part, in the conflict perspective, which considers how power and resources shape the creation or social construction of definitions of deviance and the application of those definitions to particular people. Relationships exist between resources and the ability to make or impose rules, and between resources and the ability to resist deviant labels. Rather than being universally agreed upon, rules and laws result from a political process characterized by conflict and disagreement. Conflict also characterizes the application of rules and laws. Labeling theorists have argued that "delinquent" or "criminal" labels are disproportionately applied to less powerful members of society, such as racial minorities or those from lower social classes (Farrell and Swigert 1988; Becker 1963).

We turn now to critical criminologies, which share with the labeling perspective the view that power and conflict shape how society defines and reacts to crime and criminals. Critical criminologies also place power and conflict within the political and economic structures from which they originate.[5]

Critical criminologies

In 1916, Willem Bonger offered the first explanation of how capitalism generates crime. He maintained that capitalism creates a pervasive mental state of "egoism" or ruthless competition, which he contrasted with the altruism of precapitalist societies. By emphasizing profit and the accumulation of wealth, capitalism ignites greed and competition. According to Bonger, crime is a natural outcome of such competition. He used Marxist ideology to develop a theory to explain both the crimes of the powerless working class and those of the powerful upper classes (Bonger 1969). Ideology is a set of ideas and beliefs that together form a social, political, or moral agenda and that attempt to justify a particular social or political order.

It was not until the late 1960s that interest in the structural forces that breed crime, found first in Bonger's work, reemerged in theoretical criminology. The social and political unrest that fueled labeling theory in the 1960s also led to a variety of critical interpretations of crime and delinquency that examined how the political and economic structures of society influenced criminal behavior. We briefly describe the major themes of critical criminologies and then examine three critical interpretations of delinquency.

Major themes of critical criminologies

Because a variety of distinct perspectives are housed under the roof of "critical criminologies," it is difficult to describe the central themes of the critical approach. Francis Cullen and his colleagues, however, have distilled this realm of thought down to the following five core themes (Cullen et al. 2014: 285–286).

First, the concepts of power and inequality are essential to any understanding of crime and its control. Critical criminologies focus on the distribution of power in society and on inequalities among members of different groups, including social classes. Differences in power produce conflict as members of different groups pursue their own interests. Conflict between the "haves" and the "have-nots" is an inherent part of the capitalist economic structure.

Second, crime and delinquency are politically defined. Laws do not necessarily reflect social consensus. Instead, political and economic power are used to shape definitions of what is crime and who is criminal.

In general, the injurious acts of the poor and powerless are defined as crime, but the injurious acts of the rich and powerful – such as corporations selling defective products or the affluent allowing disadvantaged children to go without health care – are not brought within the reach of the criminal law.

(Cullen et al. 2014: 285; see also Reiman and Leighton 2013)

Third, both law and the criminal justice system protect the interests of the most powerful members of society. Mechanisms of social control, including socialization (which is constrained by social forces), informal controls, law, and the criminal justice system, are necessary to maintain the existing social order and preserve the advantages of those with economic and political power. In addition, in enforcing social order, agents of control sometimes commit crimes themselves, such as excessive use of force by police.

Fourth, capitalism is the root cause of crime. The capitalist economic system leads powerless members of lower social classes, whose needs are ignored, to commit crimes out of economic necessity or resentment and frustration brought on by the "demoralizing" conditions of their disadvantaged lives. Capitalism also leads powerful members of upper classes to commit crimes to increase profits, with relatively little chance that these crimes will be punished severely or at all.

Fifth, the solution to the problem of crime is the creation of a more just and equitable society. Only by understanding how the inequalities inherent within capitalism create crime can we begin to resolve the crime problem. Those who take a critical view of law and crime argue that criminologists should advocate policies that promote social justice.

With these five themes in mind, we turn to three examples of critical approaches to delinquency: Mark Colvin and John Pauly's integrated structural–Marxist theory, John Hagan's power-control theory, and David Greenberg's Marxist interpretation of delinquency.

Colvin and Pauly's integrated structural-Marxist theory of delinquency

According to the structural-Marxist view of the causes of crime, as important as economic structures and inequality are, they alone cannot explain crime. Instead, structural Marxists try to situate microlevel explanations of crime, such as theories that focus on family and peer influences, within a broader social, political, and economic context that takes into account class distinctions inherent in capitalism (Lynch and Michalowski 2006). An excellent example of this approach is Colvin and Pauly's *integrated structural-Marxist theory* of delinquency. Colvin and Pauly begin their analysis with the structure of social relations grounded in capitalism, and then integrate elements from traditional theories of delinquency, including the emphasis of social control theory on family and school and the emphasis of social learning theory on peers (Colvin and Pauly 1983).

Workplace control structures

Structural Marxists conceptualize classes in terms of relations to the means of production – the system by which goods are produced and distributed. The capitalist class owns and controls the means of production, and the working class sells its labor to capitalists. Colvin and Pauly (1983) examine different mechanisms of control that workers experience within the workplace in a capitalist economy. They describe three "fractions" of the working class.

Fraction I workers typically labor in low-skill, "dead-end jobs" characterized by high turn-over of employees and little opportunity for advancement, such as food service and retail sales jobs. Control of these workers is coercive and is achieved through the threat of dismissal from the job. This coercive control creates a negative, alienated orientation on the part of the worker toward the employer and authority in the workplace.

Fraction II consists of organized workers who have gained some wage and benefit advantages and job protection through union representation, such as workers in the auto and steel industries. Control of these workers involves the manipulation of material rewards such as pay raises. This type of control creates an unstable bond between workers and employers that rests on workers' advancement up the pay ladder and involves limited worker loyalty to the employer.

Fraction III workers hold jobs that require independent initiative and self-motivation, such as middle-level supervisors, foremen, skilled craftsmen (e.g., electricians, plumbers), and sal-aried professional workers (e.g., accountants, teachers). Control of these workers is achieved through formal standards of professional conduct and through the manipulation of statuses and symbols to promote commitment to the organization, such as advancement to a more prestigious job title (even if that new position offers little advancement in terms of pay). This type of control creates a positive orientation toward workplace authority and the employer.

Family control structures

The cornerstone of Colvin and Pauly's theory is their analysis of how these three forms of workplace control and the orientation to authority they produce translate into mechanisms of control within the family. According to Colvin and Pauly, parents who experience greater external control in the workplace stress (either consciously or unconsciously) conformity to external authority in their childrearing practices. Parents who experience less external control and have more autonomy in the workplace stress to their children the value of self-control, initiative, and creativity (Colvin and Pauly 1983; Kohn 1977). Thus, children learn to act toward parental authority either out of fear of external consequences or out of a sense of internalized commitment and respect. Through the mechanism of parental control, parents' bonds to workplace authority are reproduced in children's bonds to parental authority.

Colvin and Pauly (1983: 536) offer these hypotheses about the links between controls and orientations to authority in the workplace and controls and orientations to authority in the family:

- Fraction I workers tend to use coercive, arbitrary, and inconsistent discipline that is some-times lax and at other times highly punitive. The result is an "alienated" bond between children and parental authority.
- Fraction II workers tend to use compliance structures that involve parental manipulation of external rewards and children's calculations of self-interest. Children can dependably predict the external consequences of their actions, and they form moderate bonds to parental authority.
- Fraction III workers tend to use compliance structures that involve parental manipulation of symbolic rewards, resulting in children's positive bonds to parental authority.

Colvin and Pauly cite research that indicates that family control structures are related to delinquency. For example, studies have shown that erratic and punitive disciplinary practices, as well as weak bonds between parents and children, are positively associated with children's involvement in delinquency (e.g., Sampson and Laub 1993; Loeber and Stouthamer-Loeber 1986; Hirschi 1969).

School control structures

According to Colvin and Pauly, schools use various control structures to create a skilled and disciplined workforce, amenable to the compliance required of workers under capitalism. School control structures parallel those in the family and the workplace through multiple mechanisms. First, children's orientation to authority, developed within family control structures, affects their behavior, which elicits controlling responses from teachers and other school authority figures. A child who is negatively bonded to parental authority may behave in school in ways that teachers interpret and label as disruptive. This labeling process may create a "self-fulfilling prophecy" of a disruptive child who is then subjected to even greater coercive controls.

Second, children take IQ and aptitude tests that are used to place them in "tracks." Colvin and Pauly argue that these tests may measure motivation and orientation to authority more than they measure cognitive ability. Students who earn high IQ scores are likely to be self-motivated – a quality achieved through positive orientation to authority within family compliance structures that involve symbolic rewards. They are likely to be placed in higher tracks that emphasize initiative, self-direction, and creativity. Students who earn low IQ scores are likely to have a more negative orientation to authority and are likely to be placed in lower tracks that emphasize strict discipline and conformity to external authority.

Colvin and Pauly cite research that indicates a relationship between school control structures and delinquency. For example, studies have shown a negative association between IQ scores and involvement in delinquency. Similarly, research suggests that placement in lower-level educational tracks is positively related to delinquency. Studies also indicate that strong positive bonds to school decrease the likelihood of delinquent behavior (e.g., Hirschi and Hindelang 1977; Schaefer, Olexa, and Polk 1972; Hirschi 1969).

Peer associations and control structures

Adolescents do not form peer groups randomly. Instead, they are drawn to one another based on common experiences and beliefs. Colvin and Pauly's theory assumes that adolescents with similar orientations to authority (based on school and family experiences) will be drawn together. Colvin and Pauly (1983: 539–540) offer the following hypotheses:

- Students in higher educational tracks, which reinforce positive bonds to authority, will form peer groups that offer symbolic rewards, reinforce positive bonds, and "insulate" group members from delinquency.
- Students in intermediate tracks, whose bonds to authority are precarious and based on the calculation of material rewards, will form peer groups centered around the pursuit of external rewards. These peer groups will reinforce occasional involvement in delinquency intended to achieve material gains, such as theft.
- Students in lower educational tracks, with alienated bonds to authority, will form peer groups characterized by coercive control (because they lack material resources and legitimate opportunities to achieve status, which are needed for other types of control). These peer groups will reinforce serious, patterned delinquency.

In summary, Colvin and Pauly argue that workplace control structures shape the forms of control parents use to discipline and reward their children. Children's socialization experiences within the family then influence the forms of control they encounter in school and peer groups. The more coercive the controls children experience in families, schools, and peer groups tend to be, the more alienated their bonds to authority will be, and the more likely they are to engage in serious, patterned delinquency.

Hagan's power-control theory of delinquency

In the mid-1980s, John Hagan, A. R. Gillis, and John Simpson developed *power-control theory*, a structural explanation for common delinquency that focuses on the intersection of social class and gender (Hagan et al. 1985, 1987). This theory combines the macro-level concept of power, derived from relations to the means of production and authority in the workplace, with the micro-level concept of control established within relationships such as family interactions. Hagan and his colleagues argue that both the presence of power and the absence of control contribute to adolescents' freedom to violate social norms. Their objective is to explain gender differences in delinquency based on gender differences in experiences of power and control. Power-control theory is explicitly intended to explain common, minor forms of delinquency, not serious, violent delinquent behavior Hagan et al. 1985).

Like Colvin and Pauly, Hagan and his colleagues begin with the premise that parents' workplace experiences, which are grounded in class, influence parental control and children's socialization experiences within families. Power-control theory contends that parents who have relatively little authority and who experience greater controls in the workplace will exercise greater controls over their children (Hagan 1989; Hagan et al. 1985, 1987).

Hagan and his colleagues (1985, 1987) define social class first in terms of relations to the means of production (e.g., employers who are owners and workers who are non-owners), and later in terms of relations to authority in the workplace (e.g., a command class that exercises authority and an obey class that is subject to the authority of others). They then distinguish ideal types of families (or abstract statements of the essential characteristics of different types of families) based on husbands' and wives' relations to authority.[6] In **patriarchal families**, family class relations are "unbalanced." Husbands exercise greater authority in the workplace than do wives, who are either unemployed or employed in positions of less authority than those of their husbands. In **egalitarian families**, family class relations are "balanced." Husbands and wives are employed in positions of similar authority, in either the command class or the obey class (Hagan et al. 1987).[7]

How, then, do differences in parents' workplace experiences of authority translate into gender differences in delinquency among sons and daughters? Hagan and his colleagues argue that, relative to fathers, mothers assume greater responsibility for the socialization and control of children. In patriarchal families, women reproduce gender imbalances in power by exerting greater control over daughters than over sons. In egalitarian families, on the other hand, daughters are subjected to controls similar to those imposed on sons. Thus, in egalitarian families, "as [wives] gain power relative to husbands, daughters gain freedom relative to sons" (Hagan et al. 1987: 792).

Power-control theory proposes that the amount of control daughters and sons experience within families influences their attitudes toward risk taking. Risk taking is contrary to the emphasis on "passivity" that characterizes patriarchal views of women's and girls' roles. Thus, in patriarchal families, parents (particularly mothers) teach daughters to avoid risk. In egalitarian families, parents encourage both daughters and sons to be more open to taking risks, in part in preparation for the kinds of entrepreneurial activities these children are expected eventually to perform in the workplace (Hagan et al. 1987).

Delinquency can be regarded as a form of risk taking. Power-control theory predicts that attitudes toward risk taking influence delinquent behavior, in part through their effect on perceived risks of sanctions for engaging in delinquency. The theory also predicts that both "taste for risk" and the deterrent effect of perceived risks of sanctions will vary by gender as a result of differences in familial controls for daughters and sons. Compared to males, females are more strongly socialized by parents (especially mothers) to avoid risks, and so will be more strongly deterred by the risk or threat of legal sanctions (Hagan et al. 1985).

In 2007, Hagan and his colleagues developed a revised version of power-control theory that includes adolescents'"dominance ideologies" as a predictor of gender differences in delinquency (Hadjar et al. 2007).[8] These dominance ideologies consist of preferences for patriarchal gender roles and "hierarchic self-interest," which includes a preference for competitiveness and a willingness to further one's own interests at the expense of others. Patriarchal gender-role preferences were measured by questions such as "It is more important for a woman to support her husband in his career than to pursue a career of her own" (Hadjar et al. 2007: 41–42). Greater hierarchic self-interest among males than females and patriarchal gender-role preferences indicate a strong male-dominance ideology. In this revised version of power-control theory, Hagan and his colleagues hypothesize that adolescents' dominance ideologies will partially mediate the effects of patriarchal workplace structures and differences in parental control on children's risk preferences and involvement in delinquency (Hadjar et al. 2007).

The model of gender and delinquency presented in the revised version of power-control theory is depicted in Figure 12.3. In sum, power-control theory argues that social class and gender together create the conditions of freedom that lead to common delinquency. Both class and gender, by determining the presence of power and the absence of control, structure

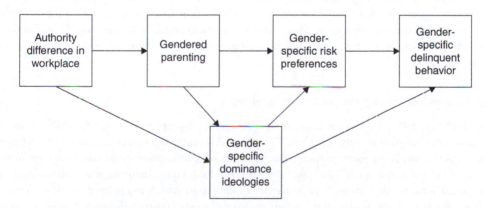

Figure 12.3 Hagan's revised model of power-control theory.
This revised model depicts how differences in power and authority in the workplace (which are structured by social class), differences in parental control of sons and daughters, children's acceptance of patriarchal dominance ideologies, and children's gendered risk preferences combine to predict gender differences in delinquent behavior.
Source: Hadjar et al. (2007: 38). Copyright © 2007, Sage Publications. All rights reserved. Reproduced with permission of the publisher.

the socialization experiences of children that contribute to delinquency. Parental power and control also influence children's dominance ideologies, which, in turn, affect children's risk preferences and delinquent behavior. Hagan and his colleagues predict that in patriarchal families, there will be large gender differences in common delinquency, while in egalitarian families there will be smaller gender differences in offending (Hadjar et al. 2007; Hagan et al. 1985, 1987).

Research support for power-control theory has been mixed. Hagan and his colleagues, as well as other researchers, have found support for the theory, including the revised version of the theory (Hirtenlehner et al. 2014; Hadjar et al. 2007; Blackwell 2000; Uggen 2000; Hagan et al. 1985, 1987, 1990).[9] A study by Christopher Uggen (2000), for example, incorporated direct measures of workplace freedom and control for both parents and working youths. Uggen found strong support for power-control theory. Other research, however, has not supported the theory (e.g., Morash and Chesney-Lind 1991; Jensen and Thompson 1990). In addition, power-control theory has been criticized for its limited definition of patriarchal control, which is reduced to parental supervision, for its hypothesis that mothers' work contributes to daughters' delinquency, and for its view of female-headed households as equivalent to egalitarian families (Chesney-Lind and Shelden 2014; Chesney-Lind and Pasko 2013).[10]

Greenberg's Marxist interpretation of delinquency

David Greenberg (1981) offers a *Marxist interpretation* of the disproportionate involvement of adolescents in crime, based on the view that youth occupy a precarious status position in capitalist societies. Greenberg begins by noting that the peak ages for involvement in crime have declined over time as a result of the changing position of juveniles in capitalist industrial societies. He argues that traditional theories of delinquency are unable to explain both this historical shift in the age distribution of crime and the decline in involvement in crime during late adolescence and early adulthood (the "aging out of crime" we discussed in Chapter 5). Greenberg's critical approach accounts for both of these patterns through two primary components. First, he attributes the motivation to engage in delinquency to the structural position of adolescents in American society. Second, he argues that the willingness to act on this motivation is different across age groups because the costs of engaging in crime vary by age.

Adolescent labor force participation and social life

Greenberg (1981) begins his analysis of delinquency by observing that American adolescents share a common status problem. Over time, American teenagers have been increasingly excluded from labor force participation through laws restricting child labor and establishing mandatory education. The result has been twofold. First, changing work and education patterns have resulted in an "age-segregated" society in which peers have become increasingly important for adolescents. Sensitivity to peer expectations, desire for peer approval, and participation in teenage social activities have become significant forces in the lives of adolescents. Participation in teenage social life, however, requires financial resources. This brings us to the second result of the exclusion of adolescents from the labor force. The decline of the teenage labor market has left adolescents less capable of financing costly social lives, which gain importance as the age segregation of society increases. Greenberg explains delinquent acts of financial gain, such as theft, in terms of this financial problem. As adolescents age, they gain more legitimate opportunities to acquire needed resources (e.g., through work in early adulthood), and the motivation to engage in delinquent acts of financial gain decreases.

School experiences and delinquency

How, then, do we explain delinquent acts that provide no financial reward, or "non-utilitarian" delinquency, such as vandalism or violence? Here, Greenberg (1981) turns to the status problems of adolescents caused by school experiences. He argues that two features of the school experience contribute to non-utilitarian delinquency: its denial of student autonomy and its humiliation of students who do not perform well academically.

First, schools are filled with rules and restrictions about everything from attendance to acceptable clothing styles. At a time when adolescents are gaining increased autonomy within the family and elsewhere, schools continue to deny student autonomy. For those who do well in school, the resentment caused by this denial of autonomy tends to be offset by rewards associated with school success. However, for those who are less successful academically, the school setting offers only frustration. It brings no gratification in the present and no promise of future reward.

According to Greenberg, class distinctions exist in this process.

> Middle and upper class children are supervised more closely than their working class counterparts, and thus come to expect and accept adult authority, while working class youths, who enter an unsupervised street life among peers at an early age, have more autonomy to protect.
>
> (Greenberg 1981: 126)

Also, middle-class adolescents may be more likely to believe that future opportunities are tied to school success, and thus may accept restrictions on autonomy more readily than will lower-class adolescents. Greenberg (1981: 126) also argues that, compared to middle-class youth, upper-class adolescents may be less concerned with conformity to school requirements because "their inherited class position frees them from the necessity of doing well in school to guarantee their future economic status."

Second, schools are places where teachers and other personnel evaluate and make distinctions among students and where respect is not universally granted to students. According to Greenberg (1981), those who are "relatively powerless," such as failing students and members of lower social classes, are shown less respect than others. Student evaluations are communicated through grades, honor rolls, track positions, privileges, and praise for academic achievement. In addition, teachers are sometimes explicit in their criticism of failing students as "stupid or lazy." The experiences of humiliation suffered by some students in the evaluation process only increase their frustrations regarding school.

Greenberg argues that non-utilitarian delinquency, such as property destruction and violence, can be understood as a response to the status frustrations associated with school. Through these delinquent acts, adolescents display independence and reject authority, restore self-esteem lost to school failure, and preserve moral character by demonstrating a willingness to take risks.

Masculine status anxiety

Greenberg (1981) contends that school requirements of submission to authority are inconsistent with social expectations about masculinity, but not those about femininity. Thus, the status problems caused by school experiences might help explain gender differences in delinquency in early adolescence. In late adolescence, individuals begin to consider occupational prospects and adult role expectations. In American society, the ability to fulfill traditional male roles centered on work and providing for a family are central to male identity. For those who face structural barriers to fulfilling these roles, such as limited employment prospects based on social class and school failure, the result can be **masculine status anxiety**. Greenberg explains crimes that are exaggerated displays of masculinity and toughness, such as rape, homicide, and assault, as attempts to alleviate masculine status anxiety.

In summary, Greenberg's Marxist interpretation of delinquency is based on the constraints of a capitalist economic system that generally excludes adolescents from workforce participation. This exclusion deprives youth of the monetary resources needed to finance teenage social activities. In addition, the status problems caused by school experiences tend to vary by social class, and they account for involvement in non-utilitarian delinquency. Finally, masculine status anxiety also varies by class and accounts for lower-class involvement in violent crime.

We turn now to feminist criminology, which shares with critical criminologies an emphasis on power and inequality within society, a focus on the structural determinants of behavior, and a view that crime and delinquency can be understood in terms of differences in power.

Feminist criminology

For most of its history, the discipline of criminology ignored the issue of gender. Feminist scholars typically attribute this neglect of gender to one of two causes. First, because crime – especially serious crime – is disproportionately committed by males (see Chapter 5), criminologists tended to view female offending as marginal to the crime problem and of little consequence for an understanding of crime and delinquency (Cullen et al. 2014). Second, criminology was a male-dominated discipline, and male criminologists tended to focus on male offenders and to ignore women and girls both as offenders and as victims of crime. Feminist criminologists have lamented not only the historical neglect of women in the discipline of criminology, but also the marginal place historically given to feminist perspectives within theoretical criminology (e.g., Naffine 1997).

Challenges to "male-centered" criminology began in the 1970s, as the women's movement gained momentum and feminist perspectives emerged. **Feminism** is not a single theory, but rather "a set of theories about women's oppression and a set of strategies for social change"[11] (Daly and Chesney-Lind 1988: 502; see also McDermott 2002). As criminologist Sally Simpson (1989: 606) writes, "Feminism is best understood as both a world view and a social movement." In its various forms, feminism tries to illuminate the origins and mechanisms of gender inequality and to propose strategies for abolishing it. Feminist perspectives place gender at the center of attempts to understand human behavior, including delinquency. Kathleen Daly and Meda Chesney-Lind (1988: 504) present five elements of feminist thought that distinguish it from other schools of social thought. "Expanding ideas: core elements of feminist thought" lists these five elements. Feminist perspectives have in common "the recognition of gender as a central organizing component of social life," the recognition of imbalances in power and value granted to males and females, and the realization that males and females inhabit different social worlds (Curran and Renzetti 2001; see also Moore 2008).

Expanding ideas: core elements of feminist thought

Kathleen Daly and Meda Chesney-Lind (1988: 504), noted feminist criminologists, describe the complexities involved in defining feminism and suggest that feminist thought is distinguished by five core elements:

1. "Gender is not a natural fact but a complex social, historical, and cultural product; it is related to, but not simply derived from, biological sex difference and reproductive capacities."
2. "Gender and gender relations order social life and social institutions in fundamental ways."
3. "Gender relations and constructs of masculinity and femininity are not symmetrical but are based on an organizing principle of men's superiority and social and political–economic dominance over women."
4. "Systems of knowledge reflect men's views of the natural and social world; the production of knowledge is gendered."
5. "Women should be at the center of intellectual inquiry, not peripheral, invisible, or append-ages to men."

Source: Daly and Chesney-Lind (1988: 504). Reprinted with permission of the publisher.

Early feminist critiques of criminology and the criminal justice system

In the 1970s, Dorie Klein (1973) and Carol Smart (1976) examined the ways in which scholars in the early twentieth century described and explained female crime.[12] On the rare occasions when scholars paid attention to female offending, they tended to attribute involvement in crime or delinquency to individual-level biological or psychological factors, rather than to social, political, or economic forces. In the early and middle 1900s, writers who considered female crime typically portrayed female offenders as somehow deviating from the true nature of women. Early explanations for female offending were interwoven with moral judgments about the behaviors of "good" or "normal" women who did not commit crime and "bad" women who did. Crime was viewed as behavior that violated both the law and the "inherent nature of women" (Klein 1973: 4; see also Belknap 2010). The focus of early explanations on individual characteristics diverted attention away from social structural factors, including gender inequality, that might account for female offending.

For over four decades, Meda Chesney-Lind has offered a feminist critique of the criminal justice system (Chesney-Lind and Shelden 2014; Chesney-Lind and Pasko 2013; Stevens, Morash, and Chesney-Lind 2011; Chesney-Lind, Morash, and Stevens 2008; Gavazzi, Yarcheck, and Chesney-Lind 2006; Chesney-Lind 1973, 1977, 1989, 1999).[13] During the 1970s and 1980s, she drew attention to the way the juvenile justice system "sexualized" female offend-ing – especially female involvement in status offenses. As we noted in Chapter 5, females are more likely than males to be arrested for status offenses, such as running away, incorrigibility, and curfew violations, even though males are more likely to report engaging in status offenses (Canter 1982; Teilmann and Landry 1981; Chesney-Lind 1977). Chesney-Lind documents how police and juvenile courts respond more harshly to female status offenses than to more serious offenses committed by females or to status and other delinquent offenses commit-ted by males (MacDonald and Chesney-Lind 2001; Chesney-Lind 1977). She attributes this "double standard of juvenile justice" to threats to parental authority and female chastity posed by female status offenses.

> The juvenile justice system is concerned that girls allowed to run wild might be tempted to experiment sexually and thus endanger their marriageability. The court involves itself in the enforcement of adolescent morality and parental authority through the vehicle of status offenses.
>
> (Chesney-Lind 1977: 122–123)

Chesney-Lind's critique is supported by evidence of juvenile court practices, such as ordering physical examinations of females brought before the court in Hawaii from 1929 to 1955, to determine if the girls were sexually active (Chesney-Lind 1973: 56).

In more recent research, Chesney-Lind and her colleagues (Stevens et al. 2011; Chesney-Lind and Irwin 2008; Irwin and Chesney-Lind 2008) have examined responses to girls' violent behavior. They argue that increases in female arrests for violent offenses such as assault are more a function of changes in policing and school policies than changes in girls' actual behavior (Stevens et al. 2011; Brown, Chesney-Lind, and Stein 2007). Increases in formal policing of girls' behavior in family and school settings have resulted in dramatic increases in the arrest, detention, and incarceration of girls for relatively minor offending behaviors that were previously ignored by the juvenile justice system (Chesney-Lind and Irwin 2008; Chesney-Lind, Morash, and Irwin 2007).

Early feminist critiques of criminology and the criminal justice system also challenged the separate spheres assumptions operating in criminological theory and criminal justice practices. Separate spheres ideology, which emerged during industrialization in the United States in the early 1800s, placed men in the public sphere of paid work, politics, and law, and women in the private sphere, responsible for the household and family life. Laws and legal practices were based on separate spheres ideology. During the 1960s and 1970s, feminists began to challenge the oppression of this ideology for women and the gender-based laws derived from separate spheres ideology (Daly and Chesney-Lind 1988). The goal of reform was equality for females and males, and it found expression primarily in liberal feminism.

Liberal feminism

Liberal feminism is based on ideals of equal opportunity and freedom of choice for females. Advocates of this perspective view gender inequality as rooted in separate spheres ideology and in attitudes favoring traditional male and female roles, reinforced through discrimination against women in the public sphere (e.g., in work, education, and politics) (Simpson 1989). Liberal feminists advocate using laws, such as those prohibiting gender-based discrimination, and the legal system as tools for achieving gender equality.

Within criminology, liberal feminist views were first expressed by Freda Adler (1975) and Rita Simon (1975). Both Adler and Simon moved away from notions of female offending as grounded in biology or psychology and focused instead on social factors. They argued that females' relatively limited involvement in crime was linked to limited opportunities for women in the public sphere. In what has been called the "liberation hypothesis," Adler and Simon argued that the liberation brought about by the women's movement would change gender socialization experiences and opportunities for women, and that both would have an effect on women's involvement in crime.

More specifically, Adler (1975) argued that women were becoming more like men – not only through growing similarity of gender roles and increasing opportunities in the work world, but also in the types of criminal offenses they were committing. Simon's argument was more complex. She linked increases in female offending primarily to their entry into the paid workforce. Women's increased participation in the labor market was accompanied by increased opportunities for participation in crimes linked to work, such as fraud and embezzlement. Unlike Adler, Simon (1975) did not argue that liberation would bring with it increases in violent crimes by women.

Adler and Simon's works are important because they proposed that women's crime was a valid topic of inquiry within criminology, and focused on social factors in explaining women's offending. But empirical evidence has not supported their hypotheses. As we discussed in Chapter 5, the gender gap in crime has not narrowed in the way or to the extent that Adler and Simon predicted.

Radical feminism

Radical feminism developed, in part, in response to criticisms of liberal feminism. Liberal feminists believe that gender equality can be achieved through changes in traditionally gendered socialization experiences and the provision of equal opportunities for women through legal reform, such as laws prohibiting discrimination based on gender. Radical feminists see this approach as inadequate because it ignores the structural roots of gender inequality. They argue that, because of the patriarchal biases of the legal system, it cannot be used as a means of achieving gender equality.

Radical feminists focus on **patriarchy** as the root of women's oppression, and they explore the structurally based imbalance of power between men and women. Patriarchy is "a social structure of men's control over women's labor and sexuality" (Daly and Chesney-Lind 1988: 511). Radical feminists focus on sexual aggression as a mechanism that men use to exert power. Catharine MacKinnon (1991, 1994, 2002, 2007), for example, contends that male dominance is maintained primarily through the control of female sexuality and reproduction, and the threat or use of sexual violence (e.g., rape, pornography, sexual abuse, sexual harassment, and partner battering).

Given their emphasis on the sexual control of women, it is not surprising that radical feminists have focused on females as victims of crime (particularly sexual violence), rather than on females as offenders (Curran and Renzetti 2001). Scholars have also shed light on the ways in which female victimization and female offending are often intertwined (Chesney-Lind and Pasko 2013; Tasca, Zatz, and Rodriguez 2012; Pasko 2008; Makarios 2007; Belknap and Holsinger 2006; Gaarder and Belknap 2002). Chesney-Lind and her colleagues (Chesney-Lind and Shelden 2014; Chesney-Lind and Pasko 2013; Irwin and Chesney-Lind 2008; Brown et al. 2007), for example, argue that in order to understand girls' delinquency, we must first understand girls' everyday lives. Gender socialization experiences, the sexual double standard (which encourages or at least condones male sexual exploration, but prohibits and punishes female sexual behavior), and female victimization in patriarchal society combine to create a reality for girls that is very different from that of boys.

Chesney-Lind's research shows that many girls who are brought into the juvenile justice system have histories of victimization, especially physical and sexual abuse (Chesney-Lind and Shelden 2014; Chesney-Lind and Pasko 2013).

> According to a study of girls in juvenile correctional settings ... a very large proportion
> of these girls ... had experienced physical abuse (61.2%), and nearly half said that they
> had experienced this abuse 11 or more times ... More than half of these girls (54.3%) had
> experienced sexual abuse and for most this was not an isolated incident; a third reported
> that it happened 3 to 10 times and 27.4% reported that it happened 11 times or more.
>
> (Chesney-Lind and Pasko 2013: 27)

More than 80 percent of these girls eventually ran away from home – a coping strategy
that violates the law and results in juvenile justice system contact for many girls who resort
to it. Female runaways are far more likely than male runaways to cite abuse as their reason
for leaving home (Chesney-Lind and Shelden 2014). Once on the street, girls often resort
to "survival" offenses such as theft, shoplifting, and prostitution, which increase the risk of
contact with the juvenile justice system. Thus, the mechanisms that girls often use to escape
victimization are themselves "criminalized" (Chesney-Lind and Pasko 2013; Chesney-Lind
1999). "Case in point: Barbara's victimization and delinquency" offers one girl's story of victimization and offending.

Case in point: Barbara's victimization and delinquency

Regina Arnold describes the relationship between abusive home environments and delinquency
among young black women. Arnold (1994: 174) illustrates this relationship with Barbara's story:

> I was with this foster lady who was very cruel. She was abusive, and I was no more than a maid as
> a child. That was my purpose. She received welfare for foster kids, that was her purpose. I stayed
> there 'til I was thirteen, then ran away. I was tired of the physical abuse. I ran to my mother's. The
> man she lived with sexually abused me, and I ran away again. I was on the street. I got arrested for
> shoplifting. I was picked up for vagrancy when I was almost fifteen. The judge gave my mother
> an option to take me home or he would have no other choice but to send me away. She says,
> "Send her away, I don't want her." So they sent me away. I went to a state home for girls.

Feminist criminologists maintain that, because of the different life experiences of girls and
boys, attempts to explain female delinquency cannot simply begin with traditional theories
developed to explain male delinquency. Daly and Chesney-Lind (1988) call this the "generalizability problem," which concerns the question: can theories of male offending be generalized
and applied to female offending? Because most traditional theories have attempted to explain
only the behavior of males, they have not considered the subordination and victimization of
girls that often contribute to girls' delinquency. Chesney-Lind and Pasko (2013: 32) write:

> Delinquency theory has all but ignored girls and their problems. As a result, few attempts
> have been made to understand the meaning of girls' arrest patterns and the relationship
> between these arrests and the very real problems that these arrests mask.

However, as we noted in Chapter 5, some studies have shown that the processes leading
to delinquency are similar for males and females (e.g., Steffensmeier and Allan 1996; Smith

and Paternoster 1987). These studies, however, should not be used to justify ignoring the unique life experiences of females and males. It would be a mistake to ignore the potential of gender-specific theories to illuminate unique causes of offending for females and males, just as it would be a mistake to assume that traditional theories have nothing of value to say about female offending (Cullen et al. 2014; see also Daigle, Cullen, and Wright 2007).

In addition to considering the generalizability of traditional theories and the link between female victimization and offending, radical feminist criminologists have also examined the patriarchal biases of the criminal justice system. According to radical feminists, the double standards of the criminal justice system signify how it is used for the perpetuation of male power. For example, the harm of crimes against women, such as domestic violence, has often been overlooked or downplayed by a system that devotes itself to fighting other types of crime (MacKinnon 1991, 2007; Daly and Chesney-Lind 1988). In addition, in crimes such as rape, female victims are sometimes treated as though they must prove their innocence by justifying, for example, their attire and sexual histories. Chesney-Lind (Chesney-Lind and Shelden 2014; Chesney-Lind and Pasko 2013; MacDonald and Chesney-Lind 2001; Chesney-Lind 1973, 1977, 1999) has also revealed the paternalistic attitudes of police and juvenile court judges, who typically have been less concerned with girls' serious delinquent offenses than with their sexual behavior (or even the potential for it, suggested by status offenses such as running away or incorrigibility, which indicate that girls are beyond parental control). Girls are also more likely than boys to be institutionalized for status offenses, and studies reveal that girls are some-times further victimized while in custody (Chesney-Lind and Shelden 2014; Chesney-Lind and Pasko 2013).

Summary and conclusions

The study of juvenile delinquency typically begins with the assumption that delinquency is behavior that violates the law, and then attempts to answer the question, "Why do they do it?" In this chapter, we examined approaches that try to answer a different question: how and why do certain behaviors and individuals get labeled "delinquent" or "criminal"? The labeling perspective and critical criminologies both focus on social and societal reactions to delinquency.

The labeling perspective is concerned with the social construction of deviance and maintains that defining what is delinquency and who is delinquent results from dynamic social processes. We described early statements of these processes offered in Tannenbaum's discussion of the dramatization of evil and Lemert's work on primary and secondary deviance. Both argued that, as a result of societal reactions to initial acts of deviance, individuals come to see themselves as "bad" and behave according to that label, enacting a self-fulfilling prophecy in which they become what they are said to be. Becker considered the importance of rule creation and enforcement in this process.

In discussing the labeling perspective, we considered both formal and informal reactions to deviance. Matsueda examined how informal labels by significant others, such as parents, peers, and teachers, are perceived and how they influence subsequent behavior, including delinquency. We explored the consequences of both formal and informal labeling. The labeling perspective contends that societal reactions to deviance have a stigmatizing effect that increases the likelihood of future deviance. In contrast, deterrence theory argues that societal reactions constitute a form of punishment that deters future deviance. Results of research on the effects of formal labels have been mixed, but several studies support the labeling perspective. Research on the effects of informal labels also offers support for the labeling perspective and demonstrates the influence of informal labels on delinquency.

We turned next to critical criminologies, which view capitalism as the root cause of crime and delinquency and the determinant of social responses to offending. Critical perspectives share a focus on power and inequality in understanding crime and crime control, a view that defining crime and delinquency is a political process that reflects conflict and power imbalances, and a view that law and the criminal justice system protect the interests of the powerful or the capitalist system as a whole.

Colvin and Pauly, Hagan and his colleagues, and Greenberg all offer critical approaches to delinquency that are based on the role of capitalism in producing delinquent behavior. Colvin and Pauly, in their integrated structural-Marxist theory, and Hagan and his colleagues, in their power-control theory, share an emphasis on the way in which control and authority in the workplace, as determined by social class, shape parental control of children and socialization processes within the family. Integrated structural-Marxist theory also considers class differences in control structures in schools and peer groups and their contribution to delinquency. Power-control theory considers how the translation of workplace control and authority to family control differs for sons and daughters in patriarchal and egalitarian families, and the ability of these gender differences to explain gender differences in delinquency. Greenberg takes a slightly different approach, explaining delinquent behavior in terms of status problems created for adolescents by the structure of work opportunities under capitalism. These status problems include frustrations associated with school experiences and masculine status anxiety regarding work and traditional male roles, both of which vary by social class.

Finally, we explored the critical understanding of crime and delinquency offered in recent decades by feminist criminologists. Feminist approaches share a view that gender must be at the center of attempts to understand human behavior, including delinquency. Early feminist critiques of criminology and the criminal justice system examined (1) how scholars had explained female crime in terms of individual biological and psychological factors, rather than social, political, or economic forces, and (2) the "sexualization" of female delinquency, particularly status offenses, by the juvenile justice system. We considered liberal and radical feminist approaches and their application to delinquency. These approaches are distinguished primarily by their views of the ability of law and the legal system to promote gender equality and accomplish social change and their emphasis on patriarchy as the root of female oppression.

Critical-thinking questions

1. What ideas do the labeling perspective and critical criminologies have in common that distinguish them from other theories discussed in previous chapters?
2. Explain the distinction between primary and secondary deviance.
3. What do critical criminologists mean when they say that crime and delinquency are grounded in the capitalist economic system?
4. Explain the distinction between liberal and radical feminism.
5. Consider the story of Rocky Sullivan and Jerry Connelly presented at the beginning of this chapter. Given what you have read in this chapter, do you think that the experience of being apprehended, labeled a "delinquent," and formally sanctioned "made a criminal out of Rocky"? Why or why not?

Suggested reading

Braithwaite, John. 1989. *Crime, Shame and Reintegration*. Cambridge University Press.
Chesney-Lind, Meda and Randall G. Shelden. 2014. *Girls, Delinquency, and Juvenile Justice*. 4th edn. Hoboken, NJ: Wiley-Blackwell.
Daly, Kathleen and Meda Chesney-Lind. 1988. "Feminism and Criminology." *Justice Quarterly* 5: 497–538.
Greenberg, David F. 1981. "Delinquency and the Age Structure of Society." Pp. 118–139 in *Crime and Capitalism*, ed. D. F. Greenberg. Palo Alto, CA: Mayfield.
Hagan, John. 1989. *Structural Criminology*. New Brunswick, NJ: Rutgers University Press.
Paternoster, Raymond and Leeann Iovanni. 1989. "The Labeling Perspective and Delinquency: An Elaboration of the Theory and an Assessment of the Evidence." *Justice Quarterly* 6: 359–394.

Useful websites

For further information relevant to this chapter, go to the following websites.

*   Deinstitutionalization of status offenders, Coalition for Juvenile Justice (www.juvjustice.org/juvenile-justice-and-delinquency-prevention-act/deinstitutionalization-status-offenders)
*   Restorative Justice Online (www.restorativejustice.org/)
*   National Public Radio, "This American Life" podcast on restorative justice in a high school setting (www.npr.org/sections/ed/2014/12/17/347383068/an-alternative-to-suspension-and-expulsion-circle-up)

Glossary of key terms

Communitarianism: The societal-level counterpart to interdependency. Shaming is more widespread and effective in communitarian societies than in other societies.

Critical criminologies: Criminologies that explore the structural bases of inequality in society and the way in which inequality and social status influence definitions of crime and criminals and reactions to behaviors.

Deviance amplification: A process whereby societal reactions to initial acts of deviance lead to the development of a deviant identity, which increases the likelihood of subsequent deviance among those who have been labeled "deviant."

Dramatization of evil: A process in which others react to delinquent acts of youth as though these acts and the youth are "evil" and through these reactions create a self-fulfilling prophecy in which the youth become what they are said to be.

Egalitarian families: According to power-control theory, families in which class relations are balanced and husbands and wives are employed in positions of similar authority.

Feminism: Theories about women's oppression and a set of strategies for social change. Feminism places gender at the center of attempts to understand human behavior.

Interdependency: "The extent to which individuals participate in networks wherein they are dependent on others to achieve valued ends and others are dependent on them" (Braithwaite 1989: 98, 100). The concept of interdependency is similar to attachment, commitment, and social bonding in control theory.

Labeling perspective: Focuses on social reactions to delinquency and crime and considers how definitions of what is crime and who is criminal result from dynamic social processes.

Liberal feminism: Maintains that gender equality can be achieved through (1) changes in socialization experiences and gender roles acquired through socialization and (2) the provision of equal opportunities for women through the elimination of discriminatory policies and practices and the development of policies that promote equal rights.

Masculine status anxiety: Anxiety about one's ability to fulfill traditional male roles centered on work and providing for a family, caused by structural economic and political constraints on male status attainment.

Patriarchal families: According to power-control theory, families in which class relations are unbalanced and husbands exercise greater authority in the workplace than do wives.

Patriarchy: A social structure in which men control women's labor and sexuality.

Primary deviance: Initial acts of deviance, many of which go undetected.

Radical feminism: Focuses on patriarchy as the root of women's oppression and explores the structurally based imbalance of power between men and women. Contends that male dominance is maintained, in part, through the control of female sexuality and reproduction.

Reflected appraisals of self: The view of self that one develops by taking the role of others and appraising oneself from the perspective of those others.

Reintegrative shaming: Shaming followed by "efforts to reintegrate the offender back into the community ... through words or gestures of forgiveness or ceremonies to decertify the offender as deviant" (Braithwaite 1989: 100–101).

Secondary deviance: Deviance that occurs in response to problems created by societal reactions to primary deviance.

Stigma: A deeply discrediting attribute or "spoiled identity" that can result from being labeled for prior deviant behavior, such as delinquency, or for personal characteristics that others sometimes perceive as deviant, such as mental illness.

Stigmatization: Disintegrative shaming where no effort is made to reconcile the offender with the community.

Notes

1. Lemert (1972: 15) offers a list of the primary works that defined "labeling theory" in the 1960s.
2. Matsueda's initial analyses included only males from the National Youth Survey sample. With his colleague, Dawn Jeglum Bartusch, Matsueda explored how well his interactionist theory explained female delinquency (Bartusch and Matsueda 1996). They found a similar pattern of results for males and females. Despite this similarity, Bartusch and Matsueda found that their model of informal labeling and reflected appraisals was able to account for a substantial portion of the gender gap in delinquency. See also Ray and Downs (1986), who examine gender differences in the labeling process, and Schur (1983), who explores the process through which women are labeled deviant.
3. See Kaplan and Johnson (1991) for a brief review of research on the effects of formal sanctions on subsequent offending.
4. See also Brezina and Aragones (2004), who argue that positive labeling by others may also promote delinquency under certain conditions by increasing opportunities for offending.
5. Within criminology, several terms have been used to describe the general approach that is an alternative to traditional criminology: *radical, critical, Marxist, socialist, humanist,* and the *new criminology.* Proponents of this new approach eventually settled on the term *critical* because "it was more inclusive of sympathizers and less offensive to critics," and because it was broad enough to include the many approaches represented by the "criminological left" (Barak 1998: 35). Thus, we use the term *critical.* We speak of *critical criminologies,* rather than the singular *criminology,* to indicate that this umbrella term includes a variety of perspectives that share a common core, but are, nonetheless, theoretically distinct.

6. In this use of the term, *ideal* does not mean good or best. Rather, ideal types are descriptive devices for characterizing and categorizing elements of the social world, such as families.
7. Hagan et al. (1987: 793) consider female-headed households to be "a special kind of egalitarian family" because they are characterized by "freedom from male domination" and an absence of power imbalances between parents. This categorization of female-headed households has drawn criticism from scholars who object to the equating of "upper-status" egalitarian families with female-headed households that are often characterized by poverty and economic deprivation (Chesney-Lind and Shelden 2014).
8. See also Hagan, Boehnke, and Merkens (2004), who show that the relationship between structural patriarchy and differences in parental control is mediated by patriarchal gender-role beliefs.
9. For additional revisions and extensions of power-control theory, see Blackwell (2000); McCarthy, Hagan, and Woodward (1999); Grasmick et al. (1996); and Hagan, Gillis, and Simpson (1990).
10. Chesney-Lind and Shelden (2014) argue that the limited definition of patriarchal control found in power-control theory leads Hagan and his colleagues to argue that mothers' work outside the home increases the likelihood of daughters' delinquency because supervision of female children is diminished in egalitarian families. Research, however, does not support the idea that girls' delinquency has increased as women's labor force participation has increased.
11. Copyright © Academy of Criminal Justice Sciences, reprinted by permission of Taylor & Francis Ltd, www.tandfonline.com on behalf of Academy of Criminal Justice Sciences.
12. This section is based on Daly and Chesney-Lind's (1988: 508–510) discussion of early feminist critiques.
13. See Belknap (2004) for a biography of Chesney-Lind and a discussion of her significant influence on the field of criminology.

References

Adams, Mike S. and T. David Evans. 1996. "Teacher Disapproval, Delinquent Peers, and Self-Reported Delinquency: A Longitudinal Test of Labeling Theory." *The Urban Review* 28: 199–211.

Adams, Mike S., James D. Johnson, and T. David Evans. 1998. "Racial Differences in Informal Labeling Effects." *Deviant Behavior: An Interdisciplinary Journal* 19: 157–171.

Adams, Mike S., Craig T. Robertson, Phyllis Gray-Ray, and Melvin C. Ray. 2003. "Labeling and Delinquency." *Adolescence* 38: 171–186.

Adler, Freda. 1975. *Sisters in Crime: The Rise of the New Female Criminal.* New York: McGraw-Hill.

Ahmed, Eliza and John Braithwaite. 2005. "Forgiveness, Shaming, Shame and Bullying." *Australian and New Zealand Journal of Criminology* 38: 298–323.

Arnold, Regina. 1994. "Black Women in Prison: The Price of Resistance." Pp. 171–184 in *Women of Color in U.S. Society*, ed. M. Baca Zinn and B. Thornton Dill. Philadelphia: Temple University Press.

Barak, Gregg. 1998. "Time for an Integrated Critical Criminology." Pp. 34–39 in *Cutting the Edge: Current Perspectives in Radical/Critical Criminology and Criminal Justice*, ed. J. I. Ross. Westport, CT: Praeger.

Bartusch, Dawn R. Jeglum and Ross L. Matsueda. 1996. "Gender, Reflected Appraisals, and Labeling: A Cross-Group Test of an Interactionist Theory of Delinquency." *Social Forces* 75: 145–176.

Becker, Howard S. 1963. *Outsiders: Studies in the Sociology of Deviance.* New York: Free Press.

Beirne, Piers and James W. Messerschmidt. 2011. *Criminology: A Sociological Approach.* 5th edn. New York: Oxford University Press.

Belknap, Joanne. 2004. "Meda Chesney-Lind: The Mother of Feminist Criminology." *Women and Criminal Justice* 15: 1–23.

Belknap, Joanne. 2010. "'Offending Women': A Double Entendre." *Journal of Criminal Law and Criminology* 100: 1061–1098.

Belknap, Joanne and Kristi Holsinger. 2006. "The Gendered Nature of Risk Factors for Delinquency." *Feminist Criminology* 1: 48–71.

Bernburg, Jon Gunnar and Marvin D. Krohn. 2003. "Labeling, Life Chances, and Adult Crime: The Direct and Indirect Effects of Official Intervention in Adolescence on Crime in Early Adulthood." *Criminology* 41: 1287–1317.

Bernburg, Jon Gunnar, Marvin D. Krohn, and Craig J. Rivera. 2006. "Official Labeling, Criminal Embeddedness, and Subsequent Delinquency: A Longitudinal Test of Labeling Theory." *Journal of Research in Crime and Delinquency* 43: 67–88.

Blackwell, Brenda Sims. 2000. "Perceived Sanction Threats, Gender and Crime: A Test and Elaboration of Power-Control Theory." *Criminology* 38: 439–488.

Bonger, Willem. 1969. *Criminality and Economic Conditions*. Abridged edn. Bloomington, IN: Indiana University Press.

Braithwaite, John. 1989. *Crime, Shame and Reintegration*. Cambridge University Press.

Brezina, Timothy and Amie A. Aragones. 2004. "Devils in Disguise: The Contribution of Positive Labeling to 'Sneaky Thrills' Delinquency." *Deviant Behavior* 25: 513–535.

Brown, Lyn Mikel, Meda Chesney-Lind, and Nan Stein. 2007. "Patriarchy Matters." *Violence Against Women* 13: 1249–1273.

Canter, Rachelle J. 1982. "Sex Differences in Self-Reported Delinquency." *Criminology* 20: 373–393.

Chesney-Lind, Meda. 1973. "Judicial Enforcement of the Female Sex Role: The Family Court and the Female Delinquent." *Issues in Criminology* 8: 51–69.

Chesney-Lind, Meda. 1977. "Judicial Paternalism and the Female Status Offender: Training Women to Know Their Place." *Crime and Delinquency* 23: 121–130.

Chesney-Lind, Meda. 1989. "Girls' Crime and Women's Place: Toward a Feminist Model of Female Delinquency." *Crime and Delinquency* 35: 5–29.

Chesney-Lind, Meda. 1999. "Challenging Girls' Invisibility in Juvenile Court." *Annals of the American Academy of Political and Social Science* 564: 185–202.

Chesney-Lind, Meda and Katherine Irwin. 2008. *Beyond Bad Girls: Gender, Violence and Hype*. New York: Routledge.

Chesney-Lind, Meda, Merry Morash, and Katherine Irwin. 2007. "Policing Girlhood? Relational Aggression and Violence Prevention." *Youth Violence and Juvenile Justice* 5: 328–345.

Chesney-Lind, Meda, Merry Morash, and Tia Stevens. 2008. "Girls' Troubles, Girls' Delinquency, and Gender Responsive Programming: A Review." *Australian and New Zealand Journal of Criminology* 41: 162–189.

Chesney-Lind, Meda and Lisa Pasko. 2013. *The Female Offender: Girls, Women, and Crime*. 3rd edn. Thousand Oaks, CA: Sage.

Chesney-Lind, Meda and Randall G. Shelden. 2014. *Girls, Delinquency, and Juvenile Justice*. 4th edn. Hoboken, NJ: Wiley-Blackwell.

Colvin, Mark and John Pauly. 1983. "A Critique of Criminology: Toward an Integrated Structural-Marxist Theory of Delinquency Production." *American Journal of Sociology* 89: 513–551.

Cullen, Francis T., Robert Agnew, and Pamela Wilcox. 2014. *Criminological Theory: Past to Present*. 5th edn. New York: Oxford University Press.

Curran, Daniel J. and Claire M. Renzetti. 2001. *Theories of Crime*. 2nd edn. Boston: Allyn & Bacon.

Daigle, Leah E., Francis T. Cullen, and John Paul Wright. 2007. "Gender Differences in the Predictors of Juvenile Delinquency: Assessing the Generality-Specificity Debate." *Youth Violence and Juvenile Justice* 5: 254–286.

Daly, Kathleen and Meda Chesney-Lind. 1988. "Feminism and Criminology." *Justice Quarterly* 5: 497–538.

De Li, Spencer. 1999. "Legal Sanctions and Youths' Status Achievement: A Longitudinal Study." *Justice Quarterly* 16: 377–401.

DeLisi, Matt, Andy Hochstetler, Gloria Jones-Johnson, Jonathan W. Caudill, and James W. Marquart. 2011. "The Road to Murder: The Enduring Criminogenic Effects of Juvenile Confinement among a Sample of Adult Career Criminals." *Youth Violence and Juvenile Justice* 9: 207–221.

Empey, LaMar T., Mark C. Stafford, and Carter H. Hay. 1999. *American Delinquency: Its Meaning and Construction*. 4th edn. Belmont, CA: Wadsworth.

Erikson, Kai T. 1962. "Notes on the Sociology of Deviance." *Social Problems* 9: 307–314.

Erikson, Kai T. 1966. *Wayward Puritans: A Study in the Sociology of Deviance*. New York: John Wiley.

Farrell, Ronald A. and Victoria Lynn Swigert. 1988. "A Hierarchical Systems Theory of Deviance." Pp. 391–407 in *Social Deviance*. 3rd edn., ed. R. A. Farrell and V. L. Swigert. Belmont, CA: Wadsworth.

Gaarder, Emily and Joanne Belknap. 2002. "Tenuous Borders: Girls Transferred to Adult Court." *Criminology* 40: 481–517.

Gavazzi, Stephen M., Courtney M. Yarcheck, and Meda Chesney-Lind. 2006. "Global Risk Indicators and the Role of Gender in a Juvenile Detention Sample." *Criminal Justice and Behavior* 33: 597–612.

Goffman, Erving. 1961. *Asylums*. New York: Anchor.

Goffman, Erving. 1963. *Stigma: Notes on the Management of Spoiled Identity*. Englewood Cliffs, NJ: Prentice Hall.

Grasmick, Harold G., John Hagan, Brenda Sims Blackwell, and Bruce J. Arneklev. 1996. "Risk Preferences and Patriarchy: Extending Power-Control Theory." *Social Forces* 75: 177–199.

Greenberg, David F. 1981. "Delinquency and the Age Structure of Society." Pp. 118–139 in *Crime and Capitalism*, ed. D. F. Greenberg. Palo Alto, CA: Mayfield Publishing.

Hadjar, Andreas, Dirk Baier, Klaus Boehnke, and John Hagan. 2007. "Juvenile Delinquency and Gender Revisited: The Family and Power-Control Theory Reconceived." *European Journal of Criminology* 4: 33–58.

Hagan, John. 1989. *Structural Criminology*. New Brunswick, NJ: Rutgers University Press.

Hagan, John. 1993. "The Social Embeddedness of Crime and Unemployment." *Criminology* 31: 465–491.

Hagan, John, K. Boehnke, and H. Merkens. 2004. "Gender Differences in Capitalization Processes and the Delinquency of Siblings in Toronto and Berlin." *British Journal of Criminology* 44: 659–676.

Hagan, John, A. R. Gillis, and John Simpson. 1985. "The Class Structure of Gender and Delinquency: Toward a Power-Control Theory of Common Delinquent Behavior." *American Journal of Sociology* 90: 1151–1178.

Hagan, John, A. R. Gillis, and John Simpson. 1990. "Clarifying and Extending Power-Control Theory." *American Journal of Sociology* 95: 1024–1037.

Hagan, John, John Simpson, and A. R. Gillis. 1987. "Class in the Household: A Power-Control Theory of Gender and Delinquency." *American Journal of Sociology* 92: 788–816.

Harris, Anthony R. 1975. "Imprisonment and the Expected Value of Criminal Choice: A Specification and Test of Aspects of the Labeling Perspective." *American Sociological Review* 40: 71–87.

Heimer, Karen and Ross L. Matsueda. 1994. "Role-Taking, Role Commitment, and Delinquency: A Theory of Differential Social Control." *American Sociological Review* 59: 365–390.

Hirschfield, Paul J. 2008. "The Declining Significance of Delinquent Labels in Disadvantaged Urban Communities." *Sociological Forum* 23: 575–601.

Hirschi, Travis. 1969. *Causes of Delinquency*. Berkeley, CA: University of California Press.

Hirschi, Travis and Michael J. Hindelang. 1977. "Intelligence and Delinquency: A Revisionist Review." *American Sociological Review* 42: 571–587.

Hirtenlehner, Helmut, Brenda Sims Blackwell, Heinz Leitgoeb, and Johann Bacher. 2014. "Explaining the Gender Gap in Juvenile Shoplifting: A Power-Control Theoretical Analysis." *Deviant Behavior* 35: 41–65.

Irwin, Katherine and Meda Chesney-Lind. 2008. "Girls' Violence: Beyond Dangerous Masculinity." *Sociology Compass* 2: 837–855.

Jensen, Gary F. and Kevin Thompson. 1990. "What's Class Got to Do with It? A Further Examination of Power-Control Theory." *American Journal of Sociology* 95: 1009–1023.

Johnson, Lee Michael, Ronald L. Simons, and Rand D. Conger. 2004. "Criminal Justice System Involvement and Continuity of Youth Crime: A Longitudinal Analysis." *Youth and Society* 36: 3–29.

Kaplan, Howard B. and Robert J. Johnson. 1991. "Negative Social Sanctions and Juvenile Delinquency: Effects of Labeling in a Model of Deviant Behavior." *Social Science Quarterly* 72: 98–122.

Kim, Hee Joo and Jurg Gerber. 2012. "The Effectiveness of Reintegrative Shaming and Restorative Justice Conferences: Focusing on Juvenile Offenders' Perceptions in Australian Reintegrative Shaming Experiments." *International Journal of Offender Therapy and Comparative Criminology* 56: 1063–1079.

Kirk, David S. and Robert J. Sampson. 2013. "Juvenile Arrest and Collateral Educational Damage in the Transition to Adulthood." *Sociology of Education* 86: 36–62.

Kitsuse, John I. 1962. "Societal Reaction to Deviant Behavior: Problems of Theory and Method." *Social Problems* 9: 247–256.

Klein, Dorie. 1973. "The Etiology of Female Crime: A Review of the Literature." *Issues in Criminology* 8: 3–30.

Kohn, Melvin L. 1977. *Class and Conformity*. University of Chicago Press.

Kurlychek, Megan C., Robert Brame, and Shawn D. Bushway. 2007. "Enduring Risk? Old Criminal Records and Predictions of Future Criminal Involvement." *Crime and Delinquency* 53: 64–83.

Lemert, Edwin M. 1951. *Social Pathology: A Systematic Approach to the Theory of Sociopathic Behavior*. New York: McGraw-Hill.

Lemert, Edwin M. 1972. *Human Deviance, Social Problems, and Social Control*. 2nd edn. Englewood Cliffs, NJ: Prentice Hall.

Liu, Xiaoru. 2000. "The Conditional Effect of Peer Groups on the Relationship Between Parental Labeling and Youth Delinquency." *Sociological Perspectives* 43: 499–514.

Loeber, Rolf and Magda Stouthamer-Loeber. 1986. "Family Factors as Correlates and Predictors of Juvenile Conduct Problems and Delinquency." Pp. 29–149 in *Crime and Justice: An Annual Review of Research*, vol. 7, ed. M. Tonry and N. Morris. University of Chicago Press.

Lopes, Giza, Marvin D. Krohn, Alan J. Lizotte, Nicole M. Schmidt, Bob Edward Vasquez, and Jon Gunnar Bernburg. 2012. "Labeling and Cumulative Disadvantage: The Impact of Formal Police Intervention on Life Chances and Crime During Emerging Adulthood." *Crime and Delinquency* 58: 456–488.

Losoncz, Ibolya and Graham Tyson. 2007. "Parental Shaming and Adolescent Delinquency: A Partial Test of Re-integrative Shaming Theory." *Australian and New Zealand Journal of Criminology* 40: 161–178.

Lynch, Michael J. and Raymond Michalowski. 2006. *Primer in Radical Criminology: Critical Perspectives on Crime, Power and Identity*. 4th edn. Monsey, NY: Criminal Justice Press.

McCarthy, Bill, John Hagan, and Todd S. Woodward. 1999. "In the Company of Women: Structure and Agency in a Revised Power-Control Theory of Gender and Delinquency." *Criminology* 37: 761–788.

McDermott, M. Joan. 2002. "On Moral Enterprises, Pragmatism, and Feminist Criminology." *Crime and Delinquency* 48: 283–299.

MacDonald, John M. and Meda Chesney-Lind. 2001. "Gender Bias and Juvenile Justice Revisited: A Multiyear Analysis." *Crime and Delinquency* 47: 173–195.

MacKinnon, Catharine A. 1991. *Toward a Feminist Theory of the State*. Cambridge, MA: Harvard University Press.

MacKinnon, Catharine A. 1994. *Feminism Unmodified: Discourses on Life and Law*. Cambridge, MA: Harvard University Press.

MacKinnon, Catharine A. 2002. *Only Words*. Cambridge, MA: Harvard University Press.

MacKinnon, Catharine A. 2007. *Women's Lives, Men's Laws*. Cambridge, MA: Belknap Press.

Makarios, Matthew D. 2007. "Race, Abuse, and Female Criminal Violence." *Feminist Criminology* 2: 100–116.

Matsueda, Ross L. 1992. "Reflected Appraisals, Parental Labeling, and Delinquency: Specifying a Symbolic Interactionist Theory." *American Journal of Sociology* 97: 1577–1611.

Matsueda, Ross L. and Karen Heimer. 1997. "A Symbolic Interactionist Theory of Role-Transitions, Role-Commitments, and Delinquency." Pp. 163–213 in *Developmental Theories of Crime and Delinquency*, ed. T. P. Thornberry. New Brunswick, NJ: Transaction.

Moore, Dawn. 2008. "Feminist Criminology: Gain, Loss and Backlash." *Sociology Compass* 2: 48–61.

Morash, Merry and Meda Chesney-Lind. 1991. "A Reformulation and Partial Test of the Power Control Theory of Delinquency." *Justice Quarterly* 8: 347–377.

Morris, Robert G. and Alex R. Piquero. 2013. "For Whom Do Sanctions Deter and Label?" *Justice Quarterly* 30: 837–868.

Murphy, Kristina and Nathan Harris. 2007. "Shaming, Shame and Recidivism: A Test of Reintegrative Shaming Theory in the White-Collar Crime Context." *British Journal of Criminology* 47: 900–917.

Murphy, Kristina and Irene Helmer. 2013. "Testing the Importance of Forgiveness for Reducing Repeat Offending." *Australian and New Zealand Journal of Criminology* 46: 138–156.

Naffine, Ngaire. 1997. *Feminism and Criminology*. Philadelphia: Temple University Press.

Pasko, Lisa. 2008. "The Wayward Girl Revisited: Understanding the Gendered Nature of Juvenile Justice and Delinquency." *Sociology Compass* 2: 821–836.

Paternoster, Raymond and Leeann Iovanni. 1989. "The Labeling Perspective and Delinquency: An Elaboration of the Theory and an Assessment of the Evidence." *Justice Quarterly* 6: 359–394.

President's Commission on Law Enforcement and Administration of Justice. 1967a. *The Challenge of Crime in a Free Society*. Washington, DC: GPO.

President's Commission on Law Enforcement and Administration of Justice. 1967b. *Task Force Report: Corrections*. Washington, DC: GPO.

Ray, Melvin C. and William R. Downs. 1986. "An Empirical Test of Labeling Theory Using Longitudinal Data." *Journal of Research in Crime and Delinquency* 23: 169–194.

Rebellon, Cesar J., Nicole Leeper Piquero, Alex R. Piquero, and Stephen G. Tibbetts. 2010. "Anticipated Shaming and Criminal Offending." *Journal of Criminal Justice* 38: 958–997.

Reid, Sue Titus. 2012. *Crime and Criminology*. 13th edn. New York: Oxford University Press.

Reiman, Jeffery H. and Paul Leighton. 2013. *The Rich Get Richer and the Poor Get Prison: Ideology, Class, and Criminal Justice*. 10th edn. Boston: Pearson.

Sampson, Robert J. and John H. Laub. 1993. *Crime in the Making: Pathways and Turning Points Through Life*. Cambridge, MA: Harvard University Press.

Sampson, Robert J. and John H. Laub. 1997. "A Life-Course Theory of Cumulative Disadvantage and the Stability of Delinquency." Pp. 133–161 in *Developmental Theories of Crime and Delinquency*, ed. T. P. Thornberry. New Brunswick, NJ: Transaction.

Schaefer, Walter E., Carol Olexa, and Kenneth Polk. 1972. "Programmed for Social Class: Tracking in High School." Pp. 33–54 in *Schools and Delinquency*, ed. K. Polk and W. E. Schaefer. Englewood Cliffs, NJ: Prentice Hall.

Schaible, Lonnie M. and Lorine A. Hughes. 2011. "Crime, Shame, Reintegration, and Cross-National Homicide: A Partial Test of Reintegrative Shaming Theory." *Sociological Quarterly* 52: 104–131.

Schur, Edwin M. 1969. "Reactions to Deviance: A Critical Assessment." *American Journal of Sociology* 75: 309–322.

Schur, Edwin M. 1971. *Labeling Deviant Behavior: Its Sociological Implications*. New York: Harper & Row.

Schur, Edwin M. 1983. *Labeling Women Deviant: Gender, Stigma, and Social Control*. Philadelphia: Temple University Press.

Siennick, Sonja E. 2007. "The Timing and Mechanisms of the Offending-Depression Link." *Criminology* 45: 583–615.

Simon, Rita J. 1975. *Women and Crime*. Lanham, MD: Lexington Books.

Simpson, Sally S. 1989. "Feminist Theory, Crime, and Justice." *Criminology* 27: 605–631.

Smart, Carol. 1976. *Women, Crime, and Criminology: A Feminist Critique*. Boston: Routledge & Kegan Paul.

Smith, Douglas A. and Robert Brame. 1994. "On the Initiation and Continuation of Delinquency." *Criminology* 32: 607–629.

Smith, Douglas A. and Patrick R. Gartin. 1989. "Specifying Specific Deterrence: The Influence of Arrest on Future Criminal Activity." *American Sociological Review* 54: 94–105.

Smith, Douglas A. and Raymond Paternoster. 1987. "The Gender Gap in Theories of Deviance: Issues and Evidence." *Journal of Research in Crime and Delinquency* 24: 140–172.

Steffensmeier, Darrell and Emilie Allan. 1996. "Gender and Crime: Toward a Gendered Theory of Female Offending." *Annual Review of Sociology* 22: 459–487.

Stevens, Tia, Merry Morash, and Meda Chesney-Lind. 2011. "Are Girls Getting Tougher on Girls? Probability of Arrest and Juvenile Court Oversight in 1980 and 2000." *Justice Quarterly* 28: 719–744.

Stewart, Eric A., Ronald L. Simons, Rand D. Conger, and Laura V. Scaramella. 2002. "Beyond the Interactional Relationship between Delinquency and Parenting Practices: The Contribution of Legal Sanctions." *Journal of Research in Crime and Delinquency* 39: 36–59.

Sweeten, Gary. 2006. "Who Will Graduate? Disruption of High School Education by Arrest and Court Involvement." *Justice Quarterly* 23: 462–480.

Tannenbaum, Frank. 1938. *Crime and the Community*. New York: Columbia University Press.

Tasca, Melinda, Marjorie S. Zatz, and Nancy Rodriguez. 2012. "Girls' Experiences with Violence: An Analysis of Violence against and by At-Risk Girls." *Violence Against Women* 18: 672–680.

Teilmann, Katherine S. and Pierre H. Landry, Jr. 1981. "Gender Bias in Juvenile Justice." *Journal of Research in Crime and Delinquency* 18: 47–80.

Triplett, Ruth A. and G. Roger Jarjoura. 1994. "Theoretical and Empirical Specification of a Model of Informal Labeling." *Journal of Quantitative Criminology* 10: 241–276.

Uggen, Christopher. 2000. "Class, Gender, and Arrest: An Intergenerational Analysis of Workplace Power and Control." *Criminology* 38: 835–862.

Ward, David A. and Charles R. Tittle. 1993. "Deterrence or Labeling: The Effects of Informal Sanctions." *Deviant Behavior* 14: 43–64.

Ward, Jeffrey T., Marvin D. Krohn, and Chris L. Gibson. 2014. "The Effects of Police Contact on Trajectories of Violence: A Group-Based, Propensity Score Matching Analysis." *Journal of Interpersonal Violence* 29: 440–475.

Wellford, Charles F. and Ruth Triplett. 1993. "The Future of Labeling Theory: Foundations and Promises." Pp. 1–22 in *New Directions in Criminological Theory. Vol. 4: Advances in Criminological Theory*, ed. F. Adler and W. S. Laufer. New Brunswick, NJ: Transaction.

Westermann, Ted D. and James W. Burfeind. 1991. *Crime and Justice in Two Societies: Japan and the United States*. Pacific Grove, CA: Brooks/Cole.

Wiley, Stephanie Ann, Lee Ann Slocum, and Finn-Aage Esbensen. 2013. "The Unintended Consequences of Being Stopped or Arrested: An Exploration of the Labeling Mechanisms through Which Police Contact Leads to Subsequent Delinquency." *Criminology* 51: 927–966.

Zhang, Lening and Sheldon Zhang. 2004. "Reintegrative Shaming and Predatory Delinquency." *Journal of Research in Crime and Delinquency* 41: 433–453.

Part IV

Responding to juvenile delinquency

Chapter 13

Delinquency prevention, assessment, and early intervention

Chapter preview

Topics:

* Responding to delinquency: the role of theory and research
* Delinquency prevention
* Assessment and early intervention

Terms:

* causal analysis
* problem behavior
* risk factors
* static risk factors
* dynamic risk factors
* resiliency
* protective factors
* implementation fidelity
* universal prevention
* selective prevention
* indicated prevention

* evidence-based practice
* meta-analysis
* risk/need assessment
* cost–benefit analysis
* assessment
* early intervention
* internalizing behavior
* externalizing behavior
* oppositional defiant disorder
* attention–deficit/hyperactivity disorder

Chapter learning objectives

After completing this chapter, students should be able to:

* Explain the central role that theory and research play in delinquency prevention and intervention.
* Identify and describe the key concepts and contexts that are predictive of delinquency.
* Describe the key elements of risk-focused delinquency prevention.

- Explain the innovation of evidence-based practice in delinquency prevention and early intervention.
- Offer examples of delinquency prevention programs that have been evaluated as "model programs."
- Describe the use of assessment in early intervention efforts.
- Describe the major service sectors involved in early intervention.

Case in point: breaking the lure of the streets through delinquency prevention

Melissa was a 13 year-old girl who persistently ran away from home. Home was a small rural town in Oregon. Her destination was always the streets of Portland. Melissa's parents had given up hope for a "normal teenage daughter," and their relationship with her was cold and brittle. In fact, they did not always call in a runaway report to the police when she left home. But her probation officer (PO) was determined in her efforts to break Melissa's persistent pattern of running away. In addition to running away, Melissa also displayed an array of other status offenses, including curfew violations, truancy, and underage drinking. Based on this pattern of behavior, the Youth Court adjudicated Melissa a "youth in need of intervention" – the legal declaration of a status offender – and through the informal intervention of the PO, the Youth Court tried to reform her behavior.

On one of Melissa's runs – one that lasted three weeks – a "street crime officer" with the Portland Police Department took her into custody for prostitution. Apparently Melissa had connected with a pimp and he was enjoying a lucrative profit from her trade. Melissa was transported to Juvenile Hall (the city detention center) and her PO was called to transport her back to her home jurisdiction for juvenile court processing. Given Melissa's unstable behavior, the Juvenile Court decided to place her in the protective custody of a short-term, semi-secure proctor home, used in lieu of secure confinement in a detention center (in this small rural town, the local jail). During this time, the PO advocated for Melissa with the Youth Court, seeking to involve the family in an intensive form of family therapy, called Multisystemic Therapy (MST). The PO was able to convince the Juvenile Court to use MST as a pre-petition diversion program: if the family successfully completed the program, the charges would not be petitioned for formal juvenile court processing, thereby providing incentive for program participation.

While the program will be described more fully later in this chapter, MST works with chronic juvenile offenders who have a long history of arrests. Highly trained MST therapists work intensely with delinquent youth and their families – they are on call 24/7. MST therapy seeks to improve parenting skills, especially family management and parent–child interaction, enhance school involvement and performance, and build job skills. The therapist and parents also introduced the youth to pro-social activities as an alternative to antisocial activities.

Over the course of several months of therapy, Melissa's parents made considerable progress in parenting skills, and they reestablished a relationship with their daughter. In so doing, they reclaimed hope for her and they became invested in her. Melissa's behavior stabilized rather quickly in the context of caring and more effective parents, and she began to develop a stronger relationship with them. How might this outcome be different had formal adjudication and commitment to some type of juvenile custodial institution occurred instead of this more preventive intervention?

Melissa's case study begs the questions, *Why? Why was Melissa drawn to the streets? Why did she develop such a persistent pattern of status offending?* The case also demands that something be done to stop Melissa's downward spiral of delinquency – for her own good and the good of the community.

Hopefully, in reading this book you have gained insight into the question of *Why?* That has been our goal throughout this book: to *define, describe,* and *explain* delinquent behavior. The study of delinquency also informs efforts to *respond* to delinquent behavior. The final section of this book describes the strategies, policies, and programs that have been developed to respond to delinquency. This chapter deals with delinquency prevention and early intervention strategies, and Chapter 14 describes contemporary juvenile justice, including juvenile policing, courts, and corrections.

Responding to delinquency: the role of theory and research

To reiterate (because it's important!), delinquency theory and research are useful to the degree that they can help us understand and respond to delinquency. Delinquency theories are central to this task because they highlight a particular set of concepts that are thought to be causally related to delinquency. Delinquency theories also attempt to explain how these concepts are interrelated in causing delinquent behavior. Delinquency research, too, is essential to the task of understanding and responding to delinquency. Research is used to empirically identify the key factors that are associated with delinquent behavior; we can then say that these factors predict delinquency. In addition, delinquency research is used to test theories that have been developed to explain delinquency. In this way, research is used to analyze the causal connections between the concepts specified in theory.

Psychologists Terrie Moffitt and Michael Rutter have argued that while research has documented a wide range of factors that predict delinquent behavior, few studies have used designs that are able to provide causal analysis of the complex processes that lead to delinquency (Moffitt 2005; Rutter 2003; Rutter et al. 2001; see also Farrington and Welsh 2007). As we saw in Chapter 1, **causal analysis** tries to move beyond demonstrating an association between two variables to an analysis of multiple causal variables, their temporal ordering, and possible spurious relationships. As such, causal analysis seeks to provide a thorough understanding of the causal processes that lead to delinquent behavior. An inadequate understanding of causation has significant consequences for delinquency prevention and intervention. For instance, if school experiences have a causal effect on delinquency, then programs designed to improve school experiences should reduce delinquency. However, if the association between school experiences and delinquency is *spurious* (due to a third factor that is related to both, such as attachment to parents) or *reciprocal* (school experiences affect delinquency and delinquency affects school experiences), then such programs will have limited effectiveness (Agnew and Brezina 2015). "Theory into practice: the need for understanding causal processes" provides more examples of the critical need to understand causation so that delinquency prevention and intervention efforts can be effective.

Theory into practice: the need for understanding causal processes

Terrie Moffitt is adamant about the need to move beyond the "risk factor stage," in which factors predictive of delinquent behavior are identified, to an understanding of causal processes. In the passage below, Moffitt (2005: 534 [references omitted]) provides a list of unsuccessful intervention efforts, which failed to adequately understand causation.

> Valuable resources have been wasted because intervention programs have proceeded on the basis of risk factors without sufficient research to understand causal processes. For example, mentoring programs are based on evidence that poor adult–child bonding is a risk factor for antisocial outcomes. Family preservation programs are based on evidence that family dissolution is a risk factor. Peer-group skills programs are based on evidence that peer delinquency is a risk factor. However, mentoring programs and family preservation have not worked, and peer-group programs have been shown to exacerbate adolescent offending. Similarly, Drug Abuse Resistance Education (DARE), gun buybacks, boot camps, outward-bound-type programs, after-school leisure-time programs, youth job programs, and neighborhood watch programs were all originally designed to correct known risk factors for delinquent offending, but formal evaluation has revealed that none of these interventions work to reduce antisocial behavior and some of them have marked iatrogenic [unintended outcomes of an intervention] effects. Simply put, the cost of getting causation wrong is not trivial.

Key theoretical concepts and contexts

Delinquency theory and research are usually embedded in particular contexts that are held to be of special importance. Biosocial criminology, for example, considers *individual traits* and the environmental context in which they are expressed. Theories that emphasize the *situational context* of delinquency focus on the activities, social dynamics, and the immediate setting that surround offending decisions. Social control theories focus on the central importance of *family relations*, and social learning theories give attention to the importance of *peer group influences*. The larger social context of *schools*, *neighborhoods*, and *communities* are the focus for social structure theories of delinquency. When we think about the practical application of delinquency theory and research, it is useful to be mindful of the different contexts that various theories emphasize.

So what does theory and research reveal that might be useful in trying to respond to delinquency? As a first step in answering this question, we offer a brief inventory of the key concepts and contexts of delinquency that have been offered in theory and research, as described in earlier chapters. These key theoretical concepts are italicized.

Individual traits (drawn from Chapter 7)

- **Neurological deficits.** Deficits associated with the prefrontal cortex that reduce *executive functioning* have been studied extensively. Low executive functioning results in poor self-regulation of impulses, emotions, and behaviors. Another neurological deficit is autonomic system underarousal, which has been associated with risk-taking, sensation-seeking, and impulsive actions.
- **Biochemical factors.** Several key neurotransmitters and the hormone testosterone have been associated with antisocial behavior. Neurotransmitters are the chemical compounds

that carry signals between neurons in the intricate communication system of the brain. Their concentration and metabolism play a critical role in how various parts of the brain evoke and regulate behavior, especially as part of the fight-or-flight response. Testosterone levels have been implicated in displays of dominance and control.

- **Behavioral genetics.** The study of behavioral genetics seeks to establish the contributions of heredity and environment to individual traits such *as impulsivity, risk-taking, self-control, aggressiveness*, and *negative emotionality*. These traits, in turn, are associated with delinquent behavior.

- **Personality.** Theory and research have established clearly that antisocial individuals are socially indifferent, self-centered, and hostile (low *agreeableness*) and that they lack self-control (low *conscientiousness*). Thus, delinquent youth tend to be "hostile, self-centered, spiteful, jealous and indifferent to others," and "they tend to lack ambition, motivation and perseverance, have difficulty controlling their impulses and hold nontraditional and unconventional values and beliefs" (Miller and Lynam 2001: 780; see also Caspi et al. 1994).

- **Intelligence and school performance.** IQ scores are most accurately viewed as a measure of *academic preparedness* and *aptitude* rather than of innate intellect. As such, low IQ places youth at risk for poor school performance and frustration, leading indirectly to delinquency. Low IQ also contributes to delinquency by inhibiting the development of self-control and increasing the likelihood of experiencing pressure from deviant peers.

Situational contexts (drawn from Chapter 8)

- **Adversity and strain.** The immediate situation can sometimes motivate and provide opportunity for delinquency by "imposing negative experiences such as frustration, threats, humiliation, and boredom; by offering positive attractions such as money, property, image-building, thrills, and sexual satisfaction; or by providing models to be imitated" (Birkbeck and LaFree 1993: 129–130). Furthermore, experiencing adverse situations, such as homelessness and abuse, and the situational strains of daily adolescent life may provoke delinquent acts.

- **Situational opportunity and reward.** The *routine activities* of adolescents and young adults provide *situational opportunities* for delinquency. Youths' daily lives tend to expose them to situations that provide opportunity and reward for deviance, because their routine activities involve both time with peers (who may increase the situational potential for deviance) and unstructured, unsupervised leisure activities that are beyond the direct control of authority figures.

- **Rational choice.** The element of *rational choice* in delinquent offending involves a range of considerations, including material gain, legal consequences, normative controls associated with relationship ties, moral beliefs, and guilt and shame. Rational choice is not simply a matter of getting caught and punished.

Family relations (drawn from Chapter 9)

- **Informal social controls.** Social control theories emphasize the important role that social relationships play in controlling behavior, especially relationships within the family. Social controls that originate from family relationships are called *informal social controls*. These are characteristics of social relationships that encourage and persuade people to conform, such as parental supervision, emotional attachment, and sensitivity to others' expectations.

- **Social bonds.** Travis Hirschi's social bond theory attempts to explain conformity in terms of four elements of the social bond: *attachment*, *commitment* to conventional lines of action, *involvement* in conventional activities, and *belief* in the moral validity of law. Sampson and Laub's life-course theory examines social bonds over the life course and explores how informal social controls in adulthood involve obligations and restraints that are attached to particular roles, such as marriage and work.
- **Self-control.** Gottfredson and Hirschi's self-control theory focuses on controls within individuals and examines how self-control develops through effective childrearing practices. Individuals with *low self-control* are "impulsive, insensitive, physical (as opposed to mental), risk taking, short-sighted, and nonverbal" (Gottfredson and Hirschi 1990: 90). Low self-control fosters problems in social relations, social activities, and involvement in social institutions, such as family, school, and work.
- **Characteristics of family life.** Characteristics of family life have significant impact on informal social controls. Research documents that the quality of the parent–child relationship, family management techniques (especially monitoring, supervision, and discipline), parental efficacy (involving both support and control), family social class, and parental criminality all influence informal social controls and subsequently delinquent behavior.

Peer group influences (drawn from Chapter 10)

- **Social learning.** Social learning theories point to peer groups as the social context in which delinquent behavior is learned and reinforced. Peer group associations vary in frequency, duration, priority, and intensity, and these four elements influence the learning process. Social learning includes both techniques for committing crime and attitudes and beliefs (*definitions*) that support involvement in crime. Social learning theory also includes the concepts of *differential reinforcement*, which refers to learning processes that involve rewards and punishments, and *imitation*, which involves copying behaviors modeled by others.
- **Peers, drugs, and delinquency.** Youth who use drugs tend to choose friends who also use drugs, and once friendships are established peer group interactions promote attitudes and behaviors that encourage continued drug use. Although drug use and delinquency are associated (the frequency and seriousness of drug use are related to the frequency and seriousness of delinquency), the causal ordering and causal processes are not clearly understood (Elliott, Huizinga, and Ageton 1985).
- **Street gang membership.** Gang members commit more frequent and more serious crime, compared to delinquent youth who are not gang members. Group processes related to group cohesion, status within the group, and the threat of violence are central to understanding how gangs influence the behavior of members. In addition, group characteristics such as gang culture and organizational structure provide the social context for group processes.

School experiences (drawn from Chapters 7, 9, and 11)

- **School performance.** As mentioned earlier, low IQ places youth at risk for poor *school performance* and frustration, leading indirectly to delinquency.

- **Attachment to school.** From a social bond perspective, students who are strongly attached to school – who "feel a part of their school" and care what teachers think of them – are less likely than others to engage in delinquency. Research supports this hypothesis and also finds that the relationship between *attachment to school* and delinquency is reciprocal – attachment influences delinquency and delinquency influences attachment.
- **Commitment to education.** Also from a social bond perspective, weak *commitment to school* is related to school misconduct and various forms of delinquency, including violence. Commitment to education is likely related to academic performance as well. Students who perform well academically are likely to be more committed to education and have higher aspirations and expectations for success than those who perform poorly.
- **Truancy and dropping out of school.** Truancy and dropping out of school are manifestations of weak social bonds to school, especially lack of commitment to academic achievement. Research has shown that truancy is a precursor to more serious delinquency (both violent and non-violent offenses) and is also related to substance abuse and marital and job problems later in life.
- **School characteristics.** A number of school characteristics have been found to be related to high rates of delinquency, including large schools with limited resources, ineffective discipline, low expectations and few opportunities for student achievement, a negative and unpleasant work space, lack of cooperation between the administration and teachers, and low levels of community involvement (Agnew and Brezina 2015).

Neighborhood and community influences (drawn from Chapter 11)

- **Structural characteristics.** Social disorganization theory emphasizes three key structural characteristics – *low economic status*, *ethnic heterogeneity*, and *residential mobility* – as being disruptive of a community's social organization. Urban areas characterized by these structures typically lack effective social control and, as a result, experience high rates of crime and delinquency.
- **Collective efficacy.** The willingness of community residents to be involved with each other and to exercise informal social control – *collective efficacy* – influences the degree to which a disadvantaged environment produces crime and delinquency.
- **Anomie.** *Anomie* is a societal condition in which the goal of economic success is emphasized without a corresponding emphasis on the legitimate means to achieve success. When norms are no longer binding – "anomie" – people are free to pursue economic success by whatever means necessary, including crime.
- **Strain.** According to general strain theory, the strains of adolescent life can lead to delinquency. Three types of *strain* are most common: (1) losing something of value; (2) being treated by others in an aversive or negative manner; and (3) being unable to achieve goals. These strains may increase the likelihood of delinquency because they may breed negative emotions (e.g., anger, frustration, jealousy, depression, and fear); they may produce personality traits such as negative emotionality and low constraint; they may reduce levels of social control; and they may foster the social learning of crime (Agnew 2006).

These key theoretical concepts and contexts that have been substantiated in research *should* form the foundation for delinquency prevention and intervention. Over the last 50 years, this has increasingly been the case. As a result, both our understanding of juvenile delinquency and the effectiveness of our response to it have improved substantially. We now turn to the practical application of theory and research to delinquency prevention and early intervention.

Delinquency prevention

Although juvenile justice systems are the primary mechanism by which communities respond to delinquent acts, delinquency prevention programs represent a proactive approach to juvenile crime, attempting to prevent it before it occurs. In the late 1960s, the President's Commission on Law Enforcement and the Administration of Justice issued a series of important reports. One of them, the *Task Force Report on Juvenile Delinquency and Youth Crime*, concluded:

> In the last analysis, the most promising and so the most important method of dealing with crime is by preventing it – by ameliorating the conditions of life that drive people to commit crime and that undermine the restraining rules and institutions erected by society against antisocial conduct.
>
> (President's Commission 1967: 4)

Similarly, in 1973 the National Advisory Commission on Criminal Justice Standards and Goals recommended that "first priority ... be given to preventing juvenile delinquency, to minimizing the involvement of young offenders in the juvenile and criminal justice system, and to reintegrating delinquent and young offenders into the community" (Howell 1997: 18). Delinquency prevention became a national priority through the Juvenile Justice and Delinquency Prevention (JJDP) Act of 1974. The JJDP Act also created the Office of Juvenile Justice and Delinquency Prevention (OJJDP), whose charge was, and still is, to assist states and local communities in developing policies, practices, and programs directed at delinquency prevention. The resulting prevention perspective stands in sharp contrast to formal processes of juvenile justice.

Risk-focused delinquency prevention

As a developmental stage, adolescence is a period of maturation, change, and unrest. The word *adolescence* is derived from the Latin verb *adolēscere*, meaning "to grow up" or "come to maturity."[1] In her book *Adolescents at Risk*, Joy Dryfoos (1990: 25) offers seven critical tasks of adolescence that are drawn from the psychological literature on adolescent development: (1) the search for self-definition; (2) the search for a personal set of values; (3) the acquisition of competencies necessary for adult roles, such as problem-solving and decision-making; (4) the acquisition of skills for social interaction with parents, peers, and others; (5) the achievement of emotional independence from parents; (6) the ability to negotiate between the pressure to achieve and the acceptance of peers; and (7) experimentation with a wide variety of behaviors, attitudes, and activities.

The developmental tasks of adolescence take place during a time in life that is often characterized by "storm and stress" (Hall 1904). According to G. Stanley Hall, an early psychologist, the turmoil of adolescence is caused by hormonal changes and the accompanying growth spurts and mood swings. These changes, he said, are at the root of adolescent misbehavior, including delinquency. Contemporary research, however, indicates that the majority of teenagers weather the challenges of the adolescent years without developing significant social, emotional, or behavioral difficulties (Steinberg and Morris 2001; Lerner and Galambos 1998).

Nonetheless, adolescence is inherently a period of *dependency* and *risk* because of the pivotal importance of adolescent development and the tremendous influence that the social environment has on such development. Psychologist Richard Jessor (1992: 22) describes successful adolescent development as:

> the accomplishment of normal developmental tasks, the fulfillment of expected social roles, the acquisition of essential skills, the achievement of a sense of adequacy and competence, and the appropriate preparation for transition to the next stage in the life trajectory – young adulthood.

Problem behaviors

During the adolescent years, involvement in **problem behaviors** compromises successful development (Steinberg and Morris 2001; Lerner and Galambos 1998; Jessor 1992). As described in Chapter 6, research suggests that juvenile delinquency is a component of a larger group of problem behaviors that tend to occur together – behaviors such as drug and alcohol use, mental health problems, behavior problems and underachievement in school, and precocious sexual activity. Although many delinquent youth are "multiple problem youth," the origins and development of these problems are distinct (Thornberry, Huizinga, and Loeber 2004; Huizinga et al. 2000; White 1992; Elliott, Huizinga, and Menard 1989). Youth who display problem behaviors early in life are more likely to develop persistent and serious patterns of problem behaviors (Broidy et al. 2003; Loeber, Farrington, and Petechuk 2003a). Therefore, delinquency prevention programs seek to reduce the occurrence of problem behaviors because problem behaviors compromise successful adolescent development.

Risk factors

Research has consistently identified a number of risk factors that increase the likelihood of problem behaviors and, ultimately, negative developmental outcomes. A **risk factor** is any individual trait, social influence, or environmental condition that leads to greater likelihood of problem behaviors and ultimately negative developmental outcomes during the adolescent years (Hoge, Vincent, and Guy 2013). Exposure to multiple risk factors significantly increases the risk of future problem behaviors (Green et al. 2008). The OJJDP Study Group on Serious and Violent Juvenile Offenders and the Study Group on Very Young Offenders reviewed this literature and concluded that a limited number of risk factors are commonly identified through research (Loeber et al. 2003a; Wasserman et al. 2003; Hawkins et al. 2000; see also Tanner-Smith, Wilson, and Lipsey 2013; Hawkins et al. 2009; Green et al. 2008). These risk factors are listed in "Research in action: risk factors predictive of juvenile delinquency." These risk factors are grouped into five categories: individual, family, peer group, school, and neighborhood and community factors. Contemporary approaches to delinquency prevention argue that these risk factors must be first identified through research and then addressed through evidence-based practice (Welsh et al. 2013; Farrington and Welsh 2007; Wasserman et al. 2003).

Two types of risk factors can be distinguished: static and dynamic (Hoge et al. 2013; Vincent, Guy, and Grisso 2012; Andrews and Bonta 2010). **Static risk factors** are background characteristics of the youth that cannot be changed through prevention programs, including the early age of onset of problem behaviors, history of aggressive behavior and violence, and parental criminality. **Dynamic risk factors** are characteristics of the youth and his/her environment that can be changed through intervention, such as antisocial attitudes and values, association with delinquent peers, dysfunctional family relationships, and antisocial personality traits (impulsiveness, risk-taking, and low self-control). Delinquency prevention programs naturally focus on the latter because of their potential for change.

Research in action: risk factors predictive of juvenile delinquency

Individual factors

- verbal deficits (affecting listening, reading, problem-solving, speech, writing, and memory)
- impulsiveness, inattentiveness, and hyperactivity
- difficult temperament/limited agreeableness (disagreeable, oppositional, defiant, rebellious)
- limited conscientiousness
- low intelligence and academic failure
- limited behavioral inhibition (self-control)
- risk-taking/sensation seeking
- early onset of problem behaviors
- aggression
- social withdrawal
- attitudes favorable to problem behaviors

Family factors

- poor family management and direct controls (monitoring and supervision, standards for behavior, recognizing and responding to problem behaviors)
- lax, harsh, and inconsistent discipline
- child maltreatment (especially neglect)
- low levels of parental involvement
- weak family attachment and indirect controls
- parental attitude favorable to deviance
- parental criminality, substance abuse, psychopathology
- family and marital conflict
- family disruption, including divorce and separation
- residential mobility

School and academic factors

- early and persistent classroom disruption and antisocial behaviors
- poor academic performance
- weak social bonds to school
- limited academic aspirations

- truancy and dropping out
- frequent school transition
- school with high rate of delinquency
- low academic quality of school
- low parent and community involvement in school

Peer-related factors

- association with delinquent peers
- peer rejection
- delinquent attitudes and behaviors are modeled, imitated, and reinforced in a delinquent peer group
- delinquent values and attitudes
- learned techniques for committing crimes
- gang membership

Neighborhood and community factors

- concentrated disadvantage (concentrated poverty, social isolation, joblessness)
- social disorganization (poverty, cultural heterogeneity, and residential mobility)
- ineffective social control (collective efficacy)
- delinquent and criminal subculture (tradition of crime, socialization, availability of drugs and access to weapons)

> *Sources*: Drawn primarily from Hawkins et al. (2000). See also Tanner-Smith et al. (2013); Hawkins et al. (2009); Green et al. (2008); Farrington and Welsh (2007); Loeber et al. (2003a); Wasserman et al. (2003).

Protective factors and resiliency

Not all youth exposed to risk factors become delinquent. In fact, some flourish despite these detriments and adversities (Bartol and Bartol 2009; Hawkins et al. 2009; Werner 2005). Understanding such **resiliency** provides a unique angle from which to approach delinquency prevention and intervention: to build strengths and skills that allow youth to resist the pressures and temptations for delinquency. *Strength-based* approaches to prevention and intervention seek to promote protective factors that have been found in research to prevent involvement in delinquency. **Protective factors** are those individual traits and social circumstances that allow youth to adapt positively to adverse environments. After reviewing the research literature on resiliency, Curt Bartol and Anne Bartol (2009: 97) identify nine key competencies that are strongly substantiated as protective factors (see also Vincent et al. 2012; Hawkins et al. 2009; Farrington and Welsh 2007).

1. Connections to competent, emotionally warm, caring adults
2. Social experiences with supportive, prosocial peers
3. Language skills and cognitive ability

4. Self-regulation skills
5. Interpersonal skills
6. Attention and focus skills
7. Positive attitude and emotions
8. Positive views of self and abilities
9. Intrinsic motivation to be effective

"Risk-focused prevention is based upon the simple premise that to prevent a problem [behavior] from occurring, we need to identify the factors that increase the risk of that problem developing and then find ways to reduce the risk" (Lehman, Hawkins, and Catalano 1994: 94; see also Welsh et al. 2013; Farrington and Welsh 2007). Nonetheless, the task of identifying and reducing risk factors is not simple or easy. Only in the last 20 years have researchers been able to clearly identify "both the risk factors that produce delinquency and the interventions that consistently reduce the likelihood that it will occur" (Greenwood 2008: 186; see also Welsh et al. 2013; Howell 2009; Greenwood 2006, 2008; Farrington and Welsh 2007; Thornberry et al. 2004; Burns et al. 2003).

Evidence-based practice in delinquency prevention

Contemporary delinquency prevention and intervention efforts are increasingly driven by evaluation research that tries to establish whether particular strategies, methods, and programs effectively reduce the likelihood of delinquent offending. Greenwood and Welsh (2012: 495) summarize this approach: "**Evidence-based practice** involves the use of scientific principles to assess the available evidence on program effectiveness and to develop principles for best practice in any particular field." As discussed in Chapter 2, evidence-based practice is one of the most significant movements in contemporary juvenile justice reform (McKee and Rapp 2014; Greenwood and Welsh 2012; Lipsey and Howell 2012).

While the rigor of evaluation research standards varies, five standards are key (Mihalic and Elliott 2015: 127–128; see also Blueprints 2015; Dodge and Mandel 2012; Greenwood and Welsh 2012; Byrne and Lurigio 2009; Greenwood 2006, 2008; Welsh and Farrington 2007):

1. **Intervention specificity:** The program clearly identifies a specific behavioral outcome that is sought, the mechanisms by which the outcome is achieved, and the target population for the intervention.
2. **Evaluation quality:** The effectiveness of the program must be established using a strong research design, including random assignment of subjects and experimental or quasi-experimental design.
3. **Intervention impact:** Evidence from scientifically sound evaluation research shows "significant positive change in intended outcomes that can be attributed to the program" (Mihalic and Elliott 2015: 128).
4. **Dissemination readiness:** "The program is available for dissemination and has the necessary organizational capability, manuals, training, technical assistance and other support required for implementation with fidelity in communities and public service systems" (Mihalic and Elliott 2015: 128). Cost–benefit analysis is also available
5. **Sustained outcomes:** The intervention program has lasting positive effects for a minimum of 12 months post-intervention.

Using these standards, the Center for the Study and Prevention of Violence at the University of Colorado has developed a guide to delinquency intervention programs that have demonstrated effectiveness through evaluation research (Mihalic and Elliott 2015). The program guide is called "Blueprints for Healthy Youth Development." Blueprints currently identifies eight "Model Programs" and nine "Promising Programs" in terms of effective "program outcomes" for "delinquency and criminal behavior" (Blueprints 2015). The number of Model and Promising Programs changes as new programs are added after review. Several of the Model Programs will be described more fully in the following section on delinquency prevention. Two other model program guides to evidence-based practice have been developed and are widely accepted in the field of juvenile justice: OJJDP's *Model Program Guide*, created by the Office of Justice programs, and the *National Registry of Evidence-Based Programs and Practices*, sponsored by the Substance Abuse and Mental Health Services Administration (SAMHSA). "Research in action: model program guides" provides the links to websites of these program guides. A perusal of these sites provides insight into the model program approach to evidence-based practice in delinquency prevention and intervention – take a look!

Research in action: model program guides

Here are links to three of the most widely-accepted guides to model programs. These links identify and describe model programs that have been found through evidence-based research to be effective. Sometimes these program guides are referred to as "registries for evidence-based programs" (Mihalic and Elliott 2015). As a word of caution: these model program guides use different criteria for assessing program effectiveness and different terminology to classify the degree of effectiveness (Mihalic and Elliott 2015: 126).

- **Blueprints for Healthy Youth Development**, Center for the Study and Prevention of Violence at the University of Colorado Boulder (www.blueprintsprograms.com/)
- **Model Programs Guide**, Office of Juvenile Justice and Delinquency Prevention (www.ojjdp.gov/mpg/). The Model Program Guide is integrated with **CrimeSolutions.gov** (www.crimesolutions.gov/) (under "Topic" use "Juveniles" and then "Delinquency Prevention").
- **National Registry of Evidence-Based Programs and Practices**, Substance Abuse and Mental Health Services Administration (www.samhsa.gov/nrepp)

The model program approach to evidence-based practice seeks to identify particular programs of proven effectiveness, and then guide implementation for successful results. The model programs that have been identified are sometimes referred to as "brand name" programs because they are often "developed by a single investigator or team over a number of years and proven through careful replications, supported by millions of dollars in federal grants" (Greenwood 2008: 192). Well-known evidence-based programs include Functional Family Therapy, Multisystemic Therapy, Multidimensional Treatment Foster Care, and Nurse–Family Partnership (Greenwood and Welsh 2012).

In contrast to this model program approach, evidence-based practice can also be "generic" when research is used to uncover strategies and methods, rather than particular programs, which are effective at reducing future offending (Greenwood and Welsh 2012; Lipsey and Howell 2012; Lipsey et al. 2010). This approach to evidence-based practice is usually accomplished through a statistical technique called **meta-analysis**, which estimates the effects found across evaluation studies of the intervention methods and strategies. The most prominent criminologist in this effort is Mark Lipsey who, in 1992, conducted the first meta-analysis focusing on juvenile justice. Lipsey found that effective strategies shared a number of common features, including targeting high-risk offenders who, even though they have high re-offense rates, have the most room for improvement (Lipsey et al. 2010: 23). Effective intervention methods are therapeutic, rather than controlling, and they are based on a number of key features:

- **Skill building:** cognitive-behavioral techniques, social skills, academic and vocational skills;
- **Counseling:** individual, group, and family counseling, mentoring;
- **Multiple coordinated services:** case management and service referrals;
- **Restorative justice:** restitution, victim–offender mediation;
- **Behavioral monitoring:** observation to detect bad behavior, intensive probation or parole supervision (Lipsey et al. 2010: 23–25; Lipsey 2006, 2009; Lipsey and Cullen 2007).

Lipsey and his colleagues (2010) have also offered a practical guide for local communities to progressively evaluate and refine prevention programs according to the methods that have been found to be effective in meta-analysis research. The Standardized Program Evaluation Protocol (SPEP) is an evaluation tool that assigns points (maximum overall score is 100 points) to delinquency prevention and intervention programs according to how closely their characteristics match those associated with programs found to be effective in meta-analysis (Lipsey et al. 2010: 29). Higher scores indicate greater correspondence, and each of the characteristics used in the tool can be assessed in order to refine the program for greater effectiveness, based on what has been shown to work in similar programs.

Evidence-based practice has increasingly embraced two additional dimensions of effectiveness: risk/need assessment and cost–benefit analysis. **Risk/need assessment** involves the use of standardized assessment instruments to identify the likelihood or "risk" of future offending or reoffending, and the "criminogenic needs" of the youth – those factors that lead to delinquency and can be changed through intervention.

Risk/need assessment is often viewed as the foundation to evidence-based practice because the effectiveness of an intervention approach depends on its appropriateness to the criminogenic needs of the youth and to the likelihood of reoffending. In this way, risk/need assessments can be used to guide intervention planning – to get the delinquent youth involved in the "right" program – one that can address the needs of the youth and the risk for reoffending (Hoge et al. 2013; Greenwood and Welsh 2012; Vincent et al. 2012; Lipsey et al. 2010; Schwalbe 2008). We will consider the contemporary use of risk/need assessments later in this chapter when we discuss early intervention.

Cost–benefit analysis of delinquency intervention programs seeks to "comprehensively identify and measure the benefits and costs of a program," including those that occur during and after participation in the program (National Research Council 2013: 167; see also

Dodge and Mandel 2012). Cost–benefit analysis "may be viewed as a way to calculate society's return from investing in an intervention"[2] (National Research Council 2013: 167; see also Rocque et al. 2014; Dodge and Mandel 2012; Cohen and Piquero 2009; Farrington and Welsh 2007). The Washington State Institute for Public Policy is unquestionably the pace-setter in cost–benefit analysis, conducting evaluation research of programs in order to inform funding decisions by the Washington state legislature.

Whether one chooses to intervene with juvenile offenders when they are institutionalized, in group or foster homes, or on probation, states and localities can adopt programs that produce remarkably large economic returns. The same is true for programs that seek to divert juveniles before they are convicted of further crimes. Indeed, some programs deliver $10 or more of benefits for each $1 of cost (National Research Council 2013: 168; based on Washington State Institute for Public Policy 2011 and Drake, Aos, and Miller 2009).

As the effectiveness of delinquency prevention programs receives increasing attention, so, too, does the drive to implement model programs in the most effective manner. As a result, identifying and implementing evidence-based practices has become a priority for both governmental and private agencies (Rocque et al. 2014; Dodge and Mandel 2012; Greenwood and Welsh 2012; Lipsey and Howell 2012; Lipsey et al. 2010; Greenwood 2006, 2008; Mihalic et al. 2004a).

Although some scholars have offered a list of the common features shared by effective programs, such generalizations fail to appreciate what makes different prevention programs effective (Lerner and Galambos 1998; Dryfoos 1990). The wide array of risk and protective factors makes it almost impossible to address them all, and different programs target different problem behaviors and contexts (Mihalic and Elliott 2015). For example, some prevention programs that focus on bullying in schools have been found to be effective because they target a particular risk factor – early aggressiveness – which predicts later violence. The effectiveness of bullying prevention is likely to be determined by program characteristics that are quite different from other forms of delinquency prevention, even those that are applied in school contexts.

Beyond program features, effective delinquency prevention depends on **implementation fidelity** – "the degree to which a program's core services, components, and procedures are implemented as originally designed" (CrimeSolutions.gov 2015). Even programs that have been evaluated as effective through research must be implemented fully to produce the desired effects. The Blueprints project conducted an evaluation of implementation quality, looking at aspects of program implementation rather than program features (Mihalic et al. 2004b). Nine model programs at 147 sites were part of the study. Questionnaires were administered at each site every four months, over a two-year period. The study revealed six key elements of program implementation (Mihalic et al. 2004b: 3–9):

1. **Effective organization.** Successful programs depend on strong administrative support for the implementing staff; agency stability; a shared vision of program goals; and inter-agency links, especially with other programs involved in clients' treatment plans.
2. **Qualified staff.** Program success is fostered by staff who support the program and who are motivated to implement the program day in and day out. Program staff must also be skilled, experienced, and have the necessary credentials to carry out the program. They must also be given the time necessary to implement the program, especially a new program. Paid staff has been found to be more effective than volunteers.

3. **Program champion(s).** Every successful program needs a person who champions the program – who motivates, innovates, guides, and fosters program delivery.
4. **Program integration.** Success is most likely when a program is integrated into a larger organizational structure, in which the prevention program supports and augments the host agency's goals and objectives. Bullying prevention, for example, is most effectively implemented within a school context in which student safety and security are taught as part of the academic curriculum.
5. **Training and technical assistance.** A strong training program followed with technical assistance cultivates employee confidence and ability and allows for more effective program implementation.
6. **Implementation fidelity.** Sometimes referred to as *integrity*, fidelity has to do with the degree to which the program is actually delivered as it was designed. Successful programs tend to be those that closely follow the goals and methods of the program's design.

Delinquency prevention programs

Delinquency prevention programs can be classified into three main approaches: (1) universal prevention; (2) selective prevention; and (3) indicated prevention (Farrington and Welsh 2007). **Universal prevention** programs (or primary prevention) target the general population of youth and include campaigns to prevent smoking and drug use, to promote problem-solving and dispute resolution skills through classroom education, and to provide classes on parenting skills to all parents.[3] **Selective prevention** programs (or secondary prevention) target youth or groups of youth who are "at risk" due to multiple risk factors in their lives. **Indicated prevention** programs (or tertiary prevention) target identified juvenile offenders in order to prevent or eliminate a serious pattern of delinquent offending. As mentioned earlier in this chapter, one of the fundamental principles of evidence-based practice is that intervention is more effective with high-risk offenders who, even though they have high re-offense rates, have the most room for improvement (Lipsey et al. 2010: 23). As a result, indicated prevention programs have received greater public policy attention in recent years than in the past (Dodge and Mandel 2012; Greenwood and Welsh 2012; Lipsey and Howell 2012).

The best way to gain insight into delinquency prevention programs is through case examples. Here we offer several descriptions of prevention programs that have been evaluated as "Model Programs" through Blueprints for Healthy Youth Development. "Research in action: learn more about the Blueprints' Model Programs for prevention and intervention of 'delinquency and criminal behavior'" provides brief program descriptions of the eight Model Programs directed at prevention and intervention of "Delinquency and Criminal Behavior." Also provided are links to the webpages of each of these Model Programs. You may also wish to explore other prevention programs that have been evaluated as effective by the other two program guides identified in "Research in action: model program guides."

Research in action: learn more about the Blueprints' Model Programs for prevention and intervention of "delinquency and criminal behavior"

Program	Impact	Summary
Functional Family Therapy (FFT) (www.fftinc.com)	Delinquency and Criminal Behavior, Illicit Drug Use	A short-term family therapy intervention and juvenile diversion program helping at-risk children and delinquent youth to overcome adolescent behavior problems, conduct disorder, substance abuse, and delinquency. Therapists work with families to assess family behaviors that maintain delinquent behavior, modify dysfunctional family communication, train family members to negotiate effectively, set clear rules about privileges and responsibilities, and generalize changes to community contexts and relationships.
Life Skills Training (LST) (www.lifeskillstraining. com)	Alcohol, Delinquency and Criminal Behavior, Illicit Drug Use, Sexual Risk Behaviors, STIs, Tobacco, Violence	A classroom-based, three-year, middle school substance abuse prevention program to prevent teenage drug and alcohol abuse, adolescent tobacco use, violence and other risk behaviors. The life skills curriculum teaches students self-management skills, social skills, and drug awareness and resistance skills.
Multidimensional Treatment Foster Care (MTFC) (www.mtfc.com)	Delinquency and Criminal Behavior, Illicit Drug Use, Teen Pregnancy, Tobacco, Violence	A therapeutic foster care program that serves as an alternative to residential treatment by placing chronic delinquents in foster homes in the community with the goals of reuniting the families, reducing delinquency and teen violence, and increasing prosocial behavior and participation in prosocial activities. The program includes behavioral parent training and support for foster parents, family therapy for biological parents, skills training and supportive therapy for youth, and school-based behavioral interventions and academic support.
Multisystemic Therapy – Problem Sexual Behavior (MST-PSB) (www.mstpsb.com)	Academic Performance, Adult Crime, Delinquency and Criminal Behavior, Illicit Drug Use, Mental Health – Other, Prosocial with Peers, Sexual Risk Behaviors, Sexual Violence	A juvenile sex offender treatment program to reduce criminal and antisocial behavior, especially problem sexual behavior, by providing intensive family therapy services in the youth's natural environment over a 5–7 month period.

Multisystemic Therapy (MST) (http://mstservices.com/)	Close Relationships with Parents, Delinquency and Criminal Behavior, Illicit Drug Use, Internalizing, Mental Health – Other, Positive Social/Prosocial Behavior, Violence	A juvenile crime prevention program to enhance parenting skills and provide intensive family therapy to troubled teens and delinquent teens that empower youth to cope with the family, peer, school, and neighborhood problems they encounter – in ways that promote prosocial behavior while decreasing youth violence and other antisocial behaviors.
Nurse–Family Partnership (www.nursefamilypartnership.org/)	Child Maltreatment, Delinquency and Criminal Behavior, Early Cognitive Development, Internalizing, Mental Health – Other, Physical Health and Well-Being, Preschool Communication/ Language Development, Reciprocal Parent–Child Warmth	A nurse home visiting program for first-time pregnant mothers that sends nurses to work one-on-one with the pregnant women to improve prenatal and child rearing practices through the child's second birthday.
Parent Management Training (Oregon Model) (www.isii.net)	Antisocial-aggressive Behavior, Conduct Problems, Delinquency and Criminal Behavior, Externalizing, Internalizing	A group- or individual-based parent training program that teaches effective family management strategies and parenting skills, including skill encouragement, setting limits/positive discipline, monitoring, problem-solving, and positive involvement, in order to reduce antisocial and behavior problems in children.
Positive Action (www.positiveaction.net)	Academic Performance, Alcohol, Anxiety, Bullying, Delinquency and Criminal Behavior, Depression, Emotional Regulation, Illicit Drug Use, Positive Social/ Prosocial Behavior, Sexual Risk Behaviors, Tobacco, Truancy – School Attendance, Violence	A school-based social emotional learning program for students in elementary and middle schools to increase positive behavior, reduce negative behavior, and improve social and emotional learning and school climate. The classroom-based curriculum teaches understanding and management of self and how to interact with others through positive behavior, with school climate programs used to reinforce the classroom concepts school-wide.

Source: Blueprints for Healthy Youth Development (2015). Program search using "Delinquency and Criminal Behavior" filter. Retrieved February 5, 2015 (www.blueprintsprograms.com/allPrograms.php). "Impact" and "Summary" descriptions are derived from this source.

Life Skills Training: drug use prevention curriculum

Life Skills Training (LST) is a universal prevention program that provides a three-year drug use prevention curriculum to sixth or seventh graders, with booster sessions during the following two years. The curriculum is "designed to prevent or reduce gateway drug use (tobacco, alcohol, and marijuana) by providing social resistance skills training to help students identify pressures to use drugs and resist drug offers" (Mihalic et al. 2004a: 47). LST is implemented primarily in school classrooms by teachers using direct instruction, discussion, and positive reinforcement. The first year involves 15 lessons, and the booster sessions include ten lessons in year two and five lessons in year three. Lessons have three basic skill-training components: (1) Personal Self-Management Skills teaches students to examine self-image and how it influences behavior, and to develop skills in goal-setting, problem-solving, decision-making, and stress management; (2) Social Skills teaches students communication skills, including assertiveness and making and refusing requests; and (3) Resistance Skills teaches students to recognize common misconceptions about drugs and violence, and through coaching and practice, students learn resistance and refusal skills in dealing with peers and media pressure to use drugs (Blueprints 2015).

In numerous evaluations, LST has been found to reduce alcohol, tobacco, and marijuana use by 50–75 percent for students completing the curriculum, compared to control group students. Reductions in smoking and the use of inhalants, narcotics, and hallucinogens were demonstrated through the 12th grade. The effectiveness of LST on violence and delinquency has also been established. "Studies testing LST have not only demonstrated short-term effects, but also provide evidence of its long-term effectiveness, with several studies providing 5–6 year follow-up data, and one study providing 10-year follow-up data" (Blueprints 2015; see also Mihalic et al. 2004a).

Nurse–Family Partnership: prenatal and infancy home visits by nurses

Nurse–Family Partnership is a selective prevention program designed for low-income, first-time single mothers. The nurse visitation program targets three risk factors associated with the development of early antisocial behavior in children: adverse maternal health-related behaviors during pregnancy, child abuse and neglect, and troubled maternal life course. Nurse visitation programs are selective prevention programs because they target a particular at-risk group.

Public health nurses with small caseloads make prenatal and infancy home visits every one to two weeks and continue home visitation until the child is 2 years old. Nurses provide support and instruction on prenatal health, infancy caregiving, personal health, child development, parenting, pursuing education, and career development. Extensive evaluation shows that the program reduced rates of child abuse and neglect by helping mothers learn effective parenting skills and personal controls. Mothers receiving nurse home visits had fewer months on welfare, fewer behavioral problems, and lower arrest and conviction rates than mothers who did not participate in the program. Adolescents whose mothers participated in the nurse visitation program were less likely to run away, be arrested, or be convicted of a crime. Compared to the children of non-participants, these adolescents smoked fewer cigarettes, consumed less alcohol, and had fewer behavioral problems related to alcohol and drug use. By the time a child reached age 15, cost savings were estimated at four times the original investment, as a result of reductions in crime, welfare and health care costs, and taxes paid by working parents (Blueprints 2015; Mihalic et al. 2004a; Olds, Hill, and Rumsey 1998).

Multisystemic Therapy: intensive treatment for chronic juvenile offenders

Multisystemic Therapy (MST) is an indicated prevention program that targets chronic juvenile offenders, providing intensive family- and community-based treatment. Highly trained therapists with small caseloads and 24/7 availability provide direct therapeutic services to youth and their families, addressing "the known causes of delinquency on an individualized, yet comprehensive basis." MST seeks to generate positive change in the youth's "natural settings – home, school, and neighborhood – in ways that promote prosocial behavior while decreasing antisocial behavior." Within the youth's natural setting, MST seeks to "empower parents with the skills and resources needed to independently address the inevitable difficulties that arise in raising teenagers, and to empower youth to cope with the family, peer, school, and neighborhood problems they encounter" (Blueprints 2015).

> Several types of interventions are typically identified for serious juvenile offenders and their families. At the family level, MST interventions aim to remove barriers to effective parenting (e.g., parental substance abuse, parental psychopathology, low social support, high stress, and marital conflict), to enhance parenting competencies, and to promote affection and communication among family members. Interventions might include introducing systematic monitoring, reward, and discipline systems; prompting parents to communicate effectively with each other about adolescent problems; problem solving day-to-day conflicts; and developing social support networks. At the peer level, interventions frequently are designed to decrease affiliation with delinquent and drug-using peers and to increase affiliation with prosocial peers. Interventions in the school domain may focus on establishing positive lines of communication between parents and teachers, parental monitoring of the adolescent's school performance, and restructuring after-school hours to support academic efforts. Individual level interventions generally involve using cognitive behavior therapy to modify the individual's social perspective-taking skills, belief system, or motivational system, and encouraging the adolescent to deal assertively with negative peer pressure.
>
> (Blueprints 2015)

MST is supported by numerous evaluations that consistently demonstrate positive outcomes for serious juvenile offenders, including violent offenders, substance abusing offenders, and juvenile sex offenders. MST has been shown to impact serious delinquency behavior, drug use, arrests, incarceration, family relations, peer relations, and psychiatric problems (Blueprints 2015).

As these delinquency prevention programs illustrate, prevention programs operate at various levels – individual, family, school, and community – and they are based in varying service sectors – mental health, public health, education, child welfare, and juvenile justice. Regardless of where they occur, prevention programs seek to keep youth out of the juvenile justice system and they attempt to integrate youth into the family, school, and community (Farrington and Welsh 2007; Howell 1997).

Assessment and early intervention

Prevention efforts at the individual, school, and community levels are designed to address risk factors so that they do not transform into problem behaviors that compromise adolescent development. However, when antisocial behavior and initial delinquent acts come to the attention of parents, teachers, or the juvenile justice system, they are sometimes addressed through assessment and early intervention, before the juvenile justice system takes formal action. Assessment and early intervention encompass a wide range of methods, some informal, some formal. **Assessment** involves systematic methods of appraisal and evaluation that are used to identify and classify antisocial and disruptive behaviors, and then inform intervention. **Early intervention** consists of individual-level therapies and programs that seek to reduce or eliminate antisocial behavior when it is observed during childhood and early adolescence. Whereas delinquency prevention efforts seek to reduce or eliminate risk factors in the lives of youth, early intervention is directed at changing antisocial and delinquent behavior in its early stages, after it occurs. Even though early intervention may eventually involve various components of the juvenile justice system, a number of other service delivery systems are often utilized first.

Assessing behavioral problems of children and adolescents

Three methods of assessing antisocial and disruptive behaviors of youth have received growing attention in relation to the early onset of delinquency: clinical diagnosis of externalizing disorders, mental health and substance use assessment, and risk/need assessment.

Clinical diagnostic categories of externalizing disorder

Antisocial behavior is often divided into internalizing disorders and externalizing disorders (Bartol and Bartol 2009). "**Internalizing disorders** are characterized by mood problems, such as depression, or by behavior featuring anxiety, social withdrawal, and isolation, hypersensitivity, low self-esteem, and eating disorders" (Bartol and Bartol 2009: 8). **Externalizing disorders** are problematic attitudes and behaviors, including lying, cheating, deceitfulness, stealing, fire-setting, aggressiveness, and physical aggression. Externalizing problem behaviors are usually represented by three diagnostic categories within the *Diagnostic and Statistical Manual of Mental Disorders* (DSM-5) published by the American Psychiatric Association (APA 2013): oppositional defiant disorder (ODD), attention-deficit/hyperactivity disorder (ADHD), and conduct disorder (CD) (Bartol and Bartol 2009: 8; see also Morrison 2014; Schubert and Mulvey 2014; Liu 2004).[4] Mental health professionals use this tool to categorize psychiatric disorders based on identified diagnostic criteria.

Oppositional defiant disorder (ODD) is indicated by an ongoing pattern of behavior that is uncooperative, defiant, disobedient, and hostile, especially toward authority figures such as parents (Bartol and Bartol 2009: 175–176). While most children are oppositional from time to time, ODD involves a persistent pattern of defiance that is significant enough to interfere with the child's ability to function at home, in school, and in the community. The essential features of ODD include:

- Often loses temper
- Often argues with adults
- Often actively defies or refuses to comply with adults' requests or rules
- Often deliberately annoys people
- Often blames others for his or her mistakes or misbehavior
- Is often touchy or easily annoyed by others

- Is often angry and resentful
- Is often spiteful or vindictive (Morrison 2014; APA 2013).

Attention-deficit/hyperactivity disorder (ADHD) is the most commonly diagnosed childhood externalizing problem behavior, affecting 3–5 percent of elementary school-age children.[5] ADHD encompasses three main problem behaviors: inattentiveness, impulsivity, and hyperactivity (excessive motor activity) (APA 2013; Morrison 2014). ADHD is associated with impaired executive functions in terms of poor self-regulation of impulses, emotions, and behaviors, and autonomic system underarousal, resulting in impulsiveness and stimulation-seeking behavior. ADHD is also linked with cognitive problems in language and communication, resulting in social and academic difficulties. In the context of social interaction, the hyperactive behavior of ADHD children is often viewed as annoying by peers, leading to peer rejection. Research has found consistently that ADHD youth are more likely than non-ADHD youth to be arrested and adjudicated delinquent and to become adult offenders (Bartol and Bartol 2009: 66–68).

Conduct disorder (CD) is the diagnostic category most closely associated with delinquency (Morrison 2014; Bartol and Bartol 2009). CD encompasses a range of 15 different problematic behaviors that can be categorized into four groups: (1) aggression, (2) destruction, (3) lying and theft, and (4) rule violations (Morrison 2014: 382). Some of the more specific diagnostic criteria of CD include:

- Often bullies, threatens, or intimidates others
- Often initiates physical fights
- Has been physically cruel to people or animals
- Has deliberately engaged in fire-setting with the intention of causing serious damage
- Use of dangerous weapons
- Has broken into someone's house, building, or car
- Often stays out at night despite parental prohibitions
- Is often truant from school
- Chronic disrespect for rules and other people's rights (Morrison 2014; APA 2013).

According to Bartol and Bartol (2009: 10):

> Conduct disorders account for the majority of referrals to outpatient child and adolescent mental health clinics in America. Overall, between 2% and 6% of children and adolescents in the United States show behavioral patterns that may be diagnosed as a CD. Boys are diagnosed with the disorder more frequently than girls by a ratio of roughly four to one. CD is found to be more common in lower-socioeconomic class families, among boys with a biological parent known to be antisocial and among boys with attention-deficit/hyperactivity disorder.

ADHD and CD tend to occur together and children with both disorders show a high probability of consistent serious delinquency and adult criminality. It is estimated that approximately 25–50 percent of all ADHD children are involved in some form of conduct disorder as a child, serious delinquency as an adolescent, and criminal behavior as an adult (Bartol and Bartol 2009: 68; see also Pratt et al. 2002). In fact, psychologist Donald Lynam (1996: 211) argues that children with ADHD and CD are impulsive and show a lack of constraint, leading to an inability to reflect on their actions, empathize with others, and feel guilt and remorse. He describes these children as "fledgling psychopaths."

"Expanding ideas: a summary of antisocial behaviors – clinical and legal definitions" provides a brief description of the three clinical diagnostic categories representing externalizing disorders, together with legal definitions of three forms of juvenile delinquency. Each of these terms, however, has distinct meaning, and *clinical definitions* of antisocial behavior must be distinguished from *legal definitions* of juvenile delinquency.

Expanding ideas: a summary of antisocial behaviors – clinical and legal definitions

Externalizing disorders	A form of antisocial behavior that involves problematic attitudes and behaviors, including lying, cheating, deceitfulness, stealing, fire-setting, aggressiveness, and physical aggression, that lead to social and legal difficulties.
• *Oppositional Defiant Disorder*	An ongoing pattern of behavior that is uncooperative, defiant, disobedient, and hostile, especially toward authority figures such as parents.
• *Attention-Deficit/ Hyperactivity Disorder*	A persistent pattern of inattentiveness, impulsivity, and hyperactivity (excessive motor activity). Symptoms include difficulty staying focused and paying attention, difficulty controlling behavior, and hyperactivity.
• *Conduct Disorder*	Habitual misbehavior, including aggression toward people or animals, destruction of property (including fire setting), frequent deceitfulness, stealing, serious violation of rules, and hostile and defiant behavior.
Juvenile delinquency	Actions that violate the law, committed by a person under the legal age of majority.
• *Delinquent Youth*	A youth who is "adjudicated" under formal proceedings of a youth court act, who has committed an offense that, if committed by an adult would constitute a criminal offense.*
• *Status Offender*	A youth who is "adjudicated" under formal proceedings of a youth court act, who has committed an offense that is illegal for a juvenile but not an adult. Status offenses include acts such as running away, truancy, ungovernability, and liquor law violations.
• *Serious Juvenile Offender*	A youth who is "adjudicated" under formal proceedings of a youth court act, who has committed an offense that would be considered a felony offense if committed by an adult; that is, an offense against a person, an offense against property, or an offense involving dangerous drugs.*

* Based on *Montana Code Annotated 2014*. 41-3-102.

Mental health and substance use assessment

Based on an extensive study, the National Center for Mental Health and Juvenile Justice (NCMHJJ) has recently stressed the need for mental health and substance abuse assessment of youth displaying antisocial behavior (Skowyra and Cocozza 2007). Targeting youth in contact with the juvenile justice system, assessment was deemed essential to the task of more accurately identifying mental health needs of these youth. The NCMHJJ also advocated for the use of mental health and substance use assessment to guide treatment strategies in individual cases.

Screening and assessment are usually distinguished in terms of time frame and scope. *Screening* is a brief process of evaluation that seeks to identify youth who are especially troubled and for whom relatively immediate attention is necessary. Although various instruments have been created, the Massachusetts Youth Screening Instrument (MAYSI-2) is used widely to provide efficient identification of mental health and substance use problems of youth. The MAYSI-2 is a 52-item self-report instrument that was developed specifically for use in juvenile justice systems. Scales within the MAYSI-2 include angry-irritable, depressed-anxious, somatic complaints, suicide ideation, thought disturbance, and traumatic experiences (Skowyra and Cocozza 2007; Grisso and Underwood 2004).

Mental health *assessment* is used when screening indicates the need for further evaluation. Assessment uses multiple sources of information, including a diagnostic interview, examination of case records, and family interviews. The most frequently used assessment instrument is the Voice Diagnostic Interview Schedule for Children (Voice DISC). This instrument was designed specifically for use with youth in juvenile justice settings. The Voice DISC is a computer administered, self-report interview that provides provisional diagnosis of a range of mental health disorders according to DSM-IV-R categories, including anxiety disorders, mood disorders, disruptive disorders (ODD, ADHD, and CD), and substance use disorders. The instrument also provides assessment of the youth's relationships with family, peers, and school personnel (Skowyra and Cocozza 2007; Wasserman, Ko, and McReynolds 2004).

Risk/need assessment

The NCMHJJ also emphasizes that mental health screening and assessment should be performed in conjunction with an assessment of risk for future violence and delinquent offending (Skowyra and Cocozza 2007: 27). Predictions of delinquency have traditionally relied on "subjective assessments, professional judgments, intuition, or 'gut-level feelings'" (Gottfredson and Moriarty 2006: 180). Much research shows, however, that predictions of delinquency based on human judgments are far less accurate and valid than those based on risk assessment instruments that classify youth according to their likelihood of delinquent offending (Andrews and Bonta 2010: 312–314).

Risk/need assessment instruments use items that measure key factors found to statistically predict the likelihood of future delinquency – the "risk" element of these assessment tools. Not surprisingly, common risk factors in risk/need assessment instruments include prior delinquent offending, substance abuse, family problems, peer delinquency, and school-related problems (Schwalbe 2008: 1368). These risk factors also identify "criminogenic needs" when the predictors that are identified can be changed through intervention. Earlier in the chapter we referred to these as "dynamic risk factors." Examples of dynamic risk factors include antisocial attitudes and values, association with delinquent peers, dysfunctional family relationships, and antisocial personality traits (impulsiveness, risk-taking, and low self-control) (Vincent et al. 2012; Andrews and Bonta 2010). In contrast, "static risk factors" also predict the likelihood of future delinquency, but cannot be changed through intervention. Examples of static risk factors include the early age of onset of problem behaviors, history of aggressive behavior and violence, and parental criminality.

"Expanding ideas: Revised Wisconsin Delinquency Risk Assessment" provides an example of a delinquency risk/need assessment instrument. The straightforward scoring of the instrument provides a total numeric score, which is used to group youth into risk categories ranging from low to high risk. Until recently, most risk assessment instruments have been utilized in the context of juvenile corrections, especially for probation case classification. But new instruments, tailored to particular processes in juvenile justice are readily being developed to inform a wide variety of juvenile justice decision points, such as diversion, detention, eligibility for alternative programs, transfer to adult court or mental health proceedings, and dispositions (Hoge et al. 2013: 3; Andrews and Bonta 2010).

Expanding ideas: Revised Wisconsin Delinquency Risk Assessment

Revised Wisconsin Delinquency Risk Assessment

NAME OF YOUTH		DATE OF BIRTH	DATE OF REPORT
SEX	ETHNIC GROUP	COUNTY	
OFFENSE			

Complete the assessment using the best available information. Total the points to determine initial level of risk. SCORE

1. **Age at First Referral to Juvenile Court Intake** "Delinquent" defined per statute (see definitions).
   Age referenced to 15th anniversary of birth date. Juvenile is "Under 15" if first referral occurred <u>prior</u> to 15th birthday.

Under 15	2
15 or Over	0 _____

2. **Prior Referrals to Juvenile Court Intake** "Delinquent" defined per statute (see definitions).

None	-1
One or Two	0
Three or More	2 _____

3. **Prior Assaults** (includes but is not limited to use of a weapon).
   "Assaults" are defined as any assaultive behavior, whether physical or sexual, and any weapon or weapon possession arrest/offense as evidenced by any reliable source including prior referrals, policy/professional reports, or other confirmed reports. "Prior" excludes current intake offense.

Yes	2
No	0 _____

4. **Prior Out of Home Placements.**
   Determine the total number of previous <u>court-ordered</u> out of home placements. Do not count a change in foster family, without an intervening return home, as a separate placement.

None or One	0
Two or More	1 _____

5. **Prior Runaways (from home or placement).**
   History of previous runaways from home or any placement. Runaways
   are defined as absconding from home or any placement and not voluntarily
   returning within twenty-four (24) hours.

None or One	0
Two or More	2 _____

6. **School Behavior Problems** (includes habitual truancy) (see definitions).

None	1
Minor Problems	0
Serious Problems or Habitual Truancy Noted	2 _____

7. **History of Physical or Sexual Abuse, or of Neglect, as a Victim.**
   Physical or sexual abuse or neglect victimization suspected by professionals
   whether or not substantiated. Professionals are those listed under s.48.987,
   Wis. Stats.

Yes	1
No	0 _____

8. **History of Alcohol or Other Drug Abuse.**
   Abuse is defined as use resulting in some prolonged disruption of
   functioning.

Yes	1
No	0 _____

9. **History of Serious Emotional Problems** (see definitions).

Yes	1
No	0 _____

10. **Peer Relationships** (see definitions).

Good Support and Influence	-1
Negative Influence; Some Companions Involved in Delinquent Behavior; or Lack of Peer Relationships	1
Strong Negative Influence, Most Peers Involved in Delinquent Behavior such as Gang Involvement	2 _____

    TOTAL RISK SCORE

    _____

Total Score	Classification
−3 to 1	LOW RISK
2 to 4	MODERATE RISK
5 to 8	HIGH RISK
9 or above	VERY HIGH RISK

Source: Wisconsin Department of Corrections, Division of Juvenile Corrections, Madison, WI, and National Council on Crime and Delinquency. Revalidated and issued 1997. Retrieved January 11, 2015 (http://dcf.wi.gov/wisacwis/knowledge_web/training/template-mapping/templates/TM_sm07b_Deliquency_Risk_Assessment_54.pdf).

Risk/need assessment instruments have evolved with use and evaluation, providing better predictive validity and reliability, and becoming more theoretically informed and more relevant and applicable to intervention efforts (Hoge et al. 2013; Vincent et al. 2012; Andrews and Bonta 2010; Andrews, Bonta, and Wormith 2006). As such, risk/need assessment instruments have taken on the dual task of predicting further delinquency (risk assessment) and informing intervention ("criminogenic need" assessment). With this evolution, risk assessment instruments have grown substantially, from the 8 to 12 predictive factors common in early versions, to anywhere from 50 to 120 risk factors in more recently developed instruments. The Youth Assessment and Screening Instrument (YASI), for example, includes 33 items in its prescreen version and 88 items in its full version. The full assessment instrument measures risks, needs, and strengths (protective factors) across ten domains: legal history, family, school, community and peers, alcohol and drugs, mental health, aggression/violence, attitudes, skills, and employment/use of free time (Vincent et al. 2012).

Christopher Baird (2009) of the National Council on Crime and Delinquency has questioned this dual focus of assessment instruments, arguing that risk assessment and need assessment should not be combined in a composite instrument. He contends that this dual purpose confuses both assessment of risk and assessment of need. Factors that predict future delinquency may be irrelevant to intervention needs, and intervention needs may not be predictive of future delinquency. He suggests that assessment instruments separate risk and need and that they utilize a separate, much smaller set of predictive factors that are empirically relevant to each (see also Andrews and Bonta 2010; Gottfredson and Moriarty 2006).

Baird and his colleagues (2013) have recently evaluated nine different risk/need assessments used in ten jurisdictions by comparing their assessment accuracy and appropriateness. Their comparison examined the instruments' predictive validity, reliability, equity, and cost, finding both strengths and weaknesses for each of the instruments. Even with mixed results, the authors concluded that risk/need assessment is an important tool to assess, classify, and treat juvenile offenders.

Early intervention

The case for early intervention when delinquent behavior occurs at a young age is well documented (Cullen and Jonson 2012; Green et al. 2008; Farrington and Welsh 2007; Loeber et al. 2003a).

> Generations of studies in criminology show that the best predictor of future behavior is past behavior. Children showing persistent disruptive behavior are likely to become child delinquents and, in turn, child delinquents are likely to become serious, violent, or chronic juvenile offenders.
>
> (Loeber et al. 2003a: 3–4; see also Loeber, Burke, and Pardini 2009; McCord, Spatz, and Crowell 2001).

In particular, those who engage in delinquent behavior in childhood (age 12 and younger) are two to three times more likely to become chronic offenders than youth who first engage in delinquency in their adolescent years (Burns et al. 2003: 1–2; see also Cullen and Jonson 2012; Farrington and Welsh 2007; Loeber et al. 2003b).

Despite these consistent findings, extensive research also documents that a substantial portion of the children who display disruptive behaviors do not receive adequate intervention to derail the development of delinquent behavior. In an important longitudinal study of youth in Pittsburg, Loeber and his associates found that "between 50% and 70% of the caretakers of the most seriously delinquent boys had never sought help [for disruptive behaviors], and only about a quarter had ever sought help from a mental health professional" (Stouthamer-Loeber,

Loeber, and Thomas 1992: 173; see also Huizinga et al. 2000; Stouthamer-Loeber et al. 1995). Cullen and Jonson (2012: 179) take this problem of non-intervention a step further:

> Year after year, children are manifesting psychological, behavioral, and criminological problems. Their careers in crime are blossoming and nothing is being done. Part of the problem, of course, falls on the shoulders of parents. But the reality is that many parents of at-risk youngsters are at risk themselves. They lack the health insurance, money, education, transportation, and ability to take time off work to haul a resistant child off to a help provider on a weekly basis. They also are living in at-risk neighborhoods where effective services may not be close at hand (Guerra 1997).

Early intervention attempts to address antisocial behavior at an early age so that it does not continue and progress into delinquent behavior at a later age. The Study Group on Very Young Offenders, a group of 39 experts on child delinquency and child psychopathology convened by the Office of Juvenile Justice and Delinquency Prevention, observed that:

> juveniles who commit serious and violent offenses most often have shown persistent disruptive behavior in early childhood and committed minor delinquent acts when quite young. Therefore, comprehensive intervention programs should encompass children who persistently behave in disruptive ways and child delinquents, in addition to young juvenile offenders who have committed serious and violent crimes.
>
> (Burns et al. 2003: 2)

Early intervention occurs most commonly in four service sectors: mental health (including substance use), education, child welfare, and juvenile justice.

Mental health and substance use

Early-onset offenders frequently develop multiple mental health problems early in life (Burns et al. 2003). As noted previously, research strongly and consistently indicates that conduct disorders, attention-deficit hyperactivity disorder, and their co-occurrence are related to the likelihood of delinquent behavior. Substance use disorder also is associated with continued offending during adolescence and during the transition to adulthood (Grisso 2008). Mental health experts contend that effective intervention requires integrated, community-based intervention that provides services across mental health, education, child protective, and juvenile justice agencies (Schubert and Mulvey 2014; Grisso 2008).

Early intervention must address the symptoms associated with these mental health disorders, especially anger and impulsiveness. "Research shows that certain treatments can reduce these symptoms and that certain interventions can reduce delinquency in youth with mental disorders" (Grisso 2008: 146). Among the most common and effective treatments are pharmacological intervention influencing psychological functioning, professional clinical care involving psychotherapy, and therapeutic intervention that structures the youth's environment.

Several specific therapies have been substantiated as effective interventions with mental health disorders. Cognitive behavioral therapy (CBT) is a therapeutic intervention that effectively reduces future delinquency for youth with depression and anxiety disorders. CBT teaches youth better awareness of social cues and promotes delayed gratification, problem-solving, and non-aggressive responses (Grisso 2008: 153–154; see also Burns et al. 2003). Two of the Blueprints' Model Programs, Functional Family Therapy (FFT) and Multisystemic Therapy (MST), provide family-based intervention that reduces the likelihood of delinquent behavior for youth with a wide range of mental health disorders, including conduct disorders and substance use disorder. These therapies seek to control and reduce child disruptive behaviors through structured, family-based intervention that promotes positive family relations and skill training in communication, parenting, problem-solving, and conflict management (Chassin 2008; Grisso 2008; Mihalic et al. 2004a). Multidimensional Treatment Foster Care (MTFC), another Blueprints' Model Program, provides therapeutic community placement in a well-supported foster home with specially trained foster parents. The foster home provides placed youth with intensive supervision at home, in school, and in the community. The biological or adoptive family is also offered family therapy, with the goal of returning the youth to their home. The parents are supported and taught to use behavior management methods that are used in the MTFC foster home, and closely supervised home visits are conducted during the youth's placement in MTFC (Blueprints 2015).

Education

Despite the effectiveness of early intervention in the mental health sector, schools play a much more central role in responding to the early onset of antisocial behavior. This is largely because schools, both preschools and elementary schools, are frequently the social context in which disruptive behavior first becomes evident, often through bullying, physical aggressiveness, and difficult temperament. Schools are also the context in which services are most frequently offered. In a North Carolina study, between 70 and 80 percent of the children who received services for mental health problems were seen by providers in the education sector, usually guidance counselors and school psychologists (Grisso 2008: 153). "However, the adequacy of school-based mental health services has been questioned, largely because school personnel, such as guidance counselors, have limited mental health training" (Burns et al. 2003: 4).

Beyond individualized attention from guidance counselors and school psychologists, early intervention in the school context may involve individualized education plans (IEPs) and alternative schools. An IEP is developed by parents and a school-based team, including the school psychologist, special education teacher, and other educational specialists relevant to the needs of the student. The IEP team conducts an assessment and develops a written plan that provides individualized support services offered in the traditional classroom and/or special education classroom. Support services may include special education, speech, occupational or physical therapy, counseling, medical services, vision or hearing therapy, and other services. Alternative schools are used for students who cannot function effectively in the traditional classroom. Alternative schools often operate in separate buildings, and they are usually highly individualized. Some alternative schools provide classes that are necessary for graduation; others prepare students to take the exams necessary to earn a GED (General Educational Development), which certifies that the student has acquired high school-level skills.

Early intervention in the school sector most commonly takes the form of *universal prevention* with programs that seek to change the social climate of schools and to enhance academic performance and the social skills of all students (Burns et al. 2003). One of the Blueprints' Model Programs described earlier – Life Skills Training – is designed to promote prosocial norms and social competence and to teach problem-solving and conflict resolution skills through a curriculum that has been proven effective. Several other model programs identified in the Blueprints Violence Prevention project are also school-based prevention programs.

Child welfare

Youth enter the child welfare system primarily because of maltreatment, most commonly in the form of abuse and neglect. Maltreatment is associated with both mental health problems and delinquency (Burns et al. 2003; Wiig, Widom, and Tuell 2003). Several child welfare studies indicate that between one-half and two-thirds of the children entering foster care have behavioral problems serious enough to warrant mental health services (Burns et al. 2003). The child welfare system, however, currently provides mental health services to relatively few children.

> Little is known about how the child welfare system identifies child delinquents and potential child delinquents and refers them to mental health services. These children are a critical population for early intervention because of their exposure to trauma and other risk factors and their consequent externalizing (or acting out) behavior.
>
> (Burns et al. 2003: 4)

Of particular concern for early intervention is the "dual status youth" who comes into contact with both the child welfare and juvenile justice systems. In 2004, the National Center for Juvenile Justice (NCJJ) published a call for action, observing that:

> research has established the strong correlation between child maltreatment and subsequent delinquency and violence. The literature is replete with well-designed longitudinal and prospective studies that consistently confirm the impact of child abuse or neglect on a host of behavior problems, the higher risks of future criminality and violence posed by youth with histories of childhood maltreatment, and the need for effective prevention and early intervention efforts that precede court involvement. ...What happens when a single youth becomes involved with both systems simultaneously? In too many instances, the two kinds of cases weave their way down separate paths, before separate judges, in pursuit of separate goals, and without any coordination, cooperation, or even communication.
>
> (Siegel and Lord 2004: 1)

The report focused on the need to coordinate and integrate intervention for dual status youth, especially in terms of case screening and assessment, case management (assignment, planning, and supervision), and inter-agency collaboration.

More recently, the NCJJ has observed that "efforts intended to improve services in cases involving dual-status youth have gained considerable momentum" (Fromknecht 2014: 1). The Office of Juvenile Justice and Delinquency Prevention and the MacArthur Foundation have co-sponsored demonstration sites for integrating child welfare and juvenile justice. A number of integration tactics have been utilized, including data sharing, advisory committees, formal inter-agency memorandums of understanding, informal inter-agency agreements, and statutory and/or court rules. In addition, the Robert F. Kennedy Children's Action Corps and the Center for Juvenile Justice Reform at Georgetown University (CJJR) provide education and technical assistance on systems integration for child welfare and juvenile justice (Fromknecht 2014).

Juvenile justice

Traditionally, juvenile courts have intervened with child delinquents only when families, schools, and social welfare agencies have failed to provide necessary services (Burns et al. 2003). In fact, the federal Juvenile Justice and Delinquency Prevention Act of 1974 emphasized the importance of diversion of status offenders and young, first-time offenders from juvenile court processing. This approach suggests that young offenders should not be subject to dispositions normally given to older or more serious offenders. Yet juvenile court dispositions of young offenders differ little from older offenders because of the limited availability of service options and programs specifically designed for the unique circumstances and needs of child delinquents (Burns et al. 2003).

In recent years, however, juvenile justice systems have begun to provide early intervention with child delinquents. A number of early intervention programs have been developed (Burns et al. 2003). As an example, the Minnesota Delinquents Under 10 Program in Hennepin County, Minnesota, involves coordinated case planning and intervention among several county departments, including Children and Family Services, Economic Assistance, Community Health, and the County Attorney's Office. A screening team reviews police reports and then determines appropriate early intervention for children considered to be at the highest risk for future delinquency. A "wraparound network" is developed for each targeted child, including

> a community-based organization to conduct in-depth assessments, improve behavior and school attendance, and provide extracurricular activities; an integrated service delivery team made up of county staff who coordinate service delivery and help children and family members access services; a critical support person or mentor; and a corporate sponsor that funds extracurricular activities.
>
> (Burns et al. 2003: 8)

Summary and conclusions

This chapter described the central role that theory and research play in delinquency prevention and early intervention. We began by reviewing the major concepts and contexts of delinquency that have been offered in theory and research. Delinquency theory and research are useful to the degree that they help us understand and respond to delinquency. Therefore, theory and research must provide the foundation for delinquency prevention and intervention.

Delinquency prevention programs represent a proactive approach to juvenile crime, attempting to keep delinquency from occurring. Research has established that juvenile delinquency is a component of a larger group of problem behaviors that tend to occur together, including drug and alcohol use, mental health problems, behavior problems and underachievement in school, and precocious and risky sexual behavior. "Research in action: risk factors predictive of juvenile delinquency" listed a number of risk factors that have been found to be related to these problem behaviors. Contemporary approaches to delinquency prevention argue that these risk factors must first be identified through research and then addressed through a broad range of prevention programs at the individual, family, school, and community levels (Coolbaugh and Hansel 2000). Delinquency prevention programs can be classified as *universal*, targeting the general population of youth; *selective*, targeting individual youth or groups of youth who are "at risk" due to multiple risk factors in their lives; and *indicated*, targeting juvenile offenders in order to prevent or eliminate a serious pattern of delinquent offending. We also considered several delinquency prevention programs that have been evaluated as successful and identified as "model programs."

Early intervention is sometimes based on mental health assessment that systematically evaluates and classifies disruptive behaviors and mental health problems. Three externalizing disorders are associated with later delinquent behavior: oppositional defiant disorder (ODD), attention-deficit/hyperactivity disorder (ADHD), and conduct disorder (CD). Risk/need assessment involves the use of standardized assessment instruments to identify the needs of the youth and to determine the likelihood of reoffending. We also considered early intervention in four different service sectors: mental health, education, child welfare, and juvenile justice.

Delinquency prevention and early intervention efforts are increasingly driven by evaluation research that tries to establish whether particular strategies, methods, and programs effectively reduce the likelihood of delinquent offending, an approach called evidence-based practice. Several model program guides are available that identify delinquency prevention and intervention programs of demonstrated effectiveness. Another form of evaluation research called meta-analysis estimates the effectiveness of particular intervention strategies and methods across a number of evaluation studies. Evidence-based practice also involves risk/need assessment, to identify the criminogenic needs of youth and to determine their likelihood of reoffending, and cost-benefit analysis, to comprehensively measure the financial impact of programs.

Critical-thinking questions

1. Referring back to the case at the beginning of the chapter, what concepts and contexts are important in explaining Melissa's delinquent offending?
2. What does the term *adolescents at risk* mean and how is it related to delinquency prevention efforts?
3. Briefly characterize the evidence-based practice approach to delinquency prevention and early intervention.
4. What are some of the dangers of ignoring evidence-based delinquency prevention practices?
5. In your study of model programs, which program appeals to you most? Why?
6. How are oppositional defiant disorder, ADHD, and conduct disorder related to juvenile delinquency?
7. Why is assessment important to early intervention?
8. Argue the need for early intervention.
9. What is a "dual status youth"?

Suggested reading

Burns, Barbara J., James C. Howell, Janet K. Wiig, Leena K. Augimeri, Brendan C. Welsh, Rolf Loeber, and David Petechuk. 2003. *Treatment, Services, and Intervention Programs for Child Delinquency*. Washington, DC: Office of Juvenile Justice and Delinquency Prevention.

Farrington, David P. and Brandon C. Welsh. 2007. *Saving Children from a Life of Crime*. New York: Oxford University Press.

Greenwood, Peter. 2008. "Prevention and Intervention Programs for Juvenile Offenders." *The Future of Children* 18: 185–210.

Loeber, Rolf, David Farrington, and David Petechuk. 2003. *Child Delinquency: Early Intervention and Prevention.* Washington, DC: Office of Juvenile Justice and Delinquency Prevention.

Mihalic, Sharon F. and Delbert S. Elliott. 2015. "Evidence-Based Programs Registry: Blueprints for Healthy Youth Development." *Evaluation and Program Planning* 48: 124–131.

Welsh, Brandon C. and David P. Farrington. 2007. "Scientific Support for Early Prevention of Delinquency and Later Offending." *Victims and Offenders* 2: 125–140.

Useful websites

For further information relevant to this chapter, go to the following websites.

- Blueprints for Healthy Youth Development, Center for the Study and Prevention of Violence at the University of Colorado Boulder (www.blueprintsprograms.com/)
- Model Programs Guide, Office of Juvenile Justice and Delinquency Prevention (www.ojjdp.gov/mpg/)
- National Center for Juvenile Justice and Mental Health (www.ncmhjj.com/)
- National Registry of Evidence-based Programs and Practices, Substance Abuse and Mental Health Services Administration (http://www.samhsa.gov/nrepp)
- Robert F. Kennedy National Resource Center for Juvenile Justice (juvenile justice and child welfare coordination) (http://rfknrcjj.org/)

Glossary of key terms

Assessment: Systematic methods of appraisal and evaluation that are used to identify and classify problem behaviors.

Attention–deficit/hyperactivity disorder: A persistent pattern of inattentiveness, impulsivity, and hyperactivity (excessive motor activity). Symptoms include difficulty staying focused and paying attention, difficulty controlling behavior, and hyperactivity.

Causal analysis: Tries to move beyond demonstrating an association between two variables to an analysis of multiple causal factors, their temporal ordering, and possible spurious relationships.

Conduct disorder: Habitual misbehavior, including aggression toward people or animals, destruction of property (including fire setting), frequent deceitfulness, stealing, serious violation of rules, and hostile and defiant behavior.

Cost–benefit analysis: In evaluating delinquency intervention programs, cost–benefit analysis seeks to "comprehensively identify and measure the benefits and costs of a program," including those that occur during and after participation in the program (National Research Council 2013: 167).

Dynamic risk factors: Characteristics of the youth and his/her environment that can be changed through intervention, such as antisocial attitudes and values, association with delinquent peers, dysfunctional family relationships, and antisocial personality traits (impulsiveness, risk-taking, and low self-control).

Early intervention: Therapies and programs that seek to reduce or eliminate antisocial behavior once it is observed.

Evidence-based practice: "Involves the use of scientific principles to assess the available evidence on program effectiveness and to develop principles for best practice in any particular field" (Greenwood and Welsh 2012: 495).

Externalizing disorders: Problematic attitudes and behaviors, including lying, cheating, deceitfulness, stealing, fire-setting, aggressiveness, and physical aggression, that lead to social and legal difficulties. Externalizing disorders are categorized by the DSM-IV-R into three broad diagnoses: conduct disorder, oppositional defiant disorder, and attention–deficit hyperactivity disorder.

Implementation fidelity: "The degree to which a program's core services, components, and procedures are implemented as originally designed" (CrimeSolutions.gov 2015).

Indicated prevention (or tertiary prevention): Targets identified juvenile offenders in order to prevent or eliminate a serious pattern of delinquent offending.

Internalizing disorders: Problematic moods and behaviors characterized by anxiety, social withdrawal and isolation, hypersensitivity, low self-esteem, and eating disorders.

Meta-analysis: A statistical technique which estimates the effects found across evaluation studies of intervention methods and strategies.

Oppositional defiant disorder: An ongoing pattern of behavior that is uncooperative, defiant, disobedient, and hostile, especially toward authority figures such as parents.

Problem behaviors: Behaviors that compromise successful adolescent adjustment, such as drug and alcohol use, mental health problems, underachievement in school, precocious and risky sexual behavior, and delinquency.

Protective factors: Individual traits, abilities, and social circumstances that allow youth to adapt positively to adverse environments.

Resiliency: Achieving healthy psychosocial development and positive functioning despite stress, hardship, and adversity (risk factors).

Risk factor: Any individual trait, social influence, or environmental condition that leads to greater likelihood of problem behaviors and ultimately negative developmental outcomes during the adolescent years.

Risk/need assessment: Standardized assessment instruments to identify the likelihood or "risk" of future offending or reoffending, and the "criminogenic needs" of the youth – those factors that lead to delinquency and can be changed.

Selective prevention (or secondary prevention): Prevention programs target youth or groups of youths who are "at risk" due to multiple risk factors in their lives.

Static risk factors: Background characteristics of the youth that cannot be changed through prevention programs, including the age of onset of problem behaviors, history of aggressive behavior and violence, and parental criminality.

Universal prevention (or primary prevention): Prevention programs that target the general population of youth and include campaigns to prevent smoking and drug use, to promote problem-solving and dispute resolution skill through classroom education, and classes on parenting skills offered to all parents.

Notes

1. "Adolescence." *Wikipedia* (http://en.wikipedia.org/wiki/Adolescence), accessed January 11, 2015. See also *Oxford English Dictionary* (http://dictionary.oed.com), accessed January 11, 2015.
2. Reprinted with permission from the National Academies Press, Copyright © 2013, National Academy of Sciences.
3. Farrington and Welsh (2007: 94) point out that there are very few truly "universal" programs, provided to all youth and families because prevention programs are a limited resource that usually must be targeted to those in greatest need. Thus, universal programs are often applied selectively.

4. ODD, ADHD, and CD were classified in the DSM–IV (1994) as "Disorders Usually First Evident in Infancy, Childhood, and Adolescence." The latest version, DSM-V (2013), now includes ODD and CD in a chapter entitled "Disruptive, Impulse-Control, and Conduct Disorder." ADHD has been moved to the chapter "Neurodevelopmental Disorders," even though it is comorbid with the ODD and CD (Morrison 2014). Our coverage will discuss the disorders collectively because they are so closely linked to juvenile delinquency.

5. A recent survey from the Center for Disease Control and Prevention estimates that almost 11 percent of children in the United States are affected by ADHD (Morrison 2014: 33).

References

Agnew, Robert. 2006. *Pressured into Crime: An Overview of General Strain Theory*. Los Angeles: Roxbury.

Agnew, Robert and Timothy Brezina. 2015. *Juvenile Delinquency: Causes and Control*. 5th edn. New York: Oxford University Press.

American Psychiatric Association (APA). 2013. *Diagnostic and Statistical Manual of Mental Disorders, Fifth Edition* (DSM-5). Arlington, VA: American Psychiatric Association.

Andrews, D. A. and James Bonta. 2010. *The Psychology of Criminal Conduct*. 5th edn. Cincinnati, OH: Anderson.

Andrews, D. A., James Bonta, and J. Stephen Wormith. 2006. "The Recent Past and Near Future of Risk and/or Need Assessment." *Crime and Delinquency* 52: 7–27.

Baird, Christopher. 2009. "A Question of Evidence: A Critique of Risk Assessment Models Used in the Justice System." Special Report. National Council on Crime and Delinquency. Retrieved February 7, 2015 (http://nccdglobal.org/sites/default/files/publication_pdf/special-report-evidence.pdf).

Baird, Chris, Theresa Healy, Kristen Johnson, Andrea Bogie, Erin Wicke Dankert, and Chris Scharenbroch. 2013. *A Comparison of Risk Assessment Instruments in Juvenile Justice* (NCJ 244477). National Council on Crime and Delinquency. Retrieved February 5, 2015 (www.ojjdp.gov/publications/PubAbstract. asp?pubi=266558).

Bartol, Curt R. and Anne M. Bartol. 2009. *Juvenile Delinquency and Antisocial Behavior: A Developmental Perspective*. 3rd edn. Upper Saddle River, NJ: Pearson Prentice Hall.

Birkbeck, Christopher and Gary LaFree. 1993. "The Situational Analysis of Crime and Deviance." *Annual Review of Sociology* 19: 113–137.

Blueprints for Healthy Youth Development (Blueprints). 2015. Center for the Study and Prevention of Violence at the Institute of Behavioral Science, University of Colorado Boulder. Accessed January 20, 2015 (www.blueprintsprograms.com/).

Broidy, Lisa M., Daniel S. Nagin, Richard E. Tremblay, John E. Bates, Bobby Brame, Kenneth A. Dodge, David Fergusson, John L. Horwood, Rolf Loeber, Robert Laird, Donald R. Lynam, Terrie E. Moffitt, Gregory S. Pettit, and Frank Vitaro. 2003. "Developmental Trajectories of Childhood Disruptive Behaviors and Adolescent Delinquency: A Six-Site, Cross-National Study." *Developmental Psychology* 39: 222–245.

Burns, Barbara J., James C. Howell, Janet K. Wiig, Leena K. Augimeri, Brendan C. Welsh, Rolf Loeber, and David Petechuk. 2003. *Treatment, Services, and Intervention Programs for Child Delinquency*. Washington, DC: Office of Juvenile Justice and Delinquency Prevention.

Byrne, James M. and Arthur J. Lurigio. 2009. "Separating Science from Nonsense: Evidence-Based Research, Policy, and Practice in Criminal and Juvenile Justice Settings." *Victims and Offenders* 4: 303–310.

Caspi, Avashalom, Terrie E. Moffitt, Phil A. Silva, Magda Stouthamer-Loeber, Robert F. Krueger, and Pamela S. Schmutte. 1994. "Are Some People Crime-Prone? Replications of the Personality–Crime Relationship across Countries, Genders, Races and Methods." *Criminology* 32: 163–195.

Chassin, Laurie. 2008. "Juvenile Justice and Substance Use." *The Future of Children* 18: 165–183. Retrieved February 12, 2015 (www.princeton.edu/futureofchildren/publications/docs/18_02_08.pdf).

Cohen, Mark A. and Alex R. Piquero. 2009. "New Evidence on the Monetary Value of Saving a High-Risk Youth." *Journal of Quantitative Criminology* 42: 89–109.

Coolbaugh, Kathleen and Cynthia J. Hansel. 2000. *The Comprehensive Strategy: Lessons Learned From Pilot Sites.* Washington, DC: Office of Juvenile Justice and Delinquency Prevention.

CrimeSolutions.gov. 2015. "Glossary." National Institute of Justice. Retrieved January 31, 2015 (www.crimesolutions.gov/Glossary.aspx).

Cullen, Francis T. and Cheryl Lero Jonson. 2012. *Correctional Theory: Context and Consequences.* Los Angeles: Sage.

Dodge, Kenneth A. and Adam D. Mandel. 2012. "Building Evidence for Evidence-Based Policy Making." *Criminology and Public Policy* 11: 525–534.

Drake, Elizabeth K., Steve Aos, and Marna G. Miller. 2009. "Evidence-Based Public Policy Options to Reduce Crime and Criminal Justice Costs: Implications for Washington State." *Victims & Offenders* 4: 170–196.

Dryfoos, Joy G. 1990. *Adolescents at Risk: Prevalence and Prevention.* New York: Oxford University Press.

Elliott, Delbert S., David Huizinga, and Suzanne S. Ageton. 1985. *Explaining Delinquency and Drug Use.* Beverly Hills, CA: Sage.

Elliott, Delbert S., David Huizinga, and Scott Menard. 1989. *Multiple Problem Youth: Delinquency, Substance Use, and Mental Health Problems.* New York: Springer-Verlag.

Farrington, David P. and Brandon C. Welsh. 2007. *Saving Children from a Life of Crime.* New York: Oxford University Press.

Fromknecht, Anne. 2014. "Systems Integration: Child Welfare and Juvenile Justice." JJGPS StateScan. Pittsburgh, PA: National Center for Juvenile Justice.

Gottfredson, Michael R. and Travis Hirschi. 1990. *A General Theory of Crime.* Stanford University Press.

Gottfredson, Stephen D. and Laura J. Moriarty. 2006. "Statistical Risk Assessment: Old Problems and New Applications." *Crime and Delinquency* 52: 178–200.

Green, Amy E., Ellis L. Gesten, Mark A. Greenwald, and Octavio Salcedo. 2008. "Predicting Delinquency in Adolescence and Young Adulthood: A Longitudinal Analysis of Early Risk Factors." *Youth Violence and Juvenile Justice* 6: 323–342.

Greenwood, Peter W. 2006. *Changing Lives: Delinquency Prevention as Crime Control.* University of Chicago Press.

Greenwood, Peter W. 2008. "Prevention and Intervention Programs for Juvenile Offenders." *The Future of Children* 18: 185–210. Retrieved February 7, 2015 (www.princeton.edu/futureofchildren/publications/docs/18_02_09.pdf).

Greenwood, Peter W. and Brandon C. Welsh. 2012. "Promoting Evidence-Based Practice in Delinquency Prevention at the State Level: Principles, Progress, and Policy Directions." *Criminology & Public Policy* 11: 493–513.

Grisso, Thomas. 2008. "Adolescent Offenders with Mental Health Disorders." *The Future of Children* 18: 143–164. Retrieved February 7, 2015 (www.princeton.edu/futureofchildren/publications/docs/18_02_07.pdf).

Grisso, Thomas and Lee A. Underwood. 2004. *Screening and Assessing Mental Health and Substance Use Disorders among Youth in the Juvenile Justice System: A Resource Guide for Practitioners.* Washington, DC: Office of Juvenile Justice and Delinquency Prevention.

Guerra, Nancy G. 1997. "Intervening to Prevent Childhood Aggression in the Inner City." Pp. 256–312 in *Violence and Childhood in the Inner City*, ed. J. McCord. Cambridge University Press.

Hall, G. Stanley. 1904. *Adolescence: Its Psychology and its Relations to Physiology, Anthropology, Sociology, Sex, Crime, Religion and Education.* New York: Appleton.

Hawkins, J. David, Todd I. Herrenkohl, David P. Farrington, Devon Brewer, Richard F. Catalano, Tracy W. Harachi, and Lynn Cothern. 2000. "*Predictors of Youth Violence.*" *Juvenile Justice Bulletin.* Washington, DC: Office of Juvenile Justice and Delinquency Prevention.

Hawkins, Stephanie R., Phillip W. Graham, Jason Williams, and Margaret A. Zahn. 2009. "Resilient Girls – Factors that Protect Against Delinquency." Girls Study Group: Understanding and Responding to Girls' Delinquency. Washington, DC: Office of Juvenile Justice and Delinquency Prevention.

Hoge, Robert D., Gina Vincent, and Laura S. Guy. 2013. "Bulletin 4: Prediction and Risk/Needs Assessment" (NCJ 242934). Study Group on the Transitions between Juvenile Delinquency and Adult Crime. Washington, DC: National Criminal Justice Reference Service. Retrieved October 6, 2014 (https://ncjrs.gov/pdffiles1/nij/grants/242934.pdf).

Howell, James C. 1997. *Juvenile Justice and Youth Violence*. Thousand Oaks, CA: Sage.

Howell, James C. 2009. *Preventing and Reducing Juvenile Delinquency: A Comprehensive Framework*. 2nd edn. Thousand Oaks, CA: Sage.

Huizinga, David A., Rolf Loeber, Terence P. Thornberry, and Lynn Cothern. 2000. "Co-Occurrence of Delinquency and Other Problem Behaviors." *Juvenile Justice Bulletin*. Washington, DC: Office of Juvenile Justice and Delinquency Prevention.

Jessor, Richard. 1992. "Risk Behavior in Adolescence: A Psychosocial Framework for Understanding and Action." Pp. 19–34 in *Adolescents at Risk: Medical and Social Perspectives*, ed. D. E. Rogers and E. Ginzberg. Boulder, CO: Westview.

Lehman, Joseph D., J. David Hawkins, and Richard F. Catalano. 1994. *Corrections Today* (August): 92–100.

Lerner, Richard M. and Nancy L. Galambos. 1998. "Adolescent Development: Challenges and Opportunities for Research, Programs, and Policies." *Annual Review of Psychology* 49: 413–446.

Lipsey, Mark W. 1992. "Juvenile Delinquency in Treatment: A Meta-Analytic Inquiry into the Variability of Effects." Pp. 83–127 in *Meta-Analysis for Explanation: A Casebook*, ed. T. D. Cook, H. Cooper, D. S. Cordray, H. Hartmann, L.V. Hedges, R. J. Light, T. A. Louis, and F. Mosteller. New York: Russell Sage Foundation.

Lipsey, Mark W. 2006. "The Effects of Community-Based Group Treatment for Delinquency: A Meta-Analytic Search for Cross-Study Generalizations." Pp. 162–184 in *Deviant Peer Influences in Programs for Youth: Problems and Solutions*, ed. Kenneth A. Dodge, Thomas J. Dishion, and Jennifer E. Lansford. New York: Guilford Press.

Lipsey, Mark W. 2009. "The Primary Factors That Characterize Effective Interventions with Juvenile Offenders: A Meta-Analytic Overview." *Victims & Offenders* 4: 124–147.

Lipsey, Mark W. and Francis T. Cullen. 2007. "The Effectiveness of Correctional Rehabilitation: A Review of Systematic Reviews." *Annual Review of Law and Social Science* 3: 297–320.

Lipsey, Mark W. and James C. Howell. 2012. "A Broader View of Evidence-Based Programs Reveals More Options for State Juvenile Justice Systems." *Criminology & Public Policy*, 11: 515–523.

Lipsey, Mark, James C. Howell, Marion R. Kelly, Gabrielle Chapman, and Darin Carver. 2010. *Improving the Effectiveness of Juvenile Justice Programs: A New Perspective on Evidence-Based Practice*. Washington, DC: Center for Juvenile Justice Reform. Retrieved January 17, 2015 (http://cjjr.georgetown.edu/pdfs/ebp/ebppaper.pdf).

Liu, Jianghong. 2004. "Childhood Externalizing Behavior: Theory and Implication." *Journal of Child and Adolescent Psychiatric Nursing* 17: 93–103.

Loeber, Rolf, Jeffrey D. Burke, and Dustin A. Pardini. 2009. "Development and Etiology of Disruptive and Delinquent Behavior." *Annual Review of Clinical Psychology* 5: 293–312.

Loeber, Rolf, David Farrington, and David Petechuk. 2003a. *Child Delinquency: Early Intervention and Prevention*. Washington, DC: Office of Juvenile Justice and Delinquency Prevention.

Loeber, Rolf, David Farrington, Magda Stouthamer-Loeber, Terrie E. Moffitt, Avshalom Caspi, Helen R. White, Evelyn H. Wei, and Jennifer M. Beyers. 2003b. "The Development of Male Offending: Key Findings from Fourteen Years of the Pittsburg Youth Study." Pp. 79–111 in *Taking Stock of Delinquency: An Overview of Findings from Contemporary Longitudinal Studies*, ed. T. P. Thornberry and M. D. Krohn. New York: Kluwer Academic/Plenum.

Lynam, Donald R. 1996. "The Early Identification of Chronic Offenders: Who is the Fledgling Psychopath?" *Psychological Bulletin* 120: 209–234.

McCord, Joan, Cathy Spatz Widom, and Nancy A. Crowell, 2001. *Juvenile Crime, Juvenile Justice*. Washington, DC: National Academy Press.

McKee, Esther Chao and Lisa Rapp. 2014. "The Current Status of Evidence-Based Practice in Juvenile Justice." *Journal of Evidence-Based Social Work* 11: 308–314.

Mihalic, Sharon F. and Delbert S. Elliott. 2015. "Evidence-Based Programs Registry: Blueprints for Healthy Youth Development." *Evaluation and Program Planning* 48: 124–131.

Mihalic, Sharon, Abigail Fagan, Katherine Irwin, Diane Ballard, and Delbert Elliott. 2004a. *Blueprints for Violence Prevention*. Washington, DC: Office of Juvenile Justice and Delinquency Prevention.

Mihalic, Sharon, Katherine Irwin, Abigail Fagan, Diane Ballard, and Delbert Elliott. 2004b. *Successful Program Implementation: Lessons from Blueprints*. Washington, DC: Office of Juvenile Justice and Delinquency Prevention.

Miller, Joshua D. and Donald Lynam. 2001. "Structural Models of Personality and Their Relation to Antisocial Behavior: A Meta-Analytic Review." *Criminology* 39: 765–798.

Moffitt, Terrie E. 2005. "The New Look of Behavioral Genetics in Developmental Psychopathology: Gene–Environment Interplay in Antisocial Behaviors." *Psychological Bulletin* 131: 533–554.

Morrison, James. 2014. *DSM-5 Made Easy: The Clinician's Guide to Diagnosis*. New York: Guilford Press.

National Research Council. 2013. *Reforming Juvenile Justice: A Developmental Approach*, ed. Richard J. Bonnie, Robert L. Johnson, Betty M. Chemers, and Julie A. Schuck. Committee on Law and Justice, Division of Behavioral and Social Sciences and Education. Washington, DC: National Academies Press.

Olds, David, Peggy Hill, and Elissa Rumsey. 1998. *Prenatal and Early Childhood Nurse Home Visitation*. Washington, DC: Office of Juvenile Justice and Delinquency Prevention.

Pratt, Travis, Francis T. Cullen, Kristie Blevins, Leah Daigle, and James Unnever. 2002. "The Relationship of ADHD to Crime and Delinquency: A Meta-Analysis." *International Journal of Police Science and Management* 4: 344–360.

President's Commission on Law Enforcement and Administration of Justice. 1967. *Task Force Report: Juvenile Delinquency and Youth Crime*. Washington, DC: GPO.

Rocque, Michael, Brandon C. Welsh, Peter W. Greenwood, and Erica King. 2014. "Implementing and Sustaining Evidence-Based Practice in Juvenile Justice: A Case Study of a Rural State." *International Journal of Offender Therapy and Comparative Criminology* 58: 1033–1057.

Rutter, Michael. 2003. "Crucial Paths from Risk Indicator to Causal Mechanism." Pp. 3–24 in *Causes of Conduct Disorder and Juvenile Delinquency*, ed. Benjamin B. Lahey, Terrie E. Moffitt, and Avshalom Caspi. New York: Oxford University Press.

Rutter, Michael, Andrew Pickles, Robin Murray, and Lindon Eaves. 2001. "Testing Hypotheses on Specific Environmental Causal Effects on Behavior." *Psychological Bulletin* 127: 291–324.

Schubert, Carol A. and Edward P. Mulvey. 2014. "Behavioral Health Problems, Treatment, and Outcomes in Serious Youthful Offenders." *Juvenile Justice Bulletin*. Washington, DC: Office of Juvenile Justice and Delinquency Prevention.

Schwalbe, Craig S. 2008. "A Meta-Analysis of Juvenile Justice Risk Assessment Instruments: Predictive Validity by Gender." *Criminal Justice and Behavior* 35: 1367–1381.

Siegel, Gene and Rachael Lord. 2004. "When Systems Collide: Improving Court Practices and Programs in Dual Jurisdiction Cases." Pittsburgh, PA: National Center for Juvenile Justice. Retrieved January 12, 2015 (www.ncjj.org/publication/When-Systems-Collide-Improving-Co urt-Practices-and-Programs-in-Dual-Jurisdiction-Cases.aspx).

Skowyra, Kathleen R. and Joseph J. Cocozza. 2007. *Blueprint for Change: A Comprehensive Model for the Identification and Treatment of Youth with Mental Health Needs in Contact with Juvenile Justice*. National Center for Mental Health and Juvenile Justice. Delmar, NY: Policy Research Associates.

Steinberg, Laurence and Amanda Sheffield Morris. 2001. "Adolescent Development." *Annual Review of Psychology* 52: 23–45.

Stouthamer-Loeber, Magda, Rolf Loeber, and Christopher Thomas. 1992. "Caretakers Seeking Help for Boys with Disruptive and Delinquent Behavior." *Comprehensive Mental Health Care* 2: 159–178.

Stouthamer-Loeber, Magda, Rolf Loeber, W. van Kammen, and Q. Zhang. 1995. "Uninterrupted Delinquent Careers: The Timing of Parental Help-Seeking and Juvenile Court Contact." *Studies on Crime and Crime Prevention* 4: 236–251.

Tanner-Smith, Emily E., Sandra Jo Wilson, and Mark W. Lipsey. 2013. "Risk Factors and Crime." Pp. 89–111 in *The Oxford Handbook of Criminological Theory*, ed. F. T. Cullen and P. Wilcox. New York: Oxford University Press.

Thornberry, Terence P., David Huizinga, and Rolf Loeber. 2004. "The Causes and Correlates Studies: Findings and Policy Implications." *Juvenile Justice* 9: 3–19.

Vincent, Gina M., Laura S. Guy, and Thomas Grisso. 2012. "Risk Assessment in Juvenile Justice: A Guidebook for Implementation." Models for Change: System Reform in Juvenile Justice. MacArthur Foundation. Retrieved April 25, 2014 (www.modelsforchange.net/publications/346).

Washington State Institute for Public Policy. 2011. "Return on Investment: Evidence-Based Options to Improve Statewide Outcomes." Olympia, WA: Washington State Institute for Public Policy. Retrieved September 30, 2014 (www.wsipp.wa.gov/rptfiles/11-07-1201.pdf).

Wasserman, Gail A., Kate Keenan, Richard E. Tremblay, John D. Cole, Todd I. Herrenkohl, Rolf Loeber, and David Petechuk. 2003. *Risk and Protective Factors of Child Delinquency*. Washington, DC: Office of Juvenile Justice and Delinquency Prevention.

Wasserman, Gail A., Susan J. Ko, and Larkin S. McReynolds. 2004. "Assessing the Mental Health Status of Youth in Juvenile Justice Settings." *Juvenile Justice Bulletin*. Washington, DC: Office of Juvenile Justice and Delinquency Prevention.

Welsh, Brandon C. and David P. Farrington. 2007. "Scientific Support for Early Prevention of Delinquency and Later Offending." *Victims and Offenders* 2: 125–140.

Welsh, Brandon C., Mark W. Lipsey, Frederick P., Rivara, J. David Hawkins, Steve Aos, Meghan E. Peel, and David Petechuk. 2013. "Bulletin 6: Changing Lives: Prevention and Intervention to Reduce Serious Offending" (NCJ 242936). Study Group on the Transitions between Juvenile Delinquency and Adult Crime. Washington, DC: National Criminal Justice Reference Service. Retrieved January 13, 2015 (https://ncjrs.gov/pdffiles1/nij/grants/242936.pdf).

Werner, Emmy E. 2005. "What Can We Learn About Resilience from Large-Scale Longitudinal Studies?" Pp. 91–105 in *Handbook of Resilience in Children*, ed. Sam Goldstein and Robert B. Brooks. New York: Kluwer Academic/Plenum Publishers.

White, Helen Raskin. 1992. "Early Problem Behavior and Later Drug Problems." *Journal of Research in Crime and Delinquency* 29: 412–429.

Wiig, Janet, Cathy Spatz Widom, and John A. Tuell. 2003. *Understanding Child Maltreatment and Juvenile Delinquency: From Research to Effective Program, Practice, and Systematic Solutions*. Washington, DC: Child Welfare League of America.

Chapter 14

Contemporary juvenile justice

Chapter preview

Topics:

- Structure of juvenile justice systems: decentralized and fragmented
- Juvenile justice process: discretion, diversion, and disproportionate minority contact
- Policing juveniles
- Juvenile court processes: informal and formal
- Juvenile corrections

Terms:

- discretion
- diversion
- disproportionate minority contact
- protective role
- taking into custody
- crime–fighting role
- collaborative role
- law–enforcer role
- search and seizure
- arrest
- custodial interrogation
- referral
- intake
- petition

- informal disposition
- detention
- adjudication
- formal disposition
- predisposition report
- commitment
- probation conditions
- probation supervision
- revocation
- residential placement
- group homes
- custodial institutions
- aftercare
- parole

Chapter learning objectives

After completing this chapter, students should be able to:

- Describe the structure of juvenile justice systems in the United States.
- Provide examples of how discretion and diversion are exercised throughout the juvenile justice process.
- Explain how disproportionate minority contact occurs throughout the juvenile justice process.
- Discuss the different roles that police take in encounters with juveniles.
- Define due process of law and describe how it affects juvenile law enforcement.
- Identify and describe the juvenile court process, including both informal and formal procedures.
- Inventory the full range of dispositional options that are authorized under state statutory law.
- Describe the three major areas of juvenile corrections: probation, community-based corrections, and residential placements.

Case in point: the juvenile court's dispositional order for Rick

The "Case in point" that opened Chapter 1 was about Rick, a teenager who was formally adjudicated a "delinquent youth" by the Youth Court in his area. Despite the efforts of the court, Rick persisted in delinquent acts, resulting in his "commitment" to the state training school. While the juvenile court disposition shown below is similar in structure and content to one that was actually handed down, the names and places are fictitious.

1 JEFFREY H. HOUSTON
2 District Judge
3 Fifth Judicial District
4 Hastings County Courthouse
5 Belfry, Minnesota
6
7 <u>FIFTH JUDICIAL DISTRICT COURT, HASTINGS COUNTY</u>
8 IN THE MATTER OF: Cause No. DJ 96 – 58
9 RICHARD A. SMITH   *ORDER OF COMMITMENT*
10
11 **A Youth Under the Age of 18**.
12   On the 1st day of October 2014, Richard Smith, a youth of this County, 17 years of age,
13 was brought before me pursuant to a Petition of Gross Criminal Mischief previously filed. The
14 youth appeared with his parents, Bernard and Mary Smith, and his attorney, Michael Langley.
15 The Court fully advised the youth and his parents of all legal rights accorded by the laws of
16 the State of Minnesota. Also present were Deputy County Attorney Jane Kline, and Juvenile
17 Probation Officer James Burfeind.
18   Upon being questioned by the Court concerning the allegations in the petition, the youth
19 admitted the allegations to make a finding of delinquency in addition to a finding that the
20 youth had violated his probation. After reviewing the predispositional report, and it having
21 been established that reasonable efforts have been made to prevent or eliminate removal of the

22 youth from the home, it is determined that removal of the youth from the home is necessary
23 at this time because continuation in the home would be contrary to the welfare of the youth.
24 The Court entered the following Order:
25   **IT IS HEREBY ORDERED** that Richard Smith is found to be a *Serious Juvenile*
26 *Offender*, having previously been found to be a *Delinquency Youth*.
27   **IT IS HEREBY ORDERED** that Richard Smith is committed to the Minnesota State
28 Department of Correction for commitment to the Minnesota State Training School.
29 1.   The youth is committed to the Department of Corrections for an indefinite period of
30   time for placement at the Minnesota State Training School.
31 2.   The youth will follow and abide by the rules of the Minnesota State Training School.
32 3.   The youth will attend school regularly, he will follow all the rules of the school, and he
33   will maintain passing grades.
34 4.   The youth will participate in treatment programs available at the Minnesota State
35   Training School.
36 5.   The youth will submit to random drug testing and UA's upon request of staff at the
37   Minnesota State Training School or the Probation Officer.
38 6.   The youth will submit to a search of his person or living area at the request of staff at the
39   Minnesota State Training School or the Probation Officer.
40 7.   The Department of Corrections will notify the Judge two weeks in advance of the
41   youth's release from the Minnesota State Training School.
42 8.   Upon release, the youth will report to his Probation Officer and be placed on
43   Intensive Supervision Probation for a ninety-day period, followed by regular proba-
44   tion supervision.
45 9.   The youth is liable for payment of restitution in the amount to be determined by the
46   Court, to be paid in full by the time the youth turns 18 years of age. The Court will
47   retain jurisdiction over the youth should he fail to pay restitution.
48 10.   The youth will not be in possession or consume any alcohol or illicit drugs.
49
50 DONE IN OPEN COURT this 1st day of October, 2014.
51 DATED this 28th day of October, 2014.
52
53 *Jeffrey H. Houston*
54 Jeffrey H. Houston
55 DISTRICT JUDGE

In Chapter 2, we saw that a series of reforms that began in the 1960s redefined the legal concept of juvenile delinquency and significantly transformed juvenile justice philosophy, policy, and practice. Through this transformation, the *parens patriae* authority of the original juvenile court was reduced substantially and the *rehabilitative ideal* was drawn into question. Detention, formal adjudication, and more punitive disposition, including incarceration, were increasingly employed to respond to serious juvenile offenders, whereas informal procedures and diversions, especially those involving community-based alternatives, were utilized for status and non-violent juvenile offenders.

In a wide-ranging critique of contemporary juvenile justice, Barry Feld (1999) examined four areas of change that are clearly evident in these reforms: (1) an increased emphasis on procedural due process with little actual gain in due process right; (2) a shift in legal philosophy from the rehabilitative ideal to punishment and criminal responsibility, especially for serious, violent juvenile offenders; (3) reforms to divert, deinstitutionalize, and decriminalize status offenders (the "soft end" of the juvenile court), thereby sending them to a "hidden," private sector treatment system of social control, administered by mental health and chemical dependency service providers; and (4) the transfer of serious juvenile offenders (the "hard end" of the juvenile court) to adult criminal court jurisdiction. As a result of these sweeping changes, the structure and process of contemporary juvenile justice systems have come to resemble those of adult criminal justice systems. Nonetheless, elements of *parens patriae* authority and the rehabilitative ideal remain, preserving some level of distinction for juvenile justice systems.

Chapter 2 also described the most recent reform effort that seeks to incorporate a developmental approach into juvenile justice reform. A growing body of research on adolescent development has questioned the punitive posture of contemporary juvenile justice systems across the United States, as expressed in get-tough policies and practices. Spearheaded by the MacArthur Foundation through its Models for Change initiative, reform efforts seek "to make juvenile justice systems more fair, effective, rational and developmentally appropriate" (Models for Change, n.d.). Accordingly, the initiative contends that:

> the overarching goal of the juvenile justice system is to support the positive social development of youths who become involved in the system, and thereby assure the safety of communities. The specific aims of juvenile courts and affiliated agencies are to hold youths accountable for wrongdoing, prevent further offending, and treat youths fairly.[1]

> (National Research Council 2013: 4)

Eight areas of reform are targeted – see "Theory into practice: adolescent development and juvenile justice reform."

Theory into practice: adolescent development and juvenile justice reform

Models for Change: Systems Reform in Juvenile Justice is grounded in theory and research on adolescent development. Eight areas of reform are targeted according to the Models for Change website:

- **Aftercare:** In a model system, youth returning to the community after a period of residential placement would be quickly connected with the programs and services they need to adjust and succeed.
- **Community-based alternatives:** In a model system, responses to delinquency would be local and informal whenever possible, and all but a limited number of youth would be supervised, sanctioned, and treated in community settings.
- **Dual status youth:** A model system would provide the kind of coordinated, multi-system integration that improves outcomes for dual status youth, those youth that move between the child welfare and juvenile justice systems.

- **Evidence-based practices:** In a model system, programs, practices and services would be based on research, having demonstrated their effectiveness or shown a strong likelihood of success in improving juvenile offenders' behavior or skills.
- **Juvenile indigent defense:** A model system would safeguard the procedural and substantive rights of all youth who come into conflict with the law.
- **Mental health:** In a model system, professionals in the fields of juvenile justice, child welfare, mental health, substance abuse, and education would work collaboratively to meet the needs of youth without unnecessary system involvement.
- **Racial and ethnic fairness/disproportionate minority contact:** In a model system, youth would receive fair treatment regardless of their race or ethnicity.
- **Status offense reform:** A model system would provide strategies to safely and effectively divert non-delinquent youth from the formal juvenile justice system.

Source: Models for Change (n.d.). Retrieved March 3, 2015 (www.modelsforchange. net/about/Issues-for-change.html).

Within the context of such juvenile justice transformation, this chapter describes contemporary juvenile justice in terms of its structure and process – how the different elements of juvenile justice are organized and how they operate. In a formal sense, the juvenile justice system comprises police, courts, and corrections. However, as we will see, a substantial amount of juvenile delinquency is dealt with informally, sometimes by agencies not usually considered a part of the "system." We begin by describing how juvenile justice is really not a "system" at all, but rather a highly decentralized and fragmented array of both public and private agencies. Moreover, each element of juvenile justice exercises tremendous discretion and relies on diversion to operate efficiently. We then briefly describe juvenile justice process in terms of discretion, diversion, and disproportionate minority contact. The bulk of the chapter examines informal and formal procedures of contemporary juvenile justice systems: police, courts, and corrections.

Structure of juvenile justice systems: decentralized and fragmented

It may surprise you to learn that there is not a single juvenile justice system in the United States. Rather, each state has a separate juvenile justice system, and they are "systems" in only a limited sense. The various parts of these systems – police, courts, and corrections – are all operated by different levels and branches of government, and sometimes even by private organizations. For example, courts with jurisdiction over juvenile matters are a judicial entity, and they operate at the federal, state, and local levels, but there is not a single, standard structure to juvenile courts. In most states, juvenile courts operate within district courts (courts of original trial jurisdiction). However, some lower courts, such as city and municipal courts, have special or limited jurisdiction in juvenile cases. Juvenile traffic violations, for example, are often handled by these lower courts. The federal court system also deals with juvenile matters, usually at the district court level, but the number of juvenile cases dealt with by federal courts is minuscule compared to state juvenile courts. Thus, the juvenile justice system is said to be *decentralized*, operating at every level of government.

The juvenile justice system is also *fragmented* among the different branches of government. Each branch of government – legislative, judicial, and executive – plays an important role in juvenile justice. For example, laws are the foundation of juvenile justice systems. Under the United States Constitution, such laws are the responsibility of legislative bodies at all levels – local, state, and federal. The structure, jurisdiction, and authority of juvenile justice systems are primarily determined by state legislatures. For instance, the law that created the first juvenile court in Chicago was enacted by the Illinois legislature in 1899. Similarly, contemporary juvenile courts are legally authorized by state youth court acts. State and federal legislatures also pass codes that regulate people's actions (criminal codes) and establish procedures to be followed (procedural codes) when someone breaks the law. Thus, legislatures play a central role in juvenile justice, even though they do not actually operate juvenile justice agencies.

Table 14.1 shows the structural elements of juvenile justice in terms of their level and branch of government. As you can see, the various parts of juvenile justice systems are spread broadly among the different levels and branches of government, making them decentralized and fragmented. Let's look at a few of these components of juvenile justice systems. Beyond statutory law, legislative units also allocate funds for the different components of juvenile justice systems. Courts, including juvenile courts, are a judicial responsibility. Juvenile courts provide both informal and formal procedures to deal with delinquency cases that are referred to them. Appellate courts at both the state and federal levels have tremendous influence on juvenile justice process, establishing due process of law in juvenile matters. The executive branch of government is responsible for law enforcement, the operation of detention centers, prosecution, departments of corrections, and sometimes probation and parole. Probation and parole are perhaps the most structurally varied components of juvenile justice. Juvenile probation is often a judicial function, but in some states it is operated by the department of corrections. In addition, parole is sometimes administratively attached to probation, in which case both operate under the same governmental unit – either the courts or the department of correction. In other states, probation is a part of the juvenile court and parole is a part of the department of correction. What can you conclude? The decentralized and fragmented organizational structure of juvenile justice in the United States is extremely confusing!

Table 14.1 Juvenile justice structure: decentralized and fragmented

	Legislative	Judicial	Executive
Local	• Ordinances • Funding	• Courts of limited jurisdiction	• Law enforcement • Detention centers • Prosecution • Corrections
State	• Statutory law (criminal codes, youth court acts, procedural codes) • Funding	• Youth courts • Probation • Appellate courts	• Law enforcement • Detention centers • Prosecution • Corrections • Probation
Federal	• Statutory law (criminal codes, procedural codes) • Funding	• District courts • Probation • Appellate courts	• Law enforcement • Detention centers • Prosecution • Corrections

Juvenile justice process: discretion, diversion, and disproportionate minority contact

The structure and procedures of juvenile justice vary considerably from state to state and from community to community. Nevertheless, a fairly common process can be identified in most juvenile justice jurisdictions, as depicted in Figure 14.1.

Two features are key to the juvenile justice process in literally every jurisdiction throughout the country: discretion and diversion. Concerns regarding discretion and diversion in contemporary juvenile justice are expressed most concertedly in widespread efforts to reduce disproportionate minority contact at the major decision points in juvenile justice systems.

Discretion and diversion

Well-known legal scholar Roscoe Pound (1960: 926) defined **discretion** as "authority conferred by law to act in certain conditions or situations in accordance with an official's or an official agency's considered judgment and conscience." Although discretion is usually discussed with regard to decision-making by the police, virtually all decisions in the juvenile justice process carry with them wide-ranging discretion. We will continually refer to this authority and latitude in decision-making as we describe the structure and process of juvenile justice.

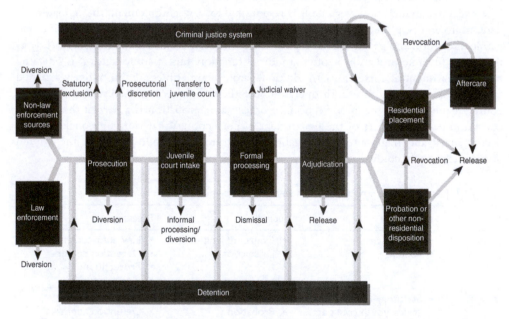

Figure 14.1 The juvenile justice process. The major decision points in this process are: (1) arrest, (2) referral to court, (3) diversion (at multiple points in the process), (4) secure detention, (5) judicial waiver to adult criminal court, (6) case petitioning, (7) delinquency finding/adjudication, (8) probation, and (9) residential placement, including confinement in a secure correctional facility.

Source: OJJDP *Statistical Briefing Book.* Juvenile Justice System Structure and Process, Case Flow Diagram. Retrieved May 28, 2014 (www.ojjdp.gov/ojstatbb/structure_process/case.html).

A second prevalent feature of the juvenile justice process is diversion. **Diversion** is the tendency of juvenile justice systems to deal with juvenile matters informally, without formal processing and adjudication, by referring cases to special programs and agencies inside or outside the juvenile justice system. Police officers commonly divert some cases to special programs within the department or to a variety of community resources such as family counseling and drug treatment. Probation officers, when screening cases that have been referred to the juvenile court, have legal authority to decide whether cases should be dealt with formally or informally. Informal handling may involve a diversionary referral to a community treatment option. Prosecutors can choose not to petition a case and instead to provide for some informal handling of a case, often involving a referral to community resources.

Disproportionate minority contact

Chapter 2 described the juvenile justice reforms that were initiated by passage of the Juvenile Justice and Delinquency Prevention (JJDP) Act of 1974. The JJDP Act authorized federal grant funding for juvenile justice system reform efforts at the state and local levels (Crank 1995). Foremost was reform in the use of secure detention in four problematic areas: (1) eliminate the use of detention for status offenders who commit offenses such as running away, truancy, and disregard of parents (incorrigibility); (2) separate detained juveniles from adult offenders being held in jails; (3) remove juveniles from adult jail facilities; and (4) reduce the disproportionate rate of minority confinement (Sickmund and Puzzanchera 2014: 87; Shepherd 1999; Crank 1995).

The 1988 amendment to the JJDP Act required states receiving grant funds through the Act to address disproportionate minority confinement – to "develop and implement plans to reduce the proportion of minority youth detained or confined in secure detention facilities, secure correctional facilities, jails, and lockups if they exceeded the percentage of minority youth in the general population" (OJJDP 2012: 1). With a growing recognition that that disparity is not limited to secure confinement and that it may occur at multiple decision points across the juvenile justice process, "DMC" was expanded in the 2002 amendment to the JJDP Act to include not only disproportionate minority *confinement*, but to encompass disproportionate minority *contact* throughout the system. "This change required participating states to address juvenile delinquency prevention efforts and systems improvement efforts designed to reduce the disproportionate number of juvenile members of minority groups who come in contact with the juvenile justice system" (Sickmund and Puzzanchera 2014: 175; see also OJJDP 2012; Leiber, Bishop, and Chamlin 2011).

Disproportionate minority contact (DMC) can be assessed at nine key contact points in the juvenile justice process: (1) arrest, (2) referral to court, (3) diversion, (4) secure detention, (5) judicial waiver to adult criminal court, (6) case petitioning, (7) delinquency finding/adjudication, (8) probation, and (9) residential placement, including confinement in a secure correctional facility (see Figure 14.1; Sickmund and Puzzanchera 2014: 175). DMC can be measured in various ways, most commonly by comparing proportions or using rates (DSG n.d.: 6). States receiving federal grant funds are required to measure DMC using the *relative rate index* (RRI). "The RRI compares the rates of processing for minority youth to the rates of processing for white youth. The RRI method describes the volume of activity from one contact point to the next and how it differs between white and minority youth" (DSG n.d.: 7). Calculation of the RRI results in a ratio that compares the minority rate at each decision point to that of white youth. An RRI value near or equal to 1.0 indicates little or no evidence of disparity, whereas values above and below 1.0 indicate more or less disparity as compared to white youth (Sickmund and Puzzanchera 2014; Leiber et al. 2011).

Empirical research on DMC has been conducted at both the national and state level. Several general findings are apparent:

- **Racial disparity.** National and state studies have consistently found minority youth to be over-represented across the points of contact in the juvenile justice process (for reviews of this literature see DSG n.d.; Kempf-Leonard 2007; Bishop 2005; Pope and Leiber 2005; Engen, Steen, and Bridges 2002; Pope, Lovell, and Hsia, 2002; see also Leiber et al. 2011).
- **Disparity across decision points.** "In most jurisdictions, disproportionate minority representation is not limited to secure detention and confinement; disparity is evident at nearly all key decision points throughout the juvenile justice system" (Sickmund and Puzzanchera 2014: 175; see also Davis and Sorenson 2013; Leiber et al. 2011; DSG n.d.). No state, however, showed consistent DMC for a particular minority group throughout all decision points (Davis and Sorenson 2013: 118). Furthermore, disparity is greatest at the earliest stages of the juvenile justice process (arrest and intake) and smallest at judicial disposition (Sickmund and Puzzanchera 2014; Leiber et al. 2011; Hartney and Vuong 2009).
- **Early disparity affects later decisions.** As youth proceed through the system, disparate treatment at early stages produces disparity at later stages (Sickmund and Puzzanchera 2014: 175). For example, Rodriguez (2010) found that youth who were detained were more likely to be petitioned into juvenile court, and subsequently more likely to be removed from the home at disposition than youth who were not detained.

Two contrasting explanations have been offered regarding DMC: the *differential offending hypothesis* and the *differential treatment hypothesis*. The differential offending hypothesis contends that minority youth are over-represented at each step of the juvenile justice process because they commit more frequent and more serious offenses, and they have more prior contacts with the juvenile justice system than do white youth. In this explanation, legal factors are the primary influence on decision points in the juvenile justice process. The differential treatment hypothesis asserts that minority youth are dealt with more formally and more harshly than white youth. Differential handling of minority youth by the juvenile justice system is the focal point in this explanation. The bulk of research evidence on these competing explanations of DMC shows persistent racial disparities after accounting for differences pertaining to legal factors. In their meta-analysis of prior state assessment studies, Pope and Leiber (2005) found that race continued to contribute to DMC even after considering legal factors in 32 of the 44 studies they reviewed (see also DSG n.d.).

As a tool of technical assistance to states, the Office of Juvenile Justice and Delinquency Prevention (OJJDP) has developed a five-stage process to reduce DMC (OJJDP 2012: 3, 4; DSG n.d.: 3; see also Cabaniss et al. 2007).[2]

1. **Identify the extent to which DMC exists.** States calculate disproportionality at nine contact points in the juvenile justice system using the relative rate index (RRI). The RRI measures the disparity at each point in terms of volume and methods of handing cases.

2. **Assess the reasons for DMC.** Assess the possible influences on any disparity observed across the contact points. Use relevant data and information to determine the degree to which these influences effect disparity.

3. **Develop an intervention plan to address DMC.** Implement appropriate delinquency prevention and systems improvement:

> Effective prevention and intervention activities include diversion, alternatives to secure confinement, advocacy, and training and technical assistance on cultural competency with youth and staffing practices. Systems improvement activities include advocating for legislative reforms; making administrative policy, and procedural changes; and implementing structured decisionmaking tools at various contact points within the juvenile justice system.
>
> (OJJDP 2012: 2)

4. **Evaluate the effectiveness of interventions.** Develop and conduct systematic, objective evaluation of the prevention and intervention activities. Assess system changes.

5. **Monitor DMC trends.** Consider demographic changes that might affect DMC rates and assess changes in DMC rates. Make adjustments to intervention strategies.

Policing juveniles

Juveniles constitute a unique population that poses a special set of challenges for the police (Walker and Katz 2005; Gaines 2003). First, police have frequent contact with juveniles. In 2011, police made nearly 1.5 million arrests of juveniles nationwide, but this number represents only a fraction of all police–juvenile encounters, many of which never result in arrest (Puzzanchera 2013). Nonetheless, juveniles account for a significant portion of the crime problem. Second, law enforcement with juveniles includes a broad array of offenses, ranging from status offenses to violent crime. Third, police commonly view juvenile delinquency as minor crime, and "taking a youth into custody" is often considered not a "real arrest." Fourth, police are often expected to take an approach with juveniles that involves prevention, protection, and rehabilitation, while at the same time they are expected to enforce the law. A report on police work with juveniles captures this dilemma: "crime prevention can be viewed as 'social work,' a role that police often see as taking time away from what they consider to be their primary role – the apprehension of criminals" (Walker and Katz 2005: 253). Fifth, juveniles must be processed through a justice system that is different from the adult system in philosophy, jurisdiction, structure, and process. This is unfamiliar terrain for many officers. Moreover, some police have little support for a system that they view as pandering – one that does not hold youth accountable for their actions. Because of this, some police officers have little interest in working with juveniles. The feeling is apparently mutual, because much research indicates that most high school students are lukewarm in their attitudes toward police (Walker and Katz 2005: 253).

Most police departments of at least moderate size have specialized juvenile units to deal with juveniles and delinquency. Criminologist Larry Gaines (2003: 286) describes the reason why juvenile units within police departments are so common.

> Although most of a department's contact with juveniles is by patrol officers, juvenile officers generally process youth who are placed in custody and coordinate programs

designed to reduce juvenile delinquency. Departments developed juvenile units because often juvenile cases are complex and many patrol officers do not remain familiar with how juvenile cases are processed. Juvenile courts have implemented specific rules to protect the juvenile, and these rules are quite different from criminal procedures. The juvenile unit maintains all files relating to juvenile cases and works with other officers in presenting their cases in juvenile court. This unit is generally housed in the criminal investigation or detective division within the department.[3]

Cops and kids: the police role

Police role refers to the expectations associated with the position of police officer. It must be noted, however, that there is much controversy over the proper police role toward juveniles.[4] "Some people favor a strict law enforcement role, emphasizing the arrest of offenders. Others prefer a crime prevention role, arguing that the police should emphasize helping young people who are at risk with advice, counseling, and alternatives to arrest" (Walker and Katz 2005: 253). Police officers sometimes struggle with the apparently inconsistent expectations of their work, believing that their primary duty is to fight crime by apprehending criminals, while at the same time they must also assist others and provide services to the public. Such role conflict can make police work difficult to manage for some individual officers and for departments as a whole. This inconsistency in role expectations seems especially pertinent to the policing of juveniles. In addition, unclear and undefined departmental policies regarding juveniles create further confusion for police officers.

Parens patriae *policing: the original protective role*

Historically, police have been viewed as an extension of the juvenile court. In fact, police officers comprised a substantial portion of the staff of the first juvenile court in Chicago, removing many distinctions between the enforcement and adjudication of laws (Wolcott 2005; Platt 1977). Although these officers were assigned to assist probation officers in supervision, their authority was derived from the court's *parens patriae* doctrine, and their role was consistent with the rehabilitative ideal that came to dominate juvenile justice. As an extension of the juvenile court, police were to deal with juveniles in an informal, parent-like fashion, acting in the "best interests of the child" (Feld 1999; Platt 1977). Recall from Chapter 2 that the early juvenile justice system was deliberately established to operate as a child-welfare system, not as a judicial system (Feld 1999). This **protective role** was adopted extensively by the police, giving them broad discretion in dealing with juveniles. In fact, the legal distinction between "taking into custody" and adult arrest was created to signify the protective approach that police traditionally have taken with juveniles. Under authority of statutory law, **taking into custody** involves gaining control of a youth, much like in an arrest, but for protective purposes; this is sometimes referred to as *protective custody*. If the police officer believes that the youth is in need of protection or has violated the law, the police officer may take control of the youth and remove the youth from his or her surroundings. This can be accomplished by physical control or by voluntary submission of the youth. The youth may be placed in the back of the squad car, told to sit in a chair in the waiting area of the police station, or placed in a holding cell. Taking into custody may or may not involve placement in a detention facility.

The degree to which individual police officers and police departments adopted this protective role is a matter of debate (Wolcott 2005; Gains 2003). Nonetheless, the protective origins of the police role established broad discretion for police in dealing with juveniles, and this discretion was exercised in a wide range of police activities related to juveniles, from prevention education and truancy reduction in school to investigation of criminal activity and arrest. Sociologists refer to this broad range of activities and expectations associated with a given position as *role diversity*, and such role diversity aptly characterizes juvenile policing.

Professional policing: the crime-fighting role

Beginning in the early 1920s, during the historical period of policing known as the Reform Era, a movement emerged that significantly influenced juvenile policing, both in terms of its structure and role (Fogelson 1977; Kelling and Moore 1988). Referred to as *professional policing*, this movement produced at least two important innovations in policing. First, bureaucratic structure and authority were implemented in local police departments across the United States (Lewett 1975). Police organization and management became more hierarchical, involving a chain and unit of command. Bureaucratic policing also resulted in specialization, in which different units performed special tasks simultaneously. Besides the creation of patrol, detective, and vice divisions, juvenile units were put in place in most medium and large police departments. Second, the protective role of policing juveniles was to a great degree replaced with the **crime-fighting role**. Enforcement of laws and crime control became the primary interest of local police. The relationship between the police and public was redefined, with the police being portrayed as the "thin blue line" that protected the lives and property of a passive and dependent public. Although the protective role of the police was not out of line with the notion of the "thin blue line," youth who formerly were viewed as dependent and at risk, requiring police protection, now began to be viewed as juvenile suspects who were most likely to violate the law.

Professional policing relied on three innovations to fight crime: motorized preventive patrol, the doctrine of rapid response to calls for emergency service, and reactive investigation of crime (Moore, Trojanowicz, and Kelling 1988). These innovations transformed the activities of police from *proactive* law enforcement to *reactive* law enforcement. The image of professional policing that emerged was that of a well-organized, tough-minded, highly trained crime fighter. Thus "professional policing" became synonymous with bureaucratic structure and authority within police departments and with the crime-fighting role.

Beginning in the mid-1960s, the due process revolution in juvenile justice introduced a variety of procedural requirements in law enforcement that can be viewed as either a limitation on crime fighting or an enhancement of professional policing. Some police officers believed that due process requirements limited their abilities to gain evidence and statements, making arrest less likely; other officers, especially supervising officers, believed that procedural requirements actually enhanced professional policing by requiring officers to know the law and to enforce it in a standardized and objective fashion. Regardless of the point of view, the introduction of due process into juvenile policing substantially reduced the protective role of police, while emphasizing the importance and quality of arrest.

Community-oriented policing: the collaborative role

Beginning in the 1960s, research, public sentiment, and changing views among the police themselves began to raise questions about professional policing. In response, community-oriented policing (COP) was born, representing a significant change in the philosophy, structure, and authority of law enforcement, especially in terms of policing juveniles (Goldstein 1990). At least four developments spurred the growth of community-oriented policing (Moore et al. 1988). First, mounting research evidence in the 1960s and 1970s showed that the strategies of professional policing were largely unsuccessful. Under scrutiny were professional policing's key strategies of motorized patrol, rapid response, and reactive investigation (Kelling 1988). Second, administrators and researchers became much more aware of role diversity in law enforcement. Despite the popularity of the crime-fighting role, it became obvious that the police role was far more diverse and included aspects of protection, public safety, order maintenance, and service. Third, the preoccupation with bureaucratic organization and the crime-fighting role seriously failed to fulfill its promises of managerial efficiency and crime control. Fourth, a long history of problematic relationships between the police and the public was worsened by the crime-fighting role when its strategies failed to control the crime problem.

Community-oriented policing is made up of four basic elements: (1) community crime prevention, (2) reorientation of patrol activities to emphasize service and public order, (3) increased accountability to the public, and (4) decentralization of command through the creation of neighborhood police centers (Moore et al. 1988). Under community-oriented policing, it is assumed that the police cannot fight crime effectively without the public's cooperation and involvement. As a result, the crime-fighting role began to be viewed as inadequate to prevent and control crime. In contrast, the **collaborative role** emphasizes that police are to engage the public in order to cooperatively prevent crime, maintain public order, and solve community problems.

To varying degrees, most police departments have incorporated the ideas of community-oriented policing, which has affected how they deal with juveniles and juvenile crime (Gaines 2003: 289; Hickman and Reaves 2001). The community-oriented policing role includes police efforts to foster relationships with neighborhood youth in order to prevent crime and maintain order. This role has been implemented most extensively through school resource officer (SRO) programs. Officers are assigned to schools (usually junior high and high schools) and provide a number of services to the school, including crime-related education in the classroom, crime prevention by walking the halls and outside the school building, and investigation of crimes on or near campus. The underlying strategy is to develop relationships with students and school personnel in an effort to prevent crime and to respond to crime committed by students:

> One of the important functions of an SRO program is for the police and schools to advise each other about criminal behavior involving students ... Historically, the police and schools have not communicated, which has led to a number of problems when students commit crimes on campus. SRO programs not only link the police with schools, they allow juvenile units to collect better information about delinquents who may be violent, possess weapons, or deal in drugs.
>
> (Gaines 2003: 287–289)

The SRO is primarily a collaborator between police, the schools, families, and the community. Thus, SRO programs provide crime prevention, order maintenance, and problem-solving collaboration between police and students, families, and school staff.

Getting tough: the law-enforcer role

Beginning in the early 1980s, the "get tough" approach to crime introduced a **law–enforcer role** for police, even as community-oriented policing was emerging in law enforcement. Greater attention has been given to public safety and holding juvenile offenders accountable for violations of law. As a result, contemporary juvenile policing is increasingly characterized by the law-enforcer role, emphasizing vigorous enforcement of laws, both criminal laws and status offense laws. Reflecting this, the legal distinction between taking into custody and arrest in statutory law has been reduced in some states, authorizing police to arrest juveniles just as adults.

Perhaps the clearest example of the contemporary law-enforcer role in juvenile policing lies in the increasing tendency of police to deal formally with juveniles taken into custody through a "referral to juvenile court" or "referral to adult criminal court." Consequently, police are also far less likely to deal informally with juveniles taken into custody through what is known as "warn and release." Figure 14.2 shows that in the early 1970s almost half of all juveniles taken into custody were handled informally within police departments and then released. In recent years, however, this has been true for only about one fifth of all juveniles that the police have taken into custody. In contrast, over two-thirds of all juveniles taken into

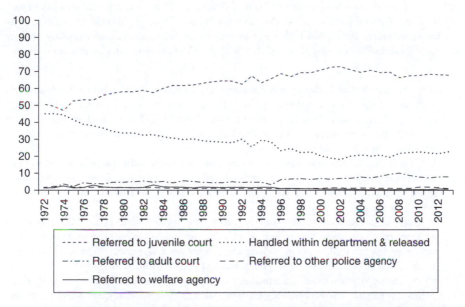

Figure 14.2 Method of handling juveniles taken into custody, 1972–2013. Over this period, local police have shown an increasing tendency to deal formally with juveniles taken into custody through "referral to juvenile court" or "referral to adult criminal court," and a decreasing tendency to deal informally with juveniles taken into custody by handling them within the department and then releasing them – a practice commonly referred to as "warn and release."

Sources: University at Albany, Hindelang Criminal Justice Research Center (2013: Table 4.26.2011). Retrieved February 19, 2015 (www.albany.edu/sourcebook/pdf/t4262011.pdf). Federal Bureau of Investigation (2013, 2014: Table 68). Retrieved January 8, 2015 (www.fbi.gov/about-us/cjis/ucr/crime-in-the-u.s).

custody are now referred to juvenile court, and a small but increasing portion are referred to adult criminal court. These trends in handling juveniles taken into custody are a clear indication of a shift in law enforcement efforts toward greater accountability and public safety.

Is the law-enforcer role beginning to wane? The Models for Change initiative, sponsored by the MacArthur Foundation, advocates a developmental model of juvenile justice reform. Reform efforts are portrayed as "system reforms," seeking to generate change across juvenile justice systems – from police to courts to corrections. These efforts are based on a growing body of knowledge on adolescent development and, corresponding to that, appropriate juvenile justice strategies and techniques (Models for Change n.d.). How might the developmental model of juvenile justice reform impact the police role with juveniles? "Theory into practice: ten strategies to improve law enforcement interactions with youth" describes tactics offered by the International Association of Chiefs of Police for police interaction with youth.

Theory into practice: ten strategies to improve law enforcement interactions with youth

The "developmental approach to juvenile justice reform" seeks to foster positive youth development in all phases of juvenile justice, including law enforcement (National Research Council 2013). The International Association of Chiefs of Police (IACP) has recently offered a brief guide called "The Effects of Adolescent Development on Policing." The guide seeks to facilitate positive law enforcement interaction with youth by promoting police officer understanding of "why teenagers think and act the way they do" (IACP 2015). Here are ten strategies that are offered.

1. Approach youth with a calm demeanor, conveying that you are there to help them. Aggression may cause the youth to shut down and make the situation worse. Refrain from pushing back (arguing). If necessary, de-escalate using a calm, focused, and non-confrontational verbal approach. Use a nonjudgmental tone. Youth are particularly attune to both verbal and non-verbal judgment from adults.

2. Establish rapport. Developing rapport is fundamental to successful youth interactions. They are not likely to open up if they feel unsupported or uncomfortable. Give them your undivided attention. Convey that you want to listen and can be trusted. Listen openly and non judgmentally.

3. Be patient. Don't act hurried, like you don't have time to talk with the youth. Give the youth a chance to ask questions and be honest with your responses. Convey that you want to hear what they have to say. Give them a chance to explain what happened. Build in extra time to assess their emotions and to work around blocked thinking due to emotion.

4. Model the respect you expect in return. Avoid criticism and lecture. Refer to them by name as much as possible. Avoid correcting them or making statements that may communicate disrespect. You may lessen their aggression and defiance by demonstrating respect and support for their autonomy, views, and choices.

5. Use age-appropriate language. Adolescents do not have adult capacity to organize thoughts. They may not fully understand what you tell them and may need time to process information. Keep it simple. Use open-ended questions and be prepared to help them sort out information. Don't expect a long attention span.

6. Repeat or paraphrase their statements. Affirm their emotions. Seek clarity and understanding through the use of these three methods. Repeating what they say gives you a chance to

confirm you heard what they said. Paraphrasing shows them you are listening. Affirming their emotions (e.g., You're frustrated with your parents) shows them genuine interest.

7. Take caution with nonverbal communication. Avoid challenging gestures. Approach youth in a natural manner, not actively seeking or avoiding eye contact. Don't demand eye contact. Convey your warmth over your authority. Get on their level (e.g., sit if they are sitting), lean in when listening, and hold your arms and body in a relaxed manner.

8. Model and praise calm confidence. Adolescents seek validation and praise while acting indifferent towards it. They act confident, even when feeling self-doubt. They tend to be most calm and cooperative when provided with adult modeling and sincere praise for their ability to make good decisions.

9. Empower them through choices. Adolescents need to feel they have choice and control over their thoughts and actions. They are sensitive to external influence and likely to feel coerced, even when there is no explicit effort to coerce them. Yet, they rely on others to validate their decisions. Provide them a range of options and explain their choices in simple terms. Give them a chance to ask questions.

10. Serve as a positive adult role model. Positive relationships with adults are a vital component of healthy youth development. Develop programs in your agency that focus on positive youth development, such as mentoring, job skills.

Discretion and diversion in juvenile law enforcement

Regardless of changes in the police role toward juveniles, it is local police (municipal and county) that have most frequent contact with juveniles. State and federal law enforcement officers have comparatively few encounters with youth. Local patrol officers are typically the first point of contact with juveniles in everyday activities and with juveniles suspected of crime. State statutory laws provide authority to police officers to stop and talk to individuals and to investigate suspicious situations and crime incidents. These laws also give police officers arrest authority and authority to take a youth into custody. The application of this statutory law enforcement authority gives police officers broad, wide-ranging discretion.

As we saw in Figure 14.2, police show a decreasing tendency to deal informally with juveniles that are taken into custody. Instead, referral to juvenile court has become far more common. However, it should be noted that these data report only those juveniles who were "taken into custody." Those contacts that were dealt with by the police in a more informal manner are not reported. We are left to speculate about the proportion of police contacts that do not result in a youth being taken into custody. We get a sense of how police respond to juveniles they come into contact with in an old but classic study by David Bordua (1967). Bordua found that in a one-year period (1964) the Detroit police had 106,000 encounters with juveniles. Only 9 percent (9,445) of these were classified as "official contacts" by the police, resulting in formal enforcement action. Bordua concluded that a majority of police–juvenile contacts are dealt with informally and never result in official action, such as issuing a ticket or citation, taking the youth into custody, or referring the youth to juvenile court (see also Piliavin and Briar 1964; Goldman 1963). Assuming that these findings are still relevant to contemporary policing, a substantial portion of all police encounters with juveniles are dealt with informally, rather than through formal referral to the juvenile court.

Informal handling of juveniles by the police involves a number of diversionary approaches intended to keep youth out of the juvenile justice system, including:

- Warn and release at the scene – a "street adjustment."
- Take the youth into custody, but release the youth to the parents at the police station – a "station house adjustment."
- Refer the case to a juvenile officer or juvenile unit within the department for further investigation or for involvement in an intervention program operated by the police department. Such referral may or may not involve taking the youth into custody.
- Refer the youth to community-based services, such as a youth services bureau, school, or church. Like in-house referrals, community-based referral may or may not involve taking the youth into custody.
- Refer the case to a child protective service agency for services, family intervention, or dependency and neglect investigation (Krisberg and Austin 1978: 83).

Whether taking a youth into custody involves the use of secure detention is also a discretionary decision. Police usually begin the initial detention decision. In most states, the decision for detention requires that the officer inform or request authorization from the probation department and provide a written report that specifies why the officer believes the youth must be held in detention. After initial authorization, statutory law typically requires that a detention hearing be held within a set time period, often within 24 hours (Sickmund and Puzzanchera 2014). The detention decision is based on the consideration of whether the youth poses a risk to him- or herself or others and whether detention is needed to ensure the youth's appearance at upcoming court hearings.

Police discretion involves much broader authority than just decisions regarding whether to take a youth into custody or make an arrest and whether to detain the youth. Patrol officers make decisions regarding where, when, and how intensely to patrol; whether to engage in high-speed pursuit; whether to stop, question, or frisk a suspect; and how much force to use in implementing an arrest. Detectives and juvenile officers make decisions related to criminal investigation, including how vigorously to investigate the case; whom to talk to; and whether to conduct surveillance, seek a warrant, or involve other police investigative agencies. Additionally, police administrators have discretion in the style of law enforcement that they encourage among their officers, the type of crimes they emphasize for enforcement, and the degree to which they emphasize supervision and accountability of officers.

Factors influencing the use of discretion

Police officers consciously or unconsciously consider a number of factors when deciding how to handle juveniles suspected of crime. Research reveals several key factors that influence police discretion:

- **Seriousness of the offense.** Perhaps the most obvious factor influencing police discretion is the seriousness of the offense. More serious offenses are more likely to lead to formal handling, including taking into custody, arrest, and referral to the juvenile court. The more serious the offense, the less police discretion is exercised. However, because a majority of all police–juvenile contacts relate to minor offenses in which the probability of arrest is very low, police discretion is extensive in juvenile matters (Gaines 2003; Lundman, Sykes, and Clark 1978; Black and Reiss 1970; Terry 1967; Piliavin and Briar 1964; Sellin and Wolfgang 1964.

- **Previous contact with the police and prior arrest.** Research documents consistently that previous contact with the police, as well as prior arrest record, influence the chance of arrest. Youths with more frequent and serious prior offenses are more likely to be arrested (Lattimore, Visher, and Linster 1995; Cohen and Kluegel 1978; Cicourel 1968; Terry 1967; Piliavin and Briar 1964; Sellin and Wolfgang 1964).

- **Attitude and demeanor of the juvenile.** The attitude and demeanor of the youth are especially important in police encounters with juveniles. One study found that 53 percent of the youths who were cooperative with the police were warned and released, and only 4 percent were arrested. In contrast, only 5 percent of the uncooperative youths were warned and released, and 67 percent were arrested (Klinger 1994; Lundman 1994, 1996; Cicourel 1968; Goldman 1963; Piliavin and Briar 1964; Sellin and Wolfgang 1964).

- **Social characteristics of the juvenile.** Race, gender, and social class appear to enter into the mix of factors considered by police officers in making discretionary decisions. However, these characteristics cannot be studied in isolation from other factors that influence discretion. The effect that any one of these characteristics has on police decision-making depends on other factors. For example, although some studies find that race significantly influences discretion, other studies indicate that race must be considered in conjunction with legal factors, such as seriousness of the offense and prior record (Sealock and Simpson 1998; Lundman 1996; Riksheim and Chermak 1993; Bishop and Frazier 1988, 1992; Fagan, Slaughter, and Hartstone 1987; Dannefer and Schutt 1982; Smith and Visher 1981; Thornberry 1979; Cohen and Kluegel 1978; Black and Reiss 1970; Ferdinand and Luchtenhand 1970; Terry 1967).

- **Source and attitude of the complainant.** A classic study of police discretion found that over three-quarters of all police–juvenile contacts resulted from citizen complaints, rather than by officer initiation. The preferences of the complainant influenced the likelihood of arrest: if a citizen initiated the complaint, remained involved, and wanted the juvenile to be arrested, the likelihood of arrest increased, compared to situations in which an officer initiated contact (Black and Reiss 1970; see also Goldman 1963; Terry 1967).

- **Community characteristics.** Various community characteristics appear to affect police discretion. Some research points to an "ecological bias" in police control of juveniles in which police are more likely to arrest juveniles in lower-class areas, in contrast to middle and upper-class areas (Sampson 1986; see also Smith, Visher, and Davidson 1984).

- **The availability of community alternatives to arrest** is of special importance regarding police discretion with juveniles. The more diversionary alternatives are available in the community, the less likely the officer is to take the youth into custody or arrest. Officers are more likely to arrest when they think that nothing else can be done (Smith and Klein 1984).

- **Organizational structures and enforcement policies of police departments.** Police departments vary extensively in how they are organized and in their enforcement policies (Wilson 1968a, 1968b). Departments that are highly bureaucratic seek to limit officer discretion through a hierarchical authority structure and through extensive rules and

regulations (Smith 1984). In contrast, departments that adopt community-oriented policing practices stress the importance of police–community cooperation in preventing and
controlling crime and delinquency. Community-oriented policing is usually decentralized,
with the use of neighborhood police stations or precincts. This organizational structure
provides much discretion to officers in their contact with local citizens, including juveniles.

Due process in juvenile law enforcement

Though police discretion in juvenile matters is broad and extensive, it is not unbridled.
During the 1960s and 1970s, the due process revolution in juvenile justice addressed several
key law enforcement methods. Drawn into question was whether constitutionally protected
due process rights apply to juveniles in a system and process that is intentionally protective
and rehabilitative in nature, operating in "the best interests of the child." Also of concern was
whether the due process revolution, as advanced by state and federal appellate courts, is binding on local law enforcement practices with juveniles. Three methods of law enforcement
have been addressed most extensively by state and federal appellate court decisions: (1) search
and seizure, (2) arrest, and (3) custodial interrogation.

Search and seizure

The Fourth Amendment to the U.S. Constitution protects citizens from unauthorized **search
and seizure**. Law enforcement may be authorized to conduct searches and to seize evidence
through warrants that are issued by courts. Warrants are based on probable cause – the reasoned conclusion, drawn from knowledge and facts, that a particular person committed a
particular crime.[5] The outcome of police violations of "unreasonable search and seizure," as
specified in the Fourth Amendment, is a case law doctrine called the *exclusionary rule*, which
requires that illegally obtained evidence be ruled inadmissible in a court of law. With several
significant exceptions, the Fourth Amendment prohibits search and seizure without a valid
search warrant.

In *State v. Lowry* (1967), the Supreme Court considered whether Fourth Amendment protections against unreasonable search and seizure apply to juveniles. The Court first acknowledged that the juvenile justice system is distinct in purpose, in that it attempts to protect and
reform youth who are dependent and at risk. Does a system that pursues "the best interests of the child" have to extend due process rights? In particular, do juveniles have Fourth
Amendment rights? The Court responded in the form of additional questions:

> Is it not more outrageous for the police to treat children more harshly than adult offend-
> ers, especially when such is in violation of due process and fair treatment? Can a court
> countenance a system, where, as here, an adult may suppress evidence with the usual
> effect of having the charges dropped for lack of proof, and on the other hand a juvenile
> be institutionalized – lose the most sacred possession a human being has, his freedom –
> for "rehabilitative" purposes because the Fourth Amendment right is unavailable to him?[6]

Without question, the Court ruled that juveniles have the right of protection from unreasonable search and seizure.

A juvenile's right against unreasonable search and seizure is conditioned in the school context, however, where school safety takes priority. In the 1985 landmark decision *New Jersey v. T.L.O.*, the Supreme Court ruled that school officials can search students and their possessions if the students are suspected of violating school rules.[7] In this case, a 14-year-old high school freshman was observed smoking in a school lavatory by a teacher. When the assistant vice-principal confronted her, she denied that she had been smoking and claimed that she did not smoke at all. The assistant vice-principal opened her purse and found a pack of cigarettes and a package of cigarette rolling papers, commonly used to smoke marijuana. Upon more thorough search of the purse, he found some marijuana, a pipe, a list of students who owed the young woman money, and two letters implicating her in marijuana dealing. Based on the need for schools to provide a safe and secure learning environment, this case grants school officials search and seizure authority beyond that of the police. In addition, evidence seized by school officials can be turned over to the police for use in their own criminal investigation (Hemmens, Steiner, and Mueller 2004).

Arrest

Most states do not have specific statutory provisions distinguishing the arrest of juveniles from the arrest of adults. Even when states maintain the legal distinction between "taking into custody" and arrest, the protective purpose of taking a youth into custody has diminished in recent years. In practice, taking into custody has come to mean almost the same as arrest. In fact, the due process rights applied to a youth taken into custody are very similar to those applied to juveniles who are arrested (see "Case in point: statutory authorization for taking a youth into custody").

Case in point: statutory authorization for taking a youth into custody

41-5-331. Rights of youth taken into custody – questioning – waiver of rights. (1) When a youth is taken into custody for questioning upon a matter that could result in a petition alleging that the youth is either a delinquent youth or a youth in need of intervention, the following requirements must be met:

(a)   The youth must be advised of the youth's right against self-incrimination and the youth's right to counsel.

(b)   The investigating officer, probation officer, or person assigned to give notice shall immediately notify the parents, guardian, or legal custodian of the youth that the youth has been taken into custody, the reasons for taking the youth into custody, and where the youth is being held. If the parents, guardian, or legal custodian cannot be found through diligent efforts, a close relative or friend chosen by the youth must be notified ...

Source: *Montana Code Annotated 2014.*

As we have seen, the police have very broad arrest authority because of the protective origins of juvenile policing and because of the extended range of juvenile offenses, particularly status offenses. Authority for arrest is granted in state statutory law (see "Case in point: statutory authorization for arrest"). **Arrest** involves the deprivation of an individual's freedom by a person of authority on the grounds that there is probable cause to believe that the individual has committed a criminal offense (Ferdico 1993). Arrest is purposive: to protect the public and to initiate a legal response to the suspected crime. The legality of arrest lies in the Fourth Amendment's "right against unreasonable ... seizures." The seizure that is specified refers to both property and people; therefore, the requirement of a warrant applies to arrest as well as to searches. However, just as there are exceptions to the constitutional requirement for search warrants, so, too, are there exceptions to the requirement that arrests be accomplished through the use of warrants (Ferdico 1993).

Case in point: statutory authorization for arrest

46-6-104. Method of arrest. (1) An arrest is made by an actual restraint of the person to be arrested or by the person's submission to the custody of the person making the arrest.

(2) All necessary and reasonable force may be used in making an arrest, but the person arrested may not be subject to any greater restraint than is necessary to hold or detain that person.

(3) All necessary and reasonable force may be used to effect an entry into any building or property or part thereof to make an authorized arrest.

Source: *Montana Code Annotated 2014.*

Use of force is the primary legal issue arising from arrest. Under Common Law tradition, most state statutes authorize that "all necessary and reasonable force may be used in making an arrest, but the person arrested may not be subjected to any greater restraint than is necessary to hold or detain that person" (see "Case in point: statutory authorization for arrest").[8] The defining Supreme Court case regarding use of deadly force involved a juvenile – a 15-year-old youth from Tennessee named Edward Garner. *Tennessee v. Garner* (1985) is a tragic case dealing with an officer's hard-pressed, spur-of-the-moment interpretation of "all necessary and reasonable force."[9] During a response to a burglary call, a Memphis police officer shot and killed a suspect attempting to flee. The officer ordered the suspect to stop, but he continued to flee over a fence. The suspect was later determined to be Edward Garner. The Supreme Court ruled that use of deadly force against an apparently unarmed and non-dangerous fleeing felon is an illegal seizure under the Fourth Amendment (Ferdico 1993: 135).

Custodial interrogation

Custodial interrogation has to do with police questioning of suspects while they are under arrest or when their freedom is restricted in a significant way. Two Constitutional Amendments are drawn into question with the practice of custodial interrogation: the Fifth Amendment's right against self-incrimination and the Sixth Amendment's right to counsel. These two fundamental rights were linked together for the first time in *Miranda v. Arizona* (1966), in which the Supreme Court ruled that in order to ensure the right against self-incrimination, it is necessary for the accused to have counsel.[10] The Miranda warning requires police to notify persons arrested that they have a right to remain silent and that any statements they make can and will be used against them; and that they have a right to counsel, and that if they cannot afford counsel, it will be provided at public expense. It should be noted, however, that Ernesto Miranda was 23 years old when he was charged with kidnapping and rape. Do these same rights apply to juveniles?

One year after the *Miranda* decision, the Supreme Court extended due process rights to juvenile court proceedings in the case *In re Gault* (1967).[11] However, the Court intentionally declined to address whether the right to counsel and the right against self-incrimination are guaranteed in pre-adjudication stages of juvenile justice, including police procedures with juveniles. Two earlier Supreme Court cases ruled that statements made by juveniles when under custodial interrogation must be considered in terms of the "totality of circumstances" – a variety of considerations including the absence of parents and lawyers, the age of the suspect, the length of questioning, and the approach used by officers.[12] In one of these cases, *Haley v. Ohio* (1948), five hours of apparently coercive interrogation, without parents or attorney present, led the Supreme Court to conclude:

> The age of the petitioner, the hours when he was grilled, the duration of his quizzing, the fact that he had no friend or counsel to advise him, the callous attitude of the police toward his rights combine to convince us that this was a confession wrung from a child by means which the law should not sanction. Neither man nor child can be allowed to stand condemned by methods which flout constitutional requirements of due process of law.[13]

After *Miranda*, the totality-of-circumstances standard was enhanced by the requirement that juveniles be given the Miranda warning by the police when questioning may extract incriminating statements. The critical question that follows is whether a juvenile is able to knowingly, intelligently, and voluntarily waive the rights stated in the Miranda warning. In most circumstances, a juvenile can waive Miranda rights only in the presence of parents or lawyers. In *California v. Prysock* (1981), the U.S. Supreme Court addressed the adequacy of the Miranda warning when it was paraphrased by a police officer to allow the youth to better understand the expressed rights.[14] The Court ruled that even though the Miranda warning was not given verbatim, its meaning was plain and easily understandable for a juvenile. Thus, an officer's attempt to make Miranda understandable for youth is permissible law enforcement practice.

Juvenile court processes: informal and formal

Police encounters with juveniles involve much discretion and rely heavily on diversion, and it is often said that the juvenile courts would collapse from the sheer number of cases referred by the police if such discretion and diversion did not exist. Even so, juvenile courts across the United States handled an estimated 1.24 million delinquency cases in 2011 (Hockenberry and Puzzanchera 2014a: 6). Juvenile courts, too, rely heavily on discretion and diversion – many cases are diverted or handled informally. The juvenile court process involves a series of discretionary decisions, including intake, petitioning, transfer to adult court, adjudication, and disposition.

Referral to juvenile court

The juvenile court process is initiated by a **referral** to the juvenile court. Referrals are written documents that request or result in court consideration of a particular juvenile matter. Referrals take various forms: police make referrals through incident reports, citations, and tickets; and parents, schools, and victims sign complaints. About 80 percnt of all delinquency referrals nationwide come from the police, almost always from local law enforcement (Sickmund and Puzzanchera 2014: 151). The remaining referrals come from probation officers, parents, schools, and victims. Compared to referrals of delinquency cases, police refer a smaller percentage of the status offense cases dealt with formally by the juvenile court. For example, in 2010, only 33 percent of the juvenile courts' truancy cases, 35 percent of the ungovernability cases, and 62 percent of the runaway cases were referred by the police (Sickmund and Puzzanchera 2014: 179). Status offense cases are more commonly referred by other entities such as schools, social welfare agencies, and relatives.

Delinquency cases in juvenile courts: extent, trends, age, gender, race

Table 14.2 shows that in 2011 almost 1.24 million delinquency cases were handled by juvenile courts across the United States. This represents a 34 percent decline in juvenile court caseloads from the peak year in 1997. When differences in the size of the juvenile population are taken into consideration by calculating an annual case rate per 1,000 juveniles, the resulting case rates increased by 46 percent between 1985 and 1996, and then declined by 39 percent through 2011 (Hockenberry and Puzzanchera 2014a: 8). The number of juvenile court cases declined between 2002 and 2011 for all types of delinquent offenses. Property offenses constituted the largest percentage of delinquency cases in 2011 at 36 percent; person offenses and public order offenses each comprised 26 percent of the juvenile court caseload, and drug violations comprised 12 percent (Hockenberry and Puzzanchera 2014a: 6–7).

Although 72 percent of all delinquency cases handled by juvenile courts in 2011 involved males, caseloads have grown at a faster rate for females than for males. During the period of greatest growth in juvenile court caseloads, 1985–1997, the female caseload grew by 98 percent, compared to a 53 percent increase for males (Hockenberry and Puzzanchera 2014a: 12). Also noteworthy is that two-thirds (64 percent) of all delinquency cases in juvenile courts involved white youth, while one-third (33 percent) involved black youth. However, a disproportionate number of delinquency cases involved black youth, given their proportion of the juvenile population (16 percent). American Indian (2 percent) and Asian (1 percent) youth constituted a very small portion of the delinquency cases in juvenile courts. In the ten-year period from 2002 to 2011, the percentage change in the number of delinquency cases decreased for all racial groups: −30 percent for white youth, −17 percent for black youth, −30 percent for American Indian youth, and −28 percent for Asian youth (Hockenberry and Puzzanchera 2014a: 18). Delinquency case rates also increase progressively with the referral age of the youth: 13-year-olds have a case rate of 27 per 1,000 juveniles, while 17-year-olds have a case rate of 91 per 1,000 juveniles (Hockenberry and Puzzanchera 2014a: 10).

Intake and petition

Intake is the initial screening of cases referred to the juvenile court that determines how they will be handled. Juvenile court intake is a discretionary decision, normally the responsibility

Table 14.2 Juvenile court delinquency caseload, 2011

Most serious offense	Number of cases	Percentage change 2002–2011	Percentage of total delinquency cases	Percentage detained	Percentage petitioned	Percentage petitioned cases adjudicated
Total	1,236,200	–26	100	21	54	59
Person offenses	317,500	–22	26	26	56	56
Property offenses	447,500	–32	36	17	51	59
Drug law violations	152,600	–17	12	15	50	58
Public order offenses	318,600	–24	26	24	57	62

Person offenses: homicide, rape, robbery, aggravated assault, simple assault, other violent sex offenses, other person offenses
Property offenses: burglary, larceny-theft, motor vehicle theft, arson, vandalism, trespassing, stolen property, other property offenses
Public order offenses: obstruction of justice, disorderly conduct, weapons offenses, liquor law violation, non-violent sex offenses, other public order offenses
Source: Hockenberry and Puzzanchera (2014a: 6, 7, 32, 36, 42).

of the juvenile probation department and, less typically, of the prosecutor's office. Four options are most common:

- Case dismissal
- Diversion for non-judicial handling, usually through community-based services
- Informal processing by the probation department
- Formal processing by the juvenile court, called *adjudication* (Sickmund and Puzzanchera 2014: 94).

In most jurisdictions, intake screening involves three key determinations. The first is a legal determination of probable cause: Are there legally admissible facts and information to warrant formal processing of the case in juvenile court? Second, do the facts of the case allow the juvenile court to have jurisdiction? This is especially important because contemporary juvenile courts do not always have original jurisdiction in juvenile matters. Recall that two recent trends limit the original jurisdiction of many juvenile courts: statutory exclusion of certain offenses and offenders and concurrent jurisdiction, which allows prosecutors discretion in filing certain types of cases in either juvenile or criminal court. Third, is formal processing by the juvenile court in the best interests of the child? Although this determination was the overarching concern of the traditional juvenile court, the contemporary emphasis on offender accountability and public safety has introduced a second question: Is formal processing by the juvenile court in the best interests of the community?

In some jurisdictions, intake screening is based on a *preliminary inquiry*, conducted by a probation officer under authority of statutory law. A preliminary inquiry collects pertinent information about the alleged offense and the youth. Information about the youth is sometimes referred to as a "youth assessment" and includes chemical dependency evaluation, educational assessment, and determination of mental health and family service needs. Thus, the preliminary inquiry provides information relevant for determining probable cause, juvenile court jurisdiction, and the "best interests" of the youth and community.

Petition: extent, trends, age, gender, race

If intake screening determines that the case should be dealt with formally by the juvenile court, a **petition** is written by the prosecutor's office to initiate the formal juvenile justice process. The petition is a legal document that specifies the facts of the case, the charges, and basic identifying information on the youth and his or her parents. Figure 14.3 indicates that 54 percent of all delinquency cases handled by juvenile courts in 2011 were petitioned and 46 percent were not petitioned. Compared to cases that are not petitioned into juvenile court, formally processed cases tend to "involve more serious offenses, older juveniles, and juveniles with longer court histories" (Sickmund 2003: 20). In addition, males are more likely than females and blacks are more likely than individuals of other races to have their cases petitioned (Hockenberry and Puzzanchera 2014a: 37; Sickmund 2003: 21).

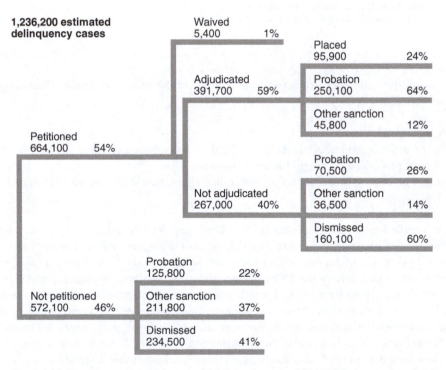

Figure 14.3 Juvenile court processing of delinquency cases, 2011. While a majority of cases (54%) referred to juvenile courts are petitioned, a sizable proportion (46%) are not petitioned and are either dismissed or provided some form of informal disposition. Of the cases that are petitioned, almost 6 out of 10 (59%) result in adjudication.
Sources: Hockenberry and Puzzanchera (2014a: 52). Used with permission of the National Center for Juvenile Justice.

Delinquency cases that are not petitioned are either dismissed or dealt with informally by the juvenile court (see bottom portion of Figure 14.3). Even though these cases are not formally petitioned, almost 60 percent receive some form of **informal disposition** by the juvenile court. Informal disposition is usually based on the youth's admission of a delinquent act or acts. A variety of disposition options are then possible, including referral to another agency for services (e.g., chemical dependency treatment or counseling), community service, restitution, and informal probation through the probation department (Sickmund 2003). These informal dispositions usually involve a *consent adjustment without petition*, a voluntary agreement between the youth and his or her parents that is approved by a juvenile court judge. The written agreement is given legal authority under statutory law and, in terms of informal probation, the consent adjustment involves rules or conditions that the youth is expected to follow, under supervision of a probation officer.

Juvenile Court Statistics provides information about status offenses only for cases that are petitioned. Therefore, we have no indication of how many or what types of status offense cases are referred to juvenile courts or what portion are petitioned. Instead, *Juvenile Court Statistics* reports on the case processing of five major categories of petitioned status offenses: running away, truancy, curfew violations, ungovernability, and underage liquor law violations (e.g., minor in possession of alcohol and underage drinking). In 2011, 116,200 status offense cases were petitioned into juvenile courts nationwide. Of these cases, 40 percent involved truancy, 20 percent liquor law violations, 12 percent ungovernability, 10 percent curfew, 9 percent runaway; the remaining 9 percent were categorized as miscellaneous (Hockenberry and Puzzanchera 2014a: 66). "Between 1995 and 2000, the formally handled status offense caseload increased considerably (55%) and then declined 40% through 2011" (Hockenberry and Puzzanchera 2014a:66). Although males accounted for 59 percent of all petitioned status offense cases in juvenile courts, females (41 percent) made up a substantially larger portion as compared to the delinquency caseload (Hockenberry and Puzzanchera 2014a: 71). Almost two-thirds of petitioned status offense cases involve juveniles younger than age 16 at the time of referral (Stahl 2008: 1). Truancy cases made up the greatest portion of the petitioned status offense caseloads for white (42 percent), black (36 percent), and Asian youth (46 percent), while truancy and liquor law violations were the greatest proportion of the caseload for American Indian juveniles (34 percent each) (Hockenberry and Puzzanchera 2014a: 74).

Detention

One of the most crucial decisions at intake is whether to detain the youth pending further court action. In most states, initial authorization for **detention** is provided by probation officers in response to police officers' request for use of secure detention. Police officers are usually required to provide a written report that describes why they believe the youth must be held in detention. Continued detention requires court authorization, usually through a judicial hearing within a statutorily specified period of time, commonly 24 hours. In cases involving detention, the detention hearing is the first court action. As specified in statutory law, the detention hearing must establish probable cause that the youth is a delinquent youth or status offender. The detention hearing follows procedural rules, also set forth in statutory law. The juvenile court's detention decision is sometimes informed by the preliminary inquiry, done by the probation officer at intake. The basic decision is whether continued detention is necessary "to protect the community, to ensure a juvenile's appearance at subsequent court hearings, to secure the juvenile's own safety, or for the purpose of evaluating the juvenile" (Puzzanchera and Sickmund 2008: 29; see also Sickmund and Puzzanchera 2014).

Statutory authorization for detention was tested in the U.S. Supreme Court case *Schall v. Martin* (1984).[15] In this case, Martin was arrested for first-degree robbery, second-degree assault, and criminal possession of a weapon. At issue was whether the statutory provisions for preventive detention provided adequate due process of law under the Fourteenth Amendment of the Constitution. The statutory provisions in question here were part of the New York Family Court Act, which allowed for preventive detention of juveniles charged with delinquent acts, pending completion of juvenile court adjudication. The Supreme Court ruled that the use of preventive detention was constitutional because the Family Court Act provided specific procedures that must be followed for a juvenile to be detained (Hemmens et al. 2004).

Detention: extent, trends, age, gender, race

Most delinquency cases handled by juvenile courts do not involve detention. In 2011, 256,800 delinquency cases involved detention between referral and disposition – 21 percent of the delinquency cases processed by juvenile courts (see Table 14.2). The number of delinquency cases involving detention increased by 7 percent between 1985 and 2011. This increase was largest for person offense cases (84 percent), but also grew for public order cases (40 percent) and drug offense cases (35 percent). In contrast, the portion of property offense cases involving detention declined (−39 percent) during this period (Hockenberry and Puzzanchera 2014a: 32). Despite this growth in the number of delinquency cases that were detained, the proportion of delinquency cases that are detained has remained relatively constant since 1985, at about 21 percent. Table 14.2 shows the variation in the use of detention across different categories of delinquency, ranging from 26 percent of all person offenses to 15 percent of all drug law violations.

Males were more likely than females to be detained for all types of delinquency, and youth age 16 or older were more likely to be detained than youth age 15 or younger (Hockenberry and Puzzanchera 2014a: 34). Of serious concern is the *disproportionate minority contact* at the point of detention: "While black youth represented 33% of the overall delinquency caseload in 2011, they made up 38% of the detention caseload." This overrepresentation was greatest for drug offense cases: "on average, between 1985 and 2011, black youth accounted for 30% of all cases involving drug offense violations but represented 46% of such cases detained" (Hockenberry and Puzzanchera 2014a: 33). Although the problem of disproportionate minority contact at the point of detention has been clearly identified and documented for over 40 years, the problem persists.

Compared to delinquency cases, a much lower proportion of petitioned status offenses involved detention: 8 percent of petitioned status offense cases versus 21 percent of delinquency cases. Of the detained status offense caseload, the largest portion involved liquor law violations (24 percent), followed by truancy (23 percent), runaway (17 percent), ungovernability (14 percent), curfew violations (11 percent), and miscellaneous status offenses (11 percent) (Hockenberry and Puzzanchera 2014a: 77). For most status offense categories, males were more likely to be detained than females, and racial minorities were more likely to be detained than whites. The percentage of petitioned status offense cases involving detention did not vary for adolescents of different ages (Puzzanchera and Sickmund 2008: 83).

Detention reform

As described in Chapter 2, the Juvenile Justice and Delinquency Prevention (JJDP) Act of 1974 sought to provide federal assistance to states in dealing with juvenile delinquency. Of particular concern were problematic detention practices across the United States. In particular, the Act sought to: (1) remove status offenders from detention or secure confinement, (2) promote sight and sound separation of juveniles from adults while in detention, (3) remove juveniles from adult jail facilities, and (4) reduce the number of minorities in secure facilities – "disproportionate minority confinement." The Office of Juvenile Justice and Delinquency Prevention (OJJDP) provided technical assistance, consultation, and grants money to deal with these problematic detention practices (Sickmund and Puzzanchera 2014; Hsia, Bridges, and McHale 2004).

Evaluation research indicates that federal initiatives through OJJDP significantly changed state and local juvenile detention practices in each of the areas addressed in the JJDP Act: (1) the number of status offenders held in secure detention or secure corrections was reduced substantially; (2) new and remodeled state and local detention facilities provided greater levels of sight and sound separation of juveniles from adults while in detention; (3) the number of juveniles held in adult jails declined considerably; and (4) the number of minorities held in secure detention facilities was reduced (Hsia et al. 2004; Pope, Lovell, and Hsia 2002). Despite notable progress, the problem of disproportionate minority confinement continues to demand attention, indicating the existence of disparities and biases in juvenile justice processing (Sickmund and Puzzanchera 2014; Pope et al. 2002).

At the forefront of detention reform is the Annie E. Casey Foundation's Juvenile Detention Alternative Initiative (JDAI) that began in 1992. JDAI promotes changes to policies, practices, and programs in an effort to reduce reliance on secure detention and to reduce racial disparities and bias in the use of secure detention. The Annie E. Casey Foundation provides funds to nearly 300 local JDAI sites in 39 states and the District of Columbia (Annie Casey Foundation 2014). JDAI site strategies focus on: (1) developing risk assessment instruments; (2) using screening teams for detention decision; and (3) increasing community-based alternatives for detention, including shelter care, home detention, and day reporting centers. JDAI sites submit Annual Results Reports to the Foundation in order to assess local detention reform progress and to provide information about reform efforts across JDAI sites (Annie Casey Foundation 2014: 1).

Transfer to criminal court

Intake screening may also result in the decision to transfer juvenile cases to adult criminal court. As we discussed in Chapter 2, several transfer provisions have become increasingly popular, including judicial waiver, concurrent jurisdiction, and statutory exclusion (Redding 2008; Kupchik 2006; Sickmund 2003). These statutory mechanisms allow juvenile court judges, prosecutors, and the legislature to designate the types of offenders and offenses that are beyond the jurisdiction of the juvenile court. *Judicial waiver* is the oldest transfer provision, providing statutory authority for juvenile court judges to waive the court's original jurisdiction and transfer cases to criminal court. Although judicial waiver provisions vary from state to state, the basic rationale is that certain types of offense and offenders, especially violent ones, are beyond the scope of the juvenile court, and juvenile court judges should be given authority to transfer these cases to adult court (Fagan and Zimring 2000). *Concurrent jurisdiction* gives statutory authority to prosecutors to file certain types of offenses in either juvenile or adult court. Some states, for example, allow prosecutors, at their discretion, to file felony offenses directly in adult criminal courts. Under *statutory exclusion*, state statutes exclude certain juvenile offenders and offenses from juvenile court jurisdiction, and these cases originate in criminal, rather than juvenile, court. State statutes providing for statutory exclusion usually set age and offense limits for excluded offenses.

Judicial waiver: extent, trends, age, gender, race

Though all states have expanded their statutory provisions for transferring juvenile cases to adult court, the actual number of juvenile cases transferred is relatively small (Sickmund 2003). Judicial waiver remains the most common transfer provision, and it is the only one for which data are available from the *Juvenile Court Statistics* (Hockenberry and Puzzanchera 2014a).[16] In 2011, juvenile courts waived less than 1 percent of all petitioned delinquency cases (see Figure 14.3). The number of juvenile cases judicially waived to adult court peaked in 1994 with 13,600 cases, a number 132 percent greater than the number waived in 1985. This increase was followed by a decline to a low of 5,400 cases judicially waived in 2011, 61 percent fewer cases than in 1994 (Hockenberry and Puzzanchera 2014b: 1–2; Sickmund and Puzzanchera 2014: 173).

Judicial waiver targets serious violent and drug offense cases. Juvenile court data show that for most years since 1985, "person offense cases were the most likely type of case to be waived to criminal court. The exception was 1989–1992, when drug offense cases were the most likely to be waived" (Sickmund and Puzzanchera 2014: 173). Corresponding to this change, the number of property offense cases waived to criminal court declined 41 percent since 1985 (Sickmund and Puzzanchera 2014: 173). Judicial waiver is more common for older juveniles than for younger juveniles, for males than for females, and for black youth than for youth of other races (Sickmund and Puzzanchera 2014: 174).

Adjudication

When formal court intervention is deemed necessary, cases proceed through a series of hearings, with varying names, that serve particular purposes. The adjudication process is initiated by the petition. The first adjudication hearing is often referred to as a *probable cause hearing*. This hearing makes an initial determination about whether sufficient information and evidence exist to substantiate that a youth was likely involved in activity that violated state criminal or status offense law. Determinations of continued detention are also made by judges in probable cause hearings. An *arraignment* normally follows at a separate time in order to advise the youth of his or her rights and obligations, to read the petition, and to allow the youth to admit or deny the petition. The vast majority of juveniles admit the petition at arraignment. (This is similar to pleading guilty in adult criminal court.) However, if the youth denies the petition, a *fact-finding* or *adjudicatory hearing* follows. This hearing comes closest to an adversarial trial in adult court, but the youth has fewer due process rights than an adult would. The outcome of this fact-finding process is a legal determination by the judge about whether the juvenile committed the offense(s). This is sometimes referred to as a *finding of fact* or a *finding of delinquency*. If the youth admitted to or was found to have committed the offense(s), the judge then decides if the youth should be **adjudicated** a *delinquent youth* or adjudicated a *status offender* (or some equivalent term). Both terms designate a legal status that results from the juvenile court's determination that the youth has in fact violated criminal law (delinquent youth) or status offense law (status offender) and that the youth is in need of juvenile court assistance. Recall from Chapter 2 that most state statutes now refer to a status offender as a youth in need of supervision (YINS), minor in need of supervision (MINS), youth in need of intervention (YINI), or some equivalent term.

Adjudication: extent, trends, age, gender, race

Figure 14.3 indicates that 59 percent of petitioned delinquency cases resulted in adjudication (391,700 out of 664,100 cases) and 40 percent were not adjudicated (267,000 out of 664,100 cases). The largest portion of delinquency cases that were not adjudicated were dismissed by the juvenile court (60 percent). The remaining non-adjudicated cases resulted in probation (26 percent) or some other sanction (14 percent). Thus, even when a youth is not adjudicated delinquent, the court can impose a mixture of dispositions, including out-of-home placement, probation, restitution, and community service. The various dispositions of non-adjudicated cases are often based on a *consent decree with petition* – an agreement between the juvenile court judge, parents, youth, and probation officer.

In 2011, 32 percent of all delinquency cases handled by juvenile courts resulted in delinquency adjudications – a proportion that has changed little since 1997 (Hockenberry and Puzzanchera 2014a: 42). Surprisingly, person offense cases were least likely to be adjudicated delinquent (56 percent), while public order offense cases (62 percent) were most likely to be adjudicated delinquent (see Table 14.2). Younger juveniles (15 years old or younger) were more likely than older juveniles to be adjudicated delinquent. Also, petitioned delinquency cases involving males were more likely to be adjudicated delinquent than those involving females, and cases involving black and Asian youth were less likely to be adjudicated delinquent than those involving white or American Indian youth (Hockenberry and Puzzanchera 2014a: 45).

Most petitioned status offense cases result in adjudication. Figure 14.4 shows that in 2011, 57 percent of the petitioned status offense cases were adjudicated, and 43 percent were not. "Among status offense categories in 2011, adjudication was least likely in petitioned runaway cases (47%) and most likely in cases involving liquor law violations (63%)" (Hockenberry and Puzzanchera 2014a: 79). The proportion adjudicated was similar for petitioned truancy, ungovernability, and curfew violations (54–55 percent). The likelihood of adjudication in status offense cases was about the same for males and females, and for younger and older status offenders. However, adjudication was less likely for black and Asian status offenders than for white and American Indian status offenders (Hockenberry and Puzzanchera 2014a: 79).

Formal disposition

Once a youth is adjudicated a delinquent youth or a status offender, the court decides the most appropriate sanction – referred to as **formal disposition**. Disposition is similar to sentencing in adult courts. Traditionally, disposition has been one of the key decision points at which the court considers "the best interests of the child." Disposition is imposed at a *dispositional hearing*, which is separated in time from adjudication hearings. After adjudication but before the dispositional hearing, a **predisposition report** is usually written by a probation officer. Authorized by court order and statutory law, the report provides an evaluation of the youth and his or her background and social environment. Even with contemporary initiatives

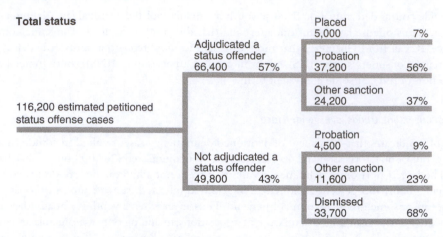

Figure 14.4 Juvenile court processing of petitioned status offense cases, 2011.
 Sources: Hockenberry and Puzzanchera (2014a: 84). Used with permission of the National Center for Juvenile Justice.

for punishment and accountability, the predisposition report attempts to provide assessment information to the judge so that disposition can be individualized and directed at rehabilitation. The predisposition report is commonly organized with three major sections: the offense section, a social history, and a summary and recommendation. The offense section covers four main areas: (1) an official version of the offense, usually provided by the police report; (2) commentary regarding the juvenile's version of the offense; (3) prior record, including previous arrests, petitions, adjudications, and dispositions; and (4) a victim impact statement (required by some states). The social history section provides observations about the juvenile and his or her family background, educational experiences and achievements, friends, employment, and neighborhood context. The final section, the summary and recommendation, is the shortest, but perhaps most important section because it is sometimes the only section that the judge reads. Two areas of concise discussion are included. First, an evaluative summary highlights and summarizes the key findings of the assessment. Second, the probation officer offers a recommendation regarding disposition that is followed by the judge in most cases. In addition to the predisposition report, various supplemental assessments can be ordered by the court, including psychological, educational, chemical dependency, and family assessments.

Formal disposition is distinct from adjudication in purpose and process. The dispositional hearing is not a fact-finding or adversarial process; rather it maintains an individualized and rehabilitative focus. Rules of evidence do not strictly apply, nor are due process rights fully extended. As the subject areas of the predisposition report suggest, non-legal factors become the center of attention in the dispositional hearing. The youth's attitude, family background, school experiences, and friends all have an important influence on disposition. Disposition attempts to fulfill multiple, seemingly inconsistent, goals: public safety, nurturance, deterrence, accountability, and rehabilitation. Disposition results in a court order prescribing sanctions, and the order usually involves more than one disposition. For example, probation is commonly included with restitution and community service. Under state statutory law, a full range of dispositions is possible, including the following:

- Probation
- Foster or group home placement
- Placement in a residential treatment center
- Restitution
- Community service
- Counseling for the youth, parents, or guardians
- Further medical or psychological evaluation of the youth, parents, or guardian
- Services that the court may designate, provided by parents or guardians
- Commitment to a mental health facility
- Home arrest
- Confiscation of the youth's driver's license
- Fine
- Payment of court costs
- Payment of victim counseling
- Deferred imposition of sentence
- Mediation
- Placement in a secure facility
- Placement in a youth assessment center[17]

A disposition of out-of home-placement usually involves a court order of **commitment**. Commitment is the juvenile court's legal authorization for out-of-home placement of a youth who has been adjudicated a delinquent youth. Legal custody is transferred to "the state" – to some state agency such as the juvenile court or department of corrections.

Disposition: extent, trends, age, gender, race

Probation was the most restrictive disposition given in 64 percent of delinquency cases that were adjudicated in 2011 (250,100 cases; see Figure 14.3). Out-of-home placement was used in 24 percent of adjudicated cases, resulting in residential placement at a training school, drug treatment center, boot camp, private treatment center, or group home (Sickmund 2003). The proportion of adjudicated cases with a disposition of out-of-home placement has declined over the last 26 years, from 31 percent in 1985 to 24 percent in 2011. Over the same time period, the proportion of probation dispositions increased from 57 percent to 64 percent). Other sanctions, including drug court, non–residential community programs, restitution, and community service, were used in 12 percent of the adjudicated cases in 2011. Once adjudicated, juveniles age 15 or younger were more likely than older juveniles to be placed on probation. In contrast, adjudicated cases involving older juveniles were more likely to result in out-of-home placement than were cases involving younger juveniles. Adjudicated cases involving females were more likely to be placed on probation than were cases involving males, whereas delinquency cases involving males were more likely to result in out-of-home placement. The disposition of probation was used at a lower rate for blacks than for other racial groups, and black youth adjudicated delinquent were more likely than youth of other races to be ordered into residential placement (Hockenberry and Puzzanchera 2014a: 46–51).

Figure 14.4 shows that probation is also the most common dispositional order in adjudicated status offense cases. Juvenile court data from 2011 show that probation was the most restrictive disposition in 57 percent of adjudicated status offense cases. The percentage of adjudicated status offense cases resulting in probation was higher for youth 15 or younger

(59 percent) than 16 or older (53 percent), for females (58 percent) than males (55 percent), and for Asian youth (72 percent) than for black (58 percent), white (56 percent), or American Indian (47 percent) youth (Hockenberry and Puzzanchera 2014a: 83).

Juvenile courts ordered out-of-home placement in 7 percent of all adjudicated status offense cases (see Figure 14.4). The offense profile of adjudicated status offense cases resulting in residential placement shows that 22 percent involved truancy, followed by 21 percent involving liquor law violations, 18 percent runaway, 17 percent ungovernability, 17 percent miscellaneous, and 5 percent curfew violations. The percentage of adjudicated status offenses cases resulting in out-of home placement was fairly equal across age and gender, and for white and black youth, with the exception of runaway offenses, in which a higher percentage of youth 16 or older and males were placed out-of-home (Hockenberry and Puzzanchera 2014a: 80–81).

Juvenile corrections

Juvenile court disposition is the gateway to corrections because it legally establishes how the court wants to deal with a case. Regardless of whether a case is adjudicated, juvenile court disposition seeks correctional options that are individualized, rehabilitative, and least restrictive. Reflecting the "rehabilitative ideal," juvenile court disposition has traditionally involved a wide range of correctional options. These correctional options can be organized into three categories: probation, community-based corrections, and residential placement. Before describing these forms of juvenile corrections, it is first necessary to briefly describe how juvenile justice reform has changed juvenile corrections.

Juvenile corrections and the rehabilitative ideal

In Chapter 2, we described four areas of juvenile justice reform, beginning in the mid-1960s, that dramatically transformed juvenile justice philosophy, policy, and practice: (1) the due process revolution, (2) the enactment of the JJDP Act of 1974, (3) "getting tough" – initiatives for punishment and accountability, and (4) contemporary juvenile justice reform and the return to rehabilitation. Common among the first three reforms was a questioning of the *rehabilitative ideal*, which was the foundation of the original juvenile court. Rehabilitation was called into question by a number of studies in the 1970s that examined the effectiveness of juvenile and adult corrections (Lipton, Martinson, and Wilks 1975; Lerman 1975; American Friends Service Committee 1971). Summarizing a large body of evaluation research, these studies yielded limited evidence of rehabilitative effectiveness of correctional treatment for both juveniles and adults. Even though researchers found that several treatment programs and approaches were successful, the general conclusion drawn was that "nothing works." Although considerable debate followed, the "nothing works" view of rehabilitation was widely adopted by the public and criminal justice professionals (Cullen and Jonson 2012). The questioning of rehabilitation was much stronger with regard to adult corrections than it was for juvenile corrections; nonetheless, the contemporary "get tough" approach, advocating punishment and accountability in juvenile justice, was fueled by this questioning of the rehabilitative ideal.

These reforms introduced a number of additional goals beyond rehabilitation into juvenile corrections. No longer was it assumed that "matters of treatment and reform of the offender are the only questions worthy of serious attention" (Allen 1959: 226). Instead, public safety, deterrence, punishment, accountability, competency development, and due process of law displaced rehabilitation as the first and foremost goal of juvenile corrections.

Probation

Probation is the most frequently imposed disposition in juvenile courts. It is used informally in cases that are not petitioned and in cases that are not adjudicated, and it is the most common formal disposition for adjudicated cases. In 2011, probation supervision was the most severe disposition in just over one-third of all delinquency cases handled by juvenile courts and in almost two-thirds of all adjudicated delinquency cases (see Figure 14.3).

Probation has its origins in the innovative work of John Augustus, a Boston shoemaker, who in the mid-1800s convinced a judge to release juvenile and adult offenders to him with the promise that he would provide moral guidance to them: he would establish certain expectations and rules for them to follow, and he would supervise their daily activities and progress. Thus, probation, as conceived by Augustus, involved the conditional release of an offender into the community, under supervision. Today, conditions and supervision are still the core of probation (Cromwell, del Carmen, and Alarid 2002).

Probation conditions

Probation conditions are court-imposed rules that juveniles must obey in order to live in the community and avoid confinement. In this way, probation involves conditional release into the community. Probation conditions are written into a legal document. In some juvenile court jurisdictions, probation conditions are a part of the court order of disposition; other juvenile courts use a standardized supervision agreement.

Probation conditions are of two types: *general conditions* that apply to everyone on probation and *special* or *individualized conditions*. General conditions involve common rules of probation such as abiding by all state laws, attending school regularly, and obeying parents. Individualized conditions are often based on specific needs identified in the predisposition report. Urinalyses, participation in various treatment programs, counseling, and restitution are examples of special conditions. A major reason for the extensive use of probation is that probation conditions serve multiple purposes – they provide public safety through supervision, they render punishment through restriction of freedom, they deter future crime, and they promote offender accountability and rehabilitation. Thus, probation has adapted to the changing philosophies of the juvenile justice system.

Juvenile courts have extensive discretion when imposing conditions of probation (Cromwell et al. 2002). Although a wide range of probation conditions have been authorized under appellate court review, the basic standard is that they be *reasonable and relevant*. Probation conditions must be clear and not excessive (reasonable), and they must be related to the offense, the prevention of future delinquency, or to public safety (relevant). For example, is a probation condition restricting freedom of association constitutional? A Florida appellate court case called *In the Interest of D. S. and J. V. Minor Children* (1965) dealt with two juveniles who were found guilty of simple assault and placed on probation.[18] One of the conditions of their probation was that they were not to associate with gang members, under the rationale that this would prevent further delinquency. Their appeal alleged that such restriction of freedom of association was unconstitutional. The appellate court ruled that this condition was reasonable and relevant (Hemmens et al. 2004).

Probation supervision

Probation supervision refers to the assistance and monitoring of probationers by probation officers. The approach to supervision taken by probation officers determines the relative emphasis given to offender rehabilitation or enforcement of probation rules. Styles of supervision have varied over the history of juvenile probation.

A descriptive typology of probation supervision can be constructed based on two important dimensions: rehabilitation and control, as shown in Figure 14.5 (Jordan and Sasfy 1974; see also Seiter and West 2003; Klockers 1972; Ohlin, Piven, and Pappenfort 1956). *Rehabilitation* refers to the degree to which probation officers emphasize reform and the role they take in bringing about offender change. *Control* refers to the level of monitoring and surveillance by probation officers and how closely they enforce probation conditions. The relative emphasis on these two important aspects of supervision influences probation officers' views and approaches to: (1) probation conditions as a vehicle for change, (2) enforcement of conditions through monitoring and surveillance, and (3) readiness to revoke probation (Czajkoski 1973; Klockers 1972).

The *moral-reformer* style of supervision was the original approach used in probation. Like many others of his day, John Augustus viewed crime and delinquency as a moral problem, requiring moral guidance. Augustus worked closely with the offenders released to him, getting involved in many aspects of their lives – family, work, church, recreation – and providing assistance. He believed that with proper guidance, offenders could be morally reformed. Following this tradition, early juvenile probation officers often used a moral-reformer style of supervision. Active involvement in the daily lives of juvenile offenders was meant to promote rehabilitation and high levels of control.

The professionalization of the juvenile court beginning in the 1920s was associated with the increasing use of full-time, highly trained probation officers rather than volunteers. State

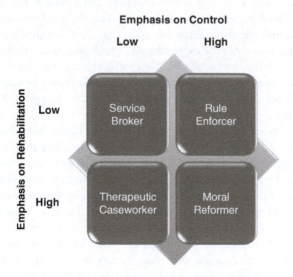

Figure 14.5 A model of probation supervision.
Source: Adapted from Jordan and Sasfy (1974: 29).

statutes began to require probation officers to have a college degree. Consistent with the child-savers' view that the juvenile court should be more of a welfare system than a judicial system, professional probation officers emphasized a *therapeutic-casework* supervision style (Feld 1999). Probation officers engaged in case assessment, in which they evaluated the needs of their "clients" and developed rehabilitative goals based on their assessment. Probation officers also provided direct services – they engaged in therapeutic counseling, including individual, family, and peer counseling.

Beginning in the 1960s, growing consideration was given to the community's role in generating and responding to crime and delinquency. In this context, a community-based approach to probation supervision developed. Rather than having probation officers engage in therapeutic casework, the *service-broker* supervision style emphasized the need to use resources in the community, including educational programs, job training, job placement, community mental health, certified counselors, and drug treatment. It was thought that by using community resources, the offender would be better able to be reintegrated back into the community. With this approach to supervision, probation officers became brokers of community services and resources.

The final supervision style to emerge was that of the *law enforcer*. Associated with the "get tough" approach to crime and delinquency during the 1980s and 1990s, the law-enforcer style of supervision seeks to provide offender accountability and public safety. The get tough approach is accomplished through supervision that emphasizes restriction of freedom, enforcement of probation conditions, monitoring and surveillance, and revocation of probation for rule violation.

Regardless of supervision style, probation supervision is accomplished primarily through three basic techniques: interviews with probationers and others, urinalysis, and records checks. These supervision techniques are used in office visits, in visits with the youth in his or her daily activities (field visits), and in contacts with people who associate with the youth (collateral contacts). As a result, probation officers conduct interviews in their offices and at probationers' homes, schools, and places of work. Most commonly, interviews are simply informal talks with the offenders, their parents, teachers, counselors, and employers. Depending on supervision style, interviews with probationers may be therapeutic, involving counseling techniques, or they may be directed at information gathering to bring about offender accountability and enforcement of conditions. Urinalysis is most commonly conducted randomly during office visits, but it may also be done during field visits at home, school, or work. Probation officers also routinely check records that are kept by various agencies, including police reports, detention intakes, school attendance records, and grades. Records information like this is normally gathered through collateral contacts with people and agencies that have relevance to the probation case. These collateral contacts supplement the probation officers' knowledge about probationers' daily activities and attitudes.

Revocation

Violations of probation conditions result in a highly discretionary decision called **revocation**. Revocation is the legal termination of probation by the court, based on the violation of probation. Violations are of two types: law violations and technical violations. *Law violations* involve the commission of a new crime, in violation of statutory law. *Technical violations* are infractions of probation conditions that do not involve violations of law, such as the failure to report to a probation officer and association with other delinquent youth (Cromwell et al. 2002). Probation conditions are imposed by the courts, and consequently the decision to revoke probation rests with the court that imposed the conditions. Nonetheless, it is the probation officer who initiates the revocation process with a revocation report to the court. The probation officer has extensive discretion in deciding whether to deal with the violation informally or formally through a revocation report that instigates a revocation hearing. Judges also have considerable discretion in deciding whether to revoke probation. The revocation hearing follows due process of law, with certain rights that have been extended through appellate court review (Cromwell et al. 2002). Upon finding that probation has been violated, the judge may continue the youth on probation, perhaps with new conditions, or the judge may revoke the probation and impose a new disposition.

Intensive supervision probation

An innovation in probation supervision, called *intensive supervision probation* (ISP), attempts to provide public safety and offender accountability through intensive monitoring and surveillance of the probationer. As an alternative to secure confinement, ISP is highly structured in terms of conditions and supervision standards. ISP officers have greatly reduced caseloads that allow for much higher levels of supervision. ISP commonly involves the use of electronic monitoring devices (at least in initial phases), a specified number of contacts per week, mandatory school and work checks, frequent urinalysis, and a required number of community service hours. Although these standards are intended to provide public safety, they are also designed to promote competency development by monitoring performance in school and work.

Community-based corrections

The rise of community-based corrections in the 1960s and 1970s coincided with the transformation of the juvenile justice system during the second revolution. This was no accident. As described in Chapter 2, the President's Commission on Law Enforcement and Administration of Justice, established in 1965, recommended that non-violent offenders be handled in the community rather than the juvenile courts. The logic of this recommendation stems from the second revolution's serious questioning whether the rehabilitative ideal could be accomplished: "the great hopes originally held for the juvenile court have not been fulfilled. It has not succeeded significantly in rehabilitating delinquent youth, in reducing or even stemming the tide of delinquency, or in bringing justice and compassion to the child offender" (President's Commission 1967a: 80, 1967c). In addition, the Commission emphasized the importance of dealing with delinquency in the context in which it develops – the local community:

> crime and delinquency are symptoms of failures and disorganization of the community … The task of corrections, therefore, includes building or rebuilding social ties, obtaining employment and education, securing in the larger sense a place for the offender in the routine functioning of society. This requires not only efforts directed toward changing the individual offender, which have been almost the exclusive focus of rehabilitation, but also mobilization and change of the community and its institutions.
>
> (President's Commission 1967b: 7)

Instead of rehabilitation, the major goal of community-based corrections is *reintegration* – correctional efforts designed to keep juvenile offenders in the community and to help them participate in community life.

Beginning in the second half of the 1970s, federal financial support through the OJJDP led to the development of community-based programs that utilized community resources. Community-based programs tend to be diversionary, attempting to deal with delinquency in the community rather than in the juvenile justice system. As we have already stressed, diversion occurs throughout the juvenile justice system. With regard to juvenile corrections, diversion refers to the use of community-based programs that provide needed services to delinquent youth in the local community, regardless of the point at which the case is diverted. Community-based programs also try to deinstitutionalize juvenile corrections, keeping delinquent youth in the local community, rather than placing them in correctional institutions.

A wide variety of community-based juvenile correctional programs were developed during this time period. Chief among them were youth service bureaux that provided various services to youth and families, including individual, peer, and family counseling; crisis hotlines; drop-in centers; job placement services; educational tutoring; and recreational programs (President's Commission 1967a: 83, 1967c). Foster care programs; community service programs; and various residential programs, including group homes that emphasize treatment and education, drug treatment centers, and halfway houses, were also developed. Though it originated much earlier than community-based corrections, probation is conceptually consistent with these community-based approaches because it provides conditional release into the community with supervision. From their beginning, community-based correctional programs have tried to promote delinquency prevention, diversion, and community reintegration as an alternative to placement in secure, custodial correctional institutions.

Balanced and restorative justice

Contemporary correctional efforts in balanced and restorative justice are often community-based, because they attempt to actively involve the community in delinquency prevention and intervention. This popular approach is typically non-residential and attempts to actively involve community members and use community resources. The balanced and restorative approach to juvenile justice is directed at three fundamental goals: offender accountability, public safety, and competency development. The balanced and restorative approach to juvenile corrections tries to accomplish these goals through "restorative conferencing": "a range of strategies to bring the victim, offender, and other members of the community together in a nonadversarial, community-based process"[19] (Belbott 2003: 324). Gordon Bazemore and Mark Umbreit (1997) describe four restorative conferencing models:

1. *Victim–offender mediation:* With the assistance of a trained mediator, victims voluntarily meet with offenders in a safe and structured setting. The victim is allowed to tell the offender about the crime's physical, emotional, and/or financial impact and to ask the offender questions about the crime. Together they work out a restitution plan for the offender (Belbott 2003).
2. "*Community reparative boards* are composed of small groups of citizens who have received intensive training and conduct public, face-to-face meetings with offenders who have been ordered by the court to participate. During the meeting, board members discuss with the offender the nature and seriousness of the offense" (Belbott 2003: 324). They

also develop agreements that sanction offenders, and monitor compliance and submit reports to the court.

3. *Family group conferencing model:* "To initiate a family group conference, a trained facilitator contacts the victim and the offender to explain the process and invite them to participate. The victim and offender are asked to identify key members of their support system who will also be asked to attend. Participation is voluntary. The conference usually begins with the offender describing the incident, after which the other participants describe how the incident has affected their lives ...After the discussion, the facilitator asks the victim what he or she wants the outcome of the conference to be" (Belbott 2003: 324). The group then collectively seeks to resolve the offense through an agreement that outlines what is expected of the offender.

4. *Circle sentencing* is based on traditional practices of indigenous groups in Canada and the United States. "Circle sentencing includes participation of the victim, offender, both of their families and friends, personnel from the justice agency, police department and relevant social service agencies, and interested community members who together develop a sentencing plan that addresses the concerns of all the parties" (Belbott 2003: 325).

Residential placement

Large, highly structured correctional institutions have been the hallmark of juvenile corrections in the United States since the mid-1800s. Contemporary juvenile corrections includes a wide range of residential facilities for out-of-home placement, including custodial institutions, residential treatment centers, psychiatric hospitals, foster homes, and group homes. These **residential placement** facilities vary tremendously, especially in terms of administrative control (private or public operation), size, physical setting, level of custody, length of placement, and the degree to which they pursue rehabilitation.

A one-day count in 2011 revealed that there were 41,097 youth committed to residential correctional facilities as a result of being adjudicated delinquent (Sickmund et al. 2013).[20] Table 14.3 shows that the vast majority of these youth (96 percent) were placed in residential facilities for delinquent offenses, rather than for status offenses (4 percent), with person offenses making up one-third (37 percent) of all commitments to residential placement. The number of youth committed to residential placement was 44 percent less in 2011 than in 1997 (Sickmund et al. 2013). Sixty percent of the committed youths were placed in public facilities and 40 percent were placed in private facilities, even though the number of public and private facilities is about equal (1,103 are public and 1,135 are private) (Sickmund and Puzzanchera 2014: 187). Table 14.4 shows that group homes and long-term secure facilities (e.g., state training schools) held the largest portion of committed offenders (43 percent and 36 percent, respectively), but a sizable portion were committed to detention centers (11 percent). Forty-seven percent of the youth adjudicated for person offenses were committed to long-term secure residential facilities, and 39 percent were placed in group homes. For adjudicated status offenders, commitment to a group home (72 percent) was by far the most common residential placement. Males (88 percent) and black (39 percent) and Hispanic (22 percent) youth make up a disproportionate percentage of the youth committed to residential placement (Sickmund et al. 2013).

Table 14.3 Adjudicated juvenile offenders committed to residential placement, 2011

	Total	Percentage of committed	State	Local	Private
Total committed	**41,097**	**100**	**16,262**	**8,233**	**16,602**
Delinquency	**39,412**	**96**	**16,061**	**8,020**	**15,331**
Person offenses	15,303	37	7,428	2,236	5,639
Property offenses	10,375	25	4,434	2,095	3,846
Drug offenses	3,094	8	889	523	1,682
Public order	5,009	12	2,100	964	1,945
Technical violation	5,631	14	1,210	2,202	2,219
Status offenses	**1,685**	**4**	**201**	**213**	**1,271**

Source: Sickmund et al. (2013).

Group homes constitute 25 percent of all residential facilities, but they provide placement for 43 percent of all adjudicated offenders who were committed to residential facilities (Sickmund and Puzzanchera 2014: 200; Sickmund et al. 2013). Most **group homes** are privately operated and community-based. They are often located in neighborhoods, and they use community resources and services in an attempt to integrate youth into the local community.

In contrast, 36 percent of the youth committed to residential placement were placed in long-term secure facilities, most commonly state training schools (see Table 14.4). These **custodial institutions** are usually large, state facilities, providing long-term custodial placement for serious juvenile offenders (Sickmund and Puzzanchera 2014: 202; Allen-Hagen 1991). The number of commitments to custodial institutions has declined by 61 percent from 1997 (38,238) to 2011 (14,976) (Sickmund et al. 2013). State training schools vary considerably, from campus-like grounds with cottages to large, secure buildings much like adult prisons. Some state training schools are very large, housing hundreds of youths (Allen-Hagen 1991). With the "get tough" approaches to juvenile corrections of the 1980s and 1990s, many states remodeled some of their state training schools or built new high-security buildings to serve as juvenile prisons. Although contemporary state training schools tend to emphasize custody over rehabilitation, they commonly offer programs for competency development, especially education and job training. State training schools typically operate on a school-day schedule and incorporate behavior modification programs in an effort to promote behavior change and to teach daily living skills.

Other residential facilities for juveniles feature focused treatment programs such as substance abuse, mental health, and sex offender treatment. Although psychiatric hospitals and residential drug treatment centers are usually private institutions, they are sometimes used as a dispositional placement by juvenile courts. "Get tough" efforts in juvenile corrections have led to the development of boot camp programs in many states, which provide relatively short-term placement in a military-style environment. A regimented schedule stresses discipline, physical training, work, and education. More general in purpose are large residential facilities for juveniles, such as boys and girls "homes," "ranches," and "towns." These large residential centers are usually broken down into smaller units identified as cottages or houses, where house parents or a small number of staff try to provide a family-like environment.

One of the biggest issues for residential placement is **aftercare** – the assistance, services, and programs that follow residential placement upon a resident's release. The contemporary term

Table 14.4 Adjudicated juvenile offenders committed to residential placement, 2011: Number and percentage of offense types committed to different types of residential facilities

Offense type	Total	Detention center		Shelter		Reception & diagnostic		Group home		Boot camp		Ranch or wilderness camp		Long-term secure	
	Number	Number	%	Number	%	Number	%	Number	%	Number	%	Number	%	Number	%
Total	**41,097**	**4,417**	**11**	**700**	**2**	**687**	**2**	**17,696**	**43**	**469**	**1**	**2,152**	**5**	**14,976**	**36**
Committed Delinquency	**39,412**	**4,293**	**11**	**586**	**1**	**609**	**2**	**16,491**	**42**	**463**	**1**	**2097**	**5**	**14,873**	**38**
Person offenses	15,303	1,035	7	206	1	212	1	6,005	39	116	—	574	4	7,155	47
Property offenses	10,375	1,055	10	149	1	196	2	4,260	41	148	1	687	7	3,880	37
Drug offenses	3,094	267	9	56	2	41	1	1,794	58	46	—	172	6	718	23
Public order offenses	5,009	484	10	55	1	58	1	2,159	43	74	—	323	6	1,856	37
Technical violations	5,631	1,452	26	120	2	102	2	2,273	40	79	—	341	6	1,264	22
Status offenses	**1,685**	**124**	**7**	**114**	**7**	**78**	**5**	**1,205**	**72**	**6**	**0**	**55**	**3**	**103**	**6**

Source: Sickmund et al. (2013).

for aftercare programming is **reentry**. Traditionally, youth released from residential placement are placed on **parole**. Parole involves conditions and supervision, just like probation. Although similar, probation and parole are distinguished in relation to residential placement: probation is used before placement and parole afterwards. In many states, parole supervision is provided by officers who are both probation and parole officers.

New contemporary aftercare programs have been developed, including the intensive aftercare program (IAP). The IAP model is designed to reduce recidivism among high-risk parolees by combining intensive supervision with treatment, as a bridge between residential placement and reentry into the community. Five principles guide the structured reentry process:

1. Prepare youth for progressively increased responsibility and freedom in the community.
2. Facilitate youth–community interaction and involvement.
3. Work with the offender and targeted community support systems (e.g., schools, family) on qualities needed for constructive interaction and for the youth's successful community adjustment.
4. Develop new resources and supports where needed.
5. Monitor and test the youth and the community on their ability to deal with each other productively (Wiebush, McNulty, and Le 2000: 2).

IAP tries to develop individualized parole reentry plans through careful case selection, assessment, and classification. In essence, it is a balanced and restorative approach to aftercare in that it provides intensive supervision and treatment services, balanced incentives, and graduated consequences.

Summary and conclusions

The term "juvenile justice system" is misleading. There is not a single juvenile justice system; rather, each state has a separate juvenile justice system, and these are "systems" in only a limited sense. The various parts of these systems – police, courts, and corrections – are all operated by different levels and branches of government, sometimes even by private organizations. Consequently, juvenile justice is highly decentralized and fragmented. In addition, many juvenile justice cases are diverted from "the system" or dealt with informally with only limited due process of law. As a result, "justice" is highly discretionary in juvenile justice systems across the United States. In addition, research consistently shows that minority youth are over-represented across the points of contact in the juvenile justice process – from arrest to disposition. Disproportionate minority contact (DMC) has been a focal concern since passage of the Juvenile Justice and Delinquency Prevention Act of 1974 and considerable federal and state resources have been devoted to DMC reduction strategies.

Police encounters with juveniles are the usual entry point into juvenile justice systems. As is true throughout the juvenile justice process, many cases are dealt with informally through diversion, such as warn and release at the scene (a "street adjustment") and referral to various community resources and services. Formal processing of juveniles suspected of crime involves a police referral to the juvenile court. Over the last 35 years, formal juvenile court referrals by the police have become increasingly common compared to informal police processing. In recent years, over two-thirds of all juveniles taken into custody have been referred to juvenile courts.

Police have extensive discretion in dealing with juvenile matters. We described several factors that influence discretion, such as seriousness of the offense; previous police contact; prior arrest; attitude and demeanor of the juvenile; social characteristics of the juvenile; and organization, policies, and customs of the police department. The arrest of a juvenile in some states is referred to as "taking into custody" in order to convey the protective role of juvenile policing. The role of police has changed over time to include both a collaborative role, which involves the public in a collective effort to prevent crime and maintain public order, and a law-enforcer role, which emphasizes arrest and formal referral to the juvenile court. Although police discretion in juvenile matters is broad and extensive, it is not unbridled. During the 1960s and 1970s, the due process revolution in juvenile justice addressed several key law-enforcement methods related to juveniles. The case decisions that make up the due process revolution established procedural law that attempts to extend basic rights and freedoms advanced in state and federal constitutions, especially with regard to search and seizure, custodial interrogation, and arrest.

Juvenile courts, too, rely heavily on discretion and diversion – many cases are diverted or handled informally. The juvenile court process involves a series of discretionary decisions, including intake, petitioning, transfer to adult court, adjudication, and disposition. Intake by a probation officer refers to the initial screening of a case referred to the juvenile court. If secure detention is requested by the police, it must be authorized initially by a probation officer as a part of intake. Continued detention, however, requires court authorization, usually through a judicial hearing within a statutorily specified period of time. Although most delinquency cases do not involve secure detention, it is used disproportionately in cases that involve black youth. The problem of disproportionate minority confinement has been identified and documented for over 30 years, but the problem persists.

More than one-half of the delinquency cases handled by juvenile courts are dealt with formally through petition to juvenile court or transfer to adult court. Several transfer provisions are used, including judicial waiver, concurrent jurisdiction, and statutory exclusion. Less than 1 percent of all petitioned delinquency cases are waived to adult court. Even when cases are not formally petitioned, they can receive some form of informal disposition by juvenile courts. Informal disposition is usually based on the youth's admission of delinquency. A variety of disposition options are then possible, including diversionary referral to another agency for services (e.g., substance abuse treatment or counseling), community service, restitution, and informal probation through the probation department. These informal dispositions usually involve a consent adjustment without petition, a voluntary agreement between the youth and his or her parents that is approved by a juvenile court judge.

When formal court intervention is deemed necessary, cases proceed through a series of hearings that have varying names and serve particular purposes. The probable cause hearing makes an initial determination about whether sufficient information and evidence exist to substantiate that a youth was likely involved in activity that violated state criminal or status offense law. In addition, probable cause hearings determine whether continued detention is necessary. Arraignments involve the advising of rights, reading of the petition, and the youth's admission or denial of the petition. The adjudicatory hearing is a fact-finding process with due process rights that results in a judicial determination of whether the youth has in fact violated criminal law (delinquent youth) or status offense law (status offender) and whether the youth is in need of the juvenile court's assistance and supervision. If a youth is adjudicated a delinquent youth or a status offender, the court decides the most appropriate sanction at a dispositional hearing. The dispositional hearing is usually separated in time and purpose from the adjudicatory procedures that precede it. A predisposition report, written by a probation officer, informs disposition through evaluation of the youth and his or her background and social environment. A full range of dispositions are normally authorized under state statute, including probation, out-of-home placement, restitution, community service, counseling, fines, and mediation.

Juvenile court disposition is the gateway to corrections, because it legally establishes how the court wants to deal with a case. Regardless of whether a case is adjudicated, court disposition seeks correctional options that are individualized, rehabilitative, and the least restrictive option. Probation is the most frequently imposed disposition in juvenile courts. Probation is usually combined with other dispositions, such as restitution or community service, and it involves a set of court-imposed rules, called conditions, and supervision by a probation officer. Community-based corrections emphasize the community's role in causing and responding to delinquency and crime. Community corrections often utilize community resources such as counseling services, tutoring and educational programs, and job training and placement. Residential placement is the most restrictive disposition available to juvenile courts. Residential placement facilities vary tremendously, especially in terms of administrative control, size, physical setting, level of custody, length of placement, and degree of emphasis on rehabilitation. Group homes are typically small, private treatment facilities in residential neighborhoods. In contrast, custodial institutions, such as state training schools, are usually much larger and oriented far more toward security than toward rehabilitation.

Critical-thinking questions

1. In what ways are juvenile justice systems decentralized and fragmented among the different levels and branches of government?
2. Describe how discretion is used throughout the juvenile justice process.
3. Describe how diversion is used throughout the juvenile justice process.
4. Describe how disproportionate minority contact occurs throughout the juvenile justice process.
5. Identify and briefly describe the various roles that police adopt in juvenile law enforcement.
6. How does due process influence law enforcement with juveniles?
7. Outline the formal juvenile court process.
8. Provide an inventory of juvenile court dispositions.
9. What are probation conditions? What does it mean that probation conditions must be "reasonable and relevant"?
10. What is the role of the community in community-based corrections?
11. Describe how residential placement facilities vary in terms of administrative control, size, physical setting, level of custody, length of placement, and degree of emphasis on rehabilitation.
12. What is commitment? Who has legal authority to impose it? When is it used? What does it entail?

Suggested reading

Feld, Barry.2013. "Real Interrogation: What Actually Happens When Cops Question Kids?" *Law and Society Review* 47: 1–35.

Hockenberry, Sarah and Charles Puzzanchera. 2014. *Juvenile Court Statistics 2011*. Pittsburgh, PA: National Center for Juvenile Justice.

Puzzanchera, Charles. 2013. "Juvenile Arrests 2011." *Juvenile Offenders and Victims National Report Series*. Washington, DC: Office of Juvenile Justice and Delinquency Prevention.

Sickmund, Melissa and Charles Puzzanchera (eds.). 2014. *Juvenile Offenders and Victims: 2014 National Report*. Pittsburgh, PA: National Center for Juvenile Justice.

Useful websites

For further information relevant to this chapter, go to the following websites.

- Models for Change: Systems Reform in Juvenile Justice, MacArthur Foundation (www.modelsforchange.net/index.html)
- National Council of Juvenile and Family Court Judges (www.ncjfcj.org/)
- The Annie E. Casey Foundation: Juvenile Justice (www.aecf.org/work/juvenile-justice/)
- OJJDP *Statistical Briefing Book: Juvenile Justice System Structure and Process* (www.ojjdp.gov/ojstatbb/structure_process/index.html)
- Model Programs Guide, Office of Juvenile Justice and Delinquency Prevention (www.ojjdp.gov/mpg/); the Model Program Guide is integrated with CrimeSolutions.gov (www.crimesolutions.gov/) (under "Topic" use "Juveniles" and then "Delinquency Prevention")

Glossary of key terms

Adjudication: A case dealt with formally by the juvenile court goes through a series of hearings, involving determination of probable cause, arraignment, and fact finding. The purpose of this adjudication process is to determine whether the youth is responsible for the offense(s) charged in the petition and whether the youth should be legally declared a "delinquent youth" or a "status offender" by the juvenile court.

Aftercare: The assistance, services, and programs that follow residential placement upon a resident's release.

Arrest: The deprivation of an individual's freedom by a person of authority on the grounds that there is probable cause to believe that that individual has committed a criminal offense.

Collaborative role: The police and the community working together to prevent crime, maintain public order, and solve community problems.

Commitment: The juvenile court's legal authorization for out-of-home placement for a youth who has been adjudicated a delinquent youth. Commitment involves a transfer of legal custody to "the state" – some state agency such as the juvenile court or department of corrections.

Crime-fighting role: The police role associated with professional policing that emphasizes enforcement of laws and crime control. The primary strategies for crime fighting involve motorized preventive patrol, rapid response, and reactive investigation.

Custodial institutions: Closed and secure residential facilities for delinquent youth, providing long-term custody.

Custodial interrogation: Police questioning of suspects when custody involves arrest or significant deprivation of freedom, and the questioning is possibly incriminating.

Detention: The secure confinement of a youth under court authority, pending court action, disposition, or placement.

Discretion: "Authority conferred by law to act in certain conditions or situations in accordance with an official's or an official agency's considered judgment and conscience" (Pound 1960: 926).

Disproportionate minority contact: "the disproportionate number of juvenile members of minority groups who come into contact with the juvenile justice system" (OJJDP 2012: 1).

Diversion: The tendency to deal with juvenile matters informally, without formal processing and adjudication, by referring cases to agencies outside the juvenile justice system.

Formal disposition: The juvenile court's response to a youth's admission of a petition or the court's finding that a youth committed an offense(s). Dispositional options include probation, out-of-home placement, restitution, and community service.

Group homes: Typically small, private, non-secure residential facilities that emphasize rehabilitation. Group homes are located in neighborhoods and use community resources and services in their attempt to integrate youth into the local community.

Informal disposition: A juvenile court's response and handling of a case that has been referred but not adjudicated. Informal disposition may occur in cases that have not been petitioned and in cases that have been petitioned but not adjudicated. A variety of informal dispositional options are available to juvenile courts, including referral to another agency for services (e.g., chemical dependency treatment or counseling), community service, restitution, and informal probation through the probation department.

Intake: The screening of cases referred to the juvenile court, usually by the probation department. Intake screening results in a determination of how the case will be handled – formally, informally, or by dismissal.

Law-enforcer role: Associated with the "get tough" approach to crime and delinquency, the law-enforcer role emphasizes public safety and offender accountability and involves vigorous enforcement of laws through arrest and referral to the juvenile court.

Parole: The conditions and supervision provided after release from residential placement, intended to smooth the transition back into the community.

Petition: A legal document filed in juvenile court that specifies the facts of the case, the charge(s), and the basic identifying information of the youth and his or her parents.

Predisposition report: A court-ordered report written by a probation officer that provides information relevant for court disposition in an effort to make disposition individualized and rehabilitative. The report usually includes three major sections (offense, social history, and summary and recommendation) that furnish information on the adjudicated youth's prior record, current offense, and social background.

Probation conditions: Court-imposed rules that are a central part of the disposition of probation. Juveniles placed on probation by the court must obey these conditions in order to live in the community and avoid confinement.

Probation supervision: Assistance and monitoring of probationers by probation officers. The approach to supervision taken by probation officers determines the relative emphasis given to offender rehabilitation or enforcement of probation rules.

Protective role: The original role of police in dealing with juveniles in which police were expected to practice "kindly discipline" in place of parents – to function *in loco parentis*. As an extension of the juvenile court, police were to deal with juveniles in an informal, parent-like fashion, acting in the "best interests of the child."

Reentry: The assistance, services, and programs that follow release from residential placement, designed to facilitate placement and acceptance into the community.

Referral: Written documents, usually from the police, parents, or schools, that request or result in juvenile court consideration of a particular matter involving a juvenile.

Residential placement: Court-authorized or court-ordered out-of-home placement of a youth in a group living facility. Residential placement facilities vary greatly in terms of administrative control, size, physical setting, level of custody, length of placement, and degree of emphasis on rehabilitation.

Revocation: The legal termination of probation by the court that granted probation, based on the violation of the probation agreement/order.

Search and seizure: The Fourth Amendment protects against unreasonable search and seizure by the police. A search requires a search warrant, which is issued by the courts and is based on probable cause.

Taking into custody: The statutory authority given to police officers to take control of a juvenile, either physically or by the youth's voluntary submission, in an effort to separate that youth from his or her surroundings. Taking into custody is used when the juvenile has broken the law or is in need of protection.

Notes

1. Reprinted with permission from the National Academies Press, Copyright 2013, National Academy of Sciences.
2. See Leiber et al. (2011) and McCarter (2011) for assessment of the effectiveness of OJJDP's DMC mandate.
3. Republished with permission of Sage; permission conveyed through Copyright Clearance Center, Inc.
4. *Cops and Kids* is the title of a book by David B. Wolcott (see Wolcott 2005).
5. *Brinegar v. U.S.*, 338 U.S. 160 (1948).
6. *State v. Lowry*, 230 A. 2d 907 (1967).
7. *New Jersey v. T. L. O.*, 469 U.S. 325 (1985).
8. *Montana Code Annotated 2014*. 46-6-14. Method of arrest.
9. *Tennessee v. Garner*, 471 U.S. 1 (1985).
10. *Miranda v. Arizona*, 384 U.S. 436 (1966).
11. *In re Gault*, 387 U.S. 1 (1967).
12. *Haley v. Ohio*, 332 U.S. 596 (1948) and *Gallegos v. Colorado*, 370 U.S. 49 (1962).
13. *Haley v. Ohio*, 332 U.S. 596 (1948).
14. *California v. Prysock*, 453 U.S. 355 (1981).
15. *Schall v. Martin*, 104 U.S. 2403 (1984).
16. Rainville and Smith (2003) examine juvenile felony defendants in criminal courts. Our concern here is with juvenile court processes.
17. *Montana Code Annotated 2014*. 41-5-1512 and 1513.
18. *In the Interest of D. S. and J. V., Minor Children*, 652 So.2D 892 (Fla. Appl. 1995).
19. Republished with permission of Sage; permission conveyed through Copyright Clearance Center, Inc.
20. Residential facilities accommodate youth who are detained (30 percent) and committed (70 percent) (Sickmund et al. 2013; see also Sickmund and Puzzanchera 2014: 190). Normally, detained youth are said to be "held" in custody, while committed youth are said to be "placed" in a residential facility.

References

Allen, Francis A. 1959. "Legal Values and the Rehabilitative Ideal." *Journal of Law, Criminology, and Police Science* 50: 226–232.

Allen-Hagen, Barbara. 1991. *Public Juvenile Facilities: Children in Custody 1989.* Washington, DC: Office of Juvenile Justice and Delinquency Prevention.

American Friends Service Committee. 1971. *Struggle for Justice.* New York: Hill & Wang.

Annie E. Casey Foundation. 2014. "Juvenile Detention Alternatives Initiative (JDAI) 2013 Annual Results Report: Inter-site Conference Summary." Retrieved February 26, 2015 (www.aecf.org/resources/juvenile-detention-alternatives-initiative-2013-annual-results-report/).

Bazemore, Gordon and Mark Umbreit. 1997. *Balanced and Restorative Justice for Juveniles: A Framework for Juvenile Justice in the 21st Century.* Washington, DC: Office of Juvenile Justice and Delinquency Prevention.

Belbott, Barbara A. 2003. "Restorative Justice." Pp. 322–325 in *Encyclopedia of Juvenile Justice*, ed. M. D. McShane and F. P. Williams. Thousand Oaks, CA: Sage.

Bishop, Donna M. 2005. "The Role of Race and Ethnicity in Juvenile Justice Processing." Pp. 23–28 in *Our Children, Their Children: Confronting Racial and Ethnic Differences in American Juvenile Justice*, ed. D. F. Hawkins and K. Kempf–Leonard. University of Chicago Press.

Bishop, Donna and Charles Frazier. 1988. "The Influence of Race in Juvenile Justice Processing." *Journal of Research in Crime and Delinquency* 25: 242–261.

Bishop, Donna and Charles Frazier. 1992. "Gender Bias in Juvenile Justice Processing: Implication of the JJDP." *Journal of Criminal Law and Criminology* 82: 1162–1186.

Bishop, Donna M., Michael Leiber, and Joseph Johnson. 2010. "Contexts of Decision Making in the Juvenile Justice System: An Organizational Approach to Understanding Minority Overrepresentation." *Youth Violence and Juvenile Justice* 8: 213–233.

Black, Donald J. and Albert J. Reiss, Jr. 1970. "Police Control of Juveniles." *American Sociological Review* 35: 63–77.

Bordua, David J. 1967. "Recent Trends: Deviant Behavior and Social Control." *Annals of the American Academy of Political and Social Science* 369: 149–163.

Cabaniss, Emily R., James M. Frabutt, Mary H. Kendrick, and Margaret B. Arbuckle. 2007. "Reducing Disproportionate Minority Contact in the Juvenile Justice System: Promising Practices." *Aggression and Violent Behavior* 12: 393–401.

Cicourel, Aaron. 1968. *The Social Organization of Juvenile Justice.* New York: Wiley.

Cohen, Lawrence E. and James R. Kluegel. 1978. "Determinants of Juvenile Court Disposition: Ascription and Achievement in Two Metropolitan Courts." *American Sociological Review* 43: 162–176.

Crank, Kathleen Kositzky. 1995. "The JJDP Mandates: Rationale and Summary." Washington, DC: Office of Juvenile Justice and Delinquency Prevention. Available online at: www.ncjrs.gov/txtfiles/fs-9522.txt.

Cromwell, Paul F., Rolando V. del Carmen, and Leanne Fiftal Alarid. 2002. *Community-Based Corrections.* 5th edn. Belmont, CA: Wadsworth.

Cullen, Francis T. and Cheryl Lero Jonson. 2012. *Correctional Theory: Context and Consequences.* Los Angeles: Sage.

Czajkoski, Eugene H. 1973. "Exposing the Quasi-Judicial Role of Probation Officers." *Federal Probation* 37: 9–13.

Dannefer, Dale and Russel Schutt. 1982. "Race and Juvenile Justice Processing in Police and Court Agencies." *American Journal of Sociology* 87: 1113–1132.

Davis, Jaya and Jon R. Sorensen. 2013. "Disproportionate Minority Confinement of Juveniles: A National Examination of Black–White Disparity in Placements, 1997–2006." *Crime and Delinquency* 59: 115–139.

Development Services Group, Inc. (DSG). n.d. "Disproportionate Minority Contact." OJJDP Model Programs Guide. Retrieved March 5, 2015 (www.ojjdp.gov/mpg/Resource/LitReviews).

Engen, Rodney L., Sara Steen, and George S. Bridges. 2002. "Racial Disparities in the Punishment of Youth: Theoretical and Empirical Assessment of the Literature." *Social Problems* 49: 194–220.

Fagan, Jeffrey, Ellen Slaughter, and Eliot Hartstone. 1987. "Blind Justice? The Impact of Race on the Juvenile Justice Process." *Crime and Delinquency* 33: 224–258.

Fagan, Jeffrey and Franklin E. Zimring. 2000. *The Changing Borders of Juvenile Justice: Transfer of Adolescents to the Criminal Court.* University of Chicago Press.

Federal Bureau of Investigation. 2013. *Crime in the United States, 2012: Uniform Crime Reports.* Washington, DC: U.S. Department of Justice. Retrieved January 8, 2015 (http://www.fbi.gov/about-us/cjis/ucr/crime-in-the-u.s.).

Federal Bureau of Investigation. 2014. *Crime in the United States, 2013: Uniform Crime Reports.* Washington, DC: U.S. Department of Justice. Retrieved January 8, 2015 (http://www.fbi.gov/about-us/cjis/ucr/crime-in-the-u.s.).

Feld, Barry C. 1999. *Bad Kids: Race and the Transformation of the Juvenile Court.* New York: Oxford University Press.

Ferdico, John N. 1993. *Criminal Procedure for the Criminal Justice Professional.* 5th edn. Minneapolis/St. Paul: West.

Ferdinand, Theodore N. and Elmer C. Luchtenhand. 1970. "Inner-City Youths, the Police, the Juvenile Court and Justice." *Social Problems* 17: 510–527.

Fogelson, Robert M. 1977. *Big City Police.* Cambridge, MA: Harvard University Press.

Gaines, Larry K. 2003. "Police Responses to Delinquency." Pp. 286–290 in *Encyclopedia of Juvenile Justice*, ed. M. D. McShane and F. P. Williams. Thousand Oaks, CA: Sage.

Goldman, Nathan. 1963. *The Differential Selection of Juvenile Offenders for Court Appearance.* Washington, DC: National Council on Crime and Delinquency.

Goldstein, Herman. 1990. *Problem-Oriented Policing.* New York: McGraw-Hill.

Hartney, Christopher and Linh Vuong. 2009. *Created Equal: Racial and Ethnic Disparities in the U.S. Criminal Justice System.* Oakland, CA: National Council on Crime and Delinquency. Retrieved March 8, 2015 (http://nccdglobal.org/publications).

Hemmens, Craig, Benjamin Steiner, and David Mueller. 2004. *Significant Cases in Juvenile Justice.* Los Angeles: Roxbury.

Hickman, Matthew J. and Brian A. Reaves. 2001. "Community Policing in Local Police Departments, 1997 and 1999." *Special Report.* Washington, DC: Bureau of Justice Statistics.

Hockenberry, Sarah and Charles Puzzanchera. 2014a. *Juvenile Court Statistics 2011.* Pittsburgh, PA: National Center for Juvenile Justice.

Hockenberry, Sarah and Charles Puzzanchera. 2014b. "Delinquency Cases Waived to Criminal Court, 2011." Juvenile Offenders and Victims: National Report Series. Washington, DC: Office of Juvenile Justice and Delinquency Prevention.

Hsia, Heidi M., George S. Bridges, and Rosalie McHale. 2004. *Disproportionate Minority Confinement 2002 Update.* Washington, DC: Office of Juvenile Justice and Delinquency Prevention.

International Association of Chiefs of Police (IACP). 2015. "The Effects of Adolescent Development on Policing." Retrieved March 3, 2014 (www.theiacp.org/Portals/0/documents/pdfs/IACPBriefEffectsofAdolescentDevelopmentonPolicing.pdf).

Jordan, Frank and Joseph M. Sasfy. 1974. *National Impact Program Evaluation: A Review of Selected Issues and Research Findings Related to Probation and Parole.* Washington, DC: Mitre Corporation.

Kelling, George L. 1988. "Police and Communities: The Quiet Revolution." *Perspective on Policing* #1. Washington, DC: U.S. Department of Justice.

Kelling, George L. and Mark H. Moore. 1988. "The Evolving Strategy of Policing." *Perspective on Policing* #4. Washington, DC: U.S. Department of Justice.

Kempf-Leonard, Kimberly. 2007. "Minority Youths and Juvenile Justice Disproportionate Minority Contact after Nearly 20 Years of Reform Efforts." *Youth Violence and Juvenile Justice* 5: 71–87.

Klinger, David. 1994. "Demeanor of Crime? Why 'Hostile' Citizens Are More Likely to be Arrested." *Criminology* 32: 475–493.

Klockers, Carl B., Jr. 1972. "A Theory of Probation Supervision." *Journal of Criminal Law, Criminology, and Police Science* 63: 550–557.

Krisberg, Barry and James Austin. 1978. *The Children of Ishmael: Critical Perspectives on Juvenile Justice*. Palo Alto, CA: Mayfield.

Kupchik, Aaron. 2006. *Judging Juveniles: Prosecuting Adolescents in Adult and Juvenile Courts*. New York University Press.

Lattimore, Pamela, Christy Visher, and Richard Linster. 1995. "Predicting Rearrest for Violence among Serious Youthful Offenders." *Journal of Research in Crime and Delinquency* 32: 54–83.

Leiber, Michael, Donna Bishop, and Mitchell B. Chamlin. 2011. "Juvenile Justice Decision-Making Before and After the Implementation of the Disproportionate Minority Contact (DMC) Mandate." *Justice Quarterly* 28: 460–492.

Lerman, Paul. 1975. *Community Treatment and Control*. University of Chicago Press.

Lewett, Allan E. 1975. "*Centralization of City Police in Nineteenth Century United States*." PhD Dissertation, University of Michigan.

Lipton, Douglas, Robert Martinson, and Judith Wilks. 1975. *The Effectiveness of Correctional Treatment*. New York: Praeger.

Lundman, Richard. 1994. "Demeanor of Crime? The Midwest City Police–Citizen Encounters Study." *Criminology* 32: 631–653.

Lundman, Richard. 1996. "Demeanor and Arrest: Additional Evidence from Previously Unpublished Data." *Journal of Research in Crime and Delinquency* 33: 349–353

Lundman, Richard J., Richard E. Sykes, and John P. Clark. 1978. "Police Control of Juveniles: A Replication." *Journal of Research in Crime and Delinquency* 15: 74–91.

McCarter, Susan A. 2011. "Disproportionate Minority Contact in the American Juvenile Justice System: Where Are We after 20 Years, a Philosophy Shift, and Three Amendments?" *Journal of Forensic Social Work* 1: 96–107.

Models for Change. n.d. "Reform Areas." Justice Policy Institute. Retrieved March 3, 2015 (www.modelsforchange.net/index.html).

Moore, Mark H., Robert C. Trojanowicz, and George L. Kelling. 1988. "Crime and the Police." *Perspective on Policing* #2. Washington DC: U.S. Department of Justice.

National Research Council. 2013. *Reforming Juvenile Justice: A Developmental Approach*, ed. Richard J. Bonnie, Robert L. Johnson, Betty M. Chemers, and Julie A. Schuck. *Committee on Law and Justice, Division of Behavioral and Social Sciences and Education*. Washington, DC: National Academies Press.

Office of Juvenile Justice and Delinquency Prevention (OJJDP). 2012. "Disproportionate Minority Contact." *OJJDP in Focus*. Washington, DC: OJJDP.

Office of Juvenile Justice and Delinquency Prevention (OJJDP). n.d. *Statistical Briefing Book*. Juvenile Justice System Structure and Process, Case Flow Diagram. Retrieved May 28, 2014 (www.ojjdp.gov/ojstatbb/structure_process/case.html).

Ohlin, Lloyd E., Herman Piven, and D. M. Pappenfort. 1956. "Major Dilemmas of the Social Worker in Probation and Parole." *National Probation and Parole Association Journal* 2: 21–25.

Piliavin, Irving and Scott Briar. 1964. "Police Encounters with Juveniles." *American Journal of Sociology* 70: 206–214.

Platt, Anthony. 1977. *The Child Savers: The Invention of Delinquency*. 2nd edn. University of Chicago Press.

Pope, Carl E. and Michael Leiber. 2005. "Disproportionate Minority Contact (DMC): The Federal Initiative. Pp. 351–389 in *Our Children, Their Children: Confronting Racial and Ethnic Differences in American Juvenile Justice*, ed. D. Hawkins and K. Kempf-Leonard. University of Chicago Press.

Pope, Carl E., Rick Lovell, and Heidi M. Hsia. 2002. "Disproportionate Minority Confinement: A Review of the Research Literature from 1989 through 2001." Washington, DC: Office of Juvenile Justice and Delinquency Prevention.

Pound, Roscoe. 1960. "Discretion, Dispensation, and Mitigation: The Problem of the Individual Special Case." *New York University Law Review* 35: 925–937.

President's Commission on Law Enforcement and Administration of Justice. 1967a. *The Challenge of Crime in a Free Society*. Washington, DC: GPO.

President's Commission on Law Enforcement and Administration of Justice. 1967b. *Task Force Report: Corrections*. Washington, DC: GPO.

President's Commission on Law Enforcement and Administration of Justice.1967c. *Task Force Report: Juvenile Delinquency and Youth Crime*.Washington, DC: GPO.

Puzzanchera, Charles. 2013. "Juvenile Arrests 2011." Juvenile Offenders and Victims National Report Series.Washington, DC: Office of Juvenile Justice and Delinquency Prevention.

Puzzanchera, Charles and Melissa Sickmund. 2008. *Juvenile Court Statistics 2005*.Pittsburgh, PA: National Center for Juvenile Justice.

Rainville, Gerard A. and Steven K. Smith. 2003. "Juvenile Felony Defendants in Criminal Courts." Washington, DC: Office of Juvenile Justice and Delinquency Prevention.

Redding, Richard E. 2008. "Juvenile Transfer Laws: An Effective Deterrent to Delinquency?" *Juvenile Justice Bulletin*.Washington, DC: Office of Juvenile Justice and Delinquency Prevention.

Riksheim, Eric and Steven Chermak. 1993. "Causes of Police Behavior Revisited." *Journal of Criminal Justice* 21: 353–382.

Rodriguez, Nancy. 2010. "The Cumulative Effect of Race and Ethnicity in Juvenile Court Outcomes and Why Preadjudication Detention Matters." *Journal of Research in Crime and Delinquency* 47: 391–413.

Sampson, Robert J. 1986. "Effects of Socioeconomic Context of Official Reaction to Juvenile Delinquency." *American Sociological Review* 51: 876–885.

Sealock, Miriam D. and Sally S. Simpson. 1998. "Unraveling Bias in Arrest Decisions: The Role of Juvenile Offender Type-Scripts." *Justice Quarterly* 15: 427–457.

Seiter, Richard P. and Angela D. West. 2003. "Supervision Styles in Probation and Parole: An Analysis of Activities." *Journal of Offender Rehabilitation* 38: 57–75.

Sellin, Thorsten and Marvin Wolfgang. 1964. *The Measurement of Delinquency*. New York: Wiley.

Shepherd, Robert E., Jr. 1999. "The Juvenile Court at 100 Years: A Look Back." *Juvenile Justice* 6: 13–21.

Sickmund, Melissa. 2003. "Juveniles in Court." Juvenile Offenders and Victims National Report Series. Washington, DC: Office of Juvenile Justice and Delinquency Prevention.

Sickmund, Melissa and Charles Puzzanchera (eds.). 2014. *Juvenile Offenders and Victims: 2014 National Report*. Pittsburgh, PA: National Center for Juvenile Justice.

Sickmund, Melissa, T. J. Sladky, Wei Kang, and Charles Puzzanchera. 2013. "Easy Access to the Census of Juveniles in Residential Placement." Retrieved February 22, 2015 (www.ojjdp.gov/ojstatbb/ezacjrp/).

Smith, Douglas A. 1984. "The Organizational Context of Legal Control." *Criminology* 22: 19–38.

Smith, Douglas A. and Jody Klein. 1984. "Police Control of Interpersonal Disputes." *Social Problems* 31: 468–481.

Smith, Douglas A. and Christy A. Visher. 1981. "Street-Level Justice: Situational Determinants of Police Arrest Decision." *Social Problems* 31: 468–481.

Smith, Douglas A., Christy A. Visher, and Laura A. Davidson. 1984. "Equity and Discretionary Justice: The Influence of Race on Police Arrest Decisions." *Journal of Criminal Law and Criminology* 75: 234–249.

Stahl, Anne L. 2008. "Petitioned Status Offense Cases in Juvenile Courts, 2004." OJJDP Fact Sheet. Washington, DC: Office of Juvenile Justice and Delinquency Prevention.

Terry, Robert M. 1967. "Discrimination in the Handling of Juvenile Offenders by Social Control Agencies." *Journal of Research in Crime and Delinquency* 4: 218–230.

Thornberry, Terence P. 1979. "Race, Socioeconomic States, and Sentencing in the Juvenile Justice System." *Journal of Criminal Law and Criminology* 70: 164–171.

University at Albany, Hindelang Criminal Justice Research Center. 2013. *Sourcebook of Criminal Justice Statistics*. Retrieved February 19, 2015 (http://www/albany.edu/sourcebook/pdf/t4262011.pdf).

Walker, Samuel and Charles M. Katz. 2005. *Police in America: An Introduction*. 5th edn. Boston: McGraw-Hill.

Wiebush, Richard G., Betsie McNulty, and Thao Le. 2000. "Implementation of the Intensive Community-Based Aftercare Program." *Juvenile Justice Bulletin*. Washington, DC: Office of Juvenile Justice and Delinquency Prevention.

Wilson, James Q. 1968a. "The Police and the Delinquent in Two Cities." Pp. 9–30 in *Controlling Delinquents*, ed. S. Wheeler. New York: Wiley.

Wilson, James Q. 1968b. *Varieties of Police Behavior*. Cambridge, MA: Harvard University Press.

Wolcott, David B. 2005. *Cops and Kids: Policing Juvenile Delinquency in Urban America, 1890–1940*. Columbus, OH: Ohio State University Press.

Index